The Who's Who of
WEST BROMWICH ALBION

Compiled by club statistician
Tony Matthews

The Who's Who of
WEST BROMWICH ALBION

Foreword by Bryan Robson OBE

breedon **books**
PUBLISHING

First published in Great Britain in 2005 by
The Breedon Books Publishing Company
Limited
Breedon House, 3 The Parker Centre,
Derby, DE21 4SZ.

A catalogue record for this book is available from
the British Library.

ISBN 1 85983 474 4

Printed and bound by CPI Group, Bath Press,
Bath, Avon, BA2 3BL.

Contents

Foreword

by Bryan Robson OBE

Without players there can be no football club.

Some have been more gifted than others and many have certainly made their mark in more ways than one during their service with West Bromwich Albion, their names synonymous with the Throstles or the Baggies, which is now, universally, the fans' nickname for the club

Players such as Billy Bassett, Jesse Pennington, Fred Morris, 'W G' Richardson, Tommy Glidden, Ronnie Allen, Ray Barlow, Bobby Hope, Tony Brown, Jeff Astle, Laurie Cunningham and Cyrille Regis…the list is endless…were, without doubt, all brilliant footballers.

Like me, many of you supporters, even your parents, never had the opportunity to see the older stars in action. But their scoring exploits, defensive qualities, midfield skills and goalkeeping techniques have been recorded in match reports, published in books and magazines and even captured on film, thus confirming that they were among the best of their generation.

Of those who have donned the famous navy blue and white striped shirt over the last 40-50 years, many are still alive today and readily reminisce of past glories and, indeed, unhappy times, which makes the game so very interesting. But sadly there are precious few with us today who were active before the Second World War. However, the records and achievements are here for all to see and admire.

In this excellent book Tony Matthews, the club's statistician, historian and curator of The Hawthorns museum - and a friend of mine for many years - has listed all the superstars from yesteryear, plus the not-so-famous or well-known and the players who are still in the game today.

This fascinating Who's Who includes every player who has appeared in a competitive game for the club since those far-off days of West Bromwich Strollers in the late 1870s to the present day. Yes, indeed, every single player, including those who made just one appearance, even as a substitute. I can't imagine how many that is - at least 1,000.

There have been many books published on West Bromwich Albion over the years and this is another must for your bookshelf. The information contained therein is fascinating and will, I am sure, answer most if not all the questions you need to know about the players who have served the club over the last 125 years and more.

I congratulate Tony on a wonderful piece of work….let's hope the team can match his efforts out on the pitch in the forthcoming seasons.

Acknowledgements

I would like to thank the following people for their help in the production of this work:

Steve Caron of Breedon Books (Derby) who kindly agreed to produce the book; and to editor Michelle Grainger; Colin Mackenzie (Solihull Lodge) who helped considerably with my two previous Albion Who's Who books and has again supplied some valuable up-dated information this time round; Robert Bradley (West Bromwich) for his assistance regarding background information on certain players. David Barber (from the Football Association), Zoe Ward (Premier League) and Dan Slee (*Express & Star*) for their efforts. To amateur photographers and supporters Kevin Grice (West Bromwich), Lee Biddle (Stafford), Dean Walton (Leamington Spa) and Barry Marsh (London) who have generously supplied several pictures from their own private collections. To a Hawthorns steward and Baggies nut Keith Simcox (Dudley), to David Morris (Clogher, County Tyrone, Ireland) and to local author Terry Price (Yew Tree, Walsall), all of whom have also contributed with various pictures. To Albion's current official photographer and long term friend Laurie Rampling (Essex) who presented me with scores of player shots all those years ago. And finally to Albion chairman Jeremy Peace, director Joe Brandrick and club secretary Dr John Evans for giving me permission to use the official club logo and reproduce a number of pictures from the Hawthorns archive. Jim Brown (Coventry City FC), John Moody, Neil Reynolds (Bedworth), Nick Veevers (Burnley FC) and Carol Salmon all loaned photographs.

Thanks also to my stepdaughter, Cathie Smith (Tamworth), for her terrific efforts on the computer keyboard. And I must say thank you and sorry to my darling wife, Margaret, who, yet again, has had put up with me being stuck in front a computer screen with hundreds of programmes, scrapbooks and reference books scattered on the floor, ready to be thumbed.

Important Notice

Introduction

I am positively certain that all supporters of West Bromwich Albion, young and old, male and female, have, at some time or another, been involved in an argument concerning a player, whether from the past or present!

In pubs, clubs, cafés, bars and restaurants, schools, colleges and universities, at home, in the office, out walking or shopping, at a ground, in a car, on a train, bus or plane and on the beach, discussions have taken place about one or more players, even managers, who have been associated with Albion through the years.

Some of these discussions have turned into heated arguments with questions being asked but no definite answer given. As a result, wagers have been laid as to who is right and who is wrong.

The questions are varied… When did he, the player, join the club?… Where did he come from?… How many goals did he score?… Who did he join after leaving The Hawthorns?… Did he play international football?… Was he a defender or midfielder?… and did he play in a cup final?

This Who's Who will answer most, if not all, of these questions, as well as offering fans loads more information besides. It will also satisfy that laudable curiosity without a shadow of doubt.

You will find multitudinous authentic personal details of every player who has appeared for Albion in a competitive match from November 1883 when the club first entered the FA Cup up to May 2005.

There are also details of players who guested for the club during the two World Wars and of those who made the first team but failed to make an appearance in a League or major cup game. There are details, too, of the club's managers, directors, chairmen, secretaries, trainers, coaches etc. and a lot more.

The date and place of birth and death are given, if clarified, although occasionally it has only been possible to ascertain a year with regards to when the player was actually born or died.

In some instances the date of death has not been included at all, although the word deceased has been added as an alternative.

Following on from my previous books, especially those appertaining to players, with the help of many statisticians up and down the country plus families of ex-players, I have been able to add, considerably, to the biographies of several of the older stars, and some of the information obtained is quite interesting.

I have included in each player's 'biog' (if possible) details of the junior and non-League clubs he served, any transfer fees involved (if known) and any honours won at club and international level.

All the player's individual senior appearance and goalscoring records with Albion are up to the end of the 2004–05 season and given directly under the player's name, along side his preferred position.

Throughout virtually all this book, the name of the club is referred to as Albion or Baggies. Very few abbreviations have been used, but among the more common ones are the obvious: FC (Football Club), 'sub' (substitute), n/c (non-contract), c. (about).

A plus sign (i.e. 100+3 apps) indicates the number of substitute appearances made.

Where a single year appears in the text (when referring to an individual player's career) this indicates, in most cases, the second half of a season, i.e. 1975 is the 1974–75 season. However, when the figures (dates) such as 1975–80 appear this means seasons 1975–76 to 1979–80 inclusive and not 1974–80.

This is not a story book. It is a reference book and a lot of the information on the following pages has, of course, been printed before, but, like a dictionary, a book of this nature always needs up-dating and that's what I've done here. A lot of players have come and gone since my last official book back in the late 1980s and this one, I feel, is the best I've produced in terms of a Who's Who.

I know someone somewhere will criticise my efforts (they always do) but I can honestly say that if someone can do better then good luck. I've put a lot of hard work into this over the years and I am proud of what has been published.

If you spot any discrepancies, errors and/or omissions, I would appreciate if you could contact me at The Hawthorns (or the publishers) so that any amendments can be made in future publications regarding West Bromwich Albion FC. If you have anything to add, this too would be appreciated as people tend to reveal unknown facts from a variety of sources when football is the topic of conversation.

ADAMS, Amos Josiah

Full-back: 214 apps. 3 goals.

Born: West Bromwich, 10 June 1878.
Died: West Bromwich, 27 January 1941.
Career: West Bromwich Baptist & Bratt Street schools. George Salter Works. Springfields FC/West Bromwich (August 1895). ALBION (June 1897-April 1910). FC Ameins, France (coach, 1925–26, then manager, 1926–27). Later worked in industry.

■ Full-back Amos Adams spent 13 years with West Bromwich Albion before retiring in 1910 to become a sports-master at a local school. A strong tackler, he made his League debut for Albion at centre-forward in a First Division match against Notts County in March 1899 and three years later won a Second Division championship medal, having developed into a classy full-back and fine partner to England international Jesse Pennington. An intelligent, versatile and stylish footballer, whose shorts always seemed a size too big for him, Adams, besides his senior appearances, also played in over 50 second XI games for Albion.

ADAMS, James

Goalkeeper: 221 apps.

Born: Norton Canes, Cannock, 4 January 1908.
Died: West Bromwich, 19 August 1979.
Career: Cannock & District Schools. Cannock Chase Colliery (1923). Cannock Town (August 1927). ALBION (professional, July 1929, retired due to poor health, May 1945. Later club scout for five years, 1947–52).

■ Jimmy 'Doc' Adams was a hefty goalkeeper who weighed almost 15 stone at one stage during his Hawthorns career. Nevertheless, he was extremely mobile, and after coming through the reserves, and playing second fiddle to George Ashmore and England international Harold Pearson he eventually took over from the latter despite Billy Light challenging him for the number one spot in 1937. He made his Football League debut against Notts County at The Hawthorns in November 1929 and also played in 62 second-team games. Adams remained a keen supporter of the Baggies (sitting in the old Halfords Lane stand) right up until his death in 1979.

ADAMS, William

Full-back: 98 apps.

Born: Blackheath, 12 August 1892.
Died: Smethwick, 20 December 1945.
Career: Blackheath & Rowley Regis Schools. Army service. Rowley Village FC. Rowley Victoria (August 1918). ALBION (March 1919). Barrow (March 1928). Cradley Heath (December 1929, retired, May 1931). Became licensee of the Old House At Home, Smethwick.

■ An England junior international full-back who also represented the FA in 1923, Billy Adams served Albion for nine years. A stout, reliable defender with a strong kick, he served in the Army as a teenager and joined The Hawthorns' ranks initially as a reserve to Joe Smith and Jesse Pennington. He made his First Division debut against Derby County in September 1920 and also played in more than 100 second XI matches, being rewarded with championship medals for triumphs in the Birmingham & District League in 1919–20 and the Central League in 1923–24.

ADAMSON, Christopher

Goalkeeper: 13 apps.

Born: Ashington, 4 November 1978.
Career: Ashington School. ALBION (apprentice, April 1995, professional, July 1997). Moor Green (on loan, October 1997). Mansfield Town (on loan, April 1999). Halifax Town (on loan, July–September 1999). St Patrick's Athletic, Ireland (from July 2002). Sheffield Wednesday (on loan, March-May 2005, signed permanently, July 2005).

■ Generally third in line for the goalkeeping spot at The Hawthorns, Chris Adamson impressed with his handling when called up for first-team duty. He was capable enough and commanded his area well. Eighteen months after making his League debut for Albion against Stockport County (away) in April 1998, he conceded two penalties (and was ultimately sent off) while playing for Albion reserves v Stoke City in December 1999. He went on to appear in almost 70 games for the second XI.

ADDERLEY, Joseph Bernard

Full-back: one app.

Born: Harborne, Birmingham, 7 December 1922.
Deceased.
Career: Bournville Youths (from 1939). ALBION (May 1941). Non-League football from May 1946. Later worked in engineering.

■ Joe Adderley got very little opportunity in the first team at The Hawthorns. His only senior game for the club was against Aston Villa in a League North game in April 1944.

AGNEW, Paul

Full-back: 40+1 apps. 1 goal.

Born: Lisburn, North Ireland, 15 August 1965.
Career: Belfast Schools. Cliftonville FC, Belfast (semi-professional, August 1982). Grimsby Town (February 1984). ALBION (£65,000, February 1995). Ilkeston Town (August 1997). Wisbech Town (November 1997). Swansea City (non-contract, December 1997–May 2000). Whittington FC (coach, 2001–04).

■ A very competent left-back, Paul Agnew was an Alan Buckley signing. Capped by his country at schoolboy, youth and under-21 levels, he took over the captaincy from Paul Mardon at The Hawthorns. He made his debut for Albion in a League home game against Stoke City (lost 3–1) just 48 hours after moving from Blundell Park. He was

released at the end of the 1996–97 season. Agnew, who played a dozen times for Albion's second string, appeared in almost 300 games for the Mariners.

AITKEN, Andrew Fox Scott

Winger: 22 apps. 2 goals.

Born: Craigmillar near Edinburgh, 21 August 1934.
Career: Edinburgh Schools, Edinburgh Emmet, Cliftonville FC/Belfast (1951), Hibernian (professional, September 1952), ALBION (£9,000, September 1959), Falkirk (£3,000, February 1961), Raith Rovers (August 1962, retired, April 1967). Later employed by an insurance firm.

■ A useful footballer able to occupy either flank, Andy Aitken did far better north of the border than he did in England. With Alec Jackson being preferred on the right-wing and Derek Hogg on the left, he subsequently left The Hawthorns following the arrival of Clive Clark. He made his Albion debut against Newcastle United in September 1959 and appeared in 45 Central League games (19 goals).

ALBISTON, Arthur Richard

Full-back: 47 apps. 2 goals.

Born: Edinburgh, 14 July 1957.
Career: Edinburgh schoolboy football. Manchester United (apprentice, July 1972, professional, July 1974). ALBION (August 1988). Dundee (June 1989). Chesterfield. Chester City. FC Molde, Norway (1992). Droylesden (manager, 1996–97). Manchester United (School of Excellence coach, August 1997, junior coach at Old Trafford, 2000–04). Also a radio summariser (football) with Manchester Independent.

■ An exceptionally fine left-back, Arthur Albiston made his senior debut for Manchester United in the 1979 FA Cup final defeat of Liverpool – the first of more than 500 appearances for the Old Trafford club. He won two more FA Cup medals (1983 and 1985) and collected a runners'-up prize in 1979, following up with a runners'-up medal in the 1983 League Cup final. Honoured by Scotland at schoolboy, under-21 and senior levels (he won 14 full international caps), he

was recruited by his former United manager, Ron Atkinson, when he returned to The Hawthorns for a second spell. He had one very good season at The Hawthorns, missing only a handful of games. He made his debut for Albion in the League away game at Leicester City in August 1988.

ALBRECHTSEN, Martin

Defender: 24+4 app.

Born: Copenhagen, Denmark, 30 March 1980.
Career: Copenhagen junior football. FC Copenhagen (amateur, 1996, professional, September 1998). ALBION (£2.5 million, June 2004).

■ In the summer of 2004, Martin Albrechtsen, already capped three times by Denmark (but not included in Morten Olsen's Euro 2004 squad), became Albion's record signing at £2.5 million (with a further £200,000 due after an agreed number of appearances). Prior to his move to The Hawthorns the blonde defender had made over 150 appearances in Danish football, the last two-and-a-half being described as 'fantastic' as FC Copenhagen won two League titles and the domestic cup.

'Albion manager Gary Megson made me an exciting offer, which I couldn't refuse' said Albrechtsen. Tall, strong and mobile, he made his Premiership debut for Albion as a substitute (for his fellow countryman Thomas Gaardsoe) against Everton in August 2004 – having made his first appearance in a Baggies shirt on tour against Frederiocia (Denmark) the

previous month. He lost his confidence and form prior to the departure of Megson but became a key member of new boss Bryan Robson's squad, playing exceptionally well as a right wing-back.

ALDERWICK, John

Goalkeeper: 1 app.

Born: New Oscott, Birmingham, 20 February 1921.
Career: Aston and Kingstanding schoolboy football. Sutton Town (1937). New Oscott FC (1938). ALBION (October 1940). Boldmere St Michael's (May 1946). Later with Sutton Town, then worked in industry.

■ A wartime signing by Albion, Jack Alderwick's career was severely disrupted by the hostilities. He had the misfortune of conceding 10 goals in his only senior game for the club, against Walsall (Football League South) in May 1941.

ALDRIDGE, Albert James

Full-back: 15 apps.

Born: Walsall, 18 April 1864.
Died: Birmingham, 29 May 1891.
Career: Pleck Council School (Walsall). Walsall Swifts (1885). ALBION (amateur, March 1886, professional, July 1886). Walsall Town Swifts (July 1888). Aston Villa (August 1889, retired through ill-health, March 1891).

■ An England international full-back (two caps gained), Albert Aldridge presented a formidable barrier, being

hardy, resolute and unyielding. He won an FA Cup medal with Albion in 1888, having collected a runners'-up prize 12 months earlier. He made his senior debut for the club in an FA Cup tie against Bolton Wanderers in October 1886, played in 90 'other' matches for Albion and later appeared in 14 competitive games for Aston Villa.

ALDRIDGE, Norman Henry

Full-back: 1 app.

Born: Foleshill near Coventry, 23 February 1921.
Career: Coventry & District Schools. Foxford FC (1944). ALBION (December 1945, professional, May 1946). Northampton Town (£750, May 1948). Headington United (June 1949). Lockheed Leamington (May 1952, retired, May 1956). Later worked at Revo (Tipton).

■ Reserve to Jim Pemberton, Norman Aldridge was a well-built, steady and composed footballer whose only senior outing for Albion was against Plymouth Argyle (Division Two) in April 1947. He appeared in 49 Central League matches for the club and after leaving The Hawthorns played in 86 competitive games for Headington (now Oxford United).

ALLAN, Jack Stanley

Centre-forward: 20 apps. 4 goals.
Born: Wallsend-on-Tyne, 28 December 1886.
Died: Wallsend-on-Tyne, 4 May 1919.
Career: Wallsend Schools. Wallsend FC (1904). Sunderland (1907). Newcastle United (June 1908). ALBION (£150, May 1911). Nottingham Forest (£125, June 1912, retired, December 1913). Joined RAMC on outbreak of World War One and served with the No 12 'A' Platoon in Egypt. Died of pneumonia, aged 31, two weeks after his return to Tyneside.

■ An excellent centre-forward, strong and mobile, Stan Allan, a schoolteacher by profession, started his only season at The Hawthorns as leader of Albion's attack, making his debut against Notts County. He did well, but then Bob Pailor returned to the side and thereafter he was virtually a 'reserve striker', although he did help Albion reach the 1912 FA Cup

final, appearing in the semi-final replay. He was a League championship winner with Newcastle in 1909.

ALLARDYCE, Samuel

Defender: 0+1 app.

Born: Dudley, 19 October 1954.
Career: Dudley and Brierley Hill Schools. Bolton Wanderers (juniors, 1970, professional, November 1971). Sunderland (£150,000, July 1980). Millwall (£95,000, September 1981). Tampa Bay Rowdies, NASL (February 1983). Coventry City (September 1983). Huddersfield Town (July 1984). Bolton Wanderers (£10,000, July 1985). Preston North End (August 1986). ALBION (player-coach, June 1989). Preston North End (non-contract, August–October 1992, then caretaker manager and youth team coach at Deepdale). Limerick (manager, briefly). Blackpool (manager, July 1994). Notts County (manager, January 1997). Bolton Wanderers (manager, October 1999).

■ As a strong tackling, resilient defender, Sam Allardyce made well over 500 senior appearances for his eight major clubs (443 in the Football League) covering a period of almost 20 years. He made his League debut for Bolton in November 1973 and played his last competitive game for Preston North End in October 1992. His only senior outing for Albion was as a substitute in the Second Division home game against Newcastle United in November 1989 (lost 5–1). He also played in 27 Central League games (2 goals scored). After retiring, Allardyce went into management and, following a 'breaking in' period in Ireland, guided Blackpool to the Second Division play-offs in 1996, led Notts County to the Third Division title in 1998 and took Bolton into the Premiership in 2001 and UEFA Cup in 2005.

ALLEN, Ronald

Centre-forward/winger: 415 apps. 234 goals.

Born: Fenton, Stoke-on-Trent, 15 January 1929.
Died: Great Wyrley, 9 June 2001.
Career: Hanley High School. Bucknall Boy's Brigade FC. Wellington Scouts. Northwood Mission. Also played Rugby Union. Staffs County Youths (1941). Port Vale (amateur, March 1944, professional,

March 1946). Served in the RAF for two years (from October 1947). ALBION (£20,000, March 1950). Crystal Palace (£4,500, player-coach, May 1961, retired as a player, May 1965). Wolverhampton Wanderers (coach, July 1965, then manager, January 1966–November 1968). Athletic Bilbao, Spain (manager, March 1969–November 1971). Sporting Lisbon, Portugal (manager, April 1972–May 1973). Saudi Arabia (coach, briefly). Walsall (manager, June–December 1973). ALBION (scouting advisor, January–June 1977, then manager to December 1977). Saudi Arabia (national team coach, December 1977). Panathinaikos, Greece (coach/manager, June -September 1980). ALBION (manager, July 1981–May 1982, then general manager until May 1983). Sales director of Black Country engineering firm, specialising in oil rigs. Part-time coach at The Hawthorns to 1995.

■ Initially a winger, Ronnie Allen was converted into a brilliant centre-forward by Albion after scoring on his debut for the club in the 1–1 home draw with Wolves in March 1950, when a record League crowd of almost 61,000 packed in to The Hawthorns. He was an ace marksman and a superb volleyer of the ball, possessing a powerful right-foot shot. He netted 208 League goals for Albion, a total bettered only by Tony Brown. He gained five full England caps (his first against Switzerland in 1952), as well as playing for his country's 'B' team, representing the Football League and also playing for the FA XI. In 1954 he netted twice in a 3–2 FA Cup final victory over Preston North End, including a dramatic equalising penalty. In that same year he also scored a hat-trick in a 4–4 Charity Shield draw with Wolves at Molineux. Allen went on to claim a total of 276 goals in 637 League matches in his career, and in all games his record was 354 goals in 812 outings. He scored in each season from 1944–45 to 1964–65 inclusive and was the First Division's top marksman in 1954–55 with 27 goals. He also netted 21 goals in 25 Central League games for the Baggies. After becoming an Albion shareholder, he helped with part-time coaching at the club until 1996, making a brief appearance as 'substitute' in a friendly away at Cheltenham in 1995, aged 66. Allen was granted a testimonial match versus Aston Villa in August 1997. He was the 'complete footballer' and one of Albion's all-time greats.
NB: Allen, besides being a 'special' footballer was also a very competent golfer. He twice won the Professional Footballers' Golf championship in 1959 and 1961 and was runner-up in 1963 and 1964.
* His son, Russell Allen, was on Albion's books in the early 1970s and later made a name for himself as a goalscorer with Tranmere Rovers (See also under MANAGERS).

ALSOP, Gilbert Arthur

Centre-forward: 1 app.

Born: Frampton Cotterill near Bristol, 10 September 1908.
Died: Walsall, 16 April 1992.
Career: Frampton Cotterill Church of England School. Frampton Court FC. Latteridge FC (1924). Bath City (1926). Coventry City (professional, August 1929). Walsall (October 1931). ALBION (£3,000, November 1935). Ipswich Town (£2,000, May 1937). Walsall (£1,500, October 1938). Guest for Leicester City, Luton Town, Mansfield Town and Northampton Town during World War Two (retired, May 1947, then coach of Walsall's third team to May 1949). Subsequently employed as a groundsman by local firm F.H. Lloyds, for whom he played and scored when well into his 40s. Returned to Walsall as groundsman (1952) and remained at Fellows Park for a further 20 years, attending most home games for the rest of his life.

■ Gilbert Alsop was a hard, robust, never-say-die centre-forward of the short, stocky brigade. A magnificent goalscorer, he netted almost 300 goals during his career, 169 coming in 222 competitive games for Walsall plus 58 in 105 World War Two fixtures. He claimed a record 48 goals in 52 appearances in 1934–35, having been in the Walsall side that sensationally knocked Arsenal out of the FA Cup in 1933. Signed as a reserve centre-forward, he never got a chance at The Hawthorns owing to the form of W.G. Richardson and Harry 'Popeye' Jones. After just one first team outing, a Division One game against Huddersfield Town in November 1935, plus 57 Central League appearances (27 goals), he moved to Ipswich Town, whom he helped gain entry to the Football League (1938).

AMPADU, Patrick Kwane

Forward/midfield: 39+23 apps. 5 goals.

Born: Bradford, 20 December 1970.
Career: Sherrards United, Dublin (April 1987). Belvedere FC, Dublin (October 1987). Arsenal (professional, July 1988). Plymouth Argyle (on loan, October–November 1990). ALBION (£50,000, June 1991). Swansea City (£15,000, February 1994). Leyton Orient (free, July 1998). Exeter City (free, July 2000, appointed player-coach, August 2003).

■ Selected by the Republic of Ireland, via parentage qualification, at youth and

under-21 levels (four caps gained in the latter category), midfielder Kwame Ampadu made only two appearances for Arsenal (both as a 'sub') and seven for Plymouth Argyle before spending just over two-and-a-half seasons at The Hawthorns. In that time he was never a first-team regular, but when called upon gave a good account of himself, mainly occupying a wide position. He made his debut for the club against his future employers, Exeter City, at The Hawthorns in August 1991 (Albion's first ever game in Division Three) and he also participated in 32 Central League games (two goals). After leaving The Hawthorns he became a more defensive player and had 178 senior games for Swansea, 86 for Orient and well over 90 for Exeter, who lost their League status at the end of the 2002–03 season.

ANDERSON, Colin Russell

Full-back/midfield: 140+12 apps. 12 goals.

Born: Newcastle, 26 April 1962.
Career: Burnley (apprentice, June 1978, professional, April 1980). North Shields (August 1981). Torquay United (September 1982). Queen's Park Rangers (on loan, 1984). ALBION (on loan, March 1985, signed permanently for £25,000, March 1985). Walsall (free, August 1991). Hereford United (free, August 1992). Exeter City (free, July 1994–May 1996). Later with Dawlish Town (Devon League).

■ Able to play as a full-back, midfielder or wide on the left, Colin Anderson was a hard-working footballer who made over

100 appearances for Torquay before moving to The Hawthorns. He made his first division debut for Albion as a 'sub' against Everton at Goodison Park in August 1985. He also played in more than 70 second XI games for the club (4 goals scored), helping the reserves win the Pontins League championship in 1990–91.

ANDERSEN, Vitle Norland

Defender: 0+1 app.

Born: Norway, 20 April 1964.
Career: Lyngby FC, Denmark (professional, July 1982). ALBION (non-contract, November 1989–February 1990). Lyngby FC (March 1990–May 1992).

■ Signed by manager Brian Talbot as defensive cover at The Hawthorns, Vitle Andersen hardly had a look in and made just one first-team appearance, as a second half substitute for Colin Anderson against AFC Bournemouth (home) in November 1989 (Division Two). He also played in three Central League games.

ANGEL, Mark

Midfield: 5+23 apps. 1 goal.

Born: Newcastle, 23 August 1975.
Career: Walker Central FC (1991). Sunderland (professional, December 1993). Oxford United (free, August 1995). ALBION (free, July 1998). Hartlepool United (trialist, 1999–2000). Darlington (August 2000). Queen of the South (November 2000). Boston United (August 2001). King's Lynn (August 2004).

■ A pacy, wide player with good technique, Mark Angel – who made his League debut for Albion against Grimsby Town (away) in August 1998 – certainly kept the bench-seat warm when called up into the first-team squad at The Hawthorns! After failing to make an impression at Sunderland, he netted five times in 90 outings for Oxford, but after leaving Albion, for whom he scored six goals in almost 40 second-team games, he had very little success at the Feethams. Then, after helping Boston United win the Nationwide Conference, he was instrumental in seeing the Lincolnshire club establish themselves in League Division Three in season 2002–03 when he also won three semi-professional caps for England.

ANGELL, Brett Ashley Mark

Striker: 0+3 apps.

Born: Marlborough, 20 August 1968.
Career: Marlborough Boys' Club. Portsmouth (apprentice, April 1985, professional, August 1986). Cheltenham Town (1987). Derby County (£40,000, February 1988). Stockport County (£33,000, October 1988). Southend United (£100,000, August 1990). Everton (on loan, September 1993, signed for £500,000, January 1994). Sunderland (£600,000, March 1995). Sheffield United (on loan, January 1996). ALBION (on loan, March–April 1996). Stockport County (£120,000, August 1996). Notts County (on loan, December 1999). Preston North End (on loan, February 2000). Walsall (free, July 2000). Rushden and Diamonds (free, February 2002). Port Vale (free, August 2002). Queen's Park Rangers (free, November 2002). Linfield (free, July 2003). Doncaster Rovers (scout, 2003–04).

■ Much-travelled striker Brett Angell spent just four weeks at The Hawthorns, during which time he came on as a substitute in three League games against Luton Town (for his Baggies debut), Norwich City and his former club, Sunderland. In a nomadic senior career (before moving to Linfield) he scored over 270 goals in almost 450 first-team matches, helping Stockport win the Second Division championship in 2000.

APPLEBY, Arthur Benjamin

Centre-forward: 1 app.

Born: Burton upon Trent, 9 September 1878. Died: Evesham, August 1944.
Career: Burton & District Schools. Derby County (professional, August 1897). Chatham (March 1898). Burton Wanderers (August 1898). Burton United (1901). ALBION (May 1901). Bristol Rovers (April 1903). Leighton FC (Gloucestershire). Later worked on a farm.

■ Ben Appleby was a useful reserve centre-forward with Albion who, in later years, was successfully converted into a hard-tackling full-back who passed the ball with pin-point accuracy. He made his League debut against Glossop (home) in September 1901 and later in his career gained a Southern League championship medal with Bristol Rovers in 1904–05. He made over 30 second XI appearances for Albion, gaining a Birmingham & District League championship medal in 1902.

APPLETON, Michael Antony

Midfield: 38 apps.

Born: Salford, 4 December 1975.
Career: Salford Boys. Manchester United (apprentice, April 1992, professional, July 1994). Wimbledon (on loan, June 1995). Lincoln City (on loan, September 1995). Grimsby Town (on loan, January 1997). Preston North End (£500,000, August 1997). ALBION (£750,000, January 2001, retired, November 2003, appointed scout and part-time coach at The Hawthorns).

■ Hard-tackling, combative central midfielder Michael Appleton struggled to get first-team action at Old Trafford, and after three loan spells with different clubs he became a vital member of the Preston engine-room, making 140 appearances for the Lillywhites before Albion boss Gary Megson brought him to The Hawthorns. He made his debut against Sheffield United in January 2001 (won 2–1), but unfortunately ten months later, after just 18 matches had been played that season, Appleton tore his posterior cruciate ligament in his right knee during a League away game against Birmingham City. The surgeon informed the club that he would be out of action for at least

nine months. He struggled to regain fitness and, in fact, missed the whole of the 2002–03 season. His absence was a massive blow to the Baggies as they lost their Premiership status.

ARCH, William Henry

Defender: 1 app.

Born: Tipton, 29 November 1894. Died: Birmingham, April 1978.
Career: Tipton schoolboy football. Tipton Comrades (1910). Great Bridge Celtic (1912). Pensnett FC (1918). ALBION (amateur, March 1919, professional, May 1919). Newport County (£75, May 1921). Willenhall (May 1922). Grimsby Town (June 1923). Hartlepools United (August 1926–May 1927). Retired, May 1930, after three seasons in non-League football. Later worked in an iron foundry.

■ Able to occupy a full-back or wing-half position, Bill Arch, resolute in the tackle with a strong, hefty kick, was a fringe player at The Hawthorns, whose only first-team appearance was against Wolves (Midland Victory League) in March 1919. He went on to play in 96 League and cup games for Grimsby.

ARMSTRONG, Gerard Joseph

Forward: 10 apps. 1 goal.

Born: Belfast, 23 May 1954.
Career: St Paul's Swifts (1970). Cromac Albion (1971). Bangor City (1972). Tottenham Hotspur (£25,000, November 1975). Watford (£250,000, November

1980). Real Mallorca, Spain (1984). ALBION (August 1985). Chesterfield (on loan, January–March 1986). Brighton and Hove Albion (May 1986). Millwall (on loan, January–March 1987). Carlisle United. Gillingham. Crawley Town (as player-manager, 1988–89). Sussex County FA (coach, 1990s). Northern Ireland (assistant manager, 2004). Also worked as a football analyst in Spain, covering La Liga from 1990 to date.*

■ Inside or centre-forward Gerry Armstrong had one season at The Hawthorns after failing to hold down a regular place in the side. His only goal for Albion was scored in a League Cup home encounter with Port Vale in September 1985 (won 1–0), a month after making his club debut against his former club, Watford, at Vicarage Road. He also scored twice in six Central League outings. More of a forager, a workhorse rather than a marksman, he won 63 caps for Northern Ireland (four during his time at The Hawthorns) and appeared in three World Cups (1978, '82 and '86). He also helped Spurs win the Second Division championship in 1978.
* Armstrong was recruited by Celtic boss and former Northern Ireland colleague Martin O'Neill (November 2001) to give a low-down on Valencia, the Bhoys' UEFA Cup opponents.

ARTHUR, David Robert

Full-back: 5+1 apps.

Born: Bushbury, Wolverhampton, 9 March 1960.
Career: Wolverhampton Schools XI.

ALBION (apprentice, April 1976, professional, March 1978). Walsall (free, August 1982). Harrisons FC, Wolverhampton (1983–84).

■ A neat and tidy full-back, who was a permanent reserve during his four years as a professional at The Hawthorns, David Arthur appeared in 182 Central League games for the Baggies (9 goals). He made his first-team debut as a 'sub' in the League away game at Ipswich in September 1981.

ASHCROFT, Lee

Forward: 79+31 apps. 18 goals.

Born: Preston, 7 September 1972.
Career: Preston North End (apprentice, April 1989, professional, July 1991). ALBION (£250,000, August 1993). Notts County (on loan, March–April 1996). Preston North End (£150,000, September 1996). Grimsby Town (£500,000, August 1998). Wigan Athletic (£250,000, August 2000). Port Vale (on loan, October 2002). Huddersfield Town (on loan, December 2002–January 2003). Southport (non-contract, February 2003, appointed player-manager, June 2003). Kendal Town (August 2004).

■ Winger Lee Ashcroft, who could also play as a centre-forward, made almost 100 appearances for Preston North End and gained one England under-21 cap prior to joining Albion, for whom he made his League debut in the home game against Middlesbrough (drew 1–1) in September 1993. He did very well at The Hawthorns, where his pace and skill down either flank was certainly

appreciated by strikers Bob Taylor and Andy Hunt who both capitalised to the full. Called 'Peggy' and sometimes 'Piggy', he scored a smart hat-trick when Albion beat Tranmere Rovers 5–1 at home in April 1995, and besides his first-team exploits he scored 13 goals in almost 50 second XI games. Injuries occasionally affected his game but on his day he was an excellent footballer at the level he performed. He reached the milestone of 450 League and cup appearances (85 goals) before having his contract paid-up by Wigan following his return to the JJB Stadium from a loan spell with Port Vale.

ASHLEY, Harold

Defender/half-back: 13 apps. 6 goals.

Born: Smethwick, 7 January 1915.
Died: Smethwick, May 1991.
Career: West Smethwick & Cape Hill Schools, Smethwick Hall (1930), Smethwick Highfield (1931), ALBION (professional, May 1934), Derby County (£525, November 1937), Darlington (August 1938), ALBION (World War Two guest, season 1942–43), Nottingham Forest (World War Two guest), Lye Town (manager, 1948–50). ALBION (assistant trainer, June 1950-June 1964). Then worked as a publican in Leicester before becoming a steward and groundstaff assistant with ALBION (1971–81).

■ Harry 'Caggy' Ashley was a good, honest performer, who spent his initial spell at The Hawthorns in the reserves. Something of a dressing room comedian, he made his Albion debut against Leicester City in a wartime League Cup game in March 1942 at full-back. He also netted 19 goals in 38 Central League games.

ASHMORE, George Samuel Austin

Goalkeeper: 268 apps.

Born: Plymouth, 5 May 1898.
Died: Handsworth, Birmingham, 12 May 1973.
Career: South Devon & District Schools. Nineveh Wesley (Handsworth). ALBION (November 1919). Chesterfield (October 1931). Retired in May 1935. Later worked for the MEB (Birmingham) for a number of years.

■ Goalkeeper George 'Cap' Ashmore was at The Hawthorns for 12 years, during which time he amassed a fine record of appearances and in 1926 gained a full England cap against Belgium in Antwerp. He was a loyal and dedicated clubman who played under the shadow of Hubert Pearson for a number of years and then understudied his son, Harold, and after that made his League debut against Blackburn Rovers at Ewood Park in October 1920 when the Baggies lost 5–1. Undeterred, he quickly put that result behind him and developed into a fine 'keeper, being both agile and daring, a fine shot-stopper with a strong right-foot kick. He also made 114 second-team appearances for Albion, gaining both Birmingham & District and Central League championship medals in 1919–20 and 1922–23 respectively. He later played in 71 League matches for Chesterfield.

ASHURST, William

Right-back: 26 apps. 1 goal.

Born: Willington, County Durham, 4 May 1894.
Died: Nottingham, 26 January 1947.
Career: Willington Schools. Durham City (1914). Leeds City (July 1919). Lincoln City (£500, October 1919). Notts County (£1,000, June 1920). ALBION (£2,500, November 1926). Newark Town (August 1928, retired, June 1929). Later employed as a machine-operator.

■ A dour, relentless, crisp-tackling full-back, scrupulously fair and a sound header of the ball, Bill Ashurst was capped five times by England in the mid-1920s and also represented the Football League. He was made captain on joining Albion and took over from Dicky Baugh, making his debut in the League home game against Arsenal in November 1926. He did well, initially, as partner to another new signing, George Shaw, before injury caused him to miss the whole of the 1927–28 season, his position being taken by Bob Finch. He helped Notts County win the Second Division championship in 1923 and made over 200 appearances for the Magpies.
* His younger brother, Elias Ashurst, played for Birmingham (1921–25).

ASKIN, George William

Inside-forward: 1 app.

Born: West Bromwich, 15 July 1861.
Died: West Bromwich, circa 1925.
Career: Guns Village School (West Bromwich). Elwells FC (1880). ALBION (June 1882). Hednesford Town (August 1889). Kidderminster Harriers (September 1889). Retired, 1895. Later worked for the local council.

■ An able forward, hard working with a good turn off speed, Billy Askin was a regular in Albion's first-team prior to the introduction of League football in 1888. His only senior outing was against Wolves in an FA Cup tie in November

1887, although he did play in nine 'other' first-team matches.

ASTLE, Jeffrey

Striker: 361 apps. 174 goals.

Born: Eastwood, Nottingham, 13 May 1942.
Died: Burton upon Trent, 20 January 2002.
Career: Devonshire Drive Junior & Walker Street Secondary Schools. West Notts Juniors. Holy Trinity Youth Club. Notts County (trialist 1956). Coventry City (trialist). John Player FC (Nottingham). Notts County (amateur, May 1957, *professional, July 1960). ALBION (£25,000, September 1964). Hellenic FC, South Africa (May 1974). Dunstable (July 1974). Weymouth (£15,000, July 1975). Atherstone (October 1976). Hillingdon Borough (on loan, February 1977). Retired in May 1977 to run his own industrial cleaning business near Burton upon Trent, later appearing on TV in 'Fantasy Football' with ardent Baggies supporter Frank Skinner and David Baddiel. In 1996 he went into the variety business with the 'Jeff Astle Road Show'.*

■ Jeff Astle was a brilliant centre-forward with great heading ability and a

19

strong right-foot shot. Known as 'The King' by all Baggies supporters, young and old, he was groomed by the great Tommy Lawton at Meadow Lane, and after scoring 41 goals for Notts County, he went on to give Albion 10 years' excellent service, making his debut in the League away game at Leicester in September 1964 and scoring twice on his home ground soon afterwards against Wolves (won 5–1). He won five full England caps against Wales and Portugal in 1969 and Scotland, Brazil and Czechoslovakia in 1970, the last two in the World Cup finals in Mexico. He also played for England against Young England in 1969; had three games for an England XI (scoring seven goals, four of them against Liga University in 1970) and had two outings for the Football League (4 goals). A member of Albion's League Cup and FA Cup winning teams of 1965–66 and 1967–68 respectively, he scored in every round of the latter competition and, indeed, became the first player to register a goal in both the FA Cup and League Cup finals at Wembley, doing so in 1968 when his extra-time winner beat Everton and in 1970 against Manchester City. Astle, who was voted 'Midland Footballer of the Year' in 1968, scored 20 goals in 46 reserve-team matches for the club. His death was a sad loss to so many people and especially Albion supporters who saw him score some smashing and vitally important goals.

* On 21 November 2002 South Staffordshire coroner Andrew Haigh concluded that Astle died from brain injuries (dementia/footballers' migraine) caused by repeatedly heading a ball during his 20-year career.

ASTON, Harold Mason

Inside-forward: 7 apps. 3 goals.

Born: Bloxwich, 10 October 1855.
Died: West Bromwich 1914.
Career: Spon Lane School. George Salter Works FC. ALBION (September 1879). Wolverhampton Wanderers (July 1885). Burslem Port Vale (1886–87). Oldbury Town (August 1887, retired May 1891). Became a labourer in West Bromwich.

■ A speedy, wholehearted forward, good in the air and able to shoot with both feet, Harry Aston played in more than 100 first-team games for Albion (local cup competitions, friendlies etc.) and scored around 40 goals. He appeared in the club's first ever FA Cup tie against Wednesbury Town in November 1883, which was his debut at senior level.

ASTON, Henry John

Centre-forward: 26 apps. 10 goals.

Born: Redditch, Worcs. 2 February 1881.
Died: Bromsgrove, 4 February 1938.
Career: Astwood Bank School. Silver Star FC (Redditch). Redditch FC. Quinton Victoria. Coventry City (briefly, 1900). Ironbridge FC (1901). Served with the 2nd Battalion Durham Light Infantry (Aldershot), then Royal Artillery. ALBION (professional, February 1904). Walsall (June 1905). Willenhall Swifts (September 1907). Clifton Victoria FC (August 1908, retired through injury, May 1910). Later engaged in steel work.

■ No relation to the player above, Harry Aston was a positive centre-forward, slight in build, who was 'bought out' of the Army (Royal Artillery) by Albion, with whom he had a useful strike record, before losing his place to Fred Shinton. He made his League debut for the club away at Derby in April 1904 and also played in 10 second XI matches.

BACHE, Harold Godfrey

Centre-forward: 14 apps. 4 goals.

Born: Churchill near Kidderminster, 20 August 1889.
Died: France, 16 February 1916.
Career: King Edward Grammar School (Birmingham). Cambridge University (1905). The Corinthians (between 1906–14). West Bromwich Springfield FC (1908–09). Staffordshire Youths (1909–10). Eastbourne FC (1911–12). ALBION (February 1914 until his death).

■ Brilliant England amateur international centre-forward Harold Bache was tragically killed while serving with the Lancashire Fusiliers in France in 1916. He won seven amateur caps (1910–13), and in one game against France he hit seven goals in a 20–0 win. He also played for the Football League, and was a fine all-round sportsman, also excelling at rugby, cricket (he represented

Worcestershire) and athletics. He made his Albion debut in the away FA Cup tie with Aston Villa in February 1914 and scored his first goal for the club in a 4–1 League victory at Bradford in October of that same year. He also netted twice when Aston Villa were defeated 3–2 in the final of the Birmingham Charity Cup in 1915.
* Bache is remembered on Panel 33 of The Menin Gate memorial at Ypres, Belgium.

BADDELEY, George

Half-back: 157 apps. 1 goal.

Born: Fegg Hayes, Stoke-on-Trent, 8 May 1874.
Died: West Bromwich, July 1952.
Career: Fegg Hayes Church of England School. Ball Heath. Burslem Swifts. Pitshill FC (1897). Biddulph FC (1899). Stoke (May 1900). ALBION (£250, June 1908, retired, May 1914). Later worked in the upholstery trade.

■ Strong in all aspects of half-back play, George Baddeley, a former Stoke captain who made over 200 appearances for the Potters, spent six seasons with Albion, during which time he gained a Second

Division championship medal in 1911 and an FA Cup runners'-up medal a year later playing against Barnsley. When he played his last League game for Albion against Sheffield Wednesday in April 1914, Baddeley was almost 40 years of age – the oldest player ever to appear in a senior game for the Baggies. He made his debut for the club away at Grimsby Town in September 1908, and most of his last season at The Hawthorns was spent in the reserves. On his retirement, Baddeley became a publican in West Bromwich.
* Brother Sam Baddeley (born in 1884) played for Burlsem Port Vale and Stoke.

BALDWIN, Harold

Goalkeeper: 5 apps.

Born: Erdington, Birmingham, 17 July 1920.
Career: Kingsbury Road Council School (Erdington). Sutton Town (1935). ALBION (professional, January 1937). Brighton & Hove Albion (July 1939). Kettering Town (August 1952). Walsall (January 1954). Wellington Town (July 1955, retired, May 1957). Worked briefly in industry before moving to Poole, Dorset.

■ Deputy to Jimmy Adams at The Hawthorns, Harry Baldwin, who made his Baggies debut against Birmingham in the League home game in April 1938, was a safe handler of the ball who could deal with any shot efficiently. After leaving Albion, he made 164 League appearances for Brighton, saving 11 penalties out of 15 over a period of two seasons, including five in a row. He was also a fine cricketer and competent tennis player.

BALIS, Igor

Full-back: 63+12 apps. 4 goals.

Born: Zalozinik, Slovakia, 5 January 1970.
Career: FC Zalozinik (1988). Slovan Bratislava (briefly, 1994). Spartak Trnava (May, 1995). ALBION (£150,000, November 2000, retired through injury, July 2003). Returned to Slovakia.

■ Tall, rangy Slovakian international right wing-back Igor Balis netted a last minute penalty to give Albion victory at Bradford City in their penultimate League game of the 2001–02 season and as a result Premiership football was just 90 minutes away. Prior to moving to The Hawthorns, Balis had scored five goals in

136 League games for Spartak Trnava. It was almost four months before he finally dislodged Des Lyttle to claim a place in Albion's first team, having made his debut for the club against Nottingham Forest (home) in December 2000 (won 3–0). He quickly became a vital cog in the playing mechanism and was a firm favourite with the fans. Unfortunately, injury forced him to quit top-line football at the end of the 2002–03 season. He netted once in 41 full internationals for Slovakia and also appeared in two 'other' games for his country.

BALL, Horace George

Centre-forward: 16 apps. 9 goals.

Born: Great Bridge, West Bromwich, 22 April 1921.
Died: West Bromwich, c.1990.
Career: Beeches Road School. Gold's Green Methodists (1937). ALBION (amateur, January 1939, professional, July 1944). Darlaston (May 1946). Banbury Spencer (August 1949, retired through injury, May 1953). Later worked in industry in Tipton.

■ A big, strong, courageous centre-forward, Horace Ball's career was ruined by World War Two, during which time he made all his senior appearances, his debut coming against Aston Villa in the Football League North in October 1943.

He scored 19 goals in only 23 Central League games for the Baggies.

BAMFORD, John Arthur Edward

Outside-left: 3 apps.

Born: Weedon near Aylesbury, Bucks, 12 December 1880.
Died: Northampton, March 1941.
Career: Weedon schoolboy & junior football. Wellingborough (1900). ALBION (professional, February 1905). Wellingborough (June 1906–May 1908). Later became a publican and served as private number 189617 with the 119th Heavy Battery, BFO France, during World War One.

■ Arthur Bamford was a neat and tidy left-winger, a shade on the small side, who was initially understudy to Albert Lewis and then Ernie Perkins and Billy Law during his time at The Hawthorns. He made his Albion League debut against Glossop (home) in March 1905 and also played in 14 second-team matches.

BANKS, George Ernest

Centre-forward: 17 apps. 110 goals.

Born: Wednesbury, 28 March 1919.
Died: Wednesbury, Summer 1992.
Career: Clayhanger Villa. Brownhills Albion (1932). ALBION (amateur, June 1933, groundstaff, May 1935, professional

June 1938). *Mansfield Town (£1,200, November 1947). Hereford United (August 1949). Dudley Town. Darlaston and others before taking over as groundsman at the Revo Works (to 1974).*

■ A zealous centre-forward, George Banks's first-team outings were restricted due to the presence of so many other fine strikers who were at the club around the same time. He scored twice on his League debut against Norwich City in April 1939. He also netted 19 times in 51 Central League games for the Baggies before becoming Mansfield's top-scorer with 14 goals in 27 games in 1947–48.

BANKS, Ian Frederick

Midfield: 2+2 apps.

Born: Mexborough, 9 January 1961. Career: Mexborough Schools. Barnsley (apprentice, July 1977, professional, January 1979). Leicester City (£100,000, June 1983). Huddersfield Town (£45,000, September 1986). Bradford City (£180,000, July 1988). ALBION (£100,000, March 1989). Barnsley (July 1989). Rotherham United (July 1992). Darlington (August 1994–May 1995). Emley Town (player-coach, 1997–98). Chesterfield (assistant manager). Bradford City (coach, January 2002). Wakefield and Emley (manager, 2003–05).

■ A very competitive hard-tackling midfield player with a cracking shot, Ian Banks had already made close on 400 club appearances (including 195 for Barnsley and 102 for Leicester) before joining Albion, for whom he made his debut against Chelsea in April 1989. He failed to settle down at The Hawthorns and departed after staying for just four months. He later made a further 250 appearances at senior level before being freed from the Feethams at the end of the 1994–95 season. He helped Barnsley win promotion from the Fourth to the Second Division between 1980 and 1983 and netted more than 100 goals, including a hat-trick for the Tykes in a 5–3 Zenith Data Systems Cup victory at The Hawthorns in November 1990. He also made three appearances for the Baggies in the Central League.

BANKS, John

Half-back/outside-left: 134 apps. 6 goals.

Born: West Bromwich, 14 May 1874.

Died: Barrow-in-Furness, January 1947. Career: Christ Church FC. Stourbridge (1890). Oldbury Broadwell (1891). Oldbury Town (1892). ALBION (December 1893). Newton Heath (August 1901). Plymouth Argyle (May 1903). Leyton FC (July 1906). Nottingham Forest (briefly). Exeter City (player-coach, December 1907, trainer 1910–11). Barrow (trainer/part-time coach for 26 years, 1912–38).

■ Jack Banks, an efficient, versatile player, spent seven years with Albion, making his debut in the League home game with Blackburn Rovers in January 1894 before going on to collect a runners'-up medal in the 1895 FA Cup final. He also participated in more than 120 'other' first-team games for the club and then played 44 times for Newton Heath/Manchester United before assisting Plymouth in their first season in the Southern League (1903–04). He was Exeter's first ever professional footballer and was with Barrow when the Cumbrian club gained election to the Third Division North in 1921. Just prior to him leaving The Hawthorns, one newspaper correspondent wrote: 'Banks possesses good speed, manoeuvres dexterously, covering a lot of ground, and usually passes to prime advantage'. He gave Barrow excellent service as a trainer and occasional coach.

BANNISTER, Gary

Striker: 68+13 apps. 20 goals.

Born: Warrington, 22 July 1960. Career: Coventry City (apprentice, July 1976, professional, May 1978). Sheffield Wednesday (£100,000, August 1981). Queen's Park Rangers (£200,000, August 1984). Coventry City (£300,000, March 1988). Albion (£250,000, March 1990). Oxford United (on loan, March–May 1992). Nottingham Forest (August 1992). Stoke City (May 1993). FC Seiko, Hong Kong (summer 1994). Lincoln City (September 1994). Darlington (player-coach, August 1995–May 1996). Porthleven FC, Cornwall (coach). In 2005 runs a bed and breakfast business in Cornwall.

■ A very positive, all-action goalscorer, as keen as mustard with the knack of scoring goals out of nothing, Gary Bannister had a fine career spanning 20 years, netting a total of 206 goals in well

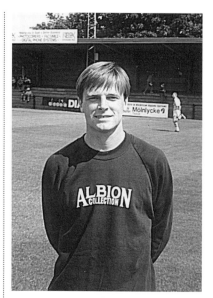

over 600 League and cup matches. He made his debut for Albion against Blackburn Rovers (away) in March 1990, and he also scored five goals in six second-team games. After leaving The Hawthorns, he helped Darlington reach the 1996 play-off final at Wembley. He was twice a runner-up in Wembley finals: with QPR in the League Cup in 1985 and Darlington in the play-offs in 1996. He had earlier gained an England under-21 cap as a Sheffield Wednesday player.

BANNISTER, Jack

Wing-half: 9 apps.

Born: Chesterfield, 26 January 1942. Career: Manor Secondary Modern School (Chesterfield). Cheshire & Chesterfield Boys (1957). ALBION (amateur February 1958, professional August 1959). Scunthorpe United (£2,700, June 1964). Crystal Palace (July 1965). Luton Town (October 1968). Cambridge United (May 1971–May 1974). Dunstable Town (June 1974, retired May 1976). Now living in Houghton Regis near Dunstable.

■ A half-back of average ability, Jackie Bannister appeared in 253 League games during his professional career. He made his First Division debut for Albion against Manchester City (away) in April 1960 and thereafter was reserve to the likes of Bobby Robson and Chuck Drury, playing in 141 Central League games and scoring seven goals. After leaving The Hawthorns, he starred with several other Albion players, including Davey Burnside, Tony

Millington, Keith Smith, Brian Whitehouse and Brian Wood, for Palace for whom he made 129 competitive appearances.

BARHAM, Mark Francis

Wide-midfield: 5 apps.

Born: Folkestone, 12 July 1972.
Career: Norwich City (apprentice, June 1978, professional, April 1980). Huddersfield Town (£100,000, July 1987). Middlesbrough (November 1988). ALBION (free, September 1989). Brighton and Hove Albion (on loan, January–March 1990, signed permanently, December 1989). Shrewsbury Town (non-contract, September–December 1992). Fakenham Town (manager, April 1997–May 1999).

■ During his time at Carrow Road, Mark Barham, who preferred the right-wing position, was capped by England at both youth and senior levels (winning two caps in the latter category, both in 1983). He had already amassed over 200 competitive appearances before joining Albion, for whom he made his League debut against Watford in October 1989. He also played in eight Central League games but unfortunately never settled down at The Hawthorns and moved to the other Albion (Brighton) after just three months. He suffered what was thought to be a crippling knee injury in December 1983 but recovered full fitness and went on to play for almost another 10 years. A fast, direct footballer with

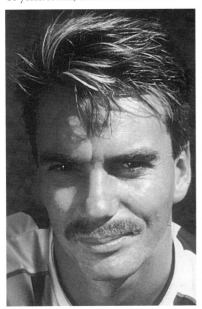

neat skills, he added a further 80 League appearances to his tally with his last two clubs.
* Barham's father won the *News of the World* amateur golf tournament and also played roller-hockey for England.

BARKER, Robert Campbell

Outside-left: 14 apps. 2 goals.

Born: Kinglassie, Fife, 1 December 1927.
Career: Kelty Public & Lower Oakfield Schools (Fife). West Burnside Rovers (1941). Kelty Rangers. Served at RAF Bovington during World War Two. ALBION (professional, September 1945). Shrewsbury Town (August 1950). Headington United (July 1951). Worcester City (January 1952). Nuneaton Borough (May 1954–May 1965). Now lives in Branksome near Poole, Dorset.

■ Bobby Barker was a ball-playing left-winger of fair speed whose crosses were often fast and accurate. He made his debut for the club against Lincoln City (away) in September 1948 and then contested the number 11 shirt with Frank Hodgetts, Roy Finch, Arthur Smith and Ernie Shepherd, and as a result his first-team outings were limited. He had the misfortune to break an arm, a wrist and a leg in the space of 12 months (1946–47). Barker did very well in non-League football later in his career, making over 200 appearances for Nuneaton.

BARLOW, Raymond John

Half-back, inside/centre-forward: 482 apps. 48 goals.

Born: Swindon, 17 August 1926.
Career: Sandford Street School (Swindon). Swindon Town (trialist, early 1942). Garrards FC (Swindon, 1942). ALBION (amateur, June 1944, professional November 1944). Swindon Town (World War Two guest, 1945–46). Birmingham City (June 1960). Stourbridge (August 1961 as experienced cover, retired, May 1962). West Bromwich Albion Old Stars (for 12 years, 1969–81). On his retirement from competitive football in 1962, Barlow took over a tobacconist and confectionary shop in West Bromwich (previously run by Albion's 1931 cup-winning skipper, Tommy Glidden) and later managed a sub-post office/newsagents business near

Stourbridge. He now lives in Pedmore near Stourbridge.

■ One of the finest footballers ever to don an Albion shirt, Ray Barlow was mainly a left-half but could also play equally as well at centre-half, centre-forward and inside-left. He made his debut for the club against Walsall in a wartime League Cup game in February 1945, following up with his League debut against Newport County (away) in September 1946, when he scored in a resounding 7–2 win. A wonderfully gifted footballer, elegant in style and long-striding, he could pass a ball with pin-point accuracy and possessed a strong right-footed shot. The driving force in Albion's midfield during the early part of the 1950s, he served the club for a total of 16 years, during which time he appeared in 403 League games. He won an FA Cup medal in 1954 and in that same year gained his only full England cap against Northern Ireland in Belfast (starring in a 2–0 win). He also represented England 'B', the Football League and the FA XI and netted 10 goals in 41 Central League games for Albion.

BARNES, Peter Simon

Left-winger: 90+2 apps. 25 goals.

Born: Manchester, 10 June 1957.
Career: Chorlton High Grammar School (Manchester). Manchester & District Schools. Gatley Rangers (1970).

■ A fast-raiding left-winger, Peter Barnes had a fine career that spanned some 25 years. Starting out initially as a schoolboy with Manchester City, he moved to The Hawthorns for a record fee in 1979, signed by manager Ron Atkinson as a straight replacement for Laurie Cunningham and Willie Johnston. Indeed, it was Barnes who had kept Cunningham out of the England team. He made his League debut on the opening day of the 1979–80 campaign against Derby County, having already scored in Albion's Centenary match victory over Ajax a week earlier. He did well with Albion, having an excellent first season when he netted 16 goals in 45 games, including a hat-trick in a 4–4 League home draw with Bolton. After that, he became something of a soccer nomad, serving a number of clubs while accumulating a tremendous record of almost 320 League appearances and 47 goals. A former schoolboy and youth international, he went on to win 22 full caps for England, played once for the 'B' team and had nine outings at under-21 level. He helped Manchester City win the 1976 League Cup, scoring in the final against Newcastle United. A year earlier he had been voted the PFA's 'Young Footballer of the Year'.

BARNSLEY, Geoffrey Robert Thomas

Goalkeeper: 1 app.

Born: Bilston, 9 November 1935.
Career: Bilston Schools. Birmingham

Manchester City (schoolboy forms, apprentice, June 1971, professional, August 1974). ALBION (£748,000, July 1979). Leeds United (£930,000, August 1981). Real Betis, Spain (on loan, August 1982). West Ham United (briefly). Melbourne JUST (for one month, April 1984). Manchester United (on loan, May 1984). Coventry City (£65,000, October 1984). Manchester United (July 1985). Manchester City (£30,000, January 1987). Bolton Wanderers (on loan, October 1987). Port Vale (on loan, December 1987). Hull City (March 1988). Drogheda United (April–May 1988). Sporting Farense, Portugal (August–September 1988). Bolton Wanderers (November 1988). Sunderland (February 1989). Tampa Bay Rowdies, NASL (April–August 1990). Northwich Victoria (August 1990). Wrexham (one week, September 1990). Radcliffe Borough (November 1990–May 1991). Mossley (July–October 1991). Cliftonville, Ireland (November 1992–93). Stockport County. Hamrun Spartans, Malta. Manchester City (part-time coach and Youth Development officer, August 1994). Runcorn (manager, August 1996–March 1997). Later employed as a part-time coach at the Manchester City School of Excellence (1997–98 – with three more ex-Albion players, Len Cantello, Asa Hartford and Gary Owen). Also coached in Norway and worked as a broadcaster (on football) with Piccadilly Radio (Manchester).

County Youths. Erdington Albion (1949). Wolverhampton Wanderers (amateur trialist, 1950). ALBION (amateur, May 1951, professional, December 1952). Plymouth Argyle (June 1957). Norwich City £2,000, May 1961). Torquay United (December 1962). Dudley Town (July 1964). Hednesford Town (November 1964). Bilston Town, Dudley Town (1969). Darlaston (August 1970, retired, May 1973). Brierley Hill (manager, 1979–80). Oldswinford (assistant manager, 1980–81). Tipton Town (manager, 1981–86). Oldswinford (manager, October 1986–May 1987). Also assisted West Bromwich Albion All Stars, 1979–81. He now lives in Tipton.

■ Quick in movement and commendably smart but a poor kicker of a dead ball, light-weight Geoff Barnsley was unfortunate to be with Albion at the same time as two other fine goalkeepers, Norman Heath and Jimmy Sanders. His only First Division outing for the club was at Preston in January 1955, although he did play in 34 Central League matches. After leaving The Hawthorns, he made almost 150 appearances for Plymouth and briefly managed Steve Bull at Tipton Town.

BARRON, Paul George

Goalkeeper: 73 apps.

Born: Woolwich, London, 16 September 1953.
Career: Erith Grammar School. Borough Road College (Isleworth). Kent Schoolboys. Kent Youth. Welling United (1971). Wycombe Wanderers (1973). Slough Town (1975). Plymouth Argyle (full-time professional, July 1976). Arsenal (£70,000, July 1978). Crystal Palace (£140,000 + Clive Allen and Kenny Sansom, August 1980). ALBION (£60,000, December 1982). Stoke City (on loan, January–February 1985). Queen's Park Rangers (£35,000, March 1985). Reading (on loan, December 1986). Welling United (August 1988–May 1989). Cheltenham Town (August 1990). Welling United (November 1990–January 1991). After two years running his own fitness club in Birmingham and a spell with Cheltenham Town, Barron was appointed coach at Aston Villa and later held a similar position with Middlesbrough before taking over as fitness/specialist coach at The Riverside Stadium, accompanied by

another ex-Albion 'keeper, Bob Ward, 'Boro's trainer.

■ Goalkeeper Paul Barron, 6ft 2in tall and 13st 6lb in weight, qualified as a PE instructor before becoming a professional footballer. He spent one season at Home Park before attracting the attention of Arsenal. He failed to establish himself in the first team at Highbury but played in 90 League games for Palace prior to taking over from Tony Godden at The Hawthorns, making his Albion debut away at Manchester United in January 1983. He also played in 13 second XI games. A safe handler of the ball, he was ever-present in 1983–84 (making 50 appearances) but then lost his place to a revitalised Godden the following season. During his career Barrow played in more than 300 first-team matches.
* His father, George, played as an amateur for Tottenham Hotspur.

BARTLETT, Kevin Francis

Forward: 31+12 apps. 11 goals.

Born: Portsmouth, 12 October 1962.
Career: Portsmouth schoolboy football. Portsmouth (apprentice, 1978, professional, October 1980). Fareham Town. Cardiff City (September 1986). ALBION (£100,000, February 1989). Notts County (March 1990). Port Vale (on loan, September 1992). Cambridge United (March–May 1993).

■ A pacy striker with an eye for goal, Kevin Bartlett joined Albion at a time

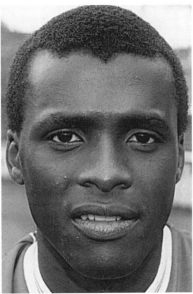

when a place in the Second Division play-offs was still a possibility. He made his debut against Bradford City (away) in February 1989 and certainly added a spark to the attack but struggled to hold down a place in the side the following season, and after less than 50 outings for the club (plus another 16 in the reserves) he moved to Meadow Lane. During his League career he scored 69 goals in 244 appearances, helping Cardiff win promotion from the Fourth Division in 1988.

BASSETT, Idris Charles Henry

Full-back: 100 apps.

Born: Brithdir, Glamorgan, 12 March 1915.
Died: Birmingham, 7 September 1979.
Career: Sutton Town (1933). ALBION (professional, October 1936, retired through injury/ill-health, January 1944).

■ No relation to Billy Bassett, Idris Bassett was a tough-tackling, never-say-die full-back, who played most of his football for Albion during World War Two, having made his League debut against Wolves at Molineux in May 1938 when the Baggies were on their way into the Second Division. He also played in 55 Central League games (one goal scored).
* His brother, William Edward George Bassett, played for Wolves, Cardiff City and Crystal Palace.

BASSETT, William Isaiah, JP

Outside-right: 311 apps. 77 goals.

Born: West Bromwich, 27 January 1869.
Died: West Bromwich, 9 April 1937.
Career: Christ Church School (West Bromwich). Oak Villa (1883). West Bromwich Strollers (not Albion, 1884). Old Church Club (1885). ALBION (professional, August 1886, retired, April 1899, appointed coach at The Hawthorns, looking after the younger players). Entered the licensing trade, while also taking an interest in the cinema. ALBION (director, August 1905, then chairman from 1908, a position he retained until his death). In 1903–04 he qualified as a Football League linesman.

■ One of the club's all-time greats, Billy Bassett was, for 13 years, the star of

club (as player, coach, shareholder, director and chairman). From 1930 to 1937 he was a member of the Football League management committee, being on the international selection panel in 1936–37. Bassett, who was appointed Justice of the Peace in 1935, died shortly before the Baggies FA Cup semi-final defeat by Preston North End at Highbury in 1937, and in an obituary the Albion programme editor described him as 'a guide, philosopher and friend' to the club, and the Football League secretary, Fred Howarth, declared him to be 'the most popular man in the game.'

* Billy Bassett's son, Norman, and his brother, Harry, were both associated with Albion. Norman was a director of the club (1937–52 – following Billy into office) and Harry was a reserve inside-right who partnered Billy for the first time on the wing against the Birmingham & District side in April 1892.

BASTOCK, Archibald Middleship Esmond

Forward: 34 apps. 13 goals.

Born: Brecon, Wales, 7 April 1869.
Died: Eastleigh, Hampshire, 13 October 1954.
Career: Singers FC (Coventry). Smethwick FC (1886). Birmingham St George (1888). Shrewsbury Town (1890). ALBION (July 1892). Burton Swifts (May 1894). Eastleigh FC (1896–1922) while also working for a Hampshire-based railway company, a job he did for many years.

■ Welsh international (one cap gained against Ireland in 1892 as a Shrewsbury player) Archie Bastock was earning around £2.50 per week at Albion for whom he made his League debut against Bolton Wanderers (away) in September 1892. A shade on the slow side, he was nevertheless a neat and compact forward with strong right-foot shot, who helped Albion win the Birmingham Senior Cup in 1894 and Eastleigh complete the Salisbury League and Cup double in the early 1900s. Bastock, who also played in 30 'other' first-team matches for Albion and scored twice in the drawn final of the Birmingham Cup v Wolves in 1894, made his final appearance on a football field at the age of 53.

NB: Some reference books list this player's surname as Bostock.

Albion's forward-line, firstly at inside-right (he made his debut in that position against Wednesbury Old Athletic in the FA Cup in October 1887) and then more predominantly on the right-wing. Quick, direct and highly effective, he possessed superb ball-control and could score goals as well as make them. He averaged a goal every four games for Albion, claiming a total of 135 in 560 first-team appearances, with 77 coming in 311 major competitive matches. He gained two FA Cup winners medals: in 1888 against Preston North End and in 1892 against Aston Villa, as well as playing in the 1895 losing final, also against Villa. He scored twice when Albion beat Great Bridge Unity 10–1 in the final of the West Bromwich Charity Cup in 1888. Bassett won a total of 16 full caps for England (eight in successive international matches against Scotland). He also represented the Football League in three Inter-League matches between 1891 and 1897, played for an England XI, a Football League XI and an FA XI, as well as appearing in several international trials. After retiring and becoming a director and then chairman of the club for a period of 27 years, from 1905 to 1932, he rarely missed a board meeting and his influence at Albion was incalculable. At the club's AGM in 1936 he was presented with a silver casket and splendid 'illuminated' scroll/address on the occasion of his completion of 50 years' service with the

BATSON, Brendon Martin, MBE

Right-back: 220 apps. 2 goals.

Born: St George, Grenada, Windward Islands, 6 February 1953.
Career: Arsenal. Cambridge United. ALBION (£30,000, February 1978, retired, May 1984). Joined PFA, rising to the position of deputy chief executive. Witton Albion (1984–85) and West Bromwich Albion All Stars (1984–87). ALBION (as managing director, July 2002–June 2003). Now working as a consultant for the FA.

■ Brendon Batson was a very efficient footballing right-back, keen to overlap, who amassed more than 400 appearances at club level, helping Cambridge win the Fourth Division title and Albion reach two major cup semi-finals and qualify for the UEFA Cup. He was manager Ron Atkinson's first signing for Albion, having made his League debut against the Baggies in 1971 when playing for Arsenal, with whom he won an FA Youth Cup winners medal that same year. His Albion debut came in the local derby away at

Birmingham City a few days after joining. He also played in seven Central League games for the club. Capped three times by England 'B' in 1980, Batson's career came to an end at the age of 31, and after his testimonial match he immediately joined the PFA. Returning to The Hawthorns in 2002, he was placed in charge of Footballing Matters, a position he held for just 12 months. He was awarded the MBE in 2001.

BAUGH, Richard Horace

Full-back: 65 apps.

Born: Wolverhampton, 6 March 1896.
Died: Wolverhampton, 1972.
Career: Stafford Road School. Stafford Road FC (1914). Wolverhampton Wanderers (professional, August 1918). Cardiff City (April 1921). Wolverhampton Wanderers (May 1921). ALBION (£500, June 1924). Exeter City (£137, May 1929). Kidderminster Harriers (January 1932, retired, April 1936).

■ Stocky full-back Dicky Baugh was a dogged performer and the dressing room comedian, who had one excellent season out of the five he spent at The Hawthorns, that of 1925–26 when he made 33 appearances, mainly as partner to Joe Smith. He had earlier made his senior debut in the First Division away game at Preston in February 1925. He also played in 93 second XI games for the club, gaining a Central League championship medal in the 1926–27 seasonwhen he partnered Bob Finch. Baugh was the subject of a 'cancelled'

transfer in 1921 when, after missing that season's FA Cup final through injury, he was induced by an agent to sign for Cardiff City. However, a joint FA/Welsh FA Commission investigated the deal and subsequently the move was declared null and void, fining Cardiff £50 and Baugh £20.
* His father Dicky Senior made 227 appearances for Wolves, played in three FA Cup finals and won two England caps.

BAYLISS, Albert Edward James Matthias

Forward: 95 apps. 36 goals.

Born: Tipton, 14 January 1863.
Died: West Bromwich, 19 August 1933.
Career: Great Bridge & Horseley Heath Council Schools. Great Bridge Unity (1878). Tipton Providence (1879). Wednesbury Old Athletic (1880). ALBION (August 1884, professional August 1885, retired March 1892). Walsall Town (guest, 1884–85). ALBION (director 1891–1905, appointed life member of club in August 1909).

■ Gentleman 'Jem' Bayliss ('Jem' was derived from the initials of three of his Christian names) was still an active player when appointed as a director when the club became a limited company in August 1891. He remained on the board for 14 years, until replaced by his former playing colleague Billy Bassett. During his eight years as an Albion player, Bayliss – a quality footballer – played in almost 300 first-team matches for Albion (mainly friendlies and local Cup competitions)

and averaged more than a goal every two games, claiming an overall total of 158, including 121 in three seasons, 1885–88. He scored on his senior debut against Derby Street Junction (away) in the FA Cup in October 1884 and appeared in three successive FA Cup finals – 1886, 1887 and 1888 – gaining a winners' medal in the latter. He also grabbed four goals in Albion's 10–1 West Bromwich Charity Cup final win over Great Bridge Unity in 1888 and scored in three Staffordshire Cup final victories – claiming two when Stoke were beaten 4–2 in 1886; two more in a 4–0 victory over Walsall Swifts in 1887 and another when Leek lost 2–1 in 1889. Initially an out-and-out centre-forward, he was successfully converted into a right-half and gained his only full England cap in that position against Ireland in March 1891 (won 6–1). Six years later he actually read his own obituary in a local paper after returning from a holiday in Gibraltar. It was rumoured that while abroad he had developed typhoid fever and died of the ailment at his Great Bridge home. Bayliss, despite being rather upset at what he had read, quickly reported himself fit and well and, in fact, lived for another 36 years.

BEDFORD, Lewis

Left-winger: 3 apps.

Born: Erdington, Birmingham, 26 March 1904.
Died: Walsall, August 1975.
Career: Icknield Street Council School (Hockley). ALBION (amateur, November 1920, professional, March 1921). Walsall (June 1922). Sheffield Wednesday (June 1925). Walsall (September 1926). Nelson (March 1927). Luton Town (August 1928). Walsall (December 1929). Bloxwich Strollers (May 1931). Walsall Wood (1933, retired, August 1940). Later worked as a shop manager.

■ A midget winger, fast and tricky, Lewis Bedford made his Albion League debut at the age of 17 against Arsenal in March 1921. He found it difficult to get into the first XI at The Hawthorns (owing to the form and presence of Howard Gregory), but he certainly did well with Walsall, appearing in 140 games for the Saddlers during his three spells at Fellows Park. He scored once in 14 Central League games for Albion.

BEESLEY, Paul

Defender: 8 apps.

Born: Liverpool, 21 July 1965.
Career: Marine FC (Liverpool). Wigan Athletic (free, professional, September 1984). Leyton Orient (£175,000, October 1989). Sheffield United (£375,000, July 1990). Leeds United (£250,000 August 1995). Manchester City (£500,000, February 1997). Port Vale (December 1997–January 1998). ALBION (on loan, March–May 1998). Port Vale (free, August 1998). Blackpool (free, July 1999). Chester City (free, July 2000). Ballymena United (August 2001). Stalybridge Celtic (November 2001–May 2002).

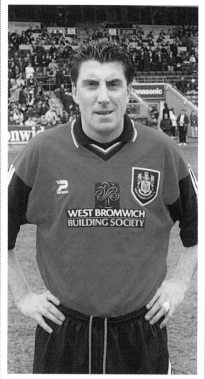

■ Paul Beesley, a rugged, quick-tackling defender, made almost 200 appearances for Sheffield United. Hugely popular with the Bramall Lane fans, he missed out on an FA Cup semi-final appearance in 1993 before his subsequent transfer to Elland Road. He made 155 League appearances for Wigan but only eight with Albion at the end of the 1997–98 season, his debut coming against Norwich City (away).

BELL, George

Outside-left: 16 apps. 7 goals.

Born: West Bromwich, 4 March 1861.

Died: West Bromwich, May 1959, aged 89.
Career: Beeches Road School. George Salter Works. ALBION (November 1878, professional, August 1885). Kidderminster Harriers (June 1888–May 1890). Also played briefly for Wednesbury Old Athletic. Returned to the factory floor after retiring from football.

■ Although an Albion player prior to the introduction of League football (1888), George Bell was a regular in the side for almost a decade and, overall, played in more than 150 games for the club, scoring at least 50 goals, including the winner in the 1883 Staffordshire Cup final against Stoke (Albion's first trophy success). An elusive player, quick and willing, he delivered accurate crosses and certainly had an eye for goal. He was in the very first 'Albion' team against Hudson's in November 1878, and five years later he made his senior debut against Wednesbury Town, the Throstles' first ever FA Cup tie.
* George was cousin to Harry (see below).

BELL, Harry

Full-back: 14 apps.

Born: West Bromwich, 18 April 1862.
Died: South Africa, 18 January 1948.
Career: Beeches Road School. George Salter Works. ALBION (September 1879, professional, August 1885, retired through injury, June 1887). Later Albion's assistant trainer (1905–07) and gateman at The Hawthorns prior to emigrating to South Africa in 1921.

■ A steady, reliable full-back and one of the strongest tacklers of his era, Harry Bell was a fitness fanatic, who also played in well over 100 first-team games for Albion with his 14 senior outings all coming in the FA Cup, the competition in which he made his first-team debut against Wednesbury Town in November 1883.

BELL, Stanley Lawrence Thomas

Utility forward: 17 apps. 6 goals.

Born: Langbank, Renfrewshire, 5 May 1875.
Died: Glasgow, Scotland, 1955.
Career: Langbank Schools. Langbank

(1891). Dumbarton (1892). Third Lanark (1893). Sheffield Wednesday (August 1895). Everton (August 1897). Bolton Wanderers (July 1899). Brentford (July 1903). ALBION (June 1904). Hibernian (May 1905, retired, May 1912). Later worked at a shipyard in Scotland.

■ Lawrie Bell was a much-travelled, constructive utility forward who preferred the centre-forward position. Having done well north of the border, he gained an FA Cup medal with Sheffield Wednesday (1896) and netted 13 goals in 54 games for the Owls, following up with nine in 48 appearances for Everton and 45 in 103 outings for Bolton. After his one season with Albion, when he suffered a few injury problems after making an impressive debut against Burnley (away) in September 1904, he returned to Scotland where he ended his career with well over 300 appearances to his credit. He was rewarded with Scottish League representative honours (against the Irish League) as a Third Lanark player in 1895 and was twice named as reserve to the full international side.

BELL, Thomas

Inside-forward: 15 apps. 5 goals.

*Born: Airth, Falkirk, 14 February 1917.
Died: Scotland, May 1980.
Career: Airth Schools. Airth Bluebell (1933). Forth Rangers (1935). Cambuslang Rangers (1936). ALBION (£125, professional, August 1939, retired through injury, May 1946). Returned to live and work in Scotland.*

■ A clever exponent of the best type of Scottish football, Tommy Bell, it was thought, would have developed into a classy inside-forward but was sadly forced to retire prematurely after suffering serious back injuries during World War Two. He made his Albion debut in a Wartime Regional League game against Leicester City (home) in November 1939.

BENJAMIN, Ian Treacy

Midfielder/striker: 1+1 apps.

*Born: Nottingham, 11 December 1961.
Career: Nottingham schoolboy football. Sheffield United (apprentice, April 1977, professional, May 1979). ALBION (£125,000, May 1979). Notts County*

(February 1982). Peterborough United (August 1982). Northampton Town (August 1984). Cambridge United (October 1987). Chester City (July 1988). Exeter City (February 1989). Southend United (March 1990). Luton Town (November 1992). Brentford (September 1993). Wigan Athletic (September 1994). Bury Town (1995). Ilkeston Town. Kettering Town (July 1996–May 1997). Chelmsford City (briefly). Corby Town (player-manager, September 1997–January 1998). Raunds Town (February 1998). Warboys Town (player, August 1999, later manager to December 2001). Soham Town Rangers (January–May 2002). Wisbech Town (August 2002–April 2003).

■ Tall midfield/striker Ian Benjamin did exceedingly well in the lower divisions, amassing over 560 appearances and scoring 149 goals, this after just two first-team outings for Albion following his £125,000 transfer from Bramall Lane. His debut was against Ipswich Town (away) in November 1980 (as a 'sub'). He also played in 90 Central League games (12 goals scored). An England youth international, he helped Northampton win the Fourth Division championship in 1987, when he was also voted the Cobblers' 'Player of the Year.' Over an eight-year period, 1995–2003, Benjamin served with no fewer than nine different non-League clubs.

BENJAMIN, Trevor Junior

Striker: 0+3 apps. 1 goal.

*Born: Kettering, 8 February 1979.
Career: Kettering schools. Cambridge United (apprentice, April 1995, professional, February 1997). Leicester City (£1 million, July 2000). Crystal Palace (on loan, December 2001). Norwich City (on loan, February 2002). ALBION (on loan, March–May 2002). Gillingham (on loan, September 2003). Rushden and Diamonds (on loan, November–December 2003). Brighton and Hove Albion (on loan, January 2004). Northampton Town (on loan, December 2004, signed permanently, January 2005). Coventry City (February 2005). Peterborough (free, July 2005).*

■ Powerfully-built, England under-21 international striker Trevor Benjamin was recruited by Albion manager Gary Megson towards the end of the 2001–02 promotion-winning campaign. He

blotted his copybook to a certain degree by getting himself sent off in a 1–0 win at Coventry, having earlier made a scoring debut for the club against Barnsley (won 3–1). He helped Leicester regain their Premiership status the following season when he also took his tally of career League and cup appearances past the 200 mark (50 goals).

BENNETT, Dean Alan

Midfield: 0+1 app.

*Born: Wolverhampton, 13 December 1977.
Career: Aston Villa (juniors, April 1995). ALBION (trialist, February 1996, apprentice, April 1996, professional, December 1996). Bromsgrove Rovers (free, September 1998). Kidderminster Harriers (£30,000, January 1999). Wrexham (on loan, July 2004, signed 2005).*

■ Dean Bennett, a lively attacking midfielder, was introduced to League football by manager Ray Harford as an 85th minute substitute in Albion's final League home game of the 1996–97 season against Grimsby Town, and, therefore, must be regarded as one of the players with the shortest senior careers ever at the club. He did, however, have 15 outings in Albion's Central League side.

An England semi-professional, he made 173 first-team appearances for Kidderminster before teaming up with former Albion boss Denis Smith at Wrexham. He helped Wrexham win the LDV Vans trophy in 2005.

BENNETT, Martyn

Defender: 217+1 apps. 10 goals.

Born: Great Barr, Birmingham, 4 August 1961.

Career: Pheasey Junior & Aldridge Comprehensive Schools. Birmingham & Aston Boys. Aldridge & Brownhills Schools. Walsall & District Schools. West Midland County Schools. Streetly FC (1976). ALBION (apprentice, August 1977, professional, August 1978). Worcester City (1990–91). Cheltenham Town (1991–92). Later managed both Worcester City and Cheltenham. Retired from football in 1994. Now living and working in Ireland.

■ Martyn Bennett was an excellent central defender who also played at right-back and in midfield. After understudying Ally Robertson and John Wile for a number of years, he finally established himself in Albion's back division during the 1980–81 campaign and quickly caught the eye of former Chelsea and Spurs striker Jimmy Greaves, who said: 'He's one of the fastest defenders I've ever seen'. Injuries, however, plagued him over the next few years (especially to his back) and there's no doubt that his absence from first-team action denied him senior international honours at least at under-21 level (having already been capped nine times as a schoolboy). Sadly, after being named club captain, his senior career was halted in 1990 through injury. He graduated through the junior ranks at The Hawthorns and made his League debut against Everton in April 1979. Bennett, who made close on 140 appearances in the Central League side, left the club after a deserved testimonial match against Birmingham City in 1990.

BENTLEY, Alfred

Centre-forward: 106 apps. 47 goals.

Born: Alfreton, Derbyshire, 15 September 1887.
Died: Alfreton, 15 April 1940.
Career: Alfreton (1905). Derby County (£50, professional, December 1906). Bolton Wanderers (£250, May 1911). ALBION (£500, June 1913). Burton Albion (May 1922). Alfreton Town (August 1924, retired, May 1926). Later worked in the steel industry.

■ An eager beaver utility forward, Alf Bentley (known affectionately as 'Nobby' or 'Snobby' in some cases) scored almost a goal every other game for Albion, whom he served for nine years following his League debut against Burnley (home) in September 1913. Partnering Fred

Morris 'up front', he helped the Baggies win the League championship in 1920 when he netted 15 important goals. He scored four times on his Albion debut against Burnley in September 1913 and hit two goals in 16 outings for the Central League side. He then went on to net a total of 99 goals in 151 League games for Derby. Serving as a private with the 4th Leicestershire Regiment, based in France, during World War One in 1918, Bentley was wounded and returned to Alfreton, then his home.

BERTHE, Sekou Lata

Defender: 3+1 apps.

Born: Bamako, Mali, 7 October 1977.
Career: AS Monaco, France (1997). Troyes, France (August 1999). ALBION (trialist, July–August 2003, signed permanently, September 2003, placed on transfer list, December 2004, contract cancelled, February 2005).

■ A tall, solid, well-built defender, Sekou Berthe – who has been capped twice by Mali – made his first appearance in an Albion shirt against Odense B1909 during the club's pre-season tour to Denmark in July 2003. Standing 6ft 3in tall and weighing a fraction over 13st, he played his first senior game for the club in a 2–1 Carling Cup win at Hartlepool on 23 September 2003 and followed up by making his League debut against Stoke City at The Hawthorns four days later. He

then battled it out in the second team for long periods and when new boss Bryan Robson arrived he was quickly placed on the transfer list, having made just four first and nearly 20 second-team appearances for the club.
* Berthe was awarded French nationality on 30 August 2003.

BETTELEY, Richard Harold

Full-back: 89 apps.

Born: Bradley near Bilston, 14 July 1880. Died: Wolverhampton, 3 August 1942. Career: Bilston Council School. Bradley Athletic (1895). Priestfield Albion (1897). Bilston St Leonard's FC (1898). Bilston United (1900). Wolverhampton Wanderers (professional, August 1901). ALBION (May 1906). Bilston United (May 1912, retired, May 1914). Later employed by a Wolverhampton brewery.

■ Dick Betteley was a full-back of some calibre, who spent six years at The Hawthorns, having earlier appeared in 123 competitive matches for Wolves. He won a Second Division championship medal with Albion, as partner to Jesse Pennington in 1911, but missed out in the 1912 FA Cup final, being replaced by Arthur Cook. His debut for the Baggies was against Burnley (away) in September 1906 (Division Two). He spent most of his last two full seasons at The Hawthorns playing in Albion's second team.

BETTERIDGE, Raymond Michael

Wing or inside-forward: 5 apps.

Born: Redditch, 11 August 1924. Career: Redditch & District Schools. Loughborough College (1939). Walsall Wood (1940). Leicester City (amateur, 1942). Warslow Celtic (1947). ALBION (amateur, April 1948, professional, November 1948). Swindon Town (July 1951). Chester (March 1954–May 1955). Burton Albion (August 1955). Banbury Spencer (August 1956, retired, April 1960).

■ A promising outside-right or inside-forward, Mike Betteridge was given few opportunities at The Hawthorns owing to the presence of so many other talented forwards. He made his debut for the club

in the League home game against Stoke City in January 1950 and also scored 21 goals in 71 second-team games before going on to claim 23 goals in 108 League outings for Swindon, later gaining a Welsh Cup runners'-up medal with Chester (1954).

BIDDLESTONE, Samuel Isaac

Goalkeeper: no senior apps.

Born: West Bromwich, 12 February 1857. Died: Canada, 15 August 1938. Career: Black Lake & Swan Village Schools. George Salter Works (1871). ALBION (September 1879-June 1881). Later emigrated to Canada where he ran his own business.

■ One of Albion's first established goalkeepers, Sammy Biddlestone was a fitness freak who possessed both agility and courage, a worthy 'custodian' who, at times, was willing to try his luck as an outfield player.

BILLINGHAM, Peter Arnold

Wing-half: 7 apps.

Born: Pensnett, 8 October 1938. Career: Brierley Hill Schools. Dudley Technical College. Brierley Hill Boys. Dudley Schools. Worcester City (March 1953). Brierley Hill Alliance (January 1954). Hednesford Town (May 1954). Walsall (professional, October 1955). ALBION (£7,000, May 1960). Worcester City (June 1962). Lye Town (1963). Kidderminster Harriers (August 1965, retired, May 1967). Became a greyhound trainer and later breeder (based at Swindon near Kingswinford), a field in which he later excelled, his dogs winning several top races, one of them, Skippy, being owned by Albion striker Jeff Astle.

■ Peter Billingham was a tall, lanky, red-haired wing-half, who joined Albion at the same time as Stan Jones, making his debut for the club in the League away game against Birmingham City in August 1960. He also played in 62 Central League games for the Baggies and made over 100 senior appearances for Walsall, whom he helped win the Fourth Division championship in 1960. Unfortunately, he wasn't quite top-flight material.

BISSEKER, William Myles

Centre-forward: 1 app.

Born: West Bromwich, 11 November 1863. Died: West Bromwich, 5 March 1902. Career: Hill Top County School. George Salter Works (1877). ALBION (September 1878, served as the club's treasurer, 1882–84, retired as a player through injury, May 1884, appointed club's official umpire, 1885). Later returned to work at Salter's.

■ A very useful centre-forward, Billy Bisseker could also play on the wing. He was the club's first 'named' captain and remained with Albion for six years making one FA Cup appearance, lining up in the club's first ever game in the competition against Wednesbury Old Athletic in 1883. He scored 56 goals in more than 50 other matches, and when he finally hung up his boots through injury he became Albion's official umpire, a position he held for at least five seasons. Bisseker died after a short illness.
* His elder brother, John Bisseker, was Albion's secretary during the 1880–81 season.

BLAGDEN, Jonathan

Inside-forward: 20 apps. 4 goals.

Born: Sheffield, 12 April 1900. Died: Dover, Kent, 1964. Career: Mansfield & District Schools. Cresswell Colliery (1919). ALBION (professional April 1921). Worksop Town (June 1923, retired, May 1930).

■ A clever, purposeful inside-right, Jonathan Blagden had Joe Carter and two Welshmen, Ivor Jones and Stan Davies, to compete with for a place in Albion's forward-line during the early 1920s. He managed one decent spell in the first XI, appearing in 16 out of 17 League games halfway through the 1921–22 season. He made his debut against Bolton Wanderers (home) in November 1921 and also scored 11 goals in 53 second-team outings during his two years at The Hawthorns, gaining a Central League championship medal in 1922–23.

BLISSETT, Luther Loide

Centre-forward: 3 apps. 1 goal.

Born: Jamaica, 1 February 1958. Career: Watford (juniors, April 1973, professional, July 1975). AC Milan (£1

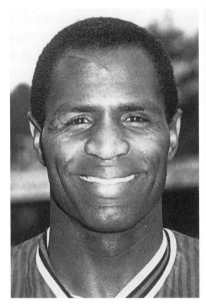

million, June 1983) Watford (£550,000, August 1984). AFC Bournemouth (£60,000, November 1985). Watford (£40,000, August 1991). ALBION (on loan, October 1992). Bury (free, August 1993). Mansfield Town (December 1993). Southport (on loan, March–May 1994). Fakenham Town (free, August 1994). Watford (assistant manager/coach, August 1997). York City (coach, May 2002–May 2003). Portsmouth (coach, 2003–05).

■ During a wonderfully exciting career, striker Luther Blissett scored 207 goals in 554 games in the Football League alone, and he also appeared in one 'B', four under-21 and 14 full internationals for England. A strong, mobile attacker with a flair for goals, he had a month loan spell at The Hawthorns (under Ossie Ardiles) and netted one goal in a 3–1 home win over Hartlepool United, having earlier made his debut against Rotherham United. Blissett holds the Watford League record for most appearances (415) and the most goals (148), helping the Hornets win the Fourth Division title in 1978.

BLOOD, Robert

Centre-forward: 53 apps. 26 goals.

Born: Harpur Hill, Buxton, 18 March 1894.
Died: Buxton, 12 August 1988.
Career: Buxton. Buxton Lime Firms. Leek Alexandra. Leek United (1914). Served with the 7th & 16th battalions of the Sherwood Foresters during World War One. Port Vale (trial, October 1918). Leek

Alexandra (December 1918). Port Vale (£50, November 1919). ALBION (£4,000, February 1921). Stockport County (£2,500, December 1924). Winsford United (May 1927). Mossley (August 1928). Ashton National FC (June 1929). Buxton (February 1930, retired, May 1931). Later worked on a farm near Buxton.

■ Bobby Blood was an all-action, courageous, hard-shooting and sometimes dynamic centre-forward who, despite having one leg shorter than the other, found goalscoring easy. Unfortunately, World War One severely interrupted his career, yet he still managed to score over 70 goals in less than 150 League games for his three major clubs, including 47 in 66 outings for Port Vale with whom he won the Staffordshire Cup in 1920. At all levels of football (from 1909 to 1931) it is believed he netted over 400 goals, including 100 in two seasons immediately prior to entering the Football League with Port Vale in 1919 (when they replaced Leeds City in Division Two). He scored a penalty on his debut for Albion in a 3–1 League home win over the subsequent FA Cup winners for that season, Tottenham Hotspur, in February 1921. He played very well alongside Fred Morris and, at times, Stan Davies and Charlie Wilson, but lost his way in 1924 when George James and Joe Carter were paired together in the front-line. He also netted 73 goals in 72 second XI games for Albion, having his best season with the reserves in 1923–24 when his total of 32 goals helped the Baggies retain the Central League championship, Blood having netted 29 the previous campaign when he also gained a winners medal. He was 94 years of age when he died in a Salvation Army Hostel in Buxton in 1988.
* During World War One Blood received serious injuries to both legs. He was left with a hole in his right limb where a bullet had passed clean through. Thankfully, he regained full fitness (after an operation to shorten the leg) and continued to play football until he was 37 years of age.

BOERE, Jeroen Willem

Striker: 5 apps.

Born: Arnhem, Holland, 18 November 1967.

Career: FC Arnhem (1984). Go Ahead Eagles (1986). West Ham United (£250,000, September 1993). Portsmouth (on loan, March 1994). ALBION (on loan, September–October 1994). Crystal Palace (£375,000, September 1995). Southend United (£150,000, March 1996). NN Kanto, Japan (July 1998–May 1999). Omiya Adrija, Japan (1999–2000).

■ Jeroen Boere, a 6ft 3in striker, had less than 30 outings with West Ham and five on loan with Portsmouth before spending a short loan spell at The Hawthorns. In that, he failed to make any impression after making a moderate debut in a 2–2 draw at Millwall in September 1994, when he partnered Bob Taylor up front. Skilful in the air (when he put his mind to it), he later produced his best form with Southend, scoring 25 goals in 82 games for the Shrimpers.

BOOKMAN, Louis James Arthur Oscar

Winger: 18 apps. 1 goal.

Born: Dolphin Bar, Dublin, 8 November 1890.
Died: Dublin, 10 June 1943.
Career: Cabra Junior & Dublin Grammar Schools. Belfast Celtic (1910). Bradford City (February 1912). ALBION (£875, June 1914). Luton Town (£250, May 1919). Port Vale (£250, July 1923). Shelbourne, Ireland (August 1924–April 1927).

■ Real name Buckhalter (his surname was changed on leaving School) Louis Bookman was a brave, determined winger, who in later years performed remarkably well at full-back. He scored on his League debut for Albion against Newcastle United (away) in September 1914 but was never regarded as a first-team regular at The Hawthorns. He gained four international caps for Ireland either side of World War One (1914–22).

BORTOLAZZI, Mario

Midfield: 26+10 apps. 2 goals.

Born: Verona, 10 January 1965.
Career: Mantova FC (1980–81). Fiorentina (July 1982). AC Milan (during 1985–86). Parma (1986–87, Serie 'B'). AC Milan (1987–88). Verona (1988–89). Atalanta (1990–91). Genoa (August 1991). ALBION (August 1998–May 1999). Livomo, Italy (July 1999). Lecce, Italy (November 2001).

■ Mario Bortolazzi became the first Italian to sign professional forms for Albion, doing so on 11 August 1998, a fortnight before his compatriot and fellow midfielder Enzo Maresca became a Baggies player. He made his debut in Italy's Serie 'C' in 1980 and later helped Genoa reach the semi-final of the UEFA Cup (beaten by Barcelona). In all, he appeared in well over 300 'league' and 'cup' games in Italy prior to joining Albion, for whom he scored twice before his release at the end of the 1998–99 season following a series of niggling knee and ankle injuries. He had the ill-luck to get sent off playing against Wolves reserves in a Pontins League game (September 1998).

BOSTON, Henry James

Outside-right: 27 apps. 6 goals.

Born: Nantwich, Cheshire, 20 October 1899.
Died: Cheshire, Decenber 1973.
Career: Ravensmoor & Wistanton Schools.

Shavington Town (1919). Nantwich FC (1921). Bolton Wanderers (January 1924). ALBION (£550, June 1929). Swansea Town (May 1931). Nantwich FC (August 1932, retired, May 1938). Later worked in engineering.*

■ Harry Boston was an adventurous footballer who was signed as cover for Tommy Glidden. He had his best spell with Albion towards the end of the 1929–30 season and at the start of the following one when Glidden switched to inside-right. He also made 32 appearances for the club at Central League level, scoring six goals. He netted three times in 39 outings for Bolton and made 19 League appearances for Swansea.

BOURNE, Richard Arthur

Outside-left: 9 apps. 1 goal.

Born: Roundle, 12 January 1881.
Died: Darlaston, 1944.
Career: Roundle Council School. Roundle FC (1897). Sheffield United (October 1900). Barnsley (March 1902). Preston North End (March 1903). Clapton Orient (April 1905). ALBION (£135, February 1907). Walsall (as player-trainer, April 1908, retired, May 1920). Later employed as a part-time groundsman and gardener.

■ Dickie Bourne was a useful left-winger who won a Second Division championship medal with Preston in 1904. He had to fight for a first-team place at The Hawthorns with Tommy

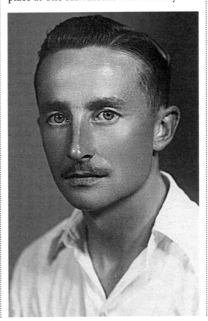

Dilly and Joe Brooks, and after 14 months of basically being a reserve (making 23 second XI appearances) he moved to Walsall. Throughout his career, Bourne appeared in well over 150 League games and as well as being a competent footballer he was also a fine cricketer, oarsman and basketball player.

BOWDEN, James William

Centre-half: 8 apps.

Born: Wolverhampton, 15 August 1882.
Died: Wolverhampton, 25 May 1951.
Career: Yardley Wood School (Birmingham). Yardley Methodists. Erdington FC (1902). Aston Villa (amateur, January 1903). Handsworth Rovers (1903–04). ALBION (June 1904). Southampton (August 1906). Grimsby Town (August 1907). Hyde United (March 1909). Stourbridge (July 1912, retired, August 1916). Later worked for an upholstery form.

■ Although handicapped by the lack of height, Jim Bowden was a strong tackling half-back, neat in style, who spent two seasons at The Hawthorns (adding 21 second XI appearances to his first XI tally) before moving to The Dell. Prior to his transfer to Saints, he had a lucky escape when he was involved in a shooting accident and a bullet passed through his left arm.

BOWEN, Stewart Anthony

Left-back/midfield: 8 apps. 1 goal.

Born: West Bromwich, 12 December 1972.
Career: ALBION (apprentice, April 1989, professional, July 1991, released, May 1992). Coventry City (trialist, season 1992–93). Now lives and works in West Bromwich.

■ A small, compact footballer with a big heart, Stewart Bowen was certainly enthusiastic, but he lacked technique and quickly drifted out of the game. He scored once in 44 Central League appearances. His only goal for Albion came in a 4–0 League home victory over Peterborough United in September 1991.

BOWEN, Thomas Henry

Forward: 6 apps. 2 goals.

Born: Great Bridge, West Bromwich, 21 August 1924.

Career: Swan Village School. Ratcliffe FC (1938). West Bromwich Athletic (1939). ALBION (amateur, October 1941, professional, April 1944). Newport County (£250, May 1946). Walsall (July 1950, retired, May 1953).

■ A dashing inside-forward, Tommy Bowen's career with Albion was ruined by World War Two, although he did score on his debut in a 3–1 League South win over his future club Walsall in May 1942. He did reasonably well with Newport County (six goals in 37 games) and Walsall (seven in 94).

* His father, Tommy senior, also played for the Saddlers (1921–23) as well as serving Wolves and Coventry City.

BOWSER, Sidney

Inside-left/centre-half: 371 apps. 72 goals.

Born: Handsworth, Birmingham, 6 April 1891.
Died: Birmingham, 10 February 1961.
Career: Astbury Richmond (1905). Willenhall Town (July 1906). Birmingham (trialist, April–May 1907). Willenhall Town (August 1907). ALBION (July 1908). Belfast Distiller (April 1913). ALBION (February 1914). Walsall (August 1924, retired May 1927). Became a licensee in Dudley, a job he held for over 25 years.

■ The tenacious, resilient and hard-working Sid Bowser had two excellent spells with Albion. He divided his

immense talents between two completely different roles – those of inside-forward and centre-half – and he excelled in both. He was a goalscorer in his first period at The Hawthorns, having learned that while playing locally. He netted twice on his League debut as a 17-year-old in a 7–2 home win over Grimsby Town in January 1909, becoming the club's youngest ever League marksman, and he held this record until Geoff Richards beat it against Luton Town in December 1946. He helped the Baggies win the Second Division title in 1911 and reach the FA Cup final 12 months later (beaten in a replay by Barnsley). When he returned after eight months in Ireland he was converted into a redoubtable, no-nonsense defender. He became a key figure at the back as Albion won the First Division title in 1920 when he obliged with a total of 10 goals, also netting a hat-trick (two penalties) in a 4–1 home victory over Bradford City. Bowser gained his only England cap against Ireland in October 1919 (1–1 draw), having earlier represented the Irish League as a distillery player. He left Albion, second time round, for Walsall, retiring at the end of the 1926–27. Bowser was born just a stones throw from The Hawthorns and as a lad stood on the Handsworth side of the ground, attending his first match in 1900 having previously watched a few games at Villa Park with his father.

BOWSER, William

Forward: 1 app.

Born: Handsworth, Birmingham, 12 November 1886.
Died: Hockley, Birmingham, 9 September 1975.
Career: Wattville Road School. Everton (trialist, 1903). Dudley Town (August 1904). ALBION (April 1907). Walsall (October 1909). Birmingham (1911–12). Shrewsbury Town (August 1913, retired, May 1925). Subsequently worked in engineering.

■ Bill Bowser, older brother of Sid, was a utility forward and a junior international (capped in 1907), who played reserve team football at The Hawthorns for two seasons, appearing in over 30 matches. His only League game was against Stockport County in October 1907 when he helped Albion to a 2–0 victory.

BOYD, Henry

Inside-forward: 10 apps. 2 goals.

Born: Pollockshaws, Scotland, 6 May 1868.
Died: Scotland, July 1935.
Career: Satley Boys. Sunderland Albion (1890). Burnley (professional, August 1892). ALBION (October 1892). Royal Arsenal (May 1894). Newton Heath/Manchester United (£45, January 1897). Falkirk (August 1899–May 1900). Later employed by Falkirk district council.

■ A powerfully built forward, Henry Boyd had a fiery temper and unfortunately his disciplinary problems marred his career. During his spell with Albion he went missing from training at least three times, and in April 1893 'disappeared' prior to a scheduled court appearance and was subsequently suspended. After leaving Stoney Lane he received a 14-day ban after failing to turn up for a game for Newton Heath, sending a telegram to his club (from Glasgow) requesting leave of absence. He was subsequently placed on the transfer list. Boyd had earlier netted twice on his debut for Newton Heath, and in 1897–98 he became the first player to score 20 League goals in a season for the Manchester club, claiming a hat-trick in each of the first two matches. He broke his right leg playing for Arsenal in October 1894 against Newton Heath. Besides his senior appearances for Albion, Boyd also played in 12 'other' first-team games.

BOYD, Jack

Full-back: 1 app.

Born: Consett, County Durham, 10 April 1925.
Career: Westwood Council & Derwent Valley Schools. Blackhill Juniors. Medomsley Juniors (July 1939). Sunderland (professional, May 1945). ALBION (£1,500, May 1948). Consett Town (June 1949, retired, May 1952).

■ A right-back of reasonable tact, Jack Boyd was signed as cover for Jim Pemberton. He made just one League appearance for the club against Tottenham Hotspur (home) in September 1948 (2–2 draw). He made 22 appearances for the Central League side.

BOYES, Walter Edward

Inside and outside-left//left-half: 165 apps. 38 goals.

Born: Killamarsh, Sheffield, 5 January 1913.
Died: September 1960.
Career: Sheffield Boys. Woodhouse Mills United (1929). ALBION (professional, February 1931). Everton (£6,000, February 1938). Guest for Aldershot, Brentford, Clapton Orient, Leeds United, Manchester United, Middlesbrough, Millwall, Newcastle United, Preston North End and Sunderland during World War Two. Notts County (player-coach, June 1949). Scunthorpe United (player-trainer, 1950–53). Retford Town (player-manager, 1954). Hyde United (player-manager, 1958). Swansea Town (trainer, 1959, retired through illness, May 1960). Also sports-master at Oakwood Collegiate School, Sheffield (1952–58) and later worked as an assistant at various schools in and around the Sheffield area.

■ Standing a fraction under 5ft 4in tall, Wally 'Titty' Boyes was a diminutive but well-built footballer, who occupied three different positions for Albion, always giving 100 percent. He made his League debut in front of almost 60,000 fans in the local derby against Aston Villa nine months after signing, lining up at inside-left in a 3–0 victory. He gained a regular place in the side towards the end of that season, mainly occupying the left-half position before finally bedding down on the left-wing from January 1934 after taking the place of Stan Wood. Just over a year later he scored in the 1935 FA Cup final defeat by Sheffield Wednesday, the team he supported as a lad. Boyes also scored 24 goals in almost 100 games for Albion's second string, gaining a Central

League championship medal in 1932–33 and helping the team retain the title the following season. At the end of his first full season at Goodison Park he collected a League championship medal. Boyes gained three full England caps (one while at Albion, two while at Everton) and also played in the Jubilee international, England against Scotland, in 1938. As a youngster he once scored 17 goals in one game, which his team won 31–2.

BRADLEY, Charles Henry

Inside-right: 3 apps.

Born: Smethwick, 19 January 1882.
Died: Hockley, Birmingham, 1949.
Career: Rolfe Street School (Smethwick). Invention Street Boys' Club (1903). ALBION (professional, February 1905). Dudley Town (April 1905, retired, May 1908). Became an engineer in Smethwick.

■ Charles Bradley spent just eight weeks at The Hawthorns, taking over from Billy Smith in the inside-right position for League games against Bristol City, Manchester United and Glossop. He played on the right-wing for Dudley.

BRADLEY, Darren Michael

Defender/wing-half/midfield: 270+18 apps. 13 goals.

Born: Kings Norton, Birmingham, 24 November 1965.
Career: St Thomas Aquinas School (Birmingham). Kings Norton Boys. West Midland County Schools. South Birmingham Schools. Broadmeadow All Stars (1981). Aston Villa (apprentice, July 1982, professional, November 1983). ALBION (£90,000 plus Steve Hunt, March 1986). Cape Town Spurs, South Africa (guest, summer 1988). Hibernians, Malta (guest). Walsall (May 1995). MV Meffen, Germany (trialist, June 1997). Solihull Borough (1997–98).

■ Albion's manager, Alan Buckley, released Darren Bradley on a free transfer at the end of the 1994–95 season after a nine-year spell at The Hawthorns. Albion's skipper at Wembley two years earlier when promotion was achieved to the First Division, Bradley often played with vision and tact, although occasionally his temper got the better of him with suspensions blighting his progress from time to time. As a teenager

he captained both Villa and the England youth team and also played in more than 60 second-team games (3 goals scored) for Albion.

BRADLEY, Donald John

Full-back: 2 apps.

Born: Annessley, Notts, 11 September 1924.
Died: Mansfield, 26 June 1997.
Career: Dukeries School. Clipstone Colliery (1939). ALBION (September 1943). Mansfield Town (guest 1944–45, signed permanently for £500, August 1949). Alfreton Town (May 1962, retired, April 1964). Later worked as an engineer in Mansfield.

■ Having played as an inside-forward or outside-left and even goalkeeper as a schoolboy, Don Bradley developed into a very fine full-back but managed only two wartime appearances for Albion, plus 87 for the Central League side, before going on to amass a record 385 in the League for Mansfield. His long-standing partnership with Sammy Chessall at Field Mill is regarded as one of the best in the Stags history. He helped Mansfield to the runners'-up spot in the Third Division North in 1951.

BRADLEY, Eli John

Wing-half/utility forward: 27 apps. 6 goals.
Born: Dudley, 24 December 1882.
Died: Dudley, May 1962.

Career: Castle Hill School (Dudley). Bilston Town (January 1898). ALBION (professional, July 1905). Luton Town (July 1908). Coventry City (August 1909). Heart of Midlothian (1912–13). Dudley Town (July 1914, retired, May 1919). Became a licensee of the Woolpack public house in Dudley Market Place and later ran his own Turf Accountancy business (his office also being in Dudley).

■ A junior international (capped in 1905), Eli Bradley was a versatile performer, quick-witted and judicious, who spent three seasons at The Hawthorns, having his best run in the first team during the second half of the 1905–06 season when he occupied three different positions. He captained the Baggies second team many times during his 54 appearances and later skippered the Southern League XI on three occasions in 1911–12 as a Coventry player. He scored 20 goals in 116 appearances for the Sky Blues.
* In the 1930s Bradley bought some diamonds from a gentleman named William Hill who needed money to become a bookmaker. Before his death, Bradley took a trip on an ocean liner to see a heavyweight boxing title fight in Madison Square Garden.

BRADLEY, Ronald John

Defender: 13 apps.

Born: Bilston, 24 April 1939.
Career: Ettingshall Primary. Harrison Junior and Stonefield Secondary Modern Schools. Bilston Boys. South-East Staffs Boys. ALBION (amateur, April 1954, professional, June 1956). Norwich City (July 1964). Wolverhampton Wanderers (coach, October 1966). Olympiakos, Greece (manager/coach, 1970–72). Scunthorpe United (coach, July 1972, manager, 1973–74). Lybia National coach (1975–76). Derby County (coach, 1976–78). Scunthorpe United (coach, 1979–81). Wolverhampton Wanderers (coach, October 1982). Also ran successful soccer camps in the US (1981–87) and in August 1986 was appointed FA coach. Returned to the Midlands in 1988 to coach junior and intermediate teams in Stourbridge and later in Halesowen Town and Bewdley.

■ An England youth international (capped in 1955–56), Ron Bradley was a

well-built defender who could occupy the full-back and wing-positions to good effect. He made his League debut in 1962 against Manchester City but found it hard to establish himself in the Albion first XI, yet made 169 second-team appearances and scored four goals. He was at Molineux when Wolves gained promotion to the First Division in 1967 and guided Olympiakos to victory in the 1971 Greek Cup final. He gained a fine reputation as a coach.

BRADSHAW, Paul William

Goalkeeper: 14 apps.

Born: Altrincham, Cheshire, 28 April 1956.
Career: Altrincham & District Schools. Altrincham & Cheshire Boys. Manchester United (trialist, 1971). Blackburn Rovers (apprentice July 1972, professional, July 1973). Wolverhampton Wanderers (£150,000, September 1977). Vancouver Whitecaps (August 1984). ALBION (free, February 1985). Walsall (coach, July 1986). Bristol Rovers (March 1987). Newport County (July 1987). ALBION (August 1988). Peterborough United (July 1990, retired, May 1991). Later worked as a security officer in Wolverhampton.

■ Goalkeeper Paul Bradshaw, tall and fearless with a safe pair of hands, was capped four times by England at under-21 level. He won the League Cup with Wolves (1980) and during his time at Molineux appeared in exactly 200 senior games for the Wanderers. He understudied Stuart Naylor at The Hawthorns, playing the first of his 14 games for the club against Brighton and Hove Albion in the Full Member's Cup in October 1985. He also played in 63 second-team games for the club.

BRETT, Ralph Samuel

Forward: 12 apps. 3 goals.

Born: Chester, 22 June 1878.
Died: London, 1940.
Career: Chester City School. Southport Central (1894). Royal Army Medical Corps (1896). ALBION (£28, professional, August 1898). Wellingborough (May 1899). Brentford (April 1903). Stoke Newington (August 1905, retired, May 1908). Became a metalworker.

■ Albion paid to get Ralph Brett released from the Army in 1898. He had been

producing some excellent performances at centre-forward during his time in the 'forces', but unfortunately he was suspended on three separate occasions between January and March 1899 and was subsequently released by the club at the end of the season. He scored on his League debut in a 3–3 draw at Bolton in September 1898 and, besides his senior outings, he also played in several 'other' first-team matches for Albion before moving to Wellingborough.

BRETT, Samuel Stephen

Forward: 10 apps. 3 goals.

Born: St Asaph near Rhyl, North Wales, 25 December 1879.
Died: London, 1938.
Career: Mold Road Junior School (St Asaph). St Asaph YMCA (1896). Southport Central (1897). ALBION (August 1898). Wellingborough (June 1902). Brentford (May 1903, retired, April 1910). Later took employment in the engineering trade.

■ Brother of Ralph (above), Sammy Brett was also a utility forward, who spent four seasons with Albion, appearing in just 10 senior games. He made his League debut in the local derby against Wolves in December 1898 and made 15 'other' first-team appearances for Albion.
NB: The Bretts did not appear in the same Albion team together but they did link up on several occasions with Brentford in the Southern League.

BRIEN, Anthony James

Defender: 4 apps.

Born: Dublin, 10 February 1969.
Career: Leicester City (apprentice, April 1985, professional, February 1987). Chesterfield (£90,000, December 1988). Rotherham United (£10,000, October 1993). ALBION (free, July 1995). Mansfield Town (on loan, February 1996). Chester City (on loan, March 1996). Hull City (free, July 1996). Stalybridge Celtic (January 1998). Bromsgrove Rovers (August 1999). Stourbridge (briefly, 2000). Alfreton Town (2000–02).

■ A Republic of Ireland youth international (capped as a Leicester player), Tony Brien was an experienced campaigner when he joined Albion, having already appeared in well over 300 competitive games. A strong, efficient

tackler, perhaps sometimes over-aggressive, he never settled in at The Hawthorns and after two loan spells and 15 second XI appearances he moved on to pastures new.

BRITTAIN, John Walter

Left-back: 10 apps.

Born: Wednesbury, 16 January 1880.
Died: Wolverhampton, 2 February 1960.
Career: Highfield Road School (Wednesbury). Wednesbury Old Athletic (1897). ALBION (professional, December 1902). Willenhall Swifts (August 1906). Hollington Rangers (August 1910, retired, May 1912). Served in World War One but was badly wounded and never worked again.

■ Jack Brittain was a cool, uncompromising defender who cleared his lines well with some first-rate kicking. He deputised for both Jesse Pennington and Jack Kifford during his four years at The Hawthorns and made his League debut against Derby County in April 1903. He also played in over 50 second-team matches.

BROAD, Thomas Higginson

Outside-right: 15 apps. 1 goal.

Born: Stalybridge, 31 July 1887.
Died: February 1966.
Career: Redgate Albion. Denton Wanderers. Openshaw Lads' Club (1903). Manchester City (trialist, 1904). ALBION (September 1905). Chesterfield Town (February 1908). Oldham Athletic (May 1909). Bristol City (May 1912).

Manchester City (March 1919). Stoke (May 1921). Southampton (July 1924). Weymouth (September 1925). Rhyl Athletic (June 1926, retired, May 1928). Later worked at a seaside fun fair.

■ A junior international winger with pace and power, Tommy Broad had an interesting and nomadic career, which saw him appear in well over 350 games (35 goals scored). At times he found it hard to produce his best form at The Hawthorns, having his best spell in a Baggies shirt during the early part of the 1906–97 season when he partnered Fred Buck on the right-wing. He represented the Football League in 1910, and in 1925 (at the age of 37) became the oldest player ever to appear in a senior game for Southampton.
NB: Broad's brother, Jimmy, served with 16 different clubs at various levels between 1908 and 1930. He scored 62 goals in 108 League games for Stoke.

BROCKHURST, William James

Defender: 5 apps.

Born: Brownhills, 25 November 1913.
Deceased.
Career: Chadsmoor School. Cannock Chase Colliery (1930). ALBION (amateur, March 1935, professional, October 1935). Hednesford Town (May 1938, retired during World War Two).

■ Relatively small for a centre-half (5ft 9in), Bill Brockhurst was steady and hardworking with good judgement and deputised for Bill Richardson and Alf Ridyard during his time at The Hawthorns. He made 31 appearances for the second XI.

BROMAGE, Enos

Outside-left: 10 apps. 2 goals.

Born: Mickleover, Derby, 22 October 1898.
Died: Derby, 9 April 1978.
Career: Mickleover County School. Stapleford Town (1919). Sheffield United (August 1922). Derby County (August 1923). Gillingham (August 1926). ALBION (March 1928). Nottingham Forest (January 1929). Chester (summer 1930). Wellington Town (August 1931, retired, May 1932). Later worked in engineering in Mickleover.

■ A sturdy, direct outside-left, Enos Bromage travelled the country in search of League action, having his longest spell with Derby (six appearances in three seasons) but perhaps playing his best football with Gillingham (6 goals scored in 21 outings).

BROOKES, William Amos

Left-half: 20 apps.

Born: Dudley, 19 April 1931.
Career: Churchfields Villa. Erdington Albion (1945). ALBION (groundstaff, June 1947, professional, 1949). Allen's Cross FC

(July 1958). Lower Gornal. Stourbridge. Kendrick and Jefferson Works FC. Lower Gornal (again). Retired in 1968 to concentrate on working for the probation service. Returned to the game later as general manager of Halesowen Town (2000). Now living in Lichfield.

■ Billy Brooks, a very useful and composed wing-half, was understudy to Ray Barlow at The Hawthorns and consequently got limited first-team call-ups, making only 20 senior appearances compared with a total of 158 in the Central League side in his 11-year association with the club. He has now retired and lives in Lichfield.

BROOKS, Joseph

Outside-left: 22 apps. 1 goal.

Born: Stairfool near Barnsley, 11 November 1886.

Died: Barnsley, April 1955.
Career: Ardesley Nelson (1902). Barnsley (professional, December 1904). ALBION (£400, April 1907). Barnsley (June 1908). Rotherham County (August 1909). Served in the Army during World War One and was forced to retire, May 1916. Employed as an mining engineer in the 1920s.

■ A short outside-left, Joe Brooks had good pace and a strong shot. He spent just one season at The Hawthorns before returning to Barnsley. He later served with Rotherham County and retired during World War One.

BROWN, Alistair

Striker: 331+28 apps. 85 goals.

Born: Musselburgh near Edinburgh, 12 April 1951.
Career: Edinburgh & District Schools. Leicester City (apprentice, October 1966, professional, April 1968). ALBION (£61,111, March 1972). Portland Timbers (on loan, May–August 1981). Crystal Palace (March 1983). Walsall (August 1983). Port Vale (July 1984, retired, May 1986 with a knee injury). Became a licensee, initially in Great Barr, and in 1995 was appointed steward of The Halfords Lane Throstle club, opposite The Hawthorns (until 2003).

■ A key figure in Albion's attack during the 1970s and early 1980s, Ally Brown played alongside some fine marksmen, including Jeff Astle, his namesake Tony Brown and Cyrille Regis. He scored his fair share of goals (85) in 11 years at The

Hawthorns (surprisingly and annoyingly never receiving a testimonial for his efforts). He also netted 38 goals in 109 Central League games. Brown, who top-scored for Leicester in 1970–71 when the 'Foxes' won the Second Division title, netted on his debut for the Baggies against Crystal Palace (home) in March 1972 and played his part in helping the team gain promotion in 1976, having had a couple of lean seasons under Don Howe's management (1973–75). He was, however, a vital cog in Albion's attack under Johnny Giles, Ronnie Allen and Ron Atkinson. He was voted 'Midland Footballer of the Year' (jointly with Tony Brown) in 1978–79. He helped Port Vale gain promotion from the Third Division in 1986 along with two other ex-Albion players, Wayne Ebanks and Alan Webb.
* Unlucky not to receive a testimonial, Brown was, nevertheless, presented with the 'Mecca Loyalty Award' by former Wimbledon tennis star and Baggies fan Ann Jones.

BROWN, Anthony

Striker/midfield: 704+16 apps. 279 goals.

Born: Oldham, 3 October 1945.
Career: St Columba's (Manchester). St Peter's (Wythenshaw) & St Clare's (Blakey) Schools. Manchester District & Lancashire Boys. ALBION (amateur, April 1961, professional, October 1963). Jacksonville Tea Men, NASL (summer 1981). Torquay United (October 1981). Jacksonville Tea Men (summer 1982). Stafford Rangers (February–April 1983). Worked as a sales representative for an electrical company in West Bromwich. ALBION (schoolboy/junior coach, February 1984, senior coaching staff, June 1984–May 1986). Birmingham City (coach, June 1987–May 1989). Also played for West Bromwich Albion All Stars (1979–88). Later had two hip replacements, now lives with his wife Irene in Walsall and is a regular visitor to Albion's home matches as well as being a columnist in a local sports paper and capital radio summariser (covering his beloved Albion).

■ One of the greatest footballers in the club's history, Tony 'Bomber' Brown appeared in more first-team games (826) and scored more goals (313) than any other Albion player during his 20 and a half years at The Hawthorns (1961 to

1981). In fact, he played in more senior matches at The Hawthorns than anyone else – 361 – including 282 in the Football League alone. His League record for the club was outstanding: 218 goals in 574 appearances, 459 of them coming in the First Division and 115 in the Second. And you can also include 66 outings for the reserves, plus a further 51 goals as well as his efforts at intermediate level. Brown, a penalty-expert, who scored 51 goals from 61 spot-kicks in all matches, had two excellent years as an apprentice before joining the professional ranks at The Hawthorns on his 18th birthday (signing in manager Jimmy Hagan's office shortly after making a scoring League debut in a 2–1 win over Ipswich Town at Portman Road in September 1963). He quickly established himself in the first team and was a regular for 15 years, from 1964 to 1979, helping Albion win both the League Cup (at the first attempt in 1966) and the FA Cup (1968). He also played in two losing League Cup finals: versus Queen's Park Rangers in 1967 and against Manchester City three years later. He played his last League game for Albion in the Midlands derby against Coventry City in December 1979 and his farewell appearance for the club followed soon afterwards, in the 2–1 FA Cup defeat at West Ham in January 1980 when he celebrated the occasion with his final goal. Capped by England at youth team level, he appeared in only one full international match (it should have been more), playing for 74 minutes in the goalless draw with Wales in front of 85,000 spectators at Wembley in May 1971. Twice a Football League representative against the Irish League, at Norwich in September 1970, when he and his teammate Jeff Astle both scored in a resounding 5–0 win, and versus the Scottish League at Hampden Park in March 1971, which was won 1–0. He was also named an England reserve. Voted 'Midlands Footballer of the Year' on three separate occasions – in 1969, 1971 and 1979 – he had the pleasure, and indeed honour, of topping the First Division scoring charts in season 1970–71 with a total of 28 goals. Besides his Albion exploits, Brown also scored 17 goals in 69 games in the NASL, netted 11 in 50 outings for Torquay United (having his last game in the Football League in December 1982 away to Port Vale) and

BROWN, Frederick

Goalkeeper: 11 apps.

*Born: Stratford, London, 6 December 1931.
Career: Leytonstone Schools. Leyton
Amateurs (1947). Leytonstone (1950).
Aldershot (professional, June 1952).
ALBION (May 1955). Portsmouth
(£1,500, June 1958). Poole Town (July
1960). Tunbridge Wells Rangers (August
1963, retired, May 1965).*

■ After making 106 League appearances
for the 'Shots', giant goalkeeper Fred
Brown was signed by Albion manager Vic
Buckingham as cover for Jimmy Sanders.
He occasionally pulled off some
wonderful saves but was inconsistent and
sometimes lost concentration. He made
his Baggies debut away at Manchester
City in October 1955 and also played in
90 Central League games for the club.

BROWN, Harry

Forward: 36 apps. 5 goals.

*Born: Northampton, 15 November 1883.
Died: Basingstoke, 9 February 1934.
Career: Kingsthorpe School
(Northampton). St Sepulchre's FC
(Northampton). Northampton Town
(1900). ALBION (£200, November 1903).
Southampton (£150, April 1905).
Newcastle United (£380, May 1906).
Bradford Park Avenue (£250, October
1907). Fulham (March 1908).
Southampton (September 1911). Woolston
FC (November 1913, retired, May 1914 to
become licensee of the Kingsland Tavern, St
Mary's Street, Southampton). During
World War One he worked in motor
transport and afterwards took over a
greengrocers shop in Padwell Road,
Southampton. In 1933 he developed a virus
that attacked his optic nerve causing him
to lose his sight. Within a few months the
illness spread and he sadly died in 1934,
aged only 50.*

■ A clever ball player, industrious and
unselfish, Harry Brown had a deceptive
style that often disconcerted his
opponents and gave colleagues either side
of him opportunities in front of goal. He
was no mean goalscorer himself, netting
65 during his career including 31 in his
two spells at The Den. He made his debut
for Albion in the League game against
Everton (home) in November 1903 and
he also played in 29 second XI matches.

claimed another three in 11 outings for
Stafford Rangers – and you can add to
that an extra 40 more strikes while
assisting the WBA All Stars in various
charity matches. Brown was coach at The
Hawthorns under managers Johnny Giles
(first), then Nobby Stiles and finally Ron
Saunders, and at the Blues under ex-

Baggies defender Garry Pendrey. Tony
Brown was one heck of a player, certainly
one of the best I've ever seen in an Albion
shirt. I know that hundreds more agree,
including his former boss Ron Atkinson,
who said that the club should erect a
monument to the 'Bomber' in the centre
circle at The Hawthorns.

BROWN, James Frederick

Inside-forward: 8 apps.

Born: Brierley Hill, 23 February 1886.
Died: Wolverhampton, May 1939.
Career: Jubilee Park Junior School (Tipton). Great Bridge Celtic (1902). Kidderminster Harriers (August 1903). Stoke (April 1907). ALBION (£210, May 1908). Kidderminster Harriers (May 1910). Willenhall Swifts (May 1914, retired, April 1919). Later worked in the carpet trade.

■ Fred Brown was a quick-moving, relaxed player whose only drawback was that he lacked courage and conviction in 50–50 situations. Nevertheless, he had a useful career, mainly in non-League football.

BUCK, Frederick Richard

Inside-forward/centre-half: 319 apps. 94 goals.

Born: Newcastle-Under-Lyme, Staffs, 12 July 1880.
Died: Stafford, June 1952.
Career: Stafford Wesleyans (August 1895). Stafford Rangers (July 1897). ALBION (November 1900). Liverpool (May 1903). Plymouth Argyle (January 1904). ALBION (April 1906). Swansea Town (May 1914, retired May 1917). Served in the Army in France during World War One. Later became a licensee in Stafford, remaining in the trade for 24 years.

■ The smallest centre-half ever to don an Albion shirt and, indeed, to play in an FA Cup final, Fred Buck, at 5ft 4in tall, was a real tough-nut, who gave Albion

tremendous service during the second of two spells with the club, during which time he took his club record to an impressive 319 appearances and 94 goals, mostly scored as an inside-forward before he moved to centre-half from where he skippered the team. Buck represented the Football League in 1910–11, the same season that Albion won the Second Division title, and the following year he gained a runners'-up medal when Barnsley beat the Baggies 1–0 in the FA Cup final replay at Bramall Lane, Sheffield. Buck also played in 22 second XI games for Albion, gaining a Birmingham & District League championship medal in 1902, and he scored both goals when Albion defeated Stoke 2–0 in the final of the Staffordshire Cup in 1903. He served as a private in the Army during World War One (based in France).
NB: Fred Buck's relatives now reside in Devon and Stafford respectively and they have kindly loaned some of his footballing memorabilia to The Hawthorns museum.

BULL, Stephen George, MBE

Striker: 5+4 apps. 3 goals.

Born: Tipton, West Midlands, 28 March 1965.
Career: Brunswick Park School. Bustleholme Boys, West Bromwich (1977–78). Tipton Town (August 1979). Newey Goodman FC (briefly, September 1983). Tipton Town (October 1983). ALBION (amateur, July 1984 but still allowed to play for Tipton). ALBION (professional, September 1984). Wolverhampton Wanderers (£70,000, with Andy Thompson, November 1986). Hereford United (as player-coach, July 1999, retired as a player, July 2001). Wolverhampton Wanderers (PR officer, August 2001).

■ He is a player Albion (or rather manager Ron Saunders) allowed to escape – and to Molineux of all places. After starting off his professional career pretty well with some excellent goals for the Baggies, Steve Bull (Black Country born and bred) went on to create record after record during his time with Wolves, for whom he rattled in no fewer than 306 goals in 559 first-team appearances. He won a total of 13 full England caps,

played in the 1990 World Cup finals in Italy and gained further honours at 'A', 'B' and under-21 levels. He helped Wolves win promotion from the Fourth to the Second Division in double-quick time and was a Wembley winner as well, when Burnley were defeated in the Final of the 1988 Sherpa Van Trophy. Manager Saunders indicated that Bully's first touch 'wasn't good enough'. Wolves boss Graham Turner (who signed him) said: 'that didn't matter, he usually scores with his second', and so it proved. During his time at The Hawthorns he scored 20 goals in 50 Central League games and four more in seven friendlies. He made his debut at senior level as a substitute against Crystal Palace (home) in the Full Member's Cup in October 1985. Certainly one that got away as far as Albion and the supporters were concerned.
NB: As a footballer (all levels including non-League action) 'Bully' scored 507 goals in 858 matches… beat that.

BUNN, Abel Thomas Frederick

Centre-half: 12 apps. 1 goal.

Born: West Bromwich, 7 February 1861.
Died: Southampton, 20 November 1921.
Career: Christ Church School, George Salter Works, ALBION (September 1879, professional, August 1885). Crosswell's Brewery (May 1886). Oldbury Town (August 1887, retired, April 1888). Later returned to work for George Salter's.

■ A powerful and fearless defender, a shade slow at times but nonetheless a grand competitor despite his height (he was barely 5ft 3in tall and weighed just 11 stones), Fred Bunn – known as 'Little Bunny' to his teammates – appeared in well over 125 games for Albion, including all their early cup-ties, and he scored in the 3–2 win over Stoke in the final of the Staffordshire Cup in 1883, the club's first trophy success. Unfortunately, he left Albion after a disagreement with certain committee members.

NB: Two of Bunn's brothers, Walter (1885–86) and Abraham (1883–90), also played for Albion. Abraham died of consumption in December 1903, aged 42.

BURGESS, Daryl

Defender: 359+18 apps. 13 goals.

Born: Birmingham, 24 January 1971.
Career: ALBION (apprentice, April 1987, professional, July 1989). Northampton Town (free, July 2001). Rochdale (August 2003).

■ Daryl Burgess was a regular in Albion's defence for a decade. He made his debut at Port Vale in 1989 and was still an important member of the side 10 years later. Starting out as an orthodox right-back, he later played in the middle of the back-four and also as a sweeper. A strong-tackling player, he always maintained a steady level of performance and received a well-deserved testimonial match (against Newcastle United) before becoming a 'Cobbler'. He also played in 120 second XI games for Albion, including reserves and the Birmingham Cup, scoring six goals. In all he made 457 first-team appearances (332 in the Football League). In October/November 2004 Burgess had the misfortune of being

sent off twice in the space of four games playing for Rochdale (once against his former club Northampton when he also conceded an own-goal and gave away a penalty).

BURGIN, Meynell

Inside-forward: 16 apps. 9 goals.

Born: Sheffield, 29 November 1911. Deceased.
Career: St Phillip's School (Bramall, Sheffield). Rossington Main Colliery (May 1919). Sheffield Wednesday (trialist, 1932). Huddersfield Town (trialist, 1932). Bradford City (trialist, 1933). Wolverhampton Wanderers (professional, May 1933). Tranmere Rovers (on loan, October 1934). Bournemouth (May 1935). Nottingham Forest (July 1936). ALBION (£1,065, May 1938). Guest for Chesterfield and Sheffield Wednesday during early part of World War Two. Retired due to cartilage trouble, May 1943.

■ Meynell Burgin was a powerfully built inside-forward, hard and aggressive, whose body strength enabled him to withstand the fiercest of challenges. Difficult to knock off the ball, he loved to be involved in the action and only the conflict of World War Two prevented him from becoming a really top-class player. He made his debut for Albion against Luton Town in August 1938 (Division Two) and also played in five second-team games, scoring two goals. He gained a Welsh Cup-winners medal with Tranmere in 1935 and amassed over 70 senior appearances and scored more than 40 goals. He failed to get into Wolves' first team, however.

BURNS, James Alfred

Outside-left: 17 apps. 5 goals.

Born: Liverpool, 20 June 1865.
Died: Hampstead, London, 16 September 1957.
Career: Liverpool & District Schools. Lancashire Boys (cricket and football). Essex Schools (seniors). London Caledonians FC (1883). ALBION (amateur, December 1889, professional, October 1890). Notts County (October 1891). ALBION (1894–95). South Weald FC (August 1895, retired two years later to concentrate on playing County Cricket). He served with Lancashire from 1884–86

and Essex for 10 years, 1897–97. He also played for the MCC in 1890 and worked in a London bookshop for many years either side of World War One.

■ Signed to replace Joe Wilson on Albion's left-wing, Alfred Burns, after scoring twice in his first three matches, failed to make much of an impact and in the end turned his allegiance to the cricket field where, as an all-rounder, he averaged 17.18 with the bat (his highest score was 114) and took 15 wickets at an average of 30.68 apiece.

BURNS, John Amos

Inside-forward: 1 app.

Born: Walsall, June 1871.
Died: Wolverhampton, July 1933.
Career: Pleck County School. Fairfield Villa (Walsall). ALBION (professional, July 1892). Stafford Rangers (August 1894). Bilston United (August 1900, retired c.1908). Later worked in a hospital for five years.

■ A diminutive forward, able to play in any position, Jack Burns was never cut out to be a professional footballer and, although he spent two seasons with Albion, he made only one senior appearance, lining up against Newton Heath (away) in October 1893. He also played in 24 'other' first-team matches.

BURNSIDE, David Gort

Inside-forward: 235 apps. 42 goals.

Born: Bristol, 10 December 1939.
Career: Bristol City (Schoolboy forms).

ALBION (amateur, 1955, professional, February 1957). Southampton (£17,000, September 1962). Crystal Palace (£5,000, December 1964). Wolverhampton Wanderers (£2,500, September 1966). Plymouth Argyle (March 1968). Bristol City (December 1971). Colchester United (March 1972). Bath City (player-manager, April 1972). Walsall (assistant manager, August–December 1973). Cadbury Heath (as a player-coach, 1974–75). Bridgwater Town (player-manager, August 1975–May 1979). Taunton Town (August 1979, retired, May 1980). A qualified FA coach, he later managed the England youth team and remained on the England coaching staff until 1999 when he returned to Bristol City as Youth Development Officer. Cheltenham Town (coach, January-October 2003).

■ A highly skilful inside-forward, Davey Burnside had a long career in League football, amassing a total of 403 League appearances and scoring 88 goals. While at The Hawthorns, he represented England youths, won two under-23 caps and played for the FA XI while also appearing in 57 Central League games (18 goals). He was later a member of Wolves' Second Division promotion-winning side of 1966–67. An adhesive ball juggler (perhaps more so off the field than on it), he received a fee for his artistry when, during the half-time interval of Albion's friendly game with the Russian Red Army side in 1957, he did some trickery in front of the 52,000 crowd and live TV audience. Three years later, after turning down a lucrative 'stage' deal, Burnside entered a sponsored 'Get-a-Header' competition and finished runner-up, with 495 clean headers, to the Austrian star George Kaul, who accumulated a staggering tally of 3,025.

BURROWS, David

Left-back: 43+10 apps. 1 goal.

Born: Dudley, 25 October 1968.
Career: St Martin's Junior & Alexandra High Schools (Tipton). West Bromwich District and West Midlands County Schools. Bustleholme Boys, West Bromwich. ALBION (apprentice, April 1985, professional, October 1986). Liverpool (£625,000, October 1988). West Ham United (September 1993). Everton (September 1994). Coventry City (£1.1

million, March 1995). Birmingham City (free, July 2000). Sheffield Wednesday (free, March 2002, retired, May 2003). Studley FC (2003–04). Emigrated to France (summer 2004). Also coached Alexandra FC (Tipton) on Sundays (1987–88).

■ A Black Country man, David Burrows made his League debut for Albion against Sheffield Wednesday in April 1986. After that he developed quickly, made 40 appearances in the second XI and in 1988, when playing superbly well, Kenny Dalglish signed him for Liverpool. He went from strength to strength, gained three England 'B' caps and seven at under-21 level. He won FA Charity Shield (1989), League Championship (1990) and FA Cup (1992) winners' medals at Anfield, making almost 200 appearances during his five years with the Reds. Burrows, who preferred the left-back position but could also occupy a central defensive berth, had made 486 senior appearances (at club level) when he retired in May 2003.

BURTON, Edward Charles

Outside-right: 1 app.

Born: Edgbaston, Birmingham, 23 June 1881.
Died: Walsall, 22 November 1963.
Career: City Road Council School (Rotten Park). Hockley Brook United (1899). Walsall (September 1902). ALBION (March 1905). Walsall (June 1905). Burton United (August 1906). Walsall (August–October 1907). Walsall Wood (1908). Darlaston (1911, retired, May 1915). Served in World War One and was later employed as a warehouseman.

■ During his relatively short stay at The Hawthorns, Ted Burton made only one first team appearance for Albion, lining up against Chesterfield (away) in March 1905.

BURTON, Henry Arthur

Full-back: 36 apps.

Born: West Bromwich, 17 January 1882.
Died: Sheffield, 20 August 1923.
Career: Tinsworth and Brinsley Schools (Sheffield). Attercliffe FC, Sheffield (1901). Sheffield Wednesday (professional, August 1902). ALBION (£850 with George Simpson, March 1909). Scunthorpe and Lindsey United (May 1911 to May 1914). Served in

the Army during World War One and later became a businessman in Sheffield.

■ A very competent full-back, Harry Burton was a well-built footballer who used his physique to good effect. He made 198 appearances for Wednesday, helping them win the League title in 1904 and FA Cup three years later. Rewarded with his Albion League debut against Blackpool in April 1909, he made only a handful of appearances in the Baggies second XI. He won both League championship and FA Cup winners' medals in 1904 and 1907 and made 198 appearances for the Owls.

BUSHELL, George Phocion

Forward: 1 app.

Born: Wednesbury, 20 March 1864.
Died: West Bromwich, May 1945.
Career: Black Lake County School, West Bromwich FC (1881). ALBION (May 1883, professional, August 1885). Wednesbury Old Athletic (May 1889, retired, May 1890).

■ George Bushell, one of Albion's early, robust players, was a heavyweight who was plagued by injuries during his six years with the club. His only senior game was against his future employers, Wednesbury Old Athletic, in the FA Cup in November 1885. He also played in 12 'other' first-team matches for the club.

BUTLER, Harry Edward

Centre-forward: 1 app.

Born: Eastwood, Notts, 18 November 1911.
Died: Bestwood, Notts, June 1984.
Career: Quarry Road Old Boys FC. Bestwood Colliery. Birmingham (amateur, May 1933, professional, August 1933). Crewe Alexandra (August 1938). ALBION (August 1939). Dudley Town (May 1943). Guest for Crewe Alexandra during World War Two. Continued to play non-League football until 1957.

■ A strong and willing reserve centre-forward, Harry Butler played in one wartime game for Albion against Stoke (away) in November 1942 and made 11 appearances for the Blues. Besides playing football, he was also a very fine crown green bowler.

BUTLER, Peter James

Midfield: 55+11 apps.

Born: Halifax, 27 August 1966.
Career: Huddersfield Town (apprentice, April 1983, professional, August 1984). Cambridge United (on loan, January–March 1986). Bury (free, July 1986). Cambridge United (free, December 1986). Southend United (£75,000, February 1988). Huddersfield Town (on loan, March–April 1992). West Ham United (£125,000, August 1992). Notts County (£350,000, October 1994). Grimsby Town (on loan, January-February 1996). ALBION (on loan, March 1996, signed after a week for £175,000). Halifax Town (free, player/assistant manager/coach, August 1998, retired as a player, May 2000). Later player-coach with the Australian club Sorrento FC then coach in Brunei (2003–04).

■ An aggressive midfielder, Peter Butler had all the battling qualities that the fans loved. A serious knee injury, suffered against Swansea City in March 2000, forced him into retirement. During his career he amassed well over 500 competitive appearances and had the ill-luck to be red-carded when making his debut for his home-town club, Halifax, against Wrexham in a League Cup tie in 1998. He was sent off playing for the Shaymen against Albion in a League Cup game in August 1999.

BUTLER, Philip Anthony

Defender: 76+6 apps. 1 goal.

Born: Stockport, 28 September 1972.
Career: Gillingham (apprentice, April 1989, professional, May 1991). Blackpool (£225,000, July 1996). Port Vale (£115,000, March 1999). ALBION (£140,000, March 2000). Bristol City (on loan, August 2002, signed on a free transfer, September 2002).

■ Strong-tackling central defender Tony Butler, 6ft 2in tall and weighing 12st 3lb, appeared in 179 games for the 'Gills' and 114 for the 'Seasiders' before moving to Vale Park. Recruited by his former boss at Blackpool, Gary Megson, he played initially at the heart of the Baggies defence, alongside Matt Carbon and James Chambers and later with Larus Sigurdsson and Phil Gilchrist. However, he was sent off in the away game at Watford early in the 2001–02 season and a subsequent suspension let in Darren Moore. After that, Butler, determined and hard-working as ever, never really got a look in, acting mainly as a substitute, although he did return briefly when Moore was sidelined, only to be sent off against his former club Gillingham inside the first five minutes in December 2001. In his first season at Ashton Gate he helped the Robins secure a place in the Second Division play-offs and win the Auto-Windscreen Shield. Then, in January 2005, he lost eight teeth after being involved in an off-the-field tussle with Peterborough striker Clive Platt as the two players went down the tunnel at half-time during a League game at Ashton Gate.

BUTLER, Stanley

Forward: 36 apps. 8 goals.

Born: Stillington, Stockton-on-Tees, 7 January 1919.
Died: Autumn 1969.
Career: Flixborough Town (1935). Scunthorpe & Lindsey United (1937). ALBION (May 1938). Bolton Wanderers (World War Two guest). Liverpool (World War Two guest). Scunthorpe and Lindsey United (trialist). Southport (World War Two guest, signed permanently, June 1947). Appleby Frodingham FC (1950). Ashby Institute (1951). Appleby Frodingham FC (1952). Later worked for a steel company.

■ A lightweight outside-left, Stan Butler's career at The Hawthorns was severely disrupted by World War Two. However, he made an impressive debut at West Ham in April 1939 and also scored 16 goals in 27 Central League games besides his first-team activity. He won a wartime League Cup runners'-up medal with Bolton in 1945 as a guest when on leave from the RAF. He died after a short illness.
* Butler's brother, Ken, was also associated with Albion (1942) as a reserve.

BYERS, John Edwin

Outside-left: 111 apps. 12 goals.

Born: Selby, Yorkshire, 12 August 1897.
Died: Worcester, 18 November 1931.
Career: Selby Schools. Knaresborough (Harrogate). Selby Town (1919). Huddersfield Town (professional, April 1921). Blackburn Rovers (April 1923). ALBION (£1,750, January 1924). Worcester City (July 1928). Torquay United (May 1929). Kidderminster Harriers (August 1931 until his sudden death).

■ An outstandingly quick, direct winger, Jack Byers had loads of skill and a powerful shot but was inconsistent. He was signed as cover for Howard Gregory (looking to retire) and Arthur Fitton and, in fact, went straight into Albion's League side (against Burnley) but thereafter was in and out of the line-up like nobody's business. However, he stuck to his guns and established himself in the team the following season when the runners'-up spot was claimed in the First Division (behind his former club Huddersfield). He scored in the final of the Birmingham Charity Cup in 1925 when Albion beat neighbours the Blues 3–1, and he also played in 39 second team games for the Baggies (13 goals scored). He moved into non-League football at the age of 34, having appeared in more than 150 competitive games since his debut for Huddersfield against Tottenham Hotspur in March 1922.

BYTHEWAY, George Samuel

Outside-right: 16 apps. 2 goals.

Born: Shuttlewood near Bolsover, Derbyshire, 22 March 1908.
Died: Chesterfield, October 1979.
Career: Staveley & Empton Village and Bolsover High Schools. Mansfield Woodhouse Comrades. Mansfield Labour Club. Seymour FC (1924). Staveley Town (1925). ALBION (£600, October 1927). Coventry City (£100, May 1933). Mansfield Town (£100, December 1933). Guildford City (June 1936–April 1939). Arnold Town (May 1939). Grimsby Town (World War Two guest, retired, May 1945). Later employed in the coal industry.

■ Quoted at the time as being 'one of the fastest wingers in the game who cuts in from the wing and makes for goal', George Bytheway suffered numerous injuries during his varied career, including three broken legs, two broken ankles, a fractured collarbone and one broken wrist – rather vulnerable, it would seem, to a strong challenge. He made his Albion debut against Leeds United in November 1927 and besides his first-team outings he also appeared in 91 Central League games, scoring 21 goals. He acted as a stand-in goalkeeper early in his career and ended it as a wing-half. He struck 23 goals in 87 games for Mansfield.

CAMERON, John Robert

Forward: 15 apps. 2 goals.

Born: Currie near Edinburgh, 14 August 1875.
Died: Edinburgh, 1944.
Career: Currie & Colinton Council Schools. Bathgate FC (1894). Everton (briefly, as an amateur, 1895). ALBION (£50, professional, November 1896). Blackburn Rovers (August 1897–February 1898).

■ A brave, determined centre-forward, Jack Cameron gave as good as he got. Unfortunately, he struggled with his form during his time with Albion after making a decent enough start by scoring on his home debut against Sunderland soon after joining the club. He also played in a further 12 or so 'other' first-team matches.
NB: There were six other Scottish-born players by the name of Cameron around at the same time (all with the Christian name John and/or Robert, who all played League football). Therefore, it is quite possible that the Albion man (here) may well have played for several more clubs, including Ayr Parkhouse, Chelsea, Govan FC, Hibernian, Lincoln City, Linthouse FC, Liverpool, Queen's Park (Glasgow). Rangers, Renton, St Mirren, Stoke, Tottenham Hotspur and even Burslem Port Vale (late in career).

CAMPBELL, Daniel

Centre-half: 11 apps.

Born: Manchester, 3 February, 1944.
Career: Droylsden (1959). ALBION (junior, September 1961, professional, November 1962). Los Angeles Wolves (£5,600, March 1968). Stockport County (January 1969). Bradford Park Avenue (March 1970). Port Elizabeth City, South Africa (May 1974, retired, April 1975, through injury). Was still resident in South Africa in 2004.

■ Centre-half Danny Campbell (replacing Stan Jones) made his Albion debut in the first leg of the 1966 League Cup final against West Ham United at Upton Park. He duly collected a winners' tankard after the second leg victory and then made his League debut at Stoke in mid-March – more than a fortnight after that cup triumph. He also played in 107 second-team matches for the club. A tall, curly-haired defender, perceptive in the

tackle, he was allowed to leave The Hawthorns after failing to dislodge John Talbot.

CAMPBELL, James Charles

Outside-right: 31 apps. 9 goals.

Born: St Pancras, London, 11 April 1937.
Died: Sedgley, June 1994.
Career: Reading (amateur, March 1952). Queen's Park Rangers (amateur, July 1952). Maidenhead Miners FC (August 1952). Maidenhead United (June 1953). ALBION (professional, June 1954, professional, July 1955). Portsmouth (£6,000, June 1959). Lincoln City (May 1962). Wellington Town (June 1964). Hednesford Town (coach, December 1966–October 1967). Warley (November 1967–May 1969). Also played for the Albion All Stars Charity team (1977–82). Later worked as a painter and decorator.

■ Right-winger Jimmy Campbell broke his right leg playing for Albion against Spurs in April 1958, a month after making his debut against his future club Portsmouth. He regained full fitness but had to fight for his place in the first team before he moved on, having also made 51 Central League appearances and scoring 11 goals. After leaving The Hawthorns, Campbell did well with both Pompey (12 goals in 50 games) and Lincoln (16 goals in 63). Sadly, he was only 57 years of age when he died.

CAMPBELL, Kevin Joseph

Striker: 17+1 apps. 3 goals.

Born: Lambeth, London, 4 February 1970.
Career: Arsenal (apprentice, June 1986, professional, February 1988). Leyton Orient (on loan, January–April 1989). Leicester City (on loan, November–December 1989). Nottingham Forest (£3 million, July 1995). Trabzonspor, Turkey (£2.5 million, August 1998). Everton (on loan, March–May 1999, signed for £3 million, June 1999). ALBION (January 2005).

■ Capped once by England 'B' and four times at under-21 level, Kevin Campbell was Everton's top scorer for three seasons running in the League and cup in 1998–2000 and again in 2002–03 before a tedious hamstring injury set in and sidelined him for quite a while. He had

earlier scored 59 goals in 228 games for Arsenal, helping the Gunners win the FA Youth Cup in 1988 and complete the League and FA Cup double in 1993, followed by European Cup-winners' Cup glory 12 months later. He then netted 35 times in 96 outings for Forest, whom he helped to gain promotion to the Premiership before having a decent spell in Turkey. He returned to England and made his debut for Everton against Liverpool in April 1999 when he was sent off in a 3–2 defeat at Anfield. A strong, purposeful player, he netted over 50 goals for Everton before joining Albion soon after the transfer window had opened in January 2005. He made his first start for the Baggies in the televised Premiership game against Fulham seven days after joining the club and then celebrated with a goal on his home debut, also on live TV, in a 2–0 victory over Manchester City, which was also Bryan Robson's first victory in the Premiership as Baggies manager. He was named skipper of the side and signed an 18-month contract with Albion.

CANTELLO, Leonard

Midfield: 365+4 apps. 21 goals.

Born: Newton Heath, Manchester, 11 September 1951.
Career: Albert Memorial School (Manchester). Manchester & District Boys. Newton Heath Schools. ALBION (apprentice, July 1967, professional, October 1968). Dallas Tornados, NASL (on loan, May–August 1978). Bolton

Wanderers (£350,000, June 1979). Eastern Athletic, Hong Kong (May 1982). Burnley (trialist, August 1982). Altrincham (September 1982). Stafford Rangers (November 1982). Hereford United (non-contract, January 1983). Bury (non-contract, February 1983). SC Cambuur, Holland (player-coach, July 1984). Peterborough United (trialist, July–August 1985). Northwich Victoria (October 1986). Stockport County (assistant manager to Asa Hartford, August 1987–March 1989). Stafford Rangers (April 1989–May 1990). Radcliffe Borough (manager, season 1990–91). Later scouted for Peterborough United (1995–96). Wigan Athletic (1996–97). Blackpool (1997–98). Also assisted on a part-time basis with evening coaching classes at Manchester City's School of Excellence along with two other ex-Albion players, Peter Barnes, Asa Hartford and Gary Owen.

■ Len Cantello donned 10 different shirts at first-team level for the Baggies. Playing with style, artistry and total commitment, he was mainly a midfielder but also filled in at left-back and occasionally as a forward. He won six schoolboy, four youth and eight under-23 caps for England and played for Albion in the 1970 League Cup final at the age of 18. Six years later he helped the Baggies win promotion from the Second Division and in December 1978 scored ITV's 'Goal of the Season' in a thrilling 5–3 win over Manchester United at Old Trafford.

Cantello, who scored 10 goals in 85 Central League games for Albion, left the club immediately after his testimonial match for what was then a record fee for an outgoing player.

CARBON, Matthew Phillip

Defender: 117+9 apps. 5 goals.

Born: Nottingham, 8 June 1975.
Career: Aston Villa (Schoolboy forms). Lincoln City (apprentice, June 1991, professional, April 1993). Derby County (£385,000, March 1996). ALBION (£800,000, January 1998). Walsall (free, June 2001, retired, August 2003, re-engaged by Walsall, October 2003). Lincoln City (on loan, October-November 2003). Barnsley (on loan, March 2004, signed permanently, June 2004).

■ Central defender Matt Carbon, 6ft 2in and 13st 6lb, made 83 appearances for Lincoln and 22 for Derby before joining Albion, following an injury to Paul Mardon. He made his debut alongside Shaun Murphy in a 3–2 home defeat by Ipswich Town and over the next two seasons produced some excellent displays, his power in the air and speed over the ground shining through as Albion battled hard and long to retain their First

Division status. Injuries interrupted his progress and after almost three and a half years at The Hawthorns he moved to nearby Walsall, released on a free transfer by manager Gary Megson. An England youth international at Sincil Bank, he went on to gain four under-21 caps before moving to Albion. Carbon surprisingly quit League football in August 2003 – only to re-sign for the Saddlers three months later.

CARR, Franz Alexander

Right-winger: 1+3 apps.

Born: Preston, 24 September 1966.
Career: Blackburn Rovers (apprentice, July 1982, professional, July 1984). Nottingham Forest (£100,000, August 1984). Sheffield Wednesday (on loan, December 1989). West Ham United (on loan, March 1991). Newcastle United (£250,000, June 1991). Sheffield United (£120,000, January 1993). Leicester City (£100,000, September 1994). Aston Villa (£250,000, February 1995). Reggiana, Italy (1996). Bolton Wanderers (October 1997). ALBION (non-contract, February–May 1998). Grimsby Town (trialist, August–September 1998). Runcorn (1999–2000).

■ Mercurial right-winger Franz Carr was never given a chance at Ewood Park, but after moving to Nottingham Forest he developed into a fine player, winning nine England under-21 caps to go with those he gained for his country at youth-team level. He appeared in over 150 games under Brian Clough's management, but then lost his way and after loan spells at Hillsborough and Upton Park he left The City Ground for St James' Park in the summer of 1991. Long periods in the wilderness disrupted Carr's progress at Bramall Lane, and in 1994 he moved again, this time to Filbert Street. Five months later he arrived at Villa Park, but again he struggled with his form and after just four outings he left for a spell in Italy. He eventually wound down his League career with Bolton and Albion and also had a trial with Grimsby, managed at the time by former Baggies boss Alan Buckley. Denis Smith brought him to The Hawthorns as a stop-gap and three of his four outings were as a substitute when he deputised, in effect, for Sean Flynn and Ian Hamilton, showing only fleeting glimpses of his once-famed ability. His

senior career realised more than 260 appearances.

CARTER, Geoffrey

Outside-left: 25 apps.

Born: Moulton, Cheshire, 14 February 1943.
Career: Moulton & Bostock Green Schools. Cheshire Boys. Northwich Victoria. Moulton FC (1958). ALBION (amateur May 1959, professional, February 1960). Bury (£4,000, July 1966). Bradford City (August 1967). Darlaston (1969–70). Parkdale FC (1970–7). ALBION (groundsman, Spring Road training ground, 1974–78). Greaves FC. West Bromwich Albion Old Stars (1975–80). Later groundsman Accles and Pollock (Oldbury).

■ Geoff Carter was a well-built, left-winger with good speed and a powerful shot. Unfortunately, owing to the excellent form of Clive Clark, his first-team outings were limited. He made his League debut with Bobby Hope against Arsenal at The Hawthorns in April 1960 and did well for the second XI, scoring 37 goals in 187 Central League games.

CARTER, Joseph Henry

Inside-forward: 451 apps. 155 goals.

Born: Aston, Birmingham, 27 July 1899. Died: Handsworth, Birmingham, 7 January 1977.
Career: Farm Street Council & Hockley Hill Schools (Birmingham). Westbourne Celtic (1918). ALBION (April 1921). Sheffield Wednesday (for six days, February 1936). ALBION (February 1936). Tranmere Rovers (£450, May 1936). Walsall (November 1936). Vono Sports FC (player-manager, 1938, retired, May 1942). Later licensee of the Grove in Handsworth, Birmingham.

■ Joe Carter, a wonderfully balanced, upright player with a fine dribbling technique, great body-swerve and exceptional positional sense, gave Albion 15 years' loyal service as a quality inside-right, making more than 450 first-team appearances and averaging a goal every third game. As partner to his captain, Tommy Glidden, he helped Albion achieve the unique FA Cup and promotion double in 1930–31, played in the 1935 FA Cup final and between 1926–29 gained three England caps (scoring 4 goals). In fact, Carter and Glidden played together in more than 350 first-team matches, while Carter also scored 34 goals in 57 Central League matches, gaining successive championship medals in 1922–23 and 1923–24. He left Albion for Hillsborough in 1936, but returned to The Hawthorns after just six days as he failed a medical.

He was then transferred to Tranmere three months later but didn't settle down with the Birkenhead club and quickly joined Walsall. Carter died of dehydration in 1977.

CARTER, Wilfred

Inside/centre-forward: 61 apps. 12 goals.

Born: Wednesbury, 4 October 1933.
Career: Wednesbury High School. South East Staffs Boys. Birmingham & District Schools. Birmingham County Youths (1948). ALBION (amateur April 1949, professional, January 1951). Plymouth Argyle (£2,525, May 1957). Exeter City (May 1964). Bath City (June 1966, retired, May 1970). Now living in Bath.

■ After leaving The Hawthorns, unable to gain a regular place in the first XI owing to the form of first Ronnie Allen and Johnny Nicholls and then Derek Kevan and Bobby Robson, plus a few others, inside/centre-forward Wilf Carter (who occasionally filled in at left-back for the injured Len Millard in 1957) became a prolific marksman, scoring 148 goals in 274 games for Plymouth, whom he helped win the Third Division South championship in 1959, having earlier represented the Division in the annual challenge match against the 'North'. A goalscorer from his early days at school, Carter made his League debut for Albion against Fulham in September 1951 and had five outings during the successful

1953–54 season. He claimed 63 goals in 143 Central League games for the Baggies.

CARTWRIGHT, Neil Andrew

Midfield: 5+7 apps.

Born: Stourbridge, 20 February 1971.
Career: High Park School. Wollaston Hales FC (1985). ALBION (apprentice, July 1987, professional, July 1988). Kidderminster Harriers (June 1993). Telford United. Worcester City (trialist). Halesowen Town (August 2000). Redditch United (2001–02). Stourbridge (August 2002).

■ Initially a striker, Neil Cartwright was switched into the midfield but failed to establish himself at The Hawthorns despite some enterprising displays in the second team, scoring 10 goals in over 75 appearances and claiming a Pontins League championship medal in 1990–91. He had a metal plate inserted in his foot during his time with Albion. His manager at non-League Stourbridge was former Albion winger Gary Hackett.

CASTLE, John Birket Richard

Wing-half: 4 apps.

Born: Hall Green, Birmingham, 20 February 1871.
Died: Dudley, August 1929.
Career: Yardley Wood Vics (1880). Birmingham St George's (August 1883). ALBION (October 1891). Brierley Hill (June 1892). Darlaston (1898). Cordley Swifts (1900, retired, May 1905). Became a licensee in Dudley.

■ A reserve half-back, Jack Castle spent just nine months with Albion, making his League debut at home to Preston North End in November 1891. He also played in half-a-dozen 'other' first-team games before developing into a solid full-back with Brierley Hill.

CAVE, George Henry

Full-back: 83 apps.

Born: Great Bridge, West Bromwich, 15 June 1874.
Died: Dudley, 28 June 1904.
Career: Whitehall Road School. Horseley Heath (1891). Great Bridge Unity

(1893–95). ALBION (July 1895, retired through injury and illness, June 1901).

■ A Black Country man through and through, George Cave was a short, stocky defender with good positional sense and a strong tackler. He made his League debut against Blackburn Rovers (away) in February 1896 when he replaced Jack Horton, and he gained a regular place in the first XI as partner to Billy Williams in 1897–98 when he was an ever-present, as he was the following season before losing out to Amos Adams. Besides his senior appearances, Cave played in more than 40 'other' first and 50 second XI games for the club. He died of consumption in a Dudley hospital, aged 30.

CHADBURN, John Lucas

Right-back/outside-right: 48 apps. 4 goals.

Born: Mansfield, 12 February 1873.
Died: Mansfield, 10 December 1923.
Career: Mansfield & District Schools. Mansfield Greenhalgh's (1891). Lincoln City (July 1893). Notts County (September 1894). Wolverhampton Wanderers (June 1897). ALBION (January 1900). Liverpool (May 1903). Barnsley (briefly). Reading (briefly). Plymouth Argyle (March 1904). Swindon Town (August 1906). Mansfield Town (July 1907, retired, January 1908).

■ Able to play at right-back and outside-right, the moustached Jack Chadburn had speed and stamina but also a volatile temperament. In a lengthy career he served in both the Football League and Southern League and played in the first game at The Hawthorns for Albion against Derby County on 3 September 1900. He made his debut for the club against Burnley (home) soon after joining from Wolves, and he also played in several 'other' first-team matches as well as a number of second XI games (helping the team win the Birmingham & District League in 1902) before transferring to Liverpool. He was a real character both in the dressing room and on the training pitch.

CHAMBERLAIN, Hubert George

Full-back: 4 apps.

Born: Langley, Oldbury, 10 November 1899.

Died: Kent, 1975.
Career: Langley Hall Council School.
Langley St Michael's (1918). Cradley
Heath (1919). ALBION (£100, April
1922). Brighton & Hove Albion (May
1926). Dartford (1928). Shoreham (1929,
retired, May 1930 through injury). Later
ran holiday chalets in Margate.

■ A finely built full-back, reserve to Joe
Smith, Billy Adams and Arthur Perry at
The Hawthorns, Bert Chamberlain won
junior international honours against
Scotland in 1925. Making his Football
League debut against Tottenham Hotspur
(away) in October 1922, he also played in
120 reserve-team matches (scoring one
goal), gaining successive Central League
championship medals in 1922–23 and
1923–24.

CHAMBERS, Adam

Midfield: 47+23 apps. 1 goal.

Born: Sandwell, West Midlands, 20
November 1980.
Career: Grove Vale FC (1996). ALBION
(apprentice, July 1997, professional,
January 1999). Sheffield Wednesday (on
loan, February–May 2004). Placed on
transfer list by Albion (December 2004,
contract cancelled, January 2005).
Kidderminster Harriers (March 2005).

■ After some enterprising second-team
performances, Adam Chambers came to
the fore in November 2001 following an
injury to Albion's hard-tackling
midfielder Michael Appleton. He stepped
confidently into the breach and did very

well, his eager-beaver approach and
tremendous work-rate earning him the
high praise of his fellow teammates and
manager alike. He has both England
youth and under-20 honours under his
belt and has played in almost 100 second-
team games for the club.
* Chambers had the misfortune to be
sent off twice in a matter of months early
in the 1999–2000, each time playing for
Albion's second team against rivals
Wolves.

CHAMBERS, James

Defender: 60+20 apps.

Born: Sandwell, West Midlands, 20
November 1980.
Career: Grove Vale FC (1996). ALBION
(apprentice, July 1997, professional,
January 1999). Watford (on loan, August
2004, signed for £75,000, September 2004).

■ Versatile defender James Chambers
(twin brother of Adam, above) was given
very few opportunities during the course
of the 2001–04 seasons after having had a
pretty useful campaign prior to that. With
Albion blessed with several experienced
and capable defenders, he only started
one game in the promotion-winning
season of 2001–02, lining up in a 2–0
defeat at Norwich City in October, and
the following year he made just nine first-
team appearances. He signed for the club
a minute before his twin brother and
made 80 senior appearances for the
Baggies, while also figuring in England
youth and under-20 internationals. He
asked for a transfer in March 2004 but
was recalled to the first team (at the
expense of Bernt Haas) as Albion
prepared for a final charge at gaining
promotion for the second time in three
years. Finally leaving The Hawthorns in
2004, having also played in more than 90
second-team games, he was a League Cup
semi-finalist with Watford in 2005.
*In season 1998–99 Adam and James
Chambers became the first set of twins
ever to represent England at any level
when they appeared together for their
country in the World Youth Tournament
in Nigeria. They were also the first twins
ever to play for Albion, lining up together
for the first time in a Football League
game against Stockport County at
Edgeley Park in September 2000 (a 0–0
draw). Three months later they became

the first twins to play in the Premiership,
playing for Albion against Arsenal at
Highbury in December 2002.

CHAMBERS, Henry

Inside-forward: 46 apps. 5 goals.

Born: Willington Quay, Northumberland,
17 November 1896.
Died: Shrewsbury, 29 June 1949.
Career: Tynemouth Schools. Willington
United Methodists. North Shields Athletic
(1913). Liverpool (April 1915). Guest for
Belfast Distillery and Glentoran during
World War One. ALBION (£2,375, March
1928). Oakengates Town (player-manager,
June 1929). Hereford United (player-
manager, January 1933, retired as a full-
time player, May 1934, stayed on as
manager until May 1948, appearing in his
last game at the age of 51).

■ Nicknamed 'Smiler', Harry Chambers,
with his distinctive bandy-legs, was a
player of ice-cool temperament with a
brilliant footballing brain. He played at
inside-left for most of his career, but
during his spell with Albion he also
occupied the centre-half, moving there
after scoring on his debut against Fulham
in March 1928. He collected an Irish Cup
runners'-up medal with Glentoran in
1919 and then helped Liverpool win the
League title twice in successive seasons:
1922 and 1923. Scorer of 151 goals for the
Merseysiders in 338 appearances – a
splendid record – he was predominantly
left-footed and was top marksman for
Liverpool in each of the first five post-war
seasons. Capped eight times by England,
he also represented the Football League

on five occasions and was honoured by his country at schoolboy level. Chambers, who was a shipyard worker by trade, is listed in the top 10 of Liverpool's greatest-ever players.

CHAPLOW, Richard David

Midfield: 3+1 apps.

Born: Accrington, 2 February 1985.
Career: Burnley (apprentice, April 2001, professional, September 2003). ALBION (£1.5 million, January 2005).

■ Signed to bolster Albion's midfield department by manager Bryan Robson on the transfer deadline in 2005, Richard Chaplow – an England youth and under-21 international – made his debut in the Premiership against Charlton Athletic after moving to The Hawthorns. A non-stop competitor, always involved in the action, he possesses good passing skills and loves to shoot from a distance. He made over 75 appearances for Burnley. He represented England at under-21 level, versus Holland in February 2004, to become Burnley's first capped player at this level. He became Albion's most expensive teenager when he joined from Burnley, his place at Turf Moor going to former Baggies star James O'Connor. He had to wait 22 days before making his premiership debut as a substitute in a 4-1 win at Charlton in March 2005.

CHAPMAN, George

Inside-forward: 14 apps. 2 goals.

Born: Moira near Burton upon Trent, 8 October 1920.
Career: Moira Village School. Burton Town Boys. Moira FC (March 1936). Donisthorpe (1937). ALBION (amateur September 1938, professional, December 1938). Guest for Norwich City and Nottingham Forest during World War Two. Brighton and Hove Albion (October 1946, retired through injury, May 1948). Later worked in engineering.

■ Basically a wartime footballer with Albion, George Chapman served in the RAF during the hostilities, attaining the rank of Corporal. A steady, adequate player, he scored 12 goals in 43 League appearances for Brighton. He made his Albion debut against Blackburn Rovers (away) in May 1940.

CHARSLEY, Christopher Charles

Goalkeeper: 1 app.

Born: Leicester, 7 November 1864.
Died: Weston-super-Mare, 10 January, 1945.
Career: St Patrick's Court (Stafford). Stafford Town (1881). Stafford Rangers (from 1883). Aston Villa (as a guest in 1886). Small Heath (September 1886). ALBION (August 1891). Small Heath (December 1891 and December 1893–May 1894). Served in the Birmingham Police Force (from 1884) and later became Chief Constable of Coventry (August 1899). Retiring in 1980, he then moved to Weston-super-Mare and was elected to the town council, rising to Deputy Mayor in 1939–40 and remaining on the council until his death.

■ A Second Division championship winner with Small Heath Division in 1892–93 and an England international (one cap against Ireland, February 1893), Chris Charsley was an amateur goalkeeper who played brilliantly for Stafford before becoming Small Heath's first full international. Well over six feet tall, he had a safe pair of hands and strong kick, and his only senior appearance for Albion was against Preston North End (home) in November 1891 when, with Joe Reader sidelined, he took over from Bob Roberts in a 2–1 defeat.
*His brother, Walter Charsley, also played briefly for Small Heath.

CHILDS, Gary Paul Colin

Midfield: 2+1 apps.

Born: Kings Heath, Birmingham, 19 April, 1964.
Career: Maypole & Brantwood Schools (Kings Heath). South Birmingham Boys. ALBION (apprentice, June 1980, professional, February 1982). Walsall (on loan, October 1983, signing permanently for £15,000, November 1983). Birmingham City (£21,500, July 1987). Grimsby Town (July 1989). Grantham Town (briefly). Wisbech Town (player-manager, 1997–98). Winterton Rangers (briefly). Boston United (1999–2001).

■ An England youth international, Gary Childs did well in Albion's intermediate and reserve teams but had limited

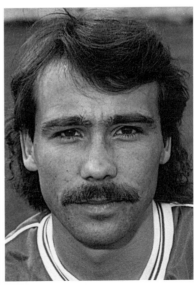

opportunities in the League side. He went on to play in over 150 games for Walsall and more than 250 for Grimsby, helping the Mariners win promotion in two successive seasons under the management of former Blues striker Alan Buckley (from Division Four in 1990 and Division Three in 1991). A ball-playing midfielder, he was a firm favourite at Fellows Park but was often criticised for his unwillingness to get stuck in at St Andrew's. Making his Albion debut against Everton (home) in February 1982, he played in 70 Central League games (9 goals scored), gaining a championship medal at this level in 1982–83.

CLARK, Benjamin

Outside-left: 1 app.

Born: Wednesbury, 13 January 1900.
Died: Wednesbury, 1970.
Career: St John's Church of England School. Seaforth Highlanders (1916). Wednesbury Old Athletic (1917). ALBION (£200, November 1919). Blakenhall (November 1920). Wednesbury Old Athletic (June 1921, retired, mid-1930s). Later worked in a glass-making factory.

■ He impressed as a teenager during his service with the Highlanders and was subsequently signed by Albion after a brief spell in local non-League football. Unfortunately, he never really got a chance to show his skills at The Hawthorns with so many other players at the club who could occupy a wing position. His only League outing was

THE WHO'S WHO OF WEST BROMWICH ALBION

against Blackburn Rovers (away) in October 1920 when he deputised for Howard Gregory. He did, however, have a handful of outings with the second XI.

CLARK, Clive

Outside-left: 351+2 apps. 98 goals.

Born: Leeds, 19 December 1940.
Career: Huddersfield Town (trialist, 1956). Leeds United (junior, August 1957, professional, January 1958). Queen's Park Rangers (August 1958). ALBION (£20,000, January 1961). Queen's Park Rangers (player-exchange deal involving Allan Glover, June 1969). Preston North End (£25,000, January 1970). Southport (July 1973). Telford United (August 1974). Washington Diplomats. Dallas Tornados and Philadelphia Fury, NASL (1974–77). Skegness Town (August 1977, retired, May 1978). Now resident in a Filey nursing home, suffering with ill-health.

■ Dashing left-winger Clive Clark could score goals as well as make them. Nicknamed 'Chippy', he became an instant success at The Hawthorns and over a period of eight and half years he netted almost 100 goals in more than 350 League and cup appearances for the Baggies, figuring in both the 1966 League Cup and 1968 FA Cup winning teams. He also played in the 1967 losing League Cup

final, scoring twice against his former club Queen's Park Rangers. Capped by England at under-23 level while with Albion, Clark also scored three times in 10 second XI games.

CLARKE, Dennis

Full-back: 25+1 apps.

Born: Stockton-on-Tees, 18 January 1948.
Career: Birmingham City (trialist, 1962). ALBION (junior, April 1963, professional, February 1965). Huddersfield Town (£35,000, January 1969). Birmingham City (September 1973, retired through injury, May 1975). Later worked in the building trade before moving to Marbella, Spain. In 2004, he sold his personal football memorabilia at auction.

■ Full-back Dennis Clarke had the honour of being the first substitute to be used in an FA Cup final, coming on for the injured John Kaye at the end of Albion's subsequent 1968 victory over Everton at Wembley. He found it hard to get a first-team game at The Hawthorns, owing to the presence of so many other full-backs (Bobby Cram, Graham Williams, Ray Fairfax and Doug Fraser), and after six years at the club he was sold to Huddersfield, for whom he appeared in 172 League games. He made his League debut for Albion against Tottenham Hotspur (home) on Boxing Day 1966. He also made 128 second XI appearances for the Baggies.

CLARKE, Isaac

Inside/centre-forward: 213 apps. 98 goals.

Born: Tipton, 9 January 1915.
Died: Canterbury, 2 April 2002.
Career: Princes End Boys School. Boys Brigade FC. Princes End Baptists. Coseley Juniors (1934). Toll End Wesley (1935). ALBION (amateur, January 1937, professional, April 1937). Guest for Nottingham Forest and Walsall during World War Two. Portsmouth (£5,000, November 1947). Yeovil Town (August 1953). Sittingbourne (manager, July 1955). Canterbury City (manager, May 1961–February 1968). Ashford Town (manager, August 1968, retiring from football, May 1973). After leaving football he worked as a fundraiser for Kent CCC while living in Herne Bay.

■ Fearless inside or centre-forward with boundless energy, solid frame and terrific goalscoring technique, Ike Clarke spent over 10 years at The Hawthorns, helping Albion win the Midland Wartime Cup in 1944. He netted 55 of his 98 goals for the club in 96 World War Two games and also contributed eight more in 26 Central League matches. After leaving The Hawthorns (unable to dislodge Dave Walsh from the central forward position), he helped Pompey win the First Division championship twice, in 1949 and 1950, and also represented the FA in five tour games against Australia in 1951. He died from a chest infection in hospital.

CLEMENT, Neil

Left wing-back: 215+15 apps. 22 goals.

Born: Reading, 3 October 1978.
Career: Aston Villa (School of Excellence, July 1994). Chelsea (apprentice, April 1995, professional, October 1995). Reading (on loan, November–December 1998). Preston North End (on loan, March–April 1999). Brentford (on loan, November–December 1999). ALBION (on loan, March 2000, signed for £150,000, August 2000).

■ Neil Clement gained England schoolboy and youth recognition as a teenager while also making steady progress with Chelsea. After loan spells with Reading, Preston North End and Brentford, he was signed on the same

basis by Albion manager Gary Megson, who then signed him permanently five months later. With a superb left foot, Clement gained a huge reputation with his free-kicks and penalties and has already scored 22 goals for Albion in 230 senior appearances. He was named in the PFA's Division One team for season 2001–02, when the Baggies gained promotion to the Premiership and returned to the top flight again two seasons later.

* His father, the late Dave Clement, played for Queen's Park Rangers, Bolton, Fulham, Wimbledon and England (5 caps).

CLEMENTS, Harold Walter

Outside-right: 10 apps.

Born: Worcester, 22 July 1883.
Died: West Bromwich, 15 February 1939.
Career: City Council School (Worcester). Worcester City (August 1900). ALBION (January 1903). Worcester City (May 1904). Shrewsbury Town (July 1905). Paisley St Mirren (August 1907). Third Lanark (1911, retired, June 1920). Became a local councillor.

■ Albion's reserve outside-right for a season and a half, Harry Clements failed to hit the headlines in English football but made a big impact north of the border. He made his Albion League debut against Aston Villa (away) in September 1903 and he also played in a dozen second XI matches.

COEN, Lawrence

Winger: 9 apps. 4 goals.

Born: Lowestoft, 4 December 1914.
Died: West Bromwich, 4 June 1972.
Career: Lowestoft Council School. Milford Haven FC (1930). ALBION (amateur, August 1932, professional, October 1932). Coventry City (£1,000, June 1938). Guest for Nottingham Forest, Notts County, Stockport County and Wrexham during World War Two. South Liverpool (briefly season 1948–49). Later worked in a iron foundry in West Bromwich.

■ A sprightly winger with an easy running action, 'Lol' Coen had to fight for a place in Albion's front-line along with Wally Boyes, Walter Robbins and Stan Wood, and in his six years at The Hawthorns he played in less than 10 first-team matches, making his League debut against Charlton Athletic (home) in February 1937. A junior international (capped in 1934), he also scored 36 goals in 108 second XI games for Albion, gaining a Central League championship medal in 1934–35. He was converted into a full-back at Coventry (1946–47) after being awarded the DFC during World War Two.

COLDICOTT, Stacy

Midfield: 81+46 apps. 4 goals.

Born: Redditch, 29 April 1974.
Career: Redditch schoolboy and junior football. ALBION (apprentice, June 1990, professional, March 1992). Cardiff City (on

loan, August-September 1996). Grimsby Town (£125,000, August 1998).

■ A highly competitive, strong tackling midfielder, Stacy Coldicott made his League debut during Albion's promotion-winning season of 1992–93, but was never really a regular in the side, having his best season in 1995–96, when he made 43 appearances, 14 of them as a substitute. He also played in 27 Central League games and eventually followed his manager, Alan Buckley, to Blundell Park. He passed the career milestone of 300 first-team games in 2003.

COLE, Harold John Samuel

Forward: 9 apps. 3 goals.

Born: Hill Top, West Bromwich, 23 February 1885.
Died: West Bromwich, 12 April 1933.
Career: Wood Green School (Wednesbury). Bloxwich Strollers (August 1900). ALBION (amateur, January 1902, professional, November 1902). Wellingborough (July 1904). Northampton Town (August 1906, retired, May 1915). Later worked as a farmhand.

■ A reserve inside-right at The Hawthorns, John Cole possessed neat skills and a strong shot. He deputised for 'Chippy' Simmons during his brief association with the club and made his League debut against Bolton Wanderers (away) in January 1903. He also played in 32 second XI matches.

* His brother, Herbert Cole, broke a leg playing for Albion's second team in September 1902 and never appeared in competitive football again.

COLLARD, Ian

Full-back/midfield: 90+7 apps. 8 goals.

Born: South Hetton, County Durham, 31 August 1947.
Career: South Hetton Primary & Senior Schools. Durham Boys. ALBION (junior, June 1962, professional, November 1964). Ipswich Town (£55,000 plus Danny Hegan, May 1969). Portsmouth (on loan, September–October 1975). Retired through injury, November 1976. Kuwait Sporting Club (coach, 1978–79). Then US, taking over soccer coaching at Duke University, North Carolina, and later at Luther

College, South Carolina University. Also coached Sunshine George Cross, Australia, was coaching organiser at the Des Moines Youth Soccer Club, Iowa, USA (responsible for the Under-11 to Under-19 age groups), and ran a Leisure Centre in Ipswich. Latterly Ipswich Town (coach).

■ A footballing inside-forward or wing-half who also competed as a left-back, Ian Collard helped Albion win the FA Cup in 1968, having played in the 1967 League Cup final defeat by Queen's Park Rangers a year earlier. He made his senior debut against Burnley in September 1964. He also appeared in 121 Central League games (19 goals scored) before leaving The Hawthorns for Ipswich for whom he played in over 100 senior games.
* Ian's brother, Bruce, was an Albion reserve (1969–73) who also played for Scunthorpe United.

COLQUHOUN, Edmund Peter Skiruing

Defender: 54 apps. one goal
Born: Prestonpans, Edinburgh, 29 March 1945
Career: YMCA (Prestonpans). Edinburgh Norton (1961). Bury (professional, March 1962). ALBION (£25,000, February 1967). Sheffield United (£27,500, October 1968). Detroit Express, NASL (May 1978). Washington Diplomats, NASL (player-coach, June 1980, retired as a player, 1982).

Later ran a sub post-office in Connisborough, South Yorkshire, and is now a night-club owner in Doncaster.

■ Initially a right-back, Scotsman Eddie Colquhoun developed into a fine central defender. As a left-half he played superbly well in Albion's defence, but then he suffered a broken leg in a League game at Newcastle in April 1968. He subsequently missed the FA Cup final and, following the switching of John Kaye to partner John Talbut, never really challenged for a first place again. He then moved to Sheffield United for whom he appeared in over 400 games, skippering the Blades to the Second Division championship in 1971. The recipient of Scottish youth and under-23 caps, he played in nine full internationals for his country and also made 12 second XI appearances for Albion.

COMYN, Andrew John

Defender: 3 apps.
Born: Wakefield, 2 August 1968.
Career: Wakefield & District Schools. Blackburn Rovers 'A' (1984). Manchester United (junior, 1985). Birmingham University (graduate, 1986). Alvechurch (briefly, 1987–88). Aston Villa (£34,000, August 1989). Derby County (£200,000, August 1991). Plymouth Argyle (£200,000, August 1993). Exeter City (trial). Northampton Town (trial). Preston North End (briefly). Rotherham United (reserves). ALBION (non-contract, March 1996). Hednesford Town (August 1997). Halesowen Town (May 2000). Nuneaton Borough (2002–04).

■ Versatile defender Andy Comyn was given a surprise Football League debut by Aston Villa manager Graham Taylor against Liverpool just a few days after walking into Villa Park as a university graduate. He went on to make 20 first-team appearances for Villa before transferring to Derby. In September 1992, with the first touch of the ball nine seconds after coming on as a substitute, he conceded an own-goal as the Rams lost 4–3 at home to Bristol City. He made 63 League appearances for Derby and followed up with 76 for Plymouth before his brief association with Albion. He made his debut for the Baggies in a 1–0 home win over Millwall on 6 April 1996, later playing in successive away games at

Sunderland (0–0) and Barnsley (1–1).
* As a gesture following the signing of Comyn, Aston Villa presented Birmingham University with a bag of football kit including jerseys and match balls.

CONNELLY, Edward John

Inside-forward: 61 apps. 15 goals.
Born: Dumbarton, 9 December 1916.
Died: Luton, 16 February 1990.
Career: Dumbarton & District Schools. Rosslyn Juniors (June 1934). Newcastle United (£90, professional, March 1935). Luton Town (£2,100, March 1938). ALBION (£4,150, August 1939). Guest for Blantyre Celtic, Dunfermline Athletic and Luton Town during World War Two. Luton Town (£2,000, April 1946). Leyton Orient (June 1948). Brighton and Hove Albion (October 1949). Dumbarton (briefly, May–October 1950, retired through injury, February 1951). Took employment as a warehouseman.

■ Blessed with heaps of talent, Eddie Connelly was a marvellous ball player, typical of the many celebrated Scots of the 1930s/early 1940s. He was, however, criticised for over-doing the clever stuff and for occasionally losing his cool on the pitch (he was sent off at least seven times during his career). On 9 November 1940 (as an Albion player) he was banned for life (sine die) by the FA after being dismissed twice for wartime misdemeanours, which were then heavily punished. He was reinstated on appeal on 25 October 1941 having been sidelined for virtually 12 months. Later he resided in Luton. He made his Albion debut in the Football Jubilee Fund game against Aston Villa (away) in August 1939 and scored 38 goals in a career total of 151 League appearances.

CONNOR, Maurice Joseph John

Outside/inside-right: 10 apps.

Born: Lochee, Ireland, 14 July 1880.
Died: Ireland, August 1934.
Career: Lochore Welfare School. Dundee Fereday FC (August 1894). Glentoran (1895). Queen's Gordon Highlanders (1896). ALBION (amateur, March 1898, professional, April 1898). Walsall (June 1899). Bristol City (July 1901). Woolwich Arsenal (May 1902). Brentford (December 1902). New Brompton (March 1903). Fulham (October 1903). Blackpool (August 1905). Glentoran (July 1915). Treharris FC, Wales (August 1918, retired, May 1919, aged 39). Returned to Ireland where he worked as a groundsman at a major golf course.

■ An Irish international (capped three times), Joe Connor was a graceful, methodical footballer, who spent just over a season with Albion, during which time he appeared in only 10 League games as partner to Billy Bassett on the right-wing. He made his debut in March 1898 against Notts County (away). He also played in several 'other' first-team matches for Albion and later scored 13 goals in 299 games for Blackpool, who converted him into a versatile half-back able to occupy all three middle positions.

CONTRA, Cosmin

Right-wing-back/midfield: 6 apps.

Born: Timisoara, Romania, 15 December 1975.
Career: Dinamo Bucharest (amateur, April 1993, professional, December 1995).

Deportivo Alaves, Spain (May 1998). AC Milan, Italy (August 2001). Atletico Madrid, Spain (£5 million, September 2002). ALBION (loan, September 2004–May 2005 with an agreed fee being paid to Atletico per appearance). Returned to Athletico Madrid (February 2005, contract cancelled). Returned to Athletico Madrid.

■ The versatile Cosmin Contra – the first Romanian to play for Albion – had already netted five goals in 43 internationals for his country and claimed 15 goals in 230 League appearances when he moved to The Hawthorns. He played for Alaves in the 2001 UEFA Cup final (beaten by Liverpool). Able to occupy as a right wing-back or midfield position, manager Gary Megson added him to the Baggies Premiership squad three weeks into the 2004–05 season. Standing 5ft 9in tall, he made his debut in English football against Colchester United (away) in a League Cup game but had to wait until new boss Bryan Robson arrived before making his debut in the Premiership, a 2–1 home defeat by Middlesbrough in November 2004. He has 34 Romania caps to his credit.

COOK, Arthur Frederick

Full-back: 55 apps.

Born: Stafford, 14 September 1890.
Died: Doxey, Stafford, February 1930.
Career: Cannock Road Council School (Stafford). Old Wesleyans (1905). Stafford Rangers (September 1906). Wrexham (professional, August 1910). ALBION (May 1911). Luton Town (August 1921). Swansea Town (June 1922). Whitchurch

FC (August 1923, retired, May 1925). Became a licensee in Stafford.

■ Less than a year after joining Albion, easy-going and fluent full-back Arthur Cook, difficult to pass and with boundless enthusiasm, played in the 1912 FA Cup final, replacing the injured Joe Smith. A very drilled, competent defender, he made his first division debut against Notts County (away) in December 1911, and as well as his senior outings he also played in over 50 second XI matches, including 16 in the Central League, and twice helped the Baggies reserves win the Birmingham & District League (1913 and 1920). Cook died under tragic circumstances after falling from the bedroom window above his licensed premises, The Doxey Arms, in Stafford in 1930. He was only 39.

COOK, Charles Frederick William

Goalkeeper: 29 apps.

Born: Rugby, 12 November 1880.
Died: Irthlingborough, Northants, January 1934.
Career: Rugby Council School. Northampton Town (professional, May 1898). ALBION (August 1903). Portsmouth (April 1905). Northampton Town (August 1908). Newport County (September 1909–May 1914). Served in the Army during World War One. Later employed in the rag trade.

■ Fred Cook, 6ft tall and weighing over 12st, was a capable goalkeeper with a good technique. He stood in for Ike Webb during his three seasons at The Hawthorns before leaving following the arrival of Jim Stringer. He made his League debut for Albion against Small Heath (away) in November 1903 and he also played in 27 second XI matches. He went on to appear in over 50 first-team games for Portsmouth.

COOKSON, James

Centre-forward: 131 apps. 110 goals.

Born: Manchester, 6 December 1904.
Died: Warminster, December 1970.
Career: South Salford Lads' Club (1919). Clayton FC (1920). Manchester North End (1921). Manchester City (professional, August 1923). Southport (trialist, August–September 1924). Chesterfield (April 1925). ALBION (£2,500, August 1927). Plymouth Argyle (August 1933). Swindon Town (August 1935, retired, May 1938, to become a publican, turning out in local charity matches until 1952). ALBION (scout, 1943–53).

■ Jimmy Cookson was a magnificent marksman, a goal-poacher of the highest quality, whose scoring record for Albion was excellent. He had been a prolific scorer prior to arriving at The Hawthorns, netting 85 League goals in three years at Saltergate. Three months after joining Albion, for what was to prove a bargain fee, he hit a double hat-

trick in a 6–3 home win over Blackpool in a Second Division match, and four years later he helped the Baggies win promotion to the First Division, having set a new club record of 38 goals in 1927–28, which was later beaten by his strike partner W.G. Richardson in 1935–36. He also netted 95 times in 92 second XI games for Albion, helping them win the Central League title in 1932–33 (when he top-scored with 29 goals). The previous season he had netted seven goals in a 10–1 win over Chesterfield's reserves. After leaving Albion he continued to score well for both Plymouth and Swindon before retiring in 1938. In a 15-year professional career, Cookson hit 256 League goals (in 392 games). He was leading scorer in Division Three North in 1925–26 and Division Two in 1927–28 and his 100th League goal came up in his 89th match, playing for Albion against South Shields in December 1927; a record for the quickest-ever century of goals. Cookson toured Canada with the FA in the summer of 1931. It was Cookson who spotted Ray Barlow, sending him to Albion in 1944.

* Jimmy Cookson's elder brother, Sammy, played right-back for Stalybridge Celtic, Macclesfield, Manchester City (285 League outings), Bradford Park Avenue (136 League games) and Barnsley in a career that lasted over 20 years (until 1935). The Cooksons worked together at Maine Road (1923–24).

CORBETT, Francis James

Full-back: 12 apps.

Born: Willenhall, 2 August 1903.
Died: Cannock, 1970.
Career: Willenhall Council School. Hednesford Prims (1920). Hednesford Town (August 1924). ALBION (£50, June 1926). Coventry City (May 1931). Hednesford Town (July 1933, retired, May 1938). Later employed by the coal board.

■ Frank Corbett was a solid defender, reserve to George Shaw, Bob Finch and Bert Trentham during his five years at The Hawthorns. Making his League debut against Liverpool at Anfield in November 1926, he also appeared in well over 200 second-team matches, 152 in the Central League, helping the reserves win the championship in 1926–27.

CORBETT, George

Full-back/outside-left: 1 app.

Born: North Walbottle near Newcastle, 11 May 1925.
Career: North Walbottle & Middlestone Moor Schools. Shildon Juniors (1943). Sheffield Wednesday (professional, May 1945). Spennymoor United (August 1946). ALBION (£800, March 1951). Workington (June 1953, retired, May 1954). Later worked at the docks.

■ A full-back by nature, George Corbett's only first-team outing for Albion was on the left-wing in a 4–1 League victory over Wolves at Molineux in April 1952. He also played in 43 Central League games (15 goals scored) but never settled in the Midlands and later played in nine League games for Workington.

CORBETT, Richard Sebastian

Left-back: 3 apps.

Born: Wolverhampton, 30 March 1887.
Died: Wolverhampton, December 1933.
Career: Stafford Road School (Wolverhampton). Willenhall Swifts (August 1905). ALBION (£40, professional, October 1909). Walsall (May 1911). Bilston United (before and after World War One). Became a licensee in Wolverhampton.

■ Reserve to Jesse Pennington and Arthur Cook, Dick Corbett won junior international honours against Scotland in 1910 but never really looked like making the grade in League football. He made his debut against Glossop (home) in March 1911.

CORFIELD, Sidney John

Centre-half: 8 apps.

Born: Tipton, 24 June 1883.
Died: West Bromwich, 1941.
Career: St Martin's School (Tipton). Toll End Wesley (April 1900). ALBION (professional, November 1902, retired, May 1904). Returned to football with Wolverhampton Wanderers (July 1905). Wrexham (August 1909). Tipton Victoria (August 1911, retiring 'second time', May 1914). Served in the Army during World War One and was later employed by a steel company.

■ Sid Corfield looked like a very good prospect before his parents decided against him turning professional. He returned to the game with Wolves, for whom he appeared in 44 League games, and later gained two Welsh Cup winners' medals with Wrexham in 1910 and 1911. He made his League debut for Albion at Middlesbrough in January 1904, and he also played in 33 second XI matches. Besides his footballing exploits, Corfield was also a very useful cricketer, playing for West Bromwich Dartmouth in 1913 and 1914.

CORK, David

Midfield/forward: 1+3 apps.

Born: Doncaster, 28 October 1962.
Career: Doncaster Schools. Doncaster Rovers (trialist, 1977). Arsenal (apprentice, July 1978, professional, June 1980). Huddersfield Town (July 1985). ALBION (on loan, September–October 1988). Norwich City (trialist, November–December 1988). Scunthorpe United (non-contract, February 1989). Darlington (July 1989–May 1992).

■ Able to play in midfield or as an out-and-out attacker, David Cork came to The Hawthorns during an injury crisis and was named as a substitute on six occasions during his short stay, coming off the bench when making his Albion debut against Walsall in September 1988. He also scored three goals in five Central League appearances for the Baggies before going on to find the net 25 times in 110 League games for Huddersfield, following up with 11 more strikes in 64 outings for Darlington.

COWDRILL, Barry James

Left-back: 144+5 apps. 1 goal.

Born: Castle Bromwich, Birmingham, 3 January 1957.
Career: Bentley Road & Castle Bromwich Schools. Sutton Coldfield Town (April 1975). ALBION (£5,000, professional, April 1979). Rotherham United (on loan, October–November 1985). Bolton Wanderers (July 1988). Rochdale (February–May 1992). Sutton Coldfield Town (August 1992). West Bromwich Albion All Stars (1993–96).

■ Barry 'Basil' Cowdrill was signed by Albion boss Ron Atkinson as a left-winger, but after a few games in that position for the second team he was

successfully converted into a competent left-back and went on to appear in almost 150 first-team matches for the club, scoring one goal against Grimsby Town in an FA Cup tie. He made his League debut for Albion against Norwich City (away) in March 1980, played in 170 second XI games, scoring 18 goals, and as captain he helped the Baggies win the Central League title in 1982–83. He was also a Sherpa Van Trophy winner with Bolton at Wembley in May 1989 and went on to make 160 senior appearances for the Trotters.

COX, Frederick James Arthur

Wing-forward: 4 apps. 1 goal.

Born: Reading, 1 November 1920.
Died: Bournemouth, 7 August 1973.
Career: Redlands Senior School (Reading). Reading Schoolboys. St George's Lads' Club (Reading). Tottenham Hotspur (amateur, August 1936, semi-professional, June 1937). Northfleet (briefly). Tottenham Hotspur (professional, August 1938). Guest for Fulham, Manchester City, Reading and Swindon Town during World War Two. Arsenal (£12,000, September 1949). ALBION (£2,000, player-coach, July 1953, then assistant manager from August 1954). Bournemouth and Boscombe Athletic (manager, April 1956). Portsmouth (manager, August 1958–February 1961). Gillingham (manager, June 1962–December 1964). Bournemouth and

Boscombe Athletic (manager, April 1965–April 1970). While serving in the RAF during World War Two, he represented the Civil Defence as a player, was awarded the Distinguished Flying Cross and reached the rank of Flight Lieutenant, clocking up over 2,000 air miles by flying transport planes in and out of the Far East. He also played for the Combined Services in India and later became a fully qualified FA coach. On leaving football in 1970, he took over a newsagents business in Bournemouth.

■ After scoring 23 goals in 138 games for Spurs, winger Freddie Cox – fast and direct – moved across North London to Highbury where he gave the Gunners excellent service for four years, netting 16 goals in 94 outings. He played in two FA Cup finals (a winner in 1950, a runner-up in 1952) and helped Arsenal win the League title in 1953 before joining his former White Hart Lane playing colleague, Vic Buckingham, at The Hawthorns. He served Albion for three years making just four first-team appearances, his debut coming in a 2–1 League home win over Middlesbrough in October 1953. He also played in 27 second-team fixtures (7 goals scored) and was Albion's first officially appointed assistant manager. He eventually moved into management himself at Bournemouth in 1956, doing well in his initial spell as the Cherries knocked his old team, Spurs, out of the FA Cup a year later. Also in charge at Fratton Park and The Priestfield Stadium, he guided Gillingham to the Fourth Division title in 1964 before returning to Dean Court where he ended his footballing career.

COX, Samuel

Full-back: 2 apps.

Born: Mexborough, 30 October 1920.
Died: 1985.
Career: Mexborough and Wath-on-Deane Schools. Denaby United (1946). ALBION (£750, May 1948). Accrington Stanley (£1,250, July 1951). Scunthorpe United (July 1952, retired through injury, May 1954). Later engaged in the licensing trade.

■ Sammy Cox was a steady, well-built reserve full-back who never quite developed the basic ingredients to perform at the highest level. His Albion debut was against Leicester City in

September 1948 when he deputised for Jim Pemberton. He made 74 appearances in the Central League side. At Accrington, he took over from Stan Lynn (previously sold to Aston Villa) and made 43 League appearances for the Peel Park club but managed only three for Scunthorpe.

CRABTREE, Frederick William

Outside-right: one app. 1 goal.

Born: West Bromwich, 6 January 1865. Died: London, 1939. Career: Walsall Street School (West Bromwich). Christ Church FC (1886). ALBION (May 1887). Old Stephen's of Shepherd's Bush FC, London (August 1889, retired May 1894). Later became a Football League referee and also coached football (and cricket) at various London Schools.

■ A small, nimble outside-left, reserve to Billy Bassett, Fred Crabtree scored in his only League game of his career for Albion against Everton (away) in February 1889. He also played in five 'other' first-team matches.

CRAM, Robert

Full-back/right-half: 163 apps. 26 goals.

Born: Hetton-le-Hole, County Durham, 19 November 1939. Career: ALBION (amateur, September 1955, professional, January 1957). Bromsgrove Rovers (August 1967). Vancouver Royals, Canada (1968). Vancouver All Stars, Canada (1969). Paul Taylor's FC (coach, late 1969). Colchester United (January 1970). Royal Canada FC, Canada (1972). Bath City (player-coach, March 1973). Returned to Canada (during 1973–74) where he set up a successful coaching school in Vancouver.

■ Hard-tackling defender and Albion's spot-kick expert, Bobby Cram became only the second full-back ever to score a hat-trick (including two penalties) in a First Division League game, doing so for the Baggies against Stoke City in September 1964 (won 5–3). Stan Lynn of Aston Villa had earlier netted three goals against Sunderland in 1958. Cram, strong and mobile with a terrific engine, made his League debut at Bolton (with Jock Wallace) in October 1959 and his last appearance for Albion came in the 1967

League Cup final defeat by Queen's Park Rangers at Wembley. He had a testimonial at The Hawthorns in 1967, and four years later starred for Colchester when they knocked the favourites, Leeds United, out of the FA Cup. He also helped the Layer Road club (with future Albion goalkeeper, Graham Smith) win the Watney Cup (at Albion's expense) at the start of the 1971–72 season. Cram appeared in 206 Central League games for Albion (23 goals) and is the uncle to former British Olympic athlete Steve Cram. He now lives in Canada.

CRAWFORD, Campbell Hackett Rankin

Right-back: 14 apps.

Born: Alexandria, Scotland, 1 December 1943. Career: Alexandria Schools. Vale of Leven FC. Alexandria Academy. Drumchapel Amateurs (1958). Dumbarton West & Scotland Boys. ALBION (amateur, June 1959, professional, February 1960). Exeter City (July 1967). Kidderminster Harriers (July 1974). Wednesbury Athletic (August 1977). Rushall Olympic (1979–80). Also played for West Bromwich Albion All Stars (1979–93). Now living in Walsall.

■ A small, boyish-looking right-back who had Don Howe and Bobby Cram ahead of him in Albion's reckoning,

Campbell Crawford did far better with Exeter City, for whom he made 259 senior appearances before stepping down into non-League football. He joined Albion with fellow Scots Ken Foggo, Bobby Hope and Bobby Murray shortly after playing for his country in a schoolboy international. Crawford's League debut for Albion was against Manchester United in September 1963 in front of more than 50,000 spectators. He made 157 appearances for the Baggies Central League side.

CRAWFORD, Raymond

Centre-forward: 17 apps. 7 goals.

Born: Portsmouth, 13 July 1936. Career: Hilsea Modern & Portsmouth Senior Schools. Portsmouth (amateur, July 1952, professional, December 1954). Ipswich Town (September 1958). Wolverhampton Wanderers (September 1963). ALBION (£30,000, February 1965). Ipswich Town (£15,000, March 1966). Charlton Athletic (March 1969). Kettering Town (November 1969). Colchester United (June 1970). Durban City, South Africa (August 1971). Brighton and Hove Albion (coach, November 1971). Portsmouth (coach, June 1973). FC Eden, New Zealand (coach, August 1974). Portsmouth (Youth team coach, July 1975). Fareham Town (manager, August 1978). Winchester City (manager, May 1981–June 1983). Also

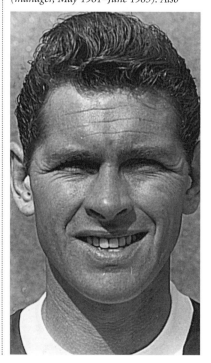

represented the Malaysian FA when on National Service in the mid-1950s. Now lives in Portsmouth.

■ Centre-forward Ray Crawford had a knack of turning half-chances into important goals. An exuberant opportunist, he netted well over 350 times in more than 600 games (289 in 475 at League level) during a playing career that spanned some 20 years. He helped Ipswich win the Second and then First Division titles in successive seasons (1961 and 1962) and claimed five goals in a 10–0 European Cup win over Fiorentina of Malta in September 1962. Following an 18-month spell at Molineux, he moved to The Hawthorns, joining fellow strikers Jeff Astle, John Kaye and Tony Brown. Surprisingly, he never really settled into manager Jimmy Hagan's plans despite scoring on his debut against Aston Villa and in the second leg of the 1966 League Cup semi-final against Peterborough, plus 17 in 19 second XI games. He returned to his former club, Portsmouth, after 13 months at The Hawthorns. Capped twice by England, he also represented the FA XI and played twice for the Football League. He is still Ipswich's record scorer of all-time with a total of 228 goals, 203 in League action.

CRESSWELL, Frank

Inside-forward: 31 apps. 6 goals.

Born: South Shields, 5 September 1908.
Died: December 1979.
Career: Stanhope Road & Westoe Central Schools (South Shields). South Shields & England Boys, South Shields (professional, August 1925). Sunderland (£400, July 1926). ALBION (£975, June 1929). Chester (June 1930). Notts County (July 1933). Chester (August 1934–May 1939). Did not play after World War Two and became a shopkeeper.

■ Frank Cresswell possessed neat and deft footwork and was a good finisher, scoring 68 goals in a total of 232 League games in a career that spanned 14 years, but spent just one season at The Hawthorns. After making his Albion debut against Wolves (away) in August 1929, he did well in an attack-minded side that scored 105 League goals while also having eight outings (4 goals) for the second XI. An injury, suffered against

Nottingham Forest in mid-March, allowed Jimmy Edwards in and, as a result, Cresswell's Albion career was over. He went on to gain a Welsh Cup winners' medal (1933) and a runners'-up prize in the same competition two years later with Chester. As a schoolboy he was capped by England against Wales and Scotland in the 1922–23 season.
* His brother, Warney Cresswell, played for Manchester United, Hibernian, Sunderland, South Shields, Everton and England.

CRICHTON, Paul Andrew

Goalkeeper: 34 apps.

Born: Pontefract, 3 October 1968.
Career: Nottingham Forest (junior, April 1984, professional, May 1986). Notts County (on loan, September–October 1986). Darlington (on loan, January–February 1987). Peterborough United (on loan, March–April 1987). Darlington (on loan, September–October 1987). Swindon Town (on loan, December 1987–January 1988). Rotherham United (on loan, March 1988). Torquay United (on loan, August–October 1988). Peterborough United (£3,000, November 1988). Doncaster Rovers (free, August 1990). Grimsby Town (free, July 1993). ALBION (£250,000, September 1996). Aston Villa (on loan). Burnley (on loan, August 1998, signed for £100,000, November 1998). Norwich City (£150,000, June 2001). York City (free, July 2004). Leigh RM (October 2004).

■ Nomadic goalkeeper Paul Crichton was an Albion player for two years after being signed by manager Alan Buckley. He made his debut in the fifth match of the 1996–97 season at home to Reading (replacing Nigel Spink) and held his place in the side until the arrival of Alan Miller in February. He also played in 16 second XI games. An excellent shot-stopper, at times he performed well but was prone to mistakes. In 2004, following his release by First Division champions Norwich City, he had accumulated a grand total of 472 appearances at club level, his best spell by far coming at Blundell Park (150 games).

CRISP, John

Winger: 124 apps. 23 goals.

Born: Hamstead, Birmingham, 27 November 1896.

Died: Birmingham, 20 February 1939.
Career: Hamstead Council School. Walsall (briefly, 1912). Aston Villa (trialist, April–May 1913). Leicester Fosse (professional, August–September 1913). Ordnance FC (October 1913). ALBION (professional, May 1914). Served in the Royal Navy during World War One (on HMS Erin). Ward End Works FC (guest, 1918–19). Blackburn Rovers (£3,125, March 1923). Coventry City (1926–27). Birmingham (1927–28). Stourbridge (1928–30). Bromsgrove Rovers (August 1930). Cheltenham Town (March 1933, retired, May 1935). Licensee of the Scott Arms, Queslett Road, Great Barr, Birmingham until his death.

■ Winger Jack Crisp was a key figure in Albion's thrustful attack of 1919–20 when they won the League championship. That season he appeared in 38 games, scored eight goals and created at least another dozen for his colleagues. A spirited forward with good pace and a strong shot, he won junior international honours, represented the Football League and scored on his League debut for Albion in a 2–1 win at Everton in December 1914. He made over 250 first-team appearances during his career. Crisp died of consumption at the age of 42.
* A relative of Crisp's, John Shell, played for Aston Villa in the late 1930s.

CRONE, Robert

Full-back: 51 apps.

Born: Belfast, 4 January 1897.
Died: Barrow-in-Furness, January 1943.
Career: Belfast Schools. Distillery (August

1885). Middlesbrough (August 1892). ALBION (March 1893). Burton Swifts (August 1895). Notts County (August 1896). Bedminster (September 1897). Bristol City (trainer, 1901–03). Brentford (trainer, 1903–08). ALBION (trainer/coach, 1908–09). Workington (trainer, August 1909, retired from football, May 1912). Later took employment in the steel industry.

■ Bob Crone was a lusty full-back, typical of defenders at the time. He always put his heart and soul into his performances and gave Albion just over two years' excellent service, first partnering Mark Nicholson and then Billy Williams in front of goalkeeper Joe Reader. He made his Albion debut against Sheffield Wednesday (home) in March 1893. Capped four times by Ireland (1889–90), he gained an Irish Cup winners' medal in 1889 having collected a runners'-up prize the previous season. He made a total of 102 League appearances during his career, having been with Middlesbrough in their pre-League days. He also played in 47 'other' first-team matches for Albion.

CROOKS, Garth Anthony, OBE

Forward: 49 apps. 21 goals.

Born: Stoke-in-Trent, 10 March 1958.
Career: St Peter's Comprehensive School, (Penkhull, Stoke-on-Trent). Stoke City (apprentice, July 1974, professional, March 1976). Tottenham Hotspur (£600,000). Albion (£100,000, July 1985). Charlton Athletic (March 1987). Manchester United (on loan, November 1983–January 1984). Retired through injury, May 1990, having already been appointed as chairman of the PFA (1988). Nowadays Crooks works for the media, covering Premiership football.

■ Having already netted 60 goals in 164 senior games for Stoke and 75 in 175 outings for Spurs, with whom he won successive FA Cup winners' medals in 1981 and 1982 as well as collecting a League Cup runners'-up prize in 1983, Garth Crooks moved to The Hawthorns as manager Johnny Giles strengthened his squad following a rather disappointing 1984–85 season. Unfortunately, he was injured on his debut against First Division newcomers Oxford United and was out of action for three weeks. He

returned to a struggling team and, although he scored his fair quota of goals, relegation was suffered at the end of the campaign, which in fact had been Albion's worst on record. Crooks, who also scored three times in 11 Central League games for the Baggies, was capped four times by England at under-21 level, netting a hat-trick against Bulgaria on his international debut at Leicester in the 1979–80 season. In fact, he also scored a treble for Stoke in a League game against Albion at The Victoria Ground in 1979 and found the net for Spurs against the Baggies in a 1983 FA Cup tie. He was awarded the OBE in October 1999 for services to the Institute of Professional Sport.

CROSS, David George

Striker: 61+1 apps. 23 goals.

Born: Heywood near Bury, Lancashire, 8 December 1950.
Career: Heywood Grammar School. Rochdale (apprentice, April 1967, professional, August 1969). Norwich City (£40,000, October 1971). Coventry City (£150,000, November 1973). ALBION (£150,000, November 1976). West Ham United (£200,000, December 1977). Manchester City (£125,000, August 1972). Vancouver Whitecaps, NASL (£75,000, April 1983). Oldham Athletic (£20,000, September 1983). Vancouver Whitecaps, NASL (£10,000, April 1984). ALBION (free, October 1984). Bolton Wanderers (free, June 1985). Bury (on loan, January–May 1986). Blackpool (non-contract, July–August 1986). Heywood Old

Boys (April 1988). Oldham Athletic (part-time coach, 1990, senior youth-team coach, 1995–2002, assistant manager, 2002–03). Rochdale (scout, 2003–04). Also scouted for a variety of other clubs in the Lancashire area (mid-1990s) and is president of the Heywood Cricket Club.

■ A fine goalscorer on his day, David Cross had two spells with Albion, signed each time by manager Johnny Giles and making his 'first' debut against his former club, Manchester City, at Maine Road. He initially partnered Ray Treacy in attack and also played alongside Ally Brown and Cyrille Regis, moving on when the latter established himself in the side. On his return to The Hawthorns (just after Regis had left for Coventry City), Cross joined Garry Thompson up front but had a lean time in the scoring stakes, although he did score four goals in 10 second XI games. In all, he netted well over 200 goals in more than 600 League and cup games as a professional and gained an FA Cup winners' medal with West Ham in 1980 and two Second Division championship medals, with Norwich in 1972 and the Hammers in 1981. He also received a League Cup runners'-up prize in 1981 and helped the Whitecaps win the NASL (Western) title in 1984.

CROSS, Nicholas Jeremy Rowland

Utility forward: 79+40 apps. 19 goals.

Born: Shirley, Birmingham, 7 February 1961.

Career: Langley Junior & Sharman's Cross Senior Schools. Solihull Boys. Peterbrook FC. Solihull Borough (1975). Woodbank Albion (1976). ALBION (apprentice, July 1977, professional, February 1979). Walsall (£48,000, August 1985). Leicester City (£80,000, January 1988). Port Vale (£125,000, June 1989). Hereford United (free, July 1994). Solihull Borough, Redditch United (player/caretaker manager, August 1999, then player-manager, 2000–02). Studley FC (manager, season 2003–04). Also assisted West Bromwich Albion All Stars (late 1990s/early 2000s). Moved to France in 2004.

■ Utility forward Nicky Cross, who was at The Hawthorns for eight years, probably spent more time sitting on the substitute's bench than any other Albion player. A third of his first-team appearances came as a 'sub' and overall he donned six different numbered shirts while on first-team duty. An eager, bustling, all-action and well-balanced player, he loved to attack defenders on the outside when possible and was good at shielding and turning with the ball in tight situations. He made his senior debut for Albion at Old Trafford in April 1981 when 44,442 fans saw Manchester United win 2–1. He netted the first of his 19 senior goals in his second game a fortnight later, a 4–2 win over the FA Cup finalists, Tottenham Hotspur, at The Hawthorns. His best spell in the first team came during the 1982–83 season when he scored four times in 32 League outings. He also claimed 60 goals in 161 Central League games for Albion. He helped Vale reach the final of the Autoglass Trophy in 1993 and the

following season played his part as the Potteries club gained promotion from the Second Division, and all this after he had been out of action for 14 months with damaged knee ligaments. During his League career, Cross scored 128 goals in 491 appearances, including 45 in 109 games for the Saddlers and 39 in 144 for the Valiants.

CROWE, Edward Wilfred

Goalkeeper: 16 apps.

Born: Stourport-on-Severn, 27 November 1911.
Died: Stourport, 20 March 1982.
Career: Stourport Council School. Worcestershire County Youths. Stourport Swifts (1926). ALBION (amateur, May 1930, professional, October 1930). Swansea Town (£375, June 1936). Aldershot (August 1937). Wilden FC (August 1939, retired, May 1942). Later worked on narrowboats (Stourport canal basin).

■ A very useful goalkeeper signed as cover for Harold Pearson and George Ashmore, Ted Crowe made his League debut for Albion against Blackburn Rovers (home) in January 1934. An England junior international (capped in 1931), he was restricted to just 16 first-team outings during his time at The Hawthorns, but he did gain three Central League championship medals in successive seasons, 1932–35, being an ever-present in the first season. He went on to make a total of 157 second-team appearances, having toured America with the Worcestershire FA party in 1928.

CROWSHAW, Allan Alfred

Winger: 11 apps. 2 goals.

Born: Willenhall, 12 December 1932.
Career: South East Staffs Schools. Bloxwich Wesley. Bloxwich Strollers (April 1946). ALBION (amateur, October 1946, professional, May 1950). Derby County (£1,000, May 1956). Millwall (May 1958). Sittingbourne FC (July 1960, retired, 1968). Chose to live and work in Kent.

■ An orthodox outside-left, able to play on the opposite flank, Allan Crowshaw made a bigger impact after leaving The Hawthorns. As an Albion reserve, he deputised for George Lee and occasionally Frank Griffin, making his League debut against Charlton Athletic at

The Valley in November 1954 (with Alec Jackson). He scored 28 goals in 113 Central League games for the Baggies. Unfortunately, he broke his leg playing for Derby but regained full fitness and went on to amass a career record of 18 goals in 78 League games.

CRUMP, Arthur Wilbert Benjamin

Right-back: 1 app.

Born: Smethwick, 22 August 1886.
Died: Stourbridge, August 1960.
Career: Cape Hill School (Smethwick). Birmingham Casuals FC (1902). Smethwick Old Church (1903). Manchester City (professional, March 1905). Reading (August 1905). ALBION (June 1909). Dudley Town (October 1910). Shrewsbury Town (April 1912). Wellington Town (May 1914, served in the Army during World War One, retired from football, May 1921). Later became a shopkeeper.

■ Defender Arthur Crump played his best football with Reading but unfortunately never looked like making the grade in the Football League. He appeared in just one game for Albion against Lincoln City (home) in April 1910, standing in for Harry Burton to partner Dick Corbett at full-back. He had already played in over 20 second XI matches for the club.

CUMBES, James

Goalkeeper: 79 apps.

Born: Didsbury, Manchester, 4 May 1944.
Career: Didsbury County School. Manchester Boys (trialist). Whalley Grange FC (Manchester Amateur League). Runcorn (1963). Southport (briefly, 1964). Tranmere Rovers (professional, September 1965). ALBION (£33,350, August 1969) Aston Villa (£36,000, November 1971). Portland Timbers, NASL (March 1976). Coventry City (non-contract, September 1976). Runcorn (semi-professional, August 1977). Southport (non-contract, January 1978). Worcester City (August 1978–May 1981). Kidderminster Harriers (August 1982–May 1984). West Bromwich All Stars (1980s). Played cricket for Lancashire (1963–67 and 1971), Surrey (1968 and 1969), Worcestershire (1972–81) and Warwickshire (1982) as well as for West

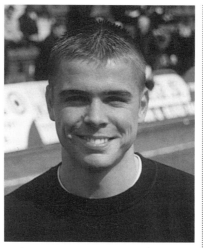

Bromwich in the Dartmouth/Birmingham League (1982–84). Retired from active sport in October 1984 to become Commercial Manager of Warwickshire CCC, a position he held until August 1987 when he switched to Lancashire CCC where he's now employed as commercial executive, based at Old Trafford.

■ A tall, agile and competent goalkeeper with good technique, who was also a very fine fast bowler on the county cricket scene, Jim Cumbes won a Cheshire Bowl winners' medal with Runcorn, played in 137 League games for Tranmere and then, after his debut against Arsenal, contested the number one position with John Osborne at The Hawthorns and made 32 second XI appearances before transferring to Villa Park in 1971. He spent five years with Villa, making 183 appearances and gaining a Third Division championship medal (1972) and a League Cup winners' prize (1975) in the process. Cumbes amassed over 400 League and cup appearances during his career. As a cricketer he won both County championship and knockout Cup medals with Worcestershire. In all, he played in 161 first-team cricket matches, averaging 7.56 with the bat and taking 379 wickets at 30.20 each with a best return of 6–24. He also took 38 catches.

CUMMINGS, Warren

Left wing-back: 7+12 apps.

Born: Aberdeen, 15 October 1980.
Career: Chelsea (apprentice, April 1997,

professional, July 1999). Bournemouth (on loan, October–November 2001). ALBION (on loan, March–May 2001 and July 2001–March 2002). Dundee (on loan, August–September 2002 and again November–December 2002). AFC Bournemouth (free, February 2003).

■ A strong, able-bodied, Scottish youth and under-21 international left-back (9

caps gained in the latter category), Warren Cummings was signed twice by manager Gary Megson as cover for Neil Clement, making his debut as a substitute in the home game against Tranmere Rovers just 24 hours after signing in March 2001. A very talented player, he made almost 20 second XI appearances for the Baggies and in May 2003 helped AFC Bournemouth win the Third Division play-off final at Cardiff's Millennium Stadium.

CUNNINGHAM, Laurence Paul

Winger: 106+8 apps. 30 goals.

Born: Archway, London, 8 March 1956.
Died: Near Madrid, Spain, 15 July 1989.
Career: Stroud Green School (Highgate). Highgate Wood Boys. Haringey Schools. South East Counties Schools. North London Boys. Leyton Orient (apprentice, August 1972, professional, July 1974). ALBION (£110,000, March 1977). Real Madrid, Spain (£995,000, June 1979). Manchester

United (on loan, March–April 1983). Sporting Gijon, Spain (on loan, August–September 1983). Olympique Marseille (on loan, August 1984–March 1985). Leicester City (on loan, November 1985–May 1986). Rayo Vallecano, Spain (August 1986–June 1987). Real Betis, Spain (trialist, August–September 1987). RSC Charleroi, Belgium (October–December 1987). Wimbledon (non-contract, January–May 1988). Rayo Vallecano (August 1988 until his death).

■ Laurie Cunningham was tragically killed in a road accident on the outskirts of Madrid during the early hours of 15 July 1989, at the age of 33. Known as the 'Black Pearl' and 'Black Beauty', he stayed for two years at The Hawthorns, averaging a goal every three-and-half games. He made a fine debut at Tottenham (with Tony Godden) and later helped Albion reach the FA Cup semi-final (1978) and the UEFA Cup quarter-final (1979), and was the first black player to don an England jersey in a major international, lining up for the under-21 side against Scotland at Bramall Lane, Sheffield, soon after joining Albion. He added another five under-21 and six senior caps to his collection as well as playing for his country at 'B' team level. Cunningham left Albion for Real Madrid in a record £995,000 deal in the summer of 1979 and was inspirational as Real completed the League and cup double in his first season in Spain. He later played in the 1981 European Cup final defeat by Liverpool and, as a substitute, was an FA Cup winner with Wimbledon (against Liverpool) in 1988. He was a brilliant footballer: superbly skilful, confidently confrontational and who, with his electrifying pace and extrovert but very effective and exciting footballing skills plus his shooting power and charisma, genuinely lit up The Hawthorns and put more than a smile or two on the faces of the Baggies supporters.

CUNNINGTON, Shaun Gary

Midfield: 11+7 apps.

*Born: Bourne, 4 January 1966.
Career: Wrexham (junior, April 1982, professional, January 1984). Grimsby Town (£55,000, February 1988). Sunderland (£650,000, July 1992). ALBION (£220,000,*

August 1995). Notts County (£25,000, March 1997). Kidderminster Harriers (June 1998, later player-coach from August 2000, then youth-team coach, 2003, appointed caretaker manager, November 2004).

■ Tough-tackling, defensive or right-sided midfielder Shaun Cunnington had already made more than 500 senior appearances by the time manager Alan Buckley brought him to The Hawthorns. He struggled with injuries during his 20 months with Albion and played in only 18 first-team games (making his debut against Charlton Athletic on the opening day of the 1996–97 season) and 20 or so in the second XI before moving to Meadow Lane, duly helping Notts County win the Third Division championship in 1998. Earlier he gained a Welsh Cup winners' medal with Wrexham (1986).

CUTLER, Reginald Victor

Outside-left: 5 apps.

*Born: Blackheath, 17 February 1935.
Career: Rowley Regis Boys. Blackheath. Smethwick & District Schools. Birmingham County Youths. ALBION (amateur, May 1950, professional, February 1952). Bournemouth and*

Boscombe Athletic (£500, June 1956). Portsmouth (September 1958). Stockport County (July 1962). Worcester City (August 1964). Dudley Town (June 1966). Bromsgrove Rovers (February 1967, retired, May 1970). Later moved to the Kidderminster area where he began his own market-garden business (Oakvale Nurseries). He now lives in Wolverley village (near Kinver) and his son resides in Australia.

■ A determined winger, 5ft 7in tall and 10st in weight, Reg Cutler was reserve to George Lee at The Hawthorns and was called up for first-team duty on five occasions, making his debut against Derby County (home) in April 1952, two months after turning professional. He also netted four goals in 74 Central League games for Albion, followed up with 21 in 96 Division Three South games for Bournemouth and 13 in 100

outings for Pompey, whom he helped win the Third Division championship in 1962 along with another ex-Albion player, Jimmy Campbell, on the right wing and future Baggies manager Ron Saunders at centre-forward. In 1957 Cutler broke a goal post in an FA Cup tie against Wolves at Molineux and then scored the winning goal to cause a major upset. That same year he represented the Third Division North against the South in the annual challenge match. Ex-Albion winger Freddie Cox, as manager, signed him for Portsmouth having earlier coached him at Bournemouth.

DALE, Richard Armstrong

Half-half: 21 apps.

Born: Willington, County Durham, 21 March 1896.
Died: County Durham, 1970.
Career: Walton School (Durham). Walbottle & Tow Law Schools. Walbottle Juniors. Tow Law Town (1914). North Walbottle FC (1919). Stanley United (August 1921). West Hartlepool (briefly). Birmingham (£250, March 1922). ALBION (£1,500, November 1928). Tranmere Rovers (£400, June 1931). Crook Town (October 1932). Tow Law Town (August 1933, retired, May 1934). ALBION (scout, 1949–52).

■ Defender Dicky Dale represented Staffordshire County FA in 1925 and made 150 appearances for the Blues before moving to The Hawthorns. A shade uncertain at times, he was, nevertheless, a fine player who could perform in either of the three half-back positions. Owing to the presence of Len Darnell and Bill Richardson and then Joe Evans and Jimmy Edwards, his first-team appearances for Albion were restricted to a meagre 21, his first coming against Preston North End (home) 48 hours after joining the club. He also played in 66 Central League matches (4 goals scored).

DARBY, Julian Timothy

Midfield: 37+7 apps. 1 goal.

Born: Bolton, 3 October 1967.
Career: Bolton Wanderers (apprentice, April 1984, professional, July 1986). Coventry City (£150,000, October 1993). ALBION (£200,000, November 1995). Preston North End (£150,000, June 1997).

GUESTS
WEST BROMWICH

Rotherham United (on loan, March–April 1998). Carlisle United (free, August 2000, later player-coach, retired, July 2001). Preston North End (coach, 2004–05).

■ An England schoolboy international, Julian Darby had a fine career amassing a total of 526 League and cup appearances and scoring 63 goals for the six clubs he served, with by far his best years coming at Bolton, for whom he played in 346 first-team matches and netted 52 goals, helping the Trotters with the Freight Rover Trophy at Wembley in 1989. After making his Albion debut against Sunderland soon after moving from Highfield Road, he had a few injury problems that seriously jeopardised his first-team ambitions, although he did appear in more than 30 second XI games.

DARNELL, Leonard

Wing-half/inside-left: 62 apps.

Born: Irchester, 14 September 1905.
Died: Wallingford, November 1968.
Career: Irchester & Wymington Schools. Higham Ferrers FC. Irthlingborough (1920). Rushden Town (1922). ALBION (amateur, May 1924, professional, October 1925). Reading (June 1930). Carlisle United (player-coach, August 1934, retired, May 1940).

■ Len Darnell, 6ft tall, was a forceful, hard-tackling, tireless player, who won junior international honours for England a year after making his Albion debut against Notts County (away) in March

1926. He also played in 91 Central League games for Albion (31 goals scored) collecting a championship medal in 1926–27.

DARTON, Scott Richard

Full-back: 21 apps. 1 goal.

Born: Ipswich, 27 March 1975.
Career: ALBION (apprentice, April 1991, professional, October 1992). Blackpool (on loan, January–March 1995, signed permanently for £7,500, March 1995). Cambridge City (briefly, 1996). Heybridge Swifts (December 1997). St Albans City (August 1998).

■ Scott Darton did reasonably well during his early years at The Hawthorns, but the fans started to get on his back early in the 1994–95 and as a result he moved clubs. He made his League debut against Brighton (home) in April 1993 as the promotion race hotted up. His only goal for the Baggies was in the Anglo-Italian Cup win over Peterborough in September 1993. He also played in almost 60 Central League games, scoring three goals.

DAVENPORT, Arthur

Right-half: 1 app.

Born: Springfield, Wolverhampton, 15 June 1924.
Career: Springfield Green School. Heath Town (Wolverhampton). ALBION (August 1942–May 1946). Did not play at competitive level after World War Two.

■ A wartime signing, Arthur Davenport's only first-team game for Albion was against Birmingham (home) in a League North fixture in April 1943.

DAVIES, Arthur

Outside-right: 12 apps. 1 goal.

Born: Bod Howell near Wrexham, 10 January 1880.
Died: Overton, 12 November 1949.
Career: Grove Park Council School. Wrexham St Giles (1895). Wrexham (professional, August 1898). Druids (August 1903). ALBION (June 1904). Middlesbrough (January–April 1905). Wrexham Nomads (1909–11). Ruabon Town (August 1914, retired, May 1917). Druids (club secretary, 1920s). Wrexham (director, 1933–35). Later a partner in the building firm Davies & McCord. Found

drowned in the River Dee in 1949, the inquest heard evidence of accumulating business problems and an open verdict was returned.

■ A Welsh international (two caps gained, both against Scotland in 1904 and 1905), Arthur Davies was a solid player with good acceleration and a powerful kick. Unfortunately, his promising career was brought to an abrupt halt by illness and he spent several years out of the game. He regained his fitness by playing tennis, another of his sporting loves. He spent just over six months at The Hawthorns, contesting the right-wing berth with Lawrie Bell. He made his Albion debut against Blackpool (away) in September 1904 and netted his only goal in a 2–0 home win over Lincoln in his 11th outing. He also played in 12 second XI games. A Welsh Cup winner in 1904 (with Druids) and 1910 (with Nomads), he made only six appearances for Wrexham in five years.
* His brother, Llewellyn Davies, also played for Albion in 1904.

DAVIES, Cyril

Centre-half: 15 apps.

Born: Cordley, West Bromwich, 13 May 1917.
Died: Tantany, West Bromwich, 1975.
Career: Swan Village School. Greets Green Wesley (1933). Kidderminster Harriers (July 1934). ALBION (amateur, January 1935, professional, March 1937). Stourbridge (June 1947). Cordley Victoria (August 1953, retired, May 1955). Later employed by an engineering firm in West Bromwich.

■ An England junior international, (capped in 1938) Cyril Davies, a reserve defender, found it hard to establish himself at The Hawthorns and made only seven League appearances, plus another eight in wartime football and 26 in the Central League. His senior debut was against Wolves (away) in May 1938 when relegation was staring the Baggies in the face.

DAVIES, Llewellyn Charles

Full-back: 3 apps.

Born: Wrexham, 29 July 1881.
Died: Ealing, West London, 10 February 1961.

Career: St Giles School (Wrexham). Ruabon Druids (1896). Wrexham (April 1901). Druids (1903–04). Wrexham (August–October 1904). ALBION (November 1904). Wrexham (March 1905). Northern Monads (guest, briefly in 1908). Everton (May 1910). St Helens FC, (August–November 1911). Flint Town (briefly). Wrexham (November 1911, retired, May 1920). Later worked as a clerk with the Ministry of Pensions.

■ Llewellyn Davies was a highly efficient Welsh international defender, capped 13 times at senior level. Able to occupy four different positions, he was the only player to dislodge left-back Jesse Pennington from the Albion team, making his debut at left-back against Blackpool (home) in November 1904, the same month that he joined Albion. He also played in eight second XI games for the club. A Welsh Cup winner in 1903, 1905, 1909, 1910, 1914 and 1915 with Wrexham, in 1904 with Druids and a runner-up in 1902, Davies also made 381 first-team appearances for Wrexham. He was also a fine tennis player and represented North Wales and Shropshire in the sport.
NB: His brother, Arthur Davies, also played for Albion and Wales.

DAVIES, Reginald Walter

Goalkeeper: 4 apps.

Born: Tipton, 10 October 1933.
Career: Tipton Green Junior & Senior Schools. Palethorpe's FC. ALBION

(amateur, May 1949, professional, January 1951). Walsall (£400, July 1955). Millwall (May 1958). Leyton Orient (July 1963). Port Vale (July 1964). Leyton Orient (March 1965, retired May 1966). Later employed at Jersey international airport before returning to live in Tipton.

■ A plucky goalkeeper who possessed greater muscular strength than one imagined, Reg Davies played in only four first-team games for Albion (owing to the presence of Norman Heath and Jimmy Sanders) and in 37 second team games. He conceded 10 goals in a testimonial match against Hereford United in 1954. After leaving The Hawthorns, Davies appeared in more than 350 League games, 199 for Millwall with whom he won a Fourth Division championship medal (1961–62).

DAVIES, Stanley Charles

Inside/centre-forward: 159 apps. 83 goals.

Born: Chirk near Oswestry, 24 April 1898.
Died: Birmingham, 17 January 1972.
Career: Chirk Council Schools. Chirk Schools representative. Chirk FC. Army Signals School (Dunstable). Manchester United (trialist, 1918). Rochdale (professional, January 1919). Preston North End (£800, April 1919). Everton (£4,000, January 1921). ALBION (£3,300, November 1921). Birmingham (£1,500, November 1927). Cardiff City (£1,000, August 1928). Rotherham United (player-manager, March 1929). Barnsley (August 1930). Manchester Central (October 1930). Dudley Town (1933). Chelmsford City (trainer, April 1938–May 1941). Shorts

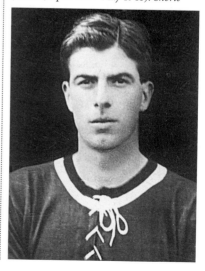

FC, Rochester (manager during World War Two). Later licensee of the Crown and Cushion, Lloyd Street, Dwygyfylchi, Penmaenmawr, North Wales, and played for and captained Amateurs FC (Penmaenmawr).

■ Stan Davies was a big, strong, forceful player (5ft 10in tall, 12st 12lb), who starred in six different positions for his country including goalkeeper (against Scotland 1922), a clear indication of his tremendous versatility. He gained 18 full caps (plus one 'other') and netted five international goals as well as touring Canada in 1930 with the Welsh FA. He possessed a cracking shot, could head a ball hard and, in a fine career, scored well over 100 goals in some 250 appearances for his seven major clubs. He made his Albion debut at centre-forward (in place of Bobby Blood) against Manchester City soon after joining the club and held his position (injury and international duty apart) until February 1924 when George James took over as leader of the attack. He came back strongly during the 1925–26 campaign, linking up superbly well with Charlie Wilson and Joe Carter and occasionally James, but following the arrival of Jimmy Cookson he went into the reserves and subsequently moved to St Andrew's. He also scored 51 goals in only 55 Central League games for Albion. As a manager, he guided Shorts FC to successive Kent Senior Cup final victories. When World War One broke out Davies, registered with the Volunteers in Aberystwyth, was immediately sent for training and by November 1914 found himself in France on the Western Front with the Royal Welch Fusiliers. He was wounded at Cambrai, and on his discharge from hospital he joined the Army Signalling School in Dunstable. He was later awarded the Military Medal and the Belgian Croix de Guerre. Davies was a teetotaller and Sunday School teacher.
* Davies' son, John, worked as a reporter for the Daily Express newspaper for many years (based in Birmingham and Bristol).

DAVIES, William Charles

Winger: 55 apps. 4 goals.

Born: Forden near Welshpool, April 1883.
Died: Caersus, May 1960.
Career: Rhayader and Llandrindod Schools. Knighton FC (1899). Shrewsbury Town (amateur, August 1903). Stoke (professional, July 1905). Crystal Palace (October 1907). ALBION (£700, August 1908). Crystal Palace (May 1910–May 1916). Did not play after World War One.

■ Fleet-footed winger Billy Davies had attracted the attention of a number of clubs, but Albion were first to step in and he gave the Baggies useful service for two seasons, making over 50 appearances before returning to Palace soon after George Simpson had arrived at The Hawthorns. Capped four times by Wales, two while with Albion, against England in 1910 and Scotland in 1910, Davies was a strong, bold performer who excelled in pinpoint crosses and was one of the first footballers to emerge from the newly-formed Mid-Wales League. He made his Albion debut against Grimsby Town (away) in September 1908.

DAWES, John Luther

Outside-left: 1 app.

Born: Smethwick, 5 June 1891.
Died: Worcester, June 1933.
Career: St Matthews School (Smethwick). Smethwick Centaur FC (1899). ALBION (August 1903). Smethwick Centaur (June 1905). Redditch Albion (1907, retired, c.1920, after serving in World War One).

■ Quick-moving, reserve left-winger Jack Dawes played in over 40 games for Albion's second XI during his time at The Hawthorns. His only League outing was against Barnsley (home) in December 1904 when he deputised for Albert Lewis in a 4–1 win.

DEACY, Charles Edward

Centre-forward/centre-half: 19 apps. 1 goal.

Born: Wednesbury, 6 October 1889.
Died: Merthyr, 2 December 1952.
Career: St Phillip's School (Wednesbury). Wednesbury Town (August 1904). Wednesbury Old Athletic (July 1907). ALBION (May 1910). Hull City (£200, June 1914). Grimsby Town (£750, December 1920). Pontypridd (July 1923). Merthyr Town (June 1924, retired, May 1925). Took casual work in a slate mine until World War Two.

■ A quiet, unobtrusive footballer, Charlie Deacy worked hard at his game and, although a regular in the second team with over 60 outings to his credit gaining a Birmingham & District League championship medal in 1913, he managed less than 20 appearances for the first team. He made his senior debut against Clapton Orient (away) in November 1910. After leaving The Hawthorns he was transformed into a very efficient centre-half and made 75 League appearances for Hull and 60 for Grimsby.

DEAN, Alfred

Outside-right/centre-forward: 8 apps. 3 goals.

Born: West Bromwich, 2 January 1877.
Died: Walsall, August 1959.
Career: West Bromwich Baptist School. Walsall (April 1894). ALBION (May 1896). Walsall (September 1898). Nottingham Forest (£120, February 1901). Grimsby Town (£100, May 1901). Bristol City (April 1902). Swindon Town (August 1905). Millwall Athletic (May 1906). Dundee (July 1907) Millwall Athletic (August 1908–May 1909). Later Wellington Town (April 1910, retired, 1916). Became a licensee in Walsall.

■ A much-travelled footballer, short in stature yet not negligible in weight, possessing pace and dribbling ability, on his day Alf Dean was one of the most dangerous forwards in the game. He made a scoring debut for Albion in a 1–0 win over his future club, Nottingham Forest, in January 1897. He also played in over 220 'other' first-team games for Albion and during his career amassed more than 180 appearances in the Football League and over 100 more in the Southern League.

DEEHAN, John Matthew

Striker: 47+3 apps. 5 goals.

Born: Solihull, 6 August 1957.
Career: St Peter's School Solihull. Olton British Legion FC. Arsenal (trialist, 1972). Aston Villa (apprentice, July 1973, professional, April 1975). ALBION (£424,000, September 1979). Norwich City (£175,000, November 1981). Ipswich Town (June 1986). Manchester City (player-coach, July 1988). Barnsley (player-coach, January 1990). Norwich City (assistant manager/coach, 1991, then manager,

January 1994-June 1995). Wigan Athletic (manager, November 1995–July 1998). Huddersfield Town (coach). Sheffield United (chief scout). Aston Villa (coach, 2001–June 2003). Ipswich Town (scout, July-September 2003). Northampton Town (Director of Football, also caretaker manager, October 2003). Also served on the PFA Management Committee in the 1980s. Northampton Town (director of football, 2004–05).

■ John 'Dixie' Deehan had an Irish father but chose to play for England and won three youth and seven under-21 caps for his country, and was also a non-playing substitute for the senior side against Brazil in 1981. A very competent striker, Deehan scored 51 goals for Villa in 139 appearances before transferring to The Hawthorns a month or so into the 1979–80 season. In just over two years with Albion he made 50 appearances – his first against Tottenham Hotspur (away) shortly after signing – yet he netted only five goals. He failed to reproduce the form he had shown with the Baggies' arch rivals, although he did net 10 times in 25 Central League games. After that he did exceedingly well with Norwich (70 goals in 199 games), played more than 50 times for Ipswich and was positive during his coaching appointments at Maine Road and

Oakwell. He then returned to Carrow Road as assistant manager/coach and was given the managers job at Norwich in place of Mike Walker before taking over as team boss of Wigan Athletic in 1995, guiding the Latics to the Third Division championship in 1996. As a player, he helped the Canaries win the League Cup in 1985 and the Second Division title 12 months later. His career went full circle when, in 2001, he was back at Villa Park. * When he joined Albion, Deehan became the first player to move from Villa Park to The Hawthorns in 70 years (since George Abner Harris switched clubs back in 1909).

DeFREITAS, Fabian

Striker: 40+28 apps. 10 goals.

Born: Surinam, 28 July 1972.
Career: FC Volendam, Holland (professional, August 1990). Bolton Wanderers (£400,000, August 1994). Osasuna, Spain (free, September 1996). ALBION (free, August 1998). SC Cambuur, Holland (September 2000). FC Den Bosch, Holland (2002–03). NEC Nijmegan, Holland (August 2004).

■ After a decent enough first season at The Hawthorns, 6ft striker Fabian DeFreitas struggled with his form in 1999–2000 and was named as a substitute more times than he actually started a

match. He had a spell of 23 games without a goal and as the weeks rolled by he became more and more frustrated, eventually leaving the club for Holland. He scored eight goals in 14 second-team games for Albion, having earlier netted nine times in 49 outings for Bolton.

DENNISON, Robert

Winger: 12+7 apps. 1 goal.

Born: Banbridge, Northern Ireland, 30 April 1963.
Career: Gilford & Craigavon Schools (Banbridge). Sunnypark FC. Gilford FC (August 1977). Glenavon (amateur, August 1978, professional, April 1980). ALBION (£40,000, September 1985). Wolverhampton Wanderers (£20,000, March 1987). Swansea City (on loan, October–November 1995). Hednesford Town (July 1997). Hereford United (December 1998). Warley Borough (200–01). Warley Rangers (coach, 2001–02).

■ A youth and 'B' international, winger Robbie Dennison went on to gain 17 full caps with Northern Ireland and, during an excellent career, amassed almost 600 senior appearances for clubs and country, scoring over 100 goals, including 52 in 184 outings for Glenavon. A direct touchline player, he spent 18 months at The Hawthorns, making his debut

against Newcastle United (away) in September 1985. He also went on to score six goals in 38 Central League games. Producing some excellent displays at times, Dennison was perhaps surprisingly transferred to Black Country rivals Wolves after Robert Hopkins had established himself as Albion's wide-man. At Molineux he teamed up with his former colleagues Steve Bull and Andy Thompson and soon afterwards was joined by Ally Robertson. He was a Sherpa Van Trophy winner with the Wanderers, whom he also helped gain promotion from the Fourth to the Second Division in successive seasons (1988 and 1989). He received a testimonial after 11 years service with Wolves and later in his career was reunited with the man who signed him from Albion, Graham Turner, at Hereford. Dennison now works in the sports trophy business, selling them not winning them. He scored 49 goals in 353 games for Wolves.

DERVELD, Fernando

Left wing-back: 1+1 apps.

Born: Vlissingen, Holland, 13 May 1976
Career: Haarlem/Holland (professional, July 1994). Norwich City (£150,000, March 2000). ALBION (on loan, February-March 2001). Odense BK/Denmark (trialist, June-November 2001, signed permanently, December

2001). Preston North End (£160,000, July 2005).

■ Signed by manager Gary Megson as cover for the left side of Albion's defence, Dutchman Fernando Derveld had earlier played a cracking game for the canaries against the Baggies at The Hawthorns. He made 25 appearances during his time at Carrow Road.

DIBBLE, Andrew Gerald

Goalkeeper: 9 apps.

Born: Cwmbran, 8 May 1965.
Career: Cardiff City (apprentice, June 1981, professional, August 1982). Luton Town (£125,000, July 1984). Sunderland (on loan, February–March 1986). Huddersfield Town (on loan, March–April 1987). Manchester City (£240,000, July 1988). Aberdeen (on loan, October–November 1990). Middlesbrough (February 1991). Bolton Wanderers (on loan, September–October 1991). ALBION (on loan, February–April 1992). Glasgow Rangers (free, March 1997). Middlesbrough (trialist, July 1997). Luton Town (free, September 1997). Middlesbrough (free, January 1998). Altrincham (July 1998). Hartlepool United (free, March 1999). Carlisle United (on loan, October 1999). Stockport County (free, August 2000). Wrexham (July 2002).

■ After winning caps for Wales as a schoolboy and youth team player, goalkeeper Andy Dibble went on to add six more to his tally, collecting three at both under-21 and senior international levels. Standing 6ft 3in tall and eventually topping the 16 stone mark, he was signed as experienced cover by Albion manager Bobby Gould when Stuart Naylor was injured. Dibble reached the career milestone of 400 senior appearances in 2003.

DICHIO, Daniele Salvatore Ernest

Striker: 59+17 apps. 18 goals.

Born: Hammersmith, Central London, 19 October 1974.
Career: Forest United, London (junior, 1990). Queen's Park Rangers (apprentice, June 1991, professional, May 1993). Barnet (on loan). Sampdoria, Italy (July 1997). Lecce (on loan, December 1997).

Sunderland (£750,000, January 1998). ALBION (on loan, August–September 2001, signed permanently for £1.25 million, November 2001). Derby County (on loan, October–November 2003). Millwall (on loan, January 2004, signed for £500,000, February 2004). Preston

■ Danny Dichio, born of Italian parents, won England schoolboy honours and later added one under-21 cap to his tally. The 6ft 3in, 12st 4lb striker scored 22 goals for Queen's Park Rangers but failed to do the business in Italy, Peter Reid bringing him back into English football in 1998. He had his ups and downs on Wearside and in the end was struggling to get into the first team ahead of Kevin Phillips and Niall Quinn. After netting 18 goals he was loaned out to Albion and celebrated with a goal on his debut against Sheffield Wednesday. Three months later he was signed on a permanent basis by the Baggies boss, Gary Megson, and went on to score some important and match-winning goals as Albion went on their way into the Premiership. After that he had mixed fortunes with injuries causing him to miss several games. When loaned out to Derby and then Millwall during the 2003–04 season he scored on his debut for both clubs and after signing permanently for the Lions he helped them reach the FA Cup final for the first time in the club's history, but unfortunately for him he missed the final against Manchester United at The Millennium Stadium, Cardiff after being sent off in a preceding League game against Nottingham Forest. Dichio also scored seven goals in 11 second-team games for Albion.

DICKEN, Harold John

Half-back: 1 app.

Born: Wednesbury, 19 November 1890.
Died: Birmingham, April 1965.
Career: Hill Top School. Hill Top Brotherhood FC. Hill Top United (1906). Bilston United (1907). ALBION (May 1909). Bilston United (July 1910). Bradley Rangers (1912–14). Served in the Army during World War One, later worked in a local market.

■ A tall, well-built half-back with limited ability, Harry Dicken was reserve to George Baddeley, Ted Pheasant,

Sammy Timmins and Jack Manners during his one season at The Hawthorns. He made over 20 second XI appearances but only one in the first team, lining up against Leeds City (away) in October 1909.

DICKENS, Alan William

Midfield: 4 apps. 1 goal.

Born: Plaistow, London, 3 September 1964. Career: Plaistow & District Schools. West Ham United (apprentice, April 1981, professional, August 1982). Chelsea (£650,000, August 1989). ALBION (on loan, December 1992–January 1993). Brentford (February 1993). Colchester United (September 1993–May 1994). Chesham Town (August 1994). Hayes (briefly). Collier Row FC (1995). Billericay Town (August 1996). Purfleet FC (August 1997–May 1998). Later employed as a London taxi driver.

■ England youth and under-21 international midfielder Alan Dickens scored 30 goals in 234 appearances for West Ham during his eight years at Upton Park. He struggled on and off at Stamford Bridge and after a loan spell at The Hawthorns (signed to bolster the squad by manager Ossie Ardiles, who handed him his debut against Mansfield Town at Field Mill 24 hours later), he wound down his senior career with Brentford and Colchester.

DICKINSON, Martin John

Midfield: 51+4 apps. 2 goals.

Born: Leeds, 14 March 1963. Career: Wykebank Infants & Foxford High Schools (Leeds). Leeds City & Yorkshire County Boys. Yorkshire Amateurs (March 1978). ALBION (trialist, July 1978). Leeds United (apprentice, July 1979, professional, March 1981). ALBION (£40,000, February 1986). Sheffield United (free, June 1988, retired through injury, May 1989). Now lives and works in his native Leeds.

■ Yorkshireman Martin Dickinson had a trial at The Hawthorns under manager Ron Atkinson and played alongside Stuart Naylor in the Yorkshire Amateurs team of 1977. He was a strongly-built midfielder who could also play in defence (if required). He spent just over two years at The Hawthorns, having his best spell for the side between August 1986 and

March 1987. He had a debut to forget for Albion, being on the wrong end of a 5–0 drubbing at Tottenham in March 1986. He then scored the first of his two goals in a 3–0 win at Sunderland 10 months later, his second followed in January 1988 against his former club Leeds (lost 4–1). He also appeared in six Central League games for the Baggies.
* Dickinson went to the same school as Paul Madeley (ex-Leeds United and England).

DILLY, Thomas

Outside-left: 37 apps. 10 goals.

Born: Arbroath, 12 November 1882. Died: Scotland, 1960. Career: Arbroath & Marwell Schools. Forfar County (1898). Arbroath (1899). Heart of Midlothian (1900). Everton (November 1902). ALBION (March 1906). Derby County (£250, October 1907). Bradford Park Avenue (June 1908). Walsall (August 1909). Shrewsbury Town (July 1910). Worcester City (September 1911). Kidderminster Harriers (April 1914). Cadbury Works FC (1918, retired May 1919).

■ An outside-left who could also play at centre-forward or on the right-wing, Tommy Dilly was rather slim-looking but good on the ball and loved to hug the touchline. He left The Hawthorns unwittingly after upsetting club chairman

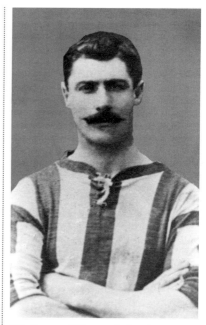

Billy Bassett. Dilly was the last Scotsman to play for Albion for 30 years – until George Dudley arrived on the scene in 1937. He represented Forfar against Perthshire in 1899–1900 and won prizes for sprinting in various races between 100 and 300 yards.

DIXON, Robert

Outside-left: 7 apps. 1 goal.

Born: Felling-on-Tyne, 11 January 1936. Career: Felling & Gateshead Schools. Newburn Boys Club. Crook Town (April 1952). Arsenal (professional, August 1957). Workington (October 1957). ALBION (£5,000, May 1959). Hereford United (June 1960). Kidderminster Harriers (July 1964). Cinderford Town (July 1966). Abergavenny Thursday (February 1967). Hereford United (coach, August 1972, retired, May 1974). Later ran his own business in Hereford where he now lives.

■ Signed by Albion manager Vic Buckingham as a possible replacement for George Lee, Bobby Dixon found himself out of his depth in the First Division and, after a season at The Hawthorns, dropped down the scale into non-League football. He made his debut for the Baggies in a 3–2 home win over Manchester United on the opening day of the 1959–60 season and scored his only goal in a 5–0 win over Leicester a fortnight later. He scored twice in 21 Central League games for the Baggies and then appeared in almost 100 games for Hereford, whom he later coached under Colin Addison's management.

DOBBINS, Lionel Wayne

Right-back/midfield: 40+15 apps.

Born: Bromsgrove, 30 August 1968.
Career: Birchen Coppice Infants & Middle Schools and Harry Cheshire High School (Bromsgrove). Habberley Hotspur FC. St David's FC. Burlish Olympic (1893). ALBION (apprentice, June 1984, professional, September 1986). Torquay United (July 1991). Yeovil Town (August 1992). Gloucester City (1994–96). Redditch United (August 1996). Stourbridge (1997–98). Evesham United (1998–2000). Brintons FC, Cheltenham (2001–04).

■ Basically a midfielder, Wayne Dobbins was a shade on the small side but was a totally committed footballer. He made his League debut for Albion against Sheffield United (home) in August 1986 as a substitute. He also played in 98 Central League games for the club, scoring three goals.

DOBIE, Robert Scott

Striker: 64+63 apps. 25 goals.

Born: Workington, 10 October 1978.
Career: Carlisle United (apprentice, June 1995, professional, May 1997). ALBION (£150,000, July 2001). Millwall (£350,000, November 2004). Nottingham Forest (£525,000, March 2005).

■ In August 2000 striker Scott Dobie

played as a 'sub' for Carlisle United against Halifax Town in a Third Division match in front of less than 4,500 fans at Brunton Park. Twelve months later he made his League debut for Albion at Walsall, when the crowd doubled to 9,000, and shortly afterwards scored in a 4–0 home win over Manchester City when the turnout was well over 24,000. He netted 26 goals in 156 appearances for the Cumbrian club before transferring to Albion for a bargain fee of just £150,000. Fast and decisive, his first touch perhaps lets him down at times, but he had a fine first season with the Baggies, top-scoring with 12 goals in 50 outings as Premiership football came to The Hawthorns. He also gained the first of six full caps for Scotland against South Korea in 2002 and had the pleasure of becoming the first ever Baggies player to score for the Scots during that game. Two years later he helped Albion regain their top-flight status but then, with Kanu, Hulse, Earnshaw and Horsfield seemingly ahead of him for a place in the first team, Dobie was left out in the cold, subsequently joining his former Hawthorns colleague Danny Dichio at Millwall. This enabled Albion to make a substantial profit on his original fee, with Carlisle also benefitting

from the deal by receiving £37,500 as an agreed share of any sell-on price. He scored seven goals in 21 outings for Albion's second team. He failed to save Forest from relegation.

DOBSON, Anthony John

Defender: 8+7 apps.

Born: Coventry, 5 February 1969.
Career: Coventry City (apprentice, April 1985, professional, July 1986). Blackburn Rovers (£300,000, January 1991). Portsmouth (£150,000, September 1993). Oxford United (on loan, December 1994–January 1995). Peterborough United (on loan, January–February 1996). ALBION (trialist, July–August 1997, signed permanently, September 1997). Gillingham (on loan, September 1998). Northampton Town (£25,000, September 1998). Forest Green Rovers (June 2000). Nuneaton Borough (player-coach). Coventry City (part-time coach). Rugby United (manager, August 2001).

■ An England under-21 international defender (4 caps gained), Tony Dobson's League career was coming to an end by the time he joined Albion as an extra squad member and experienced cover for the likes of Daryl Burgess, Paul Mardon and Shaun Murphy. He had more than

180 senior appearances under his belt when he made his debut for manager Ray Harford against Cambridge United (home) in the Coca-Cola Cup in September 1997.

DONAGHY, Barry

Outside-right or left: 4+2 apps. 1 goal.

Born: Consett, County Durham, 21 March 1956.
Career: Consett & Shotley Bridge Schools. ALBION (apprentice, August 1971, professional, May 1973). Workington (December 1975). Consett (1977–79). Worked 25 years for Npower (to 2003).

■ An England youth international (10 caps gained in 1973–74), winger Barry Donaghy was far too diminutive to make any real impression in League football and quickly disappeared from the scene after leaving The Hawthorns. He made his Albion debut against Nottingham Forest (home) in September 1973 and scored his only goal in a 2–0 win at Cardiff in October 1974. He also claimed nine goals in 55 Central League matches and later scored three times in 44 outings for Workington before the Cumbrian side lost its League status in 1977.
In 1974 Donaghy played on his home ground, The Hawthorns, for England against the Netherlands in a qualifying round of the UEFA International Youth tournament, lining up against future Albion player Maarten Jol.

DONNACHIE, Charles Alexander

Half-back: 2 apps.

Born: Invergowie, Strathmore, 18 April 1869.
Died: Perth, Scotland, May 1923.
Career: Longforgan School (Perth). Dundee (August 1887). ALBION (November 1889). Cambuslang Rangers (June 1890–April 1892).

■ A reserve with Albion during the 1889–90 season, Charlie Donnachie made his Football League debut against Accrington (home) in December 1889.

DONOVAN, Kevin

Rightside midfield: 170+33 apps. 32 goals.
Born: Halifax, 17 December 1971.

Career: Huddersfield Town (apprentice, April 1988, professional, October 1989). Halifax Town (on loan, February–March 1992). ALBION (£70,000, October 1992). Grimsby Town (£300,000, July 1997). Barnsley (July 2001). Rochdale (November 2003). York City (on loan, March 2004, signed free transfer, June 2004).

■ Right-sided midfielder Kevin Donovan – nicknamed 'Jason' – helped Albion win promotion via the Wembley play-off final in 1993, scoring the third goal against Port Vale. A skilful, thoughtful player with a strong right-foot shot, he made over 200 appearances for Albion before being reunited with his former manager, Alan Buckley, at Grimsby in 1997. In his first season with the Mariners he went back to Wembley and gained an Auto-Windscreen Shield winners' medal. After switching to Oakwell he suffered disappointment with the Tykes when they were relegated to the Second Division. He made his debut for Albion against Port Vale in October 1992, and the following month he netted a hat-trick in an 8–0 FA Cup victory over non-League side Aylesbury United. He also played in almost 30 Central League games (scoring 9 goals). He was close to a career milestone of 500 senior appearances in 2004.

DORSETT, George

Outside-left: 100 apps. 22 goals.

Born: Brownhills, 9 August 1881.
Died: Manchester, 15 April 1943.
Career: Brownhills & District Schools. Shireoaks Athletic. Small Heath (trialist, 1898). Shrewsbury Town (amateur, January 1899). Brownhills Albion (August 1899). ALBION (professional, November 1901). Manchester City (£450, December 1904, retired through injury, May 1912).

■ George 'Sos' Dorsett, a ball-playing left-winger, was a Second Division championship winner with Albion in 1902, and eight years later he collected another winners' medal in the same division with Manchester City after switching to left-half. A Football League representative (in 1905–06), he possessed splendid control, had an unflurried demeanour, was always confident and, altogether, a cultured footballer. He replaced Ben Garfield in Albion's front-line and was succeeded by Albert Lewis following his record transfer (for a winger) to Manchester City. Making his Albion debut against Preston North End (away) in January 1902, he also played in a dozen or so second XI games and later appeared in the same Manchester City team as his brother, Joe. He scored 65 goals in 211 first-team games for City.

DORSETT, Joseph Arthur Harold

Outside-right or left: 18 apps. 3 goals.
Born: Brownhills, 19 April 1888.
Died: Eccles, Manchester, 15 March 1951.

Career: Brownhills Albion (1904). ALBION (professional, January 1907). Manchester City (May 1910). Colne FC (January 1920). Southend United (August 1920). Millwall Athletic (July 1921, retired, May 1923).

■ Like his elder brother, Joe Dorsett was a nimble winger with a neat touch, who made his senior debut for Albion in Jesse Pennington's benefit match versus Leeds City (home) in Division Two in October 1908. Working hard to gain a place in the first XI, he did well in the reserves, making over 30 appearances before going on to play in almost 145 games for City (scoring 20 goals). He later played in 35 League games for Southend and 55 for Millwall.

NB: George and Joe Dorsett's nephew, Dicky Dorsett, played for Aston Villa and Wolves, scoring in the 1939 FA Cup final for the latter club.

DRURY, Charles

Half-back: 160 apps. 1 goal.

Born: Darlaston, 4 July 1937.
Career: Slater Street Secondary Modern School (Darlaston). Darlaston & Wednesbury Schools. South East Staffs Boys. FH Lloyds FC (1952). ALBION (amateur, September 1954, professional, February 1955). Bristol City (£7,500, June 1964). Bradford Park Avenue (March 1968). Tamworth (August 1969). Warley (September 1972). Bromsgrove Rovers (August 1973, retired, May 1974). Now lives in the village of Acton Trussell, Staffordshire.

■ A rugged, determined, hard-tackling wing-half, 'Chuck' Drury scored just one goal for Albion – and it was a real 'cracker', belted home from a distance against Wolves at Molineux in 1962 (a game Albion won 5–1). An England youth international, he made his League debut against Bolton Wanderers (away) in February 1958 and established himself in the side during the second half of the 1959–60 season (after replacing Maurice Setters). He also made 93 Central League appearances for the Baggies and later had 51 League outings for Bristol City and 31 for Bradford.

DRURY, George Benjamin

Inside-forward: 31 apps. 9 goals.

Born: Hucknall, Notts, 22 January 1914.
Died: Sheffield, Yorkshire, 1972.
Career: Hucknall Park County School. Hucknall & Linby Boys. Hucknall Colts (1931). ALBION (trialist, August–September 1932). Hucknall Congregationalists. Hucknall Villa. Loughborough Corinthians. Heanor Town (April 1934). Sheffield Wednesday (£1,000, September 1934). Arsenal (£7,000, May 1938). Guest for Aberdeen, Burnley, Bury, Distillery, Doncaster Rovers, Liverpool, Nottingham Forest and Sheffield Wednesday during World War Two. ALBION (£2,500, October 1946). Watford (£2,500, June 1948). Darlaston (August 1950). Linby Colliery (August 1951). South Normanton FC (August 1952, retired, May 1954). Returned to mining in Yorkshire.

■ George Drury was a consistent performer with each of his four senior clubs, making 44 League appearances for Wednesday, 38 for Arsenal, 29 for Albion and 35 for Watford, scoring a total of 23 goals. He also netted seven times in 24 games for Albion's second XI. An inside-forward of innate footballing skill, shrewd and gutsy, he had a trial at The Hawthorns as a 19-year-old but was not offered a contract. His playing career (after leaving school) spanned 23 years. He twice represented the Irish Regional League against the League of Ireland in 1943–44 and was top-scorer for Forest (17 goals) in 1939–40 and Bury (16 goals) in 1944–45.

DUDLEY, George

Inside-forward: 25 apps. 5 goals.

Born: Gartcosh, Glasgow, 12 February 1916.
Died: West Bromwich, December 1979.
Career: Gartcosh & Glasgow Central Schools. Albion Rovers (June 1932). King's Park, Stirling (March 1937). Vono Sports FC (July 1937). Coventry City (trialist, 1936). ALBION (professional, October 1937). Guest for Bromsgrove Rovers, Leicester City, Oldham Athletic and Walsall during World War Two. Banbury Spencer (October 1946). Dudley Town (August 1947). Netherton (April 1951). Cradley Heath (August 1952). Accles and Pollock Works (1954–55, retired, June 1955). Later became Aero Department's Chief Planning Engineer at the Broadwell Works depot.

■ George Dudley was a player who

relied on skill rather than strength and effort. He spent nine years at The Hawthorns and when he signed for the club he became the first Scottish-born player on Albion's books since Tommy Dilly 30 years earlier. He had a scoring League debut for Albion against Bury (away) in November 1938 and also netted 18 goals in 51 Central League games. His younger brother, Jimmy Dudley, also played for Albion.

DUDLEY, James George

Wing-half/inside-forward: 320 apps. 11 goals.

Born: Gartosh, Glasgow, 24 August 1928.
Career: Burnt Tree Mixed School (Dudley). Hill Top School (West Bromwich). Walsall Conduits FC. Albright Youth Club (1943). ALBION (amateur, August 1944, professional, August 1945). Walsall, (£4,000, December 1959). Stourbridge (August 1964). Guest Motors FC (West Bromwich). Retired as a player in 1967, remained an employee at Guests until 1990.

■ Able to play at inside-forward or wing-half, Jimmy Dudley settled into the latter berth superbly for Albion and became a key player in the side during the 1950s. He actually started out as a goalkeeper, switched to inside-right in 1947 and established himself in Albion's Central League side in 1949 before becoming the club's regular right-half two years later. He occupied that berth (number 4) until 1959, during which time he appeared in well over 30 matches, including 166 in succession in 1952–56, which was a new club record that stood for more than 20 years until bettered by

Ally Robertson in 1979. His most vital goal for the Baggies was, without doubt, that vital equaliser against Port Vale in the 1954 FA Cup semi-final at Villa Park. He made his Albion debut against Manchester City (away) in December 1949 and was to become part of two terrific middle-lines, first with Joe Kennedy and Ray Barlow as his centre-half and left-half colleagues and then with Jimmy Dugdale as pivot and Barlow alongside. He also played in 115 Central League games for the Baggies, was capped by Scotland 'B' and in 1954 gained an FA Cup winners' medal. He later played in 175 League and cup games for Walsall, helping the Saddlers win both the Fourth and Third Division championships in successive seasons (1960–61 and 1961–62). He now lives in Great Barr.
* George and Jimmy were cousins of the former Albion wing-half of the 1930s, Jimmy 'Iron' Edwards.

DUGDALE, James Robert

Centre-half: 74+1 apps.

Born: Liverpool, 15 January 1932.
Career: Harrowby FC (Liverpool). ALBION (amateur, January 1950, professional, May

1952). Aston Villa (£25,000, February 1956). Queen's Park Rangers (retired through injury, May 1963). Later worked as a steward (at Moseley rugby club and the Hasbury Conservative Club, Halesowen) and also as a licensee, running the Lion's Club for Aston Villa. Now lives in Acocks Green, Birmingham.

■ Jimmy Dugdale was an excellent centre-half who shared the number 5 shirt at Albion with Joe Kennedy during the early 1950s. Making his League debut against Bolton Wanderers in December 1952 (when he completely blotted out the threat of England's Nat Lofthouse), he was an FA Cup winner two years later, gained three England 'B' caps and also represented the Football League. With Kennedy taking priority at the heart of defence, Dugdale – who also made 71 Central League appearances for Albion – was sold to Aston Villa in 1956 and the following year collected his second FA Cup winners' medal when double-chasing Manchester United were defeated 2–1 in the Wembley final. He then helped Villa win the Second Division title in 1960 and the Football League Cup 12 months later, before seeing out his career with Queen's Park Rangers. Sadly, Dugdale had a leg amputated in 1993.

DUGGAN, James

Inside-forward: 27 apps. 8 goals.

Born: Droitwich, Worcs. 17 November 1920.
Died: Droitwich, April 1982.
Career: Droitwich Spa Old School. Droitwich Town. Droitwich Old Boys. West Ham United (trialist, November 1934). Bromyard (briefly, early 1935). Droitwich Old Boys (August 1935). ALBION (amateur, December 1935, professional, December 1938). Guest for Bradford City, Chelmsford City, Cowdenbeath, Heart of Midlothian, Luton Town, Newport County and Worcester City during World War Two. Hereford United (June 1947). Worcester City (1949). Bromsgrove Rovers (August 1951). Swan Athletic, Australia (1952–53). Bromyard (August 1954, retired, April 1958). Later worked in general stores in Bromyard.

■ An anxious but very adaptable inside-forward, Jimmy Duggan, the 'Joker in the Pack', had his career severely disrupted by the hostilities of World War Two. A great

pal of Albion's 1930s star Tommy Green, he had to wait until August 1946 before making his League debut against Swansea Town. He also scored 13 goals in 38 Central League games.

DUNN, Archibald

Full-back/wing-half/centre-forward: 81 apps. 3 goals.

Born: Bridgetown, Glasgow, 14 December 1876.
Died: Glasgow, February 1943.
Career: Bothwell School (Glasgow). Avenue Thistle FC (Glasgow). Queen's 2nd Gordon Highlanders (from 1893). ALBION (professional, April 1898). Millwall Athletic (May 1901). Grimsby Town (May 1902). Wellingborough (July 1904). Later Motherwell (briefly).

■ Archie 'Soldier' Dunn was a gritty, hard-working full-back or wing-half who occasionally lined up at centre-forward. As a defender he was awkward to pass, always keeping close to his opponent. He spent three years with Albion, making his League debut against Blackburn Rovers (away) in April 1898. He also played in 25 or so 'other' first-team matches for Albion and later starred in 50 League and cup games for Millwall and 45 for Grimsby. In 1895 he had helped the Gordon Highlanders win the Army Cup.

DURNIN, John Paul

Inside-forward/midfield: 5 apps. 2 goals.

Born: Bootle, 18 August 1965.
Career: Bootle/Merseyside & District Schools. Waterloo Dock FC (1981). Liverpool (apprentice, July 1983, professional, March 1986). ALBION (on loan, October–November 1988). Oxford United (£275,000, February 1989). Portsmouth (£200,000, July 1993). Blackpool (on loan, January 1999). Carlisle United (December 1999). Kidderminster Harriers (free, October 2000–May 2001). Rhyl Athletic (August 2001). Port Vale (free, December 2001–April 2002). Accrington Stanley (free, August 2003).

■ Unable to get into Liverpool's first team, John Durnin had just five games on loan with Albion, making his debut against Bradford City (home) in October 1988 before embarking on an excellent career that realised more than 470 senior appearances. Known to most as 'Johnny

Lager', he was sent off playing for Oxford United against Albion in January 1991.

DUTTON, Henry Robert

Half-back: 60 apps. 2 goals.

Born: Edmonton, London, 16 January 1898.
Died: Sussex, 1972.
Career: Edmonton and Tufnell Park Schools. Tufnell Park FC, London (1919). ALBION (professional, November 1922). Bury (£1,300, May 1927). Brighton and Hove Albion (October 1928). Shoreham FC (August 1932, retired, May 1935). Later worked in the stationery business.

■ A very durable left-half, Harry Dutton was a tremendous clubman who gave nothing less than 100 percent and his appetite for the game was first-class. He made the first of his 60 appearances for Albion in a League home game against Cardiff City in December 1922, deputising for Bobby McNeal, the player he eventually replaced in the half-back line before moving on following the arrival of Nelson Howarth. Dutton also played in 114 second XI games for the Baggies, gaining three Central League championship medals in 1922–23, 1923–24 and 1926–27.

DYER, Frank George

Half-back: 46 apps. 3 goals.

Born: Bishopbriggs, Strathclyde, 5 August 1870.
Died: 1940.
Career: Bishopbriggs & Clydebank Schools. Chryston FC. Bolton Wanderers (professional, August 1888). Warwick County (September 1889). ALBION (July 1890). Woolwich Arsenal (July 1892). Ardwick/Manchester City (August 1893, retired through ill-health and injury, May 1898).

■ A diligent, dexterous and hard-pressing half-back, Frank Dyer often amused spectators with his war cry of 'that's mine' when going for the ball. He made his Albion debut against Everton (home) in September 1890 and also played in over 60 other first-team games for the club.

DYER, Lloyd

Left-winger: 4+20 apps. 2 goals.

Born: Aston, Birmingham, 13 September 1982.

Career: Aston Villa (apprentice, April 1999). ALBION (free, professional, July 2001). Kidderminster Harriers (on loan, August–December 2003). Coventry City (on loan, March–May 2005).

■ After failing to make headway at Villa Park, enthusiastic and pacy left-winger Lloyd Dyer was snapped up by Baggies manager Gary Megson, who gave him his senior debut in the away Worthington Cup tie against Wigan Athletic in October 2002. Later the following season he was mainly used as a second-half substitute and turned games in Albion's favour with important assists and two vital goals as the Baggies regained their Premiership status. In 2005 he was fast approaching the milestone of 100 second-team appearances for Albion.

DYSON, Paul Ian

Centre-half: 69 apps. 5 goals.

Born: Kings Heath, Birmingham, 27 December 1959.
Career: Coventry City (apprentice, April 1976, professional 1978). Stoke City (£150,000, July 1983). ALBION (£60,000, March 1986). Darlington (March 1989). Crewe Alexandra (August 1989). Telford

United (July 1990). Solihull Borough (player-coach 1996, later manager, 2000–03)

■ A well-built, sturdy centre-half, Paul Dyson – who was capped by England at under-21 level as a Coventry player – joined Albion immediately after the team had been hammered 5–0 by Tottenham Hotspur as Second Division football was destined to return to The Hawthorns for the first time in a decade. He made his debut, alongside Martin Dickinson and Mickey Forsyth, in a 2–2 home draw with Leicester City, and he held his place at the heart of the defence until the end of the 1986–87 season. He returned briefly after injury but left the club when Chris Whyte became first choice in the pivotal position. He made over 35 second-team appearances for the Baggies.

EARNSHAW, Robert

Striker: 20+14 apps. 14 goals.

Born: Zambia, 6 April 1981.
Career: Junior football in Zambia (1987–90). Schoolboy football in Caerphilly (Wales). Cardiff City (apprentice, June 1997, professional, August 1998). Greenock Morton (on loan, January–February 2000). ALBION (£3.6 million, August 2004).

■ A record signing by Albion on transfer deadline day in August 2004, Rob Earnshaw joined fellow Welsh international teammates Jason Koumas and Andy Johnson at The Hawthorns. He always said that he wanted to play in the Premiership and Baggies boss Gary Megson granted his wish when he handed him his debut (as a second-half substitute) against Liverpool at Anfield 12 days after moving from Cardiff City. Unfortunately, just a week later, he missed a penalty in the 1–1 draw with Fulham on his home debut. Fast and direct with a positive style and a splendid right-foot shot, he scored over 100 goals in more than 200 first-team games during his time at Ninian Park, helping the Bluebirds gain promotion to the First Division in 2002–03 when, in all games, he bagged 35 goals (31 in the League). Now a regular in the Welsh national side with almost 20 full caps to his credit, he scored a hat-trick against Scotland in February 2004. Earnshaw has also played for the under-21 team on 10 occasions as well as gaining youth honours. Voted as 'Welsh Footballer of the year' in October 2004, 'Earnie' came on as a substitute and scored Albion's first Premiership hat-trick in a 4-1 win at Charlton in March 2005. He ended the season as the Baggies leading marksman with 14 goals. He also took part in the BBC TV programme *A Question of Sport*.

* His manager, Bryan Robson, had also featured on the same programme some years earlier, as a player with Manchester United.

EASTER, Graham Paul

Midfield: 0+1 app.

Born: Epsom, 26 September 1969.
Career: Bramhall Schools (Stockport). Cheshire County Boys. Manchester City (schoolboy trialist). ALBION (apprentice, July 1986, professional, May 1989). Huddersfield Town (March 1989). Crewe Alexandra (July 1989). Played in Finland (briefly). Preston North End (October–December 1990). Later with SFB Svendborg, Denmark (from 2003).

■ Sprightly performer Graham Easter was spotted by Nobby Stiles yet he failed to make an impression at The Hawthorns and moved to Huddersfield after just one first-team outing, as a substitute against Peterborough United in an away Littlewoods Cup game in September 1988. He scored six goals in 30 Central League games for Albion.

EASTOE, Peter Robert

Inside-forward: 33+1 apps. 9 goals.

Born: Dorden near Tamworth, 2 August 1953.
Career: Glascote Highfield. Warton Hatters (1969). Wolverhampton Wanderers (apprentice, June 1970, professional, June 1971). Swindon Town (on loan, November 1973, signed permanently for £88,000, January 1974). Queen's Park Rangers (March 1976). Everton (player-exchange deal March 1979). ALBION (£250,000
plus Andy King, July 1982). Leicester City (October 1983). Huddersfield Town (on loan, March 1984). Walsall (on loan, August 1984). Leicester City (on loan, October 1984). Wolverhampton Wanderers (on loan, February 1985). Sporting Farense, Portugal (July 1985). Atherstone Town (August 1986). Bridgnorth Town (player-coach, 1989–90). Atherstone (again, 1990–91). Alvechurch (manager, 1991–92). Nuneaton Borough (assistant manager, 1992–93). Bridgnorth Town (coach). Became a rep. for a printing company and now lives in Stourbridge.*

■ A very capable goalscorer, Peter Eastoe had a decent career that spanned 15 years. His nomadic wanderings took him all over the country and further, and he netted well over 100 goals, including 95 in 330 League games. As a teenager he won eight England youth caps (1971–72) and made his League debut for Wolves against Manchester United in 1982, top-scored for Everton in 1980–81 and appeared in FA Cup semi-finals for both the Merseysiders and Queen's Park Rangers. His first outing for Albion was away to Liverpool in August 1982, losing 2–0 in front of almost 36,000 fans. He also scored seven goals on 24 second-team games for the Baggies.

EBANKS, Michael Wayne Anthony

Full-back: 6+1 apps.

Born: Longbridge, Birmingham, 2 October 1964.

Career: Turves Green Primary &
Secondary Modern Schools (Birmingham).
Southern Cross FC (1979). ALBION
(apprentice, June 1980, professional, April
1982). Stoke City (on loan, August 1984).
Port Vale (on loan, March 1985, signed
permanently, June 1985–May 1987).
Cambridge United (trialist, August 1987,
then non-contract September–November
1987). Oldbury United (December
1987–May 1990). Later joined the
Staffordshire Police Force, and played for
the force soccer team.

■ Albion reserve full-back Wayne
Ebanks, who appeared in over 80 second
XI games, gained a Central League
championship medal in 1982–83 and
made his First Division debut against
Sunderland (away) in December 1983,
but left the field early due to an injury.
He later made 10 senior appearances for
Stoke, 48 for Port Vale and three for
Cambridge.

EDWARDS, Clifford Ivor

Wing-half: 102 apps. 3 goals.

Born: Chase Terrace, Cannock, 8 March
1921.
Died: West Bromwich, March 1989.
Career: Rawnsley School. Chase Terrace
United. Cannock Town (August 1936).
ALBION (amateur, October 1938,
professional, May 1939). Guest for Bath
City, Blackpool and Carlisle United during
World War Two. Bristol City (player-
exchange deal involving Cyril Williams

plus £500, June 1948). Gravesend and
Northfleet (retired, 1950). Returned to
West Bromwich and later ran his own
business (Tek Rubber and Plastics Ltd).
ALBION (director, August 1971, retired
through poor health, July 1986).

■ A short, thickset half-back, strong in
the tackle and very reliable, Cliff Edwards
spent 10 years as a player at The
Hawthorns, making his League debut in a
Second Division game against
Birmingham City in August 1946, having
earlier broken into the first team during
World War Two, playing against
Blackburn Rovers in a 1940 Cup tie. He
also scored once in 45 Central League
games for the Baggies. When he left the
Board in 1986 Edwards broke a sequence
that had been running since 1891, that of
an ex-player always being on the club's
Board of Directors.

EDWARDS, Ernest Arthur James

Inside-forward: 10 apps. 6 goals.

Born: Dudley Port, Tipton, 28 March 1893.
Died: West Bromwich, 1962.
Career: Great Bridge Schools. Old Hill
Unity (August 1912). ALBION (amateur,
May 1913, professional, November 1913).
Guest for Tipton Excelsior during World
War One. Walsall (March 1920). Merthyr
Tydfil (1921). Dudley Town (1922, retired,
May 1923). Later worked in engineering
(Tipton).

■ Stockily-built, straight-haired, centre-
forward Ernie Edwards was initially
signed as reserve to Alf Bentley and Fred
Morris at The Hawthorns. He broke his
leg in a League game at Newcastle in
January 1914, a month after scoring twice
on his debut against Sheffield Wednesday
(away). He never really performed after
that injury, although he did have a few
outings in the second XI, helping the
reserves win the Birmingham & District
League championship in 1920 before
joining the Saddlers.
* Ernie was the brother of Jimmy
Edwards.

EDWARDS, Robert Ian

Striker: 19+3 apps. 3 goals.

Born: Wrexham, 30 January 1955.
Career: Rhyl Junior & Mold Grammar

Schools. Flintshire Boys. Rhyl FC (August
1971). ALBION (£5,000, professional,
February 1973). Chester (£20,000,
November 1976). Wrexham (£125,000,
November 1979). Crystal Palace (July
1982, retired, May 1983). Ran his own
milk business for a while before returning
to the game with the Welsh League side
Mold FC (player-manager, August 1983).
Porthmadog Town (July 1984). Chorley
Town (1986–88). Then hotelier in Criccieth
(February 1989). Portmadoc FC (player-
manager, May 1989, retired as a player,
injured, May 1990, continued as manager
until January 1995). Then back into hotel
business. He had seven knee operations in
all.

■ A tall, blonde, well-built striker, yet
not the most fluid of movers, Ian
Edwards scored a fine goal on his League
debut for Albion in a 4–0 home victory
over Sheffield Wednesday in March 1975.
Unfortunately, following the arrival of
player-manager Johnny Giles, he hardly
figured in the first team again and duly
left for Sealand Road, having also netted
32 goals in 86 Central League games,
including one 35-yard header against
Liverpool reserves at The Hawthorns in
March 1976. Edwards gained two under-
23 and four full caps for Wales for whom
he netted four times in a European
championship qualifier against Malta in
1978. His League career realised more
than 200 appearances and 60 goals,

including 36 in 104 outings for Chester and 20 in 75 for Wrexham. He scored the BBC's *Match of the Day* 'Goal of the Month' for Wrexham against Derby County in September 1980.

EDWARDS, James

Left-half/inside-left: 202 apps. 9 goals.

Born: Tipton, 11 December 1905.
Died: West Bromwich, April 1982.
Career: Horseley Bridge & Tipton Schools. Tipton Park FC. Newport Foundry FC (West Bromwich). Stourbridge (August 1924). Great Bridge Celtic. Stourbridge (August 1925). ALBION (£350, May 1926). Norwich City (£750, May 1937). Bilston United (December 1937). Kingswinford (March 1939). Dudley Town (August 1939, retired, May 1944). Later worked in industry (Tipton).

■ Known affectionately as Jimmy 'Iron' Edwards, this tough-tackling defender gave Albion tremendous service at all levels for 11 years, during which time he accumulated over 200 first-team appearances after making his League debut against Hull City in March 1928. Initially an inside-forward, he reverted to left-half and was a key figure during Albion's double-winning season of

1930–31 and again in 1934–35, when the Baggies reached the FA Cup final. He also played in 184 second-team games (63 goals scored), gaining a Central League championship medal in 1926–27. He represented the Football League XI and was close to an England call up in 1934.
* Albion's half-back line in the early 1930s was Sankey, W Richardson and Edwards, known as 'salt, pepper and mustard', while Edwards and Richardson were referred to as 'iron and steel'.
* Jimmy Dudley was Jimmy Edwards's cousin.

EDWARDS, Paul Ronald

Full-back: 57+3 apps.

Born: Birkenhead, 25 December 1963.
Career: Altrincham (semi-professional, 1983). Crewe Alexandra (professional, January 1988). Coventry City (£350,000, March 1990). Wolverhampton Wanderers (£100,000, August 1992). ALBION (£80,000, January 1994). Bury (on loan, February–March 1996). Hednesford Town (briefly, August 1997–98).

■ Normally an orthodox left-back, ginger-haired Paul Edwards was drafted into a more central-defensive position (alongside Paul Mardon) during his time at The Hawthorns. A good, clean kicker of the ball, he perhaps lacked that extra yard of pace when opposing a tricky and

speedy winger. Nevertheless, in a senior career that spanned almost a decade, he amassed a fine record of 269 appearances. He made his debut for Albion against Millwall (home) in January 1994, after five other players had already been used in the left-back position that season. He made 20 second XI appearances for the Baggies.

EDWARDS, Samuel Conrad

Half-back: 1 app.

Born: Wolverhampton, 5 June 1885.
Died: 6 February 1959.
Career: Stafford Road School (Wolverhampton). Brades Park FC (August 1900). ALBION (£50, June 1901). Stafford Rangers (July 1905–May 1909). Later had a spell as assistant groundsman at The Hawthorns.

■ Albion's reserve right or centre-half for one season, Sammy Edwards appeared in one League game, taking the place of Harry Hadley in the away fixture with Bristol City in October 1894. He also made over 25 appearances in the second XI, gaining a Birmingham & District League championship medal in 1902.

ELLIOTT, William Bethwaite

Outside-right: 303 apps. 157 goals.

Born: Harrington, Cumberland, 6 August 1919.
Died: Canary Islands, July 1966.
Career: Harrington Junior & Carlisle Grammar Schools. Carlisle United (amateur, August 1935). Dudley Town (briefly, late 1935). Wolverhampton

Wanderers (professional, March 1936). Bournemouth (July 1937). ALBION (£4,000, December 1938). Bilston United (July 1951, later player-manager, August 1952, retired, May 1954). Became licensee of The Farcoft Hotel in Handsworth, Birmingham, later assuming the role of licensee of the Red Lion (Smethwick). Elliott, who helped found the first Albion Supporters Club in 1951, sadly died while holidaying in the Canary Islands in 1966. He was 47.

■ Billy Elliott was a brilliant outside-right, fast and clever with incredible close ball control and a powerful shot. He was rejected by Wolves manager Major Frank Buckley as a 16-year-old and went on to play for Albion for 13 years, appearing in more than 300 games and scoring over 150 goals in all competitions. He made his debut for the club in a Second Division League game against Luton Town (away) in December 1938 and also played in 13 Central League games. During the 1939–45 World War Two hostilities he was quite superb, netting 117 times in just 148 outings. He also played for England against Wales and Scotland in Wartime and Victory internationals and against Combined Services at Stoke in April 1944, as well as representing the Western Command, the Army and the FA. If it hadn't been for a certain Stanley Matthews then Elliott would have surely gained full England recognition. He helped Albion win promotion from the Second Division in 1948–49 and was in tip-top form until he suffered an Achilles tendon injury in 1951, effectively ending his League career. A fully qualified FA coach and members of the Players' Union Committee, he retired in 1954.

ELMORE, George Victor

Utility forward: 4 apps. 1 goal.

Born: Wednesbury, 27 September 1884. Died: 1952.
Career: Kings Hill Council School (Wednesbury). Wednesbury YMCA (1900). Broadheath FC (Manchester). ALBION (professional, December 1902). Bristol Rovers (£40, August 1903). Witton Albion (September 1904). Altrincham (August 1905). Glossop (August 1907). Blackpool (July 1909). Partick Thistle (August 1911, retired after World War One). Later became a policeman.

■ George Elmore, short and stocky, made his debut for Albion in a home FA Cup tie against Tottenham Hotspur in February 1903. An energetic footballer, brave and able to withstand considerable buffeting, he never really settled at The Hawthorns, yet during his career amassed well over 200 appearances at competitive level, playing his best football with Glossop (14 goals in 34 League outings). He appeared in 23 second XI matches for Albion.

EHIOGU, Ugochuka

Defender: 0+2 apps.

Born: Hackney, London, 3 November 1972. Career: ALBION (apprentice, April 1988, professional, July 1989). Aston Villa (£40,000, July 1991). Middlesbrough (£8 million, October 2000).

■ Undoubtedly the 'one that got away' as far as Albion are concerned! Ugo Ehiogu had appeared in just two first-team matches for the club (both as a substitute) before former Baggies boss Ron Atkinson snapped him up for peanuts in July 1991 (a month after he had taken over at Villa Park). Standing 6ft 2in tall and weighing well over 14st, Ehiogu went on to win 15 caps for England at under-21 level, played once for the 'B' and followed up with four appearances for the senior side. He made over 300 appearances for Villa, helping them win the League Cup in 1996, and, following his big-money move to Middlesbrough, he is now well in sight of the century mark in games for the Riverside club. A junior player on Hackney Marshes, Ehiogu made his Albion debut (taking over from Tony Ford) in a 1–1 draw at Hull City in September 1990. He also made 24 appearances for the Baggies in the Pontins League, gaining a championship medal at this level in 1990–91 when he partnered Paul Raven in defence.
* When Ehiogu was transferred from Villa Park to Middlesbrough, Albion benefitted by £2 million as a result of a sell-on agreement in his contract.

EVANS, Albert James

Full-back: 40 apps.

Born: Barnard Castle, County Durham, 12 March 1874.

Died: Warwick, 24 March 1966.
Career: Startforth & West Auckland Schools. Eggleston Abbey Boys. Barnard Castle FC (1894). Small Heath (trialist, 1895). Aston Villa (professional, August 1896). ALBION (October 1907, retired, June 1909, to take over as coach for two seasons, until May 1911). Coached in Norway until World War One. Coventry City (manager, June 1920–November 1924). After this he travelled the world, doing many different jobs including gold mining in the Yukon and sheep farming in Canada. Returning to England in 1950, he became a scout for Aston Villa (until 1956) and lived in Coventry for many years until his death in a Warwick nursing home at the age of 92, the last survivor of Villa's double-winning side.

■ Strong-tackling full-back Albert Evans made over 200 senior appearances for Aston Villa before joining Albion, for whom he made his debut against Blackpool (away) in November 1907 (as partner to Jesse Pennington). As a 'Villain' he won three League championship medals and an FA Cup winners' medal, helping them complete the double in 1896–97. Evans had the misfortune to suffer four broken legs during his career: in 1901, 1903, 1906 and 1908, but he always came back for more. After serving as a sapper and then sergeant in the 16th Royal Warwickshire Regiment during World War One, he became Coventry's third manager in three months when he took over the reins at Highfield Road in 1920.

EVANS, Alun James

Inside-forward/wing-half: 29 apps. 2 goals.

Born: Penrhycadery, South Wales, 1 December 1922.
Career: Ynysboeth Council School (Wales). Hounslow West Senior School (London). Wilden FC (Stourport). ALBION (amateur, January 1941, professional, May 1948, retired, eyesight failure, May 1948). Now almost blind, he resides in Kidderminster and is one of the oldest ex-Albion players alive today.

■ Alun 'Bungo' Evans started out as an aggressive left-half and made his debut in that position for Albion against Stoke City (away) in a World War Two League North match in November 1942. He was later converted into a diligent, steady inside-forward, yet still played occasionally as a wing-half, tackling keenly and always inspiring his teammates with his determination and willpower. Unfortunately, after less than 30 senior outings for the Baggies, he was forced to retire at the age of 25 with failing eyesight after taking a knock on the head playing against Doncaster Rovers in April 1948. He received just £350 in compensation, the accrued share of his benefit. He represented Wales against the RAF at Wrexham in September 1944 and played three times for his Army regiment in friendlies against sides from India. A fully qualified PE instructor and Drill training officer, he is the father of Alun Evans, the former Wolves, Aston Villa, Liverpool and Walsall forward.

EVANS, Charles John

Inside-forward: 130 apps. 31 goals.

Born: West Bromwich, 4 February 1923.
Died: Romsley near Halesowen, February 1998.
Career: Gunn's Lane Junior & George Salter Council Schools (West Bromwich). Hawthorn United. Cordley Vics (1936). ALBION (amateur, May 1937, professional, July 1941). Guest for Chelsea (1944–45). Stafford Rangers (July 1950). Nuneaton Borough (August 1952). Dudley Town (May 1953). Stourbridge (trainer-coach, 1962–64). Retired from football to work as an oil blender with the Eclipsol Oil Company.

■ World War Two interrupted Charlie Evans's playing career with Albion. Nevertheless, as a utility forward he gave the club tremendous service, scoring almost a goal every four games. He scored on his debut at Cardiff City in a League South game in May 1941 (4–4 draw), having made excellent progress through the local League. In 1944 he was the recipient of a Midland Cup winning medal after Albion had beaten Nottingham Forest 6–5 in the final over two legs. He also scored 14 goals in 41 Central League games for Albion.

EVANS, Elfed Ellison

Inside-forward: 17 apps. 3 goals.

Born: Ferndale, Glamorgan, 28 August 1926.
Died: Cardiff, 1988.
Career: Ferndale Council School. Cardiff City (amateur, June 1943). Treharris Athletic (August 1947). Cardiff City (amateur, May 1948, professional, May 1949). Torquay United (on loan, March-May 1951). ALBION (£5,000, June 1952). Wrexham (£1,250, June 1955). Southport (December 1956). Burton Albion (August 1957, retired through injury, May 1959). Later associated with the coal mining industry in the Rhondda Valley.

■ Owing to the presence of Ronnie Allen and Johnny Nicholls, Wilf Carter and Kenny Hodgkisson, Elfed Evans's first-team opportunities were limited at The Hawthorns, although at times he showed a fine goalscoring technique. Indeed, he netted 43 times in his 70 appearances for Albion's Central League side as well as his efforts in the senior XI. During his career he claimed 42 goals in 122 League matches, perhaps having his best spell at Ninian Park, top-scoring for the Welsh club in 1949–50. He made his debut for Albion against his former employers, Cardiff City, in September 1952.

EVANS, George Clement

Inside-forward: 16 apps. 8 goals.

Born: Sutton-in-Ashfield, 18 December 1865.
Died: West Bromwich, 1930.
Career: Sutton-in-Ashfield Junior and Derby Council & Central Schools. Derby Midland. St Luke's FC (1883). Derby County (July 1884, professional, August 1885). ALBION (May 1889). Brierley Hill Alliance (May 1890). Oldbury Town (August 1892). Oldbury St John's (July 1895, retired, May 1901). Later worked for a brewery.

■ A fiery player, normally occupying the inside-right position, George Evans had a cracking right-foot shot and made his Albion debut against his former club, Derby County, in September 1889. Unfortunately knee injuries affected his game considerably, although he did continue to play, albeit at a lower level, and actually appeared in 25 'other' games for Albion. He retired at the age of 35.

EVANS, Joseph Thomas

Defender: 90 apps. 8 goals.

Born: Darlaston, 12 February 1906.
Died: Walsall, 1971.
Career: Darlaston Central School. Darlaston FC (1921). ALBION (amateur October 1922, professional, October 1923, retired through injury, May 1931). Entered into engineering in 1934.

■ Joe Evans captained England as a schoolboy in 1922 and also played in a junior international (1925) before making his League debut for Albion against West Ham United (away) in March 1926. He remained a loyal servant at The Hawthorns, making 110 appearances for the Central League side, before quitting the game with a serious knee injury at the age of 25. A powerfully built centre-half, strong in the air, he would surely have made more appearances if the likes of Bill Richardson, Fred Reed and Ted Rooke hadn't been around at the same time. He played in 110 games for the second team, helping them win the Central League title in 1926–27.

EVANS, Michael James

Striker: 40+33 apps. 9 goals.

Born: Plymouth, 1 January 1973.
Career: Plymouth Argyle (apprentice, June 1989, professional, March 1991). Southampton (£500,000, March 1997). ALBION (£750,000, October 1997). Bristol Rovers (£250,000, August 2000). Plymouth Argyle (£30,000, March 2001).

■ Hard-working striker Micky Evans suffered far too many injuries during his

time with Albion to make any real impact. Nevertheless, he still made over 70 first-team appearances, with a fair proportion coming as a substitute – plus 22 in the reserves (13 goals scored). He made his senior debut in a 1–0 defeat at Middlesbrough in November 1997 and remained at The Hawthorns for almost three years before moving down the ladder to join Bristol Rovers. Capped once by the Republic of Ireland v Romania in October 1997 (as a Saints player), he helped Plymouth win the Third Division title in 2002 and the following year reached the milestones of 600 club appearances and 120 career goals.

EVANS, Stewart John

Inside-forward: 16+1 apps. 1 goal.

Born: Maltby, Yorkshire, 15 November 1960.
Career: Maltby Schools. Rotherham United (apprentice, April 1977, professional, November 1978). Gainsborough Trinity (August 1979). Sheffield United (November 1980). Wimbledon (March 1982). ALBION (£60,000, August 1986). Plymouth Argyle (£50,000, March 1987). Rotherham United (November 1988). Torquay United (on loan, March–May 1991). Crewe Alexandra (September 1991–May 1993). Denaby United (1995–96). Later Parkgate FC (manager, 2003 onwards).

■ Initially a tall striker who later became a dogged defender, Stewart Evans found himself completely out of his depth when

he played for Albion, despite scoring on his home debut, following his first outing against Hull City in August 1986. He also netted four goals in 13 Central League games for the club. A Fourth Division championship winner with Wimbledon (1983), he then helped the Dons secure promotion again the following season, was top-scorer for the Plough Lane club in 1984–85 (Division Two) with 14 goals and three seasons later gained promotion again, this time with Rotherham. Surprisingly, he went on to net over 100 goals in more than 400 competitive appearances before dropping into non-League football in 1993.

EVANS, Thomas Taylor John

Full-back: 22 apps.

Born: Wolverhampton, 12 September 1872.
Died: 1950.
Career: Essington & Featherstone Council School. Fairfield FC (Wolverhampton). ALBION (£75, professional, June 1896). Wellington Town (briefly, November 1897). Tottenham Hotspur (£25, December 1897, retired through injury, May 1896).

■ A hard-tackling full-back, yet somewhat unreliable, especially under pressure, Tom Evans was never at home with Albion and left the club in a huff

after several disputes with the directors, being suspended four times in 1897. He made his League debut for the Baggies against Blackburn Rovers (away) in September 1896, and as well as his senior outings for the club he also played in over 20 'other' first-team matches.

EVENSON, Isaac

Forward/wing-half: 8 apps. 1 goal.

Born: Manchester, 20 November 1882.
Died: Nottingham, July 1954.
Career: Gorton & Audenshawe Schools. Manchester Tonge FC (1897). Glossop North End (professional, August 1898). Stockport County (April 1901). Leicester Fosse (July 1903). Clapton Orient (July 1905, later caretaker manager for three months in 1906). ALBION (£75, April 1907). Plymouth Argyle (May 1908). Nottingham Forest (August 1910, retired after World War One).

■ Signed as a centre-forward by Leicester Fosse after top-scoring for Stockport, Ike Evenson was switched to inside-left where he did exceptionally well, netting 16 goals in 56 outings for the Foxes before his transfer to Clapton Orient whom he assisted in their first ever League campaign. He was referred to as a 'middle line schemer' with Albion, whom he spent just one season with before entering the Southern League. He made his debut for the Baggies against Oldham Athletic (away) in September 1907 and, in all, hit 32 goals in a career total of 147 League appearances, playing his best football with Orient (8 goals in 63 outings). He also had a handful of games for Albion's second XI.

FACEY, Delroy Michael

Striker: 2+7 apps.

Born: Huddersfield, 22 April 1980.
Career: Huddersfield Town (apprentice, April 1996, professional, May 1997). Bolton Wanderers (July 2002). Bradford City (on loan, November–December 2002). ALBION (January 2004). Hull City (free, July 2004). Gillingham (January 2005). Oldham Athletic (March 2005).

■ A fast and powerful striker, signed by Albion boss Gary Megson to boost the front-line early in 2004, Facey made 82 appearances for Huddersfield (15 goals) and a dozen for Bolton (nine in the

Premiership) as well as having a handful of outings during his time at Bradford. He made his Albion debut as a substitute against Watford soon after joining but, after failing to establish himself in the side, was released at the end of the season.

FAIRFAX, Raymond

Full-back: 90+2 apps. 1 goal.

Born: Smethwick, 13 November 1941.
Career: Corbett Street Junior & James Watt Technical Schools (Smethwick). Smethwick and Birmingham Boy. Staffs County FA. ALBION (junior, May 1959, professional, August 1959). Northampton Town (June 1968). Wellingborough (July 1971). Olney Town (September 1972, retired, May 1974). Later returned to ALBION as assistant to commercial manager Gordon Dimbleby (1974, taking over as assistant secretary a year later). Then Port Vale (secretary, August 1985–June 1987). Aston Villa (ticket office clerk, 1988–2002). ALBION (ticket office clerk/administrator, May 2003). Also represented West Bromwich Albion All Stars (1975–82). He now lives in Sutton Coldfield.

■ Stern-tackling full-back Ray Fairfax scored once for Albion – a terrific long range effort in the Fairs Cup clash against Bologna at The Hawthorns in March 1967. Honoured by the Staffordshire County FA before joining Albion, he had to wait four years for his League debut (which came at Liverpool in March 1963) and three years later, having taken over the left-back position from Graham

Williams (who moved into the half-back line), he helped the Baggies win the League Cup in 1966. Fairfax left The Hawthorns a month after Albion had won the FA Cup in 1968. He also had 194 outings for Albion's Central League side and after leaving the club amassed more than 120 first-team appearances for Northampton. He was the player on the receiving end of George Best's trickery when the Manchester United and Irish international winger scored six goals against the Cobblers in an 8–2 FA Cup victory at The County Ground in February 1970.

FARRINGTON, Samuel George

Forward: 1 app. 1 goal.

Born: Burslem, Stoke-on-Trent, 11 July 1884.
Died: Bristol, 1946.
Career: Burlsem County School. Stoke Priory. Glossop (amateur, August 1901). Hanley Swifts (March 1902). ALBION (professional, March 1903). Castleford Town (June 1904). Southampton (December 1908). Bristol City (April 1909, retired through injury, May 1914). Did not play after World War One. Later worked in the docks.

■ A quick and active centre-forward, Sammy Farrington was far too light to make any impression in top-class football. He did, however, have the pleasure of scoring in his only League game for Albion – a 3–0 win over Derby County in April 1903. He played in 12 second XI matches.
* Two of Sammy's brothers – George and Fred Farrington – both played professionally, the former briefly for Albion's reserve side and Preston North End (1906–07) and the latter for Burlsem Port Vale between 1888–94.

FELLOWS, James Ernest

Forward: 14 apps.

Born: West Bromwich, 12 February 1870.
Died: Birmingham, 1933.
Career: Beeches Road School (West Bromwich). Copper's Hill Methodists (1888). ALBION (April 1892). Kings Heath FC (July 1897). ALBION (April 12899). Studley Rovers (November 1899, retired May 1907). Became a licensee

(briefly) and later worked in the painting and decorating business.

■ A very handsome man and a useful footballer to boot, Ernie Fellows was a roving forward able to occupy all five positions, although he was never a regular in Albion's line-up during his two spells with the club. An amateur throughout his career, he made his League debut against Wolverhampton Wanderers in December 1892, setting up Roddy McLeod for his goal in the 1–1 draw at Molineux. He made eight 'other' first-team appearances for the club.

FENTON, Frederick

Forward: 6 apps. 1 goal.

Born: Gainsborough, 2 November 1878.
Died: Hackney, London, 1944.
Career: Gainsborough & Lincoln Council Schools, Gainsborough Trinity (1898). Stoke (March 1900). West Ham United (August 1900). Gainsborough Trinity (January 1901). Preston North End (March 1902). ALBION (April 1903). Bristol City (£50, September 1904). Swindon Town (August 1907). Croydon Common (May 1910, retired through injury, May 1911). Later ran an ironmonger's ship in London.

■ Able to occupy both wing positions and occasionally the centre-forward berth, Fred Fenton had a varied career. His style was a mixture of flair and cleverness and during his playing days he gained a Second Division championship medal with Bristol City (1906) and amassed over 150 Football League and Southern League appearances, playing in West Ham's first ever Southern League game (against Gravesend in 1900). He made his Albion debut against Small Heath (away) in November 1903 and he also played in 14 second XI games for the club.

FENTON, Graham Anthony

Inside-forward/midfield: 7 apps. 3 goals.

Born: Wallsend-on-Tyne, 22 May 1974.
Career: Aston Villa (apprentice, June 1990, professional, February 1992). ALBION (on loan, January–February 1994). Blackburn Rovers (£1.5 million, November 1995). Leicester City (£1.1 million, August 1997).

Walsall (free, March 2000). Stoke City (free, August 2000). St Mirren (free, September 2000). Blackpool (free, August 2001). Darlington (on loan, September–October 2002). Blyth Spartans (June 2003).

■ A very skilful and active footballer, Graham Fenton had an excellent loan spell at The Hawthorns and thousands of Albion supporters were bitterly disappointed when he didn't sign permanently for the club. He made his debut against his future club, Leicester City, at Filbert Street in January 1994 and scored in his last game for Albion, the return fixture with the Foxes, before returning to Villa Park. A League Cup winner in 1994, he passed the milestone of 150 senior appearances at club level in 2002. He also helped Leicester City reach the League Cup final in 2000 and was capped once by England at under-21 level.

FENTON, Ronald

Inside-forward: 66 apps. 18 goals.

Born: South Shields, County Durham, 2 September 1940.

Career: South Shields & District Schools. Durham Boys. ALBION (trialist, April–May 1955). South Shields (August 1955). Burnley (junior, April 1956, professional, September 1957). ALBION (£15,000, November 1962). Birmingham City (£7,500, January 1965). Brentford (January 1968). Notts County (July 1970, retired in May 1971, became coach at Meadow Lane, later manager, 1975–77). Nottingham Forest (assistant trainer, then coach, October 1977, promoted to assistant manager under Brian Clough in 1987 after 10 years' service at The City Ground, resigned, May 1993, when Clough also left). Later an England scout and coach in Malta.

■ Ronnie Fenton was a battler, a player who gave his all. He grafted hard and long and never really fulfilled his true potential with Albion despite playing in almost 70 first-team matches, his first being against West Ham United at Upton Park in December 1962. He also scored eight times in eight second XI games and during his career he scored 43 goals in 194 League games.

FEREDAY, Wayne

Full-back/winger: 43+10 apps. 3 goals.

Born: Warley, West Midlands, 16 June 1963.

Career: Queen's Park Rangers (apprentice, June 1979, professional, September 1980).

Newcastle United (£400,000, May 1989). Bournemouth (£150,000, November 1990). ALBION (on loan, December 1991, signed permanently, £20,000, February 1992). Cardiff City (free, March 1994). Telford United (October–December 1995). Christchurch FC (briefly). Broadstone Albion (manager/coach, Under-10s, 2001–04). Christchurch FC (briefly, 2002–03). Also worked for the Southampton branch of URO in 1997–98 – the company owned by the then Albion chairman Tony Hale – and has been associated with the PFA and worked as a football reporter/summariser. Now lives in Poole, Dorset.

■ In 1980–81 Wayne Fereday made a name for himself as a new teenage superstar with Queen's Park Rangers. He netted twice on his League debut and quickly gained England under-21 honours, later representing the Football League (1988) while still with QPR. Lithe and extremely quick, he was one of the fastest players in the game and made almost 250 appearances for the London club before transferring to Newcastle, being reunited with his former manager Jim Smith. He rarely showed his best form at St James' Park and, after 41 outings, moved to Bournemouth in a player-exchange deal involving Gavin Peacock. He made over 50 appearances for Albion including 20 in the promotion-winning campaign of 1992–93. However, injuries started to

interfere with his game and on transfer deadline day in 1994 he moved to Cardiff. Fereday made his debut for Albion in a 1–0 defeat at Bradford City in December 1991. He also played in over 20 Central League matches, netting two goals.

FETTIS, Alan William

Goalkeeper: 3 apps.

Born: Belfast, 1 February 1971.
Career: Ards (semi-professional, March 1989). Hull City (£50,000, August 1991). ALBION (on loan, November–December 1995). Nottingham Forest (£250,000, January 1996). Blackburn Rovers (£300,000, September 1997). York City (free, March 2000). Hull City (free, January 2003). Sheffield United (on loan, November–December 2003). Grimsby Town (on loan, March–May 2004). Macclesfield Town (July 2004).

■ Goalkeeper Alan Fettis joined Albion on loan when Stuart Naylor was injured. A very competent performer, he now has 25 full caps under his belt for Northern Ireland, having also represented his country in three 'B', schoolboy and youth internationals. Standing 6ft 1in tall and weighing almost 13st, he has now amassed well over 350 senior appearances at club level, half with Hull City.

FIELDING, Alec Ross

Outside-right: 10 apps. 1 goal.

Born: Trentham, Stoke-on-Trent, 7 January 1880.
Died: Stoke-on-Trent, March 1952.
Career: Silverdale Council School (Stoke). Stoke Priory (1888). Florence Colliery. Stoke (amateur, March 1902). Nottingham Forest (September 1902). Stoke (March 1903). ALBION (September 1908). Stoke (February 1909). Burton United (August 1909, retired, May 1913). Returned to work on his father's estate.

■ Right-winger Ross Fielding was a ebullient winger with excellent dribbling skills and a wonderful body-swerve. He did far better with his other clubs than he did at The Hawthorns and in his three spells with Stoke notched up more than 100 appearances. He was signed by Albion while out hunting on his father's estate in North Staffordshire and made his debut at Burnley 24 hours after joining. His only goal for the club came in a 5–1 home win over Blackpool in April 1909. His brother, Arthur John Fielding, also played for Stoke in 1908–10 and for Port Vale.

FINCH, Ernest Abel Robert

Full-back: 234 apps.

Born: Hednesford, 31 August 1908.
Died: Hednesford, December 2000.
Career: Hill Top & West Hill Council Schools (Hednesford). Hednesford Prims (1922) Hednesford Town (1923). ALBION (amateur, April 1925, professional, September 1925). Swansea Town (May 1939). Hednesford Town. Tamworth (as a guest during World War Two). For 14 years, from 1942 to 1956, served in the Police Force as PC 475 Finch in the Cannock Division of the Staffordshire County Force.

■ Bob 'Able' Finch was a redoubtable full-back who spent 14 years at The Hawthorns, appearing in more than 230 League and cup games, but failed to score a single goal, although he did concede three past his own 'keeper. He netted twice in 231 appearances for the second XI with whom he won four Central League championship medals in 1926–27, 1932–33, 1933–34 and 1934–35, skippering the side in the last three. Quick-witted, zealous, alert and confident in his kicking, Finch had to compete for a first-team place with so many other fine full-backs and missed out on Albion's two FA Cup final

appearances in the 1930s. He played for Albion against Arsenal in a sixth round FA Cup tie when a record crowd of 64,815 packed into The Hawthorns, but was a loser one step from Wembley when the Baggies lost to Preston North End at Highbury! Finch, who played in two England international trials, made his League debut against Leicester City in February 1926 (aged 17). He was also a very keen golfer, playing right up until 1997. He was 92 years of age when he died in a Hednesford hospital.

FINCH, Royston Arthur

Inside or outside-left: 22 apps. 2 goals.

Born: Barry Island, Glamorgan, 7 April 1922.
Career: Glaston Road Boys' School (Barry). Barry Shop Assistants' FC. Barrians FC (Cardiff & District League). Swansea Town (amateur, July 1938). Blackburn Rovers (trialist, February–April 1939). Stoke City (trialist, May–June 1939). Swansea Town (amateur, August 1939). ALBION (amateur, June 1944, professional, September 1944). Lincoln City (£3,000, February 1949, retired through injury, May 1959). Played for East End Athletic (briefly, 1961–62). Ran a newsagents in Winn Street, Lincoln, for many years.

■ Roy Finch made soccer history in February 1949 when he flew to Southampton to sign in time to play for Lincoln at The Dell (a 4–0 defeat). He went on to score 56 goals in 275

appearances for the Imps, helping them win promotion to the Second Division in 1952. He was a regular in the first XI at Sincil Bank for 11 years, having spent almost five seasons at The Hawthorns, during which time he served in World War Two. He made his Albion debut in a League North game against Walsall in April 1945 and lost his place in the team early in the 1948–49 promotion season when challenged by Frank Hodgetts, Bobby Barker and new signing Ernie Shepherd, so he left to join the Imps. He scored 22 goals in 56 Central League games for Albion.

FITTON, George Arthur

Outside-left: 99 apps. 11 goals.

Born: Melton Mowbray, Leicestershire, 3 May 1902.
Died: Worcester, 15 September 1984.
Career: Melton Mowbray Junior School. Kinver Council School. Kinver Swifts. Cookley St Peter's (1919). Kidderminster Harriers (August 1920). ALBION (£400, October 1922). Manchester United (March 1932). Preston North End (December 1932). Coventry City (May 1935). Kidderminster Harriers (October 1937, retired, May 1938 to become third-team trainer at Highfield Road). ALBION (assistant trainer-coach, October 1948, then first-team trainer July 1951–June 1956). Later game warden at Kinver National Park.

■ Arthur 'Mother' Fitton, a former bricklayer's labourer, was a penetrative outside-left who gave Albion distinguished service both on and off the field for a total of 18 years – first as a player and then as assistant trainer-coach and first-team trainer. In his 10 years' service as a player, he made almost 100 first-team appearances before giving way to Stan Wood, and he also registered a record 261 outings for the reserves, netting 56 goals. He helped the second string win the Central League championship on three occasions: 1922–23, 1923–24 and 1926–27. Later Fitton gained a Third Division South winners' medal with Coventry (1936) and during his League career scored a total of 55 goals in 232 appearances. Fitton was also a fine cricketer, a left-handed batsmen and able wicketkeeper, who finished fourth in the Staffs County batting averages in 1928 with a highest score of 112. He also played regularly for West Bromwich Dartmouth CC.

FLAVELL, Arthur Edwin

Goalkeeper: 2 apps.

Born: West Bromwich, 15 June 1875.
Died: 1939.
Career: Guns Village School (West Bromwich). Mitchell St George's. West Bromwich Baptist (1895). ALBION (professional, September 1896). Bournbrook FC (June 1898). Millwall Athletic (September 1899, retired through injury, May 1900). Later became a gardener.

■ A safe and supple goalkeeper, reserve to Joe Reader, Edwin Flavell was given just two League outings by Albion, both were away defeats in March 1898: the first at Sunderland, the second at Bury. A regular in Albion's second XI for two seasons, he also played once for Millwall, another defeat 1–0 (home) by Spurs in September 1899 in the Southern League.

FLEWITT, Albert William

Inside-forward: 80 apps. 23 goals.

Born: Beeston, Notts, 10 February 1872.
Died: Nottingham, 1943.
Career: Stamford (1890). Mansfield Greenhalgh's FC (1892). Lincoln City (professional, August 1893). Everton (August 1895). ALBION (January 1896). Bedminster FC (June 1899–May 1900). Was a licensee before serving in World War One.

■ Inside-forward Albert Flewitt scored a goal every four games for Albion, but, after representing the Football League in November 1895, he fell foul of the management and was suspended six times between August 1898 and March 1899 for breaches of club rules, which led to his departure. Signed by Lincoln with another future Albion player, John Chadburn, Flewitt was reported to have a terrific shot, to work hard and, at times, produce a touch of elegance. He was top-scorer for the imps in 1894–95 with 17 goals and went on to score 30 in 56 outings before joining Everton. He made his Albion debut against Blackburn Rovers (away) in February 1896 and his efforts in the test matches at the end of that season helped keep Albion in the First Division. Besides his senior appearances for the club, Flewitt also starred in more than 80 'other' first-team matches (20 goals scored) and partnered Billy Bassett on the right-wing for most of the time he was at Stoney Lane.

FLYNN, Sean Michael

Midfield: 110+12 apps. 9 goals.

Born: Birmingham, 13 March 1968.
Career: Halesowen Town (August 1988).

Coventry City (£20,000, December 1991).
Derby County (£250,000, August 1995).
Stoke City (on loan, March–May 1997).
ALBION (£260,000, August 1997).
Tranmere Rovers (free, July 2000).
Halesowen Town (June–July 2002).
Kidderminster Harriers (August
2002–September 2003). Evesham United
(October 2003). Redditch United (July
2004).

■ Never-say-die midfielder Sean Flynn
skippered the Baggies several times and
made over 120 first-team appearances for
the club before becoming surplus to
manager Gary Megson's requirements at
the end of the 1999–2000 season. He
spent just two seasons at Prenton Park
before returning to his first club,
Halesowen Town, for the briefest of
spells, then moved to nearby
Kidderminster. Purposeful, aggressive and
a thoroughly honest competitor, 'Flynny',
who had 105 outings for Coventry and 65
for Derby, reached the career milestone of
350 senior appearances in 2003.

FOGGO, Kenneth Taylor

Right-winger: 136 apps. 29 goals.

*Born: Perth, Scotland, 7 November 1943.
Career: Peebles High School. Peebles &
Scotland Schools. Peebles YMCA. St
Johnstone (trialist, April 1958). ALBION
(amateur, August 1959, professional,
November 1960). Norwich City (£15,000,
October 1967). Portsmouth (£25,000,
January 1973). Brentford (on loan,
June–August 1973). Southend United
(September 1975). Chelmsford City
(August 1976). Brereton Social Club
(briefly, 1980–81). Retired from the sport
to go into the laundry and dry-cleaning
business, later having a stall on London's
Petticoat Lane. Now lives in London.*

■ Impish Scottish right-winger Ken
Foggo came down to The Hawthorns
with three other Scots, Campbell
Crawford, Bobby Hope and Bobby
Murray, in the summer of 1959, having
played in a schoolboy international for
his country. He progressed through the
ranks and developed a strong physique,
extra pace and stability before making his
League debut against Fulham in
September 1962, assisting in three of the
goals in a 6–1 win. Replacing Alec
Jackson on the right-wing, he went on to
make almost 140 senior appearances for

Albion and was 'sub' for the 1967 League
Cup final against Queen's Park Rangers.
He also notched up 50 goals in 114
Central League games. During his career
Foggo accumulated a fine record, playing
in 432 first-team games and netting 100
goals, including 92 in 406 League outings.
He won a Second Division championship
medal with Norwich in 1972 when he
was their leading scorer.

FOLKS, William Thomas

Forward: 1 app.

*Born: Tottenham, North London, 9
September 1886.
Died: London, 15 April 1944.
Career: Wood Green & Haringey Schools.
Waltham Forest Boys. Clapton FC (August
1902). ALBION (March 1904). Clapton
(June 1904–April 1908). Later, with
Dulwich Hamlet. Became a university
lecturer.*

■ An amateur outside-right, Billy
Crabtree spent just a few months at The
Hawthorns, during which time he
appeared in one Football League game, at
home to Sheffield United in April 1904,
and in five reserve-team matches. He
later played in the 1905 FA Amateur Cup
final for Clapton.

FORD, Ernest Frederick

Inside-forward: 1 app.

*Born: Chingford, 9 January 1896.
Died: Essex, April 1960.*

Career: Chingford Council & Buckhurst
Hill Schools. Woodford Town. Ilford FC.
ALBION (amateur, December 1922).
Retired, May 1923, to concentrate on his
business interests in Woodford, Essex.

■ An amateur left-winger signed as a
squad member, Ernie Ford made his only
League appearance for Albion against
Sheffield United at The Hawthorns in
March 1923 when he took over from
Howard Gregory.

FORD, Tony, OBE

*Outside-right/midfield: 127+1 apps. 15
goals.*

*Born: Grimsby, 14 May 1959.
Career: Grimsby Town (apprentice, July
1975, professional, May 1977). Sunderland
(on loan, March–May 1986). Stoke City
(£35,000, July 1986). ALBION (£145,000,
March 1989). Grimsby Town (£50,000,
November 1991). Bradford City (on loan,
September–October 1993). Scunthorpe
United (free, August 1994). Barrow (free,
August 1998). Mansfield Town (free,
October 1996, later player/assistant
manager). Rochdale (free, July 1999).
Barnsley (£70,000 paid in compensation to
Rochdale, November 2001, as assistant*

manager/coach, sacked October 2002), re-appointed as Rochdale assistant manager, December 2003, under former Albion player Steve Parkin).

■ Tony Ford – described as a 'Model T Ford' – has been associated with professional football for almost 30 years, and, as a player, accumulated more than 900 League appearances (1,000 plus in all competitions), the second highest tally behind Peter Shilton. He was signed by Albion manager Brian Talbot with whom he had played while at Stoke, and did exceptionally well as a right-sided forward, racing up and down the pitch and generally giving a good account of himself. He made 128 appearances for Albion, his first against Swindon Town (away) in March 1989. He was assistant manager/coach to ex-Baggies player Steve Parkin at Barnsley. He made 469 appearances in his two spells with Grimsby and amassed 135 for the Potters. He won two England 'B' caps (against Switzerland and Norway) as an Albion player, having earlier helped Grimsby twice gain promotion, winning the Third Division title in 1980 and the Football League Group Cup in 1982. Ford, who was awarded the OBE in 2000 (for services to football), also played in three Central League games for Albion. Ford is Grimsby Town's youngest-ever first-team player, making his League debut as a substitute against Walsall in October 1975, at the age of 16 years and 143 days.
* In November 2001 Ford became the most costly 47-year-old footballer when Barnsley were forced to pay Rochdale £70,000 for his services because he was still registered as a player at Spotland. He was sacked along with another ex-Albion player, Steve Parkin, after 11 months at Oakwell.

FORD, William Gracey

Centre-forward: 12 apps. 1 goal.

Born: Dundee, Scotland, 7 May 1876.
Died: Dundee, 21 February 1948.
Career: Invergowrie & Newport-on-Tay Schools. Lochee FC (1891). Dundee (August 1892). ALBION (£50, June 1896). Hereford Thistle (December 1896). New Brompton (1897–98). Luton Town (1898–99). Gravesend United (August 1899). Chatham (January 1901, retired 1902). Returned to Scotland to take on a business in Dundee.

■ Lightly built centre-forward Billy Ford played in Albion's front-line during the first half of the 1896–97 season but was then left in the cold following the arrival of John Cameron. He made his debut in a 2–1 League home win over Blackburn Rovers in September 1896 and scored his only goal for the club in a 3–1 defeat at Sheffield Wednesday in his third game. He played in more than 20 'other' first-team games for Albion and netted seven goals in 23 League outings for Luton.

FORRESTER, Anthony Charles

Outside-right: 6 apps. 3 goals.

Born: Parkstone, 14 January 1940.
Career: Bournemouth Junior & Poole Grammar Schools. Dorset & District Boys. ALBION (amateur, September 1955, professional, January 1957). Southend United (£1,000, April 1959). GKN Sankey's (August 1962). Kettering Town (March 1965, retired, May 1966). Later emigrated to New Zealand where he coached FC Whenaupai (Auckland).

■ A reserve outside-right at The Hawthorns, it was hoped that raven-haired Tony Forrester would eventually take over the number 7 shirt from Frank Griffin, but it was not to be and after a very respectable record of a goal every two games, including one on his debut against Tottenham Hotspur in November 1958 (won 4–2) plus three more in 35 Central League games, he was transferred to Southend United, for whom he made 10 senior appearances before drifting into non-League football.

FORSYTH, Michael Eric

Defender: 31+1 apps. 1 goal.

Born: Liverpool, 20 March 1966.
Career: Woodrush High School (Liverpool). Earlswood Juniors. ALBION (apprentice, June 1982, professional, November 1983). Northampton Town (on loan, March 1986). Derby County (£20,000, March 1986). Notts County (£200,000, February 1995). Hereford United (on loan, September 1996). Wycombe Wanderers (£50,000, December 1996). Burton Albion (June 1999, retired, May 2001). Derby County (coaching staff). Wycombe Wanderers (Youth-team manager from August 2003).

■ Given his Football League baptism at Highbury in December 1983, Micky Forsyth developed into a very efficient covering defender who preferred the left-back position. Honoured by England at youth level, he later added 'B' and under-21 caps to his collection and spent five years at The Hawthorns, playing mainly in the second team (48 appearances), before transferring to Derby County. He appeared in 408 senior games for the Rams, helping them win the Second Division championship in 1987. When he moved to Burton in 1999, Forsyth had well over 500 appearances behind him.

FOSTER, Adrian Michael

Inside-forward: 14+19 apps. 2 goals.

Born: Kidderminster, 19 March 1971.
Career: ALBION (apprentice, June 1987, professional, July 1989). Torquay United (free, July 1992). Gillingham (£60,000, August 1994). Exeter City (on loan, March–April 1996). Hereford United (August 1996). Rushden and Diamonds (August 1997). Yeovil Town (August 1999). Forest Green Rovers (August 2000). Yeovil Town (on loan, April–May 2001). Bath City (August 2001). Taunton Town (July 2004).

■ A short, nippy, hard-working utility forward, Adrian Foster spent five years at The Hawthorns playing under three different managers before being released by Ossie Ardiles. He made his League debut against Oldham Athletic (home) in February 1990 and had the pleasure of scoring in the local derby against Wolves at Molineux the following month. He also netted 25 goals in 90 Central/Pontins League appearances for the Baggies,

gaining a championship medal at this level in 1990–91 when he netted 11 times.

FOSTER, John Jabez

Utility forward: 1 app.

Born: Rawmarsh, Yorkshire, 19 November 1877.
Died: York, August 1946.
Career: Rotherham Church Institute. Thornhill United. Darlaston (briefly). Berwick Rangers, Worcester (August 1894). ALBION (September 1898). Blackpool (July 1901). Rotherham Town (July 1902). Stockport County (1904). Watford (1905–06). Sunderland (£800, December 1907). West Ham United (briefly, May–September 1908). Southampton (in exchange for former Albion player Fred Costello, March 1909). Huddersfield Town (May 1909). Castleford Town (1910–11). A back injury crippled him at the age of 45.

■ After failing to make headway with Albion, Jack Foster (sometimes referred to as Jabez) developed quite a reputation as a dashing centre-forward with Watford. A decline in his health saw his form slump at Sunderland, he failed to make much of an impression with West Ham and appeared in just six games for Saints and was a huge disappointment at Huddersfield. He made his League debut for Albion against his future club, Sunderland, in October 1898.

FOULKES, Hugh Edward

Full-back: 15 apps.

Born: Llandudno, 13 April 1909.
Died: Harborne, Birmingham, 16 December 1981.
Career: Llandudno Council & Rhos-on-Sea Schools. Llandudno Town (April 1928). ALBION (amateur, March 1930, professional, May 1930). Guildford City (£100, May 1937). Darlington (June 1938, retired during World War Two, c.1940). After World War Two he became an exceptionally fine semi-professional golfer with a handicap of 10.

■ A former schoolboy international and Welsh amateur trialist, full-back Hugh Foulkes was thoughtful and gifted with a fair degree of ability and positional sense. He was capped once at senior level against Ireland in 1932 and also played in two junior internationals against Ireland

in 1929 and 1930. He was an Albion player for seven years, during which time, as fourth choice full-back behind George Shaw, Bert Trentham and Bob Finch, he appeared in only 15 first-team games, his first against Sunderland (away) in September 1931, but he did gain three successive Central League championship medals: 1933, 34 and 35. Indeed, he made 229 appearances for Albion's second string, scoring one goal.

FOX, Ruel Adrian

Forward: 44+23 apps. 2 goals.

Born: Ipswich, 14 January 1968.
Career: Norwich City (apprentice, June 1984, professional, January 1986). Newcastle United (£2.25 million, February 1994). Tottenham Hotspur (£4.2 million, October 1995). ALBION (£250,000, August 2000, released, May 2002). Southend United (part-time coach, August 2002). Stanway Rovers (briefly, 2003).

■ Initially an orthodox winger (preferring the right side of the park),

Ruel Fox later became an exceptionally fine midfielder with good close control, splendid vision, neat passing and a will to win. He made 219 appearances for the Canaries (25 goals scored) before moving to Newcastle. He spent 18 months at St James' Park, adding a further 70 appearances to his tally (14 goals) and then in almost five years with Spurs amassed 129 appearances and claimed another 15 goals. Gary Megson was delighted to bring Fox to The Hawthorns and in his first season saw him play some excellent football, having made his Baggies League debut as a 'sub' against Barnsley (away) in August 2000. After sitting on the bench for most of the 2001–02 promotion-winning season, Fox was released, having scored only twice in 67 senior outings. Earlier in his career Fox gained two England 'B' caps and was a League Cup winner with spurs in 1999.

FRASER, Douglas Michael

Wing-half/full-back: 325 apps. 12 goals.

Born: Busby, Lanarkshire, Scotland, 8 December 1941.
Career: Busby Junior & Senior Schools. Rolls Royce FC. Eaglesham Amateurs. Blantyre Celtic. Celtic (trialist, 1956). Leeds United (trialist, 1957). Aberdeen (amateur, August 1957, professional, January 1959). ALBION (£23,000, September 1963). Nottingham Forest (£35,000, January 1971). Walsall (£8,000, July 1973, then manager from January 1974–March 1977). Later served as a prison officer at Nottingham Gaol (until 1996). Now lives in retirement in Ilkeston, Derbyshire.

■ A craggy Scot, Doug Fraser immediately established himself in the English First Division after joining Albion in 1963 and making his debut against Birmingham City (home) shortly after moving south. A stern-tackling wing-half who eventually switched to full-back, he helped Albion win the League Cup and FA Cup in 1966 and 1968 respectively, and skippered the side in the 1970 League Cup final defeat by Manchester City, having earlier played in the 1967 losing final against Queen's Park Rangers. He made well over 300 senior and 12 second XI appearances for Albion in eight years with the club. He later

FREDGAARD, Carsten

Midfield: 5 apps.

*Born: Hillesod, Denmark, 20 May 1976.
Career: Lyngby FC, Denmark (professional, June 1994). FC Copenhagen, Denmark (1997). Sunderland (£800,000, July 1999). ALBION (on loan, February–March 2000). Bolton Wanderers (on loan, November–December 2000). FC Copenhagen (three-year contract, July 2001).*

■ A tall, pacy, left-sided player with one Danish cap to his credit, Carsten Fredgaard made little impact at Sunderland, and after loan spells at The Hawthorns and Bolton he returned to his home country in 2001 having appeared in just 15 first-team matches in England. He made his debut for Albion in a 1–0 home win over Crewe Alexandra in February 2000.

FREEMAN, Ronald Peter

Centre-forward: 2+1 apps.

*Born: Newark, Notts, 4 July 1945.
Career: Newark State School. Alvechurch Church of England School. Astwood Bank (August 1960). Alvechurch (January 1962). Stourbridge (August 1964). ALBION*

became manager at Fellows Park and quit soccer in 1977 to join the Nottingham prison service. Fraser, who was capped twice by Scotland while at The Hawthorns, played 70 times for Aberdeen (1960–63).

(£2,500, professional, April 1968). Lincoln City (£2,500, June 1970). Reading (£11,500, January 1973). Lincoln City (£1,500, January 1975). Bradford City (on loan, briefly 1975). Boston FC (August 1977, retired, November 1977). Nettleham FC (manager, July 1989–May 1991). Boston (manager, August 1991). Stamford Town (manager, December 1993). Also managed Ivy Tavern FC (Lincoln Sunday League team). He returned to his former job as a lorry/transport driver, which he did prior to joining Albion.

■ 'Percy' Freeman, as strong as an ox with a big heart, was a robust centre-forward who never really got a look in at The Hawthorns, making just three first-team appearances, the first on the left-wing against Southampton (away) in August 1969. He did, however, score 29 goals in almost 50 Central League games. He went on to find the net on 74 occasions in 171 first-team matches for Lincoln, helping the Imps win the Fourth Division championship in 1976 when he claimed 23 goals.

FRYER, Edward Reginald

Wing-half: 23 apps.

Born: South Yardley, Birmingham, 12 August 1904.
Died: Bury St Edmunds, 1987.
Career: Yardley Wood School. Foleshill St George's FC. Harborne Lynwood (1921). ALBION (amateur, April 1923, professional, May 1924). Shrewsbury Town (May 1930). Wellington Town, retired, May 1935). Became an office worker after World War Two.

■ A neat, stylish wing-half, clever at timing his tackle, Reg Fryer was reserve to Nelson Howarth and Len Darnell during his time at The Hawthorns. He made his first-team League debut against Grimsby Town (home) in September 1927, having gained a Central League championship medal the previous season when he appeared in 15 games.

FUDGE, Michael Henry

Inside-forward: 16 apps. 5 goals.

Born: Bristol, 5 December 1945.
Career: Carlton Park School (Bristol). Bristol Boys (1960–61). ALBION (amateur, May 1961, professional, December 1963). Exeter City (June 1967).

Wellington Town (August 1968). Telford United. Kidderminster Harriers (June 1976). Malvern Town (July 1977). Brierley Hill (July 1978). Brereton Town (as player-manager, August 197) Retired in 1981 to become licensee of the Lord Hill Public house at Dawley, Shropshire.

■ Inside-forward Micky Fudge made his League debut for Albion against Sheffield United in December 1963. He played in the next six games and scored just one goal (in a thrilling 4–4 draw with Spurs). When he came back into the side against the reigning First Division champions, Everton, at the end of March 1964, he cracked in a hat-trick as the Baggies stormed to an impressive 4–2 victory. Basically a reserve forward at The Hawthorns, he netted 38 goals in 96 Central League games before being released by manager Alan Ashman in 1967. He went on to score six times in 34 League games for Exeter.

GAARDSOE, Thomas

Defender: 78+4 apps. 4 goals.

Born: Randers, Denmark, 23 November 1979.
Career: AAB Aalborg (junior, April 1995, professional, December 1996). Ipswich Town (£1.3 million, August 2001). ALBION (£520,000, July 2003).

■ Capped 10 times by Denmark at under-21 level, Thomas Gaardson has

now played in three full internationals for his country. Known as 'The Viking' at The Hawthorns and standing 6ft 2in tall and weighing in at 12st 8lb, he struggled with his form and suffered niggling injuries during his two seasons at Portman Road, appearing in only 49 first-team matches, having made, prior to that, almost 70 for Aalborg (five goals scored). A very skilful defender with the ability to keep calm under pressure, he made his debut for Albion in a 4–0 Carling Cup home win over Brentford in August 2004 and thereafter produced some exquisite performances while also netting some vitally important goals, including two late winners in promotion encounters with Sheffield United (away) and Wigan Athletic (home). He had the misfortune of getting sent off in the last minute of Albion's promotion clash with Millwall in April 2004, but that red card was subsequently rescinded by the FA. Voted Albion's 'Player of the Year' as the baggies reclaimed their place back in the Premiership, he missed out on Euro 2004 and was looking forward to partnering fellow countryman Martin Albrechtsen in defence during 2004–05. He scored his first international goal in his second game for Denmark versus Poland in August 2004.

GABBIDON, Daniel Leon

Full-back: 26+1 apps.

Born: Cwmbran, Gwent, 8 August 1979.
Career: Cwmbran & District Schools. ALBION (apprentice, November 1996, professional, July 1998). Cardiff City (£175,000, August 2000).

■ A versatile defender, cool and composed and able to occupy a variety of positions, Danny Gabbidon was surprisingly transferred by Albion in 2000 after making just 27 senior appearances, the first against Ipswich town (home) in March 1999 (in place of Andy McDermott). He also starred in more than 30 second-team games. However, after moving to Ninian Park his career blossomed. He took his tally of under-21 caps to 17 (to go with those he won at youth team level), established himself in the Welsh senior side (four outings) and helped Cardiff twice win promotion, from the Fourth to the First Division in just three years, in 2001–03.

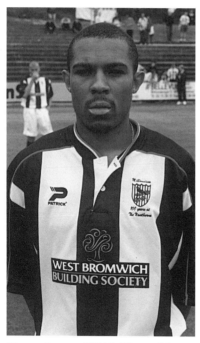

He was also voted Welsh 'Player of the Year' in 2003.

GALE, Arthur Reuben

Forward: 29 apps. 12 goals.

Born: Salford, 16 November 1904.
Died: Trafford Park, Manchester, 20 May 1976.
Career: Salford Lads' Club (1921). Sedgley Park (1923). Bury (professional, January 1926). Chester (1930). ALBION (£1,000, June 1931). Chester (£800, December 1936). Macclesfield (March 1938). Altrincham (coach, August 1938–May 1952). Accrington Stanley (World War Two guest, 1939–40). Chester (scout, 1952–60). Later Northern Nomads (manager, 1967–68). Quit football in 1969 and returned to full-time teaching.

■ A schoolteacher by profession, outside-right or centre-forward Arthur Gale spent five and a half years at The Hawthorns, during which time he appeared in less than 30 first-class games yet scored a dozen goals. He made his senior debut against Newcastle United in April 1932 and was desperately unlucky not to make Albion's 1935 FA Cup final line-up. He played in every round up to the semi-final and scored in the first four, including a brilliant diving header (the winner) in the quarter-final against Preston North End. Fast and direct, he netted 146 goals in only 136 appearances

for Albion's second team during the 1930s, including hauls of 25, 39 and 41 respectively in seasons 1932 to 1935 when he collected successive Central League winners' medal. Prior to joining Albion, Gale scored 73 goals (out of 170) for Chester in the Cheshire Combination County League in season 1930–31. He coached football at various venues until he was 70.

GALLAGHER, Michael

Forward: 1 app.

Born: Cambuslang near Glasgow, 16 January 1932.
Died: Glasgow, July 1975.
Career: Cambuslang & Flemington Schools. Rutherglen Boys. Benburb FC. Royal Marines. Plymouth Argyle (trialist, 1949). Bolton Wanderers (amateur, May 1951, professional, January 1952). ALBION (£2,000, December 1952). Selkirk FC (June 1953). Hibernian (briefly, retired, May 1955, through ill-health). Later worked as a casual labourer.

■ Mick Gallagher, a reserve left-winger with Albion, played in only one League game, away at Burnley in January 1953 when the Baggies lost 5–0.

GARFIELD, Benjamin Walter

Outside-left: 117 apps. 38 goals.

Born: Higham Ferrers, 18 August 1872.
Died: Kent, 10 December 1942.
Career: Finedon FC, Wellingborough

(1891). Kettering Town (1892). Burton Wanderers. ALBION (£200, May 1896). Aston Villa (guest player, 1900). Brighton & Hove Albion (£100, August 1902). Tunbridge Wells Rangers (1905–06). Became a publican in Kent.

■ A rare bundle of energy on Albion's left-wing, Ben Garfield was always involved in the action and he gave the club six years of excellent service. He made his senior debut in a League game against Blackburn Rovers at Ewood Park in September 1896, and besides his senior outings for the club he also played in more than 120 'other' first-team matches plus a dozen or so second XI games. Capped once by England in 1898, he helped Brighton win the Southern League championship in 1903.

GARNER, Simon

Striker: 35+10 apps. 9 goals.

Born: Boston, Lincolnshire, 23 November 1959.
Career: Blackburn Rovers (amateur, 1976, professional, July 1978). ALBION (£30,000, August 1992). Wycombe Wanderers (free, February 1994). Torquay United (January 1996). Woking (July 1996). Wealdstone (February 1997). Dagenham and Redbridge (on loan, season 1997–98). Windsor and Eton (1998). Flackwell Heath FC (August 1999). Kirkham Prison FC (briefly, before retiring, May 2000). Also employed as a postman in Maidenhead (late 1990s). Played for Blackburn Rovers Old Stars and did PR work and worked as a match summariser for Sky Sports and BBC Radio Lancashire.

■ Striker Simon Garner became a legend in Blackburn's history by scoring 192 goals in 565 first-team matches, helping them win the Full Member's Cup at Wembley in 1987. He was signed by Albion boss Ossie Ardiles and during his time at The Hawthorns netted nine goals in 45 outings, helping the Baggies gain promotion to the First Division. He also scored four goals in seven Central League games. An impulsive smoker, Garner, who was almost 40 when he retired, was the first ever Wycombe player to score a hat-trick in the FA Cup, obliging against Hitchin Town in December 1994 when he took over the central scoring berth from another former Albion player, Cyrille Regis (out injured).

GARRATT, George

Outside-right: 30 apps. 3 goals.

Born: Byker, County Durham, 5 April 1882.
Died: Birmingham, June 1926.
Career: Cradley St Luke's (1899). Brierley Hill Alliance (1902). Crewe Alexandra (1904). Aston Villa (£500, March 1905). Southampton (briefly, February 1907). Plymouth Argyle (March 1907). ALBION (£300, May 1907). Crystal Palace (in exchange for Bill Davies, May 1908). Millwall (October 1913). Kidderminster Harriers (1919–20). Later worked in the carpet trade and also as a carpenter.

■ Extremely well built, perhaps a shade overweight at times, and completely blind in his left eye, George Garratt was basically an outside-right, who played his best football with Crystal Palace, for whom he netted eight goals in 185 appearances. He made his Albion debut on the opening day of the 1907–08 season in a 2–1 win over Wolves at Molineux and scored his first goal on his home debut five days later against Burnley. He was replaced on the right-wing after just one season by Bill Davies whose position he took in the Palace side.

GARRATY, William

Centre/inside-forward: 59 apps. 22 goals.

Born: Saltley, Birmingham, 6 October 1878.
Died: Birmingham, 6 May 1931.
Career: Church Road & Saltley St Saviour's Schools (Birmingham). Ashted Swifts. St Saviour's FC. Highfield Villa. Lozells FC. Aston Shakespeare (1896). Aston Villa (professional, August 1897). Leicester Fosse (£150, September 1908). ALBION (£270, October 1908). Lincoln City (£100, November 1910, retired, May 1911). Aston Villa (trainer, briefly, April–May 1913). Fell seriously ill with pneumonia in April 1915, recovered and thereafter was a beer-delivery driver for Ansells Brewery until his death.

■ An excellent goalscorer throughout his career, Bill Garraty – with his dashing moustache – finished up as top-scorer in the whole country in season 1899–1900 when his 27 goals (in only 33 matches) helped Villa win the League title for the fifth time. He later added an FA Cup winners' medal to his collection (1905)

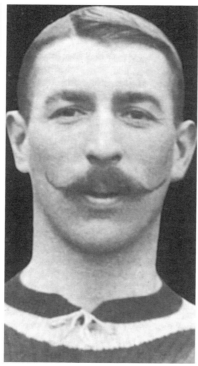

and also gained one full England cap (against Wales in 1903). A positive forward, always looking to get in a shot on goal, he netted 112 times in 259 first XI outings for Villa and was part of a brilliant Villa attack in the late 1890s/early 1900s. He skippered Albion on several occasions and during his time at The Hawthorns produced some exciting performances. He was, without doubt, a very fine player – pity Albion didn't spot him in 1897!

GEDDES, Alfred John

Outside-left: 93 apps. 38 goals.

Born: West Bromwich, 14 April 1871.
Died: Bristol, October 1927.
Career: Causeway Green Villa (1889). ALBION (September 1891). Clapham Rovers (April 1894). Millwall Athletic (September 1894). ALBION (April 1895). Millwall Athletic (May 1895). Bedminster (May 1899). Later served briefly with Bristol City and Bristol Rovers. Retired May 1908. Later worked as a storeroom assistant.

■ Alf 'Jasper' Geddes was a mercurial outside-left, fast and energetic with a powerful shot. He was also a temperamental player, a little greedy at times but, nevertheless, was still an

outstanding footballer who, in 1892, scored a vital goal as Albion beat Aston Villa 3–0 to win the FA Cup. On his return to the club in 1895 he immediately helped the team escape relegation, scoring twice in a dramatic last-match 6–0 home win over Sheffield Wednesday. As well as his senior appearances for Albion, Geddes also played in 80 'other' first-team fixtures. He was Millwall's first professional footballer, and skippered the Lions to two Southern League championships in the mid-1890s. Geddes represented the Southern League against the London FA in 1897.

GERA, Zoltan

Midfield: 35+7 apps. 6 goal.

Born: Pecs, Hungary, 22 April 1979.
Career: Pecs District XI (1995). Pecs FC (1996). PMSC, Hungary (1997). Ferencvaros (August 2000). ALBION (£1.5 million, July 2004).

■ Albion's first senior professional from Hungary – semi-pro Alex Kirally was at The Hawthorns in the 1960s – Zoltan Gera made his debut for the Baggies as a second-half substitute in the Premiership game at Ewood Park against Blackburn Rovers in August 2004, and he scored his first goal in England in the 1–1 home draw with Tottenham Hotspur soon afterwards. Captain of Hungary's national team, preferring the right side of midfield, where he performs with aggression, skill and commitment, he won his first senior cap in 2001, having previously represented his country at under-21 level. Voted Hungary's

'Footballer of the Year in 2004 and Baggies supporter's player of the year in 2005, he scored within three minutes of starting his first Premiership game for Albion versus Spurs (home) in August 2004.

GILBERT, David James

Midfield: 60+16 apps. 6 goals.

Born: Lincoln, 22 June 1963.
Career: Lincoln City (apprentice, July 1979, professional, June 1981). Scunthorpe United (September 1982). Boston United (October 1982). Northampton Town (£5,000, June 1986). Grimsby Town (£55,000, March 1989). ALBION (£50,000, August 1995). York City (on loan, March–April 1997). Grimsby Town (non-contract, August–September 1998). Grantham Town (October 1998–September 1999). Spalding United (2001–03). Lincoln United (August 2003).

■ Small in stature with good, close dribbling skills, left-sided midfielder Dave Gilbert – an Alan Buckley signing – spent three years at The Hawthorns. Earlier in his career he appeared at Wembley with Boston United in the 1985 FA Trophy Final and made a total of 303 senior appearances for Grimsby (two spells), helping them win the Fourth Division title in 1987. During his senior career Gilbert amassed a fine record of 573 League and cup appearances and 82 goals. He made his Albion debut against Charlton Athletic (home) in the opening League game of the 1995–96 season and celebrated the

occasion by scoring the only goal of the game to earn the Baggies victory in front of 14,688 spectators. He also played a dozen games in the second XI.

GILCHRIST, Philip Alexander

Defender: 121+5 apps.

Born: Stockton-on-Tees, 25 August 1973.
Career: Nottingham Forest (apprentice, April 1989, professional, December 1990). Middlesbrough (free, January 1991). Hartlepool United (free, November 1992). Oxford United (£100,000, February 1995). Leicester City (£500,000, August 1999). ALBION (£500,000, March 2001). Rotherham United (on loan, March–May 2004, signed permanently, free, June 2004).

■ A solid, left-sided defender, Phil Gilchrist has excellent positional sense and a positive approach. He had a superb 2001–02 season with Albion, his experience showing through time and time again. Always composed, solid in the tackle, resilient and hard working, he suffered a broken wrist at Barnsley early in that campaign and then received a nasty facial injury just before Christmas in the home clash with Sheffield Wednesday, but he bounced back each time, determined as ever to help Albion into the Premiership ahead of Wolves. Unfortunately, he was plagued by more injuries during the 2002–03 season when

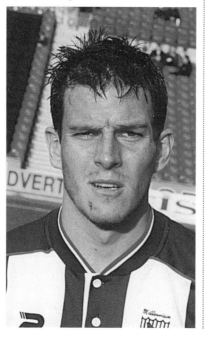

he appeared in only 24 competitive matches. A League Cup winner with Leicester in 2000, he made his Albion debut in a 2–1 League home win over Tranmere Rovers in March 2001 and followed up with the 450th competitive appearance of his career, during the first half of the 2003–04 season but, unfortunately, niggling injuries meant long periods in the treatment room and at the end of the campaign, following a loan spell at Millmoor, he was released by manager Gary Megson. He made almost a dozen second-team appearances during his three years at The Hawthorns.

GILES, Michael John

Midfield: 87+1 apps. 5 goals.

Born: Cabra, Dublin, 6 November 1940.
Career: Brunswick Street School (Dublin). St Columbus FC. Dublin Schools Select. Dublin City (later Munster Victoria). Stella Maris Boys. Leprechauns FCX (Dublin). Home Farm (schoolboy forms, March 1955). Manchester United (professional, November 1957). Leeds United (£35,000, August 1963). ALBION (£48,000, June 1975). Shamrock Rovers (June 1977–February 1983). Philadelphia Fury/NASL (guest, May–June 1978). Vancouver Whitecaps (coach, November 1980–December 1983, while retaining his position with Shamrock Rovers). ALBION (manager, February 1984–September 1985). Retired from football and later became a soccer writer for a national newspaper and then a journalist and TV presenter in Ireland. Was player-manager of the Republic of Ireland national team (October 1973–April 1980). Played for West Bromwich Albion All Stars (1984–89) and was also guest for Worcester Ramblers (in charity matches). Now lives in Edgbaston, Birmingham, and pens a regular soccer column in the Daily Express.

■ Johnny Giles was Albion's first player-manager, signed to replace Don Howe in 1975 shortly after appearing for Leeds United against Bayern Munich in the European Cup final. Making his debut against Chelsea (home) in August 1975, he succeeded in getting Albion out of the Second Division in his first season in charge and then took them to the brink of European football before leaving The Hawthorns to become player-manager of Shamrock Rovers, much to the dismay of the supporters. In fact, he had threatened

to quit after a year but was persuaded to stay longer after irate fans made their opinions heard in no uncertain terms. Giles had earlier starred as a right-winger for Manchester United, gaining an FA Cup winners' medal v Leicester City in 1963. He was then converted into a splendid scheming midfielder by manager Don Revie at Leeds United, with whom he collected medals galore, including winners' prizes for both the First and Second Division championships, the FA Cup, League Cup and Inter-Cities Fairs Cup as well as becoming an established member of the Republic of Ireland national team. He won his first cap as an 18-year-old and went on to gain a total of 60, scoring five goals. He played in 11 FA Cup semi-final matches and five FA Cup finals (six if you count the 1970 replay), the latter equalling the inter-war record set by Joe Hulme of Huddersfield Town and Arsenal. Unfortunately, things didn't go too well for him during his second spell in charge of Albion and after 18 months he dropped out of active competitive football. One of the finest midfield players ever to pull on a Baggies shirt, Giles's playing career spanned 18 years (from 1959 to 1977), during which time he netted 99 goals in 554 League games. In all competitions, playing for club and country, he notched 125 goals in 863 outings; a fine set of statistics for an exceptionally fine footballer.
* His son, Michael, was with him during his second spell at The Hawthorns.
* The 1970s rock band Thin Lizzy dedicated a track on their 'Johnny the Fox' album to Giles.

GLIDDEN, Thomas William

Outside-right: 479 apps. 140 goals.

Born: Coxlodge, Newcastle-upon-Tyne, 20 July 1902.
Died: West Bromwich, 10 July 1974.
Career: Castletown School (Tyneside). Sunderland & District Boys. Durham Boys. Sunderland (amateur, August 1917). Bristol City (trialist, July 1919). Colliery Old Boys, Newcastle (August 1919). Bolden Villa (July 1920). Sunderland West End (April 1921). ALBION (April 1922). Retired as a player, May 1936, to become coach at The Hawthorns (to September

1939). Later ran a tobacconists shop in West Bromwich. An ALBION shareholder, he became a club director in 1951 and remained on the board until his death at the age of 72.

■ A fine captain and terrific goalscoring right-winger, Tommy Glidden served Albion admirably for more than 50 years, first as a player, then as a coach, shareholder and finally as a director. Able to play in any forward position, he made his Albion debut at outside-right against Everton (away) in November 1922 (Division One). After a few games on the opposite wing, he eventually settled down on the right flank from where he skippered the Baggies to the coveted FA Cup and promotion double in 1930–31 and in the FA Cup final again in 1935. Taking over from Jack Crisp, he formed a fine 'wing' partnership with Joe Carter and was perhaps unfortunate not to win full international recognition, although he did participate in an England trial match in 1925–26. Glidden also scored 17 goals in 91 Central League games for Albion, gaining successive championship medals in the competition in 1922–23 and 1923–24. He sadly died from a heart attack in 1974.
NB – Tommy's brother, Sidney, was an Albion reserve during the mid-1920s.

GLOVER, Allan Richard

Inside-forward/winger: 92+13 apps. 10 goals.

Born: Staines, Middlesex, 21 October 1950. Career: Windsor Church of England School. London & Middlesex Schools. Queen's Park Rangers (junior, April 1966, professional, October 1967). ALBION (June 1969, in a £70,000 exchange deal involving Clive Clark). Southend United (on loan, January 1976). Brentford (on loan, October 1976). Leyton Orient (March 1977 with Joe Mayo allowing Laurie Cunningham to transfer to The Hawthorns). Brentford (£5,000, November 1978). Staines FC (August 1980, retired, May 1981). Now lives in Berkshire.

■ A clever, witty wide-midfielder, Allan Glover spent eight seasons at The Hawthorns, during which time he appeared in more than 100 first-team matches. He was in excellent form when he suffered a severe ankle injury against

Blackpool in December 1974. He regained full fitness but not his place in Albion's starting line-up and was eventually transferred to Orient with Laurie Cunningham moving to The Hawthorns. He appeared in a total of 165 League games during his career (16 goals) but his time with Southend lasted for just 30 seconds before being carried off injured against Hereford. He made his Albion League debut as a substitute against Wolverhampton Wanderers (home) in February 1979 (a 3–3 draw). and also scored 19 goals in 149 Central League games.

GODDEN, Anthony Leonard

Goalkeeper: 329 apps.

Born: Gillingham, Kent, 2 August 1955. Career: Napier Secondary Modern School (Gillingham). Leonard Star FC. Eastcourt United. Gillingham & District Schools. Medway & Kent Schools. Gillingham (amateur, August 1969). Ashford Town (August 1971). Wolverhampton Wanderers (trialist, June–July 1975). ALBION (professional, August 1975). Preston North End (on loan, September 1976). Happy Valley FC, Hong Kong (guest, 1980). Luton Town (on loan, March–April 1983).

Walsall (on loan, October–December 1983). Chelsea (on loan, March 1986, signed for £40,000, August 1986). Birmingham City (£35,000, July 1987). Bury (on loan, December 1988). Sheffield Wednesday (on loan, March–April 1989). Peterborough United (July 1989). Leicester City. Wivenhoe Town (July 1990). Colchester United (non-contract, March–May 1991). Warboys Town (1991–92). Torquay United (1992–93). March Town (manager, July 1993). King's Lynn (manager/coach, December 1993, manager, February 1994). Bury Town (manager/coach, May 1996). Wisbech Town (manager/coach, 1997–98). Also Northampton Town (part-time coach, 1996–97). Later associated as a goalkeeping coach with Rushden and Diamonds, Lincoln City, Peterborough United, Leicester City, Derby County, Notts County and then Derby County again, the latter in 2003–04.

■ In October 1981 Albion's goalkeeper, Tony Godden, set a record that will take some beating – he appeared in his 228th consecutive first-team match and in doing so eclipsed defender Ally Robertson's previous total of successive outings by a considerable margin. Four and a half years earlier, Godden, as a 21-year-old, made his Albion debut in a 2–0 away win at Tottenham, and the media immediately described him as '…a goalkeeper with a big future'. How right they were, for he went from strength to strength and over the next nine years

amassed a tremendous record for the Baggies, helping them qualify for the UEFA Cup in 1978. A safe handler of the ball and a fine shot-stopper, he was perhaps vulnerable at times on high crosses but generally was an excellent 'keeper whose professional career realised more than 450 senior appearances. He also played in 72 Central League games for Albion, helping the team win the championship of this competition in 1982–83. He was granted a testimonial to celebrate 10 years at The Hawthorns. He once scored a goal from 90 yards when clearing his lines playing for Peterborough reserves against Northampton in 1989–90. He later helped the Cobblers reach the Third Division play-offs.

GOLLINGS, Platt

Half-back: 5 apps.

Born: Winson Green, Birmingham, 11 October 1878.
Died: Dudley, September 1935.
Career: Dudley Road Council School (Birmingham). Handsworth Old Boys. Hereford Thistle (August 1898). ALBION (professional, May 1899). Brierley Hill Alliance (June 1904). Hereford Town (September 1907, retired, c.1916). Served as a soldier in World War One. Later worked in the steel industry.

■ A League debutant for Albion against Stoke (away) in October 1899, Platt Gollings was a strong, well-built half-back, who kicked well with both feet, often helping his goalkeeper with his set pieces. He was regarded as a senior reserve at Albion, making over 70 appearances for the second XI and picking up a Birmingham & District League championship medal in 1902.

GOMM, Brian Arthur

Centre-forward: 4 apps. 1 goal.

Born: Castle Cary, Somerset, 24 June 1918.
Career: Castle Cary Schools. Yeovil & St Petters reserves (1933–34). Corinthians (August 1934). Yorkshire Amateurs (December 1934). Dudley Training College (from January 1935). ALBION (amateur, February 1935, professional, March 1937, released June 1946). Later played for Dudley Town and Brierley Hill Alliance. Retired, c.1952. Served with the Royal

Corps of Signals during World War Two and was a PoW in both Italy and Germany. He played County cricket for Somerset in 1939 and scored just seven runs in three innings, had bowling figures of 0–21 and took two catches.

■ Brian Gomm, under the supervision of W.G. Richardson and Harry Jones, looked promising in his early years at The Hawthorns, but World War Two severely disrupted his footballing career. He made his Albion debut against Coventry City (away) in a League South game in December 1945. He scored 13 goals in 19 Central League games.

GOODALL, Darren

Inside-forward: 0+1 app.

Born: Oldbury, West Midland, 9 April 1971.
Career: Britannia High School (Rowley Regis). Warley & District Boys & West Midlands Schools. Rowley Regis Boys. Stourbridge Falcons (1986). ALBION (apprentice, July 1987, professional, April 1989). Walsall (July 1989). Hereford United (October 1989). Oldbury Town (briefly). Bromsgrove Rovers (March–May 1990). Halesowen Town (1990–92). Torquay United (trialist, 1992). Oldswinford (1992–93). Oldbury United. Stourbridge. Cradley Town. Stoke City (trialist). Willenhall Town (August 1998–May 2001). Rushall Olympic (August 2003).

■ Diminutive midfielder Darren Goodall had a childhood dream come true when he made his Albion debut as a substitute in a Simod Cup tie at West Ham in September 1988. This was his only first-team outing, along with 15 Central League appearances.

GOODMAN, Donald Ralph

Striker: 163+18 apps. 63 goals.

Born: Leeds, 9 May 1966.
Career: Collingham FC (August 1982). Bradford City (professional, July 1984). ALBION (£50,000, March 1987). Sunderland (£900,000, December 1991). Wolverhampton Wanderers (£1.1 million, December 1994). San Frecce Antlers of Hiroshima, Japan (June 1998). Barnsley (on loan, December 1998–February 1999). Motherwell (March 1999). Walsall (free, March 2001). Exeter City (August 2002).

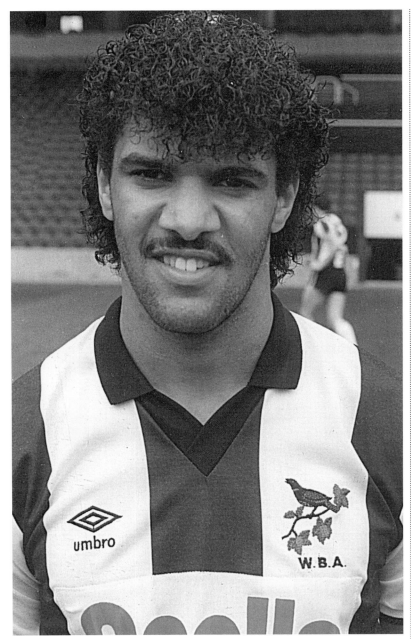

Doncaster Rovers (August 2002, released, May 2003). Stafford Rangers (September 2003, retired, December 2003). Kidderminster Harriers (fitness coach, 2004–05).

■ An exciting striker, fast and aggressive with good ability and a strong right-foot shot, Don Goodman joined Albion soon after that horrific fire disaster at Valley Parade in 1987. He became a huge hit with the Baggies fans, averaging a goal every three games before leaving The Hawthorns for Sunderland to the disappointment of hundreds of supporters. He netted over 40 goals in three years at Roker Park and then, to the dismay of diehard baggies fans, he went and teamed up with Steve Bull at Molineux, becoming Wolves' top-scorer in 1995–96. After recovering from a serious head injury, he tried his luck in Japan only to return to Football League action within six months. During an excellent career, Goodman scored almost 200 goals in some 675 appearances including a League record (in England and Scotland) of 127 goals in 435 outings. He made his Albion League debut against Oldham Athletic in March

1987, and he scored six goals in 11 Central League games for the club. Goodman helped Bradford win the Third Division championship in 1985, Walsall gain promotion to the First Division via the play-offs at Cardiff's Millennium Stadium in 2001 (scoring against Reading in the Final) and then two years later helped Doncaster reach the Nationwide Conference play-offs and ultimate promotion to the Football League.

GORDON, Dennis William

Outside-right: 30 apps. 10 goals.

Born: Wolverhampton, 7 June 1924.
Died: Brighton, May 1998.
Career: Southfield Secondary Modern School (Oxford). Headington United (August 1939). Lincoln City (World War Two guest). Tottenham Hotspur (trialist, July 1945). Oxford City (August 1945). ALBION (amateur, July 1947, professional, September 1947). Brighton and Hove Albion (£1,150, June 1952). Guildford City (August 1961). Tunbridge Wells United (May 1963, retired, June 1966). Later worked as a clerk in a Brighton office.

■ Outside-right Dennis 'Flash' Gordon was educated in Oxford and was mighty close to signing for Spurs after four goals in two games as a trialist. Signed by Albion as cover for Billy Elliott, he made his senior debut in a home FA Cup tie against Reading in January 1948, following up with his first League outing soon afterwards against Leicester City (also at home) in Division Two. He played in three different positions for Albion in 1949–50 (outside and inside-

right and centre-forward) but was never a first-team regular and after leaving The Hawthorns spent nine years with the other 'Albion', for whom he hit 63 goals in 276 League appearances. An expert sprinter as a youngster, Gordon won both the 100 and 200-yard races and competed in the national 'AAA' championships during World War Two, when he served in the RAF, initially as a pilot-observer, rising to the rank of sergeant, qualifying as a compass adjuster and teaming up with the 97th Bomber Command Squadron, flying Halifax and Lancaster bombers. He played regularly for his RAF Unit, for various RAF teams in India and was chosen to represent the Isthmian League against Denmark and China, he was also an England international trialist and scored 32 goals in 102 Central League games for Albion.

GOULD, Robert Anthony

Striker: 60 apps. 19 goals.

Born: Coventry, 12 June 1946.
Career: Coventry City (apprentice, July 1962, professional, June 1964). Arsenal (£90,000, February 1968). Wolves (£55,000, June 1970). ALBION (£66,666, September 1971). Bristol City (£68,888, December 1972). West Ham United (£80,000, November 1973). Wolverhampton Wanderers (£30,000, December 1975). Bristol Rovers (player-coach, £10,000, October 1977). FC Aaslund, Norway (coach, January–April 1978). Hereford United (£10,000, player-coach, September 1978). Charlton Athletic (coach, early-to-mid 1979). Chelsea (assistant manager, October 1979). Wimbledon (registered as a non-contract player, August 1981). Aldershot (assistant manager/coach, September–October 1981). Bristol Rovers (manager, October 1981). Coventry City (manager, May 1983 to December 1984). Bristol Rovers (manager, May 1985–May 1987). Wimbledon (manager, June 1987 to June 1990). ALBION (manager, February 1991–May 1992). Coventry City (manager, 1992–93). Queen's Park Rangers (briefly). Welsh national team manager (with ex-Albion skipper Graham Williams as his assistant, 1966, holding office for 18 months). Cheltenham Town (manager, January 2003, resigned, October 2003). Peterborough United (assistant coach/adviser, February 2004).

■ An out-and-out striker, Bobby Gould had a very interesting and nomadic footballing career. Known as the 'Wanderer', he netted around 200 goals in more than 500 appearances at various levels. He was an FA Cup winner with West Ham in 1975 (as a non-playing substitute) and in 1988 was boss at Wimbledon when they beat Liverpool in the FA Cup final. He was a Second Division championship winner with Coventry (1967) and likewise with Wolves a decade later. He also played and scored for Arsenal in their League Cup final defeat by Swindon in 1969,

the same year he represented young England against England. Signed by Don Howe, he made his Albion debut against Ipswich Town (home) in September 1971 and did well initially alongside Jeff Astle, netting 12 goals in his first season at The Hawthorns. His form then started to wane and halfway through the 1972–73 campaign he was sold to Bristol City. Although he signed Bob Taylor from his former club Bristol City, he didn't have much joy as manager at Albion, taking the Baggies down into the Third Division, and he was not a success as the Welsh boss either.

* His son Jonathan, a goalkeeper, has played for several top-class clubs including Celtic for whom he made over 150 senior appearances. He was briefly associated with Albion.

GRANT, Anthony James

Midfield: 3+2 apps.

Born: Liverpool, 14 November 1974.
Career: Everton (apprentice, April 1992, professional, July 1993). Swindon Town (on loan, January–February 1996). Tranmere Rovers (on loan, September–October 1999). Manchester City (£450,000, December 1999). ALBION (on loan, December 2000–January 2001). Burnley (£250,000, October 2001).

■ An England under-21 international midfielder (one cap), Tony Grant spent a short spell on loan at The Hawthorns halfway through the 2000–01 season when he joined the engine-room crew of Richard Sneekes, Ruel Fox and Jordao among others. Already an experienced campaigner with over 100 first-team appearances under his belt plus a Charity Shield winner's prize with Everton at Wembley in 1995, he later moved to Burnley after turning down a permanent move to The Hawthorns. Grant, a strong

tackler, good on the ball with a good passing technique, made his Albion debut as 'sub' against Wimbledon at Selhurst Park 48 hours after signing (won 1–0).

GRAY, Andrew Mullen

Striker: 34+3 apps. 11 goals.

Born: Gorbals, Glasgow, 30 November 1955.
Career: Clydebank Strollers. Clydesdale Juniors. Dundee United (amateur, April 1971, professional, May 1973). Aston Villa (£110,000, September 1975). Wolverhampton Wanderers (£1.15 million, September 1979). Everton (£250,000, November 1983). Aston Villa (£150,000, July 1985). Notts County (on loan, August 1987). ALBION (on loan, September 1987, signed for £25,000, October 1987). Glasgow Rangers (September 1988). Cheltenham Town (August 1989). Aston Villa (assistant manager/coach, July 1991 to June 1992). Now works for Sky Sports as a soccer summariser/analyst.

■ Striker Andy Gray became the most expensive footballer in Britain when Wolves paid Aston Villa more than £1 million for his services in 1979. He

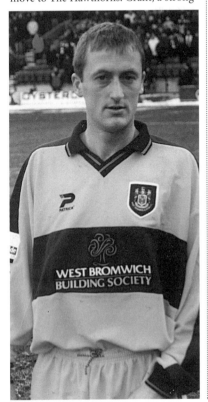

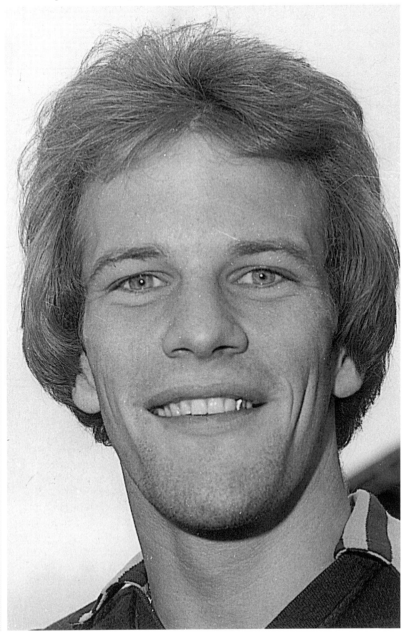

actually completed the move by signing the appropriate forms on the pitch at Molineux before Wolves' League game with Crystal Palace. Gray was certainly and a colourful figure wherever he played. Brave, determined, totally committed and a tremendous header of the ball, he helped set up scores of goals for his colleagues, while netting plenty of his own with both head and feet. He made almost 80 appearances for Dundee United, gaining a runners'-up medal in the 1974 Scottish Cup final. With Villa, he played in the two drawn games of the 1977 League Cup final v Everton and was voted 'Player of the Year' and 'Young Player of the Year' by the PFA. He scored 45 goals in 162 games for Wolves, including the 'lucky' winner against Nottingham Forest in the 1980 League Cup final. He continued doing the business with Everton, hitting 23 goals in 71 games, and during his time at Goodison Park collected winners' medals in three competitions: the FA Cup, League championship and European Cup-winners' Cup. As a stop-gap, Villa re-signed Gray in 1985, and after a loan spell at Meadow Lane he was snapped up by his former boss, Ron Saunders, for Albion, for whom he made his debut against Plymouth Argyle (away) in September 1987, claiming two goals in a 3–3 draw. Trying his luck in Scotland with Rangers, he was a Skol League Cup and Premier League title winner before hanging up his boots in the early 1990s to pursue a career in television, becoming a familiar face as a soccer summariser and analyst on Sky Sports. He also contributed a column to the *Daily Express*. In June 1997 he was linked with the vacant manager's job at his former club Everton but declined the offer, choosing to stay with Sky TV instead. Capped 20 times by Scotland, Gray also won under-23, youth and schoolboy honours for his country and netted over 200 goals in more than 600 senior club matches.

* In the space of five years, Gray scored in three major Finals: the League Cup for Wolves and the FA Cup and European Cup-winners' Cup for Everton. He actually appeared in a major final with five of his clubs: Dundee United (Scottish Cup), Villa and Wolves (League Cup), Everton (FAC and ECWC) and Rangers (Skol Cup). Also, he's one of only two players to have netted a hat-trick in a European competition for Everton.

GREALISH, Anthony Patrick

Midfield: 65+11 apps. 5 goals.

Born: Paddington, London, 21 September 1956.
Career: Wilberforce Junior & Rutherford Secondary Modern Schools (Paddington). Leyton Orient (apprentice, April 1973, professional, July 1974). Luton Town (£150,000, August 1979). Brighton and Hove Albion (£100,000, July 1981). ALBION (£80,000, March 1984). Manchester City (trialist, September 1986, signed permanently for £20,000, plus Robert Hopkins, October 1986). Rotherham United (August 1987). FC Salgueros, Portugal (on loan, 1987). Walsall (player-coach, August 1990). Bromsgrove Rovers (assistant manager/player-coach to January 1995, then manager to May 1995). Atherstone Town (assistant manager/coach, 1995–96). Also assisted Sandwell Borough (1996–97) and playing regularly for West Bromwich Albion All Stars. Now lives in Sutton Coldfield.

■ Hard-working, strong-armed and strong-limbed midfielder Tony Grealish was capped 47 times by the Republic of Ireland at senior level (8 goals scored) having earlier gained youth team honours. He joined Albion on the same day as Steve Hunt, signed by Johnny Giles, and made his debut against Spurs 24 hours later, in March 1984, which was also the 350th League appearance of his career. He did well for the Baggies but was part of a massive clear-out following the club's worst-ever season in 1985–86. He also played in 18 Central League games for the Baggies. Often graced with a healthy beard, he skippered Brighton in

the 1983 FA Cup final against Manchester United (first game) and was a Fourth Division championship winner with Rotherham. He went on to play in more than 600 competitive games as a professional (for clubs and country).

GREEN, Harry

Full-back: 65 apps.

Born: West Bromwich, 19 January 1860.
Died: West Bromwich, May 1900.
Career: George Salter Works. ALBION (June 1881). Old Hill Wanderers (May 1891, retired, 1892, through injury). Returned to work for Salter's until his death at the age of 40.

■ An excellent full-back, meaningful, sure-footed and one of the best of his era, Harry Green made three successive FA Cup final appearances for Albion: 1886, 1887 and 1888, gaining a winners' medal in the latter against Preston North End. He also played in Albion's first ever League game against Stoke in September 1888 and played in over 250 first-team games for the club, but only 65 at senior level. Green scored a rare goal in Albion's 10–1 West Bromwich Charity Cup final win over Great Bridge Unity, also in 1888.

GREEN, Thomas

Inside-forward: 8 apps. 2 goals.

Born: Kings Heath, Birmingham, 14 July 1873.
Died: Worcester, 4 October 1921.
Career: Vicarage Road School (Birmingham). Coles Farm Unity (1892). ALBION (May 1894). Small Heath Alliance (June 1896). Oldbury Town (May 1902–May 1906). Became a licensee in West Bromwich and also Dudley.

■ An effective inside-forward with heaps of stamina, Tommy Green possessed a wicked right-foot shot but somehow never really produced the consistency required at senior level. He made his League debut against his future club, Small Heath, (away) in February 1895 and also played in half-a-dozen 'other' games for Albion.

GREEN, Thomas Charles Walford

Inside/centre-forward: 16 apps. 8 goals.

Born: Worcester, 7 August 1863.
Died: Droitwich, December 1931.
Career: St Peter's School. Dreadnought FC (Worcester). Mitchell St George's (1880). Small Heath (briefly). Mitchell St George's. Aston Unity (1883). Great Lever, Bolton (August 1883). Mitchell St George's (October 1883). Wolverhampton Wanderers (guest, 1885). Church FC (guest 1885). ALBION (August 1885). Aston Villa (June 1887). Kidderminster Harriers (August 1889). Worcester Rovers (September 1892, retired, April 1901). Became a licensee, first in Worcester and later in Droitwich.

■ Tommy Green was a real character, a highly-talented forward who played the game with great verve and tenacity, although he did occasionally upset match officials with his over-keen tackling and vigorous approach. He played for Albion in the 1886 and 1887 losing FA Cup finals and represented both the Birmingham and Staffordshire FA sides as well as appearing for the North against the South in the annual challenge match in 1887. He also had the honour and indeed the pleasure of scoring Albion's first goal at Stoney Lane against the Third Lanark Rifle Volunteers in a friendly match in September 1885. He later had the distinction of claiming Villa's first ever goal in the Football League in a 1–1 draw with Wolves at Dudley Road in September 1888. In September 1889 he hit Villa's first League hat-trick against Notts County. Besides his senior outings for Albion, Green also played in at least 75 'other' first-team games for the club.
* He was the father of Tommy Green, junior.

GREEN, Thomas

Inside-forward: 16 apps. 5 goals.

Born: Droitwich, Worcestershire, 12 May 1913.
Died: Bromyard, Worcestershire, 5 February 1997.
Career: St Peter's School (Worcester). Droitwich Town. Droitwich Spa FC (1929). Droitwich Comrades (1930). ALBION (amateur, October 1931, professional, March 1932). West Ham United (£3,000, December 1936). Coventry City (March 1939). Worcester City (1941). Bromyard FC (1945). Bromyard Sports (manager, 1949–51). Quit football to

become a licensee in Bromyard, later worked as an engineer, bookmarker, timber merchant and producer of hanging-baskets.

■ A junior international (capped in 1932), Tommy Green was an enthusiastic and hard-working footballer with plenty

of skill but perhaps a shade on the light side to make a real impression in the First Division. He was given his Albion League debut against Leeds United (home) in February 1934 in place of Joe Carter, for whom he had acted as first reserve since joining the club. The recipient of two Central League championship medals in 1933–34 and 1934–35, he netted 23 goals in 79 second XI matches for the Baggies. He later scored six times in 44 first-team outings for the Hammers and twice in nine games for Coventry.

GREENING, Jonathan

Midfield: 34+3 apps.

Born: Scarborough, 7 January 1979.
Career: York City (apprentice, June 1995, professional, December 1996). Manchester United (£500,000, March 1998). Middlesbrough (£2 million, August 2001). ALBION (£1.25 million, July 2004).

■ An England youth and under-21 international (18 caps won in the latter category) and an attacking and competitive right-sided midfielder,

Jonathan Greening made 27 appearances for both York City and Manchester United before moving to Middlesbrough. After helping United reach the final of the European Champions League in 1999, he was on the 'subs' bench against Bayern Munich in Barcelona (covering for David Beckham). Five years later he was a League Cup-winner with 'Boro for whom he had 109 outings prior to his big-money transfer to The Hawthorns, a year after being voted 'Player of the Year' at The Riverside Stadium in 2002–03. He made his Albion debut in the opening Premiership game of the 2004–05 season at Ewood Park against Blackburn. He had the misfortune of being sent off (with Aston Villa's Liam Ridgewell) in the 1–1 draw at Villa Park in April 2005.

GREGAN, Sean Matthew

Defender/midfield: 83+3 apps. 2 goals.

Born: Guisborough, Cleveland, 29 March 1974.

Career: Darlington (apprentice, June 1989, professional, January 1991). Preston North End (£350,000, December 1996). ALBION (£2 million, August 2002). Leeds United (August 2004).

■ A big-money signing by manager Gary

Megson to bolster up Albion's squad for their initial Premiership campaign, defender/midfielder Sean Gregan had a reasonable first season at The Hawthorns. Captaining the side at times, he was a far better player in midfield than in defence – making too many mistakes at the back, some of which led to goals being scored. While making 162 appearances for the Quakers, he gained experience by the minute and went on to play 251 games for Preston (13 goals), becoming a talismanic figure at Deepdale and helping the Lancashire club win the Second Division championship in 2000. He linked up again with his former North End colleague Michael Appleton at The Hawthorns, and, later, left Albion for relegated Leeds at a time when the Elland Road club was in serious financial difficulty.

* In some people's minds Gregan resembles Ian Collard, Albion's midfielder from the 1960s.

GREGORY, Howard

Outside-left: 181 apps. 45 goals.

Born: Aston Manor, Birmingham, 6 April 1893.
Died: Birmingham, 15 August 1954.
Career: Gower Street & Aston Hall Schools (Birmingham). Aston Manor FC (1908). Birchfield Trinity (April 1910). ALBION (May 1911, retired through injury, May 1926). A year later became 'mine host' of the Woodman Inn (next to The Hawthorns) where he remained until 1932 and stayed in the licensing trade until 1953.

■ Known as the 'Express Man' and 'Greg', ginger-haired Howard Gregory was a fine left-winger, quick-witted, fast and plucky, who teamed up exceedingly well with Fred Morris immediately after World War One. He made his League debut against Everton at Goodison Park in April 1912 and during the next 14 years did exceedingly well, scoring over 40 goals in more than 180 first-team appearances for the Baggies, helping them win the League championship in 1920. He also contributed greatly to Albion's Birmingham & District League side during the four campaigns leading up to World War One, making over 100 appearances and gaining a Birmingham & District League championship medal in 1902. He followed up, after the hostilities,

with 22 goals in 37 outings for the Central League team. He was an invited guest at the reception following Albion's FA Cup triumph in 1954, but sadly died three months later, aged 61.

GREW, Mark Stuart

Goalkeeper: 47+1 app.

Born: Bilston, 15 February 1958.
Career: Bilston & Moxley Schools. ALBION (apprentice, June 1974, professional, June 1976). Wigan Athletic (on loan, December 1978–January 1979). Leicester City (£40,000, July 1983). Oldham Athletic (on loan, October–November 1983). Ipswich Town (£60,000, March 1984). Fulham (on loan, September–October 1985). ALBION (on loan, January 1986). Derby County (on loan, March 1986). Port Vale (June 1986). Blackburn Rovers (on loan, October 1990–January 1991). Cardiff City (August 1992–May 1993). Port Vale (Community Department, later youth and reserve-team coach and assistant manager coach to Brian Horton, sacked December 2002, re-appointed as coach, August 2004).

■ Goalkeeper Mark Grew gained an FA Youth Cup winners' medal with Albion in 1976 before becoming understudy to John Osborne and Tony Godden. A very capable 'keeper with good reflexes and a

safe pair of hands, he gained a regular place in Albion's side in 1981–82 and played in that season's FA Cup semi-final defeat by Queen's Park Rangers. He made his debut for Albion as a second-half substitute in the home game with Galatasaray in the UEFA Cup in September 1978. He also made close on 150 Central League appearances for Albion, helping them win the championship in 1982–83. He went on to play in 184 League games for the 'Valiants' and was a member of their Third Division promotion-winning side in 1989.

* Grew was dismissed initially by Port Vale as a cost-cutting exercise due to a cash crisis.

GRIFFIN, Frank Albert

Outside-right: 275 apps. 52 goals.

Born: Pendlebury, Manchester, 28 March 1928.

Career: Pendlebury Central School. St Augustine's Youth Club. Newton Heath. Hull City (trialist, March–April 1944). Bolton Wanderers (amateur, 1944–48). Eccles Town (August 1948). Shrewsbury Town (amateur, May 1950, professional, March 1951). ALBION (£9,500, April 1951). Northampton Town (£1,500, June 1959). Wellington Town (August 1960). GKN Sankey's (September 1961). Worthen United (manager, August 1962–May 1966). Now resides in Shrewsbury.

■ Scorer of Albion's FA Cup winning

goal in the 1954 final against Preston North End, Frank Griffin was, without doubt, a splendid outside-right, who took over the number 7 shirt from Billy Elliott, making his Albion debut against Sunderland (at Roker Park) in April 1951. Hugging the touchline for most of the game and keeping his full-back occupied, he possessed good pace, had excellent ball control and delivered precise crosses as well as packing a fair shot with his right foot. He spent eight years at The Hawthorns, notching a goal every five games, and was part of a wonderful forward line assembled by manager Vic Buckingham, which comprised himself, Paddy Ryan, Ronnie Allen, Johnny Nicholls and George Lee. He broke his leg playing against Sheffield United in an FA Cup replay in February 1958, never really regained full fitness and subsequently left The Hawthorns for Northampton Town in the summer of 1959. He scored five goals in 42 Central League games for Albion.

GRIMLEY, Thomas William

Goalkeeper: 30 apps.

Born: Dinnington, Sheffield, 1 November 1920.

Died: Great Barr, Birmingham, November 1976.

Career: Dinnington & Thurcroft Schools. Sheffield & South Yorkshire Boys. Barnsley (trialist, 1936). Wolverhampton Wanderers (trialist, 1937). Swallownest FC (August 1938). ALBION (amateur, September 1938, professional, April 1939). New Brighton (£500, May 1948). Hednesford

Town (June 1951). Rugby Town (May 1952, retired, March 1957). ALBION scout (August 1957–May 1962). Worked in general engineering for some years afterwards.

■ A massive goalkeeper, alert with a safe pair of hands, Tommy Grimley was not too certain with ground shots but was always in command of high crosses that floated in towards his goal. He had both Jim Sanders and Norman Heath challenging him for a first-team place directly after World War Two, and consequently his outings were restricted to a mere 30, all in Division Two, having made his debut against Fulham (home) in November 1946. He also played in 24

Central League games. Grimley spent four and a half years in the central Mediterranean area, playing for the Eighth Army and CMF, meeting up with his colleagues Cecil Shaw, Jim Pemberton and Billy Elliott during World War Two. He sadly died near his home aged 56.

GRIPTON, William Ernest

Centre-half: 208 apps. 3 goals.

Born: Princess End, Tipton, 2 July 1920.

Died: West Bromwich, July 1981.

Career: Princess End & Tipton Schools. Dartmouth Vics. Bush Rangers (March 1934). Brownhills Albion (August 1934). ALBION (amateur, June 1935, professional, November 1937). Luton Town (£3,000, June 1948). Bournemouth (July 1950). Worcester City (1952, retired, May 1956). Later groundsman at Dudley Sports Centre, Tipton, and adviser to Vono FC.

■ Billy Gripton was a hard but scrupulously fair defender. He was a superb tactician and such a domineering

character in the heart of Albion's defence, certainly during the wartime period, when he appeared in 192 competitive matches. He took over the pivotal role from Bill Tudor and Cyril Davies in 1939 and handed over his jersey in 1945 (on a regular basis) to George Tranter. Gripton, who made his League debut against Millwall (home) in April 1939, won a Midland Wartime Cup-winners' medal in 1944 and also scored four goals in 102 Central League outings for the club.

GROVES, Paul

Midfield: 30+2 apps. 5 goals.

Born: Derby, 28 February 1966.
Career: Burton Albion (May 1984). Lincoln City (on loan, August–September 1989). Leicester City (£12,000, April 1988). Blackpool (£60,000, January 1990). Grimsby Town (£150,000, August 1992). ALBION (£600,000, July 1996). Grimsby Town (£250,000, July 1997, player-manager from December 2001, sacked as manager, February 2004). Scunthorpe United (March 2004). York City (August 2004–05).

■ Signed by manager Alan Buckley, to become one of the vast army of Albion players with a Grimsby connection, during the late 1990s, Paul Groves, although adequate and totally committed, was not a success at The Hawthorns and he returned to Blundell Park at a cut

price after spending just one season with the Baggies during which time he also played in 10 second team games. Promoted and relegated with Grimsby, he also helped the Mariners win the Auto-Windscreen Shield in 1998 and seven years later was searching for a personal milestone of 750 League and cup appearances.

GROVES, William

Wing-half/forward: 69 apps. 110 goals.

Born: Leith, Scotland, 9 November 1869.
Died: Edinburgh, 13 February 1908.
Career: Thistle FC, Edinburgh (1884). Leith Harp (1885). Hibernian (August 1886). Celtic (£25, August 1888). Everton (£40, January–February 1889). Celtic (£40, March 1889). ALBION (£50, October 1890). Aston Villa (£100, four payments of £25 each, September 1893). Hibernian (£75, August 1895) Celtic (£100, November 1896). Rushden (August 1898, retired, May 1902). Suffered with TB and died at the age of 38.

■ Swarthy, well-featured and well set-up, Willie Groves was an exciting footballer who, although having no claims to greatness in heading or goalscoring, was second to none in foraging and ball distribution. He could play anywhere (even in goal) and he had immense enthusiasm and dedication for the game. In a wonderful career, which saw him converted by Albion from an eager-beaver

forward into a purposeful wing-half, he won three Scottish caps 1888–90, scoring a splendid hat-trick against Ireland in his second international. He also represented the Football League XI in 1891–92 and played for Edinburgh in an Inter-City match. In his first spell with Hibs he won a Scottish Cup winners' medal (1887) and later a runners'-up prize in the same competition in 1896. With Celtic he gained a Cup runners'-up medal in 1889 and helped Albion carry off the FA Cup in 1892, setting up two of the three goals against Aston Villa in the final at Crystal Palace. As a Villa player, he collected a First Division championship medal in 1894 and during a fine career (with Hibs, Celtic, Albion and Villa in the main) he hit over 30 goals in almost 200 matches. He did not appear in Everton's senior side and on joining Albion had to suffer a month suspension after Everton had claimed he was still registered with them. When he signed for Aston Villa in 1893 after more objections from Everton, Groves became the first player in Football history to command a transfer fee of three figures (£100). He made his Albion debut against Wolverhampton Wanderers (home) on December 1890 and besides the senior appearance record, he also played in more than 75 'other' first-team games for the club in local Cup competitions and friendlies.

GUY, Harold (1948–56)

Full-back/centre-half: 1 app.

Born: Wolverhampton, 1 January 1932.
Career: Penn Road Schools. British Rail (Stafford Road Works) of Wolverhampton. Birmingham County Youths. Springfield Old Boys FC (1947). Albion (July 1948, professional, March 1950). Peterborough United (£250, June 1956). Stafford Rangers (retired, May 1965). Now lives in Wolverhampton.

■ Harry Guy was a reserve full-back or centre-half with Albion. His only senior game was against Sheffield Wednesday in December 1950 and he'll never forget it as he was given a real roasting by the Owl's right-winger Johnny Marriott as Wednesday won the match 3–1 to spoil Guy's and Albion's Christmas. Guy also made 91 Central League appearances for the Baggies before transferring to Peterborough.

HACKETT, Gary Stuart

Winger: 30+21 apps. 4 goals.

*Born: Stourbridge, 11 October 1962.
Career: Bromsgrove Rovers (1981).
Shrewsbury Town (£5,000, July 1983).
Aberdeen (£80,000, July 1987). Stoke City
(£110,000, March 1998). ALBION
(£70,000, March 1990). Peterborough
United (£40,000, September 1993). Chester
City (free, August 1994). Bromsgrove
Rovers (August 1995, later assistant
manager). Stourbridge (player-coach,
August 1997). Stourport Swifts (2000–01).
Redditch United (player-coach, 2001, with
ex-Albion man Nicky Cross his manager).
Bromgsrove Rovers (joint manager,
2002–03). Stourbridge (joint manager
from July 2003). Also played cricket for the
Belbroughton CC.*

■ A positive winger with good skill,
Gary Hackett failed to hold down a
regular place in Albion's first team
following his arrival from The Victoria
Ground (signed by ex-Stoke player Brian
Talbot). He made his debut for the club
as a substitute in a 0–0 home draw with
Portsmouth in March 1990 and also
scored twice in almost 60 Pontins League
games, gaining a championship medal at
this level in 1990–91. During a fine career
he amassed over 400 senior appearances
and helped Shrewsbury win the Welsh
Cup in 1984.

HADLEY, Benjamin Arthur

Wing-half: 8 apps. one goal.

*Born: West Bromwich, 12 March 1871.
Died: West Bromwich, September 1931.*

HAAS, Bernt

Defender: 51+1 apps. 2 goals.

*Born: Vienna, Austria, 8 April 1978.
Career: Grasshopper Zurich, Switzerland
(amateur, August 1994, professional, April
1995). Sunderland (£750,000, August
2001). FC Basel, Switzerland (on loan,
August 2002–May 2003). ALBION
(£500,000, July 2003). Bastia/Corsica (free
transfer, February 2005).*

■ Swiss international full-back (over 20
caps gained, one goal scored) Bernt Haas
joined Albion in the summer of 2003
following the announcement that Igor
Balis had retired from top-class football.
An impressive attacking player with
blistering pace, he was unfortunate to
struggle with injuries at Sunderland, a
hamstring causing him most concern. He
appeared in more than 175 League and
cup games for Grasshopper Zurich and
29 for the Wearsiders but didn't play in a
single match in their relegation campaign
of 2002–03. He made his debut for
Albion in the Nationwide League game
against Walsall at The Bescot Stadium on
the opening Saturday in August 2003.
Representing Switzerland in Euro 2004,
Haas was sent off in the group match
against England. Hass left Albion by
mutual consent.
NB: He was once a male model for the
Armani group.

*Career: Greets Green & Great Bridge
Schools, West Bromwich. Grestone Harriers
(1889). Hereford Thistle (August 1890).
ALBION (professional, July 1892).
Hereford Town (May 1896, retired through
injury, April 1900). Became an electrician.*

■ Ben Hadley was a player of reasonable
skill who could also stand-in as an
emergency pivot. He made his Albion
League debut against Accrington (away)
in December 1892. He also played in
eight 'other' first-team games for the club.
He died from low blood pressure after 10
weeks of illness.

HADLEY, Henry

Half-back: 181 apps. 2 goals.

*Born: Barrow-in-Furness, 26 October
1877.
Died: West Bromwich, 12 September 1942.
Career: Cradley Heath & District Schools.
Colley Gate United. Halesowen (August
1893). ALBION (£100, professional,
February 1897). Aston Villa (£250,
February 1905). Nottingham Forest (April
1906). Southampton (April 1907).
Croydon Common (August 1908).
Halesowen (February 1910). Merthyr
Town (manager, May 1919–April 1922).
Chesterfield (manager, April–August
1922). Merthyr Town (three spells as
manager between 1923–27). Aberdare
Athletic (manager, November
1927–November 1928). Gillingham
(manager, briefly in 1929–30). Aberdare
Athletic (manager, April 1930–September
1931). Bangor City (manager, July
1935–April 1936). Moved back to West
Bromwich where he spent the remaining
years of his life (he was present at The
Hawthorns when a record crowd of 64,815
saw Albion beat Arsenal in an FA Cup tie
in March 1937).*

■ Harry Hadley was a good, efficient,
easy-going player, cool, calculated and
energetic, who, as a half-back, was firm in
the tackle, forceful in going forward and
determined to win. He made his debut
for Albion against Notts County (away)
in Division One in March 1898 and
gained a Second Division championship
medal in 1902. During his eight-year
association with the club, he appeared in
more than 180 senior and 25 'other' first-
team matches and was capped by
England against Ireland in February
1903. Normally filling the left-half slot, at

the turn of the century, he featured prominently in Albion's middle-line alongside Dan Nurse and Jimmy Stevenson. Brother of Ben Hadley, he became a highly-successful manager after his playing days had ended and was sought by many leading clubs including Everton and Sheffield United, but he preferred to remain in the lower divisions and did exceptionally well with Merthyr Town.

HAINES, John Thomas William

Inside-forward: 62 apps. 23 goals.

Born: Wickhamford near Evesham, Worcestershire, 24 April 1920.
Died: Evesham, March 1987.
Career: Badsey Council & Evesham Grammar Schools. Evesham Town (1935). Cheltenham Town (1937). Liverpool (trialist, 1938). Swansea Town (1939). Guest for Wrexham, Doncaster Rovers, Notts County, Bradford Park Avenue and Lincoln City during World War Two. Leicester City (£10,000, June 1947). ALBION (March 1948, in £6,000 deal involving Peter McKennan). Bradford Park Avenue (£10,000, December 1949). Rochdale (September 1953). Chester (July 1955) Wellington Town (May 1957). Kidderminster Harriers (1958–59). Evesham (August 1959). Bretforton Village (August 1960, retired, March 1961).

■ Jackie Haines was soccer-mad at school, always wanting to play football. When he became an established professional he made the game look easy. He scored on his debut for Albion against West Ham United (away) in Division Two in March 1948, and did likewise (with two goals) when appearing in his only full international cap for England in a 6–0 win over Switzerland at Highbury in 1948. He was a short, aggressive inside-forward who, in his day, was highly skilful and mobile. During the 1948–49 season he was a key player in Albion's promotion-winning outfit, scoring 14 goals in 38 League matches. He also scored five times in 10 second XI games. He played in 28 League games (7 goals) for the Swans, made 12 appearances for Leicester (3 goals), scored 34 times in 135 outings for Bradford, hit 16 goals in 60 appearances for Rochdale and eight in his 46 League matches with Chester. His full

League record was 340 appearances and 94 goals. He was the leading scorer for Lincoln in 1944–45 with 21 goals and also played for the Air Command and RAF teams during World War Two.

HALL, Paul Anthony

Forward: 4 apps.

Born: Manchester, 3 July 1972
Career: Manchester Schoolboy football. Torquay United (apprentice, July 1988, professional, July 1990). Portsmouth (£70,000, March 1993). Coventry City (£300,000, with a further £200,000 after an agreed number of appearances, August 1998). Bury (on loan, February 1999). Sheffield United (on loan, December 1999). ALBION (on loan, February 2000). Walsall (free, March 2000). Queen's Park Rangers (trialist, August 2001). Rushden and Diamonds (October, 2001). Tranmere Rovers (March 2004).

■ A Jamaican international (43 caps gained at 2004), Paul Hall joined Albion on a month loan from Coventry City, taking over on the right side of midfield. He made his debut against Crewe Alexandra (won 1–0) 24 hours after signing. During his days at Torquay and Portsmouth he was a fast, direct player with boundless energy. He lost his way at Coventry but later regained his confidence and form under ex-Albion manager Brian Talbot at Rushden and

Diamonds, whom he helped to win the Third Division championship in season 2002–03, when he also reached the milestone of 500 appearances at club level (86 goals).

HAMILTON, Ian Richard

Midfield: 266+16 apps. 28 goals.

Born: Stevenage, Herts, 14 December 1967.
Career: Southampton (apprentice, April 1984, professional, December 1985). Cambridge United (March 1988). Scunthorpe United (December 1988). ALBION (£160,000, June 1992). Sheffield United (March 1998). Grimsby Town (on loan, November 1999). Notts County (free, August 2000). Lincoln City (free, November 2001). Woking (October 2002–May 2003).

■ Able to play as a central or wide midfielder, Ian Hamilton gave Albion excellent service for six years, helping the team gain promotion from Division Two in 1993 (via the Wembley play-off final against Port Vale), also having played for Scunthorpe in the previous season play-offs. A hard-working, strong-running footballer, he initially linked up splendidly with Bernard McNally and right-winger Kevin Donovan in the engine-room and carried on the good work later with Darren Bradley, Dave Gilbert and Stacy Coldicott. He made his Albion League debut against Blackpool (home) in August 1992, and a decade later (with Lincoln) he reached the

milestone of 600 senior appearances at club level, having failed to make Southampton's first team!

HANCOCK, Henry

Inside-forward: 2 apps.

Born: Levenshulme, Manchester, 7 July 1878.
Died: Manchester, 1940.
Career: Levenshulme & District Schools. Manchester YMCA (1903). Stockport County (May 1904). Blackpool (£50, May 1905). Oldham Athletic (£75, May 1906). Manchester City (£100, May 1908). ALBION (£100, February 1909). Brierley Hill Alliance (free, April 1910, retired, May 1913).

■ Henry Hancock was a tough, aggressive inside-forward who joined Albion at the end of his professional career, staying at The Hawthorns a little over a year. Playing mainly in the second XI, he made his senior debut against Clapton Orient (home) in February 1909.

HARBEY, Graham Keith

Full-back: 113 apps. 2 goals.

Born: Chesterfield. 29 August 1964.
Career: Derby County (apprentice, April

1981, professional, August 1982). Ipswich Town (£65,000, July 1987). ALBION (£80,000, December 1989). Stoke City (£80,000, July 1992). Exeter City (trialist, June 1994). Gresley Rovers (August 1994). Burton Albion (July 1995). Brailsford FC (1997–99).*

■ Blonde-haired, clean-kicking left-back Graham Harbey made 50 appearances for Derby County and 77 for Ipswich before joining Albion halfway through the 1989–90 season, when player-manager

Brian Talbot became concerned about the number three position. He had an excellent debut as Albion crushed Barnsley 7–0, and thereafter he did well as partner to Simeon Hodson before Ossie Ardiles replaced him with Steve Lilwall. He was a Pontins League championship winner with Albion in 1990–91 (14 games played). Harbey's transfer fee to Stoke was fixed by an independent tribunal.

HARGREAVES, Christian

Forward: 0+2 apps.

Born: Cleethorpes, 12 May 1972.
Career: Grimsby Town (apprentice, June 1988, professional, December 1989). Scarborough (on loan, March–April 1993). Hull City (£5,000, July 1993). ALBION (free, July 1995). Hereford United (free, February 1996). Plymouth Argyle (free, July 1998). Northampton Town (free, July 2000). Brentford (free, June 2004).Oxford United (July 2005).

■ A versatile forward converted later in his career into a midfielder player, Chris Hargreaves was an Alan Buckley signing. Unfortunately, he never looked the part during his brief stay at The Hawthorns, making just two 'sub' appearances, the first against Sunderland in the League in

late November 1995, the second against Brescia in the Anglo-Italian Cup a fortnight later. He also played in 20 second XI games and later had over 120 outings for the Cobblers.

HARPER, William Edwin

Outside-left: 8 apps. 1 goal.

Born: Nechells, Birmingham, 19 November 1876.
Died: Birmingham, 1958.
Career: Saltley Gate Schools. Nechells Star. Smethwick Wesleyan Rovers (1897). ALBION (professional, July 1899). Leicester Fosse (£40, September 1903, retired, April 1907). Served in the armed forces during World War One.

■ A well-built outside-left of the forceful type, Billy Harper won junior international recognition for England in 1899. He possessed a worthy shot and had good pace over short distances but lacked total commitment. Basically an Albion reserve during his four years with the club, he played in more than 60 second XI games and gained a Birmingham & District League championship medal in 1902. He made his senior debut against Newton Heath (away) in Division Two in November 1901 and a year later scored in Albion's 3–0 win over Stoke in the final of the Staffordshire Cup.

HARRIS, George Abner

Half-back: 20 apps. 1 goal.

Born: Halesowen, 4 January 1878.

THE WHO'S WHO OF WEST BROMWICH ALBION

Died: Brierley Hill, 10 June 1923.
Career: Gortsy Hill School. Haden Hill Rose FC (April 1893). Coombs Wood (May 1896). Halesowen (August 1899). Aston Villa (1905). ALBION (£400 January 1909). Wellington Town (June 1910). Coventry City (June 1912, retired though injury, April 1915). Was 'Mine Host' at the Sportsman, Old Hill, for a number of years before entering into engineering. He was tragically killed in a steel works accident aged 45.

■ George Harris – a moderate smoker and sometimes heavy drinker – was a most capable and efficient defender who usually preferred the left-half berth. He was a junior international for England versus Scotland in 1905 and 1906, when he skippered the side, but never really made the grade in the top flight, although he was always a consistent performer for his minor clubs. He made his League debut for Albion against Fulham (away) in Division Two in January 1909.

HARRIS, William

Goalkeeper: 17 apps.

Born: Oakham, Dudley, 1 December 1918.
Died: Dudley, 20 February 1996.
Career: Tividale and Broadway Schools. Rowley Regis Boys. Oakham Juniors. Whiteheath FC (1934). ALBION (October 1936, professional, February 1937). Guest for Newport County, Norwich City and Shrewsbury Town during World War Two. Oldham Athletic (£150, June 1946). Accrington Stanley (August 1947). Dudley Town (player-manager, 1950–53). Bilston

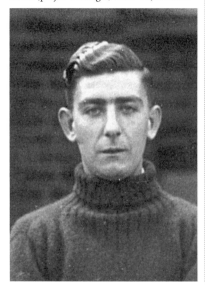

United (player-manager, 1953–55). Retired to become ALBION scout (Dudley & District League, 1956–59). Later worked for an engineering company in Tividale.

■ Bill Harris was badly wounded in Normandy (1944) but recovered to continue in League football, making 32 appearances for Oldham and 99 for Accrington. He was an unspectacular 'keeper who dealt with high crosses exceptionally well but was suspect on the ground. He made his Albion debut

against Everton (away) in Division Two in April 1938 and made 34 appearances for the club at Central League level.

HARTFORD, Richard Asa

Inside-forward: 266 + 9 apps. 26 goals.

Born: Clydebank, Scotland, 24 October 1950.
Career: Fairfley Primary School. Clydebank High School. Dunbartonshire Boys. Drumchapel Amateurs (1965). ALBION

(apprentice, April 1966, professional, October 1967). Leeds United (for 24 hours, November 1971). ALBION (November 1971). Manchester City (£225,000, August 1974). Nottingham Forest (£450,000, July 1979). Everton (record fee of £500,000, August 1979). Manchester City (October 1981). Fort Lauderdale Sun, NASL (May 1984). Wolverhampton Wanderers (trialist, August 1984). Norwich City (September 1984). Norway (coach, summer 1985). Bolton Wanderers (July 1985). Stockport County (player-manager, June 1987). Oldham Athletic (March 1989). Shrewsbury Town (coach, July 1989, manager July 1990, sacked, January 1991). Boston United (March 1991). Blackburn Rovers (coach). Stoke City (coach/assistant manager, 1993–94, under Joe Jordan). Manchester City (coach, assistant manager, later reserve-team manager and part-time coach at the club's School of Excellence, 1997–2004, released, May 2005). Played for WBA All Stars (1990s).

■ Asa Hartford made his Football League debut for Albion as a 17-year-old against Sheffield United at Bramall Lane in Division One in February 1968. He developed quickly and became a midfield dynamo – a player who darted here, there and everywhere, seeking to create chances for his colleagues. Full of energy, he was always buzzing around in midfield, and during his career he amassed well over 800 senior appearances, including 275 for Albion for whom he also starred in 38 Central League games (8 goals). In 1971 he was rejected by Leeds United (on medical advice) after agreeing to move to Elland Road. Doctors had diagnosed a 'hole in the heart'. Three years later, however, the same Asa Hartford was sold to Manchester City for almost a quarter of a million pounds. In 1979 he moved from Maine Road to Nottingham Forest for twice that amount and Everton paid £500,000 for him later in that same year. A Scottish international at youth, under-21, under-23 and full-team levels (50 caps), Hartford played for Albion in the 1970 League Cup final, later winning a medal in the same competition with Manchester City (1976) and Norwich City (1985) when his deflected 'goal' gave the Canaries victory over Sunderland. He played in the Freight Rover Trophy Final for Bolton against

Bristol City, collecting another runners'-up medal.
*He was christened Asa after the celebrated American singing star Al (Asa) Jolson.

HATTON, Sidney Edwin Oscar

Utility player: 6 apps.

Born: West Bromwich, 8 April 1891.
Died: Solihull, 7 November 1960.
Career: Beeches Road School (West Bromwich). Stourbridge (1907). West Bromwich Baptist FC (1909). ALBION (professional, November 1912). Army football. Shrewsbury Town (free, May 1922). Stourbridge (July 1925, retired, c.1927). Became a councillor and also worked for the local education department.

■ Sid Hatton was a steady player who could perform in several positions, including left-half, outside-right or inside-forward. Although a member of the club for 10 years, he only managed six first-team outings, World War One badly disrupting his career (he served with the 5th South Staffs Regiment, based in Ireland). He made his senior debut against Sheffield United (home) in Division One in February 1920 and also played in more than 50 second XI matches, competing in both the Birmingham & District and Central Leagues either side of the Great War, helping the team win the championship of the former competition in 1920.

HAWKER, Philip Nigel

Left-back: 1 app.

Born: Solihull, 7 December 1962.
Career: Langley Secondary School. Birmingham City (apprentice, June 1978, professional, June 1980). Walsall (on loan, December 1982, signed permanently, March 1983). ALBION (on loan, September–October 1990). Kidderminster Harriers (December 1990). Solihull Borough (August 1991, retired, October 1993, through injury).

■ Phil Hawker, a tall, long-striding defender, capped twice by England at youth-team level, made almost 40 appearances for the Blues and over 220 for the Saddlers before having just one outing for Albion in place of the injured Graham Harbey against Hull City (away).

He also played in 11 Pontins League games in 1990–91 when Albion's second XI team won the title. It was thought that Hawker would have developed into a central-defender but was rarely tried in that role during his career.

HAYCOCK, Frederick James

Inside-forward: 15 apps. 8 goals.

Born: Smethwick, 10 August 1886.
Died: Dudley, July 1955.
Career: West Smethwick Schools. Smethwick Victoria (1901). Coombes Wood FC (1902). ALBION (professional, June 1904). Crewe Alexandra (£50, July 1907). Leyton (briefly). Luton Town (£60, June 1908). Portsmouth (£75, August 1909). Lincoln City (£50, October 1910). Port Vale (June 1911). Dudley Town (August 1913). Shrewsbury Town (1915, retired, c.1922, after serving in World War One). Became a foreman in a steelworks.

■ Freddie Haycock was an energetic inside or centre-forward who put a lot of creativity into his play. He was alert, had a good shot but unfortunately a promising career with Albion was ruined by injury after he had scored, on average, a goal every two games. He also had a handful of games for the second XI. He moved around several clubs after leaving The Hawthorns but never settled, although he accumulated, in all, more than 200 senior appearances during his professional career, having made his Albion League debut against Burnley (home) in Division Two in December 1904.

HAYNES, George Harold

Inside-forward: 10 apps. one goal.

Born: West Bromwich, 11 November 1865.
Died: West Bromwich, April 1937.
Career: Hargate Lane School. West Bromwich. Tantany Rovers (1883). West Bromwich Sandwell (1885). ALBION (professional, July 1887). Coles Farm Unity (free, May 1892). West Bromwich United (April 1895, retired, May 1897).

■ George Haynes was a bustling forward, chiefly noted for his opportunism, which in friendly games was outstanding, although he did not achieve the same sort of success at competitive level. He was a temperamental fellow and often clashed with authority. His argumentative nature resulted in him leaving Albion. He made his League debut for the club against Preston North End (home) in December 1888. He also played in 18 'other' first-team games for the club.

HAYWARD, Archibald

Outside-left: 3 apps.

Born: Oldham, Lancs, 28 July 1878.
Died: October 1972, aged 94.
Career: Pine Villa (1893). Oldham Athletic (trialist, November 1894). Accrington Stanley (trialist, April 1895). Blackburn Rovers (trialist, August–September 1895). ALBION (professional, January 1896). Chorley (free, February 1896). Colne (August 1907, retired, April 1908).

■ Hardly the most polished of left-wingers being something of a plodder, Archie Hayward was associated with Albion for just 28 days (to 28 January 1896), having his registration cancelled after being found in possession of spirits during a game at Sunderland. He was dismissed on the spot and paid £1 to cover his expenses back to Lancashire. He made his debut for the club against Burnley (away) in Division One in January 1896.

HAYWARD, Sean

Centre-half: 1 appearance.

Born: Bloxwich, 21 July 1968.
Career: Bloxwich & District Schools. ALBION (apprentice, July 1985, professional, July 1986, released, June 1987). Derby County (trialist, August 1987). Sheffield Wednesday (non-contract, November 1987). Willenhall Town (April 1988). Halesowen Town (1989). Tamworth (January 1991). Later with Goole Town and Lichfield City.

■ Sean Hayward was a strong, well-built central-defender, who was the backbone of Albion's second-team side throughout seasons 1985–86 and 1986–87 before being released by the club after making one first-team appearance against Millwall (away) in the Full Member's Cup in October 1986. He also played in 48 Central League games, scoring three goals.

HAYWARD, Adam Seymour

Inside-forward: 67 apps. 27 goals.

Born: Horninglow, Burton upon Trent, 23 March 1875.
Died: May 1932.
Career: Anslow Gate School. Burton Ivanhoe (junior, 1893). Burton Wanderers (junior, 1894). Swadlincote (junior, 1985). Woolwich Arsenal (professional, January 1896). Glossop (May 1899). Queen's Park Rangers (August 1899). New Brompton (September 1900). Burton Swifts (March 1901). Wolverhampton Wanderers (August 1901). Albion (May 1905). Blackpool (December 1907). Crystal Palace (player-coach, 1908, retired out of football, 1912). Worked on munitions during World War One. Later a shop proprietor.

■ Adam Hayward played in both inside-forward positions for Albion and during his long career he occupied all five forward positions as well as those of right and left half. He had all the qualities these positions demanded, possessing a fierce shot and keen eye for the half-chance. Despite his size – he was only a dot – he could rough it with the biggest and strongest opponents in the game. He was an England international trialist (South against North) and during his career amassed well over 300 competitive appearances. He scored 36 goals in 91 games for Arsenal and 28 in 113 for

Wolves before switching to The Hawthorns, making his Albion debut against Burnley (home) in Division Two in September 1905.
* Some reference books have this player's surname spelt as Heywood.

HAYWOOD, Thomas Henry

Half-back: 15 apps.

Born: Walsall, 22 March 1877.
Died: Walsall, 23 March 1947.
Career: Queen Street School (Walsall). Walsall Co-op FC (1897). Stourbridge (September 1900). Aston Villa (April 1904). ALBION (£75, March 1905). Crewe Alexandra (free, November 1908). Darlaston (August 1914, retired, May 1915). Served in the Army during World War One, later employed as a civil servant in West Bromwich and Walsall.

■ Tom Haywood was a real tough-guy defender whose headwork for a small man was exceptionally good. His ground play was pretty useful too, but he never really got the opportunity his overall play deserved with Albion, being mainly a reserve to Messrs Randle, Pheasant and Manners. A junior international for England in 1904, he made his League debut for Albion against Bradford City (home) in March 1905, and he also played in over 25 second XI games. Haywood died leaving seven children.

HEASELGRAVE, Samuel Edward

Inside-forward: 163 apps. 57 goals.

Born: Smethwick, 1 October 1916.
Died: Birmingham, April 1975.
Career: Smethwick & District Schools. Bearwood Swifts. Warley Lions. Smethwick Highfield (1933). ALBION (amateur, October 1934, professional, March 1936). Walsall (guest, September 1945). Northampton Town (£750, October 1945). Dudley Town (1948). Northwich and Victoria (October 1948, retired 1949). After his playing days were over he became a solicitor in Bearwood, a business that is still in the family today. Won the All-England bowls championship in 1963.

■ Sammy Heaselgrave was a hard-working, seemingly tireless, utility forward, constantly on target with his powerhouse shooting. A junior international for England in 1936, he broke into Albion's first team in March 1937 (making his debut against Brentford at home) and was an ever-present until his departure to Northampton in 1945. He appeared in well over 160 senior matches, scoring, on average, a goal in every three. Initially, he had to bide his time before establishing himself in the senior XI but once in he stayed and did a splendid job, especially during hostilities when he played alongside some great footballers including Len Duns, Jack Acquaroff, W.G. Richardson, 'Ike' Clarke and Billy Elliott. Indeed, Heaselgrave was one of only four players to represent Albion in each of the seven wartime seasons (1939–46 inclusive), gaining a Midland War Cup medal in 1944. He also scored 15 goals in 49 Central League games for the club.

* Sammy's brother, Billy Heaselgrave, was on Albion's books as an amateur in the late 1930s.

HEATH, Norman Harold

Goalkeeper: 169 apps.

Born: Wolverhampton, 31 January 1924.

Died: Great Barr, Birmingham, November 1983.

Career: Bushbury Hill School. Wolverhampton Boys. Henry Meadows FC (1940). ALBION (amateur, May 1942, professional, October 1943, forced to retire in June 1955, following serious neck and back injuries, suffered in a League match against Sunderland at Roker Park in March 1954, where he was involved in a collision with the home centre-forward Ted Purdon). Later manager of the junior side Great Barr Gunners (1971–73).

■ In his day, Norman Heath was a fine, courageous goalkeeper whose agility and brilliant reflexes were key features of his splendid displays as Albion's last line of defence. He came to The Hawthorns during World War Two and made his first-team debut against Wolverhampton Wanderers (home) in the Football League North in September 1943, and at the end of that season he gained a Midland Cup medal after Albion had beaten Nottingham Forest 6–5 in the final over two legs. However, he had to wait another three years before making his Football League debut against Sheffield Wednesday in a Second Division

encounter at Hillsborough in December 1947, when he saved a penalty in a 2–1 win. Besides his tally of senior appearances, he also played in 138 Central League games for the Baggies. Heath understudied Jimmy Sanders for quite a while before that sickening injury in 1954 ended his career. In fact, he missed the 1954 FA Cup final – his place going, ironically, to Sanders! In November 1944 Heath joined the Army, based at Shrewsbury, before teaming up with the King's Shropshire Light Infantry at Llandrindrod Wells. He moved to India where, at Poona, he was posted to the 2nd Leicester Regiment. He represented his platoon, company and battalion and also the brigade team, playing for the Combined Services XI on several occasions. He rose to the rank of CQMS.

HEGAN, Daniel

Inside-forward: 17 apps. 2 goals.

Born: Coatbridge, Scotland, 14 June 1943. Career: Coatbridge & Bailieston Schools. Glasgow Boys. Rutherglen Youths. Sunderland (trialist, April–May 1958). Albion Rovers (June 1959). Sunderland (£6,000, September 1961). Ipswich Town (£10,000, July 1963). ALBION (£88,000, plus Ian Collard, May 1969). Wolverhampton Wanderers (£27,500, May 1970). Sunderland (November 1973). Highlands Park FC Johannesburg, South

Africa (June 1974). Partick Thistle (trialist, 1974–75). Highlands Park, South Africa (April 1975). Coleshill Town (August 1975, retired, May 1978 to become soccer coach at Butlins, Clacton). Now lives in Birmingham and works as a taxi driver.

■ Danny Hegan was a player with loads of natural ability but his hectic social life ruined a promising career as a midfield general. He was capped by Northern Ireland seven times and won a Second Division championship medal with Ipswich in 1968 after making his debut for the Portman Road club five years earlier against Bolton. He made his debut on the opening Saturday of the League programme against Southampton (away) in August 1969 and he also scored five goals in 15 Central League appearances for the Baggies. A recipient of a UEFA Cup runners'-up medal with Wolves in 1972, during his professional career in the Football League, Hegan made a total of 280 appearances and netted 42 goals; his Ipswich record was 207 appearances and 34 goals.

* Hegan was sued for libel by Billy Bremner in January 1982 and the former Leeds United player was awarded £100,000 damages.

HEGGS, Carl Sydney

Forward: 21+31 apps. 4 goals.

Born: Leicester, 11 October 1970. Career: Leicester City Boys Club. Leicester United (August 1988). ALBION (£25,000, August 1991). Bristol Rovers (on loan, January 1995). Swansea City (£60,000, July 1995). Northampton Town (£40,000,

July 1997). Rushden and Diamonds (£65,000, October 1998). Chester City (on loan, March–May 2000). Carlisle United (free, August 2000). Forest Green Rovers (July 2001). Ilkeston Town (player/assistant manager, 2003–05).

■ A tall, quick, lively utility forward with a penchant for hard work, Carl Heggs preferred the left flank but was never considered as a first-team regular at The Hawthorns. Indeed, his best season came in 1992–93 when promotion was gained to the First Division (via the play-offs). He appeared in 22 senior games, 21 as a substitute under manager Ossie Ardiles, and also starred in almost 120 Central/Pontins League games (scoring 38 goals). He later became Ian Atkins's first signing for Carlisle.

HENDRY, William Henry

Centre-forward: 18 apps. 4 goals.

Born: Dundee, Scotland, 16 June 1864.
Died: Sussex, February 1901.
Career: Dundee & Invergowrie Schools. Dunblane Thistle (1882). Dundee Wanderers (amateur, 1885). ALBION (professional, August 1888). Stoke (free, March 1889). Kidderminster Harriers (briefly). Preston North End (January 1890). Sheffield United (February 1891). Dundee (May 1895). Bury (March, 1896). Brighton United (September 1898). Watford (August 1899, retired, March 1900, due to ill-health).

■ Centre-forward Billy Hendry had qualities of speed, headwork and whole-hearted endeavour. He made his Albion debut against his future club Stoke (away) in the first ever League game in September 1888, but in truth he was never really at home at West Bromwich, although he did play in 10 'other' first-team matches for the club. After leaving the Black Country he did extremely well with Sheffield United following his conversion to the centre-half position, where he performed with aggressive commitment. He skippered the Blades for a time and helped them win promotion to the First Division in 1893, making 20 appearances (2 goals).

HERBERT, Craig Justin

Defender: 11 apps. 1 goal.
Born: Coventry, 9 November 1975.

Career: Torquay United (apprentice, April 1992). ALBION (professional, March 1994). Shrewsbury Town (July 1997). Rugby United (to 2000).

■ A hard tackling central defender, reserve to Darren Bradley, Daryl Burgess, Paul Mardon, Paul Raven and Gary Strodder at The Hawthorns, Craig Herbert made just under a dozen first-team appearances for Albion with his first League outing coming against Luton Town (away) in August 1994. His only goal for the Baggies was a close range effort against Foggia in an Anglo-Italian Cup tie in October 1995. He had some 80 outings for the second XI and went on to appear in 24 League games for Shrewsbury.

HEWITT, Charles William

Inside-forward: 64 apps. 28 goals.
Born: Greatham, Cleveland, 10 April 1884.
Died: Darlington, 31 December 1966.
Career: Greatham. West Hartlepools & Billingham Schools. Middlesbrough (professional, August 1904). Tottenham Hotspur (£100, May 1906). Liverpool (August 1907). ALBION (£75, April 1908). Spennymoor United (May 1910). Crystal Palace (£125, October 1910). Hartlepools United (May 1919, retired as a player, May 1923). Mold FC (manager, August 1923–May 1924). Wrexham (manager, November 1924–December 1926). Flint Town (manager, August 1927). Connah's Quay (manager, May 1928). Chester (manager, 1930). Millwall (manager, April 1936–April 1940). Leyton Orient (manager, January 1946–April 1948). Millwall (manager, August 1948–January 1956).

■ Charlie Hewitt was a popular, colourful character who was a big favourite with the supporters. His inside-forward play was always praiseworthy without ever being brilliant. He had only brief spells with his three major clubs prior to Albion, scoring six goals in 16 games for Liverpool in 1907–08 and 14 in 33 for Middlesbrough in 1904–6. He made his Albion debut against Fulham (home) in Division Two in April 1908. As a manager, he guided Millwall to the Third Division South championship in 1938 and was twice a Welsh Cup winner: in 1925 with Wrexham and 1933 with Chester. He was almost 72 years of age when he retired from football.
* Hewitt was awarded £4,500 damages in July 1956 after a great deal of publicity following his sacking as Millwall manager six months earlier.

HIBBERT, James William

Wing-half/inside-forward: 3 apps.
Born: Hebburn-on-Tyne, Co. Durham, 5 January 1890.
Died: Heworth, 1955.
Career: Heworth Colliery. Pelaw FC (1909). ALBION (professional, April 1910). Hartlepools United (free, June 1912). Retired at end of World War One after serving as a soldier.

■ A useful competitor who could fill either wing-half or inside-forward berth efficiently and well, Jimmy Hibbert was a reserve-team player at Albion throughout most of his two-year association with the club, making his League debut against Barnsley (away) in Division Two in October 1910. He made over 50 appearances in the second XI.

HIGGINS, John Thomas

Centre-half: 94 apps. 5 goals.
Born: Smethwick, 8 September 1874.
Died: Stockton-on-Tees, May 1916.
Career: Smethwick & District schools. Hasbury Welfare. Woodfield FC. Albion Swifts (August 1888). Stourbridge (1893). ALBION (May1894, retired through injury, September 1898). Later became a Middlesbrough publican.

■ Tom Higgins was a fine pivot, strong in all phases of half-back play, especially good in the air and a solid tackler on the ground. Twelve months after signing for Albion he played in the 1895 FA Cup final against Aston Villa, suffering a bloody head-wound that restricted his overall vision. He battled on manfully and received the princely sum of £5 for his noble efforts, despite Villa winning the contest 1–0. Higgins represented the Football League twice in 1896 and might well have gained full international honours had a cartilage operation not forced him to retire prematurely at the age of 24, after he had amassed almost 100 senior and over 50 'other' first-team appearances for Albion. He made his League debut against Aston Villa (away) in Division One in October 1894.

* Elder brother, Billy Higgins, (born in Smethwick, 1870) played for Grimsby Town (two spells), Bristol City, Newcastle United and Newton Heath between 1892 and 1912, amassing over 200 League and cup appearances, including 127 for Grimsby.

HOBSON, Alfred Frank

Utility player: 15 apps. 4 goals.

Born: Tipton, West Midlands, 26 November 1878.
Died: Darlington, May 1944.
Career: Tipton & Princess End Schools, Wednesbury Town (1898). ALBION (professional, December 1899). Brentford (free, April 1905). Crewe Alexandra (1907). Gainsborough Trinity (September 1908). Darlington (May 1914, retired c.1916). Later employed in the steel industry.

■ Alf Hobson, who made his League debut for Albion against Sunderland (away) in November 1902, was an individual who loved to go it alone from whatever position he occupied, albeit full-back, centre-half, left-half, inside-right or centre-forward. He appeared in 15 games before being suspended 'Sine Die' by the club's directors after a heated Cup tie at Nottingham for using bad language and defiance against the Albion captain Jimmy Stevenson. This ban was 'lifted' later and he started afresh with Brentford in 1905. He played over 25 times for Albion's second XI, gaining a Birmingham & District League championship medal in 1902.

HODGETTS, Frank

Outside-left: 178 apps. 34 apps.
Born: Oakham, Dudley, 30 September 1924.

Career: Rowley Regis School. St Mary's Sunday School, Accles & Pollock Works FC. ALBION (amateur, September 1939, professional, October 1942). Millwall (£6,000, May 1949). Worcester City (seasons 1953–57, retired after his Achilles tendon snapped). Returned to ALBION as coach (1958–62). Currently chairman of the Herefordshire and Worcestershire County Tennis Association, and is chief organiser of coaching. Lives in Hagley near Kidderminster.

■ Frank Hodgetts was a good old-fashioned winger, who was aged just 16 years and 26 days old when he made his first-team debut for Albion against Notts County in a wartime game in October 1940. That made him the youngest-ever player to wear a first-team strip in the club's history – and his record still holds today. Basically an outside-left, Frank was likely to bob-up anywhere in the forward line and he frequently did just that – sometimes to the annoyance of his colleagues. An ebullient character with a cannonball shot, Hodgetts played in well over 200 competitive matches during his career (Albion and Millwall) and scored 44 goals. Most of his Albion outings were made during World War Two (108 being in various League and cup tournaments, helping the Baggies win the Midland Cup in 1944). He scored on his Football League debut against Swansea Town (away) in Division Two in August 1946 (Albion won 3–2) and he netted five times in 38 Central League games.

HODGKISSON, William Kenneth

Inside-forward: 21 apps. 4 goals.

Born: West Bromwich, 12 March 1933. Career: George Salter's School, West Bromwich. Birmingham County Youths. Newtown Rangers. Church Army Social FC (1948). ALBION (amateur, May 1949, professional, April 1950). Walsall (£1,600, December 1955). Worcester City (July 1966). Dudley Town (1967, manager, August 1968–November 1971). Greets Green Prims (manager/coach, 1973). ALBION (coaching staff, 1975–79, youth-team manager, July 1981–85). Later scout for Derby County (1986–89). Played for West Bromwich Albion All Stars 1969–79. Now lives in Greets Green, West Bromwich.

■ Ken Hodgkisson was a useful inside-forward, who had to fight for his first-team place at The Hawthorns, having Ronnie Allen, Johnny Nicholls, Reg Ryan, Wilf Carter and others keen to play at the same time. He finally made his League debut against Aston Villa (away) in April 1953, in front of almost 50,000 fans, four years after joining the club. He also scored 12 goals in 82 Central League games for the Baggies before doing a lot better at first-team level with Walsall, with whom he gained a Fourth Division championship medal in 1960 and helped the Saddlers climb into Division Two a season later. He played in well over 350 games for Walsall and was their first ever League substitute, coming on against Workington in August 1965.

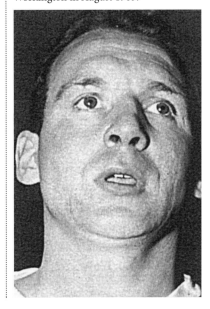

HODSON, Simeon Paul

Defender: 17 apps.

Born: Lincoln, 5 March 1966.
Career: Lincoln & District Schools. Notts County (apprentice, 1982, professional, March 1984). Charlton Athletic (April 1985). Lincoln City (January 1986). Newport County (July 1987). ALBION (£5,000 March 1988). Doncaster Rovers (non-contract, September 1992). Kidderminster Harriers (briefly). Mansfield Town (March 1993). Telford United (August–September 1997). Rushden and Diamonds (October 1997). Sutton Coldfield Town (August 2000, retired, July 2001).

■ A utility defender, quick in recovery, Simeon Hodson could also adopt a midfield role. He made 30 appearances for Notts County, five for Charlton, 66 for Lincoln and 42 for Newport before joining Albion on the transfer deadline in 1988. He suffered an injury during the 1988–89 campaign and was never the same player again, although he did go on to amass a total of 237 League appearances up to the mid-1990s. He made his debut for the Baggies against Stoke City (home) in Division Two in April 1988. He also played in more than 50 second-team matches.

HOGG, Derek

Outside-left: 87 apps. 12 goals.

Born: Stockton-on-Tees, 4 November 1930.
Career: Middleforth Church of England School (Penwerthan). Middleforth Juniors.

Preston North End (amateur trialist, August 1944). Lostock Hall FC (August 1947). Chorley (June 1950). Leicester City (professional, October 1952). ALBION (£20,000, April 1958). Cardiff City (£12,000, October 1960). Kettering Town (August 1962–May 1965). Later a Leicester publican, now retired and living in Nottingham.

■ An ingenious, fleet-footed outside-left who responded best to a ball playing inside-partner, Derek Hogg (known as 'Hoggy') had the marked tendency to hold the ball much too long! He arrived at The Hawthorns to replace George Lee and Roy Horobin and was taken to Spain to play in a game against Athletic Bilbao before settling into Albion's League side for the start of the 1958–59 season, making his debut against Luton Town (away) in Division One on 23 August. His form was on and off during the 1959–60 campaign, and, after being subsequently ousted by Geoff Carter and Andy Aitken, he left the club in October 1960. Hogg, who scored once in nine Central League games for Albion, represented the Football League XI in 1955–56 and the following season helped Leicester win the Second Division championship. In his League career (Leicester, Albion and Cardiff) he appeared in 283 matches and netted 44 goals.

HOGG, Graeme James

Defender: 8 apps.

Born: Aberdeen, 17 June 1964.
Career: Aberdeen & District Schools. Manchester United (apprentice, July 1980, professional, June 1982). ALBION (on loan, November–December 1987). Thence back to United after turning down a permanent move to The Hawthorns. Portsmouth (£150,000, August 1988). Heart of Midlothian (£200,000, August 1991). Notts County (January 1995). Brentford (January 1998). Linlithgow Rose FC (2000–02).

■ Former Scottish under-21 international (4 caps) Graeme 'Hedger' Hogg made over 100 senior appearances for Manchester United before Ron Atkinson secured him on loan in an effort to bolster up Albion's leaky defence. While at Old Trafford he battled earnestly for a regular first-team place with Gordon McQueen (1983–84) and found

it increasingly difficult to keep his place following the emergence of Kevin Moran, Billy Garton and Paul McGrath. On his return to United, however, he gained a senior place owing to the injuries to both McGrath and Moran. He missed United's FA Cup final win over Everton through injury but later helped United to First Division runners-up in 1988. He made his Albion debut against Sheffield United (home) in Division Two in November 1987.
* In July 1994 Hogg, playing for Hearts against Raith Rovers, was sent off in a pre-season friendly for fighting with his teammate Craig Levene. He was suspended for 10 months.

HOLDEN, George Henry

Outside-right: 4 apps. 1 goal.

Born: West Bromwich, 6 October 1858.
Died: March 1922.
Career: St John's School (Wednesbury). Wednesbury Old Park (1873–76), Wednesbury St James (August 1876). Wednesbury Old Athletic (September 1878). ALBION (guest, May 1883). Wednesbury Old Athletic (August 1883). Aston Villa (March–April 1885). Wednesbury Old Athletic (1985–86). ALBION (amateur, July 1886). Wednesbury Old Athletic (June 1887). Derby Midland (August 1888, retired, April 1892). Later worked as a puddler for the Patent Shaft & Axletree Company and was also a local councillor.

■ George Holden was a famous outside-right, who won four England caps (two against Scotland) between 1881–84. After a three-week spell with rivals Aston Villa, he then assisted Albion for one full season, having previously 'guested' for the club in 1883. Possessing superb skill and great enthusiasm, he provided some splendid entertainment for the supporters. He played for the Birmingham FA on at least 24 occasions, lining up against London, Sheffield, Lancashire, Glasgow, Nottinghamshire and Scottish Counties select XI's between 1878–86, and he also served the Staffordshire FA. He was obviously past his best when he joined Albion but he still revealed flashes of his brilliant dribbling ability that had earned him international stardom up and down the country. Funnily enough, he only occasionally occupied the right-flank in Albion's senior side, usually preferring to play inside. He made his senior debut for the club against Burton Wanderers (home) in the first round of the FA Cup in October 1886, scoring in a 6–0 win. He also appeared in 27 'other' first-team matches for Albion.

HOLMES, Paul

Defender: 114+1 apps. 1 goal.

Born: Stocksbridge, 18 February 1968.

Career: Doncaster Rovers (apprentice, June 1984, professional, February 1986). Torquay United (£8,000, August 1988). Birmingham City (£40,000, June 1992). Everton (£100,000, March 1993). ALBION (£80,000, January 1996). Torquay United (free, November 1999, retired as a player, June 2003, and as a coach, 2003–04).

■ Paul Holmes, a speedy defender able to occupy the right-back berth as well as that of centre-half, was cool and collected and always assured, but who perhaps lacked consistency with his crossing! He might well have become a Liverpool player before joining the Blues. He had a good spell at The Hawthorns, making 115 first-team appearances and over 30 for the reserves before moving on following the emergence of Danny Gabbidon and the presence of Andy McDermott. He later took his total number of career appearances towards the 500 mark in 2003.
* His father, Albert Holmes, made 470 League appearances for Chesterfield between 1961–76.

HOOD, Owen Glyn

Wing-half: 74 apps.

Born: Pentwyn, Monmouthshire, 12 March 1925.
Died: Coventry, 28 September 2004.
Career: Abersychan Council School. Broad Street Senior Boys' School (Coventry). AWA Bagington FC. Daimler-Aero Mechanics FC. Nuffield FC (1942). ALBION (amateur, May 1943, professional, September 1945, retired, July 1951, with an arthritic knee condition and ill-health). He died of TB and dementure aged 79.

■ Glyn Hood was a most attractive left-half, whose dainty footwork and quiet, subtle approach to the game were first class. As a lad he played rugby in the Welsh Valleys and when he turned to soccer he wanted to become a goalkeeper and played in that position for the AWA team. But it was as a dominant number 6 in the navy blue and white stripes of Albion where Hood blossomed most, and he was a key member of the 1948–49 promotion side. Then came injury, coupled with ill-health, and at the age of 26 his career ended quite abruptly. He made his senior debut for Albion against Chelsea (home) in the Football League

South in October 1945, at centre-half, starring in a comprehensive 8–1 victory. He also appeared in 75 Central League games.

HOPE, Robert

Inside-forward: 398+5 apps. 42 goals.

Born: Bridge of Allan, Stirlingshire, 28 September 1943.
Career: Clydebank High & Dunbartonshire West Schools. Drumchapel Amateurs. Sunderland (trialist). Scotland Boys. ALBION (amateur, August 1959, professional, September 1960). Birmingham City (£66,666, May 1972). Philadelphia Atoms (on loan, April 1975). Dallas Tornados (on loan, May–August 1976). Sheffield Wednesday (September 1976). Dallas Tornados (on loan, April–August 1977 and again, April–August 1978). Bromsgrove Rovers (player-coach, August 1979, appointed manager, May 1983). Burton Albion (manager, August–October 1988). Bromsgrove Rovers (manager, June 1989). ALBION (youth development officer, July 1998, then chief scout from August 2001). Also played for West Bromwich Albion All Stars (1979–88, making over 200 appearances in charity matches).

■ Bobby Hope turned down the team he had supported since he was six years of age, Glasgow Rangers, to join Albion in 1959. A player who displayed a masterly generalship in midfield, his splendid ball skills and telling passes were highlights of a wonderful association with Albion with whom he won a League Cup tankard in 1966 and an FA Cup medal two years later, as well

Imre Varadi). Birmingham City (£25,000, March 1989). Shrewsbury Town (free, July 1991). Instant Dictionary FC, Hong Kong (May 1992). Solihull Borough (September 1992). Colchester United (February 1993). Solihull Borough (player-coach, 1994–99). Bromsgrove Rovers (1999–2000). Paget Rangers (2000–01). Pelsall FC (coach, October 2003). Also played for West Bromwich Albion All Stars (late 1990s).

■ Robert Hopkins was a hard-working, aggressive yet skilful midfielder, who preferred to play on the righthand-side of the park. He joined Albion in a player/exchange deal shortly after the start of the 1986–87 season and thus teamed up with manager Ron Saunders for the third time, having initially played

as collecting runners'-up prizes in the League Cup competition in 1967 and 1970. Capped by Scotland at schoolboy, under-23 and full team levels, he appeared in over 400 games for Albion plus another 100 for the Central League side, scoring 17 goals. He had the pleasure of claiming the club's first ever goal in a European Cup competition against DOS Utrecht in Holland in season 1966–67. For Albion, the Blues and Wednesday, Hope made a total of 407 League appearances and claimed 45 goals. In all matches, including his spell in the NASL, he accumulated in excess of 525 outings and netted 60 times. He was only 16 years of age when he made his Albion debut against Arsenal (home) in

the First Division in April 1960 (won 1–0).

HOPKINS, Robert

Midfield: 92+2 apps. 12 goals.

Born: Hall Green, Birmingham, 25 October 1961.

Career: Pitmaston School. South Birmingham Schools (playing in English Schools Trophy). West Midlands County Boys. Aston Villa (apprentice, July 1977, professional, July 1979). Birmingham City (March 1983, in exchange for Alan Curbishley). Manchester City (£130,000, September 1986). ALBION (£60,000, October 1986, exchange deal involving

under him at Villa and with the Blues. He occasionally got himself into trouble with the officials but his temper eventually calmed down! He captained Villa's youth team to victory in the Southern junior Floodlit Cup final and was also a member of Villa's FA Youth Cup winning side in the same season (1979–80). He helped the Blues gain promotion to the First Division in 1985. He amassed well over 250 appearances during his professional career and scored on his Albion debut against Grimsby Town (home) in Division Two in October 1986 (1–1 draw). He also had four games for the Baggies in the Central League, scoring one goal.

HORNE, Henry Leslie

Centre-half: 16 apps.

Born: Netherton, Dudley, 2 May 1925.
Died: Dudley, February 1986.
Career: Northfield Road School Netherton. Netherton Wayfarers FC. Thompson's Works side, Dudley. Herman Smith's FC (1943). ALBION (amateur, December 1944, professional, April 1948). Plymouth Argyle (£1,650, June 1952). Walsall (November 1954). Bedford Town (August 1955). Cradley Heath (September 1956, retired, May 1957). Worked locally until his death.

■ Les Horne, with his flaming red hair, was a useful stopper centre-half, as hard as nails, tireless, tenacious in the tackle and ever-reliable. He was Jack Vernon's understudy at The Hawthorns and during his six-year stay as a 'pro' he made 16 first-team appearances, his first coming against Liverpool (home) in Division One in October 1949. He also scored three goals in 142 Central League appearances before going on to make 52 in the League for the Saddlers, eventually drifting into non-League football in 1955.

HOROBIN, Roy

Outside-left: 67 apps. 8 goals.

Born: Brownhills, 10 March 1935.
Career: Brownhills and Walsall Wood Schools. Erdington Albion. Walsall Wood FC (1949). ALBION (amateur, June 1950,

professional, October 1952). Notts County (£4,000, November 1958). Peterborough United (£5,000, June 1962). Crystal Palace (July 1964). Weymouth (October 1965–cs 1967). ALBION (October 1972 as youth team assistant, later youth development officer 1973–86). Chelsea (scout, 1987–88). Derby County (scout, 1989–91). Now living in Sutton Coldfield.

■ Roy Horobin was a useful winger who chose the number11 shirt in preference to the number 7. He had an effervescent style laced with a touch of dash and vigour. He had a good eye for goal and created many goalscoring opportunities for his colleagues. He took over from George Lee at Albion but then lost his place to Derek Hogg and subsequently left The Hawthorns for pastures new, serving in turn with Notts County (123 League appearances, 37 goals), Peterborough (80 games, 20 goals) and Palace (four outings), helping Notts County gain promotion from the Fourth

Division in 1959–60. His Albion debut was against Cardiff City (away) in Division One in March 1956. And he also scored six goals in 63 Central League games for the club.

HORSFIELD, Geoffrey Malcolm

Striker: 41+12 apps. 11 goals.

Born: Barnsley, 11 November 1973.
Career: Scarborough (apprentice, April 1990, professional, July 1992). Halifax Town (free, March 1994). Witton Albion (May 1995). Halifax Town (free, May 1997). Fulham (£325,000, October 1998). Birmingham City (£2 million, July 2000). Wigan Athletic (£1 million, July 2003). ALBION (£1 million, December 2003).

■ An all-action striker, signed on a two-and-a-half-year contract to bolster up Albion's flagging attack, Geoff Horsfield, nicknamed 'the horse', had already scored over 70 goals in some 250 first-team

matches (including a couple against Albion for the Blues and Wigan) before moving to The Hawthorns. He made his debut for the Baggies in the Midlands derby against Coventry City 48 hours after signing, and he scored his first goal in a 2–0 home win over Walsall three weeks later. Able to play in midfield (if required) and indeed as an emergency full-back, he is strong and forceful, holds the ball up well and isn't at all afraid to throw his weight around when challenging the toughest defenders in the League. He was a Conference winner with Halifax in 1988, a Second Division championship winner with Fulham in 1999, he helped the Blues reach the Premiership in 2001 and then, after his move to The Hawthorns, played a massive part in helping Albion regain their Premiership status in 2004. Horsfield has already played in five different divisions of top-flight football – the Premiership, League Divisions One, Two and Three and the Conference.

HORTON, Ezra

Right-half: 83 apps. 1 goal.

Born: West Bromwich, 20 August 1861.
Died: West Bromwich, July 1939.
Career: Christ Church & Beeches Road Schools West Bromwich, George Salter Works FC, West Bromwich FC (1880). ALBION (amateur, August 1882, professional, August 1885). Guest for Port Vale (September 1884). Aston Villa (guest, March–April 1885). Retired, June 1891. Subsequently became a referee (1895) and in later years turned out for the West Bromwich Hockey team as a centre-half and became only the second Midlander to represent England at his sport.

■ As a footballer 'Ezra' Horton, nicknamed 'Ironsides', was a very sporting player, a largely defensive right-half who was good at heading, strong with his kicking and fearsome in the tackle, hence his nickname! He played in three successive FA Cup finals for Albion (1886–88) being a 'winner' in the latter against Preston North End. He skippered Albion in 1884–85 and had the distinction of playing in each of the club's first 36 FA Cup ties. In fact, Horton played in Albion's first ever FA Cup tie, his senior debut against Wednesbury Town (home) in November 1883, and in the club's first ever Football League

match, against Stoke (away) in September 1888, being one of only two players to do so. He actually played his first game for the club against St George's (away) in September 1882. In all, he appeared in more than 350 matches for the 'Throstles' (all competitions, including local cup-ties and friendlies) during his nine-year association with the club.
* Ezra's brother, John Horton, was also a member of Albion's first XI, and they played together on many occasions.

HORTON, John Henry

Full-back: 152 apps.

Born: West Bromwich, 21 February 1866.
Died: West Bromwich, January 1947.
Career: Dartmouth School (West Bromwich). Oak Villa. Burslem Port Vale (1880–81). Wednesbury Old Athletic (1881–82). ALBION (amateur, November 1882, professional, September 1885, retired, May 1899, took charge of Albion's reserves for a time). Later a licensee in West Bromwich and also worked in a warehouse.

■ A schoolteacher by profession, 'Jack' Horton was a grand full-back who could never be faulted when it came to resolute tackling and clearing his line, which he did in fine style. A magnificent clubman – 17 years with Albion – he chalked up over 300 appearances for the Throstles (all competitions, including local cup ties and friendlies). He made his senior debut against Wednesbury Old Athletic (home) in the FA Cup second round in December 1884 and was right-back in Albion's first ever League match four years later, against Stoke in September 1888. During his long association with the club he was never critical of the way it was run. In 1895 he played in the FA Cup final against Aston Villa after missing all the previous rounds. During his playing days, he filled in as a half-back and as an emergency centre-forward, but all his best footballing was done from the two full-back positions, where he excelled on many occasions, perhaps being somewhat unlucky not to gain England international honours. Brother of Ezra Horton, he was a supporter of Albion right up until the day he died, the last game he attended at The Hawthorns being the Second Division match between Albion and Swansea on 28 December 1946.

HOULT, Russell

Goalkeeper: 195 apps.

Born: Ashby-de-la-Zouch, 22 November 1972.
Career: Leicester City (apprentice, April 1989, professional, March 1991). Lincoln City (on loan, August–September 1991). Blackpool (on loan, October 1991). Bolton Wanderers (on loan, November 1993). Lincoln City (on loan, August–October 1994). Derby County (£300,000, February 1995). Portsmouth (£300,000, January 2000). ALBION (£500,000, January 2001).

■ Goalkeeper Russell Hoult set two new Albion club records during the 2001–02 season: 27 clean-sheets (24 in the Nationwide League) and blanking out his opponents in seven successive games in January and February. Cool, composed and a terrific shot-stopper, he certainly had a wonderful campaign as the Baggies leapt into the Premiership ahead of their arch-rivals, Wolves. He was voted Albion's 'Player of the Season' and was also included in the PFA's Division One side, being rated as the best 'custodian' outside the Premiership at the time. After failing to establish himself at Filbert Street, he made 138 appearances for Derby and made his Albion debut in the League home game against his former club Portsmouth in February 2001, taking over from the Dane Brian Jensen. Voted 'Midland Footballer of the Year' in November 2002, he was in line for an England call-up during the season that David Seaman was out injured, but Sven Goran Eriksson preferred David James instead. Hoult performed well again in 2003–04 (despite a niggling back injury) and conceded only 39 goals in 44 League games as the Baggies regained their Premiership status.

* Hoult became only the second Albion goalkeeper to be sent off in a senior, competitive game when he was dismissed for a professional foul during the Premiership game against Liverpool at Anfield in September 2002. England international Joe Reader, dismissed against Bolton Wanderers (away) in a League encounter in April 1895, is the other 'keeper.

HOWARTH, Nelson

Wing-half: 63 apps. 2 goals.

Born: Irlam o'th' Heights near Eccles, Lancs, April 1905.
Died: c.1970.
Career: Hollinwood & Tilstock Schools. Urmston Old Boys FC (1920). Bolton Wanderers (professional, May 1922). ALBION (£600, July 1926, retired through injury, April 1929). Returned to the game in January 1931 to play with Runcorn after receiving the sum of £341 from the FA Player's Union Management Committee on his initial retirement. Loughborough Corinthians (September 1931–August 1932). Later employed as an office clerk.

■ Nelson Howarth was a dogged left-half, not flashy but clever at breaking up attacks and supplying his forwards with seductive passes. He was part of the Bolton Wanderers squads for the 1923 and 1926 FA Cup finals, and, in all, played 35 times for the Trotters in his four seasons at Burnden Park. He made his Albion debut against Sunderland (home) in Division One in August 1926. He also played in 18 Central League games in 1927–28.

HOWE, Donald

Right-back: 379 apps. 19 goals.

Born: Springfield, Wolverhampton, 12 October 1935.
Career: St Peter's School Wolverhampton. Wolverhampton & District Boys. Wolverhampton Wanderers (trialist, September–October 1950). ALBION (December 1950, professional, November 1952). Arsenal (£40,000, April 1964, retired, May 1967, through injury, to become coach at Highbury, then appointed assistant manager, 1969). ALBION

(manager, July 1971–April 1975). Galatasary, Turkey (coach, May 1975). Leeds United (coach, October 1975–June 1977). Arsenal (coach, August 1977, then manager, December 1983–March 1986). England 'B' team coach/assistant manager (January 1978–June 1982). England chief coach (June 1982–89, including World Cups of 1982 and 1986). Saudi Arabia (coach, 1986–87). Bristol Rovers (part-time coach, July 1987). Wimbledon (assistant manager/coach, August 1987–July 1989). Queen's Park Rangers (assistant manager, July 1989, manager/coach, November 1989–May 1991). Wimbledon (coach, May–October 1991). Barnet (coach, briefly, 1991). Coventry City (manager, January–July 1992). Chelsea (coach/assistant manager, July 1992). Covered Italian Serie 'A' football for Channel 4. Arsenal (youth team coach/advisor while also FA Technical Adviser/coaching – the latter from January 1993). Still associated with Arsenal (Technical Adviser in 2003). Now living in Hertfordshire.

■ Deft positioning, reliability and strength in kicking and acumen were generally the hallmarks of Don Howe's overall play at the right-back for Albion and, indeed, for England. Although in later years he did occupy the number 4 and number 8 shirts for the Throstles, it was as an attacking full-back that he

became such a fine footballer, winning a total of 23 caps for his country, consecutively, from October 1957 to November 1959. He took over the number 2 shirt from Welshman Stuart Williams at The Hawthorns in August 1955, making his debut (with Derek Kevan) against Everton (home) in the First Division. He established himself in the side before the end of the year and once in he remained put, going on to amass well over 370 senior appearances (plus 43 in the second XI) in a long association with the club. He was also honoured by his country at under-23 level, he represented the England 'B' team and played for the Football League side and the FA XI in 1956 and 1962, touring New Zealand with the FA party in 1961. When with Arsenal (signed incidentally by one of his boyhood heroes, Billy Wright), he fractured his right leg in March 1966 and sadly the injury ended his career. He became coach at Highbury and saw Arsenal lift the coveted League and cup double in 1971. He came back to The Hawthorns as team manager in 1971, but disaster struck two years later as Albion slumped into the Second Division for the first time since 1949. Perhaps Don's best signing while he was boss at Albion was that of Scottish international winger Willie Johnston from Rangers for a then club record fee of £138,000. When he returned to Arsenal, he coached the Gunners to three successive FA Cup finals in 1978, 1979 and 1980. He was coach with Wimbledon for their 1988 FA Cup final victory over Liverpool, when ex-Albion winger Laurie Cunningham was in the Dons side, managed by former Baggies forward and future boss Bobby Gould.

* Howe was awarded a Honorary Fellowship at Wolverhampton University in 2001.

HOWSHALL, Gerald Thomas

Wing-half: 43 apps. 3 goals.

Born: Stoke-on-Trent, 27 October 1944.
Career: Thursham United. Newton Abbot Schools. Torbay & Brixham Boys. Plymouth Argyle (amateur, April 1959). ALBION (amateur, August 1960, professional, May 1962). Norwich City (£25,000, October 1967). Nuneaton Borough (June 1971). Weymouth (August

1973). Cork Athletic (August 1975, retired, May 1977). Now living in the West Country.

■ Gerry Howshall's play certainly matched his flame-coloured hair. He was a wing-half who could also play at inside-right and a player who was totally committed to soccer, being relentless in the tackle, forcible in attack and sound in defending. He spent five years as a 'pro' at The Hawthorns, making his League debut against Aston Villa (away) in October 1964, and had to contest a first-team place with the likes of Bobby Cram, Chuck Drury, Ron Bradley, Duggie Fraser, Terry Simpson and Graham Lovett. He managed just over 40 senior outings and in each game he gave 101 percent effort. He also netted 10 goals in 102 Central League games before leaving Albion for Norwich City, for whom he played 43 times prior to entering non-League football, first with Nuneaton and then with Weymouth. He finished his playing days with the Irish club Cork Athletic before a knee injury forced him to retire in 1977. Howshall's father played for Southport and his uncle, for Stoke City.

HOYLAND, Ernest

Outside-right: 1 app.

Born: Thurnscoe near Rotherham, 17 January 1914.
Died: Pembrokeshire, Dyfed, 1988.
Career: Thurnscoe & Rotherham District

Schools, South Yorkshire Boys, Lincoln City (trialist, August 1936). Halifax Town (professional, December 1936). Blackpool (£100, February 1938). Albion (£350, May 1938). Lincoln City (£500, May 1939 with Jack Rix). Grantham (March 1946 in exchange for Jack Earnshaw). Retired, May 1946, but later returned to play for Haverford West and Milford United. Also a fine cricketer with Pembrokeshire CC. Served in the Army during World War Two.*

■ Ernie Hoyland was a well-built right-winger with good acceleration over short distances. Unfortunately, injury plagued him throughout his career and he quit the game with less than 20 senior outings to his credit. He made his League debut for Albion against Newcastle United (away) in Division Two in September 1938. He also netted five times in 17 Central League games.

HUCKER, Ian Peter

Goalkeeper: 7 apps.

Born: Hampstead, London, 28 October 1959.
Career: London & District Schools. Queen's Park Rangers (apprentice, July 1976, professional, July 1977). Oxford United (£100,000, April 1987). ALBION (on loan, January–March 1988). Manchester United (on loan, two spells, October 1988 and February 1989). Millwall, Aldershot (1990–91). Later a milkman and then ran a coaching School for youngsters in Wanstead, London (from June 2000).

■ A former England under-21 international, Peter Hucker gained a Second Division championship medal with Queen's Park Rangers in 1983, a year after appearing in the FA Cup final against Tottenham Hotspur, after thwarting Albion at Highbury in the semis. In 1986 he missed out in the Milk Cup final against Oxford United, former Albion 'keeper Paul Barron donning the green jersey. He joined Albion on loan after chalking up almost 200 competitive appearances for Rangers and Oxford. His debut for the Baggies was against Leeds United (home) in Division Two in January 1988.

HUGHES, Byron Wayne

Utility player: 3+5 apps. 2 goals.

Born: Port Talbot, 8 March 1958.
Career: Port Talbot & Maesteg Schools. Neath Boys' Club. Brinton Ferry FC. Leeds United (trialist). Everton (trialist). Manchester City (trialist, February–March 1976). Albion (apprentice, July 1974, professional, March 1976). Cardiff City (October 1979). Yeovil Town (July 1982). Played in the NASL with Tulsa Roughnecks (January 1979–September 1979, Albion receiving £50,000). Retired to become a pub landlord in Swansea, then a hotelier in Blackpool. Later Blackpool Mechanics FC (manager, North West Counties League). Also coached and played for Broomfield Veterans (Blackpool). Now a Social Worker in Leyland, Lancashire.

■ Wayne Hughes was a tall, blonde utility player, able to fulfil any 'outfield' position but in England preferred a midfield role. During his spell in the NASL, he was converted into a dashing centre-forward by the former Derby County and England winger Alan Hinton, and immediately created a new record by scoring a hat-trick of penalties against Dallas Tornados. While a Yeovil player he was in the same side as Ian Botham! Capped by Wales at youth and under-21 levels, he played almost 50 first-team games for Cardiff and won an FA Youth Cup winners' medal with Albion in 1976. Related to Emlyn Hughes (ex-Liverpool captain), he made his debut for Albion against Aston Villa (away) in Division One in May 1977 as a substitute. He also played in 112 Central League games (11 goals scored).

HUGHES, Lee Brett

Striker: 192+45 apps. 98 goals.

*Born: Smethwick, 22 May 1976.
Career: Bustleholme Boys & Charlemont
Boys, West Bromwich. Forest Falcons,
Stourbridge. Fresher FC, Oldbury (1990).
ALBION (trialist, March 1991). Walsall
(schoolboy forms, May–August 1991).
Oldbury United (August 1992).
Wolverhampton Wanderers (trialist, July
1993). Sheffield Wednesday (trialist,
August 1993). Kidderminster Harriers
(September 1993). ALBION (£250,000,
May 1997). Coventry City (£5 million +
£1, August 2001). ALBION (£2.5 million,
August 2002, contract cancelled, August*
*2004), Featherstone Prison FC (during
season 2004–05).*

■ Striker Lee Hughes – to the delight of
'thousands' of supporters – rejoined
Albion for a club record fee shortly after
the start of the 2002–03 Premiership
season. But annoyingly, not only for the
player himself but for the fans and indeed
his manager, he failed to score a single
goal in the top-flight, his only strike
coming in a poor Worthington Cup
defeat at Wigan. Nicknamed 'Ginger-
Ninja' and the 'Balti-kid', Hughes, at one
time a labourer on a building site, won
four semi-professional England caps
during his days at Aggborough when his

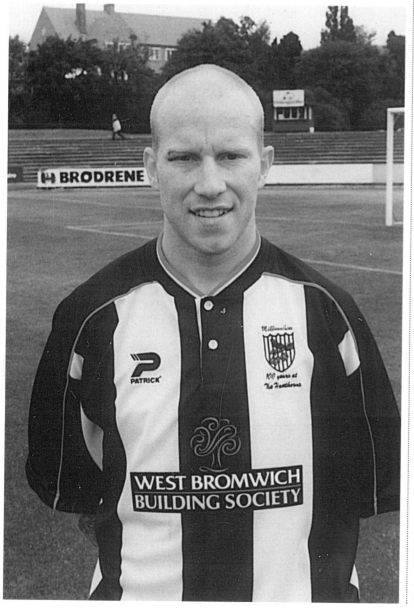

goal scoring feats made him a huge
favourite with the fans. In fact, as soon as
he set foot inside The Hawthorns the
Baggies supporters quickly made him
their hero too. He made his League debut
as a 'sub' against Tranmere Rovers
(home) on the opening day of the
1997–98 season and netted twice in his
next game, a 3–2 win at Crewe. He ended
his first full season with 14 goals to his
name and added 32 to his total in
1998–99, followed by another 16 the next
season. He found the net 85 times in 177
first-team matches in four seasons before
his big-money move to Highfield Road,
bitterly disappointed that Albion had lost
their end-season play-off semi-final to
Bolton Wanderers. Like scores of other
footballers, he desperately wanted to play
in the Premiership… and he duly made
his debut in the 'top flight' a year later,
for Albion against Fulham just a couple
of days after returning 'home'. Positive in
his approach with an eye for goal, he
admits his first touch isn't brilliant, but
he certainly knows where the framework
of the goal is, and, after his worst-ever
season as a professional, he bounced back
in style in 2003–04 by netting 12 more
goals, while helping the Baggies regain
their Premiership status. He also played
in 15 second XI games for the club (4
goals scored). Unfortunately, in August
2004 Hughes's career as a Premiership,
and indeed an Albion, footballer ended
abruptly when he was sentenced to six
years' imprisonment for causing death by
dangerous driving. The accident occurred
in Warwickshire on 22 November 2003
when his £100,000 Mercedes sportscar
crashed into a Renault Scenic. Hughes left
the scene of the accident and did not give
himself up to the police for 34 hours,
knowing that if he had remained with his
car he would have been breathalysed. He
was subsequently charged, bailed and
then found guilty at Coventry Crown
Court. As well as his gaol sentence,
Hughes was also banned from driving for
10 years, having received an 18-month
ban for drink-driving when he was an
18-year-old. He played for Featherstone
Prison FC, scored on his debut and was
later sent off and suspended for four
months (to the end of the campaign).
* Hughes's Christian name, Brett, comes
from Brett Maverick, his father's favourite
cowboy.

HUGHES, Lyndon James

Wing-half: 116 + 9 apps. 4 goals.

Born: Smethwick, 16 September 1950.
Career: Holly Lodge Grammar School (Smethwick). Smethwick & District Boys, ALBION (associated-schoolboy, September 1964, apprentice, July 1966, professional, January 1968). Peterborough United (£1,500, May 1975). Kettering Town (free, May 1978). Bromsgrove Rovers (seasons 1980–82). Later worked in Birmingham and now lives in Shirley near Solihull.

■ A former England schoolboy and youth international who went on to put into his play some grim determination as a wing-half, Lyndon Hughes could also occupy an inside-forward role. He didn't quite live up to his schoolboy promise but during his League career (with Albion and Posh) he accumulated a total of 175 appearances, scoring eight goals. Having made his Albion debut as a substitute against Queen's Park Rangers (home) in Division One in October 1968, he played with only one kidney for 20 years. He also scored 18 goals in 166 Central League games.

HULSE, Robert William

Striker: 35+11 apps. 13 goals.

Born: Crewe, 25 October 1979.
Career: Crewe Alexandra (apprentice, April 1996, professional, June 1998). ALBION (£800,000+, July 2003). Leeds United (on loan, March–May 2005, signed permanently for £1m, June 2005).

■ A 6ft 1in, 11st 4lb striker, Rob Hulse was nurtured through the ranks under the shrewd guidance of manager Dario Gradi at Gresty Road and over a period of four years scored 52 goals in 131 first-team games for Crewe, finishing up as leading marksman in successive seasons, 2001–03, as well as being voted into the PFA Second Division team for 2002–03. Chased by one or two big-name clubs, Hulse was eventually snapped up by Baggies boss Gary Megson following the transfer request by Jason Roberts. A hard-working player with an eye for goal, he made his senior debut for Albion in the League game at Walsall in August 2003 and netted 12 goals before Christmas, but then after being sent off at Burnley in early January he lost his form and his place (following Geoff Horsfield's arrival), although, in truth, he did play his part in helping the Baggies regain their Premiership status at the end of the season, finishing up as the club's top scorer. Hulse's father played for Stoke City and Nantwich Victoria in the 1960s.
* Hulse was the first player to join Albion on a direct transfer from Crewe for 52 years, since David Mountford's switch to The Hawthorns in 1951.

HUMPAGE, William Leonard Frederick

Goalkeeper: 4 apps.

Born: Balsall Heath, Birmingham, 12 February 1870.
Died: Birmingham, April 1936.
Career: Edward Road School. Coles Farm Unity. Wednesbury Juniors. Wednesbury Old Athletic (1891). ALBION (professional, August 1893). Hereford Thistle (free, May 1896, retired, May 1900). Became an engineer and served as an Army mechanic during World War One.

■ Len Humpage was a reliable goalkeeper, who spent most of his three years with Albion languishing in the reserves. A solid man, with good reflexes and large hands, capable of picking up the ball single-handed, he was Joe Reader's deputy and made his senior debut against Preston North End (away) in Division One in March 1894. He also played in seven 'other' first-team matches.

HUNT, Andrew

Striker: 228+12 apps. 85 goals.

Born: Thurrock, Essex, 9 June 1970.
Career: Ashill FC. Kings Lynn (August 1989). Kettering Town (August 1990). Newcastle United (£210,000, January 1991). ALBION (on loan, March 1993, signed for £100,000, May 1993). Charlton Athletic (free, July 1998, retired through illness, April 2000). Moved to Sanignacio, Belize to live and work (forming is own export business, The Green Dragon Company). Played for Banana Bank FC, Belize (summer 2002). Charlton Athletic (briefly, November 2003–January 2004). Returned to Belize and assisted Belmopan Bandits and Banana Bank again.

■ Andy Hunt, a tall, lean but alert and competent striker, scored a hat-trick on his Hawthorns debut for Albion against Brighton in March 1993 and proved inspirational (alongside Bob Taylor) as the Baggies surged on towards promotion that season. Hunt, in fact, netted the crucial opening goal in the play-off final at Wembley when Port Vale were defeated 3–0 as Ossie Ardiles' side clinched a place in the

First Division. Formerly a centre-half, Hunt developed into a willing front-runner who never gave up the ghost. He notched 13 goals in 51 games for the Magpies and then proceeded to hit the net regularly for Albion, claiming a goal every three games at senior level, as well as netting 12 times in 14 games for the second XI, before a 'Bosman' free transfer took him to Charlton in 1998, much to the disgust of hundreds of Baggies supporters! He did very well, it must be said, at The Valley and before he was forced to quit through illness in 2000, he bagged 32 goals in 86 outings for the London club. Hunt now lives in a seven-bedroomed wooden dome on the banks of a jungle river in Belize, Central America, where he and his girlfriend keep chickens and grow vegetables – a far cry from playing for Albion and keeping the fans happy by scoring goals!

HUNT, Stephen Kenneth

Midfield: 84 apps. 20 goals.

Born: Perry Barr, Birmingham, 4 August 1956.
Career: Yew Tree Infants & Junior Schools. Aston & Witton Boys. Warwickshire Schoolboys. Stanley Star (1971). Aston Villa (apprentice, July 1972, professional, January 1974). New York Cosmos, NASL (£50,000, February 1977, Coventry City (£40,000, August 1978). New York Cosmos (on loan, May 1982). ALBION (£80,000, March 1984). Aston Villa (£90,000 plus Darren Bradley, March 1986, retired with knee injury, May 1988). Willenhall Town (manager, June 1988). Port Vale (youth-team coach, July 1989, then community officer, June 1990). Leicester City (youth coach, 1991–92). VS Rugby Town (manager, 1994–95). AP Leamington (manager, 1996–97). Hinckley Town (coach, 1997–99). Bembridge FC, Isle of Wight (coach, 2003–05).

■ An energetic, hard-working, purposeful midfielder with a fine left foot, Steve Hunt gave his three Midland clubs excellent service. After starting his professional career with Aston Villa, he moved into the NASL with New York Cosmos, returning to England to sign for Coventry in 1979. A further spell in the NASL with the Cosmos preceded his transfer to The Hawthorns (signed by manager Johnny Giles), and, after winning two full England caps, he returned to Villa Park for what was to be

his last season in League football. He made a total of 79 senior appearances for Villa (nine goals scored) and had the misfortune to play in successive relegation teams (Albion in 1986, Villa in 1987). In his first spell in the NASL, Hunt, playing alongside Pele and Franz Beckenbauer, helped Cosmos win two Super Bowl titles, in 1977 and 1978, and was voted 'The Most Valuable Player' in the former competition. He made 216 appearances for Coventry (34 goals) and certain supporters believe that he would have become one of the Sky Blues' all-time greats if he had decided to stay at Highfield Road! He later did reasonably well as a manager in non-League football. He made his Baggies debut against Tottenham Hotspur in March 1984, and at the end of the season he became the Albion player with the least number of appearances under his belt (12) to win a full international cap when he lined up against Scotland in the Home International championship encounter at Hampden Park. Also in the England side were two future Albion players (Graeme Roberts and Luther Blissett) and a past one (Bryan Robson). He won a second cap a week later, again as a 'sub', against the USSR. In all his international career he lasted only 49 minutes!

HUNTER, Roy Ian

Midfielder/defender: 7+7 apps. 1 goal.

Born: Middlesbrough, 29 October 1973.
Career: ALBION (apprentice, April 1990,

professional, March 1992). Northampton Town (free, August 1995). Nuneaton Borough (July 2002). Oxford United (October 2002). Hucknall Town (June 2003). Northwich Victoria (August 2004).

■ A reserve midfielder at The Hawthorns, Roy Hunter scored on his League debut for Albion as a 'sub' to earn a 1–0 home win over Torquay United in February 1992. He also appeared in more than 80 Central League games (7 goals), and later made over 200 senior appearances for Northampton Town.

HURST, Sir Geoffrey Charles, MBE

Striker: 12 apps. 2 goals.
Born: Ashton-Under-Lyne, 8 December 1941.
Career: Kings Road Secondary School, Chelmsford. Chelmsford Schools Select. Halstead FC (August 1955). Chelmsford City (January 1957). West Ham United (amateur, July 1957, professional, April 1959). Stoke City (£80,000, June 1972). Cape Town City (guest, summer 1973). ALBION (£20,000, August 1975). Cork Celtic (guest, 1976). Seattle Sounders, NASL (free, February 1976). Telford United (player-manager, March 1976–May 1977). Appointed England under-21 coach/manager (September 1977). Full England team assistant coach (January 1978–June 1982). Chelsea (coach, May 1979, appointed manager, October 1979–April 1981). Al-Kuwait (coach, 1982–May 1984). Currently sales director of Motorplan, Essex.

■ Already a household name in England following his unique hat-trick at Wembley against West Germany, which helped England lift the World Cup in 1966, Geoff Hurst was signed as an experienced striker, by manager Johnny Giles, as Albion sought to gain promotion from the Second Division. He made his debut for the Baggies against Chelsea (home) in August 1975, and, besides his senior outings, he also played in seven second XI games. As a youngster, he started out as a wing-half but quickly turned himself into a big, strong, powerful striker, full of heart, thoroughly unselfish and a player able to score goals, which he did out of nothing at regular intervals and all levels. He topped West Ham's scoring charts on six separate occasions, between 1962–63 and 1979–70, with a best season tally of 29. He netted six goals against luckless Sunderland in a First Division match in 1968, and, all told, during his 15 years' association with the Hammers Hurst appeared in 411 League matches and scored 180 goals. He gained 49 England caps (24 goals) and also played in six youth internationals, four under-23 games and seven Inter-League matches. Besides winning a Word Cup medal in 1966, he also collected medals in the FA Cup final of 1964 and the European Cup-winners' Cup final of 1965, as well as receiving a League Cup runners'-up medal (against Albion) in 1966. During season 1966–67 Hurst performed the feat of scoring a hat-trick in the First Division, FA Cup, League Cup and World Cup. In his younger days he was a useful county cricketer, having one game for Essex against Lancashire, but instead of becoming a prolific run-maker or wicket-taker, he opted to reach the top as a prolific goalscorer. During his long illustrious career, Hurst found the back of his opponent's net no fewer than 296 times in a total of 716 competitive matches (for West Ham, Stoke, Albion, Seattle and Cork Celtic). Quite a record for a very fine player.

HUTCHINSON, Thomas

Centre-forward: 58 apps. 21 goals.

Born: Glasgow, 20 June 1872.
Died: Cheshire, 1933.
Career: Rutherglen & Paisley Schools. Gowan FC. Stockton. Whitfield FC (1889). Darlington (professional, August 1891). Newcastle United (October 1893). Nelson (January 1894). ALBION (£50, July 1894). Stockport County (free, July 1896, retired through injury, May 1897). Returned with Ellesmere Port (1899, retired again, 1904).

■ Tommy Hutchinson was a powerful centre-forward, good in the air, able on

the ground and steady in overall performance. He was a reserve at Newcastle and a second-team player with Nelson but as soon as he joined Albion, as a replacement for Bastock, he began to prove his worth and scored consistently during his three seasons with them, also playing in the 1895 FA Cup final against Aston Villa. In November 1895 he was omitted from Albion's first XI because of a court appearance, which brought him a fine for being drunk and disorderly. He was in trouble again for breaches of training rules between January and March 1896 and was released soon afterwards. He had made his Albion debut against Sheffield United (away) in Division One in September 1894, and, besides his senior record, he also played in over 30 'other' first-team games for the club, having the pleasure of scoring the winning goal v Aston Villa in the 1895 Birmingham Senior Cup final.

INAMOTO, Junichi

Midfield: 0+3 apps.

Born: Kagoshima, Japan, 18 September 1979.
Career: Gamba Osaka, Japan (professional, April 1997). Arsenal (on loan, July–October 2001). Fulham (on loan, July 2002–May 2004). ALBION (on loan, plus £200,000, July 2004). Cardiff City (on loan, December 2004–February 2005).

■ Japanese international Junichi Inamoto, who has won over 60 caps for his country, some as captain, made four appearances for Arsenal before scoring 9 times in 58 outings for Fulham, including a goal on his debut against Middlesbrough and the winner against Manchester United. An industrious player, able to occupy central or wide positions, he starred with Kanu at Highbury but unfortunately broke his leg playing for Japan against England at The City of Manchester Stadium in June 2004 and took time to recover. He didn't figure in Albion's plans immediately, finally making his debut for the club as a 'sub' in the 1–1 Premiership draw at Tottenham in April 2005. He has also played in eight second XI games.

INWOOD, Gordon Frederick

Outside-left: 12 apps. 1 goal.
Born: Kislingbury, Northants, 18 June 1928.

Career: Kislingbury & Rothersthorpe Schools. Rushden Town (August 1945). ALBION (£300, semi-professional, November 1946, full professional, January 1949). Hull City (£1,500, May 1950). Kettering Town (free, August 1952, retired May 1955).

■ Gordon Inwood played outside-left all his life. He exhibited qualities of smartness off the mark and good, close ball control, but perhaps lacked that extra bit of determination to reach the top. He was George Lee's deputy at Albion and made his Baggies debut against Wolverhampton Wanderers (away) in Division One in October 1949. He also played in 31 Central League games.

JACK, Walter Robert

Centre-forward: 26 apps. 13 goals.

Born: Grangemouth, Scotland, 17 November 1874.
Died: May 1936.
Career: Grangemouth & Bo'ness Schools. Marshall Boy's Club (1892). Leith Athletic (1896). Bristol Rovers (April 1902). ALBION (May 1904). Clyde (manager, July 1905–May 1909).

■ Walter Jack was an orthodox centre-forward, whose heading was first rate and shooting, spot-on. He spent just one season at The Hawthorns, scoring a goal every two games – a record he maintained to a certain degree throughout his playing career. He could also play in many other positions, including right-back, centre-half and outside-right, but leader of the attack was by far his best slot. In April 1905 he was suspended by the Albion directors for misconduct and was subsequently released. He made his debut for the club against Burnley (away) in Division Two in September 1904.
* Walter was the brother of Robert Jack, who was born in Alloa, Scotland, in 1876 and played, in turn, for Alloa Athletic, Bolton Wanderers, Preston North End, Glossop, Burslem Port Vale and Plymouth Argyle, between 1893 and 1905. He then managed Argyle for one season and Southend United for four before returning to Argyle for a second spell in charge in 1910, and remained in office until April 1938. He became a Player's Union Executive member on 1901 and died in May 1943. He recommended Walter to Clyde in 1905.

JACKMAN, Clive Edward James

Goalkeeper: 21 apps.

Born: Aldershot, 21 March 1936.

Career: Aldershot & Farnham Schools. Hampshire County Schools. Hampshire Youths. Aldershot (amateur, April 1951, professional, May 1953). ALBION (£1,000, June 1957, retired, June 1960 with serious back injury, initially received in 1958). Later worked for an insurance company and then earned a living in the clock and watch business, based in Hampshire.

■ Clive Jackman made his first-team debut for Aldershot as a 15-year-old schoolboy in 1951, his League baptism came somewhat later in season 1952–53 (Division Three South). He came to Albion shortly after another ex-Aldershot 'keeper, Fred Brown, but he did not replace Brown between the sticks, it was, in fact, veteran 'keeper Jimmy Sanders, after the Cockney had agreed to join Coventry City in the close season of 1958. A fine 'keeper, ideally built, he made his Albion debut against Portsmouth (away) in Division One in March 1958. Often brilliant in the reserve team, making 28 Central League appearances, he played in 21 consecutive League games for the Baggies before suffering a career-ending spinal injury in the Midlands derby against Aston Villa (away) in October 1958. He was only 24 years of age and in excellent form at the time, destined for bigger and better things, but just when it seemed as if he was establishing himself among the top 10 'keepers in Division One, tragedy struck. He played 38 League matches for Aldershot.

JACKSON, Alec

Winger/Inside-forward: 208 apps. 52 goals.

Born: Tipton, 29 May 1937.

Career: Park Lane Secondary Modern School (Tipton). Tipton St John's FC. W.G. Allen's FC. ALBION (amateur, May 1954, professional, September 1954). Birmingham City (£12,500, June 1964). Walsall (£1,250, February 1967). Nuneaton Borough (August 1968). Kidderminster Harriers (May 1970). Warley (1971–72). Oldbury Town (1972). Warley Borough, Darlaston (1973). Blakenhall (1974). Lower Gornal (1976). Rushall Olympic (1978). Bush Rangers (1979–80). Also assisted West Bromwich Albion All Stars (1968–85). Acted as coach to Coseley Rovers Youth Club (1980–82). Worked for Hinchliffe's (West Bromwich) for many years, now retired, living in Tipton.

■ Alec Jackson was a plucky little utility forward, fleet of foot and able to perform in any position with a great deal of success. He was a brilliant dribbler (at times) and he had a pretty useful shot. 'Jacko' chose the right-wing spot as his best choice position and it proved to be just so. He represented the Football League against the Scottish League at Villa Park in 1962, wearing the number 7 jersey, his only 'honour'. The youngest-ever player to score a League goal for Albion – obliging on his debut in a 3–1 win over Charlton Athletic at The Valley in Division One in November 1954, when he was 17 years, five months and eight days old – 'Jacko' was still playing regularly in Charity matches in 1985, aged 48. He scored, on average, a goal every four

outings for Albion, a fine record. He also bagged 30 in 135 Central League games, and, during his professional career, (with Albion, the Blues and Walsall), he amassed a grand total of 307 League appearances and netted 67 goals. He became a permanent fixture in Albion's senior side in the 1959–60 season and was an ever-present in 1961–2. In 1958, playing against Spurs at White Hart Lane in a League game, Jackson broke his leg, but he recovered quickly and served Albion, all told, for 10 full seasons. He is a very enthusiastic gardener.

JACKSON, William Hiekin

Centre-forward: 3 apps.

Born: Oldbury, 11 July 1894.
Died: France, May 1917.
Career: Oldbury & Warley Schools. Birmingham University (1911). Langley Old Church (1911–12). Olive Mount FC. Oldbury Town. Langley St Michael's FC. ALBION (February 1912, sadly killed in action during World War One).

■ An exciting amateur centre-forward, blessed with power and efficiency, Bill Jackson was sadly killed at war when only 23 years of age – a big loss to Albion and to football in general. He scored 35 goals for Langley Old Church in 1911–12 and the following season helped Albion's second team win the Birmingham & District League title. He also made his Football League debut in that campaign against Oldham Athletic (away) in Division One in March 1913.

JAMES, George Charles

Centre-forward: 116 apps. 57 goals.

Born: Oldbury, 2 February 1899.
Died: West Bromwich, 13 December 1976.
Career: Oldbury & District Schools. Bilston United (September 1917). ALBION (January 1920). Reading (£650, May 1929). Watford (£300, February 1930, retired May 1933). Became a West Bromwich licensee.

■ George James was a real character – shortish, heavily-built and fearless, a centre-forward of the bustling type with a big heart, telling shot and sometimes a fiery temper! He was a chatterbox both on and off the field, but he certainly gave Albion splendid service during his stay at The Hawthorns, scoring, on average, a goal every two matches, having made his debut for the club against Bolton Wanderers (away) in Division One in November 1921. He whipped in a goal five seconds after the start of Albion's League home game against Nottingham Forest in December 1924 and went on to claim four that afternoon (in a 5–1 win), finishing the season with 30 to his credit in 41 League and cup games, a personal record. As a 'striker', he teamed up exceedingly well with Joe Carter, Charlie 'Tug' Wilson and the Welsh international Stanley Davies, and he was forever seeking to have a crack at goal, from any distance with any foot, on the half-volley or volley. He played in one England trial in 1925, the nearest he got to an international call-up, which he certainly deserved for his all-action performances during the mid-1920s. James also scored 87 goals in 131 Central League games for Albion, gaining championship medals at this level in 1923–24 and 1926–27. He also netted twice when Albion beat the Blues 3–1 in the final of the Birmingham Charity Cup in 1925. He went on to hit seven goals in 19 League games for Reading and claimed an astonishing 69 in 83 League outings for Watford, before a knee injury forced him to give up the game he loved so much.

* His brother, Roland James, was with him at The Hawthorns in seasons 1920–22.

JAMES, Roland William

Left-half: 9 apps, 4 goals.

Born: Smethwick, West Midlands, 9 May 1897.
Died: Birmingham, April 1979.
Career: West Smethwick School. Smethwick Highfield. ALBION (professional, October 1919). Brentford (June 1922). Stockport County (August 1925–May 1928). Hyde (briefly). Manchester Central (January–May 1931). Stalybridge Celtic (1931–32). Worked in engineering until World War Two, then afterwards in a garage.

■ 'Roly' James was a useful player, who certainly put plenty of effort into his game, especially for the reserves for whom he appeared in over 30 matches, gaining a Birmingham & District League championship medal in 1920. When called into the first team he did even

better, scoring four goals in only nine outings. Brother to striker George James, after leaving Albion he served with Brentford for two seasons, appearing in 35 League games. He made his Albion debut against Derby County (away) in Division One in September 1920.

JENSEN, Brian

Goalkeeper: 51 apps.

Born: Copenhagen, Denmark, 8 June 1975. Career: BK Copenhagen (junior). AZ 67 Alkmaar (professional, April 1997). ALBION (March 2000). Burnley (free, May 2003).

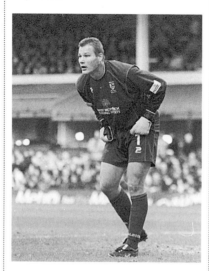

■ Brian 'The Beast' Jensen, 6ft 1in tall and 13st, made over 100 appearances in Dutch football before moving to Albion, initially as cover for Alan Miller. He made a winning start with the Baggies in the month he joined as Tranmere were defeated 2–0 at The Hawthorns, and thereafter produced some excellent displays, but looked overweight and cumbersome at times and was eventually replaced between the posts by Russell Hoult. He later became third choice at The Hawthorns, following the arrival of Joe Murphy, and, after languishing in the reserves (making over 30 appearances for the second XI), he subsequently switched to Burnley. He didn't have a happy return to The Hawthorns in August 2003 as Albion claimed a 4–1 victory.

JEPHCOTT, Alan Claude

Outside-right: 190 apps. 16 goals.
Born: Smethwick, 30 October 1891.

Died: Penn near Wolverhampton, 5 October 1950.
Career: West Smethwick School. Olive Mount FC (1906). Brierley Hill Alliance (September 1907). Stourbridge (August 1909). Brierley Hill Alliance (March 1910). ALBION (£100, April 1911, retired through injury, May 1923). Became a local businessman. ALBION (director, January 1934, remained on the Board until his death in 1950).

■ Claude Jephcott was a brilliant right-winger, full of dash and vigour. He certainly had terrific pace and was wonderfully consistent, a player who rose to the big occasion. A junior international for England in 1911, he suffered a broken leg in 1922 (against Aston Villa) and this injury eventually ended his career, somewhat abruptly, when he was perhaps in peak form. He appeared in almost 200 competitive games for Albion (plus several more for the second team in the Birmingham & District League) but managed only 16 senior goals. Yet reports indicate, quite clearly, that he probably created and made another 65–70! Jephcott appeared in the 1912 FA Cup final against Barnsley and in 1919–20 helped Albion win the First Division championship, his form during this season being quite superb. He played for the Football League XI and for an England Select XI between 1913 and 1919, and it must be said that he was unlucky not to win full international recognition for England. He made his League debut as a 20-year-old against Sunderland (away) in Division One in December 1911.

JOHNSON, Andrew James

Midfield: 124+12 apps. 7 goals.

Born: Bristol, 2 May 1974.
Career: Norwich City (apprentice, June 1990, professional, March 1992). Nottingham Forest (£2.2 million, July 1997). ALBION (£200,000, September 2001).

 A snip-of-a-signing by Baggies boss Gary Megson, midfielder Andy Johnson played a crucial role in Albion's promotion-winning campaign of 2001–02, appearing in 36 League and cup games and scoring five goals.

Capped by England at youth-team level as a teenager, he spent seven years at Carrow Road, making 75 appearances, before having a further 126 outings for Forest, with whom he won a First Division championship medal in 1998. After becoming an established Welsh international, gaining a total of 14 full caps, Johnson loves to drive forward from centre-field but admits his goal scoring record needs to improve! He signed an extension to his contract in July 2004, thus keeping him at The Hawthorns until June 2006. Johnson, who missed the last four months of the 2004–05 season with damaged medial ligaments, announced his retirement from international football in October 2004.

JOHNSON, George

Utility forward: 3 apps. 1 goal.

Born: West Bromwich, 11 November 1871.
Died: Walsall, 12 July 1934.
Career: West Bromwich Baptist & Beeches Road Schools. West Bromwich Sandwell. West Bromwich Baptist FC. Wrockwardine Wood (May 1892). ALBION (professional, May 1895). Walsall (September 1896). Aston Villa (£300, April 1898, retired through injury, December 1904). Later worked for the park's committee (Walsall).

George Johnson was a thoughtful and aggressive forward who was equally at home in any of the three central positions. He was restricted to a mere two senior games with Albion but in later years did very well with Aston Villa, appearing in more than 100 first-team games and winning a League Division One championship medal in 1899, as well as assisting the 'Villans' to retain the trophy the following season (1900). He made his Albion debut against Grimsby Town (home) in an FA Cup second round replay in February 1896.

JOHNSON, Joseph Arthur

Outside-left 145 apps. 47 goals.

Born: Grimsby, 4 April 1911.
Died: West Bromwich, August 1983.
Career: Grimsby Schools. Cleethorpes Royal Saints (August 1926). Scunthorpe & Lindsey United (professional, April 1928). Bristol City (£1,200, May 1931). Stoke City

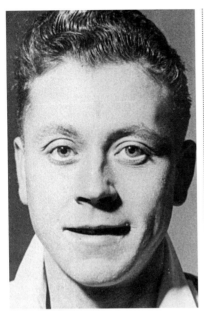

(£2,500, April 1932). ALBION (£6,500, November 1937). Hereford United (free, May 1946). Northwich Victoria (August 1948, retired 1950). Guest for Crewe Alexandra, Leicester City and Notts County during World War Two. Later ran the Dartmouth Park café-restaurant in West Bromwich for a number of years in the 1950s and 60s.

■ Joe Johnson was an excellent left-winger, who received much praise for some quite superb displays in the Stoke side of the 1930s. He had a very fine record as a goalscoring left-winger and, along with Stanley Matthews, steered the Potters to the Second Division championship in 1932–33. Capped by England on five occasions between November 1936 and May 1937 (scoring two goals against Sweden and Finland), Johnson made over 200 appearances for Stoke, 184 at League level, netting 58 goals. He added almost 150 more games to his total while with Albion (47 goals), making his debut for the Baggies against Huddersfield Town (away) in Division One in December 1937. He went on to tot up another 60 appearances in non-League football, eventually retiring with well over 450 senior outings under his belt (120 goals).

JOHNSON, Lloyd Glen

Centre-forward: 2 + 2 apps.

Born: Vancouver, 22 Canada, April 1951.
Career: Vancouver State Schools, Vancouver

Spartans (1966–69). Albion (professional, October 1969). Vancouver Royals (free, June 1972). Vancouver Whitecaps (1973–77). Still lives in Canada.

■ Glen Johnson was a swift-moving, solid striker, who, although staying in the West Midlands for three seasons, never really settled down to the English game. He later made his mark in Canada, winning nine international caps for his country (1972–76). He made his Football League debut for Albion against Blackpool (away) in Division One in August 1970, as a substitute.

JOHNSTON, William McClure

Outside-left: 254 + 7 apps. 28 goals.

Born: Maryhill, Glasgow, 19 December 1946.
Career: Fife County Schools. Fife District Schools Select. Bowhill Strollers. Manchester United (trialist, April 1961). Glasgow Rangers (amateur, July 1962). Lochore Welfare (August 1961). Glasgow Rangers (professional, February 1964). ALBION (£138,000, December 1972). Vancouver Whitecaps, NASL (£100,000, March 1979). Birmingham City (on loan, October 1979–February 1980). Glasgow Rangers (£40,000, August 1980). Vancouver Whitecaps, NASL (May 1982). Heart of Midlothian (September 1982). South China, Hong Kong (on loan, summer, 1983). Heart of Midlothian (player-coach, 1983–84). East Fife (player-coach, August 1984, retired as a player, May 1985). Raith Rovers (coach, March 1986). Later became a publican in Glasgow (June 1986) but returned to football as coach of Falkirk (July 1987). Now licensee of the Port o'Brae in High Street, Kirkcaldy, Fife.

■ With his ability to beat the defence with either footwork or speed and cap a move with a fierce shot, Willie Johnston was a welcome acquisition to Albion in a defence-orientated game. On the down side, however, Johnston, as good as he undoubtedly was, had the tendency to hold on to the ball far too long and was often in trouble with referees (he was actually sent off 17 times during his professional career, which is perhaps a record). He had just finished 67 days suspension when he joined Albion. But, nevertheless, he was a fine winger, who

played in 393 competitive games for Rangers (in two major spells at Ibrox Park) scoring 125 goals, winning medals galore in League, cup and European competitions. In November 1971 he claimed a hat-trick (two penalties and a follow up after a miss from the spot) in a League away game for Rangers at St Johnstone and six months later he scored two vitally important goals to help Rangers win the European Cup-winners' Cup (against Moscow Dynamo). For Albion, Johnston's appearance tally topped the 260 mark (plus 13 in the second XI) and, after leaving The Hawthorns after six years, he carried on adding to his personal record by appearing regularly for Birmingham, Hearts and East Fife, as well as helping the Whitecaps win the NASL title in 1979. When he retired to take on coaching, Johnston had amassed well over 700 competitive appearances in a 20-year professional career. He gained 22 Scottish caps (13 with Albion), had two games for the Scottish League side, two for the under-23 XI and also represented his country at youth-team level. He gave thousands of fans in England, Scotland and perhaps in Canada many hours of high-quality entertainment as a dashing left-winger who could sprint 40 yards in approximately five seconds from a standing start! Johnston, one of Albion's greatest post-war wingers, made his Baggies debut against Liverpool (home) in Division One in December 1972.

JOHNSTONE, William Richard

Centre-forward: 3 apps.

Born: Kirriemuir, Angus, Scotland, 18 May 1867.

Died: Scotland, c.1933.
Career: Kirriemuir and Forfar Schools. Strathmore Thistle (1885). Dundee Harp (1887). ALBION (November 1889). Alloa Athletic (April 1890). Arbroath (1893–94).

■ A centre-forward who could also play at outside-left, Willie Johnstone never settled in the Midlands and returned home to Scotland after five months and three games with Albion, having made his debut for the club against Bolton Wanderers (away) in a First Division fixture in December 1889 (Albion lost 7–0).

* His brother, Robert Johnstone, played for Renton, Sunderland and Third Lanark during the 1890s.

JOL, Maarten Cornilius

Midfield: 68 + 1 apps. 4 goals.

Born: Den Haag, Holland, 16 January 1956.
Career: The Hague Schools. ADO Den Haag (amateur, April 1972, professional, January 1974). Bayern Munich (£50,000, October 1977). FC Twente Enschede (March 1978). ALBION (£250,000, October 1981). Coventry City (June 1984). ADO Den Haag, Holland (March 1985). FC Twente Enschede, Holland (coach, from August 1989). Scheveningen, Holland (coach, July 1991). Dutch FA (Dutch Community Relations & Youth coach/Academy officer, 1995–96). Roda JC, Holland (coach, July 1996–May 1998). RKC Waalwijk, Holland (coach, July 2000–May 2004). Tottenham Hotspur (assistant manager/coach, June 2004, caretaker manager, November 2004, then appointed full-time manager within a week).

■ When Albion sold midfielders Bryan Robson and Remi Moses to Manchester United in October 1981, the Dutch duo of Maarten Jol and Romeo Zondervan were recruited by The Hawthorns to replace them. At first Jol – who turned down Arsenal initially – filled Robson's gap to a tee, the fans loved him and he was a great asset to the team, tackling strongly with a lot of aggression while also spraying passes out in all directions, some short, some long, covering 40–50 yards downfield and across it. Unfortunately, after a couple of decent seasons, his form dipped considerably and he found himself in trouble with one

or two referees, getting sent off in the home leg of the 1982 League Cup semi-final against Spurs, along with Tony Galvin. He was subsequently transferred to Coventry City, signed by ex-Albion player and future boss Bobby Gould. He only appeared in 15 League games for the Sky Blues before returning to Holland. After retiring as a player, Jol gained a reputation as an astute, technically accomplished coach. He helped his former club, Den Haag, win promotion from the Dutch Second Division in 1986 and reach the 1987 domestic Cup final, collecting a runners'-up medal against Ajax. Having earned his coaching certificate at the age of 25, Jol set his first foot on the football management ladder with Scheveningen (on the outskirts of Den Haag). He immediately brought them success with the Dutch non-League title, and then, after switching clubs, he won the Dutch Cup with Roda JC in 1997, beating Heerenveen 4–2 in the final, their first trophy success in 30 years. He then claimed two 'Coach of the Year' awards with RKC Waalwijk, in 2001 and 2002. Indeed, he did superbly well with the latter club, who had the lowest budget in the League at around £4 million, but Jol sold players for £8 million, secured some excellent youngsters and was paid 75,000 euros for his efforts. Jol, who won three full caps for Holland, all with FC Twente Enschede, when he played alongside Jan Peters and Frans Thijssen in midfield, also represented his country

at intermediate, under-21, 'B' team, youth and schoolboy levels. He made his Albion debut against Southampton (home) in Division One in October 1981. He also played in four Central League games. He returned to English football in 2004 as assistant to newly-appointed Spurs manager Jacques Santini. When Santini quit, Jol was handed the role of caretaker manager before taking over on a permanent basis within a week to become Spurs' seventh manager in seven years. His first Premiership game in charge ended in a 5–4 home defeat against arch-rivals Arsenal. In January 2005 he returned to The Hawthorns for a fourth round FA Cup tie against Albion, coming face to face with the player he replaced in the Baggies midfield 24 years earlier, Bryan Robson.

* In 1974 Jol starred for the Netherlands against England in the qualifying round of the UEFA Youth tournament at The Hawthorns.

JONES, Abraham

Centre-half: 117 apps. 10 goals.

Born: Tipton, 20 February 1875.
Died: West Bromwich, June 1942.
Career: Tipton & Great Bridge Schools. Folkestone Town Boys (August 1879). Folkestone FC (August 1891). Cameron Highlanders, Scotland (1892). ALBION (professional, September 1896). Middlesbrough (£95, May 1901). Luton Town (free, July 1906, retired, May 1910). Worked in industry, first in Bedford and later in the Black Country.

■ 'Abe' Jones was a marvellous, all-action, robust centre-half who, despite his size, was as tough as they come and he mixed it with the hardest strikers in the game, often coming out on top. He was built like a tank and had the gift of anticipation, possessed a stout tackle, could kick long and true and, above all, he was an inspiration to the rest of his players, always having his sleeves rolled up past the elbow in the coldest of weather. Always eminently strong, Jones made over 100 League appearances for Albion, for whom he also played in several 'other' first and second-team matches. In 1901–02 he helped Middlesbrough win promotion from the Second Division, and, after a brief association with Luton, he retired with more than 250 competitive outings under his belt (139 in the League with 'Boro). He left Albion following Jim Stevenson's arrival from Preston North End. Jones made his Football League debut against Bolton Wanderers (home) in Division One in November 1897, scoring once in Albion's 2–0 win.

* Abe Jones's nephew, Teddy Sandford, played for Albion during the 1930s.

JONES, Charles Leslie

Forward: 1 app.

Born: Penn, Wolverhampton, 5 April 1925.
Career: Penn Schools. Compton Colts. Penn FC (1940). ALBION (amateur, November 1941, professional, August 1946-June 1947). Then non-League football until 1958. Later worked for the park's authority.

■ A wartime signing, Charlie Jones was given just one first-team game and thereafter released into non-League football without ever showing the keenness to progress. He made his debut against Walsall (home) in the Football League South in May 1942.

JONES, Eric Norman

Outside-right: 22 apps. 7 goals.

Born: Stirchley, Birmingham, 5 February 1915.
Died: August 1985.
Career: Bournville and Selly Park Schools. Shirley FC. Kidderminster Harriers (August 1931). Wolverhampton Wanderers (professional, October 1936). Portsmouth (£150, November 1937). Stoke City (£400, March 1938). ALBION (£500, May 1939). Guest for Portsmouth, Chelsea, Southend United, Watford, Brentford, Fulham, Cardiff City, Arsenal, Queen's Park Rangers, Northampton Town, Crystal Palace, Luton Town, Aldershot, Exeter City, Leeds United and Nottingham Forest during World War Two. Brentford (£500, December 1945). Crewe Alexandra (free, July 1946). Kidderminster Harriers (free, August 1948). Egyptian National team (coach, 1955–56). Bromsgrove Rovers (manager, 1959–61). De Graaschap, Holland (coach, 1961–62). Port Vale (coach 1962–63). Remained in football until 1980 as part-time scout, acting on behalf of several European clubs.

■ Playing for a total of 17 different clubs (including his spell with Albion), Eric

Jones was one of the most travelled footballers during the 1939–45 hostilities. He was a thick-set winger who had good pace and some skill and, although the war disrupted Eric's playing career considerably, overall he appeared in well over 200 games during his playing days, top-scoring for Watford in 1942–3 with a total of 10 goals in 21 outings. After leaving Albion he made 20 appearances for Brentford and 60 for Crewe (53 at League level, 14 goals). His debut for the Baggies was against Swansea Town (away) in Division Two in August 1939 (a fixture subsequently declared null and void).

JONES, Grenville Arthur

Outside-right: 3 apps.

Born: Nuneaton, Warwickshire, 23 November 1932.
Died: Pentre Broughton, North Wales, 15 October 1991.
Career: Nuneaton Borough Schools. Erdington Albion. Birmingham County FA. ALBION (amateur, June 1947, professional, December 1949). Wrexham (£1,250 with Elfed Evans, June 1955, retired through injury, May 1961). Later employed by an insurance company in North Wales.

■ Grenville Jones, an outside-right with pace and ability, was reserve to Billy Elliott and then Frank Griffin during his eight years' association with Albion, during which time he gained schoolboy

and youth international honours for England. He made his debut for Albion at Sunderland in Division One in March 1954 (lost 2–1). He also scored 10 goals in 83 Central League games for the Baggies before moving to Wrexham, for whom he appeared in 276 first-team games (241 in the Football League), scoring 40 goals. In 1957 he gained a Welsh Cup medal when Wrexham defeated Swansea 2–1 at Ninian Park, Cardiff, and collected a second medal in the same competition in 1958, beating Chester at Bangor, also by 2–1 (after a replay).

JONES, Harold Eric

Goalkeeper: 2 apps.

Born: West Bromwich, 10 July 1881.
Died: Dudley, July 1948.
Career: West Bromwich & District Schools. Leamington Town (1896). Walsall (August 1900). Brierley Hill Alliance (September 1901). ALBION (professional, November 1902). Brierley Hill Alliance (free, June 1904). ALBION (free, August 1905). Shrewsbury Town (free, June 1907). Did not play after World War One.

■ A resourceful goalkeeper possessing any amount of courage, Harry Jones had two spells with Albion, firstly as deputy to Ike Webb, and second time round as stand-in for Jim Stringer. He made his Football League debut against Burslem Port Vale (home) in Division Two on Boxing Day in 1906. He appeared in 50 second XI matches for Albion during his two spells at The Hawthorns.

JONES, Harry Joseph

Inside-right/centre-forward: 169 apps. 104 goals.

Born: Haydock, Lancs, 26 October 1911.
Died: Preston, 22 February 1957.
Career: Haydock & Newton Le Willows Schools. Haydock Athletic (1925–28). Preston North End (professional, July 1928). ALBION (£500, May 1933, retired through injury and illness, August 1943). Guest for Blackburn Rovers and Everton during first part of World War Two. ALBION (scout 1946–42). Later, worked briefly in engineering.

■ Harry 'Popeye' Jones was a jovial, loquacious character, able to play equally well in any forward role, although he thoroughly enjoyed the centre-forward berth. He had an aggressive style, reminiscent of Trevor Ford in his hey-day. Often 'Popeye' would bundle both ball and 'keeper into the net as he tore in on goal from deep positions. He was a huge favourite with The Hawthorns' faithful, he had an appetite for goals and, during his career with Albion, netted over 100 in less than 170 first-team matches. In the 1939–40 season he rattled in 50 goals in 40 outings (all senior games) and scored at least once in 11 consecutive matches – a club record later equalled by winger Billy Elliott, his forward colleague in so many wartime fixtures with Albion. Indeed, during World War Two, 'Popeye' – who served in the Army and played for London Command and London District – scored 47 goals in just 40 Regional League and Cup games for Albion (1939–43). In February 1943, as a guest with Everton, he kept goal in a game against Burnley. Without doubt, Harry 'Popeye' Jones was a great player, a fine club man and a real prize guy when it came to goalscoring. He made his Albion debut against Sheffield Wednesday (away) in Division One in January 1935. He also scored 39 goals in 69 Central League games for the club, including 18 in 26 outings, when the title was won in 1934–35. In June 1932 he was awarded the Royal Humane Society Testimonial Medal after diving into a Haydock canal to save a child from drowning. He died of a heart attack at the age of 45. His son lives in Haydock.

JONES, Ivor

Inside-forward: 67 apps. 10 goals.

Born: Merthyr near Carmarthen, South Wales, 31 July 1899.
Died: Swansea, 24 November 1974.
Career: Merthyr & Carmarthen Schools XI. Merthyr Town (April 1915). Armed Forces (serving in France). Caerphilly (August 1918). Swansea Town (£50, August 1919). ALBION (£2,500, April 1922). Swansea Town (free, May 1926). Aberystwyth Town (player-coach, August 1927). Aldershot (free, June 1928). Thames Association (November 1928). Eastside FC (February 1930). Aberavon Harlequins (April 1933). Aberystwyth (coach, September 1933, retired out of football May 1935). Later worked for the National Coalboard of Wales.

■ Ivor Jones was a grand little inside-forward with good control over mind and ball. He was difficult to 'rob' yet his erratic play at times annoyed both himself and his colleagues! He had a decent kick, getting distance and power with his trusty right foot, but again he was far too inconsistent. However, when in form he was a classy player and between 1920 and 1926 won 10 Welsh international caps, as well as representing the Welsh League against the Southern League at Aberdare in 1921. He spent four seasons at The Hawthorns, teaming up at various times with wingers Howard Gregory, Tommy Glidden and Jack Byers. He made his debut against Newcastle United (away) in Division One in April 1922 and also played in 66 Central League games, scoring 22 goals and helping the team win the championship at this level in 1923–24.
* Ivor Jones's son, Cliff, was the star winger for Tottenham Hotspur and Wales during the 1960s. His brothers Bryn (Arsenal and Wolves), William (Merthyr Town), Emlyn (Merthyr, Everton and Southend United) and Bert (Southend and Wolves), were all talented footballers, Bryn especially, who won 17 caps for Wales and was Britain's most expensive footballer when he joined the Gunners from Wolves for £14,000 in 1938.

JONES, Stanley George

Centre-half: 267 apps. 3 goals.

Born: Highley, Shropshire, 16 November 1938.
Career: Highley Council & Bridgnorth Grammar Schools. Staffordshire Youths. Kidderminster Harriers (August 1954). Wolverhampton Wanderers (amateur, April 1955). Walsall (amateur, August 1955, professional, May 1956). ALBION (£7,000 and Peter Billingham, May 1960). Walsall (free, March 1968). Burton Albion (free, July 1973). Kidderminster Harriers (player-manager, 1974–5). Hednesford Town (March 1976). Coleshill Town (coach, 1977–80). Walsall (trainer 1980–87). Burton Albion (trainer, 1987–89). WBA All Stars XI (1979–88). Now runs sports equipment business in Walsall where he lives.

■ Stan Jones was a big, burly defender, inspiring, strong in the air, hard in the tackle and a player who rarely put a foot

wrong, although in one five-match spell in the mid-1960s he had the dubious record or scoring three own-goals! In a long and steady career, he served Walsall for 10 years in two spells, amassing 265 appearances in major competitions and gaining a Fourth Division championship medal in 1959–60. Signed by Albion as a straight replacement for Joe Kennedy, he largely held on to the number 5 shirt until Eddie Colquhoun arrived from Bury in 1967. Jones was injured and sadly missed the 1966 League Cup final victory over West Ham, but regrettably he was dropped for the 1967 final against Queen's Park Rangers at Wembley and played only once more for the Baggies after that 3–2 defeat, returning to Fellows Park on the transfer deadline of 1968. He made his Albion debut against Birmingham City (away) in Division One in August 1960 and also lined up in 41 Central League games for the club.

JORDAN, William Charles

Centre-forward: 35 apps. 18 goals.

Born: Langley, 9 December 1885.
Died: Belbroughton, Worcestershire, December 1949.
Career: Langley Junior & Infants Schools. Five Ways Grammar School (Birmingham). Birmingham City Technical School. St John's College (Oxford). Oxford University. Liverpool

(reserves, 1902). Assisted Langley Church FC, Langley Victoria and Langley St Michael's (1902–04). ALBION (amateur, November 1904–April 1909). Everton (September 1911). Wolverhampton Wanderers (July 1912, retired, January 1913). A graduate in Natural Science at Oxford University and ordained in 1907, he was curate at St Clement's Church, Nechells, Birmingham (1911–12) and thereafter devoted most of his time to the church, conducting several Sportsman's Services up and down the country, choosing to 'appear' on the soccer field whenever he could. He served the Church of Wales on the Isle of Man, at Slaidburn (West Riding of Yorkshire), in Darlington and also in Belbroughton. He was a director of Darlington FC for three years, 1936–39.

■ Billy Jordan was a brilliant amateur centre-forward, a player with precision and thought, speed and deadly marksmanship. An England amateur international, he scored six goals against France in 1907 when making his debut for his country and claimed a hat-trick for Albion on his League debut against Gainsborough Trinity in February 1907.

(JORDAO) Batista Adelion Jose Martins

Midfield: 52+19 apps. 8 goals.

Born: Malange, Angola, 30 August 1971.
Career: Benfica, Portugal (junior, 1987,

professional, August 1989). Estrala Amadora, Portugal (August 1990). Campomaiorense, Italy (1993–94). Lecce, Italy (August 1994). Estrela Amadora, Portugal (August 1995). Benfica, Portugal (August–September 1997). Sporting Braga, Portugal (October 1997). ALBION (£350,000, August 2000, released, May 2003, re-signed, July 2003). Estrala Amadora, Portugal (August 2004).

■ A strong, hard-working 6ft 2in midfielder, Jordao helped Albion win promotion to the Premiership in 2001–02, but found it increasingly difficult to get into the first team the following season and was subsequently released by manager Gary Megson. Prior to his move to The Hawthorns, Jordao had amassed over 200 senior appearances for his previous clubs. His Albion League debut was against Barnsley (at Oakwell) in August 2000 and he was certainly the hero of all Baggies fans when he scored the only goal of the Black Country derby to earn a 1–0 victory over Wolves at Molineux in December 2001. He made over 40 appearances for Albion's second XI.

JOSEPH, Roger Anthony

Defender: 0+2 apps.

Born: Paddington, London, 24 December 1965.
Career: Southall (April 1982). Brentford (professional, October 1985). Wimbledon (£150,000, August 1988). Millwall (on loan, March–April 1995). Leyton Orient (free, November 1996). ALBION (free, February 1997). Leyton Orient (free, August 1997, retired through injury, June 2000).

■ An England 'B' international defender (2 caps), Roger Joseph joined Albion on a short-term contract as cover for both full-back positions, making his debut (as a 'sub') in a 4–0 home win over Southend United, soon after arriving at The Hawthorns. A persistent calf injury led to his retirement from first-team soccer at the age of 34 after more than 400 senior appearances at club level (199 for the Dons).

KANU, Nwankwo

Striker: 23+7 apps. 3 goals.

Born: Owerri, Nigeria, 1 August 1976.
Career: Federations Works FC, Nigeria

(1991–92). Iwauanyanwu National FC, Nigeria (August 1992). Ajax Amsterdam, Holland (July 1993). Inter Milan, Italy (September 1996). Arsenal (£4.5 million, February 1999). ALBION (free, August 2004).

■ Twice a Premiership winner and also twice an FA Cup winner with Arsenal (as well as achieving Charity Shield success), Kanu had made almost 200 appearances for the Gunners before joining Albion. He was also an established Nigerian international (over 40 caps to his name and six goals) and had gained a soccer gold medal with his country at the 1996 Olympic Games in Atlanta, US. He also gained youth honours at the 1993 under-17 World Cup and was voted African 'Footballer of the Year' in 1996. At 6ft 4in tall, he is one of the tallest players ever to sign for Albion. He has exceptional close ball control, can shoot with both feet and is good in the air, but his tricks and talent can be beguiling. At times he displays outrageous ability and wonderful skills, then is can be so different, out of the game for long spells, looking disinterested. But on his day he is a top quality footballer, who turned down Aston Villa before joining Albion, for whom he made his debut in the Premiership game against Blackburn Rovers at Ewood Park in August 2004, scoring his first goal for the club to earn a point in a 1–1 draw with Fulham at The Hawthorns the following month. He had the misfortune to miss a last minute sitter (from just two feet out) in Albion's 2–1 home Premiership defeat by Middlesbrough in November 2004. After that he was not at his best and suffered a series of injuries. He played in successive European Champions League finals with Ajax, winning in 1995 versus AC Milan, losing a year later on penalties against

Juventus. After winning in 1995, he suffered a life-threatening heart problem, from which he made a full recovery.
* In 2003 Kanu was awarded the Order of Niger. His younger brother, Chris (born in 1979), plays for Peterborough United.

KAYE, John

Inside-forward/wing half: 358+3 apps. 54 goals.

Born: Goole, 3 March 1940.
Career: Goole & District Schools. Goole Town Boys. Goole United (1954). Goole Dockers FC (September 1955). Hull City (amateur, April 1956). Goole Town (August 1957). Scunthorpe United (£750, professional, September 1960). ALBION (£44,750, May 1963). Hull City (£28,000, November 1971, retired and appointed coach at Boothferry Park, August 1974, as successor to Terry Neill). Scunthorpe United (assistant manager/coach, October 1977–February 1981). Later Goole Town (manager, 1982–83). Brigg Town (manager, 1990–92). Entered the hotel business, mid-1990s, later worked as an engineer on oil rigs.

■ John 'Yorky' Kaye was a goalscoring forward with Scunthorpe when he was snapped up by Albion manager Jimmy Hagan in 1963 for a club record fee of almost £45,000. He spent his first four years at The Hawthorns as a front-runner (playing along side Jeff Astle from 1964) but then, during the team's tremendous FA Cup-run of 1968, he was successfully converted by manager Alan Ashman into a dominant, highly efficient and resourceful left-half. He helped Albion win the trophy that year, having earlier received winners' and runners'-up prizes in the 1966 and 1967 League Cup finals, and three years later he collected another runners'-up medal when Albion lost to Manchester City in the 1970 League Cup final. In 1965–66 Kaye, a battler to the last and a wholehearted player in every sense of the word, represented the Football League, and twice, in 1966 and 1970, he was voted 'Midland Footballer of the Year'. In all, he appeared in well over 350 senior games for Albion plus 12 in the Central League (3 goals) and during his career amassed a total of 433 League appearances (for Scunthorpe, Albion and Hull) claiming 79 goals, 25 for the Iron, 45 for Albion and nine for the Tigers.

Kaye made his debut for the Baggies against Leicester City (home) in Division One in August 1963.

KELLY, Anthony Gerald

Midfield: 32 apps. 1 goal.

Born: Huyton, Nr Liverpool, Merseyside, 1 October 1964.
Career: St Columbus School, Liverpool. Liverpool & Merseyside Boys. Liverpool (apprentice, April 1980, professional, September 1982). Derby County (briefly, August 1983). The Eagle FC, Liverpool. Wigan Athletic (November 1983). Stoke City (£80,000, April 1986). ALBION (£60,000, July 1987). Chester City (on loan, September–October 1988). Colchester United (on loan, October–November 1988). Shrewsbury Town (on loan, January 1989, signed permanently for £30,000, March 1989). Bolton Wanderers (August 1991). Port Vale (non-contract, September 1994). Millwall (non-contract, October 1994). Peterborough United (December 1994). Wigan Athletic (July 1995–March 1996). Sligo Rovers (player-manager/coach, 1997–99). Later worked as a scheme leader for under privileged children with special needs in Huyon. Also football coach in the same place (with 20 kids) and scout for Stoke City, 2004–05.

■ Tony 'Zico' Kelly was signed by manager Ron Saunders as a straight-replacement for Steve Mackenzie (sold to Charlton Athletic). A busy, aggressive midfield player, he failed to make the grade with Liverpool, and after a brief association with Derby County he finally made his Football League debut for Wigan in 1984, gaining a Freight Rover Trophy medal with the Springfield Park club in 1985 at Wembley. He joined Stoke in 1986 after making 137 senior appearances for Wigan (22 goals scored). He had a good first half to season 1986–87 with the Potters and was a key figure in their midfield set-up as they forced their way into the promotion reckoning. Alas, Kelly became rather 'overweight' and consequently lost his place in the side, moving to The Hawthorns during the summer of 1987. He made his Albion debut against Burton Albion (away) in the Bass Charity Vase in July 1987 and appeared in his first League game for the club against Oldham Athletic (home) the following month (0–0). He also scored once in four Central League outings. He made 419 League appearances during his nomadic career.

KELSEY, Arthur George

Left-half/inside-forward: 11 apps.

Born: Wallingford, Berkshire, 12 May 1871.
Died: Dudley, 19 October 1955.
Career: Wallingford & Abingdon Schools. Reading (August 1888). 29th Worcestershire Regt, Aldershot (from 1891). ALBION (professional, October 1895–May 1896). Brierley Hill Alliance (free, August 1896). Wolverhampton Wanderers (free, July 1897–May 1898). Willenhall Phoenix (August 1898). Walsall Falcons (1901). Willenhall Pickwick (1904, retired, 1907).

■ A wing-half or inside-forward of sound build and average ability, Arthur Kelsey acted as cover for Billy Richards and Albert Flewitt during his season with Albion, making his club debut against Aston Villa (home) in Division One in October 1895. He also appeared in 20 'other' first-team games for the club.

KENNEDY, Joseph Peter

Centre-half: 397 apps. 4 goals.

Born: Cleator Moor near Whitehaven, 15 November 1925.

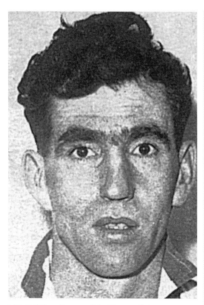

*Died: West Bromwich, September 1986.
Career: St Patrick's School (Whitehaven).
Whitehaven & District Boys'. Cleator Moor
Celtic (1941). Workington Town (1942).
Brentford (trialist, 1943). Millwall (trialist,
1944). Gravesend non-League football
(1944–45). Freelands FC (August 1945).
Altrincham (April 1946). ALBION (£750,
professional, December 1948). Chester
(free, June 1961). Stourbridge (player-
manager, August 1962). Brockhouse Works
FC. Retired, 1966, after playing his last
game of football at the age of 40. Remained
as employee of Brockhouse (West
Bromwich) until his death.*

■ Joe Kennedy began his Albion career
as an inside-right before having a decent
spell as a right-half. He was then switched
to centre-half where he performed
brilliantly, being steady, totally reliable,
consistent, superb in the air, sure and
sound on the ground. A wonderful player,
he developed into one of the club's best
post-war pivots, certainly since Jack
Vernon left in 1952. He was desperately
unlucky not to gain a full England cap.
Raven-haired, he seemed destined to play
for his country after being a permanent
reserve during the early '50s, but injury
forced him out of the reckoning at crucial
times and the only representative calls he
received were to skipper England 'B' on
three occasions and play for the FA XI.
After being injured and ultimately losing
his place in the side to a young Jimmy
Dugdale, Kennedy was drafted into the
right-back position to replace Stan
Rickaby in Albion's 1954 FA Cup winning

side. He played superbly well and started
the build up that led to Frank Griffin's
87th match-winning goal. Five years
earlier he had helped Albion gain
promotion from the Second Division,
having made his debut for the Baggies
against Luton Town (away) in April 1949.
The aforementioned Irishman, Jack
Vernon, was commanding the centre-half
position when Kennedy first arrived at
The Hawthorns, but when Vernon
returned 'home' Kennedy took over and
went on to appear in almost 400 senior
games for the Baggies, teaming up with
Jimmy Dudley (4) and Ray Barlow (6) to
form one of club's best-ever middle lines.
He also made 68 Central League
appearances for Albion and followed up
by having 35 outings for Chester, quitting
League football in 1962. Sadly Kennedy
collapsed and died while at work. He was
60 years of age.

KENT, Kevin Joseph

Utility forward: 1+1 app.

*Born: Stoke-on-Trent, Staffs, 19 March
1965.
Career: St Joseph's School, Stoke. Stoke &
Hanley Schools. Newcastle Town (Staffs).
ALBION (apprentice, June 1981,
professional, December 1982). Newport
County (free, June 1984). Mansfield Town
(free, September 1985). Port Vale (player-
exchange involving Gary Ford, plus
£80,000, March 1991, retired through
injury, January 1996, then coaching-
assistant at Vale Park, February 1996–May
1997).*

■ Kevin Kent found it difficult to make
an impact with Albion, although he did
help the reserves lift the Central League
championship in 1982–83, top scoring
with ten goals. Unfortunately, he also
failed to make much headway as a
marksman with Newport, but did
exceedingly well with Mansfield (46 goals
in 275 games) and Port Vale (7 in 138).
He gained a winners' medal in the Freight
Rover Trophy at Wembley in 1987,
scoring the Stags' first goal in their
subsequent penalty shoot-out victory
over Bristol City. He also helped
Mansfield win promotion from Division
Four in 1985–86 and eight years later was
an Auto-Windscreen Finalist and Second
Division promotion winner with the
Valiants. Making his Albion debut against

Everton (home) in Division One in
February 1984, he also scored 13 goals in
48 second XI games. He suffered a
fractured knee-cap, playing against
Wolverhampton Wanderers in February
1995, and was then hospitalised with a
serious back injury, hence his early
retirement.

KEVAN, Derek Tennyson

Centre-forward: 291 apps. 173 goals.

*Born: Ripon, Yorkshire, 6 March 1935.
Career: Ripon Secondary Modern School.
Harrogate & District Schools. Ripon
YMCA. Ripon City (1950). Sheffield
United (trialist, April–May 1951).
Bradford Park Avenue (amateur, July 1951,
professional, October 1952). ALBION
(£3,000, July 1953). Chelsea (£50,000,
March 1963). Manchester City (£35,000,
August 1963). Crystal Palace (free, July
1965). Peterborough United (free, March
1966). Luton Town (free, December 1966).
Stockport County (free, March 1967).
Macclesfield Town (free, August 1968).
Stourbridge (free, August 1969). Ansells FC
(December 1969–June 1975). West
Bromwich Albion All Stars (1972–85, later
manager, 1985–93). Also ALBION Lottery
Agent (1983–84, having 'returned' to the
club 20 years after his playing career had
taken him to Chelsea). Now retired and
living in Castle Vale, Birmingham, he had
previously worked in a pub, for a brewery,
as a delivery driver and also as a driver for
a sign-making company.*

■ Derek 'The Tank' Kevan was an Albion
great. A huge fella, standing 6ft tall and
weighing almost 13 stones, he had power
in every department, a big heart, heaps of
stamina and a lust for goals. He could
head a ball as hard as some players could
kick one and he packed a fierce shot in
his right foot and a fair one in his left! A
marvellous competitor in every sense,
'Kevvo' won 14 full caps for England
(eight goals scored), played four times for
the under-23 XI and also had outings for
the Football League side. He spent almost
10 years with Albion, scoring at the rate
of a goal every 151 minutes of playing
time for the Baggies, including five in one
League match against Everton at The
Hawthorns in 1960. Five years earlier he
had scored twice on his debut for Albion
in a 2–0 League home win over the
Merseysiders. He also netted 35 goals in

1906). Coventry City (free, August 1907, retired, June 1908). Joined Fred Karno's Circus Troop.

■ Jack Kifford was a player adept with both feet and so able to occupy either full-back berth effectively. He was a big, strong player and a useful penalty-taker, who gave Albion good service for four seasons, making almost 100 appearances, winning a Second Division championship medal in 1902. He was suspended for six weeks by the Football Association during the 1903–04 season after being sent off in the local derby against Aston Villa. During his career Kifford topped 200 senior matches for his seven major clubs. He made his Albion debut against Glossop (home) in Division Two in September 1901.

KILBANE, Kevin Daniel

Left-wing/forward: 121+1 apps. 18 goals.

Born: Preston, 1 February 1977
Career: Preston North End (apprentice, April 1993, professional, July 1995). ALBION (£1 million, June 1997). Sunderland (£2.5 million, December 1999). Everton (£2 million, September 2003).

■ After leaving The Hawthorns for a record incoming fee for Albion, well-built, fast-raiding left-winger Kevin Kilbane went on to establish himself in the Republic of Ireland team, playing his part in the success of his country in the 2002 World Cup finals in the Far East. Transferred to Albion for £1 million (a

only 45 appearances for Albion's Central League side. After leaving the Baggies, amid some controversy, Kevan created a new post-war scoring record for Manchester City with 30 League goals in season 1963–64 and in 1967 gained a Fourth Division championship medal with Stockport. During the course of his League career (1952–68) 'The Tank' netted 235 goals in 440 matches, topping the First Division scoring charts in 1961–62 with 33 to his name. Admittedly, he was a shade clumsy at times, especially when he first joined Albion, but Derek developed into one of the greatest strikers the club has ever

seen – his record proves that beyond all doubt.

KIFFORD, John

Full-back: 99 apps. 8 goals.

Born: Paisley near Glasgow, 12 August 1878.
Died: Glasgow, 1955.
Career: Neilston Thistle Paisley. Glenburn & Pollockshields Schools. Paisley FC (August 1893). Abercorn (August 1895). Derby County (June 1897). Bristol Rovers (July 1900). Portsmouth (May 1901). ALBION (£50, June 1901). Millwall (free, April 1905). Carlisle United (free, August

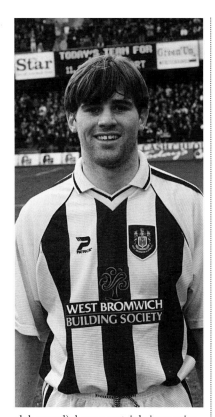

Queen's Park Rangers. (£425,000, September 1980). ALBION (£400,000, September 1981). Everton (£225,000, plus Peter Eastoe, July 1982). SC Cambuur, Holland (July 1984). Wolverhampton Wanderers (January 1985). Orebro, Sweden (on loan, April–August 1985). Luton Town (December 1985). Aldershot (August 1986). Aylesbury United (1988). Waterford (player-manager, 1988–89). Cobh Ramblers (1989). Southport (August 1989). Luton Town (Commercial Manager). Sunderland (scout, late 1990s), Grimsby Town (assistant manager, 1997). Swindon Town (coach 1998, then manager, October 2000–May 2001, returned as manager, January 2002 and appointed director of football, February 2005).

■ A former England under-21 international (two caps won) Andy King arrived at Albion soon after the start of the 1981–82 season and inside six months had appeared in both the League Cup and FA Cup semi-finals. Unfortunately, he never really fitted into the Baggies style of play as one would have liked and he left The Hawthorns after a season, returning to Goodison Park, having appeared in 38 first and five second XI games. In 1986–87, he helped Aldershot gain promotion from the Fourth Division, at the same time pushing his career appearance tally up past the 450 mark (112 goals). He also played in the 1977 League Cup final for Everton (beaten by Aston Villa) as well as lining up in three losing FA Cup semi-finals. He made his Albion debut against his former club, Everton (away), in Division One in September 1981. King top-scored for Everton in 1978–79 (12 goals) and is in the top 10 of League Cup marksmen for the Merseysiders. As a manager, he guided Swindon Town into the Second Division play-offs in 2004.

KING, Philip Geoffrey

Full-back: 5 apps.

Born: Bristol, 28 December 1967.
Career: Exeter City (apprentice, January 1984, professional, January 1985). Torquay United (£3,000, July 1986). Swindon Town (£155,000, February 1987). Sheffield Wednesday (£400,000, November 1989). Notts County (on loan, October 1993). Aston Villa (£250,000, August 1994). ALBION (on loan, November 1995).

Swindon Town (free, March 1997, later appointed player-coach). Brighton & Hove Albion (1998). Chester City (trialist, March 1999). Kidderminster Harriers (May 1999-April 2001). Bath City (2001–02).

■ A competent, attacking left-back, Phil King accumulated almost 150 senior appearances for Swindon during his first spell at the club. He played in just 23 games during his two and a half years with Aston Villa, where he became a 'forgotten player'. After his loan spell at The Hawthorns, when he deputised for Paul Edwards, making his debut in the home League game against Leicester City on 5 November, he went back to The County Ground. Capped once by England 'B', King gained a League Cup medal with Sheffield Wednesday in 1991.

KINSELL, Thomas Henry

Full-back: 158 apps.

Born: Cannock, Staffs, 3 May 1921.
Died: Dudley, 14 August 2000.
Career: Cannock Central High School. Chadsmoor FC. Cannock & District Schools. ALBION (May 1935, professional, June 1938). Bolton Wanderers (£12,000, June 1949). Reading (May 1950). West Ham United (£5,250, January 1951). Bedford Town (free, May 1956, retired, June 1957). Guest for Blackpool, Grimsby Town, Mansfield Town, Middlesbrough and Southport during World War Two, playing for Blackpool against Aston Villa in the 1944 Wartime League Cup final. Became 'mine host' of the Alma Arms in Stratford, London, 1981, later taking over

club record), he was certainly impressive at times, especially when going at defenders, his long strides, individual skill and strength seeing off many a challenge. He did, however, have the tendency to hold on to the ball just a fraction too long at times, much to the annoyance of his colleagues and, indeed, his manager and the fans! Nevertheless, he scored some cracking goals, several from distance. He was relegated with Sunderland at the end of the 2002–03 Premiership season, having taken his tally of senior appearances, at club level, to almost 300 (30 goals), but a month or so into the new campaign he moved back into the top flight with Everton. Kilbane has now played almost 50 times for Eire's senior side, having previously collected 11 caps at under-21 level.

KING, Andrew Edward

Midfield: 33 + 5 apps. 6 goals.

Born: Luton, 14 August 1956.
Career: Luton & Dunstable Schools. Bedfordshire Boys. Stopsley Youths. Tottenham Hotspur (trialist, August–September 1971). Luton Town (apprentice, August 1972, professional, July 1974). Everton (£35,000, March 1976).

an off-licence, before returning to live in Brierley Hill until his death.

■ On his day, Harry Kinsell was a wonderful left-back: fast, intelligent and a good ball-player, who won a junior international cap at the age of 18. He partnered Idris Bassett, Cecil Shaw and Jimmy Pemberton during his lengthy stay at The Hawthorns and performed admirably with all three, winning further international honours when he lined up at left-back for England in two 'Victory' games against Ireland and Wales in September/October 1945, having played for the FA Services XI against Switzerland in the summer as well as turning out for the Army, Combined Services and Western Command. After a season in the reserves, he made his Baggies debut against Walsall (home) in the Midland Regional League in May 1940 and made 67 appearances during the hostilities. A key member of Albion's 1948–49 promotion-winning side, during the course of that season he actually played one game at outside-left. In all, he accumulated almost 160 senior appearances for Albion, plus 27 for the second team, and his transfer to Bolton in 1949 was a club record pay-out for the Lancashire club. He had only 17 League outings for Bolton, 12 for Reading and 101 for West Ham, for whom he scored two goals, the first of his career!

KINSELLA, Mark Anthony

Midfield: 15+3 apps. 1 goal.

Born: Dublin, 12 August 1972.

Career: Home Farm (1986). Colchester United (apprentice, August 1987, professional, August 1989). Charlton Athletic (£150,000, September 1996). Aston Villa (£750,000, August 2002). ALBION (free, January 2004). Walsall (free, June 2004).

■ A Republic of Ireland international with five youth, one 'B', eight under-21 and over 40 full caps to his credit, Mark Kinsella, an influential right-sided midfielder and an excellent passer of the ball with a terrific shot, had already amassed more than 450 appearances at club and international level (over 60 goals scored) before signing for Albion early in 2004, having failed to gain a regular place in Villa's first team, amassing no Premiership outings during 18 months with the Birmingham club. He made his Albion debut as a substitute against Burnley (away), 48 hours after moving to The Hawthorns to boost Gary Megson's midfield options. He scored his only goal for Albion in a 3–0 home win over Coventry and then went on to play his part in helping the team regain its Premiership status.

KNOWLES, John Walter

Inside-forward: 3 apps.

Born: Wednesbury, 17 July 1879.
Died: Dudley, 1937.
Career: Kings Hill School (Wednesbury). ALBION (professional, July 1897). Dudley Town (free, May 1898). ALBION (free, May 1900). Dudley Town (free, May 1901, retired through injury, May 1908).

■ Jack Knowles had two spells with Albion, making three appearances in all as a reserve forward. He made his League debut against Nottingham Forest (away) in December 1897 and played in 20 second XI matches. He was forced to retire with a serious knee injury.

KOUMAS, Jason

Midfield: 78+16 apps. 14 goals.

Born: Wrexham, 25 September 1979.
Career: Liverpool (trialist, 1995). Tranmere Rovers (apprentice, April 1996, professional, November 1997). ALBION (£2.25 million, August 2002). Cardiff City (on loan, July 2005).

■ After long drawn-out discussions, attacking midfielder Jason Koumas joined

Albion for a club record fee in readiness for the start of the 2002–03 season. This record, however, lasted for just four hours before Albion re-signed Lee Hughes from Coventry City for £2.5 million. A driving force in centre-field, he has an enormous amount of skill, is energetic, packs a powerful right-foot shot and, above all, is an honest-to-goodness worker who never shirks a tackle. He scored 30 goals in close on 150 senior appearances for Tranmere and has now collected eight full caps for Wales. He made his Albion debut as a substitute in the Premiership home game against Fulham two days after moving to The Hawthorns, and was voted Baggies 'Player of the Year' for 2003. Unfortunately, Koumas was sent off playing against Germany in a Euro 2004 qualifier in Cardiff in September 2003 and seven months later saw red again when dismissed for two yellow cards playing against Millwall at The New Den. Nevertheless, having been voted the First Division's 'Player of the Month' for November 2003, he certainly played his part in helping Albion regain their Premiership status. He was not part of Bryan Robson's plans when he took over as manager and as a result lost his place. Koumas was still registered as a player at The Hawthorns at the start of the 2005-06 season.

KRZYWICKI, Ryzsard Lazlo

Outside-right: 60 + 4 apps. 12 goals.

Born: Penly, Flint, North Wales, 2 February 1947.
Career: Mountside Secondary Modern School (Stoke City). Leek Boys. Leek Youth Club. ALBION (apprentice, July 1962, professional, February 1965). Huddersfield Town (£45,000, March 1970). Scunthorpe United (on loan, February 1973). Lincoln City (July 1974, retired, November 1976). Settled into an engineering job at Batley, Yorkshire. Also manager of Moorlands Youth Club, Dewsbury.

■ 'Dick' Krzywicki made his League debut for Albion against Fulham (away) in Division One in December 1964, aged 17 and still an apprentice. Despite his name (he was born of Polish parents), he was a Welshman and he gained eight full caps for his country, plus three at under-23 level, the first of which ended in

complete disaster as Wales crashed 8–0 to England at Wolverhampton in October 1966. He was exceptionally quick over 20–25 yards, but alas he could not command a regular first-team place at Albion due, perhaps, to his inconsistent form. He played for Albion in the 1970 League Cup final, one of 64 senior outings for the Baggies, plus 138 in the second XI (49 goals scored). He played 47 League games for Huddersfield (seven goals), two for Scunthorpe and eight for Northampton, and he finished his career by gaining a Fourth Division championship medal in 1976 with Lincoln, for whom he made 68 League appearances, netting 11 goals. His daughter represented Wales and Great Britain in athletics.

KUSZCZAK, Thomasz

Goalkeeper: 3+2 apps.

Born: Kvonsno Ordanski, Poland, 23 March 1982.
Career: Hertha Berlin/Germany (2000). ALBION (free transfer, July 2004).

■ Signed by Albion as cover for Russell Hoult and Joe Murphy, giant, 6ft 3in, baby-faced goalkeeper Thomasz Kuszczak was on the bench for the opening Premiership game of the 2004–05 season at Blackburn. Well-built and well-proportioned, he joined The Hawthorns

ranks with two Polish caps to his name, when deputising for Liverpool's Jerzy Dudek. He appeared in his first game for Albion in a pre-season friendly against Fredericia in Denmark on 24 July 2004 – a week after his transfer – and then made his Premiership debut at home to Fulham in September 2004, playing well in a 1–1 draw.

LANGE, Anthony

Goalkeeper: 56+3 apps.

Born: West Ham, London, 10 December 1964.
Career: Charlton Athletic (apprentice, June 1981, professional, December 1982). Crewe Alexandra (on loan, November 1984). Aldershot (on loan, August 1985, signed for £2,500, July 1986). Wolverhampton Wanderers (£150,000, July 1989). Aldershot

(on loan, November 1990). Torquay United (on loan, September 1991). ALBION (free, August 1992). Fulham (£5,000, July 1995). St Leonard's, Stancroft, Sussex (August 1997, retired, May 2002).

■ One of the few Albion goalkeepers to play at Wembley, Tony Lange was signed by manager Ossie Ardiles from neighbouring Wolves to put pressure on Stuart Naylor. In fact, with Naylor struggling at times with a knee injury, Lange took over the first-team spot in mid-March 1993 and held it until the end of the season, helping Albion gain promotion to the First Division via the play-offs. He held his place, injuries aside, until January 1994 (when Naylor was recalled) but afterwards languished in the reserves playing in over 50 games, until his departure to Fulham in 1995. Understudy to Nicky Johns at Charlton, he was injury prone, suffering a broken ankle at Crystal Palace followed by a fractured wrist in 1984–85. He actually made his League debut for the Addicks against his future club, Fulham, on his 19th birthday. His first outing for Albion was against Huddersfield Town (home) in Division One in January 1993. He also played in 25 Central League matches.

LATCHFORD, Peter William

Goalkeeper: 104 apps.

Born: Kings Heath, Birmingham, 27 September 1952.
Career: Broadmeadow Junior & Brandwood Secondary Modern Schools. South Birmingham Boys. Monyhull Hospital FC. Redditch Town. Sutton Coldfield Town (1968). ALBION (apprentice, May 1969, professional, October 1969). Celtic (on loan, February–April 1975, signed permanently for £35,000, July 1975, released, June 1987). Clyde (1987–89). Went into farming in Mauchline, Scotland. Later with Forfar Athletic (part-time coach, November 2001).

■ Peter Latchford had exceptional ability for a big man and he used his height and weight to good advantage during his first five years' association with Albion for whom he made his League debut against Sheffield United (home) in August 1972. After some useful performances, his

overall form became inconsistent and he was subsequently 'sold' to Celtic after spending three months on loan at Parkhead at the end of 1974–75. He had also played in more than 50 Central League games for Albion. He comes from a footballing family with his brothers, Dave and Bob, perhaps better known nationally. Peter was at The Hawthorns at a time when Albion were well off for 'keepers and, therefore, he was never sure of first-team football, although he was an ever-present in League and cup competitions in 1973–74. With Celtic he did very well at first but then lost form – again – and dropped into the reserves. He received a testimonial at Parkhead in 1985, after gaining considerable European experience as well as winning medals in both the League (2) and major cup (3) competitions in Scotland. He was voted Celtic's 'Player of the Year' in 1977–78. As a youngster he represented England at basketball, and while with Albion he gained two caps for England at under-23 level.

LAW, Abraham

Goalkeeper: 1 app.

Born: Wealdstone, 7 February 1874.
Died: Wolverhampton, 1932.
Career: Wealdstone & Harrow Schools. Millwall Athletic (semi-professional, August 1894). ALBION (£100, May 1896). Stafford Rangers (free, May 1897).

Brewood (August 1899). Walsall Wood (1902). Willenhall Pickwick (1905, retired, 1908).

■ A goalkeeper of adequate ability, 'Abe' Law played once for Albion, replacing Joe Reader against Derby County (home) in Division One in February 1897. He understudied the England international for a full season, making over 20 appearacnes for the second team. Before joining Albion, Law helped Millwall twice win the Southern League championship, in 1894–95 and 1895–96.

LAW, William Daniel

Outside-left: 11 apps.

Born: Pleck, Walsall, 5 March 1882.
Died: May 1952.
Career: Wolverhampton Road School Pleck. Rushall Olympic. Walsall (May 1903). Doncaster Rovers (August 1904). ALBION (£25, professional, May 1905). Watford (£50, April 1906). Queen's Park Rangers (August 1908). Glossop (March 1910–May 1914). Did not figure after World War One. Became a factory worker.

■ Billy Law was a clever little winger, good at lobbing over deep crosses and doing so on the run. He joined Albion when Doncaster failed to get re-elected to the Football League in 1905. He spent just one season with Albion, acting mainly as reserve to first-choice winger Eddie Perkins. He was released when Tommy Dilly arrived from Everton in March 1906. His Albion debut was against Hull City (home) in Division Town in December 1905. He made over 100 appearances for Glossop (95 in the Football League, scoring four goals).

LEE, George Thomas

Outside-left: 295 apps. 65 goals.
Born: York, 4 June 1919.
Died: Norwich, 1 April 1991.
Career: Knavesmere School (York). York City Schools. Yorkshire County Boys. Acomb FC (1934). Tottenham Hotspur (trialist, April–May 1935). Scarborough (August 1935). York City (amateur, June 1936, professional, July 1937). Served in the Army and was a guest for Bradford Park Avenue, Lincoln City and Chester during World War Two. Nottingham Forest (£7,500 August 1947). ALBION (£12,000, July 1949). Lockheed Leamington (free,

June 1958). Vauxhall Motors (March 1959). ALBION (trainer/coach, June 1959). Norwich City (trainer/coach, May 1963–May 1987).

■ George 'Ada' Lee was a wholehearted left-winger who varied his game and style judiciously. Strongly built, he had powerful legs, a useful turn of speed and a cracking shot in his left foot. He came to Albion when the club was without a direct outside-left. Indeed, the left-wing position was causing some concern and Lee stepped in to fill the gap splendidly, being first choice for that position for seven seasons, having made his debut against Charlton Athletic (home) in Division One in August 1949. Injuries cropped up occasionally, but generally he was always the guy lined up to wear that number 11 jersey and did so wonderfully well in almost 300 senior games for the Baggies, plus 36 more in the second XI (9 goals scored). He gained an FA Cup medal in 1954, laying on Ronnie Allen's opening goal, and, after leaving The Hawthorns, he was trainer for Norwich City when they won the Second Division title in 1972. Lee gave 25 years' service to the Canaries, acting latterly as assistant trainer to the reserve side. At the end of World War Two he played for BAOR (British Army on the Rhine) in the European championships (1946).
* Lee was the first player to score 100 goals for York City, reaching the milestone against Sheffield Wednesday in a World War Two game in April 1943 (from the penalty spot).

LEE, Michael James

Outside-left: 1 app.

Born: Chester, North Wales, 27 June 1938. Career: Mold & St Asaph Schools. Saltney Juniors (Chester). ALBION (amateur, May 1956, professional, August 1956). Crewe Alexandra (free, June 1958). Flint Town United (free, August 1959). Pwllheli (March 1960). Sankey's Works (July 1961). Bethesda Athletic (August 1962). South African Football (1963–64). Dolgellau (August 1964). Colwyn Bay (July 1965). Bangor City (January 1966). Holyhead (May 1966). Ellesmere Port (August 1967). Holyhead FC (July 1968, retired, May 1970).

■ Mike Lee – son of George Lee – was a slim left-winger of fair skills who was his father's and Roy Horobin's deputy during his two years with Albion. He gained Welsh schoolboy and youth international honours but played only two League games during his career, one each for Albion and Crewe, making his Baggies debut against Sheffield Wednesday (home) in Division One in December 1956. He scored 12 goals in 45 Central League games.

LEE, William

Centre-forward: 76 apps. 25 goals.

Born: West Bromwich, 12 August 1878. Died: Walsall, 5 November 1934. Career: Guns Lane School (West Bromwich). West Bromwich Baptist FC. West Bromwich Standard. Bournville Athletic (1899). ALBION (professional, September 1901). Bournemouth Wanderers (on loan, 1903). Portsmouth (£100, September 1904). New Brompton (£50, August 1906). Chesterfield Town (£50, August 1907). Darlaston (free, October 1908, retired through injury, May 1911). Later employed as a porter at Wolverhampton railway station.

■ Billy Lee's unerring marksmanship made him a consistent scorer from the centre-forward berth. He led the line fluently, always producing maximum effort on the pitch. He arrived at Albion soon after the club had suffered relegation for the first time, and his presence in the side, plus his goalscoring ability, soon had the fans cheering promotion inside 12 months! Lee played in three junior internationals for

England and, later, was a shade unlucky not to make the full England team. He scored an average of a goal every three games for Albion – a record he kept up throughout an interesting career, which took him all over the country with various clubs. His Albion debut was against his future club, Chesterfield (away), in Division Two in September 1901. A goalscorer in Albion's 3–0 win over Stoke in the final of the Staffordshire Cup in 1903, Lee also played in 13 second XI matches for the club. During his senior career he scored 53 goals in 166 League games.

LEEDHAM, Frederick Arthur

Outside-right: 4 apps.

Born: Lye near Stourbridge, 18 February 1909.
Died: 12 January 1977.
Career: Lye Cross & Cradley Heath Schools, Cradley Heath Vics, Kidderminster Harriers (August 1925). ALBION (amateur, April 1926, professional, February 1928). Kidderminster Harriers (May 1929). Bradford Park Avenue (August 1931). Accrington Stanley (July 1933). Oldham Athletic (February 1935, released, June 1937). Played non-League football to 1939. Did not figure after World War Two. Became a part-time schoolteacher.

■ Fred Leedham was a player who exhibited fine persistence and speed in his raids from the right-wing position. He was reserve to Tommy Glidden during his stay with Albion, having just four senior outings before returning to Kidderminster Harriers. In 1931 he was brought back into League football and played in the top grade until 1937, scoring six goals in 49 appearances for Park Avenue, nine in 51 for Accrington and 11 in 48 for Oldham. He made his Albion debut at Reading in Division Two in November 1928.

LEGGE, Samuel George Frederick

Outside-left: 9 apps. 3 goals.

Born: Willenhall, 8 June 1881.
Died: Walsall, 12 August 1973.
Career: Essington & Darlaston Schools. Willenhall Swifts (1900). ALBION (professional, August 1906). Worcester City

(free, April 1907). ALBION (free, May 1908). Coventry City (free, June 1909, retired through injury, March 1911).

■ Sammy Legge was a delightful outside-left, a shade on the small side but always eager to tussle with the bigger opponents that marked him. He was mobile, passed with accuracy and could unleash a powerful shot. Had two spells with Albion, being reserve to Tommy Dilly and Edward Perkins first of all and then deputy to Bill Davies on his second visit. He made his debut for the Baggies against Nottingham Forest (home) in Division Two in February 1906, scoring in a 3–1 win. He played in over 30 second-team matches during his time at The Hawthorns but only had nine first-team outings for Coventry.

LEWIS, Albert Edward

Inside-left: 48 apps. 9 goals.

Born: Wolverhampton, 3 September 1884. Died: Northampton, 2 March 1923. Career: Heathtown School (Wolverhampton). Stafford Rovers (1902). ALBION (professional, June 1904). Northampton Town (£50, June 1906). ALBION (£50, May 1913). South Shields (£50, March 1914). Served in Army during World War One. Northampton Town (free, December 1919, retired, May 1920).

■ Albert Lewis was basically an inside-forward who could also play on the left-wing if required. He was a forager, always trying to pierce a tightly knit defence, a 100 percent trier, who had two spells with Albion. On his debut in September 1904 he hit a superb hat-trick in a 4–1 win at Burnley. He also played in 26 second XI matches. In 1908–9 he won a Southern League championship medal and the following season represented the Southern League. He scored over 100 goals for Northampton, another club he served twice.

LEWIS, Edward

Goalkeeper: 28 apps.

Born: West Bromwich, 21 June 1926. Career: Beeches Road & George Salter Schools (West Bromwich). ALBION (amateur, October 1944, professional, November 1944). Clapton Orient (£250, March 1946, retired through injury, May 1948).

■ Reserve to Jimmy Adams, Norman Heath and then Jim Sanders at Albion, Ted Lewis later played five League games for Orient. He made his Baggies debut against Stoke City (home) in the Football League North in November 1944.

LEWIS, Michael

Midfield: 30 + 3 apps.

Born: Birmingham, 15 February 1965. Career: Chilcote Primary & Moseley Comprehensive Schools (Birmingham). Hall Green St Michael's. Beeches Terriers FC. Olton Ravens. ALBION (apprentice, June 1981, professional, February 1982). Derby County (£25,000, November 1984). Oxford United (August 1988, player-exchange with Trevor Hebbard, later assistant manager/caretaker manager and player-coach, between 1996–2001).

■ Mickey Lewis was just 16 years and 10 months old when he made his senior debut as a substitute for Albion against Crystal Palace in the League Cup tie at Selhurst Park in December 1981. He was the youngest player to serve the club in this competition and the fourth youngest debutant in Albion's history, behind Frank Hodgetts, Charlie Wilson and Bobby Hope. An eager-beaver midfielder with a mop of frizzy hair, Lewis won four England youth international caps but found the challenge of first-team football too competitive at Albion, although he did appear in 66 Central League games (scoring six goals) and collected a championship medal at this level in 1982–83. He helped Derby win promotion to the Second Division in 1986.

LIGHT, William Henry

Goalkeeper: 30 apps.

Born: Woolston, Hampshire, 11 June 1913. Died: Colchester, February 1993. Career: Woolston & Bursledon Schools. Southampton Boys. Harland & Woolf FC. Thorneycrofts FC (Woolston). Winchester City (1931). Southampton (amateur, May 1932, professional, September 1933). Albion (£2,000, March 1936). Colchester United (free, June 1938, later coach and trainer at Layer Road, retired, June 1968).

■ A former joiner in a shipbuilding yard, goalkeeper Billy Light was far from

light in build! He was a massive man, one of the heaviest Albion had ever signed. Indeed, when he first arrived at The Hawthorns he tipped the scales at 15 stones and some of the fans got a shock when they saw him take the field for his Baggies debut against Wolverhampton Wanderers at Molineux in a Division One game in March 1936. However, despite his size, he never fulfilled his promise and, in fact, it was reported that he was snubbed by certain players at The Hawthorns. He was also unfortunate to stand (or rather hobble) between the sticks when Albion crashed to their heaviest League defeat ever, losing 10–3 at Stoke in 1937. He made 37 appearances for Albion's Central League side. Light played 45 League games for Southampton and was coach at Colchester when they gained entry into the Football League in 1950.

LILWALL, Stephen

Full-back: 84+2 apps.

Born: Solihull, 5 February 1970. Career: Moor Green (1988). Kidderminster Harriers (semi-professional, May 1990). ALBION (£75,000, professional, June 1992). Kidderminster Harriers (free, July 1995). Moor Green (August 1998–2001). Later Woodbourne FC (coach).

■ Bandy-legged, strong tackling full-back Steve Lilwall made a rapid rise from non-League football to Wembley Stadium

THE WHO'S WHO OF WEST BROMWICH ALBION

in just over a year! Signed by Albion manager Ossie Ardiles from Kidderminster Harriers to fill the left-back position, he was an ever-present in 1992–93 and played a big part in helping the Baggies gain promotion to the First Division via the play-offs. A player who enjoyed to overlap, he lost his place following the arrival of new manager Alan Buckley and a new left-back (Paul Agnew), and, subsequently, he returned to Aggborough after being given a free transfer, having also appeared in almost 30 second-team games.

LLOYD, John Amos

Outside-left: 46 apps. 9 goals.

Born: Pelsall near Walsall, 19 May 1889. Died: February 1943.
Career: Pelsall. Walsall Wood & Brownhills Schools. West Bromwich Wednesbury Athletic (1905). Nuneaton Town (1906). Halesowen (1908). Hednesford Town (1909). ALBION (professional, May 1910). Swansea Town (£250, June 1914, served in the Army during World War One, retired from football, May 1920).

■ Amos Lloyd was a fast and clever left-winger, whose performances were generally highlighted by his skilful cent-ring of the ball, aided by some power-house shooting. He made his debut for Albion against Hull City (away)in Division Two in September 1910 and won a Second Division championship medal that same season. He also scored 12 goals in more than 70 games for Albion's second XI in three years (1911–14), gaining a Birmingham & District League championship medal in 1902. He later added a Welsh Cup runners'-up medal to his tally when Swansea lost in the 1915 final.

LOACH, Arthur Albert

Forward: 14 apps. 9 goals.

Born: West Bromwich, 8 November 1863. Died: Rhyl, 9 February 1958.
Career: Christ Church School (West Bromwich). George Salter Works FC. ALBION (August 1882, professional, August 1885). Aston Villa (free, May 1886). Rhyl (August 1888, retired, 1896). Became a hotelier in the Welsh seaside town.

■ Arthur Loach was a speedy utility

forward who was a great team man. He played aggressively and loved to get involved in the action. A member of Albion's beaten 1886 FA Cup final side (against Blackburn Rovers), he appeared in over 80 first-team games during his four seasons with the club, making his debut against Junction Street School, Derby, (away) in the first round of the FA Cup in October 1884, scoring in an emphatic 7–1 win. He was 94 when he died.
* His brother, Albert, played reserve-team football in 1885–86 with Albion.

LONG, William Richard

Outside-right/left: 2 apps.

Born: Tividale, Tipton, 19 April 1899. Died: Dudley, 1960.
Career: Burn Tree Schools (Tipton). Tipton Excelsior FC. Hednesford Town (1917). ALBION (professional, August 1919). Hednesford Town (free, May 1921). Brierley Hill Alliance (August 1923, retired, May 1932).

■ Billy Long was a pattern-weaving winger who was reserve to Howard Gregory during his short stay with Albion, for whom he made his League debut against Blackburn Rovers (home) in October 1920. He also played a few games for the Baggies second XI, and he did very well at Hednesford, where he became a firm favourite with the Cross Keys fans.

LOVATT, John

Centre-forward: 18 apps. 5 goals.

Born: Burton upon Trent, Staffs, 23 August 1941.
Career: Uxbridge Street Junior & Burton Technical Schools. Spirella FC. Erdington Albion (1955). ALBION (amateur, January 1956, professional, December 1958). Nuneaton Borough (free, November 1963). Worcester City (June 1966). Banbury Spencer (1967, retired, May 1968). Later a businessman in Willenhall.

■ 'Shack' Lovatt was a tall, lanky striker who had good skills and a fair bit of energy and willpower but lacked that extra bit of snap. He made his League debut for Albion against West Ham United (away) in Division One in March 1961, scoring in a 2–1 win. He scored 50 goals in 124 Central League appearances for the Baggies.

LOVETT, Graham John

Midfield: 141 + 15 apps. 9 goals.

Born: Sheldon, Birmingham, 5 August 1947.
Career: Cockshutt Hill. Sheldon Heath & Camp Lane Schools (Birmingham). Birmingham & County Schoolboys. ALBION (apprentice, February 1964, professional, November 1964). Southampton (on loan,

November–December 1971). Worcester City (free, June 1972). Solihull Borough (1974–75). Greaves FC, West Bromwich (1975–76). West Bromwich Albion All Stars (1979–1986, when he retired). Later worked for the Express and Star *newspaper (promotions department). Now running a café/bar in Marbella, Spain.*

■ In the mid-1960s, Graham Lovett – nicknamed 'Shuv' – was being talked of as the 'new Duncan Edwards' of Midlands soccer. A skilful midfielder, he plied his fellow forwards with regular scoring chances, being strong in the tackle with stamina to match. Lovett won an FA Cup medal in 1968 after manager Alan Ashman gambled by naming him at outside-right in an effort to combat the overlaps of the Everton full-back Ray Wilson. It worked a treat, although he didn't have the greatest of games, missing an open goal late on. He made his League debut against Chelsea (home) in December 1964 and came back into big time football – prior to that 1968 Wembley appearance – after surviving two horrific car crashes, but the injuries he received in these accidents eventually forced him to give up competitive soccer at the early age of 26, although he did play some football for a few years afterwards. Lovett made over 150 senior appearances and 104 in the Central League (13 goals) for Albion – it would have been considerably more had those collisions not occurred when they did, so cruelly ending the career of such a fine player. In 1973, at Birmingham Crown

Court, he was awarded £14,000 damages against the West Midlands Passenger Transport Executive, after one of the accidents in Quinton, Birmingham.

LOWE, Joseph Arthur

Goalkeeper: 4 apps.

Born: West Bromwich, 15 July 1876.
Died: December 1931.
Career: Guns Village School (West Bromwich). West Bromwich Sandwell. Coombes Wood FC. ALBION (professional, June 1899). Willenhall Pickwick (July 1903). Tettenhall (1906, retired, January 1910).

■ A junior international (capped in 1899), Joe Lowe was unspectacular in style but safe and reliable when it came to the basic art of goalkeeping. Reserve to Joe Reader and Ike Webb during his four years with Albion, he made his League debut against Derby County (away) in December 1900 and, besides his four senior outings, he also appeared in 70 second XI games.

LOWERY, Anthony William

Midfield: 1 app.

Born: Wallsend-on-Tyne, 6 July 1961.
Career: Wallsend-on-Tyne & Heaton Schools. Newcastle Boys. Ashington FC (1979). ALBION (£3,500, February 1981). Walsall (on loan, February–March 1982). Mansfield Town (free, May 1983). Walsall (on loan, October-November 1990). Carlisle United (free, October 1991). Bedlington Terriers (player, August 1992, later coach from 1996, then manager, 2001–02, later assistant manager).

■ Tony Lowery was a good, hard-working midfielder who had limited opportunities at Albion but developed into an exciting player with Mansfield, helping the Stags win the Freight Rover Trophy at Wembley in May 1987 and promotion to Division Three in 1985–86. He amassed almost 300 senior appearances during his career, the majority with Mansfield (for whom he made 252 in the League). He made his Albion debut against Manchester City (away) on the opening day of the 1981–82 First Division season. He also scored seven goals in 52 Central League games, gaining a championship medal at

this level in 1982–83 when he assisted Mickey Lewis and Gary Childs in centre-field.

LOWERY, Harry

Wing-half: 44 apps.

Born: Moor Row near Whitehaven, Cumberland, 26 February 1918.
Died: c.1990.
Career: Egremont & Whitehaven Schools (Cumbria). Cleator Moor Celtic (August 1933). ALBION (amateur, November 1934, professional, May 1935). Guest for Bournemouth and Walsall during World War Two. Northampton Town (£1,250, October 1945). Bromsgrove Rovers (free, August 1949, retired, May 1955).

■ 'Snowy' Lowery was a centre-field grafter for Albion. He had an adventurous spirit, loved to attack and was polished in his overall play. Two thirds of his appearances for Albion were made during World War Two. No relation to Tony, he made his League debut for Albion against Preston North End (away) in January 1938. He also played in 60 second-team matches (one goal scored).

LUKE, Noel Emmanuel

Midfield: 11+3 apps. 1 goal.

Born: Moseley, Birmingham, 28 December 1964.
Career: Conway Junior & Moseley Comprehensive Schools (Birmingham). Moseley Colts. Beeches Terriers. Olton Ravens (1980). ALBION (apprentice, June 1981, professional, April 1982). Mansfield Town (free, June 1984). Newport County (on loan, 1986). Peterborough United (free, August 1986). Rochdale (on loan, March-April 1993). Boston United (August 1993). Holbeach United (1994). Corby Town (1995). King's Lynn (March 1996). Raunds Town (October 1996, retired, May 1997). Later ran a café/bar adjoining Peterborough's London Road ground.

■ Perhaps not First or Second Division standard, Noel Luke was, nevertheless, a player who did well after dropping down the ladder to link up with Mansfield and later with Peterborough. A Central League championship winner with Albion in 1982–83, he made over 70 appearances for the second XI and his senior debut came as a substitute against Norwich City (home) in May 1983. He

THE WHO'S WHO OF WEST BROMWICH ALBION

helped Mansfield gain promotion to the Third Division in 1985–86 and made over 300 appearances for Posh (30 goals scored).

LUNN, William John

Inside-forward: 10 apps. 5 goals.

Born: Lurgan, Northern Ireland, 8 May 1923.
Career: Lurgan & Craigavon Schools. Portadown (trialist). Waringstown FC. Shanklin FC. Distillery Ireland (1942). Glenavon, Ireland (1944). ALBION (£1,750, professional, January 1946). Bournemouth (£3,000, February 1948). Newport County (free, July 1950). Yeovil Town (free, May 1952, retired, April 1955). Now lives in Bournemouth.

■ Billy Lunn was an versatile forward of consequence, whether at inside or outside-left. Not a prolific goalscorer but a player who netted at vital times, he was a subtle schemer rather than a marksman, a player who plugged away unceasingly. Capped at schoolboy level by Northern Ireland, he made his League debut for Albion against Chesterfield (home) in Division Two in April 1947, and he also netted 25 times in 46 second XI games. After leaving The Hawthorns, he appeared in 47 League matches for Bournemouth (19 goals) and six for Newport (one goal). He is one of Albion's oldest ex-players.

LYNEX, Stephen Charles

Outside-right: 28 + 6 apps. 5 goals.

Born: West Bromwich, 23 January 1958.
Career: All Saints Junior & Churchfields Comprehensive Schools (West Bromwich). West Bromwich Town Boys. Charlemont Farm Boys. Sandwell Rangers. Aston Villa (trialist, March–April 1973). Wolverhampton Wanderers (trialist, May–June 1973). ALBION (apprentice, July 1974, professional, January 1977). Sligo Rovers (trialist, April 1977). Shamrock Rovers (free, July 1977). Queen's Park Rangers (trialist, 1978). Birmingham City (free, April 1979). Leicester City (£60,000, February 1981). Birmingham City (on loan, October–December 1986). ALBION (£5, March 1987). Cardiff City (free, June 1988). Telford United (free, March 1990). Trafford Park FC, Birmingham (March 1991–April 1992).

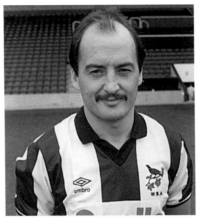

Later a publican in Birmingham and West Bromwich (licensee of the Red Lion). Also played for Ansells FC (briefly, 1992–93).

■ A fast-raiding outside-right who 'returned' home to West Bromwich 10 years after Johnny Giles had whisked him over to Ireland, Steve Lynex's presence in the side certainly went a long way towards helping Albion stave off relegation at the end of the 1986–87 season. In his first spell at The Hawthorns he won an FA Youth Cup medal (1976) but never got a chance in Albion's League side. In Ireland he gained European experience with Shamrock Rovers and won an FAI Cup medal in 1978, as well as representing the League of Ireland XI against Liverpool. He returned to England in 1979 and made over 50 appearances for the Blues, helping them win promotion to Division One in 1980. He then switched to Leicester and was a key member of their promotion-winning side from Division Two in 1983. During his career, Lynex amassed well over 400 senior appearances, netting more than 70 goals, of which a fair number have been penalties. He made his Albion debut (at senior level) against Oldham Athletic (away) in Division Two in March 1987, 13 years after first joining the club, and overall he appeared in more than 80 second XI games, scoring eight goals.
* When Lynex was licensee of the Red Lion in West Bromwich, a young boy was accidentally killed during a firework display in the grounds of the pub.

LYTTLE, Desmond

Full-back: 73+16 apps. 1 goal.

Born: Wolverhampton, 24 September 1971.
Career: Leicester City (apprentice, April

1988, professional, September 1990). Worcester City (May 1991). Swansea City (£12,500, July 1992). Nottingham Forest (£375,000, July 1993). Port Vale (on loan, November–December 1998). Watford (free, July 1999). ALBION (free, March 2000, released, June 2003). Sheffield Wednesday (trialist, May–August 2003). Chesterfield (trialist, September 2003). Stourport Swifts (one game). Northampton Town (October 2003–May 2004). Forest Green Rovers (August 2004).

■ A very steady right full-back, Des Lyttle played for Swansea against Albion in the 1993 play-off semi-final and helped Forest win the First Division championship in 1998. He had already appeared in more than 300 first-team matches before joining Albion. He went straight into the side, making his Baggies debut as a 'sub' against Portsmouth (away) in March 2000. He held his position throughout the following campaign but lost out eventually to the Slovakian international Igor Balis. He made over 30 second XI appearances for Albion.

McCALL, Andrew

Inside-forward: 32 apps. 3 goals.

Born: Hamilton, Scotland, 15 March 1925.
Career: Hamilton & East Kilbride Schools. Bent Royal Oak BSA. Blantyre Celtic (1943). Blackpool (professional, July 1947). ALBION (£8,500, January 1951). Leeds United (£2,000, August 1952). Lovells Athletic (free, July 1955). Halifax Town (free, July 1956, retired, May 1961). Now resident in Bradford.

■ Andy McCall was not the most polished of inside-forwards, but he was workman-like and combined excellently with his winger. He tended to be rather greedy at times, but occasionally he performed brilliantly, and during his career he accumulated a total of 316 League appearances and scored 41 goals. He won Scottish junior international honours in 1945 (against Northern Ireland) and made his Albion debut against Chelsea (home) in Division One in January 1951. He also scored six goals in 13 second-team games for the Baggies. * McCall was badly burned in the Bradford City fire disaster at Valley Parade in May 1985 while watching his son, Stuart, playing for City, later of Glasgow Rangers, Everton and Sheffield United.

McCULLOCH, Thomas

Full-back: 57 apps.

Born: Strathblane, Stirlingshire, 12 December 1868.
Died: Glasgow, April 1940.
Career: Strathblane & Blanefield Schools (Glasgow). Glasgow Rangers (trialist, 1887). Glasgow United (August 1888). ALBION (professional, January 1891). Stirling (free, November 1893). Burslem Port Vale (briefly, 1995). Glasgow East End (1896, retired 1898). Later worked as a teacher in Glasgow from 1900.

■ Tom McCulloch was a steady, easy-going full-back, whose displays were precociously cool, clever and mature, even in his younger playing days in Glasgow. He could play virtually anywhere, with persuasion and in 1890–91 kept goal in one match for Albion's reserve side. He formed a fine partnership with Magnus Nicholson, but in 1893–94 he was given notice to quit Albion because of neglecting to train and left the club in these sad circumstances

after two and a half years. He won an FA Cup medal (against Aston Villa) in March 1892, having made his Albion debut a little over a year earlier against Preston North End (home) in February 1891. He also played in almost 60 'other' first-team games for the club.

McKENNAN, Peter Stewart

Inside-forward: 27 apps. 17 goals.

Born: Airdrie, 16 July 1918.
Died: Troon, Ayrshire, Scotland, September 1991
Career: Whitburn Junior & Airdrie High Schools. Whitburn Juniors FC. Edinburgh Juniors. Partick Thistle (amateur, July 1935, professional, September 1935). Guest for Wrexham, Linfield, Glentoran, Chelsea, Wolves, Brentford and ALBION during World War Two. ALBION (£10,650, October 1947). Leicester City (£6,000, plus Jack Haines, March 1948). Brentford (September 1948). Middlesbrough (May 1949). Oldham Athletic (July 1951). Coleraine (player-coach, 1954–55). Later lived in Dundonald, Ayrshire.

■ Peter 'Ma Ba' McKennan twice played for the Irish Regional League (against the League of Ireland) during World War Two. He was a gifted inside-forward with a physique to withstand the heaviest of challenges. His chief assets were speed off the mark, good ball control, a thunderbolt shot and, above all, supreme confidence in possession. He cost Partick the proverbial 'song' back in 1935, and he made his debut as a 17-year-old against Dunfermline, becoming an instant 'hit' with the fans. He joined the Army in September 1939, serving first with the Royal Artillery and later with the Royal Welch Fusiliers, landing in Normandy two weeks after 'D' Day and taking part in the battle of Caen. He finished up in Hamburg in February 1946. He was one of only four survivors from his section in one engagement and was mentioned in dispatches for patrol work. He joined Albion in the face of tough competition from Aston Villa, Grimsby and Middlesbrough, but sadly never settled down at The Hawthorns, nor did he settle at Filbert Street or Brentford, making a total of just 42 League appearances for the latter two clubs. He did far better with Middlesbrough (18

goals in 40 League games) and Oldham (78 games, 28 goals), winning a Third Division North championship medal with the Latics in 1952–53. While with Partick, McKennan also represented the Scottish League XI twice (in 1937 and 1938). He made his debut for Albion as a wartime guest against Northampton Town (home) in the Football League South in December 1941, scoring a hat-trick in a 7–0 win, and his League debut followed against Bury (away) in Division Two in November 1947.

MACKENZIE, Stephen

Midfield: 179 + 5 apps. 25 goals.

Born: Romford, Essex, 23 November 1961.
Career: Havering & Essex Schools. Byron Red Star (Romford). Crystal Palace (July 1977, professional, July 1979). Manchester City (£250,000, July 1979). ALBION (£650,000, July 1981). Charlton Athletic (£200,000, June 1987). Sheffield Wednesday (February 1991). Shrewsbury Town (December 1991–April 1993). Willenhall Town (1993–94). Bromsgrove

Rovers (briefly). Stafford Rangers (1995–96). Atherstone United (player-coach 1997, then assistant manager, 1998 and manager, May 2000). Pelsall Villa (player-manager, September 2002). Gresley Rovers (player-coach, March 2004). ALBION (Academy coach, 2003–04). Later with the Press Association/PF, working on betting-related match commentary.

■ Central midfielder Steve Mackenzie joined Albion almost immediately after scoring one of the most spectacular goals ever seen at Wembley, for Manchester City against Tottenham Hotspur in the 1981 FA Cup final. By coincidence, he made his Baggies debut against his former club, Manchester City (away), in a First Division game in August 1981. He also appeared in 24 Central League games, scoring 10 goals. His first move in professional football circles – from Selhurst Park to Maine Road in 1979 – caused something of a stir because he had not figured in either a League or major cup game at senior level but still cost a quarter-of-a-million pounds when signed by Malcolm Allison. He had been a key member of Palace's youth cup teams of 1977 and 1978 but was a novice as far as competing in the big time was concerned. However, Mackenzie pulled through. He made 75 appearances for City and, after his £650,000 transfer to The Hawthorns, continued to improve and impress, although he missed virtually all of the 1982–83 campaign because of a serious pelvic injury. On the international front, Mackenzie won 15 youth caps for England and later added three under-21 level and several 'B' caps to his collection. He was a youth Cup winner with Palace in 1978 but collected a runners'-up medal in the same competition with Manchester City in 1980. On leaving Albion in 1987, he teamed up with his former colleague Garth Crooks of Charlton and was later joined at Atherstone by another ex-Albion midfielder, Tony Grealish.

McCUE, James

Forward: 0+2 apps.

Born: Glasgow, 29 June 1975.
Career: West Park United. Hamilton Thistle (schoolboy trialist, during 1990). ALBION (apprentice, January 1991, professional, February 1993). Partick Thistle (free, January 1996). Kidderminster

Harriers (free, August 1996). Hereford United (free, October 1997–May 1998). Now in Scotland

■ Scottish-born striker James McCue made his Albion debut as a substitute away to Mansfield Town (Autoglass Trophy) in January 1993 and had one more outing, also as a 'sub', against Bristol Rovers (League Cup) seven months later, as well as playing in over 80 second-team games, scoring more than 20 goals. However, owing to the form of Bob Taylor, Andy Hunt and a few others, he was hardly ever in the first-team squad during his time at The Hawthorns and returned to his homeland in 1996. He joined ex-Albion players Mark Dearlove and Neil Cartwright at Kidderminster and played alongside Lee Hughes in the Harriers attack during the 1996–97 season.

McCULLUM, William Donald

Full-back: 3 apps.

Born: Paisley, Renfrewshire, 14 June 1870. Died: Dumbarton, 1935.
Career: Paisley. Johnstone & Glenburn Schools. Glasgow Celtic (1889). ALBION (professional, January 1891). Dumbarton (free, May 1891–April 1893).

■ 'Jock' McCullum was a sturdy defender, some say he was overweight at 12 stones plus, but he could kick like a mule, tackle hard and fair and occupy several defensive positions, including both full-back berths, right half and pivot. He joined Albion along with two Mac's – McCulloch and McLeod – but, unlike his fellow countrymen, he left the club after barely five months, having made his League debut against Preston North End (home) in Division One in February 1891 as McCulloch's partner.

McDERMOTT, Andrew

Full-back: 53+4 apps. 2 goals.

Born: Sydney, Australia, 24 March 1977. Career: Australian Institute of Sport. Queen's Park Rangers (professional, August 1995). ALBION (£400,000, March 1997). Luton Town (trialist, March–April 2000). Notts County (free, August 2000). Northern Spirit FC, Australia (June 2001). Dunfermline Athletic (during 2003–04).

■ After just six League games for Queen's Park Rangers, Aussie right wing-back Andy McDermott joined Albion on transfer deadline day in 1997. He made his debut for the club against Sheffield United a week later, taking over from Paul Holmes with fellow countryman Shaun Murphy alongside him in the Baggies defence. A shade on the small side, he got forward when given the chance but lacked consistency as well as struggling with his crosses at times. He did, however, score a cracking League goal during his time at The Hawthorns – in the local derby against Wolves in October 1999 (1–1 draw). As an Albion player, he gained four under-21 caps for his country and also played in over 40 second-team games.

McINNES, Derek John

Midfield: 99+1 apps. 6 goals.

Born: Paisley, Scotland, 5 July 1971. Career: Gleniffer Thistle (August 1987). Greenock Morton (professional, August 1988). Glasgow Rangers (£250,000, November 1995). Stockport County (on loan, November 1998–January 1999). Toulouse, France (December 1999, ALBION (£450,000, August 2000). Dundee United (free, July 2003).

gaining the first of two full Scottish caps against Denmark in August 2002 (a second followed against Portugal three months later). McInnes went on to play in 100 first-team games for Albion, although he did have the misfortune of being sent off in the club's first ever Premiership game against Manchester United at Old Trafford on 17 August 2002, with over 67,500 fans present! A great competitor, nevertheless.

McKENZIE, Alexander Duncan

Inside-forward: 55 apps. 9 goals.

Born: Greenock, Scotland, 28 March 1875. Died: Glasgow, June 1950.
Career: Greenock & Port Glasgow Schools. Clyde (May 1893). Millwall Athletic (£50, August 1894). Sunderland (£125, May 1895). Millwall Athletic (£75, June 1896). ALBION (£16, July 1897). Dumbarton (free, May 1899). Third Lanark (free, August 1903). Sunderland (£25, August 1905, retired, May 1908). Later employed in the Port of Glasgow as a steelworker.

■ Alex McKenzie was a clever, scheming inside-forward whose creative gifts brought the best out of his colleagues. Teaming up well with Ben Garfield and John Nock, he appeared in over 50 senior and 20 'other' first-team games for the Baggies, making his League debut against Aston Villa (away) in September 1897 when he scored in a 4–3 defeat. After leaving the club, he gained a Scottish Cup winners' medal with Third Lanark (1905) and the following season returned to Sunderland for a second spell. Earlier in his career McKenzie represented the Southern League against a London FA XI in 1896–97, partnering Alf Geddes, an ex-Throstle, on the left-wing. He was also suspended four times during the 1898–99 season for breaches of training rules, thus hastening his departure from Albion.

MacLEAN, Hugh

Outside-left: 6 + 2 apps.

Born: Stornoway, Isle of Lewis, 20 January 1952.
Career: Achmore & Bayble Schools. Stornoway Boys. Tantallon Youth Club. West Kilbride & District Boys (1966). ALBION (apprentice, May 1967, professional, February 1969). Swindon

■ Midfielder Derek McInnes agreed to a drop in wages to join Albion from the French club Toulouse in the summer of 2000. His first season at The Hawthorns was ruined by injury but his second, as captain, was excellent as he led the Baggies into the Premiership. After making more than 250 appearances for Morton, he spent half his time at Ibrox as a substitute, playing in just 51 matches in four years, as well as having a loan spell under Gary Megson at Stockport and

Town (£20,000, July 1974). Dumbarton (free, August 1975, retired through injury, 1979). Now living and working in Scotland.

■ Hughie MacLean was tall and lanky and a good ball player but was always going to miss out because of his weight. He had 19 League outings for Swindon before switching to Scotland. His senior debut for Albion came against the League Cup holders Tottenham Hotspur (home) in a second round tie in September 1971. He also played in 120 Central League games and netted 16 goals.

McLEAN, James Charles

Outside-right: 60 apps. 10 goals.

Born: Stoke-on-Trent, 15 November 1877.
Died: Perth, Australia, 18 April 1914.
Career: Stoke City Schools. Sneyd FC. Burslem Port Vale (July 1896). Eastville Rovers (March 1897). Worcester Rovers (August 1897). Walsall (professional, November 1899). ALBION (£100, May 1901). Preston North End (£150, April 1903, retired through injury, May 1911). Emigrated to Canada where he went into business, later travelled to Australia where he died at the age of 36 after a short illness.

■ Jimmy McLean was a shrewd, stocky little right-winger who had loads of confidence, good ball control, aggression and a quick turn of foot. He joined Albion when the club had just dropped into Division Two for the first time, and his presence in the forward-line during the 1901–02 season went a long way in helping the club regain their top division status at the first attempt. McLean was, in fact, the first ever professional to sign for Eastville (1897), yet was 'fined' after his debut game for turning out as a professional! The fixture was forfeited and for a time McLean was paid for his services as a groundsman at Eastville until the club adopted professionalism legally later in 1897. He gained two Second Division championship medals, first with Albion (1902) and then with Preston (1904), for whom he netted four times in 185 League games. McLeod had the pleasure of scoring Albion's first Second Division goal against his future club Preston (home) in September 1901, having made his debut against Glossop (also at home) five days earlier. He also netted in Albion's 3–0 win over Stoke in the final of the Staffordshire Cup in 1902.

McLEOD, Roderick

Inside-forward: 185 apps. 65 goals.

Born: Kilsyth, Stirlingshire, 12 February 1872.
Died: Lambeth, London, December 1931.
Career: Kilsyth & Kirkintilloch Schools. Westburn FC. Partick Thistle (professional, April 1889). ALBION (£50, January 1891). Leicester Fosse (£50, August 1897). Brighton United (free, May 1898). Southampton (free, April 1899). Brentford (free, August 1900, retired, 1904). Worked as a civil servant for many years and also as a tiller in a London bank.

■ Roddy McLeod was a grand little player, occupying the inside-right position most of the time. He possessed intricate footwork skills and his passing and shooting ability were outstanding. He was the perfect foil to Billy Bassett with whom he performed so wonderfully well in so many games for Albion during the 1890s. McLeod's own record with Albion was exceptional – a goal every three matches – and besides scoring regularly he also set up several more scoring chances for his colleagues. He made his Albion debut against Sheffield Wednesday (away) in a third round FA Cup tie in February 1891 and appeared in two FA Cup finals, gaining a winners' medal in 1892 (against Aston Villa) and a runners'-up medal against the same opponents in 1895. Besides his first-team appearances for the club, McLeod also played in more than 125 'other' matches. He later helped Brentford win the Southern League

Second Division championship (1901). After retiring (in 1906) he fell on hard times and in March 1911 an appeal was made on his behalf to find employment. He eventually became a warehouseman, later worked in a brewery and then worked as a boiler mechanic in London, eventually retiring with rheumatoid arthritis, a legacy from his playing days.

McMANUS, Peter Thomas

Half-back: 28 apps. 1 goal.

Born: Winchburgh, West Lothian, 18 April 1873.
Died: Edinburgh, Scotland, May 1936.
Career: Winchburgh & Queensferry Schools. Hibernian (professional, June 1891). Mossend Swifts (1893–94). St Bernard's FC (August 1894). ALBION (free, June 1896). Warmley FC (June 1898). Thames Ironworks/West Ham United (free, February 1899). Retired to Scotland in the summer of 1900, having failed to recover full fitness after breaking his leg. He took employment with the forestry commission, based near Edinburgh.

■ Peter McManus was a driving, dashing half-back who knew no fear. It is said that no one defended with more gusto than this 'fella' in the 1890s, yet his first-team outings for Albion were restricted to a mere 28 owing to the presence of such fine players as Tom Perry, Tommy Higgins and Jack Banks. McManus gained a Scottish Cup winners' medal with St Bernard's in 1895 (against Renton). He made his League debut for Albion against Blackburn Rovers (away) in September 1896 and also played in 30 or so 'other' first-team matches for the club.

McNAB, Alexander

Left-half: 186 apps. 4 goals.

Born: Glasgow, 27 December 1911.
Died: West Bromwich, 19 September 1962.
Career: Glasgow & District Schools. Tuesday Waverley FC. Pollock FC (Glasgow). Sunderland (August 1932). ALBION (£6,750, March 1938). Guest for Newport County, Nottingham Forest, Northampton Town and Walsall during World War Two. Newport County (£1,000, April 1946). Dudley Town (free, December 1946). Northwich Victoria (August 1947, later player-manager, from August 1948,

retired, May 1952). Then a licensee at Carter's Green, West Bromwich, until his death.

■ 'Sandy' McNab was a marvellous, pint-sized left-half, whose tackling was done judiciously without him losing his poise. A red-head, he was brave, seemingly tireless and rallied Sunderland to victory in the 1937 FA Cup final against Preston. A year later he helped the Wearsiders win the First Division title. McNab won two full caps for Scotland (1937–39), represented the Football League and toured Canada and the US with the Scottish FA party in 1939. He was Albion's skipper during World War Two when most of his senior appearances for the club were accumulated. He helped the Baggies win the Midland War Cup (against Nottingham Forest) in May 1944 and also played in 10 second-team games. An ex-grocer, he played outside-left at School and made his Albion debut against Derby County (home) in Division One in March 1938 (at a time when Second Division football was looming at The Hawthorns).

McNALLY, Bernard Anthony

Midfield: 168 apps. 14 goals.

Born: Shrewsbury, 17 February 1963. Career: Shrewsbury Town (apprentice, April 1979, professional, February 1981). ALBION (£385,000, July 1989). Hednesford Town (free, July 1995). Telford United (briefly, 1998). Rushall Olympic (1998–2001). ALBION (youth team coach, July 2002, later youth recruitment officer). AFC Telford (manager, June 2004).

■ An industrious midfielder who scored 23 goals in over 282 League games for Shrewsbury before joining Albion in 1989, Bernard McNally spent six years at The Hawthorns, during which time he helped Albion win promotion to the First Division in 1993 (via the play-offs). He made his debut for the Baggies against Sheffield United in August 1989 and, besides his first-team outings, he played almost 50 games for the second team, scoring three goals and helping the team win the Pontins League title in 1990–91. He was capped five times by Northern Ireland. In the summer of 2002 McNally returned to The Hawthorns to assist another ex-Albion player, Craig Shakespeare, with youth development at the club, before taking his first steps into management with the reformed non-League side AFC Telford.

McNAUGHT, Kenneth

Central-defender: 50 apps. 1 goal.

Born: Kirkcaldy, Fife, 17 January 1955. Career: Everton (junior, July 1970, professional, May 1972). Aston Villa (£200,000, July 1977). ALBION (£125,000, August 1983). Manchester City (on loan, December 1984–January 1985). Sheffield United (£10,000, July 1985, retired, May 1986). Dunfermline Athletic (coach, 1986–87). Swansea City (assistant manager, briefly, 1987–88). Vale of Earn, Scotland (manager, 1988–89). Now working in the pro's shop at the famous Scottish golf course, Gleneagles.

■ Ken McNaught gained both youth and Amateur international honours for

Scotland as a teenager. After more than 65 outings for Everton he developed into an excellent centre-half with Villa, commanding in the air, positive and sure in the tackle. He was the backbone of Ron Saunders's and Tony Barton's defences during his time at the club, scoring 13 goals in 260 senior appearances, while collecting a League Championship, European Cup and Super Cup medal. Ironically, he made his Baggies debut in a 4–3 defeat at Villa Park on the opening day of the 1983–84 season, following his transfer in the summer (signed by the manager to replace John Wile). Indeed, he was an ever-present at the heart of the Baggies defence that season, before Martyn Bennett and Ally Robertson became the club's chosen defensive duo. McNaught's only goal for Albion came in a 2–0 League home win over Notts County in November 1983. He also played in 20 second XI games.

*McNaught's father, Willie, was a full Scottish international.

McNEAL, Robert

Left-half: 403 apps. 10 goals.

Born: Hobson Village, County Durham, 19 January 1891.
Died: West Bromwich, 12 May 1956.
Career: Hobson Day School (Durham). Hobson Wanderers (August 1907). ALBION (professional, June 1910, retired throuh injury, May 1925, later became club coach, 1926–27). Guest for Fulham, Middlesbrough, Notts County and Port Vale during World War One. Licensee in West Bromwich (1930s).

■ Bobby McNeal was a stylish left-half with a footballing brain. He distributed the ball accurately and defended with commendable steadiness and reliability. Arriving at The Hawthorns as a raw-boned 19-year-old in the summer of 1910, he made his debut as an inside-left against Leeds City (home) in Division Two in October of that year, but he was later switched to left-half where he became an international-class player in a relatively short period of time. Once

McNeal had bedded himself into Albion's first XI at left-half he was virtually immovable and only injuries, suffered during the 1924–25 season, resulted in him losing his place. In the end it was his left knee that finally ended his career at the age of 34. He gained two England caps (against Wales and Scotland in 1914) and also represented the Football League on five occasions (1912–14). He won four medals with Albion: Division Two champions (1910–11), FA Cup runner-up (1912), League championship (1919–20) and FA Charity Shield victors (also in 1920). He was something of a penalty expert too and would often fire in a free-kick from a full 25 yards, usually hitting the target. A magnificent club man, McNeal appeared in over 400 senior games for Albion (370 in the League) and during the first four seasons, after serving in the Army during World War One (1919–23), he missed only eight matches; such was his reliability and consistency. He also played in over 50 second-team matches. As a guest, he helped Fulham beat Chelsea in the Victory Cup final at Highbury in 1918.

McVITIE, George James

Winger: 52 apps. 5 goals.

Born: Carlisle, 7 September 1948.
Career: Petterill Bank School (Carlisle). Carlisle & District Boys. Carlisle United (apprentice, May 1964, professional, December 1965). ALBION (£33,333 August 1970). Oldham Athletic (£15,000, August 1972). Carlisle United (£12,000 December 1975). Queen of the South (1981–82). Now living and working in his native Carlisle.

■ George McVitie was a winger with many skills but a player whose ability was not always up to First Division standard. Prior to joining Albion, he won four England schoolboy caps (1963–64) and a youth cap. In the summer of 1971 he played in three games for the FA XI on tour to Ireland and later Australia, and during the course of his professional career (which spanned 17 years) he amassed a total of 502 League appearances (in England and Scotland) and scored 66 goals. His record with Carlisle (two spells) was 326 League outings and 41 goals. McVitie gained a Third Division championship medal with Oldham in

1973–74 and played for Carlisle (against Albion) in the 1970 League Cup semi-final. He made his Baggies debut against Newcastle United (home) in Division One in September 1970. He also scored five goals in 28 Central League games.

MACREADY, Brian Leslie

Outside-right: 15 apps. 1 goal.

Born: Leicester, 25 March 1942.
Career: Beverley Grammar School. Willerby Boys' Club. East Riding County Boys. Hull City (amateur, May 1957). ALBION (amateur, December 1959, professional, February 1960). Mansfield Town (£2,300, June 1964). Worcester City (June 1966). Banbury Spencer (July 1967). Lower Cornal (July 1968). Darlaston (March 1969). Lower Gornal (1969–70). Whiteheath FC (1971–72). West Bromwich Albion All Stars (1972–75). Now resident in Sutton Coldfield.

■ Brian Macready was a compact winger, not brilliant but a player who worked hard. Injury cut short his League career, although he hung on in the game until well into his 30s. He scored 11 goals in 50 League outings for Mansfield after leaving Albion in 1964. He made his Albion debut against Blackpool (home) in Division One in December 1960 and scored his only goal for the club later that month in a 3–12 defeat at Cardiff. 'Macca' also scored 24 goals in 100 Central League games for the Baggies.

MADDEN, Craig Anthony

Striker: 10 + 2 apps. 3 goals.

Born: Manchester, 25 September 1958.
Career: Cheetham Hill & Blackley Schools

(Manchester). Stockport Boys. Northern Nomads (September 1973). Bury (amateur, April 1977, professional, March 1978). ALBION (£50,000, March 1986). Blackpool (£50,000, February 1987). Wrexham (on loan, January–March 1990). York City (March 1990). Later Stockport County (coach, 2000–03).

■ A highly-successful marksman with Bury, scoring a record 152 goals in 337 appearances, Craig Madden never struck that same lethal form during his brief association with Albion, although it must be said that he was never really given the opportunity! At Gigg Lane, Madden broke Norman Bullock's club record of 124 League goals set between 1920–35. He was leading scorer for the Shakers on six occasions and in 1981–82 was the country's top-marksman with 42 League and cup goals, including 35 in the Fourth Division, a record for Bury, whom he helped gain promotion to the Third Division in 1984–85. Always alert and eager in the 'box', he left Albion for Blackpool and immediately began to find the net once again. Madden, in fact, was manager Ron Saunders's 100th signing as a League manager when he bought him

from Bury in 1986. He made his Albion debut against Ipswich Town (away) in Division One in March 1986. He scored 12 goals in 14 Central League games for the Baggies.

MAGEE, Thomas Patrick

Wing-half: 434 apps. 18 goals.

Born: Widnes, 6 May 1899.
Died: Widnes, May 1974.
Career: St. Mary's School (Widnes). Appleton Hornets (Rugby League). St Helen's Recreation Club (Rugby League). Widnes Athletic (amateur, 1914–15). ALBION (professional, January 1919). Crystal Palace (free, player-coach, May 1934). Runcorn (player-manager 1935, later coach, retired, c.1947). Returned to Widnes where he worked briefly in engineering.

■ Tommy Magee was a midget right-half, formerly an outside-right or inside-forward, who played with evident enjoyment, tenacity, wonderful consistency and constructiveness. Nicknamed 'Pocket Hercules' and the 'Mighty Atom' by the players and supporters alike, 'wee Tommy' played well over 400 games for Albion during 15 years' service with the club. He was initially signed-up while serving in the trenches in France during World War One, sending the appropriate papers back to The Hawthorns by air. As a player (you could call him a fighter too) he won five England caps, all as a right-half, against Wales and Sweden in 1923, Belgium in 1924 and Scotland and France in 1925. He also toured Canada with the FA party

in 1926 and 1931 and is the only Albion player (so far) to have won a First Division championship medal (1920) and an FA Cup winners' medal (1931) with the club. Magee also played in over 100 second XI games, helping the Baggies win the Birmingham & District League title in 1919–20 and the championship of the Central League in 1932–33 and 1933–34. Magee is reputed to be the smallest player ever to wear an England shirt at only 5ft 2½in tall, and he's certainly the smallest first-team player Albion have ever had. But what a footballer! He made his senior debut against Derby County (home) in the Midland Victory League in April 1919, scoring in Albion's 3–1 win, and followed up with his first League outing at Oldham on the opening day of that championship-winning season of 1919–20.

MAHON, John

Outside-right: 123 apps. 44 goals.

Born: Gillingham, 8 December 1911.
Deceased.
Career: Doncaster Junior & Grammar Schools. New Brompton Excelsior (1925). Doncaster Rovers (professional, August 1928). Leeds United (£1,300, May 1930). ALBION (£4,000, September 1935). Huddersfield Town (£4,250, September 1938). Guest for Aldershot, Bradford City, Chelsea, Halifax Town, Leeds United,

Millwall, QPR, Reading, Torquay United and West Ham United during World War Two. York City (£500, August 1945–September 1946). Leeds United (free, player-coach, August 1947, retired as a player, January 1948). Hull City (coach, August 1950–June 1956). Later coached in Denmark and Sweden for some eight years (to 1964).

■ 'Jack' Mahon was a resourceful and swift right-winger who made his Albion debut against Liverpool (away) in Division One in September 1935. He had a good shot and he never used robust tactics, being fair and diligent in his overall play. He came to Albion as a replacement for Tommy Glidden and appeared in well over 120 games, scoring regularly. He also made seven appearances for Albion's second string. Sadly, he made a tragic start to his career with Huddersfield, fracturing his shin-bone on his debut versus Sunderland. He bounced back, however, and toured South Africa with the FA Party in 1939, playing in one Test Match. During his career, Mahon appeared in 250 plus senior matches, including 84 for Leeds (23 goals). He was also a first-team cricketer.

MALE, Norman Alfred

Full-back: 4 apps. 1 goal.

Born: West Bromwich, 27 May 1917.
Died: Tipton, 1992.
Career: Greets Green & Horseley Heath Schools. Bush Rangers (1931). ALBION (amateur, November 1933, professional, October 1934). Walsall (£250, May 1938) ALBION (guest, World War Two). Walsall (August 1945, retired, August 1949, worked on groundstaff at Fellows Park for 20 years to 1969).

■ Norman Male was a most capable and efficient full-back who was a respected reserve during his five years' association with Albion, for whom he made his senior debut against Grimsby Town (away) in Division Two in September 1937. A salt-of-the-earth character, he won junior international honours for England in 1935 and played in 17 Central League games (one goal scored) before leaving The Hawthorns for Walsall, whom he served splendidly, first as a player, appearing in 81 League and cup matches and over 170 during World War Two, and then on the groundstaff.

MANN, John Frederick

Centre-forward: 2 apps.

Born: West Bromwich, 3 March 1891.
Died: West Bromwich, summer, 1969.
Career: Great Bridge Schools. Great Bridge Juniors (1907–11). Great Bridge Celtic (August 1911). Hurst Hill Rovers (briefly). Bilston United (January 1912). ALBION (professional, April 1912). Newport County (£195, July 1919). Walsall (£75, July 1920–May 1921). Later with Darlaston and Stourbridge. Retired through injury, April 1925. ALBION (scout, for seven years, August 1945–July 1952).

■ Jackie Mann was a direct, hard-running centre-forward, fast in action and always seeking to have a shot at goal. Twice a junior international, honoured in 1913 and 1917, he was only a small man but could take the heftiest of challenges. A former playing colleague of Sammy Richardson with Great Bridge Juniors, he made his League debut for Albion against Manchester United at Old Trafford in October 1914, stepping in for the injured Alf Bentley in a 0–0 draw. He also played in several games for the second XI, gaining a Birmingham & District League championship medal in 1913. After leaving The Hawthorns, unfortunately, he didn't make much of an impression with Newport but went on to score six goals in 29 Birmingham League games for Walsall before injuries started to disrupt his career.

MANNERS, John Albert

Half-back: 209 apps. 7 goals.

Born: Morpeth, 12 March 1878.
Died: Newcastle, May 1946.
Career: Morpeth & District Schools. Morpeth YMCA. Morpeth Harriers. ALBION (professional, May 1904). Hartlepools United (free, player, June 1913, then manager June 1924, retired out of football in July 1927). Became a licensee in Morpeth.

■ Jack Manners was a solid, strong-looking left-half with a biting tackle and good powers of distribution. He maintained a consistent level of performance during his nine years at The Hawthorns and appeared in over 200 first-team games for Albion, being the mainstay of the side for five seasons (1905–10) when he formed a fine middle-line partnership in front of his goalkeeper with first 'Ted' Pheasant and Arthur Randle, and later with George Baddeley and Sammy Timmins. He also appeared at outside-left and at centre-half but it was at left-half where he became a performer, winning a Second Division championship medal in 1911. He made his League debut against Burnley (away) in a Second Division fixture in September 1904 and also played in several second XI matches, mainly in the 1910–11 season. His best term as a manager came in 1925–26 when he took Hartlepools to sixth position in the Third Division North.

MARDON, Paul Jonathan

Defender: 140+14 apps. 3 goals.

Born: Bristol, 14 September 1969.
Career: Boco Juniors. Bristol City (apprentice, June 1985, professional, September 1987). Doncaster Rovers (on loan, September 1990). Birmingham City (tribunal-set fee of £115,000, July 1991). Liverpool (trialist, January 1992). ALBION (£450,000, November 1993). Oldham Athletic (on loan, January 1999). Plymouth Argyle (on loan, September 1999). Wrexham (on loan, October–November 2000). Retired through injury, January 2001.

■ A strong, forceful defender, 6ft and 11st 10lb, Paul Mardon had the ability to judge a last-minute tackle to perfection. He joined the Blues after failing to earn a regular place in the Bristol City team. He immediately became a firm favourite with The Hawthorns fans after a series of outstanding performances at the heart of the defence, mainly alongside Paul Raven.

He was soon made captain and in October 1995 was chosen to play for Wales against Germany (selected by former Albion player and manager, Bobby Gould) in the European Championships. He also played for the Welsh 'B' team and made close on 40 appearances in Albion's second XI. He suffered a serious facial injury towards the end of the 1994–95 season, causing him to miss the last seven matches. He regained full fitness and his first-team place before injury struck again (he suffered knee ligament damage after a horror challenge in a pre-season friendly in July 1999). After three loan spells he was forced to retire having been told that if he continued playing he could be a cripple at the age of 40.

NB: In June 2002 Mardon rocked Albion by taking legal action against the club, claiming £500,000 in damages after that knee injury (above) had ended his career. He dropped the case in May 2003.

MARESCA, Enzo

Midfield: 31+22 apps. 5 goals.

Born: Salerno, Italy, 10 February 1980. Career: Cagliari, Italy. ALBION (free, August 1998). Juventus, Italy (£4.5 million,

January 2000). Bologna (on loan, during 2001–02). Piacenza (£2.5 million, June 2002). Juventus (2003). Fiorentoina (£1.5 million, September 2004).

■ A highly-skilled Italian midfielder, Enzo Maresca never really settled down at The Hawthorns despite having his fellow countryman Mario Bortolazzi to keep him company, and after a lot of speculation he was sold to Juventus for a club record fee of £4.5 million, having appeared in just over 50 senior games for Albion. No doubt a tremendously talented footballer, he played for Juventus in the Champions League and has now represented his country at youth, under-20, under-21 and senior levels.

MARRIOTT, Andrew

Goalkeeper: 3 apps.

Born: Sutton-in-Ashfield, 11 October 1970. Career: Arsenal (apprentice, April 1987, professional, October 1988). Nottingham Forest (£50,000, June 1989). ALBION (on loan, September 1989). Blackburn Rovers (on loan, December 1989). Colchester United (on loan, March–May 1990). Burnley (on loan, August–October 1991). Wrexham (£200,000, October 1993). Sunderland (£200,000, August 1998). Wigan Athletic (on loan, January 2001). Barnsley (free, March 2001). Birmingham City (on loan, March–May 2003). FC Biera Mar, Portugal (June 2003). Coventry City (trialist, July–August 2004, signed September 2004). Colchester United (October 2004). Bury (non-contract, November 2004). Torquay United (on loan, February-May 2005).

■ Goalkeeper Andy Marriott had not played in a senior game for either Arsenal or Nottingham Forest when Albion manager Brian Talbot signed him on loan to deputise for the injured Paul Bradshaw and Stuart Naylor early in the 1989–90 season. He made his Football League debut in a 3–1 win at Leicester on 9 September, a month before his 19th birthday. As time rolled by Marriott improved, developing into a high-class 'keeper and going on to win five full caps for Wales, having earlier played for England at schoolboy, youth and under-21 levels. He was a Fourth Division championship and Zenith Data Systems Cup winner with Forest in 1992 and a Welsh Cup winner with Wrexham in

1995. Marriott, a consistent performer throughout his career, reached the personal milestone of 375 senior appearances in 2003 (266 for Wrexham).

MARSHALL, Lee Keith

Midfield: 5+5 apps. 1 goal.

Born: Islington, London, 21 January 1979. Career: Enfield (August 1995). Norwich City (March 1997). Leicester City (£600,000, March 2001). ALBION (£700,000, August 2002). Hull City (on loan, January–May 2004). Retired through injury, May 2005.

■ Lee Marshall made his debut for Albion as a second-half substitute in the club's first ever Premiership match, away to Manchester United on 24 August 2002. Signed from Leicester a few days earlier, he then scored his first and, indeed, Albion's first goal in the Premiership, in the 3–1 home defeat by Leeds United the following Saturday. A strong, well-built six-footer, he eventually replaced Andy Johnson, now a colleague at Albion, in the senior side at Carrow Road, going on to score 13 times in 132 appearances for the Canaries before his transfer to Filbert Street. He played 47 games for the Foxes but following relegation from the

Premiership moved to The Hawthorns. Unfortunately, injuries interrupted his initial season with Albion, but when fit he surprisingly never really figured in manager Megson's plans or indeed in Bryan Robson's. Marshall, who helped Hull City win promotion from the Third Division, gained one England under-21 cap in 1999 as a Norwich player. He made some 40 appearances in Albion's second XI.

MARTIN, Dennis William

Winger: 20 + 3 apps. 2 goals.

Born: Edinburgh, 27 October 1947.
Career: Edinburgh & Murrayfield Schools. Kettering Town (April 1965). Albion (£5,000 June 1967). Carlisle United (£22,222, August 1970). Newcastle United (£40,000, October 1977). Mansfield Town (£25,000, March 1978). Fremad Amager, Denmark (1979). Kettering Town (July 1980, retired, May 1981). Later worked for an insurance company in Carlisle.

■ Dennis Martin got very little opportunity at Albion as a wing-forward, but after leaving The Hawthorns he served Carlisle exceptionally well from midfield, appearing in 275 League games for Cumbrians (scoring 48 goals) and helping them win promotion to the First Division in 1974. He had a brief spell at Newcastle (11 League outings) and then played 46 games for Mansfield before going to Denmark, returning to his former club Kettering in 1980. He made his League debut for Albion against Stoke City (home) in Division One in March 1968 and he also played in 97 Central League games, scoring 34 goals.

MARTIN, Michael Paul

Midfield: 108 + 7 apps. 15 goals.

Born: Dublin, 9 July 1951.
Career: Whitehall School. St Vincent's CBS (Football & Hurling club). Reds United. Home Farm. Greenfields-in-Santry FC. Home Farm (1967). Bohemians (professional, April 1968). Manchester United (January 1973). ALBION (on loan, October 1975, signed for £30,000, December 1975). Preston North End (on loan, September–October 1978). Newcastle United (£100,000, December 1978). Wolverhampton Wanderers (on loan, September 1983). Vancouver Whitecaps,

NASL (May 1984). Willington Athletic (briefly, November 1984). Cardiff City (November 1984). Peterborough United (February 1985). Rotherham United (July 1985). Preston North End (September 1985, retired, 1987). Newcastle United (chief scout, November 1987, then assistant coach October 1990). Celtic (coach June 1991-June 1993). Later returned to Tyneside to run his own sports shop in Swalwell while also working as a local soccer pundit covering Newcastle's matches for Radio Metro.

■ Son of Con Martin, the former Aston Villa and Eire international, Mick Martin was as versatile as his father, able to play in midfield, at full-back or in the centre of the defence, but he preferred a midfield role. He spent almost five years with Manchester United without ever really establishing himself in the first team. Then Johnny Giles brought him to The Hawthorns and inside a season he had developed into a class player, helping Albion gain promotion from the Second Division – having made his Baggies debut against Oldham Athletic (home) in October 1975. He also went on to play in 14 Central League games (5 goals). In later years, Martin did a fine job at Newcastle (making over 160 appearances), and when he retired he had played in well over 500 games as a professional footballer and had been capped 52 times by the Republic of Ireland (1971–83), scoring four goals. He collected one cap at under-23 level and also received amateur international recognition as well as representing the League of Ireland when

with Bohemians. Martin was granted a testimonial match at Dalymount Park, Dublin, in August 1983, for his services mainly to Irish football and also to English football in general. Unfortunately, in 1978 he became one of only a handful of players to get sent off in an FA Cup semi-final, playing for Albion against Ipswich Town at Highbury.

MATTHEWS, Joseph

Goalkeeper: 1 app.

Born: West Bromwich, 17 May 1860.
Died: West Bromwich, 20 December 1928.
Career: Spon Lane School (West Bromwich). Handsworth Sentinels. Aston Unity. ALBION (August 1883). Crosswells Brewery (June 1885). Oldbury Town (May 1887). Chance's Glassworks FC (August 1894, retired, May 1897). Became a Football League linesman (1909–10).

■ Joe Matthews was a hefty goalkeeper with a powerful pair of shoulders, massive kick and enormous courage. He did have the tendency to balloon the ball too much, but his overall performances were rated highly. He was understudy to Bob Roberts in the Albion camp in the mid-1800s and played in just one major competitive game (his debut being against Blackburn Rovers at home in a sixth round FA Cup tie in February 1885) plus several friendlies.
* He was the father of Howard Matthews, the former Burton United, Oldham, Port Vale, Coventry City and Halifax Town goalkeeper.

MAYO, Joseph

Centre-forward: 84+6 apps. 20 goals.

Born: Tipton, 25 May 1951.
Career: Horseley Heath Junior & Tipton Grammar Schools. Braithwaites Works FC. Tipton Sports. Oxford United (trialist, 1971–72). Dudley Town (August 1972). Hawthorns Throstles Club FC. Walsall (September 1972, as professional). Albion (£17,000, February 1973–March 1977). Orient (with Allan Glover, exchange deal plus cash for Laurie Cunningham). Cambridge United (£100,000, September 1981). Blackpool (on loan, October 1982). Happy Valley United, Hong Kong (summer 1983). Caernarfon Town (1986–87). Later ran a hotel in Criccieth near Portmadog, North Wales.

Joe Mayo was a strong, bustling centre-forward, perhaps a shade clumsy at times (he certainly missed his fair share of sitters) but generally did a fine job for Albion, especially in their promotion-winning season of 1975–76 when he scored eight goals, some of them crucial. He was criticised for not using his weight more than he did, but as a 'pro' he had a good career, amassing over 300 League and cup appearances for his five English clubs, scoring 75 goals including 35 in 155 League matches for Orient. He played in the same Cambridge side as George Reilly, later to join Albion. Mayo made his debut for the Baggies against Hull City (away) in Division Two in September 1973, as a substitute. He also scored 27 goals in 73 Central League games.

MELLON, Michael Joseph

Midfield: 47+10 apps. 7 goals.

Born: Paisley, 18 March 1972.
Career: Bristol City (apprentice, June 1988, professional, December 1989). ALBION (£75,000, February 1993). Blackpool (£50,000, November 1994). Tranmere Rovers (£285,000, October 1997). Burnley (£350,000, November 1999). Tranmere Rovers (free, March 2001). Fleetwood Town (briefly). Boston United (trialist, July 2004). Kidderminster Harriers (free,

briefly, July 2004). Fleetwood Town (June 2004).

Signed by manager Ossie Ardiles to boost the midfield engine-room as Albion's promotion charge gathered momentum in 1993, Micky Mellon made a scoring debut in a 4–0 League home win over Fulham 48 hours after moving to The Hawthorns. A hard-working, forceful player, he unfortunately missed the Wembley play-off final with Port Vale that season after being sent off in the second leg of the semi-final showdown with Swansea City. He also played over 20 times for Albion's second team and in later years provided both stability and guidance to youthful midfield trios and quartets at both Burnley (to a certain extent) and Tranmere. In 2003 he reached the milestone of 500 career appearances (League and cup).

MERRICK, Alan Ronald

Defender/midfield: 156+13 apps. 5 goals.

Born: Selly Oak, Birmingham, 20 June 1950.
Career: Water Orton Junior & Coleshill Grammar Schools. ALBION (July 1966, professional, August 1967). Peterborough United (on loan, September 1975). Kidderminster Harriers (March 1976). Minnesota Kicks (July 1976). Kettering Town (on loan, November 1976–January 1977). Minnesota Kicks (till August 1979). Los Angeles Aztecs (June–September 1980).
San Jose Earthquakes (March–June 1981). Minnesota Kicks (June–September 1981). Toronto Blizzard (1981–82). Team America (1983–84). Minnesota Strikers (coach, 1985). Team America (coach, 1986). Dallas (coach, 1987). Maplewood, USA (coach, 2001–05).

Alan Merrick was a loyal club servant who showed toughness, stamina and determination in an array of defensive positions for Albion, ranging from full-back, to wing-half, to dual-centre-half, to midfield anchorman. He never really established himself as a regular in Albion's first team, but when he did play he always gave 100 percent effort. As a lad he won three England youth caps (1968) and later made a big impression in the NASL, serving no fewer than six different clubs as a player before venturing into the coaching side of the game. Merrick totted up well over 250 appearances in the NASL and over 170 in England, having made his senior debut for Albion against Peterborough United (away) in a third round League Cup tie in September 1968. He also played in 176 Central League games (8 goals) and was later capped by the USA against Haiti in 1983.
* He became a millionaire in 2003

MILLAR, James

Centre-forward: 1 app.

Born: Annbank, Ayrshire, 2 March 1870.
Died: 5 February 1907.
Career: Annbank & Tarbolton Schools. Annbank FC (1886) Sunderland (professional, August 1890). Rangers (May 1896). ALBION (signed as trainer, July 1904). Chelsea (trainer/coach, April 1905, until his sudden death at the age of 36).

In his long career with Sunderland and Rangers, Jimmy Millar appeared as a strong, mobile and aggressive centre-forward, with plenty of willpower and ability to match. He actually joined Albion as a trainer but at the age of 34 was asked to stand in as leader of the attack for a game against Burton in October 1904 – and at the same time became the first Albion player to captain the team in his only League appearance for the club. He was capped three times by Scotland (1897–98) and also made three appearances for the Scottish League side. He won four First Division

championship medals with Sunderland (1892, 1893, 1895, 1902) and while with Rangers collected two more League championship medals (1899, 1900) as well as two Scottish Cup winners' medals (1897, 1898) and a runners'-up prize (1899). For Sunderland alone, Millar scored 104 goals in his 237 League outings, and was a member of Sunderland's first ever Football League side – versus Burnley in September 1890. In one 1895 FA Cup tie for the Wearsiders he scored five goals against Fairfield.

MILLARD, Albert Robert

Defender: 5 apps.

Born: West Bromwich, 18 September 1868.
Died: West Bromwich, 1930.
Career: Swan Village & Ryder Street Schools (West Bromwich). West Bromwich Victoria. ALBION (professional, July 1888). Halesowen (free, May 1892, retired through injury, April 1896). Became a caretaker at a West Bromwich school.

■ Albert Millard was a reserve defender who could play either at full-back or wing-half. A thickset footballer, he was as tough as they come and deputised as a half-back in five senior matches, making his Albion debut against Notts County (home) in Division One in October 1888. Besides his senior appearances for the club, he also appeared in at least 24 'other' first-team games.

MILLARD, Leonard

Right-half/left-back: 627 apps. 18 goals.

Born: Coseley near Wolverhampton, 7 March 1919.
Died: Coseley, 15 March 1997.
Career: Christ Church School (Coseley). Wallbrook FC. Coseley Town. Bilston Town. Sunbeam FC (1936). ALBION (amateur, May 1937, professional, September 1942). Guest for Bilston Borough (1938–39) and Sedgley Rangers during World War Two. Stafford Rangers (manager, June 1958, retired, May 1961).

■ Len Millard was Albion's left-back for a number of years, skippering the side to success in the 1954 FA Cup final. A defender who stuck to his task, he gave fine service to several wing-halves and left-wingers he played behind, always being fair in the challenge, strong and clean with his kicks and honest in his keen and thoughtful approach to the professional game. He started off as a centre-forward, scoring two hat-tricks in wartime football. He then switched to wing-half before settling down at left-back in 1949, replacing the long-serving Harry Kinsell (sold to Bolton Wanderers). Nicknamed the 'Agitator' or 'Len the Dependable', Millard appeared in almost 650 first-team matches for Albion including friendlies, with 436 coming in the Football League – having made his debut against Northampton Town (away) in the Football League South in August 1942. Two years later he gained a Midland Wartime Cup medal (v Nottingham Forest). He also played in 17 Central League games. Without a shadow of a doubt, he was a great servant to the club, staying at The Hawthorns through thick and thin for 21 years. He missed only 13 games in the immediate 10 post-war seasons, being an ever-present twice. Sadly Len, who had a leg amputated in 1989, died in a nursing home at the age of 78.

MILLER, Alan John

Goalkeeper: 113 apps.

Born: Epping, London, 29 March 1970.
Career: Arsenal (apprentice, June 1986, professional, May 1988). Plymouth Argyle (on loan, November 1988–January 1989). ALBION (on loan, August–September 1991). Birmingham City (on loan, December 1991–February 1992).

Middlesbrough (£500,000, August 1994). Grimsby Town (on loan, January–February 1993). ALBION (£400,000, February 1997). Blackburn Rovers (£50,000, February 2000). Bristol City (on loan, August 2000). Coventry City (on loan, November 2000). St Johnstone (on loan, October 2001–February 2002). Retired through injury, April 2003.

■ Alan Miller was a first-team goalkeeper who had two spells with Albion. The first was on loan from Highbury when he took over from Stuart Naylor in the opening three games of Albion's first ever season in the Third Division in August 1991, making his debut in the 6–3 home win over Exeter City. Then, after signing for the club on a permanent basis in 1997, he replaced Paul Crichton. Miller was a big favourite with the Baggies supporters and at times his heroics between the posts kept Albion in the game. He eventually lost his place to the Dane Brian Jensen but took his career appearance tally in League and cup competitions to almost 250, before announcing his retirement. Capped by England at schoolboy, youth and under-21 levels, he helped Arsenal lift the European Cup-winners' Cup in 1994 and a year later was in Middlesbrough's First Division title-winning team.

MILLINGTON, Anthony Horace

Goalkeeper: 40 apps.

Born: Hawarden near Queensferry, North

Wales, 5 June 1943.
Career: Hawarden & Mancot Schools.
Flintshire Boys. Everton (amateur, 1958).
Connah's Quay Nomads. Queensferry FC.
Sutton British Legion. Sutton Town
(1958). ALBION (amateur, June 1959,
professional, July 1960). Crystal Palace
(£7,500, October 1964). Peterborough
United (March 1966). Swansea Town/City
(June 1969). Glenavon (October 1974,
retired in the summer of 1975 following a
car accident). A crippling disease has since
left him paralysed. Now lives in Wrexham
and in 1990 was instrumental in forming a
club for wheelchair supporters at the town's
Racecourse ground.

■ Tony Millington was a goalkeeper with guts, agility, a safe pair of hands, useful kick and self-confidence – yet he was also a player who was somewhat over elaborate in his general approach to the game, occasionally completely losing his concentration! He was capped by Wales on 21 occasions and for the under-23 team four times. He only had 40 League outings with Albion, his debut coming against Manchester City (home) in September 1961, but he did play in 73 second XI games. He followed up by appearing in 16 League matches for Palace, 118 for Peterborough and 178 for Swansea before winding down his career in Ireland with Glenavon. He gained a Third Division promotion medal with Swansea, Albion providing the opposition at Vetch Field. In season 1962–63 he played twice for Albion against Wolves at Molineux – and conceded 15 goals, seven for the senior side and eight when goalkeeping for the reserves. Sadly a car crash ended his playing days at the age of 32.

MILLS, David John

Forward: 55 + 21 apps. 6 goals.

Born: Robin Hood's Bay near Whitby,
North Yorkshire, 6 December 1951.
Career: Walker Street School (Whitby).
Thornaby School (Teeside). Stockton Boys.
North Yorkshire Boys. Scarborough &
District Youths. Middlesbrough
(apprentice, June 1967, professional,
December 1968). ALBION (£516,000
January 1979). Newcastle United (on loan,
January 1982). Sheffield Wednesday
(£30,000, January 1983). Newcastle United
(£20,000, August 1983). Middlesbrough

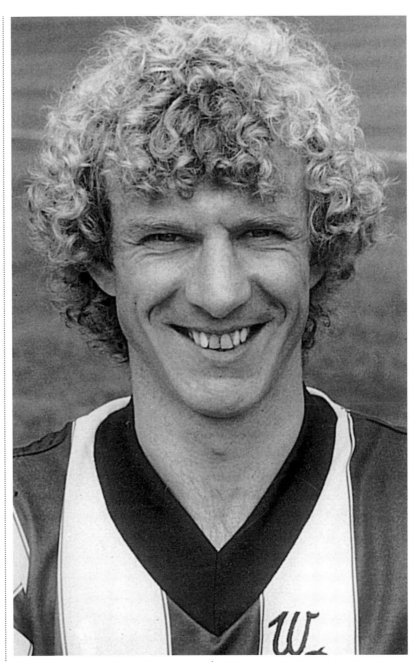

(free, May 1984). Darlington (non-
contract player, July 1986). Middlesbrough
(coach, 1986–87). Whitby Town (player-
coach, 1987–88). Then a sales executive
with a printing group based in Bishop
Auckland as well as becoming a sports
journalist for the People newspaper.
Dorman's Athletic (coach, 1997–98).
Newcastle United (scout, 2000–05).

■ David Mills was Britain's costliest footballer and the country's first half-a-million pound player when he joined Albion in January 1979. Manager Ron Atkinson gambled at the time, hoping that he would replace veteran striker Tony Brown at The Hawthorns. The gamble failed! In fact, Mills never lived up to the price-tag Albion had placed on his head – or rather tied around his feet – and Atkinson readily admitted that he made a 'serious mistake in the transfer market' when he signed Mills, especially after having a £750,000 bid for Birmingham City star Trevor Francis turned down a week or so earlier. A hard-working inside or centre-forward with a distinctive knack of scoring goals, he had netted 94 goals in over 340 games for 'Boro before moving south. It was anticipated that he would continue to find the net with Albion for whom he made his debut against Liverpool (away) in Division One in February 1979 (as a substitute). That was not so. He tried his best but didn't quite fit the bill and after four years and 76 outings for the Baggies (plus 20 goals in 40 second XI games) he switched to Sheffield Wednesday after a brief spell on loan at Newcastle. When he retired after a second spell at Ayresome Park and a brief association with Darlington, David had chalked up an impressive record – over 500 appearances and 126 goals. He gained eight England under-23 caps while with Middlesbrough, and in 1974 he helped the Ayresome Park club with the Second Division championship in a canter, scoring 11 goals in his 39 League outings. He was involved in a serious car accident in 1988 when his father was killed. He took many months to recover.

* In March 1988 Albion played Whitby Town in Mills's testimonial match. Atrocious weather conditions kept the attendance figure down to just 290 and Mills received less than £1,000 in takings. Albion won 8–0.

MINTON, Roger Christopher

Full-back: 27 + 2 apps. 1 goal.

Born: Moseley, Birmingham, 4 June 1951.
Career: Wrens Nest Secondary Modern School. Dudley Schoolboys. ALBION (apprentice, May 1966, professional, June 1969). Dunstable Town (May 1975). Bedford Town. Washington Diplomats (1975–76). Atherstone. Bedford Town (August 1978). Stourbridge (August 1978, retired through injury, May 1984).

■ Roger Minton was an adventurous right-back who loved to attack down the flank, consequently his overall play was far from satisfying to his manager! He made 26 appearances for Albion's League side and hit one goal versus Nottingham Forest in September 1973, and also played in 208 Central League matches (8 goals scored). He spent most of his last eight years in football playing at non-League level except for a brief spell in the NASL in the mid–70s. He made his Albion debut against Morton (home) in the Texaco Cup in September 1970.

MONAGHAN, Derek James

Utility forward: 17 + 7 apps. 3 goals.

Born: Bromsgrove, Worcs, 20 January 1959.
Career: Abbey High School (Redditch). Astwood Bank (May 1975). ALBION (apprentice, January 1976, professional, January 1977). Port Vale (free, July 1984). Redditch United (free, May 1985). Played for West Bromwich Albion All Stars (1987–90).

■ Derek Monaghan was a useful forward who won an FA Youth Cup winners' medal with Albion in 1976, capping a fine season, which also saw him play six times for England's youth team. He was in and out of Albion's side after initially forcing his way into the League team in 1979–80 and following a cartilage operation, and other niggling knee and thigh injuries, he was given a free-transfer at the end of the 1983–84 campaign. He made his senior debut for the Baggies in a European competition, taking the field against the East German side Carl Zeiss Jena (home) in the UEFA Cup second round, second leg clash in October 1979. He also scored 51 goals in 185 Central League games. He suffered with injuries at Vale Park.

MOORE, Darren Mark

Defender: 98+9 apps. 6 goals.

Born: Handsworth, Birmingham, 22 April 1974.
Career: James Watt School (Handsworth). Holly Lane Colts. Walsall (trialist, 1989). Torquay United (apprentice, June 1990, professional, November 1992). Doncaster Rovers (£62,500, July 1995). Bradford City (£310,000, June 1997). Portsmouth (£500,000, November 1999). ALBION (£750,000, September 2001).

■ One of the many stars of Albion's 'mean defence' in 2001–02, rock-like centre-back Darren Moore put in some superb displays (sometimes suffering pain) as Gary Megson's team charged through to clinch an automatic promotion spot after a tremendous last third to the season. He was awesome at the 'back' with his defensive colleagues Phil Gilchrist and Larus Sigurdsson in front of goalkeeper Russell Hoult. In fact, his never-say-die performances earned him a place in the PFA First Division team that season. Unfortunately, along with his fellow defenders, he struggled at times in the top flight and, in fact, due to a cruciate ligament injury, missed the last eight games of the 2002–03 campaign and the first half of the following season. but returned to play his part in helping the Baggies regain their Premiership status. Moore played 124 times for the Gulls, 84 for Doncaster, 70 for Bradford and 66 for Pompey. Physically strong and determined, he is a player who enjoys a battle. He gained four caps for Jamaica

MOORWOOD, Thomas Leonard

Goalkeeper: 33 apps.

Born: Wednesday, 6 September 1888.
Died: Dudley, 1976.
Career: Holyhead Road School (Wednesbury). Bilston United. ALBION (professional, May 1909). Burnley (£1,100, October 1920). Blackpool (£250, August 1924). Blackheath (free, July 1925, retired May 1929). Later ran a stall in both Old Hill and Cradley Heath markets.

■ Len Moorwood was a consistent and reliable goalkeeper, big and strong with a huge right-footed kick. He spent 11 years with Albion, acting mainly as reserve to Hubert Pearson, making his Football League debut against Leeds City (away) in Division Two in February 1911. He also played in more than 150 second XI matches either side of World War One, having his best seasons before the hostilities (1911–15). After leaving The Hawthorns he made 18 appearances for Burnley but failed to make Blackpool's senior side. He was 40 years of age when he retired.

MORLEY, William Anthony

Outside-left: 63 + 1 apps. 13 goals.

Born: Ormskirk, 26 August 1954.
Career: Ormskirk & District Schools. Preston North End (apprentice, July 1969, professional, August 1972). Burnley (£100,000, February 1976). Aston Villa (£200,000, June 1979). ALBION (£75,000, December 1983). Birmingham City (on loan, November–December 1984). FC Seiko, Japan (August 1985). FC Den Haag, Holland (July 1986). Walsall (trialist, June 1987). Notts County (trialist, July 1987). ALBION (August 1987). Burnley (on loan, October–November 1988). Tampa Bay Rowdies (March 1989). Hamrun Spartans, Malta (April 1990). New Zealand football (1990–91). Sutton Coldfield Town (1992). Bromsgrove Rovers (player-coach, January 1995). Stratford Town (player, March 1995). Also coach in Australia and Hong Kong. Assisted both Aston Villa and WBA Old Stars (1990s).

■ Tony Morley was a fine winger, a player able to turn the flow of a game in one sweeping run. He hugged the touchline and drew defenders to him before taking them on, crossing and

(his last as an Albion player v USA in August 2004) and represented a Rest of the World side (with teammate Jason Roberts) against an African XI at Bolton in 2002–03. He gained his fourth cap for Jamaica versus the US in August 2004. A born-again Christian from 1999, he had a spell as Albion captain in 2004.

creating chances galore for his colleagues. As a youngster he gained England youth team honours (seven caps) and later added one 'B', one under-21 and six full caps to his collection. He had 99 outings for Preston (20 goals), 100 for Burnley (7 goals) and over 180 for Villa (34 goals), helping the latter club win the First Division championship (1981), the European Cup and European Super Cup in 1982 and become World Cup championship runners'-up. He helped Den Haag win promotion from the Dutch Second Division and gained a Cup runners'-up medal in 1987, before rejoining Albion – having trained with both Walsall and Notts County in the pre-season. Morley scored the first hat-trick of his career at competitive level for Albion against Huddersfield Town in October 1987, four years after making his debut for the club against QPR (home) in Division One in December 1983, netting in a 2–1 defeat. He also scored nine goals in 34 Central League outings for the Baggies.

MORRIS, Frederick

Inside-left: 287 apps. 118 goals.

Born: Tipton, 27 August 1893.
Died: Tipton, July 1962.
Career: Great Bridge Primary School, Bell Street Primitives, Tipton Victoria, Redditch (September 1910). ALBION (professional, May 1911). Guest for Fulham (1917–19), Watford and Tipton Excelsior during World War One. Coventry City (£625, August 1924). Oakengates Town (£50, August 1925, retired, May 1930). Worked locally before and after World War Two. His relatives still live in the Great Bridge/Tipton area.

■ Fred Morris was a strongly built, courageous forward who displayed glorious talents, neat control, rapid acceleration, dynamic shooting powers and intelligent off-the-ball running. He was a great competitor and formed a wonderful left-wing partnership with Howard Gregory just after World War One. A junior international, capped in 1911, he slowly got into his stride with Albion's second XI during the 1911–12 season, scoring some superb goals. He finally made his League debut against Sunderland (home) in Division One in April 1912, netting the only goal of the

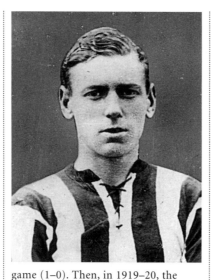

game (1–0). Then, in 1919–20, the dashing Morris claimed a club record 37 goals, including a five-timer in an emphatic 8–0 League home win over Notts County, as the Baggies won the First Division championship for the first and, so far, only time in the club's history. At the end of that season he gained two full caps for England, scoring against Scotland in a 5–4 win at Hampden Park and then doing well in his second international against Ireland (won 2–0). He also received Football League and FA honours as an Albion player. In 1921–22, Morris became the first Baggies player to reach the milestone of 100 League goals and was top-scorer for the Baggies three seasons running either side of World War One – 1914–15, 1919–20 and 1920–21. Before leaving The Hawthorns he made three appearances in Albion's Central League side, having earlier (1913) helped the Baggies second string win the Birmingham & District League. And he also scored in Albion's 1–0 win over Aston Villa in the final of the Birmingham Charity Cup in 1914 and in their 2–0 victory over the Blues in the final of the same competition eight years later. During World War One, when he served in the Ministry of Transport Base Depot in Ruislip (Middlesex), Bookham (Surrey) and France, Morris notched 24 goals in 24 outings as a guest with Fulham, whom he helped finish third in the London Combination. Some of his relatives still reside in the Great Bridge and Tipton districts of West Bromwich.

MORROW, Hugh John Eagleson

Winger: 5 apps. 2 goals.

Born: Larne, Northern Ireland, 9 July 1930. Career: Manor Park School. Courtaulds. Nuneaton Borough. Wolverhampton Wanderers (amateur, 1944). ALBION (amateur, October 1945, professional, August 1947). Nuneaton Borough (free, July 1950). Lockhead Leamington (1953). Northampton Town (free, June 1956). Kettering Town (August 1957, retired, May 1965). Larne, Ireland (coach, August 1966–March 1968). Still lives in Northern Ireland.

■ Albion's reserve winger immediately after the war, Hugh Morrow was given just a handful of senior outings plus 47 in the second team (5 goals) before being released in 1950. He went on to play in 30 League games for Northampton (3 goals). His Albion debut was against Southampton (home) in Division Two in November 1948.

MOUNTFORD, David

Forward: 5 apps.

Born: Hanley, Stoke-on-Trent, 9 January 1931.
Died: Stoke-on-Trent, 1985.
Career: Hanley & Burslem Schools. Stoke City Boys. Crewe Alexandra (amateur, April 1947, professional, November 1948). ALBION (£6,750, December 1951). Crewe Alexandra (£1,500, October 1953). Hereford United (free, August 1958, retired c.1960). Worked in the pottery trade for 10 years during the late 1960s/early 1970s.

■ Dave Mountford was a solid, well-built utility forward, broad-shouldered and mobile. He was recruited by Albion as a reserve forward and left after just five games. For Crewe he scored 12 goals in 60 League matches, accumulated in two separate spells at Gresty Road. Handed his senior debut by Albion against Chelsea (away) in a fourth round FA Cup tie in January 1953, he also scored seven goals in 41 second XI games for the Baggies.

MOSES, Remi Mark

Midfield: 73 apps. 6 goals.

Born: Miles Platting, 14 Manchester, 14 November 1960.

Career: Miles Platting School Manchester. Corpus Christi Boys' Club (Manchester). Manchester Boys. ALBION (apprentice, July 1977, professional, November 1978). Manchester United (£500,000, September 1981, as part of the deal involving Bryan Robson, forced to retire, June 1988). Is now involved with the church.

■ Born of Nigerian parents, Remi Moses was a midfield player who worked tirelessly, always on the go, prompting, teasing and harassing defenders into making mistakes. He was allowed to leave The Hawthorns (with Robson) having just established himself in Albion's 'engine-room' occupying a left-sided role. He made his debut for the club against Crystal Palace (away) in Division One in January 1980 and also appeared in 56 Central League games (8 goals scored). Capped eight times by England at under-21 level, he appeared in more than 170 games for Manchester United despite missing most of the 1985–86 season through injury. He also sat out both the 1983 and 1985 FA Cup finals through suspension and injury respectively, but did collect a runners'-up prize when finishing on the losing side for the Reds against Liverpool in the 1983 Milk Cup final. He played in the England Schools Trophy semi-final with Manchester Boys.

MULLIGAN, Patrick Martin

Right-back: 132 apps. 2 goals.

Born: Dublin, 17 March 1945.
Career: Dublin City Schools. Stella Maris. Home Farm. Bohemians (August 1963).

Home Farm. Shamrock Rovers (1964–67). Boston Rovers (July 1967). Boston Beacons, NASL (April 1968). Shamrock Rovers (1968–69). Chelsea (October 1969). Crystal Palace (September 1972). ALBION (September 1975). Shamrock Rovers (August 1979). Panathinaikos, Greece (assistant manager, 1980–81). Galway Rovers (manager, August 1981, retired, May 1982). Became an insurance agent for a company in West London and later formed his own accountancy-insurance business in Dublin.

■ Paddy Mulligan was an attacking right-back, an expert at over-lapping, steady and thoughtful – a player with ability who was never completely dominated by a winger. He was a snip-of-a-signing by player-manager Johnny Giles in 1975 and his presence in Albion's defence went an awful long way in helping the side gain promotion that season (1975–76). A Republic of Ireland schoolboy international (1960–61), Mulligan went on to gain 51 full caps for his country (1969–80), one goal scored, and he also served the League of Ireland (1965–69). He won four FAI Cup-winners' medals (1965–66–67–69) and was a member of Chelsea's League Cup final side of 1972 (losing to Stoke City at Wembley), having appeared as a substitute for the London club in the 1971 European Cup-winners' Cup final against Real Madrid in Athens. All told, in a splendid career in Ireland, England and America, Mulligan amassed more

than 350 senior appearances, including 224 in the Football League with Chelsea, Palace and Albion, making his debut for the latter against Fulham (home) in a second round League Cup tie in September 1975. He also played in nine Central League games. He was assistant to manager Ronnie Allen at Panathinaikos.
* Mulligan was granted a testimonial by FAI (mainly for services to Irish football).

MURPHY, James Patrick

Right-half: 223 apps.

Born: Ton Pentre, South Wales, 27 October 1910.
Died: Manchester, 14 November 1989.
Career: Ton Pentre Village School. Ton Pentre Boys. Treorchy Thursday FC. Treorchy Juniors. Mid-Rhondda Boys. ALBION (professional, February 1928). Swindon Town (£140, March 1939). Morris Commercial FC (July 1939–May 1940). Manchester United (coach, November 1945, assistant manager, July 1955, temporary manager, February 1958–August 1959, then assistant manager, until June 1971, remained at Old Trafford until May 1982, being employed as coach, scout and scouting advisor). Welsh international team manager (October 1956–June 1963, taking Wales to the 1958 World Cup finals in Sweden).

■ 'Spud' or 'Twinkletoes' Murphy – a church organist as a lad – was a vigorous, attacking wing-half, skilled in tackling and a glutton for hard work. He had already gained Welsh schoolboy honours (in 1924 against England at Cardiff) when Albion signed him in 1928. He developed quickly and went on to win 15 full caps for his country as well as playing in more than 220 competitive games for Albion, including an appearance in the 1935 FA Cup final against Sheffield Wednesday, receiving a runners'-up medal. He made his League debut against Blackpool (away) in Division Two in March 1930. He replaced Tommy Magee in Albion's middle-line where he did a splendid job for seven seasons (1931–38). He also scored 11 goals in 146 second XI games. During World War Two 'Spud' Murphy served overseas with the Eighth Army, and when based in Bari, Italy, in 1945, he first met Matt Busby who asked him to join United as his assistant in rebuilding the club. Indeed, all went well, and United won the First Division title three times, finished runners-up on four occasions, carried off the FA Cup and twice lifted the Charity Shield inside 10 seasons, before the tragic Munich air crash decimated the team as a whole. He took over the reins from Busby, who was badly injured in that horrific smash, and when the boss returned he and 'Spud' saw United again reach the heights of world soccer with more championships and further cup success, all culminating in that great triumph in 1968 when Manchester United won the European Cup at Wembley.

MURPHY, Joseph

Goalkeeper: 4+2 apps.

Born: Dublin, 21 August 1981.
Career: Tranmere Rovers (apprentice, April 1997, professional, July 1999). ALBION (July 2002). Walsall (on loan, October 2004–May 2005).

■ A Republic of Ireland international, capped 14 times for the under-21 side and once at senior level, as a substitute against Turkey in September 2003 (after earlier representing his country's Under-18 side), goalkeeper Joe Murphy saved a Michael Owen penalty on his Premiership debut for Albion against Liverpool at Anfield in September 2002, seconds after

coming off the bench following the dismissal of Russell Hoult. He played in three games (all won) in 2003–04 when Albion regained their place in the Premiership. A fine shot-stopper, he made 75 appearances during his five years at Prenton Park. After slipping down to fourth in line at The Hawthorns early in the 2004–05 season, he was loaned out to neighbours Walsall. He has appeared in almost 30 second-team games for Albion.

MURPHY, Shaun Peter

Defender: 67+11 apps. 7 goals.

Born: Sydney, Australia, 5 November 1970.
Career: Heildelberg United. Blacktown City. Perth Italia (all in Australia). Notts County (professional, September 1992). ALBION (£500,000, December 1996). Sheffield United (free, July 1999–May 2003). Crystal Palace (on loan, February–April 2002). Perth Glory, Australia (2003–05).

■ Australian international centre-half Shaun Murphy has now played in more than 300 Football League games since arriving in the UK to join Notts County in 1992. The black-haired, 6ft 1in, 12st defender, who made 135 appearances for

the Magpies, made his Baggies debut in a televised FA Cup tie against Chelsea shortly after moving to The Hawthorns. He did well and continued to perform with aggression and was, at times, one of the best defenders on the park. He had an 11-game loan spell with Crystal Palace in early 2002. Capped over 20 times by his country at senior level, Murphy also gained under-21 and under-23 honours for Australia earlier in his career and made almost 20 appearances for Albion's second XI. He was an Anglo-Italian Cup winner in 1995 with Notts County, having been a runner-up in the same competition the previous season. Murphy quit England and returned to Australia in 2002 due to his wife being seriously ill.

MURRAY, Maxwell

Centre-forward: 3 apps.

Born: Falkirk, Scotland, 7 November 1935. Career: Falkirk High School. Camelon Juniors (June 1953). Strollers XI. Queen's Park (amateur, September 1953). Glasgow Rangers (professional, August 1955). ALBION (£10,000, November 1962). Third Lanark (£5,250, July 1963). Clyde (1965–66). Distillery (free, August 1966, retired May 1967). Entered the insurance business in 1969.

■ Max Murray was a slimly built centre-forward with lightning speed and a good,

accurate shot. He found that playing for Albion (in the First Division) was a far greater challenge than he had anticipated and returned home to Scotland in double-quick time, after making just three First Division appearances for the Baggies, his debut coming against Nottingham Forest (home) in November 1962. He also scored 11 goals in 17 Central League games. As a Queen's Park player, Murray won four caps for Scotland as an amateur, also adding youth and under-23 honours to his collection, having earlier played for the ATC XI at Wembley in 1952. He won three Scottish League championship medals with Rangers (1956, 1957, 1959) and a Scottish Cup runners'-up prize in 1958. He scored 107 goals in 223 appearances in Scottish football, including 79 strikes in 104 outings for Rangers. His full record for the Ibrox club was 125 goals in 167 matches – excellent by anyone's standards. It was a pity he couldn't bring that sort of form with him to The Hawthorns!

NAYLOR, Stuart William

Goalkeeper: 419+1 apps.

Born: Wetherby, Yorkshire, 6 December 1962. Career: Leeds United (trialist, 1977). Yorkshire Amateurs (1978). Lincoln City (schoolboy forms, February 1979, professional, June 1980). Kettering Town (on loan, January 1983). Peterborough United (on loan, February–April 1983). Crewe Alexandra (on loan, October 1983–May 1984). ALBION (£110,000, February 1986). Crewe Alexandra (on loan, August 1994). Bristol City (free, August 1996). Mansfield Town (on loan, December 1998–January 1999). Walsall (free, March 1999). Exeter City (free, August 1999). Rushden and Diamonds (on loan, March–May 2000, signed permanently, August 2000, retired, May 2001).

■ A tall, strongly built goalkeeper with good reflexes, Stuart Naylor – a record signing for a goalkeeper by Albion – was capped by England at youth level and in 1989 represented his country's 'B' team on three occasions against Switzerland, Iceland and Norway. He made his Baggies debut at Old Trafford against Manchester United, conceding a Jesper Olsen hat-

trick, two of them penalties. Thankfully, he quickly put that disappointment behind him and went on to set a new club record by appearing in more games for Albion than any other 'keeper – 468 in the first team alone (355 League, 13 FA Cup, 22 League Cup, 20 others and 58 friendlies). He also had 25 outings in the reserves. Known as 'Bruiser', he helped Albion gain promotion from the Second Division in 1993, although he missed the play-off final against Port Vale, replaced by Tony Lange. Granted a testimonial (against Coventry City), he was released by Albion on a free transfer at the end of the 1995–96 season. He later joined Rushden and Diamonds, managed by his ex-boss at The Hawthorns, Brian Talbot. During his time with the 'Imps', he actually turned out at centre-forward in a League game against Newport County in 1982. Naylor made his 500th League appearance of his career for Bristol City against Rotherham United in March 1997.
* Naylor's father (Bill) and uncle (Tommy) played for Oldham Athletic between 1948 and 1959.

N'DOUR, Alassane

Left-wing-back: 3 apps.

Born: Dakar, Senegal, 12 December 1981 Career: Arsenal (trialist, 1998). St Etienne, France (professional, August 1999). ALBION (on loan, July 2003–May 2004). St Etienne (August 2004).

■ Senegalese international, 6ft 1in tall and star of the 2002 World Cup in South

Korea/Japan, 'Assy' N'Dour joined Albion as cover and to put pressure on Neil Clement. A positive footballer, hard but fair, he made 41 appearances in two seasons of French football and has over 20 full caps to his credit (six with Albion), helping his country reach the final of the African Nations Cup (beaten on penalties by Cameroon) and reach the quarter finals of the World Cup in Japan and Korea in 2002. He made his debut for the Baggies in the 2–2 League away draw with Crystal Palace in September 2003 and went on to appear in 14 second XI games (5 goals scored) before returning to France.

NEALE, William Steele

Centre-forward: 7 apps. 3 goals.

Born: West Bromwich, 17 January 1872.
Died: Dudley, March 1932.
Career: All Saints School (West Bromwich). Grove Hall Saints FC (1890). ALBION (professional, January 1893). Brierley Hill Alliance (free, May 1894, retired, May 1898).

■ Billy Neale was a reliable reserve utility-forward who might well have done great things had he been given the opportunity at Albion. He made his debut against Derby County (home) in Division One in April 1893.

NEVIN, John William

Wing-half: 2 apps.

Born: Lintz, County Durham, 20 February 1887.
Died: Newcastle, 12 December 1951.
Career: Gosforth & Longbenton Schools. Newcastle Boys. Gateshead United. Sunderland (professional, April 1908). Hobson Wanderers (March 1910). ALBION (free, July 1910). Bristol Rovers (£20, July 1912). Dolphin FC (Gloucester). Ayr United. West Stanley. Workington. Barrow (May 1922). West Stanley. Crewe Alexandra (August 1924). York City (reserves, 1925). Inverness Thistle. Fraserburgh. Retired, May 1927, returned to Newcastle where he became a publican.

■ Billy Nevin was a reserve wing-half, sturdy and compact, who was never defeated and one who was always determined out on the field. He made his Albion debut against Gainsborough Trinity (away) in Division Two in

October 1910 and also appeared in 24 second XI matches. He went on to play in a handful of games for Ayr, 54 in the League for Barrow and 23 for Crewe.
* His son, George William Nevin, played for Newcastle United, Sheffield Wednesday, Manchester United, Burnley, Lincoln City and Rochdale (1929–39), while two of his cousins also played professionally, George William for Sheffield Wednesday and Hartlepools United in the late 1930s and John for Crewe Alexandra and Chester.

NEWALL, John Thomas

Inside-forward: 22 apps. 3 goals.

Born: West Bromwich, 16 September 1890.
Died: West Bromwich, 10 November 1957.
Career: Ocker Hill Schools Wednesbury. Great Bridge Celtic (April 1909). ALBION (professional, May 1912, retired through injury, June 1922). Later worked for West Bromwich public library and also in the Town Hall.

■ Tom 'Nigger' Newall played anywhere in the forward-line but preferred the inside-right spot. He also loved to feature on the wing and during his 10 years' association with Albion actually lined up in eight different positions for the first and second teams, making over 40 appearances for the latter during the last two seasons before World War One, gaining a Birmingham & District League championship medal in 1920 when he top-scored with 27 goals. Forced out of the game through knee trouble at the age of 27, he made his League debut against Newcastle United (home) in September 1913, scoring in the 1–1 draw.

NEWALL, William Thomas

Outside-left: 15 apps. 2 goals.

Born: Lye, 7 March 1869.
Died: Smethwick, February 1954.
Career: Peter's Hill Primary & Lye Council Schools. Stourbridge St George. Birmingham Carriage Works FC. Stourbridge (April 1892). ALBION (professional, May 1894). Worcester Rovers (£10, May 1895). Coventry City (free, August 1898). Smethwick Wesleyan Rovers (1899–1901). Oldbury Pickwick (May 1902, retired through injury, May 1903). Became a fishmonger and later worked in a betting shop.

■ Billy Newall was a steady left-winger who played the first half of the 1894–95 season on Albion's left flank, teaming up successfully with Billy Richards. He then lost his form and place and was subsequently 'sold' to Worcester Rovers. His Albion debut was against Sheffield United (away) in Division One in September 1894.

NEWSOME, Robinson

Utility forward: 59 apps. 30 goals.

Born: Hebden Bridge near Barnsley, Yorkshire, 25 September 1919.
Died: Dudley, 2000.
Career: Kexborough & Staincross Schools. Barnsley Boys. Willington Boys' Club. Congleton Town (July 1937). ALBION (professional, March 1939). Guest for Walsall (1941–44), Manchester United (1943–45), Burnley (1942–43), Chester (1943–45) and Norwich City (1945–46) during World War Two. Coventry City (£1,500, May 1947). Hereford United (£50, August 1948). Dudley Town (free, August 1950). Gornal Wood (June 1953, retired, May 1955). Lived in Kingswinford for many years and attended The Hawthorns regularly until his death.

■ 'Bobbie' Newsome was a sprightly utility-forward, whose best positions were outside-right or centre-forward. Direct in style, he was skilful and sharp near goal and was always likely to figure on the score-sheet. He played in goal for Albion during the war and often said that he could well have made the grade as a custodian. Sadly, World War Two ruined his chances of making the bigtime with Albion, yet during the hostilities he did exceptionally well, amassing a total of 229 senior appearances for his various clubs and scoring 58 goals, top-scoring for Norwich in 1945–46 with a total of 11. He made his Albion debut against Leicester City (home) in the Midland Regional League in November 1939, and also scored twice in 19 Central League appearances.

NICHOLL, James Michael

Right-back: 67 apps. 1 goal.

Born: Hamilton, Canada, 28 December 1956.
Career: Whitehouse Primary & Belfast Central Schools. Manchester United

(apprentice, July 1972, professional, March 1974). Sunderland (on loan, February 1982). Toronto Blizzard, NASL (£250,000, March 1982, after contract cancelled by Manchester United). Sunderland (September 1982–March 1983). Toronto Blizzard (May 1983). Glasgow Rangers (on loan, October 1983). ALBION (£65,000, November 1984). Glasgow Rangers (player exchange deal involving Bobby Williamson, August 1986, appointed player-coach of Rangers second team, March 1987). Dunfermline Athletic (July 1989). Falkirk (briefly). Raith Rovers (player-manager, 1990–96). Millwall (manager, 1996–97). Dunfermline Athletic (assistant manager, April 1999, then caretaker manager, 2000–01, reverting back to assistant manager, 2001–May 2004). Aberdeen (assistant manager, August 2004).

■ Jimmy Nicholl played the easy game from the right-back position, never flashy, usually steady and always seeking to find a man with his clearances. He made his Albion debut v Stoke City (home) in Division One in November 1984, after being signed by another former Manchester United player, Johnny Giles. He later played in one second XI game. He had earlier appeared in almost 200 League games for the Old Trafford 'Reds', as well as taking part in 50 cup matches, including the 1977 and 1979 FA Cup finals at Wembley, gaining a winners' medal against Liverpool in the former. He also helped United to runners-up spot in the First Division in 1979–80. He

added 38 more outings to his tally with Sunderland and a further 30 with Rangers, helping the Ibrox club carry off the Premier League title in 1986–87 and the Skol Cup in 1986–87 and 1987–88. At international level, Nicholl won 73 full caps for Northern Ireland, plus ones at schoolboy, youth and under-21 levels. When at The Hawthorns he was the second most capped player ever to play for Albion. He helped Northern Ireland win the British Home International 'crown' in 1980 and played for his country in the 1982 and 1986 World Cup finals. He twice helped 'Blizzard' reach the Super Bowl Final in the NASL (1982, 1984), losing both contests.

NICHOLLS, Frederick

Outside-right: 7 apps.

Born: Handsworth, Birmingham, 5 November 1884.
Died: Wellington, May 1956.
Career: Handsworth New Road & Park Road Schools. Handsworth Victoria. Handsworth Rovers (August 1900). ALBION (professional, August 1904). Goldenhill Wanderers (August 1906). Served in Boer War. Shrewsbury Town (August 1914). Served in Army during World War One, retired from football, May 1921). Later involved with farming.

■ Fred Nicholls was a powerfully built right-winger, who had seven games in Albion's first XI at a time when the position was causing some concern. He made his League debut against Leicester Fosse (away) in November 1905 and also appeared in over 20 games for the reserves. Earlier in his career, Nicholls travelled abroad extensively and was captured by the Boers in South Africa.

NICHOLLS, Herbert John

Outside-left: 4 apps.

Born: Walsall Wood, 18 June 1891.
Died: Walsall, April 1921.
Career: Lichfield Road Junior & Shelfield Senior Schools (Walsall). Walsall Wood. Clayhanger Villa. Lichfield Road Juniors. Hednesford Town (July 1911). ALBION (£150, November 1913). Cannock Town (free, May 1914). Rushall Olympic (1915). Shireoak Saints (1919, retired, May 1921). Later employed as a pit labourer.

■ A useful outside-left, Jack Nicholls

deputised for Ben Shearman in four games in season 1913–14, making his League debut against Burnley (away) in Division One in December 1913. He played a few games in the second team in 1913–14.

NICHOLLS, James

Utility player: 6 apps.

Born: West Bromwich, 16 September 1867.
Died: Worcester, August 1934.
Career: Cronehills Council School (West Bromwich). St John's United (August 1888). ALBION (professional, August 1889). Kidderminster Olympic (free, June 1891). Stourport Swifts (1897). Wilden Rangers (1903, retired, May 1905). Employed in the carpet business before and after World War One.

■ A 'play-anywhere' footballer who preferred a wing-half role, Jim Nicholls occupied the centre-half and left-half positions during his two seasons with Albion and was an emergency goalkeeper in some second-team matches during 1890–91. He made his League debut against Wolverhampton Wanderers (home) in Division One in October 1889 and also starred in more than 25 'other' matches.

NICHOLLS, John

Forward: 145 apps. 64 goals.

Born: Wolverhampton, 3 April 1931.
Died: West Bromwich, 1 April 1995.
Career: Prestwood Road. Holy Trinity & Springfield Road Schools (Wolverhampton). Heath Town FC (Wolverhampton & District League). ALBION (trialist, July–September 1946). Heath Town Wesley (October 1946). Heath Town United (May 1948). Wolverhampton Wanderers (trialist, August–September 1949). ALBION (amateur, August 1950, professional, August 1951). Cardiff City (£4,000, May 1957). Exeter City (November 1957). Worcester City (August 1959). Wellington Town (February 1961). Oswestry Town (July 1961). Sankeys Works FC (1962). Henry Meadows FC (Technical Advisor, 1963–64). Red Dragon FC (West Bromwich League). Also played for West Bromwich Albion All Stars (1969–73). Lived and worked in Wolverhampton and attended The Hawthorns every game right up until his sudden death.

■ One of Albion's greatest post-war strikers, Johnny/Jack 'Poacher' Nicholls was a player who could dart into the right place at precisely the right moment and score a vital goal. He had an instructive knack of 'poaching' crucial goals and he did this so regularly during his stay with Albion. He could also unleash a cracking shot or delicately flick the ball home with either foot or head, back to goal or not. He made his senior debut against Blackburn Rovers (away) in a fifth round FA Cup tie in February 1952 and went on to form a magnificent 'twin-striking' partnership with Ronnie Allen. Indeed, he and Allen scored 105 goals between them in two seasons (1953–55). Nicholls also played alongside Allen in two full internationals for England, scoring on his debut against Scotland in front of 134,544 spectators at Hampden in April 1954. He also collected a 'B' cap and one at under-23 level. He was a key figure in Albion's attack in 1953–54 when the Baggies so very nearly carried off the coveted League and cup double. Nicholls, in fact, was in Albion's Cup-winning team at Wembley in 1954, although he admits that he had one of his worst games in a striped shirt that afternoon. His overall record for Albion was an exceptionally good one,

and he netted frequently for the reserves as well, grabbing 46 goals (in only 69 games), plus another 50 for the intermediates and 40 for the juniors. In his entire career (with Albion, Cardiff and Exeter City) Nicholls, who was also nicknamed 'Johnny on the Spot', struck 95 goals in 225 outings, a first-class record. He suffered a stroke, followed shortly afterwards by a heart-attack, in the mid-1970s but recovered and his sudden death occurred as he was driving home from Albion's League home game against Middlesbrough in 1995.

NICHOLLS, Samuel

Centre-forward: 50 apps. 17 goals.

Born: West Bromwich, 12 January 1871.
Died: 5 October 1912.
Career: Spon Lane School (West Bromwich). Kidderminster Olympic. West Bromwich Victoria (1889). ALBION (professional, February 1890). London CBC (free, June 1892). ALBION (free, July 1893, retired, July 1894, after a paralytic seizure and became permanently disabled).

■ Any lack of ball finesse was more than atoned for by Sammy Nicholls's dashing, fearless displays in and around his opponents' penalty-area. He had two spells with Albion, and during the first one helped them beat Aston Villa 3–0 in the 1892 FA Cup final, scoring one of this side's goals, having made his League debut two years earlier against Everton (away) in Division One in March 1890. Perhaps he found it hard to settle into the team early on, but once in he stuck and

was forever in the thick of the action, roughing it with the biggest and hardest defenders in the land. He actually left football for a year (1892–93), going to work in London for the County Borough Council. Besides his 50 senior outings, Nicholls also played in more than 60 'other' games for Albion.

NICHOLSON, Magnus Douglas

Full-back: 68 apps.

Born: Oakengates, Shropshire, 6 March 1871.
Died: Oswestry, 3 July 1941.
Career: Oakengates Fellowship School. Oswestry Town (April 1889). ALBION (professional, May 1891). Bedford School. Luton Town (free, May 1894). Cairo, Egypt (July 1896). First Vienna FC, Austria (summer of 1897). Became associated with the Austrian FA, coaching their national team in 1899–1900. Appointed captain for life of First Vienna FC in 1900 – the only person in the club's 110-year history to be so honoured. Later became the first President of the Austrian Football Union, having a team named after him (Nicholson FC) in 1900. Also played for Standard Athletic FC, Austria (during World War One). Was one of the pioneers of Austrian Football, playing for Cricket FC and Vienna FC. Later worked for Thomas Cooke (travel agent) in Vienna, Paris and Hamburg and was also a competent pole-vaulter.

■ Magnus (Mark) Nicholson was, indeed, a very fine, cultured full-back,

whose footwork and speed in recovery were outstanding features of his game. He was a consistent player, never in trouble with officials and seldom did he commit a foul. His three seasons with Albion coincided with those of Tom McCulloch, Seth Powell, Jack Horton and Bob Crone, and he had to be in tip-top form to hold on to his first-team place, which he did with grim determination and subtle play. He left Albion to become assistant Schoolmaster at Bedford School. His only honour in English football was collecting an FA Cup winners' medal with Albion in 1892, having earlier made his League debut against Everton (home) in Division One in September 1891. He appeared in over 30 'other' games for Albion.

NICHOLSON, Shane Michael

Full-back: 60+2 apps.

Born: Newark, Notts, 3 June 1970.
Career: Lincoln City (apprentice, June 1986, professional, July 1988). Derby County (£100,000, April 1992). ALBION (£150,000, February 1996). Chesterfield (free, August 1998). Stockport County (free, June 1999). Sheffield United (July 2001). Tranmere Rovers (free, July 2002). Chesterfield (June 2004).

■ Traditionally a left-back, Shane Nicholson had two respectable seasons at The Hawthorns before being sacked by the club for alleged misuse of drugs. He made over 150 senior appearances for Lincoln, 87 for Derby and then, after

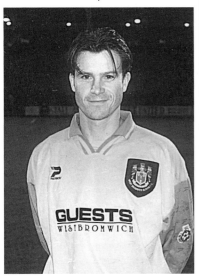

leaving The Hawthorns, added a further 200 senior appearances to his tally with his four other clubs. He was a GM Vauxhall Conference winner with Lincoln in 1988 and made his debut for Albion in the then problem left-back position, against Southend United (home) in February 1996 (won 3–1). He also played in a dozen or so second-team games for the club.

NICOL, Stephen

Full-back/midfield: 9 apps.

Born: Irvine, Scotland, 11 December 1961.
Career: Irvine schoolboy football. Ayr United (amateur, April 1977, professional December 1979). Liverpool (£300,000, October 1981). Notts County (free, January 1995). Sheffield Wednesday (free, November 1995). ALBION (on loan, March–May 1998). Doncaster Rovers (June 1998). New England Revolution, USA (May 2002).

■ When Albion signed Steve Nicol on loan from Hillsborough on transfer deadline day in 1998, he was already a vastly experienced Scottish international midfielder with 27 full and 14 under-21 caps under his belt plus four League championship, three FA Cup, a European Cup and Charity Shield medals in his

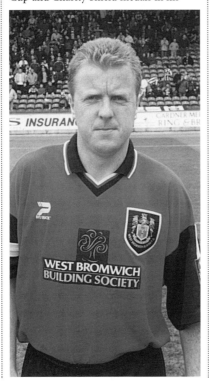

locker, all won as a Liverpool player. He served the Merseysiders for well over 13 years, amassing 469 senior appearances and scoring 46 goals, having previously had 89 outings with Ayr United as well as playing 37 times for Notts County and 54 for Wednesday. He gave Albion a touch of class in the engine-room and it was a pity they couldn't have secured his services two or three seasons earlier! He made his debut for the club against Norwich City (away) in March 1998. Nicol helped New England Revolution with the American League title in 2003.

NISBET, Gordon James Mackay

Right-back: 167 apps. one goal.

Born: Wallsend-on-Tyne, 18 September 1951.
Career: Wallsend Grammar School. Wallsend & Northumberland Boys. Willington Boys' Club. Blackpool (trialist, 1966). Leicester City (trialist, also 1966). Preston North End (trialist, 1967). Sunderland (trialist, April–May 1968). ALBION (apprentice, August 1968, professional, September 1968). Hull City (£10,000 September 1976). Plymouth Argyle (£32,000, December 1980). Exeter City (August–October 1987). Ottery St Mary (1989–90). Plymouth Argyle (youth team coach, July 1991, acted as caretaker manager, February 1992). Barnstaple Town (manager, 1994–95). Later served in and played for the Devon and Cornwall Police. Now coaches at various non-League clubs in Devon and also plays occasionally for the ex-Plymouth Argyle charity team.

■ Gordon Nisbet was a thoughtful and composed right-back who started his League career as a goalkeeper, making his debut in that position for Albion against Coventry City at Highfield Road in a First Division match in August 1969. Prior to breaking into the senior side (on a regular basis), he occupied several positions in Albion's Central League side, including those of right-half and centre-forward. But then, under Don Howe's shrewd management, he was successfully converted into a right-back and never regretted the decision to exchange a green jersey for the number 2 shirt. He won one England under-23 cap in 1972 and when he left Albion in 1976 (following the arrival of Paddy Mulligan) he had

made 136 League appearances, plus another 31 in various Cup competitions, and over 120 in the Central League. He scored his only first-team goal against Carlisle United in an FA Cup tie in January 1975. He later helped Plymouth beat Albion and reach the FA Cup semi-finals in 1984, while also assisting the Pilgrims to promotion from Division Three two years later.

* In 1993–94 'Nizza', aged 42, came on as a 'sub' and scored in a reserve-team game for Plymouth against Welton Rovers.

NOCK, Josiah Francis

Outside-left: 15 apps. 6 goals.

Born: Hagley, 22 October 1875.

Died: West Hagley, 11 November 1933. Career: Beeches Road Infants & Hollyhedge Council Schools (West Bromwich). Greets Green Boys. West Bromwich Swifts. Halesowen Town (July 1896). ALBION (professional, August 1897). Langley Richmond (June 1900). Brierley Alliance (1901–02). Old Hill Saints (August 1902, retired, c.1908). Later formed his own business in Kidderminster.

■ An outside-left of extraordinary speed over a short distance, Joe Nock had a useful shot but had the tendency to hold on to the ball far too long. He had to contest a first-team spot with the likes of Ben Garfield and Arthur Watson. He made his League debut against Liverpool (away) in Division One in January 1898 and also played in a handful of 'other' first-team matches for the club.

NORMAN, Oliver

Utility forward: 20 apps. 4 goals.

Born: West Bromwich, 15 August 1866. Died: Birmingham, 6 November 1943. Career: Hall Green School (West Bromwich). Oldbury Town (August 1888). Wednesbury Old Athletic (September 1889). ALBION (professional, June 1893–May 1896). Hereford Town (August 1896). Birmingham (trainer, 1903–07). Thereafter was sports supervisor at three Birmingham Schools in Sparkhill, Sparkbrook and Bordesley Green.

■ 'Olly' Norman filled in from time to time for Billy Bassett and Roddy McLeod on Albion's right flank. He was a useful, versatile player, always eager to try his luck at something new with a good eye and powerful shot. It was unfortunate that he was with Albion at the same time as so many other fine players. He made his League debut against Aston Villa (away) in Division One in September 1893 and also played in 15 'other' first-team matches for the club.

NORTH, Stacey Stewart

Defender: 70 apps.

Born: Luton, 25 November 1964. Career: Luton & Bedfordshire Schools. Limbury Boys' Club. Luton Town (apprentice 1981, professional, November 1982). Wolverhampton Wanderers (on loan, November–December 1985). ALBION (£120,000 December 1987). Fulham (October 1990, retired through injury, April 1992).

■ Blonde centre-back, strong in the tackle, good in the air, Stacey North joined Albion after failing to gain a

regular first-team place with Luton, for whom Steve Foster and Barry Donaghy were established performers. He made his Luton debut against Albion in May 1984 and played his first game for the Baggies against Swindon Town (away) in Division Two in January 1988. He settled in extremely well at The Hawthorns during the 1988–89 campaign, becoming the first Albion player to make 46 League appearances in a single campaign. He also played in 18 Central League games for the club. He possessed a terrific long throw. A tedious back injury forced him into early retirement.

NURSE, Daniel George

Right-half: 88 apps. 4 goals.

Born: Princes End, Tipton, 23 June 1873. Died: West Bromwich, 20 April 1959. Career: Princes End Council School. Princes End FC. Coseley FC. Wolverhampton Wanderers (professional, June 1894). ALBION (£75, May 1901, retired through injury, April 1905, became an ALBION director, August 1910, retaining his position until May 1927, elected Life Member of the club in 1920 in recognition of his sterling efforts to help keep Albion in existence during the summer of 1910).

■ Dan Nurse was a powerful right-half who was instrumental in helping Albion win promotion on the first attempt in 1901–02. He was not always at ease when

faced with intricate dribblers, but he was mighty efficient in going forward and breaking up threatening attacks aimed down the right-hand side of his defence. Nurse skippered Albion for three seasons, having made 40 appearances for Wolves in seven years at the club. He doubled his tally with Albion and in 1902–03 represented the Football League. A player who led by example, he made his Albion debut against Glossop (home) in Division Two in September 1901.

O'CONNOR, James Kevin

Midfield: 33+5 apps.

Born: Dublin, 1 September 1979.

Career: Stoke City (apprentice, April 1995, professional, September 1996). ALBION (tribunal set fee of £250,000, July 2003). Burnley (on loan, October 2004–May 2005, loan spell ended February 2005, signed permanently for £175,000, March 2005).

■ Capped by the Republic of Ireland at youth team level, midfielder James O'Connor went on to appear in nine under-21 internationals during his time with Stoke City, whom he helped win the

Auto-Windscreen Shield in 2000 and gain promotion to the First Division two years later. A totally committed performer and a firm favourite with the Stoke fans, his aggressive approach to any game has, over the years, earned him several yellow cards. A strong tackler, he appeared in 211 first-team matches for the Potters (22 goals) before moving to The Hawthorns. He made his Albion debut against Walsall on the opening day of the 2003–04 League programme and went on to play his part in helping the Baggies reclaim their place in the Premiership. However, he did not figure in manager Gary Megson's plans at the start of the following season and was subsequently loaned out to championship side Burnley. * Stoke initially wanted £1.25 million for O'Connor but a Football League transfer tribunal set the figures at a fifth of that sum.

OLIVER, Adam

Midfield: 4+24 apps. 1 goal.

Born: West Bromwich, 25 October 1980. Career: Sandwell schoolboy football. ALBION (apprentice, April 1997, professional, August 1998, retired through injury, May 2002).

■ An England youth international midfielder, strong, hard-working and mobile, Adam Oliver's career came to an abrupt end in 2002 when he was forced

to retire with severely damaged knee ligaments, this after he had signed an extended contract that would have kept him at The Hawthorns until June 2003. He was only 21 years of age at that time. Initially said to have a bright future in the game, he made his senior debut for Albion in a League Cup game against Brentford in August 1998, scoring his only goal for the club against Bolton Wanderers in a League home match in April 2000 (a 4–4 draw). He also played in more than 60 second-team games for the club.

OLIVER, Harold Sidney Milton

Full-back: 1 app.

Born: Yardley, Birmingham, 7 February 1863.
Died: Birmingham, 1935.
Career: Yardley Wood School. Kings Heath Nomads. Small Heath Alliance (1886). ALBION (professional, November 1888). Small Heath Alliance (January 1889) Bournville United (May 1889). Shirley St Luke's (1890, retired, May 1892). Later worked in Birmingham's Bull Ring market until World War One.

■ Harry Oliver was a dogged full-back who spent five years with Small Heath (now Birmingham City), making over 60 appearances before having just one solitary outing for Albion against Burnley (away) in Division One in November 1888, in two and a half months with the club.

O'REGAN, Kieran Michael

Midfield: 44+10 apps. 2 goals.

Born: Cork, 9 November 1963.
Career: Tramore Athletic (semi-professional, August 1981). Brighton & Hove Albion (professional, April 1983). Swindon Town (free, August 1987). Huddersfield Town (free, August 1988). ALBION (£25,000, July 1993). Halifax Town (free, August 1995, player-manager, July 1998–April 1999). Altrincham (free, August 2000–May 2002). Huddersfield Town (youth-team coach, from August 2003). Also soccer summariser on Radio Leeds (2002–04).

■ Besides being a competent, hard-working midfielder, Kiernan O'Regan

could also fill in at right-back, from where he produced some confident displays. He had already made close on 400 senior appearances before joining Albion in 1993, signed by manager Keith Burkinshaw. Unfortunately, niggling injuries interrupted his last season at The Hawthorns. Capped at youth-team level, O'Regan went on to win four full caps for the Republic of Ireland. He made his debut for Albion in a 1–1 League draw at Barnsley in August 1993 and, besides his first-team appearances, he also made close on 40 for the reserves (2 goals scored).

OSBORNE, John

Goalkeeper: 312 apps.

Born: Barlborough, Derbyshire, 1 December 1940.
Died: Worcester, 2 December 1998.
Career: Barlborough Junior & Staveley Netherthorpe Grammar Schools. Chesterfield Boys. North East Derbyshire & District Schools. Barlborough Colliery Miners' Welfare FC. Netherthorpe FC. Chesterfield (amateur, July 1959, professional, September 1960). ALBION (£10,000, January 1967, retired, June 1972, reinstated by ALBION, January 1973). Walsall (on loan, February–March 1973). Shamrock Rovers (July 1978). Preston North End (non-contract, 1979). Telford United (non-contract, 1979). Coventry City (non-contract, September 1979). Birmingham Post and Mail Rangers (1980–81). West Bromwich Albion All Stars (1982–87). Walsall (non-contract, December 1983). Corinthians FC (manager, 1983–84). Worked on the

promotions side at the Sandwell Evening Mail for a number of years, then commercial manager of Worcestershire CCC.

■ John Osborne, 'Ossie' to his pals and nicknamed the 'Bionic' goalkeeper (after having a strip of plastic inserted into his finger to act as an extra joint), served Albion splendidly for over 10 years, divided into two periods. A product of Chesterfield's famous goalkeeping academy, which sent out Gordon Banks among others, Osborne often performed miracles between the posts for Albion and was undoubtedly one of the finest post-war 'keepers the club has had. He had a safe pair of hands, was alert in positioning and a courageous and dedicated club man; indeed, a splendid chap all round. Initially an outfield player, winning two schoolboy caps as a left-half, Osborne appeared in the 1968 FA Cup winning side and 1970 League Cup runners-up team with Albion, and he helped the club win promotion in 1976 when he conceded only 33 goals in 42 matches (a club record). Signed to replace Ray Potter and Dick Sheppard, he was Albion's first-choice 'keeper until 1970 and then lost his place to Peter Latchford before regaining it a year later, only to drop out of contention again soon afterwards. He returned for a third spell and eventually took his tally of competitive appearances past the 300 mark, having made his debut against Nottingham Forest (home) in Division One in January 1967. He also played in

over 50 second XI games. During his professional career, Osborne, who had a great sense of humour, played in 420 senior games. He loved ornithology, sports quizzes and cricket, and once ran a sports outfitters business with fellow 'keeper Jimmy Cumbes. The first Albion goalkeeper to receive a testimonial (1978), the fund raised a total of £32,000, a record at the time for a Midland-based footballer. Ossie sadly died of cancer at the age of 58.

OWEN, Alfred George

Outside-right: 7 apps. 1 goal.

Born: Coalbrookdale, Salop, 21 March 1880.
Died: Smethwick, 1944.
Career: Coalbrookdale & Madeley Schools. Ironbridge Welfare FC. Ironbridge FC. ALBION (professional, June 1903). Walsall (£25, May 1905). Hereford Thistle (free, April 1908). Rood End FC (as secretary, 1913, retired out of football, May 1919 after serving in World War One). Later worked for an estate agent in Oldbury.

■ Despite being small and frail, Alf Owen was an extremely nippy, purposeful right-winger who possessed a strong shot in both feet. He played most of his football at Albion in the second team but was always eager to grab the opportunity of first-team action. His made his League debut against Stoke (home) in Division One in March 1904 and also played in 22 second XI matches for Albion (4 goals).

OWEN, Gary Alfred

Midfield: 225 + 4 apps. 26 goals.

Born: St. Helen's, Lancs, 7 July 1958.
Career: St Aidan's Church of England School (St Helens). Eccleston YC. Warrington & District Boys. Manchester City (apprentice, August 1972, professional, August 1975). ALBION (£465,000, May 1979). Panionios, Greece (£25,000, July 1986). Sheffield Wednesday (trialist, July 1987, signed August 1987–June 1988). Apoel Nicosia, Cyprus (August 1988, retired through injury, May 1990). Became an art dealer (Gary Owen Fine Art) in North Staffordshire/Cheshire. Later worked for Radio Picadilly, Manchester and Century radio, Manchester. Also coach at Manchester City School of Excellence.

■ Gary Owen was a skilful midfielder

OWERS, Ebenezer Harold

Centre-forward: 4 apps.

*Born: Bromley, Kent, 11 February 1889.
Died: Scotland, June 1951.
Career: Leytonstone & District Schools.
Bashwood FC (Leyton). Leytonstone FC.
Leyton FC (August 1905). Blackpool
(briefly, April 1906). Leyton FC (July
1906). ALBION (professional, November
1907). Chesterfield Town (£40, January
1909). Darlington (free, August 1911).
Bristol City (£50, March 1912). Clyde
(free, August 1913). Celtic (free, November
1913). Served in World War One, did not
play after the hostilities.*

A snappy, punchy centre-forward who
unfortunately never hit it off with Albion
like he did north of the border! 'Ginger'
Owers made nine appearances for
Blackpool, 20 for Chesterfield, 12 for
Darlington, 31 for Bristol City, a handful
for Clyde and 16 for Celtic. In January
1914 he scored four goals for Celtic
against Ayr United in a League game. He
helped Celtic complete the double in
1913–14, scoring nine goals in total
including four in a 6–0 League home win
over Ayr in December. His Albion debut
was against Derby County (away) in
Division Two in December 1907, and
when fit he also played several times for
the Baggies second team.

PADDOCK, John William

Winger: 31 apps. 5 goals.

*Born: West Bromwich, 11 July 1877.
Died: Wolverhampton, 10 April 1928.
Career: Christ Church & Lyng Schools
(West Bromwich). ALBION (professional,
April 1894). Walsall Town (free, May
1896). Brierley Hill Alliance (free, May
1898). ALBION (free, May 1899).
Halesowen (free, June 1900). Brierley Hill
Alliance (1902–04). Wellington (1905).
Burslem Port Vale (August 1906, retired
May 1907). Later worked in Stoke-on-
Trent before returning to the Black
Country.*

'Jack' Paddock was a markedly
unselfish winger who could play on
either flank. In the vicinity of goal he was
always willing to have a shot at the target,
from any angle with either foot. Son of
Jack Paddock (Albion's trainer of the
1890s), and brother of William, he had
two spells with Albion, making his

and quality ball-player, whose career with
Albion was ruined late on by a series of
niggling injuries including a fractured
shin, gashed calf (which required a skin
graft) and torn thigh muscle.
Nevertheless, he had the ability to grace
any football pitch, any match and any
competition, if he put his mind to it. He
certainly had the craft, the know-how and
indeed the confidence to dictate the
midfield arena, but he never really
enforced his authority on the game in
question. He had five excellent seasons
with Albion (1979–84), but after breaking
his shin bone (at West Ham in January
1984) he was never the same player again,
and when manager Ron Saunders arrived

at The Hawthorns Owen's days were
numbered. He eventually left the club in
1986, signing an initial two-year contract
with the sister club of Panionios in
Greece. Earlier in his career, with
Manchester City, he won England
recognition at youth and 'B' levels and
held the record for most under-21 caps
(22). He also represented the Football
League. Owen appeared in 123
competitive games (scoring 23 goals) for
Manchester City, with whom he also
gained a First Division runners'-up medal
(1977). He made his Albion debut against
Derby County (home) in Division One in
August 1979. He scored once in 31
Central League outings for the club.

League debut against Wolverhampton Wanderers (away) in Division One in December 1894. He also played in over 20 'other' games for the club and, six years after leaving The Hawthorns, he actually made his debut for Port Vale against Albion in September 1906.

* Another relative, John James Paddock, who was also associated with Albion, died in 1964.

PADDOCK, William

Outside-left: 8 apps. 3 goals.

Born: West Bromwich, 6 February 1862.
Died: West Bromwich, April 1938.
Career: Christ Church School (West Bromwich). West Bromwich Unity (1884). ALBION (professional, February 1886, retired through injury and illness, June 1888).

■ Like his brother, 'Jack', Bill Paddock was a positive winger who occasionally opted to play inside-left. He had good skills, fair speed and a useful shot. He was forced to give up football with a knee injury at the age of 26. Albion's outside-left in the 1887 FA Cup final, he made his senior debut in that competition against Burton Wanderers (home) in October 1886 and also played in 35 'other' first-team games for the club. He died two weeks after his brother.

PAILOR, Robert

Centre-forward: 92 apps. 47 goals.

Born: Stockton-on-Tees, 7 July 1887.
Died: Hartlepool, 24 January 1976.

Career: Galley Field School (Stockton-on-Tees). St Oswald's FC. West Hartlepool (1906). ALBION (professional, October 1908). Newcastle United (£1,550, May 1914, retired, May 1915 with kidney complaint). Later became a bookmaker in Hartlepool but in later years was forced to relinquish his license when his eyesight failed, and he eventually went blind.

■ Bob Pailor was a player made for scoring goals. His hefty weight allied with pace and agility made him such an effective and useful centre-forward, one of the best around at that time. He made his Albion debut against Bradford Park Avenue (away) in Division Two in January 1909 and went on to average a goal every two games, scoring 40 in 79 League outings alone, topping the club's scoring charts in successive seasons (1911–13). In 1912 he helped the Baggies reach the FA Cup final, scoring a last-gasp extra-time winner against Blackburn Rovers in the replayed semi-final. During his six years' association with Albion, Pailor won many friends, both on and off the field. He scored a lot of goals for the second team in the 1908–09 and 1909–10 seasons, but he eventually left The Hawthorns after Alf Bentley had arrived from Bolton. Then, ironically, he made his debut for Newcastle against Albion in September 1914. He was 88 when he died.

PALMER, Carlton Lloyd

Midfielder/defender: 131+8 apps. 5 goals.

Born: Rowley Regis, Warley, West Midlands, 5 December 1965.

Career: Whiteheath Infants & St Michael's Junior Schools (Oldbury). Rowley Regis & District Boys. Newton Albion (1980). Netherton Town (1981). Dudley Town (1982). ALBION (apprentice, July 1983, professional, December 1984). Sheffield Wednesday (£750,000, with striker Colin West, valued at £250,000 moving to The Hawthorns as part of the deal, February 1989). Leeds United (£2.8 million, June 1994). Southampton (£1 million, September 1997). Nottingham Forest (£1.1 million, January 1999). Coventry City (£500, September 1999). Watford (on loan, December 2000–January 2001). Sheffield Wednesday (on loan, February–May 2001 and again, September–October 2001). Stockport County (free, as player-manager, November 2001, retired as a player, February 2003, sacked as manager, September 2003). Darlington (non-contract, November 2003). Cork City (February–March 2004). Mansfield Town (temporary manager, November 2004, appointed full-time manager, March 2005).

■ A tall, long-striding utility player who looked international class from a very young age, Carlton Palmer made rapid progress after making his League debut for Albion against Newcastle United in September 1985 (as a substitute). A driving force from centre-field, he performed with total commitment match after match and it was a blow to the supporters when he left, having also appeared in over 50 Central League games (3 goals). He went on to gain a total of 18 full caps for England, played in five 'B' and four under-21 internationals and was in the Leeds side beaten by Aston Villa in the 1996 Coca-Cola Cup final. In February 2003, after receiving a red card away at Cheltenham Town, Palmer announced his retirement from first-team football, with a total of 740 senior appearances behind him at club and international level (591 in the Football League). A very likeable man, as a player he served under manager Ron Atkinson at Albion, Hillsborough and Nottingham Forest. As a manager himself, however, Palmer had a tough time at Stockport, who were relegated from the First Division in 2002. He was placed in charge at Mansfield following the suspension of the former Wolves defender Keith Curle.

PALMER, Leslie James

Forward: 5+3 apps. 1 goal.

Born: Birmingham, 5 September 1971.
Career: ALBION (apprentice, April 1988, professional, July 1990). Kidderminster Harriers (free, August 1992). Then with Bromsgrove Rovers, Oldbury United, Blakenhall (2000–02). Oldbury United (player-coach, from August 2002).

■ A reserve forward at The Hawthorns, Les Palmer made his senior debut for Albion as a 'sub' against Notts County in November 1990 (lost 4–3). He scored his only first-team goal for the club in a 2–1

home defeat by Plymouth Argyle in March 1991, yet managed to net 17 times in 62 Pontins League matches, gaining a championship medal at this level in 1990–9, when he finished as top marksman.

PARKER, Alan Eric

Full-back: 5 apps. 1 goal.

Born: Tipton, 25 February 1925.
Career: Tipton Central School. ALBION (amateur, August 1942, professional, March 1945). Hereford United (May 1947). Wrexham (briefly). Tipton Town (1948). Dudley Town (1953, retired, May 1955). Worked locally for many years, now lives on the suburbs of Wolverhampton.

■ A full-back, small in stature and build, Alan Parker was a wartime signing by Albion, who made his debut in the Black Country derby against Wolverhampton Wanderers (away) in the Football League North in September 1942.

PARKES, Harry Arnold

Outside-right: 31 apps. 4 goals.

Born: Gorsty Hill, Halesowen, 9 September 1888.
Died: 18 Basford, March 1947.

Career: Coombes Wood Junior & Halesowen Grammar Schools. Coombes Wood FC. Halesowen. ALBION (professional, February 1906). Coventry City (£50, May 1908). ALBION (£50, May 1914). Newport County (secretary-manager, June 1919). Chesterfield (secretary-manager, August 1922). Lincoln City (secretary-manager, May 1927). Mansfield Town (secretary-manager, May 1936). Notts County (manager, January 1938, from football, July 1939). After World War Two, he assisted the Nottinghamshire County FA.

■ Harry Parkes was a quiet, unassuming player and very unselfish, who was a shade too light to make any real impression at top level. He later became a very successful official, serving five clubs in the capacity of secretary-manager. In April 1920 he was forced to play one game in goal for Newport County in a Southern League match, despite his height, and he also turned out for Lincoln City reserves in the early 1930's when acting as secretary-manager at Sincil Bank. He saw the 'Imps' win promotion from Division Three North in season 1931–32, some 25 years after making his senior debut for Albion against Notts County (home) in a fourth round FA Cup tie in September 1907. He appeared in over 35 second XI matches in his two spells at The Hawthorns.

PARKIN, Stephen John

Full-back/midfield: 49+5 apps. 2 goals.

Born: Mansfield, 7 November 1965.
Career: Portland School (Worksop). Bassetlaw Schoolboys. Nottinghamshire Schools. Stoke City (apprentice, April 1981, professional, November 1983). ALBION (£190,000, June 1989). Mansfield Town (free, July 1992, manager September

1996–May 1999). Rochdale (manager, June 1999). Barnsley (manager, November 2001, sacked October 2002). Notts County (assistant manager/coach, August–December 2003). Rochdale (manager, December 2003).

■ After more than 10 years in the game as a professional, Steve 'Billy' Parkin entered management with Mansfield Town in 1996. Originally a wing-half, he played most of his 260 plus games as a full-back, first with Stoke (whom he served for six years), then Albion and finally Mansfield. He made his debut for Albion against Sheffield United (home) in August 1989 (the opening League game of that season, when another ex-Stoke player, Brian Talbot, was manager at The Hawthorns, while former Potter Tony Ford was in front of Parkin at number 7). He also played in 24 Central League games for the Baggies. Capped five times by England at under-21 level, Parkin had earlier represented his country as a schoolboy and youth team player.

PARRY, John

Outside-left: 1 app.

Born: Glanmule, Newton, mid-Wales, 4 February 1871.
Died: Ruabon, North Wales, May 1936.
Career: Newtown & Welshpool Schools. Chirbury St Luke's. Newtown FC. ALBION (amateur, January 1895). Aberystwyth (amateur, June 1895, retired, May 1900).

■ An amateur outside-left who spent six months as a trialist with Albion, Jack Parry made one League appearance for the club, lining up against Preston North End (home) in Division One in January 1895.
* Some pre World War One reference books list this player as John Perry.

PARSLEY, Neil Robert

Full-back: 43+5 apps.

Born: Liverpool, 25 April 1966.
Career: Witton Albion (semi-professional, April 1985). Leeds United (professional, November 1988). Chester City (on loan, December 1989–January 1990)). Huddersfield Town (free, July 1990). Doncaster Rovers (on loan, February–March 1991). ALBION (£25,000, September 1993). Exeter City (free, August 1995). Leeds United (trialist,

April–May 1996). Witton Albion (free, August 1996). Guiseley (free, October 1996). Witton Albion (free, November 1997). Guiseley (free, manager, from July 2001).

■ Neil Parsley was an efficient full-back who had produced some excellent displays for Huddersfield before moving to The Hawthorns, where he replaced Wayne Fereday (following the departure of Nicky Reid). He was one of three ex-Terriers' players in the Baggies side when he made his debut against Middlesbrough (home) in September 1993, the others being Kevin Donovan and Kieran O'Regan. Parsley played in almost 30 second-team games for Albion.

PASKIN, William John

Striker: 15+13 apps. 5 goals.

Born: Capetown, South Africa, 1 February 1962.
Career: Hellenic FC, South Africa (July 1980). Toronto Blizzard, NASL (May 1983). South China, Hong Kong (August 1984). FC Seiko, Hong Kong (August 1985). KV Kortrijk, Belgium (August 1986). Dundee United (trialist, July 1987). ALBION (non-contract, March 1988, professional, August 1988). Wolverhampton

Wanderers (£75,000, June 1989). Stockport County (on loan, September 1991). Birmingham City (on loan, November 1991). Shrewsbury Town (on loan, February 1992) Wrexham (free, February 1992). Bury (free, July 1994-May 1996). Returned to South Africa.

■ John Paskin was a tall, black-haired striker, signed by Albion boss Ron Atkinson, who was seeking an extra goalscorer following a rather disappointing 1988–89 campaign, when the team netted only 55 times in 49 League and cup games. Despite a few enterprising displays, he failed to make much of an impression at The Hawthorns, although he did find the net on his League debut at Leicester in August 1988 and scored 13 goals in 56 second XI appearances. Later, he did well with Wrexham, scoring 14 goals in 60 games for the Welsh club, while also helping Bury reach the play-off final in 1995. Earlier in his career he knocked in four goals in a game for Toronto Blizzard against Tampa Bay Rowdies in July 1984.

PEARS, William George

Centre-forward: 4 apps. 2 goals.

Born: Aston, Birmingham, 6 July 1922.
Died: Kidderminster, 1992.
Career: Park Lane School (Aston). Wolsley FC. ALBION (amateur, October 1943, professional, March 1944). Kidderminster Harriers (free, October 1947). Chaddesley Corbett Nomads (1951). Churchill Swifts (1953, retired, May 1954).

■ Bill Pears was a big, strapping forward who began his career as an outside-left. World War Two obviously interrupted his footballing progress and after leaving Albion he never really maintained his form, which he showed early on with the Throstles for whom he made his debut against Nottingham Forest (away) in the Midland War Cup in March 1944, scoring once in a 3–2 defeat.

PEARSON, Harold Frederick

Goalkeeper: 303 apps.

Born: Tamworth, 7 May 1908.
Died: West Bromwich, November 1994.
Career: Tamworth & Amington Schools. Glascote United. Glascote Methodists.

Belgrave YMCA. Belgrave United. Two Gates FC. Nuneaton Borough. Tamworth Castle. ALBION (amateur, April 1925, professional, May 1925). Millwall (£300, August 1937, retired, 1940 after guesting for West Ham United (1939–40). Returned to ALBION as coach, 1948–52, then scout, 1953–55. Worked for WJ and S Lees, iron founders, for many years and lived on Oldbury Road, West Bromwich until his death.

■ For a big man, Harold 'Algy' Pearson made goalkeeping look so easy. Equally adept with high or low crosses, he had tremendous reach, kicked vast distances out of his hands and he could throw the ball a fair way too. He was on Albion's books along with his father, Hubert (1925), and he went on to make over 300 senior appearances for the club, including 281 in the League, his debut coming against South Shields (home) in Division Two in December 1927. He won an FA Cup medal in 1931 and runners'-up prize in the 1935 final. Three years later he collected a Third Division South championship medal with Millwall. Earlier in his career Pearson had gained a junior international cap for England (1927) and his only full cap was against Scotland at Wembley in 1932, when he played behind his club colleague George Shaw. He also played for Tamworth Castle in the 1926–27 Bass Charity Vase final, which they won. Pearson replaced George Ashmore between the posts for

Albion and was subsequently dislodged by Billy Light (briefly) and then Jimmy Adams in 1937. In three seasons – 1930–33 inclusive – Albion played 126 League matches and Pearson appeared in 125 of them. Harold also played in almost 100 second XI games for the Baggies, helping them win the Central League title in 1933–34. A very consistent performer, and a very fine goalkeeper, he was one of Albion's best. He was the cousin of Harry Hibbs (ex-Blues 'keeper) and another cousin, Horace Pearson, kept goal for Coventry City in the 1930s.

PEARSON, Hubert Pryer

Goalkeeper: 377 apps. 2 goals.

Born: Kettlebrook, Tamworth, 15 May 1886.
Died: Tamworth, October 1955.
Career: Kettlebrook & Wilnecote Schools. Kettlebrook Oakfield. Tamworth Castle (1902). Tamworth Athletic (1904). ALBION (amateur, February 1906, professional, March 1906, retired, May 1926). Guest for Oldbury Town (1915–16) when serving in the Army. Worked in an iron works after World War One.

■ Hubert Pearson took over the goalkeeper's jersey from Jim Stringer during the 1909–10 season and was subsequently replaced by George Ashmore, who in turn handed over to Hubert's son, Harold, in 1927. Between them, Hubert and Harold Pearson won

every honour in the game at that time: First, Second and Third Division South championship medals, FA Cup winners' and runners'-up medals, FA Charity Shield winners' and runners'-up medals, junior and full England international caps, Football League and FA honours and runners'-up prizes in League Divisions One and Two (in 1925 and 1931 respectively). Hubert, a well-balanced, agile 'keeper with an abundance of confidence, made his senior debut against Birmingham (away) in the FA Cup first round replay in January 1908 and played his last first-team game 17 years later against West Ham United (away) in March 1925. Pearson had the pleasure of scoring two goals for Albion, both from the penalty spot, against Bury (home) on Boxing Day in 1911 (won 2–0) and against Middlesbrough (home) in April 1912 (won 3–1). He also played in well over 100 second-team games for Albion, 88 in the Central League, gaining a championship medal at this level in 1923–24. Pearson served in the AA Reserve Brigade, stationed on the Isle of Wight during World War One.

PEARSON, Thomas

Inside-left: 171 apps. 88 goals.

Born: West Bromwich, 20 May 1866.
Died: West Bromwich, 4 July 1918.
Career: Christ Church School. Oak Villa. West Bromwich Sandwell. ALBION (professional, April 1886, retired through injury, May 1894). He was crippled at the age of 30, being confined to a wheelchair.

■ Tom Pearson was Albion's first really great marksman, who was leading scorer in each of the first five Football League seasons, between 1888–93. He was, indeed, a brilliant inside-left, who had endurance, resolution, high quality shooting power (with both feet) and a distinctive short gait, whose senior debut was against Notts County (away) in the sixth round of the FA Cup in February 1887. He was certainly a natural goalscorer, whose alertness and presence of mind brought him well over 150 goals in more than 400 first-team games (including local Cup competitions and friendlies) during his Albion career. He played in the 1887, 1888 and 1892 FA Cup finals, picking up winners' medals in

the latter two, and in his six seasons with Albion (as a League player) he missed only 14 matches (all through injury). He would surely have earned international honours for England had his playing days not ended prematurely owing to a serious leg injury, suffered in 1894.

PEMBERTON, JAMES Henry Arthur

Right-back: 172 apps.

Born: Wolverhampton, 30 April 1916.
Died: Wolverhampton, February 1995.
Career: Willenhall Road School.
Wolverhampton & District Boys. Ward Street Clinic FC. Round Oak FC. Brownhills Albion. Birmingham (trialist, 1936). ALBION (amateur, September 1937, professional, August 1938, retired through injury and ill-health, May 1951).

■ Jimmy Pemberton was a strong, confident right-back, hard and wiry, with

a fine physique, solid kick and excellent positional sense. He was pretty quick too, one of the fastest full-backs Albion have ever signed, making his League debut against Swansea Town (away) in Division Two in August 1946. A prominent member of the Baggies' Second Division promotion side in 1948–49, he was virtually an ever-present during the first four post World War Two League seasons, missing just seven games out of a possible 168. He also played in 13 second XI games before cruelly getting injured against Aston Villa (away) in the opening League match of the 1950–51 season. He never played again. During World War Two, Pemberton served as a Lance Corporal for the Royal Fusiliers, based in North Africa and Italy. He played for the Army against Italy, Yugoslavia, England XI, Switzerland and Greece. He was almost completely blind when he died in 1995.

PEMBERTON, James Thomas

Left-back: 1 app.

Born: Kingswinford, 14 November 1925. Deceased.
Career: Brierley Hill & Pensnett Schools. Round Oak (1942). ALBION (amateur, November 1943). Round Oak (June 1944). ALBION (professional, May 1945). Stourbridge (June 1946). Luton Town (November 1947-May 1957).

■ Brother of Jimmy, Tom Pemberton (initially a full-back) played one game for Albion, against Nottingham Forest (home) in the Midland Cup in March 1944, when trialist at The Hawthorns during the second half of the 1943–44 season. Although he returned to the club after the hostilities, when he was converted into a left-winger, he failed to gain a first-team place but later did well with Luton, for whom he made almost 100 first-team appearances (8 goals scored).

PENDREY, Garry James Sidney

Defender: 18 apps.

Born: Lozells, Birmingham, 9 February 1949.
Career: Lozells Junior School (Birmingham). Handsworth Technical

College. Aston Schools. Stanley Star. Harborne Lynwood. Birmingham City (apprentice, July 1965, professional, October 1966). ALBION (£30,000, August 1979). Torquay United (free, August 1981). Bristol Rovers (free, December 1981). Walsall (free, player-coach, July 1982, appointed assistant manager, 1983–August 1986). Birmingham City (manager, June 1987–April 1989). Wolverhampton Wanderers (coach, July 1989–March 1994). Derby County (coach, briefly). Coventry City (coach, February 1995, then assistant manager, November 1996). Southampton (coach/assistant manager, October 2001). Also played over 100 games for West Bromwich Albion All Stars (1982–90).

■ Garry Pendrey supported Albion as a lad and used to stand at the Brummie Road End at The Hawthorns. He was a schoolboy trialist with England in 1964 and three years later skippered the Blues in the 1967 FA Youth Cup final (collecting a runners'-up medal). A hard, competitive defender, he served the Blues splendidly for 14 years, amassing a grand total of 357 appearances and scoring five goals, helping the side gain promotion from Division Two in 1972. In 1979 he was granted a testimonial (against Albion) for his loyal service to the St. Andrew's club, this being his last game for the Blues before his transfer to The Hawthorns. He was signed by Ron Atkinson as defensive cover, making his debut against Southampton (home) in Division One in October 1979, when he took over from the injured Derek Statham. He also played 24 times for Albion's second XI. When his playing career ended in May 1983, Pendrey had accumulated 333 League appearances for his five clubs, and in all competitive matches his career tally topped 450. He was assistant to manager Alan Buckley at Walsall and his assistant at the Blues was the former Albion striker Tony Brown. He lost his job at Wolves when the Kumar brothers took over at Molineux. He later worked under Gordon Strachan at both Coventry and Southampton.

PENNINGTON, Jesse

Left-back: 496 apps.

Born: West Bromwich, 23 August 1883. Died: Kidderminster, 5 September 1970. Career: Brasshouse Lane & Devonshire Road Day Schools (Smethwick). Summit Star (1896). Smethwick Centaur (1898). Langley Villa (1899). Langley St Michael's (1900). Dudley Town (1901). Aston Villa (amateur, August 1902). Dudley Town (November 1902). ALBION (professional, March 1903, retired, May 1922). Oldbury Town (guest 1915–16). Notts County (guest 1916). ALBION (coach, May 1922–August 1923). Kidderminster Harriers (coach, September 1923–June 1925). Also football coach to Malvern College (1938). Wolverhampton Wanderers (scout, 1938–39). Rafman FC, Kidderminster (manager, 1939–40). ALBION (scout, 1950 to 1961 when he retired from football, aged 77). Lived in the village of Hartlebury near Stourport until his death.

■ One of the greatest names in the annals of West Bromwich Albion FC, Jesse 'Peerless' Pennington was a superbly equipped left-back and scrupulously fair in his play. Notably quick in recovery and a defender with beautiful balance, a keen eye and splendid kick down the line, he was a magnificent club captain, wonderful sportsman and indeed a grand club man of the highest calibre. Pennington played in a then record 455 League games for Albion, holding the record for 54 years, until it was beaten by Tony Brown in 1976. He also appeared in 39 FA Cup matches, including the final of 1912 when Albion lost to Barnsley in a replay. A Cup winners' medal was, in fact, the only major honour that eluded

Pennington during a wonderful career. He won 25 England caps (1907–20), represented the Football League XI on nine occasions, played for an England XI five times and also appeared in five international trials (1910–12). He skippered his country twice and the League XI once (all in 1920) when aged 36. He led Albion to the Second Division championship in 1911 and nine years later was presented with the coveted First Division trophy (1920). In his entire playing career, Pennington never scored a goal, he missed a penalty aswell! He was only dropped once by Albion and his displays were always edged with genius. Universally regarded as the nonpareil of Albion and England left-backs, he formed a superb duo in international circles with Bob Crompton of Blackburn Rovers, lining up as Crompton's partner in 23 of his full internationals for his country. Pennington had the unique experience of playing his first and last League games of his career against Liverpool (his debut in September 1903 and his swan song in April 1922). In 1910 he had a dispute with Albion regarding pay and actually signed for Kidderminster Harriers. That dispute, thankfully, was soon sorted out and the appropriate forms cancelled before they found the post. Three years later, Pennington, forthright and honest, was the subject of a bribe scandal when he was approached with cash to 'fix' a League game between Albion and Everton so that Everton would not lose. A very shrewd character, he quickly

informed the police as well as the Albion directors. A trap was set and the culprit – one Samuel Johnson alias Frederick Pater from Birmingham – was arrested and later sentenced to six months imprisonment at Stafford Assize Court. In 1969 Pennington was made a Life Member of the Albion club at the age of 86, a fitting tribute to a king-size footballer, one of Albion's greatest.

PERKINS, Edward Ernest

Outside-left: 34 apps. 1 goal.

Born: Astwood Bank, Redditch, 12 December 1883. Died: Redditch, 9 June 1941. Career: Astwood Bank & Studley Schools. Astwood Bank FC (1889). Studley Rovers (1891). Feckenham Youths (1892). Astwood Bank FC (1893). Worcester City (1895). ALBION (professional, January 1904). Worcester City (free, May 1907, retired, April 1909). Became licensee of The Red Lion Pub, Redditch.

■ A mere stippling of a man, whose body swerve was first class, Ernie Perkins, a former England junior international outside-left, was fast and direct. He joined Albion as a temporary replacement for George Dorsett and made his belated League debut against Burnley (home) in Division Two in September 1905, and he appeared in several second-team matches before moving to Worcester.

PERKINS, Eric

Full-back: 2 apps.

Born: West Bromwich, 19 August 1934. Career: Hill Top & Swan Village Schools. Hill Top Foundry FC (1950). ALBION (amateur, April 1951, professional, June 1952). Walsall (June 1956). Hinckley Athletic (1960–61). Stafford Rangers (August 1962, retired, May 1964). Later worked in Walsall where he now resides.

■ Understudy to Len Millard during his four years with Albion, Eric Perkins was a steady left-back who did well with Walsall, making 67 League appearances for the Saddlers in the late 1950s. His League debut for the Baggies was against Charlton Athletic (home) in Division One in October 1955. He also played in 41 second XI matches.

PERRY, Arthur Arnold

Full-back: 81 apps.

Born: West Bromwich, 25 July 1897.
Died: May 1977.
Career: Bratt Street School. West Bromwich Baptist. ALBION (professional, February 1921). Crystal Palace (£75, May 1927). Merthyr Town (free, September 1930). Wellington Town (August 1931). Brierley Hill Alliance (1932, manager, January 1935). Dudley Town (manager, July 1935, retired 1937). Later scouted for ALBION (late 1940s–50s). Opened a motorcycle business in West Bromwich in the 1960s, this was later taken over by his youngest son, Doug, an Albion shareholder.

■ Arthur Perry was a brainy and thoughtful right-back who placed his clearances with precise timing. Part of the famous Perry family, he won junior international honours for England in 1923 and played over 80 senior games for Albion, plus 70 in the Central League, gaining successive championship medals at this level in 1922–23 and 1923–24. A serious knee injury eventually ended his League career. He did turn out occasionally for Wellington and Brierley Hill after leaving The Hawthorns but was never the same player again. He made his League debut against Everton (home) in Division One in November 1923.

PERRY, Charles

Centre-half: 219 apps. 16 goals.

Born: West Bromwich, 3 January 1866.
Died: West Bromwich, 2 July 1927.
Career: Christ Church School (West Bromwich). West Bromwich Strollers FC (not Albion). ALBION (March 1884, professional, August 1885, retired, May 1896, became club director 1896–1902). Also licensee of the 'Golden Cup' public house in Cross Street, West Bromwich, until George Woodhall took over in 1905.

■ Charlie Perry was a superb player and grand captain. He had a polished style, was determined in everything he did, cool under pressure and a man who marshalled his defence magnificently from the centre-half position, which was undoubtedly his best. Brother of Tom and Walter, he won three England caps (1890–93), had two outings for the Football League XI and appeared in four international trials (1889–91). He was

Albion's pivot in the 1886, 1887, 1888 and 1892 FA Cup finals, gaining winners' medals in the last two. He missed the 1895 final through injury, which eventually forced him to retire from top-class football when he was still a reasonably fit man. Tall and strong, Perry was Albion's first 'great' centre-half and, besides his tally of first-team appearances (219), he also played in a further 280 games for Albion in local cup competitions and friendlies, being a regular in the side for seven years, from 1888–95. He had the distinction of making his senior debut for the club in the 1886 FA Cup final against Blackburn

Rovers at the Oval, almost two years after his first appearance for the second XI.

PERRY, Michael Alexander

Striker: 17+6 apps. 5 goals.

Born: Wimbledon, London, 4 April 1964.
Career: Kontas Trinity & Dormers Wells High Schools (London). Glebe Athletic. Southall FC. Wimbledon (trialist, 1979). Kingston-upon-Thames Schools. ALBION (apprentice, June 1980, professional, February 1982). Torquay United (on loan, October 1984). Northampton Town (on loan, December 1984). Mansfield Town (on loan, January–February 1985). Torquay United

(£5,000, March 1985). Port Vale (free, October 1985). Stafford Rangers (free, August 1986). Wealdstone (1987). Worcester City (February 1988). Singh Brothers (1988–89). Redditch United (1989–90).

■ Mick Perry was a striker with good ball control who could operate wide on the right or as an out and out centre-forward. He had limited chances with Albion and, after loans spells around the country, drifted into non-League soccer in 1986. He made his debut against Watford (home) in Division One in April 1983 and also hit 14 goals in 48 Central League games, helping Albion win the title of this competition in 1982–83.

PERRY, Thomas

Half-back: 291 apps. 15 goals.

*Born: West Bromwich, 5 August 1871.
Died: West Bromwich, 18 July 1927.
Career: Christ Church School (West Bromwich). Christ Church FC (April 1886). West Bromwich Baptist (August 1887). Stourbridge (August 1888). ALBION (professional, July 1890). Aston Villa. (£100, October 1901, retired, May 1902). Later worked in accountancy.*

■ A stalwart right-half for Albion during the 10 years leading up to the club's move from Stoney Lane to The Hawthorns, Tom Perry was a capable, efficient and extremely enthusiastic performer, wholehearted in every way, whose hard graft and dedicated approach to the game made him such a key figure in the 1890s. He made his debut against Preston North End (away) in Division One in September 1890. He made his Albion debut at outside-left, but he soon became respected for his splendid displays in the half-back line where he lined up alongside his elder brother, Charlie. He gained one England cap (1898), played three times for the Football League XI (1894–98) and turned out for the League Select XI against Aston Villa in 1894. He was Albion's right-half in the 1895 FA Cup final (also against Villa) and appeared in almost 300 competitive games for the club (plus over 170 'other' first-team matches), lining up at full-back and inside-forward as well as in his best position of right-half. Perry, who made 29 appearances for Villa, died just two weeks after his brother. He had been ill for quite some time.

PERRY, Walter

Inside-forward: 15 apps. 7 goals.

*Born: West Bromwich, 11 October 1868.
Died: West Bromwich, 21 September 1928.
Career: Christ Church School (West Bromwich). West Bromwich Excelsior. ALBION (professional, August 1886). Wolverhampton Wanderers (£20, December 1889). Warwick County (May 1890). Burton Swifts (August 1891). ALBION (October 1894). Burton Swifts (November 1895, retired, May 1900). ALBION (reserve team manager, 1906–07). Later a Football League linesman (1909–12). Taken ill shortly after World War One and never quite recovered full health.*

■ A naturally gifted, versatile footballer, Walter Perry, who could occupy both wing-half and inside-forward positions, had two spells with the club as a player but never really established himself as a regular in the first team. He made his League debut against Burnley at Stoney Lane in Division One in September 1888 and had the pleasure of scoring in the club's first League home goal in their first home game (won 4–1). He also played in more than 40 'other' first-team matches for the club.

PETERS, Samuel

Wing-half: 6 apps. 1 goal.

*Born: West Bromwich, 20 October 1886.
Died: Dudley, 23 December 1957.
Career: Guns Village School (West Bromwich). Carters Green Juniors. Churchfields FC (1902). ALBION (professional, November 1904). Crewe Alexandra (free, June 1907). Served in Army during World War One. Brierley Hill Alliance (August 1919, retired, May 1920). Worked for a local transport company for many years.*

■ 'Little Sammy' Peters was a useful wing-half of the unflustered and accomplished type, always willing to try a shot at goal, unleash a 30 yard pass or beat opponents twice! Basically a reserve for Albion, he made all his senior appearances in 1905–06. He later gave Crewe yeoman service and was granted a benefit match against Albion reserves in 1912–13 as reward. He made his Football League debut against Manchester United (home) in Division Two in October 1905

and made over 40 appearances for the Baggies second XI.

PESCHISOLIDO, Paulo Pasquale

Striker: 41+10 apps. 21 goals.

*Born: Scarborough, Ontario, Canada, 25 May 1971.
Career: Toronto Blizzard, NASL. Kansas City Comets, NASL (1990–91). Toronto Blizzard, NASL (1991–92). Birmingham City (£25,000, November 1992). Stoke City (£400,000, player exchange deal involving David Regis, August 1994). ALBION (£600,000, July 1996). Fulham (£1.1 million, October 1997). Queen's Park Rangers (on loan, November–December 2000). Sheffield United (on loan, January–March 2001). Norwich City (on loan, March–April 2001). Sheffield United (£150,000, July 2001). Derby County (free, March 2004).*

■ Canadian international Paul Peschisolido, an exciting, nimble, all-action, industrious utility forward, eager inside the penalty area, certainly made a big impact at The Hawthorns and there is no doubt that several fans were bitterly disappointed when he was sold to Fulham in the Autumn of 1997. At 5ft 5in tall – one of the smallest forwards ever to

wear an Albion shirt – 'Pesch' made his debut for the club in the home League Cup encounter with Colchester United in September 1996 and, in his next game, scored his first goal for the Baggies in a 2–0 League win at Queen's Park Rangers, one of his future clubs. After leaving Albion, he helped Fulham win the Second Division championship in 1998–99 and was a key member of the Sheffield United side that reached the semi-final of both the FA Cup and League Cup and lost to Wolves in the First Division play-off final in 2003. He has played in 51 full internationals for Canada (nine as an Albion player) having earlier played in 11 under-21 games and in several youth matches. He was voted the US Major Indoor Soccer League's 'Newcomer of the Year' in 1990 and seven years later was named Canadian 'Footballer of the Year'. He is married to the Birmingham City managing-director Karen Brady.

PHEASANT, Edward

Centre-half/centre-forward: 152 apps. 22 goals.

Born: Darlaston, 15 February 1877.
Died: Wolverhampton, 15 July 1910.
Career: Joseph Edward Cox County School (Wednesbury). Wednesbury Excelsior (1892). Wednesbury Old Athletic (1893). Wolverhampton Wanderers (August 1895). ALBION (£500, November 1904). Leicester Fosse (£100, July 1910). Died of peritonitis two weeks after leaving The Hawthorns.

■ Ted 'Cock' Pheasant was a huge man and when kitted out (and wringing wet) he tipped the scales at 15 stones. Such a physique has seldom been found in a player who could occupy two completely different roles – those of centre-half and centre-forward – and perform so splendidly in both. As hard as nails and always in the thick of the action, he was a fearless competitor who made over 150 appearances for Albion. He was an ace penalty-taker, standing almost on top of the ball before letting fly with his right foot. He skippered Albion for two years after appearing in 168 senior games and scoring 17 goals for Wolves – missing only one League match in three seasons (1899–1902 inclusive). He was selected to play for the Football League but refused the honour, choosing to turn out for Wolves instead. He made his Albion debut against Manchester United (home)

in Division Two in November 1904. He played several games for Albion's second XI during his last two seasons at the club. Pheasant's hobbies included beekeeping and gardening (he loved roses).

PHELAN, Michael Christopher

Midfield: 20+3 apps.

Born: Nelson, Lancashire, 24 September 1962.
Career: Barrowfield County Primary & Colne Park High Schools. Nelson & Colne Town. Lancashire Schools. Barrowford Celtic Boys Club. Burnley (associated schoolboy, July 1977, apprentice, July 1979, professional, July 1980). Norwich City (May 1985). Manchester United (£750,000, July 1989). ALBION (free, July 1994). Norwich City (player/reserve-team coach, March 1996). Blackpool (non-contract). Stockport County (player/assistant manager). Norwich City (reserve-team manager, July 1998). Manchester United (coach, from August 1999).

■ Capped at youth-team level, hard-working midfielder Mike Phelan went on to play in one full international match for England, lining up against Italy in

November 1989 (albeit as a second-half substitute). He helped Burnley win the Third Division championship and reach the semi-final of the League Cup before moving to Carrow Road. He joined Manchester United on the same day as Neil Webb and during his time at Old Trafford won two Premiership titles (1993 and 1994), the FA Cup (1990), the League Cup and the European Cup-winners' Cup, while also receiving a runners'-up prize in the League Cup. Handed a free transfer by United, he joined Albion as an experienced campaigner and made his debut against Luton Town (away) on the opening Saturday of the 1994–95 League season. Unfortunately, he never settled at The Hawthorns, a lack of fitness and niggling injuries proving his downfall. He made over 20 second-team appearances for the club.

PHILLIPS, Stewart Gavin

Striker: 15 + 1 apps. 4 goals.

Born: Halifax, 30 December 1961. Career: Halifax & District Schools. Yorkshire Boys. Hereford United (apprentice, July 1976, professional, November 1979). ALBION (£20,000, March 1988). Swansea City (£25,000 February 1989). Hereford United (August 1990). Wrexham (non-contract, August–October 1991).

■ An enterprising forward, fast and able to shoot with both feet, Stewart Phillips scored over 100 goals in more than 300 appearances for Hereford in eight years at

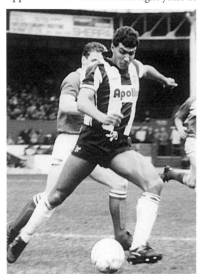

Edgar Street, before moving to The Hawthorns two-thirds of the way through the 1987–88 season, helping Albion stave off the threat of relegation to the Third Division. He made his Baggies debut against Middlesbrough (home) in March 1988. He ended his career in League football with 99 goals to his credit (in 367 games).

PICKEN, Thomas

Goalkeeper: 2 apps.

Born: Hednesford, 30 May 1883. Died: Dudley, August 1960. Career: Hednesford & Littleworth Village Schools. Hednesford Town. Wolverhampton Wanderers. Hednesford Town. Shrewsbury Town (1903). ALBION (professional, May 1905). Road End FC (June 1910). Oldbury Town (1912). Dudley Phoenix (August 1915, retired, 1918, following service in the armed forces). Later engaged in steel work before helping his wife open a clothes shop in West Bromwich.

■ A junior international goalkeeper (1905), Tom Picken had a good technique and a safe pair of hands. Able to throw a ball a full 50 yards left-handed, he deputised for Jim Stringer at Albion, having earlier appeared in Wolves' reserve side and Staffordshire in 1900. He made his League debut against Chesterfield Town (away) in Division Two in April 1906 and played in more than 60 second-team matches for Albion. He was also a good cricketer, playing mainly for Hednesford CC.

PICKERING, Thomas George

Inside-forward: 10 apps. 2 goals.

Born: Wednesbury, 21 February 1879. Died: Brierley Hill, 1934. Career: Old Park Infants & Junior Schools (Wednesbury). Wednesbury Town (1894). Brierley Hill Alliance (1897). ALBION (professional, July 1900). Kettering Town (free, June 1901). Brierley Hill Alliance (August 1903, retired through injury, April 1905).

■ A utility forward, strong in appearance, Tom Pickering spent just one season with Albion before being released after internal disputes. He made his League debut against Wolverhampton

Wanderers (away) in Division One in September 1900. He played in 15 reserve and several 'other' games for Albion.

PIKE, Richard Sidney George

Centre-forward: 1 app.

Born: Finchley, London, 15 March 1917. Died: Banbury, Oxfordshire, 24 January 1988. Career: Shoreham-by-Sea Grammar School. London & District schoolboy football. Harpenden St David. Arsenal (junior, 1932). Banbury Spencer (March 1935). Oxfordshire County (amateur championship). ALBION (amateur, March 1937, professional, £50, October 1937). Banbury Spencer (free, May 1946, retired through injury, April 1949).

■ A keen, storming centre-forward, always battling away and eager to succeed, Dick Pike had just one League outing with Albion, lining up against Nottingham Forest (away) in Division Two in April 1939. He did, however, score well over 60 goals for the club in reserve, intermediate, combination and general midweek matches, 27 coming in only 36 Central League outings. During the hostilities, while serving with the Army in France (1944), Pike was hospitalised, suffering from anaemia.

PIGGOTT, Gary David

Striker: 3+2 apps.

Born: Warley, West Midlands, 1 April 1969.

Career: Princes End United. Sandwell Borough. Oldswinford. Dudley Town. ALBION (professional, March 1991). Shrewsbury Town (non-contract, March 1993). Chesterfield (trialist). Willenhall Town (March 1994). Tamworth (1997–98). Stafford Rangers (August 1998). Halesowen Town (1999–2001). Rushall Olympic (2001–02). Later played for Sedgley White Lions FC and Causeway United.

■ Reserve striker Gary Piggott, a trier to the last, spent two years at The Hawthorns acting as cover for both Don Goodman and then Bob Taylor (and Simon Garner). He made his League debut as strike-partner to Goodman in a 1–0 win at Darlington in August 1991.

Scorer of 13 goals in 40 Pontins League games for Albion, he helped the reserves win the title of that competition in 1990–91 and later did extremely well on the non-League scene.

PITTAWAY, James

Centre-forward: 1 app. 1 goal.

Born: West Bromwich, 7 November 1867. Died: Oldbury, 1937.
Career: Hallam Junior School (West Bromwich). West Bromwich Wednesday FC. ALBION (professional, August 1889). Stourbridge (free, June 1890). Oldbury Town (May 1898, retired, August 1902).

■ Jim Pittaway was a reserve forward who had the pleasure of scoring Albion's winning goal on his Football League debut against Burnley (away) in Division One in October 1889.

POTTER, Graham Stephen

Midfield: 32+15 apps.

Born: Solihull, 20 May 1975.
Career: Solihull schoolboy football. Birmingham City (apprentice, June 1991, professional, July 1992). Wycombe Wanderers (on loan, September–October

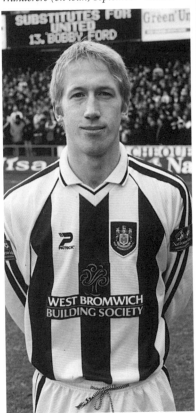

1993). Stoke City (£75,000, December 1993). Southampton (£250,000, July 19965). ALBION (£300,000, February 1997). Northampton Town (on loan, October–November 1997). Reading (on loan, December 1999–January 2000). York City (free, July 2000). Boston United (August 2003). Shrewsbury Town (on loan, November–December 2003). Macclesfield Town (free, February 2004).*

■ A former England youth international who later gained one under-21 cap, Graham Potter, 6ft 1in tall, was a useful footballer who preferred to play down the left-hand side of the pitch. He had a good technique, fair pace and delivered a telling cross, given the time and space. He suffered with injuries during the second half of his three-year stay at The Hawthorns, but, after regaining full fitness and also his appetite for the game, he went on to amass well over 125 games for York City and had made 350 appearances in total to 2005. Making his debut for Albion as a substitute in a 4–2 League win at Norwich in February 1997, he also played in more than 40 second XI games for the club.

POTTER, Raymond John

Goalkeeper: 238 apps.

Born: Beckenham, Kent, 7 May 1936.
Career: Beckenham & District Schools. Beckenham Boys. West Kent Schools. Kent Schools XI. Millwall (amateur, August 1951). Beckenham AFC (May 1951).

Crystal Palace (amateur, July 1952, professional, May 1953). ALBION (£30,000, June 1958). Portsmouth (£5,000, May 1967, retired, June 1970). Colchester United (assistant commercial manager, August 1970). Bournemouth (assistant commercial manager and PRO secretary, 1970–75). Portsmouth (administration officer for two seasons, 1975–77). Later employed as a bread delivery driver.

■ For a player who cost 'nothing', goalkeeper Ray Potter gave Albion excellent service for a number of years. Never flashy or showy, never brilliant or daring, he did his job professionally and well, appearing in almost 240 senior games for the Baggies plus another 105 in the Central League. He arrived at The Hawthorns at a time when there was a goalkeeping problem, Clive Jackman having been injured. Potter was dropped in at the deep end immediately, but he didn't let the side down, performing confidently from day one. He continued to do a fine job thereafter, gaining a League Cup winners' tankard in 1966 and keeping goal in Albion's first ever European match against DOS Utrecht in Holland in November of that same year. Potter's time was called when Albion secured the services of John Osborne in 1967, Dick Sheppard already being on the books. During his League career Potter amassed 264 appearances, 217 being in the First Division with Albion, for whom he made his debut against West Ham United (home) in the First Division in October 1958. He also played in 120 second XI games for the Baggies.

POTTER, Ronald Charles

Centre-half: 8+1 apps.

Born: Wolverhampton, 5 December 1948
Career: Highfields School (Wolverhampton). ALBION (apprentice, April 1964, professional, December 1966). Swindon Town (£5,000, November 1970, released, June 1975) Hartlepool (trialist, 1975–76). Later entered the antique business, based in Quatt near Bridgnorth.

■ Ron Potter was an enthusiastic centre-half whose outings for Albion spanned six seasons, when he covered for Stan Jones and John Talbot – making his League debut against Everton (away) in Division One in September 1968 (as a second-half substitute). After leaving The

Hawthorns he appeared in 86 League matches for Swindon.

POULTON, Alonzo

Centre-forward: 9 apps. 1 goal.

Born: Monmore Green, Wolverhampton, 28 March 1890.
Died: Merry Hill, Wolverhampton, 15 May 1966.
Career: St Luke's Junior & Moreton Senior Schools (Wolverhampton). Monmore Green FC. Priestfield Albion (1912). ALBION (professional, March 1913). Worcester City (on loan, December 1913–May 1914). Army Service. Merthyr Town (£400, October 1919). Middlesbrough (March 1920). Bristol City (September 1921). Reading (October 1922). Wolverhampton Wanderers (September 1923, retired, May 1924). Became a solicitor's clerk.

■ 'Olly' Poulton was only 16 years old when he first joined Albion. A chunky, bouncy centre-forward with good tidy skills and a fair shot, he made his League debut against Newcastle United (away) in Division One in September 1914, playing between Alf Bentley and Harold Bache. He found it hard to fit in with Albion's style of play, but after moving from The Hawthorns he did much better with his other clubs, appearing in 60 League matches (1919–24) and scoring 14 goals. Initially based in Andover, he served as a private with the 17th Middlesex Regiment (Footballers' Battalion) in France during World War One.

POWELL, David Robert

Goalkeeper: 4 apps.

Born: Cannock, Staffs, 24 September 1967.
Career: Brockmoor Middle & Buckpool Senior Schools (Hednesford). Cherry Valley FC (1983). ALBION (apprentice, September 1984, professional, August 1986). Wrexham (on loan, March 1987). Stoke City (on loan, March 1988). Retired through injury, June 1988.

■ David Powell showed ability and confidence between the posts but elected to quit football at the age of 21! He made his senior debut for Albion against Crystal Palace (home) in the Full Member's Cup in October 1985. He also played in 51 Central League games.

POWELL, Seth

Full-back: 35 apps.

Born: Cerney near Wrexham, 6 August 1862.
Died: Oswestry, 3 February 1945.
Career: Pulford & Saltney Schools. Chester City Boys. Summerhill FC, Wrexham (1882). Oswestry Town (August 1883). ALBION (trialist, December 1889, signed as a professional, January 1890). Burton Swifts (free, July 1892). Chester (May 1895). Oswestry United (August 1898, retired as a player, May 1902). From 1900 until his 68th birthday (in 1930) he was a District Relieving Officer for the Oswestry Board of Guardians. Also acted as secretary of the Oswestry United Football Club and spent 20 years as a member of the 2nd Volunteer Battalion of the King's Shropshire Light Infantry.

■ A strongly built full-back who tackled crisply and distributed the ball well under pressure, Seth Powell was capped seven times at full international level by Wales (1895–1902) and also played for his country against the Canadian tourists (1891). Able to perform in both full-back positions, prior to joining Albion (for £2-a-week) he won a Welsh Cup medal with Oswestry (1884). He made his Football League debut against Wolverhampton Wanderers (away) in Division One in December 1889 and also played in 22 'other' games for the club. When moving to Oswestry in 1883, he simultaneously became an assistant Schoolmaster at the Oswestry Board School.

POXTON, James Harold

Outside-left: 9 apps. 1 goal.

Born: Staveley, 2 February 1904.
Died: 12 Walsall, December 1971.
Career: Staveley & Chesterfield Schools. Eckington FC. Staveley Town (July 1922). ALBION (professional, June 1924). Gillingham (deal involving Enos Bromage, March 1928). Millwall (free, May 1929). Watford (£500, July 1934). Walsall (free, May 1935). Bristol City (briefly, 1936). Reading (free, October 1936, retired, May 1938). After World War Two he was engaged in maintenance work for an engineering company.

■ An outside-left with astute little flicks and clever short passes, Jimmy Poxton was reserve to Jack Byers and Arthur Fitton at The Hawthorns. Later, he appeared in 43 League games for Gillingham, 147 for Millwall, scoring 51 goals in total, 29 for the Lions. He failed to make the first team at Bristol City or Reading. An ex-miner and capable cricketer, he made his League debut for Albion against Manchester United (home) in Division One in May 1927.

POYNTON, William John

Outside-right: 2 apps. 2 goals.

Born: Hill Top, West Bromwich, 7 June 1883.
Died: West Bromwich, 1958.
Career: Tameside Council School (Wednesbury). Wednesbury Old Athletic (August 1898). Britannia Victoria (September 1900). ALBION (professional, March 1902, retired through injury, June 1907).

■ Bill Poynton replaced Jimmy McLean when called up for his two senior outings by Albion. He made his League debut against Burton United (home) in Division Two in April 1902, netting in a 2–1 win, and then he scored again in his second game against Barnsley (also won 2–0) on the last day of that season. A tactful right-winger with good skills, he made over 25 second XI appearances, helping the team clinch the Birmingham & District League title in 1902, before his career ended prematurely following a broken leg mishap in 1903, although he did attempt four unsuccessful comebacks in four years before finally hanging up his boots.
* Some reference books spell this player's name as Pointon.

PREW, James Herbert

Outside-right: 7 apps. 1 goal.

Born: Coventry, 23 February 1914.
Died: Leicester, 1986.
Career: Stoke Heath School (Coventry). Leicester City (trialist, 1929). Coventry Colliery (1929–32). Hinckley United (semi-professional, 1933). ALBION (£150, professional, September 1936). Walsall (free, February 1938). Hinckley United (August 1938, retired, April 1940).

■ Midget outside-right whose height and weight were detrimental to Jimmy Prew's playing career. He had good skills and positive touch, but the handicap of his overall stature was too great a burden. He made his Football League debut for Albion against Grimsby Town (home) in Division Two in October 1936. He did well in the Baggies second XI, scoring nine goals in 38 games.

PRICE, Gilbert Walter

Centre-forward: 1 app.

Born: Wolverhampton, 22 October 1888.
Died: Wolverhampton, February 1955.
Career: Regis Council School (Tettenhall). Deansfield High School (Wolverhampton). Chillington Rangers (1908). ALBION (professional, April 1910). Cradley St Luke's (free, February 1911). Rawmarsh Town, Sheffield (August 1913, retired, April 1914 to concentrate on teaching in Wolverhampton).

■ Gilbert Price was an amateur centre-forward who stayed with Albion for 10 months, making one senior appearance against Barnsley (away) in Division Two in April 1910, plus half a dozen in the second team.

PRITCHARD, David Michael

Forward: 1+4 apps.

Born: Wolverhampton, 27 May 1972.
Career: ALBION (apprentice, June 1988, professional, July 1990). Telford United (free, August 1992). Bristol Rovers (free, February 1994). Telford United (free, August 1998).

■ David Pritchard was a reserve right-sided midfielder whose League debut for Albion was as a substitute against Stockport County in September 1991. He

was later converted into a useful right-back, appeared in 125 League games for Bristol Rovers and was also capped by Wales at 'B' team level. He scored once in 71 Pontins League outings for Albion, helping the second XI win the championship in 1990–91.

PURSE, Darren John

Defender: 24 apps.

Born: Stepney, London, 14 February 1977.
Career: Leyton Orient (apprentice, May 1993, professional, February 1994). Oxford United (£100,000, July 1996). Birmingham City (£800,000, February 1998). ALBION (£500,000, rising to £750,000 after an agreed number of on appearances, June 2004). Cardiff City (£700,000, July 2005).

■ After more than 50 games for Orient, whom he skippered at the age of 17, over 70 for Oxford and almost 200 for the Blues, Darren Puse became Albion's second big-money defensive signing in the summer of 2004 (following the Dane,

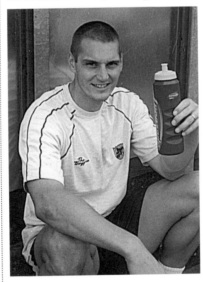

Martin Albrechtsen). Standing 6ft 2in tall and weighing 12st 8lb, he was capped twice by England at under-21 level earlier in his career and helped Birmingham gain promotion to the Premiership (with Geoff Horsfield) in 2002. Solid, resilient and nicknamed 'Pursey', he suffered a serious ankle injury during the 2002–03 season and as a result never regained his place in the first XI at St Andrew's, being replaced by Matthew Upson. He made his senior debut for the Baggies in the Premiership against Blackburn Rovers (away) in August 2004 and was sent off

against Newcastle United at St James' Park in his seventh outing. He also had the misfortune to concede two own-goals in quick succession.
* Purse turned down apprenticeships with both Arsenal and Spurs so that he could remain at school where he subsequently gained nine GCSE's. He even wanted to become a pilot but chose football instead.

QUAILEY, Brian Sullivan

Striker: 1+7 apps.

Born: Leicester, 24 March 1978.
Career: Leicester & District schoolboy football. Nuneaton Borough (semi-professional, August 1995). ALBION (professional, September 1997). Exeter City (on loan, December 1998–January 1999). Blackpool (on loan, December 1999). Scunthorpe United (free, February 2000). Halifax Town (September 2002). Tamworth (August 2003). Stevenage Borough (April 2004).

■ A very quick and direct striker, who found it tough at The Hawthorns when acting as reserve to Andy Hunt, Bob Taylor, Paul Peschisolido and Lee Hughes, Brain Quailey made his Albion debut, as a 'sub' against Manchester City at Maine Road in February 1998. He also scored 10

goals in more than 50 appearances for Albion's second XI. Capped by St Kitts and Nevis at under-21 level, he later did well with Scunthorpe, scoring 17 goals in 77 outings.

QUINN, Stephen James

Forward/midfield: 90+33 apps. 10 goals.

Born: Coventry, 14 December 1974.
Career: Birmingham City (apprentice, April 1991). Blackpool (professional for

£25,000, July 1993). Stockport County (on loan, March 1994). ALBION (£500,000, February 1998). Notts County (on loan, November–December 2001). Bristol Rovers (on loan, March–April 2002). Willen II, Holland (June 2002). Sheffield Wednesday (on loan, March–May 2005). Also columnist for The Guardian *(2003–04). Peterborough United (July 2005).*

■ Northern Ireland international James Quinn had two pretty good seasons at The Hawthorns before losing his way under manager Gary Megson, who then released him in the summer of 2002. Capped by his country at youth, 'B' and under-21 levels, he averaged a goal every two games for Albion's second XI (12 in 24) and his tally of senior caps is now edging towards the 30-mark. He made over 180 appearances for Blackpool (48 goals scored). He helped Wednesday in the 2005 play-off final.

RAMSEY, Alexander Robert

Right-back: 1 app.

Born: Collington, Hereford, 24 March 1867.
Died: 1938.
Career: Collington & Bredenbury Schools. Kidderminster Harriers (1887). ALBION (professional, May 1888). Kidderminster Harriers (free, June 1890). Middlesbrough (coach, 1900–02).

■ Father of Sir Alexander Ramsey, Mayor of West Bromwich (1931–35), Bob Ramsey was a reserve full-back for Albion in the club's first League season of 1888–89, his only senior appearance coming against Stoke (home) in December.

RANDLE, Arthur John

Right-back: 143 apps. 2 goals.

Born: West Bromwich, 3 December 1880.
Died: Coventry, 29 September 1913 (cancer).
Career: Springfield School (West Bromwich). Lyng Rovers. Oldbury Town. Darlaston (1900). ALBION (professional, April 1901). Leicester Fosse (£1,500, May 1908, retired ill-health, May 1912).

■ Arthur Randle was the perfect right-half, always foraging and possessing superb, close ball-control. He was an excellent passer, had an accurate shot and his main forte was probably his tactical genius. A junior international, capped in 1901, he joined Albion just as the team had suffered relegation from Division One for the first time. He made his Football League debut against Newton Heath (away) in Division Two in November 1901, yet spent practically two seasons in the reserves, during which time he played in over 40 matches, gaining a Birmingham & District League championship medal in 1902, before forcing his way into the limelight with 19 more League appearances in 1903–04. He finally settled into the senior side the following season, holding his place confidently for three campaigns before relinquishing his position to Sammy Timmins at the start of the 1907–08 season. He left The Hawthorns under a cloud but remained a star with the supporters.

RANKIN, Bruce

Winger: 31 apps. 6 goals.

Born: Glasgow, 21 July 1880.

Died: 1946.
Career: Walton Council & St Bernard's Schools (Liverpool). White Star Wanderers. Kirkdale FC. Tranmere Rovers (trial, August–September 1900). Everton (December 1901). ALBION (£500, February 1906). Manchester City (£500, February 1907). Luton Town (August 1907). Egremont Social Club (March 1908). Wirral FC (May 1908). Wrexham (August 1908, retired, May 1912). Later worked in the docks on Merseyside.

■ Bruce Rankin was an easy-moving, graceful-looking wing-forward, clever on the ball and a player that could let fly with a useful, telling shot. He represented The North playing against The South, in 1903, and in 1909 he gained a Welsh Cup winners' medal with Wrexham. He cost Albion a fair sum after making 38 appearances for Everton. He left The Hawthorns in a huff after being suspended and transfer-listed. He made his Albion debut against Bristol City (home) in Division Two in February 1906.

RAVEN, Paul Duncan

Defender: 294+10 apps. 21 goals.

Born: Salisbury, 28 July 1970.
Career: Doncaster Rovers (apprentice, July 1986, professional, July 1988). ALBION (£150,000, March 1989). Doncaster Rovers

(on loan, November–December 1991). Rotherham United (on loan, October–December 1998). Grimsby Town (free, July 2000). Carlisle United (free, February 2002). Barrow (player-coach, August 2004).

■ A very capable defender, Paul Raven formed fine partnerships at The Hawthorns with Daryl Burgess, Gary Strodder and also Paul Mardon. Strong in the tackle and commanding in the air, he showed good pace and ability on the ground and made over 300 senior appearances for Albion, scored seven goals in 82 outings for the second team and gained a Pontins League championship medal in 1990–91, before being released by the club at the end of the 1999–2000 season. An England schoolboy international (1985), he made his Football League debut for the Baggies at right-back against Portsmouth (away) in May 1989, played in the play-off final victory over Port Vale at Wembley four years later and was granted a deserved testimonial before his departure from The Hawthorns in 2000, when he joined his former boss Alan Buckley (and a cluster of other ex-Baggies) at Grimsby.

RAW, Henry

Wing-half/Inside-forward: 27 apps. 7 goals.

Born: Tow Law, County Durham, 6 July 1903.
Died: Durham West, November 1965.
Career: Tow Law & Crook Schools. Tow Law Town (amateur). Durham County (semi-professional, August 1923). Huddersfield Town (professional, May 1925). ALBION (£1,500, February 1931). Lincoln City (£250, July 1936, retired, May 1939). After World War Two he coached football at various schools and junior clubs and his experience proved to be a huge asset to a lot of youngsters.

■ 'Harry' Raw was a schemer with go-ahead ideas, a player of commendable steadiness, who played for Huddersfield Town in their championship-winning side of 1925–26 and was also in their FA Cup team of 1930. Bought to The Hawthorns in 1931 as a reserve for both Tommy Magee and Joe Carter, he spent most of his time in Albion's second team, gaining three Central League championship medals in the mid-1930s, to go with the two he won earlier with Huddersfield.

He skippered the reserves in 1934–35 and, all told, made 147 appearances and scored 34 goals for the second XI. As a lad, Raw represented Durham versus Huddersfield at St James' Park, Newcastle. He made his Albion debut against Millwall (home) in Division Two in March 1931.

RAWLINGS, James Dean Sidney

Outside-right: 10 apps. 1 goal.

Born: Wombwell, Yorkshire, 5 May 1913.
Died: Penarth, July 1956.
Career: Preston Central & Fulwood Schools. Dick Kerr's XI (briefly). Preston North End (professional, August 1932). Huddersfield Town (£250, February 1934). ALBION (£600, March 1935). Northampton Town (£500, June 1936). Millwall (free, December 1937). Everton (£1,000, January 1945). Plymouth Argyle (free, May 1946, retired, April 1948).

■ Son of Archie Rawlings, the former Preston North End FA Cup final winger from 1922, Sid Rawlings was a brisk, penetrative outside-right, who was signed as cover for Tommy Glidden. He travelled around a bit during his career, serving with no fewer than seven different clubs on a permanent basis, as well as guesting for Clapton Orient, Rochdale, Preston, Bury, Liverpool, Southport, Everton, and

Stockport County during World War Two. Unfortunately, he collected very few honours along the way, his only two coming with Millwall in 1937–38 when they won the Third Division South championship and when they were beaten finalists in the FA Cup South in 1945. All told, Rawlings accumulated a total of 254 appearances at competitive level (1932–48), scoring 70 goals. In wartime football his record was 120 games and 36 goals. It is a pity the hostilities interrupted his career. He made his Albion debut against Chelsea (home) in Division One in March 1935, and also scored 13 goals in 38 Central League games for the club.

REA, John Charles

Outside-left: 1 app.

Born: Lledrod, Aberystwyth, 13 February 1868.
Died: Aberystwyth, 6 February 1944.
Career: Bronant School. Artdwyn Upton Excelsiors. London Caledonians. London Welsh. Aberystwyth Town (August 1892). ALBION (amateur, September 1894). Aberystwyth Town (February 1895). ALBION (March 1896, retired, May 1898). Thereafter devoted his time to the family's hotel and grocery business in Aberystwyth. A major in the Cardiganshire Battery of the Field Artillery during World War One, he eventually reached the rank of colonel.

■ A Welsh international outside-left, nine caps gained while with Aberystwyth (1894–98), John Rea spent six months as an amateur with Albion, during which time he had one League game, lining up against Stoke (home) in Division One in December 1894. He later returned to the club as a 'reserve', when injuries were causing some concern. A founder member of London Welsh, he served as a secretary for that club for a while and did much to foster soccer among the expatriates in London. He was also a leading light in the infant club on the field of play and was recognised by the London FA as well as representing Essex, Middlesex and mid-Wales. Said to be 'very fast with a good command over the ball and a good shot', he made well over 120 appearances for Aberystwyth.
* Rea's former hotel – the White Horse – still preserves the family name in glass and coloured tiles.

READER, Josiah

Goalkeeper: 370 apps.

Born: West Bromwich, 27 February 1866. Died: West Bromwich, 8 March 1954. Career: Beeches Road & St Phillips Schools (West Bromwich). ALBION (amateur, January 1885, professional, August 1885, retired, April 1901, became trainer-coach at The Hawthorns, later serving as a ground steward until 1950). His association with Albion spanned 65 years – the longest anyone has been with the club.

■ Joe Reader was a goalkeeper to rank with the finest the game has produced. Superb in handling and with marvellous reflexes, he used his feet, as much as anything else, to divert goalbound shots or headers. He appeared in 315 League games, 39 FA Cup ties and 16 other senior games for Albion, as well as starring in more than 150 local cup matches and friendlies during his 16-year playing career with the club. He was an ever-present in five League campaigns during the 1890s. He participated in the 1892 and 1895 FA Cup finals, gained one England cap (against Ireland in 1894), represented the Football League three times and the League XI once. He was a dedicated club man, whose love for the club was enhanced when he turned out in one match with his arm in a sling. Nicknamed 'Kicker', he is the only player to have served Albion on three of their home grounds – Four Acres, Stoney Lane and The Hawthorns. He was forced to give up the game through illness rather than injury, yet he still remained an active member of the club during his spell there as coach until shortly before World War One, when he became a steward. He saw his last game at The Hawthorns two weeks before he died at the age of 88. It is believed that Joe Reader was the last of the goalkeeper's to discard the customary long white trousers, doing so in the mid–1890s. He took over between the posts for Albion from the great Bob Roberts, and in 1901 he handed over the duties to Ike Webb. He made his Football League debut against Aston Villa (away) in Division One in October 1889.

READFERN, Thomas Edward

Centre-forward: 5 apps.

Born: Crook, County Durham, 9 July 1944. Career: Crook & Durham City Schools. Liverpool (amateur). Langley Park Juniors. ALBION (amateur, May 1960, professional, July 1961). Kidderminster Harriers (July 1964). Hednesford Town (December 1965). Stourbridge (December 1966–May 1968). Later worked for British Telecom (Durham). Now retired and living in his native Crook.

■ Initially a half-back, Eddie Readfern was developed by Albion into a strong,

hard-running centre-forward. He had limited ability and never really looked the part with the Baggies, for whom he made his First Division debut in the Midlands derby against Birmingham City (away) in September 1963. He also scored 35 goals in 58 Central League games for Albion.

REECE, Paul John

Goalkeeper: 1 app.

Born: Nottingham, 17 July 1968. Career: Stoke City (apprentice, July 1984, professional, July 1986). Kettering Town, Grimsby Town (July 1988). Kettering Town, Doncaster Rovers (non-contract, September 1992). Oxford United (free, October 1992). Notts County (August 1994). ALBION (free, August 1995). Ilkeston Town (July 1996). Cliftonville, Ireland (2000–02). Woking (February 1997).

■ Signed by Albion manager Alan Buckley as cover for Stuart Naylor and Nigel Spink, goalkeeper Paul Reece made just one senior appearance for the club, lining up against his former club Grimsby Town (away) in November 1995. He also played in 17 reserve-team games. Surprisingly, during his 12-year professional career, Reece, who was a fine

shot-stopper on his day, made only 108 League appearances, including 54 for the Mariners and 39 for Oxford.

REED, Frederick William Marshall

Centre-half: 157 apps. 5 goals.

Born: Scotswood-on-Tyne, 10 March 1894. Died: West Bromwich, 12 December 1967. Career: Scotswood Central School. Newborn FC. Wesley Hall. Benwell FC. Lintz Institute (1912). ALBION (professional, February 1913, retired, July 1927). Guest for Newcastle United (1919).

Engaged as first-team trainer at The Hawthorns (July 1927 to May 1950).

■ Fred Reed's displays at centre-half for Albion were typical of a rugged North-Easterner, especially in the tackle, where he was solid, determined and so efficient. When he arrived at The Hawthorns he understudied Frank Waterhouse and Sid Bowser and, in fact, had to wait almost 10 years before establishing himself as a regular in the first team. He made his Football League debut against Tottenham Hotspur (home) in Division One in April 1915. During World War One he served as a sergeant instructor in the 2nd

Battalion of the Royal Fusiliers, based in Surrey, Northumberland and Edinburgh. He worked hard at his game in Albion's second XI before becoming a permanent fixture in the senior side as skipper. He had three-and-a-half seasons as first-team pivot, totting up 138 appearances at League level before standing down in favour of a younger man, Ted Rooke. Reed played in over 200 reserve-team matches either side of World War One. He helped the side win the Birmingham & District League title in 1920 and the Central League (as captain) in 1922–23, when he missed only one game, and again the following season. As Albion's trainer, Fred saw the team achieve that unique double in 1930–31 (FA Cup glory and promotion) from Division Two), finish runners-up in the 1935 FA Cup final and gain promotion from Division Two in 1949. He was also sponge man to the Football League in 1934–35 and trainer in two England against The Rest matches in 1927–28 and 1934–35. During the 1930's Reed was also masseur to Warwickshire CCC, based at Edgbaston. He was succeeded as Albion's trainer by Arthur 'Mother' Fitton in August 1950.
* Reed's daughter, Jill, an avid Albion supporter, was headmistress of a junior School in Aston, Birmingham, for a number of years in the 1970s. Her husband was a vicar.

REED, Hugh Dennett

Outside-right: 5 + 4 apps. 2 goals.

Born: Alexandria, Dumbarton, 23 August 1950.
Died: 12 November 1992.
Career: Bonhill and Renton Junior Schools. St Patrick's High School (Dumbarton). Drumchapel Amateurs. ALBION (apprentice, February 1966, professional, August 1967). Plymouth Argyle (£11,000, November 1971). Brentford (on loan, February–March 1973). Plymouth Argyle. Crewe Alexandra (July 1974). Huddersfield Town (September 1976). Hartlepool (October 1976). Stafford Rangers (December 1976). Shotton United (1978). Stafford Rangers (September 1981, retired, May 1982).

■ Hughie Reed was a small, energetic and courageous outside-right, whose style failed to impress The Hawthorns coaching staff. As a lad he won three

Scottish youth caps (1968) and after leaving Albion amassed 113 League appearances (and scored 19 goals) serving with his five other major clubs. He made his First Division debut against Stoke City (home) in Division One in November 1968 and also scored 48 goals in 150 Central League games for Albion.

REES, Anthony Andrew

Forward: 15+15 apps. 3 goals.

Born: Merthyr Tydfil, 1 August 1964
Career: Aston Villa (apprentice, August 1980, professional, August 1982). Birmingham City (free, July 1983).

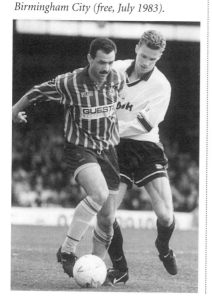

Peterborough United (on loan, October 1985). Shrewsbury Town (on loan, March 1986). Barnsley (March 1988). Grimsby Town (August 1989). ALBION (£30,000, November 1994). Merthyr Town (August 1996-May 1998).

■ An FA Youth Cup winner with Villa in 1980, Tony Rees gained successive promotions with Grimsby, from Division Four to Division Two, in 1990 and 1991, as well as representing Wales at full, under-21 cap, youth and schoolboy levels. He built up a considerable reputation in Villa's youth side until a broken leg halted his progress, causing him to miss a complete season. On recovering, he chose to join the Blues and stepped straight into the first team. Initially, he played wide on the right, where he displayed an ability to take on defenders, but he also seemed a little lacking in stamina. His career stagnated for a while, but after joining Alan Buckley at Grimsby his fortunes improved, although during his time at The Hawthorns, when his career was winding down, he was never guaranteed a first-team place and half of his senior outings came as a substitute. He made his Albion debut in a League game against Notts County at Meadow Lane in November 1994. He also played in 33 Central League games for the club (seven goals scored).

REES, Melvyn

Goalkeeper: 19 apps.

Born: Cardiff, 25 January 1967.
Died: Sheffield, 30 May 1993.
Career: Cardiff City (apprentice, April 1983, professional, September 1984). Watford (July 1987). Crewe Alexandra (on loan, August–September 1989). Leyton

Orient (on loan, January–February 1990). ALBION (£25,000, September 1990). Sheffield United (£25,000, March 1992, until his death).

■ A Welsh youth international, Mel Rees appeared in a total of 75 League games over a period of 10 years, before his sadly died of cancer at the age of 26. One of the youngest goalkeepers ever to appear in all four Divisions of the Football League, he had over 30 outings for Cardiff but was then a reserve at Watford and to a certain extent with Albion, for whom he made his debut at Ipswich Town in January 1991, replacing Stuart Naylor. He was a Pontins League championship winner with Albion in 1990–91, making 18 appearances.

REES, Ronald Raymond

Winger: 40+1 apps. 12 goals.

Born: Ystradgynlais, Brecknock, Wales, 4 April 1944.
Career: Queen's Road School (Merthyr). Merthyr Schools. Coventry City (apprentice, July 1960, professional, May 1962). ALBION (£65,000, March 1968). Nottingham Forest (£60,000, February 1969). Swansea City (£26,000, January 1972, retired, May 1975). Later worked for a large manufacturing company in Bridgend, South Wales, and also assisted in the administration offices at Cardiff City's Ninian Park ground.

■ Ronnie Rees was a two-footed winger who could play on either flank. Fast, direct in style and always eager to have a shot at goal, he joined Albion at perhaps the wrong time, Clive Clark leaving a year later. He won seven under-23 and 39 full caps for Wales and helped Coventry win the Third Division Championship in 1964 and the Second Division in 1967. During his career, Rees appeared in well over 500 competitive matches (440 in the Football League, 68 goals scored). His League record for the Sky Blues was 42 goals in 230 outings. He made his debut for Albion in a 6–2 League home defeat by Everton in Division One in March 1968. He also played in one second XI game.

REGIS, Cyrille

Centre-forward: 297 + 5 apps. 112 goals.

Born: Maripiasoula, French Guyana, 9 February 1958.

Career: Cardinal Hinsley School (Harlesden). Borough of Brent Boys. Ryder Brent Valley. Oxford & Kilburn Boys. Ryder Brent Valley (again). Moseley FC (August 1975). Hayes (semi-professional, July 1976). ALBION (£5,000, May 1977). Happy Valley FC, Hong Kong (guest, 1980). Coventry City (£300,000, October 1984, player-coach, April 1988). Aston Villa (free, July 1991). Wolverhampton Wanderers (free, August 1993). Wycombe Wanderers (free, August 1994). Chester City (May 1995–May 1996). ALBION (coach, February 1997–January 2000). Now a football agent, with his nephew, Jason Roberts, one of his 'players'.

■ Big Cyrille – 'Smokin Joe' – Regis had seven wonderful years with Albion, during which time he scored 140 goals in 370 matches (including tour and friendly fixtures). A huge favourite with the fans from his debut day when he scored twice in a 4–0 home League Cup victory over Rotherham United in August 1977, he found the back of the net on a regular basis, scoring some quite spectacular and breathtaking goals on the way. Indeed, Regis created a club record – unique if you like – by netting on his debut for Albion in five different competitions – the Football League, FA Cup, League Cup, Tennent-Caledonian Cup and Central League. He actually netted three times in his four second XI games. Strong, muscular and aggressive, he had a terrific shot, his heading ability was top-class and he could leave opponents standing with his devastating speed over 25–30 yards. He would often collect the ball around the halfway line and head towards goal, brushing aside his markers with his powerful shoulders before unleashing a cannonball shot. TV cameras have several of his classic goals on film so that we can relive his explosive style in years to come. He was certainly a snip of a signing from non-League football, spotted by Ronnie Allen. Capped by England at full, 'B' and under-21 levels, Regis was voted PFA 'Young Footballer of the Year' in 1979 and was runner-up to 'Footballer of the Year' Steve Perryman in 1982. He was voted *Evening Mail* 'Footballer of the Year', won the 'Merit Man' award in 1987 and was also chosen as the Midlands Soccer Writer's 'Player of the Year', after helping Coventry City win the FA Cup for the first time, beating Tottenham

Hotspur 3–2 in a memorable Wembley Final. His transfer to Coventry in 1984 was a shock to every Albion fan and Regis himself said it was a wrench to leave The Hawthorns. However, he soon settled down at Highfield Road and in 1985 he scored five goals against his future club, Chester, in a Milk Cup game. He is only the second player to net from the penalty spot on his senior debut for Albion (the first being Bobby Blood in 1921) and in May 1996, at the age of 37 years and 86 days, he became the oldest player ever to turn out in a League game for Wycombe. During his exciting career, Regis scored over 200 goals in more than 700 club and representative matches and he became the first 'professional' to play for Albion, Villa, Wolves and Coventry City. A born again Christian, other members of the Regis family include footballers Dave Regis and Jason Roberts and Olympic athlete John.
* Before joining Moseley, Regis was offered a trial by Chelsea but had to pull out with a hamstring injury.

REID, George Albert

Centre-forward: 13 apps. 3 goals.

Born: Handsworth, Sheffield, 3 February 1872.

Died: Sheffield, 5 December 1934.
Career: Handsworth & Woodhouse Schools (Sheffield). Attercliffe FC (1888). Sheffield Wednesday (professional, May 1896). ALBION (£100, August 1897). Warmley, Bristol (free, March 1898). Thames Ironworks (February 1899). Middlesbrough (free, May 1899–April 1900).

■ George Reid was a tough-nut centre-forward, whose career 'took off' after he had left the Midlands. He did rather better with Middlesbrough in season 1899–1900, scoring four goals in 13 matches. His League debut for Albion was against Liverpool (home) in Division One in November 1897. He also played in several 'other' first-team games for the club.

REID, Nicholas Scott

Full-back: 17+9 apps. 1 goal.

Born: Davyhulme near Manchester, 30 October 1960.
Career: Manchester City (apprentice, April 1977, professional, November 1978).

Seattle Sounders (free, May 1982). Manchester City (free, September 1982). Blackburn Rovers (free, July 1987). Bristol City (on loan, September–October 1992). ALBION (free, November 1992). Wycombe Wanderers (free, March 1994). Woking (free, July 1995). Witton Albion (September 1995). Bury (player-coach, December 1995). Sligo Rovers (player-manager, August 1997). Burnley (assistant physiotherapist, 2000–04).

■ One of the very few full-backs to score in a Wembley Cup final – doing so for Albion against Port Vale in the 1993 play-offs, Nicky Reid was an experienced campaigner when Ossie Ardiles recruited him to take over the number 2 slot at The Hawthorns and he did a fine job as the Baggies surged on towards promotion from Division Two. A tough defender who could pass a ball as well as any midfielder, he also played in 11 Central League games for Albion. He amassed 262 senior appearances for Manchester City and 209 for Blackburn, while also gaining six England under-21 caps.

REILLY, George Gerrard

Defender/centre-forward: 49 + 1 apps. 10 goals.

Born: Belshill, Lanarkshire, Scotland, 14 September 1957.
Career: St Brendan's RC School Corby.

Corby Town (May 1973). Northampton Town (professional, June 1976). Cambridge United (£140,000, November 1979). Watford (£100,000, August 1983). Newcastle United (£200,000, February 1985). ALBION (£100,000, December 1985–June 1988). Cambridge United (free, July 1988). Barnet (1989–90). Alvechurch (January 1991-April 1992). Now working as a bricklayer in Corby.

One of the tallest strikers and defenders ever to play League football (not particularly great in any position), George Reilly joined Albion having already had 10 seasons in competitive football (1976–85). He made his Baggies debut against Everton in a First Division home game in December 1985 but failed to make much of an impact at The Hawthorns. Although born in Scotland, he moved with his parents to Corby (Northants) as a lad, and it was with Corby Town where he first started to score goals and, thereafter, continued to hit the target throughout his career. In fact, 'Big George', nicknamed 'Mother' by some supporters, notched a total of 121 goals in 407 League appearances, finding the net in all four divisions, with a 'best return' of 23 in 1977–78 with Northampton. He gained an FA Cup runners'-up medal with Watford in May 1984. Awkward-looking, lanky-legged and appearing disinterested, he has certainly put the wind up a few players over the years but sadly not during his days at The Hawthorns. Reilly, who was

sent off after just 75 seconds of Albion's Bass Charity Cup tie with Burton Albion in July 1987, also played in two Central League games for the club.

REYNOLDS, John

Wing-half: 46 apps. 6 goals.

Born: Blackburn, 21 February 1869.
Died: Sheffield, 12 March 1917.
Career: Portglenone & Ballymena Schools. County Antrim (Northern Ireland). Park Road FC (Blackburn). Witton FC (Blackburn). Blackburn Rovers reserves (1884–86). Park Road FC (August 1886). East Lancashire Regiment (from December 1886, posted to Ireland, demobbed, December 1889). Guest for Distillery (May 1888–December 1899). Ulster (June 1890). ALBION (professional, March 1891). Droitwich Town (on loan, 1892). Aston Villa (£50, April 1892). Celtic (free, May 1897). Southampton (free, January 1898). Bristol St George (free, July 1898). Grafton FC, New Zealand, then coached in New Zealand (1902–03). Returned to England to play for Stockport County (free, September 1903). Willesden Town (October 1903, retired, April 1905). Cardiff City (coach, 1907–08). Subsequently worked as a miner at a colliery near Sheffield.

■ 'Jack' Reynolds, nicknamed 'Baldy' and only 5ft 4in tall, was a stumpy wee man, yet a marvellous wing-half, who sometimes bewildered his own teammates as well as the opposition. He mastered every trick in the book, and, aided by some quite remarkable ball skills, his footwork was at times exceptionally brilliant. Although born in Blackburn, he spent his youth in Ireland, returning to his home town in 1884. He joined the forces at the age of 17 and, after two years' service, signed for Distillery. When based in Ireland, Reynolds was capped five times for that country (1890–91), but after returning to England he went on to gain another eight caps, this time for the country of his birth, thus making him one of only a handful of footballers who have represented two countries at senior international level. Reynolds also played for the Football League on four occasions, for the Professionals XI three times and he appeared in one England trial (1894). As Albion's right-half, he

won an FA Cup medal in 1892, scoring a fine goal in a 3–0 win over Aston Villa, and in 1895 he was in Villa's FA Cup-winning side against Albion! The following year he won another First Division Championship medal to add to the one he had gained in 1894, and in 1897 was a key member of Villa's 'double-winning' team. He scored 17 goals in 96 League games for Villa in four successful seasons. Playing north of the border with Celtic, Reynolds helped bring the Scottish First Division crown to Parkhead in 1898. Earlier, with Ulster, he had collected an Irish Cup-winners' medal (1891), and he also had the pleasure of scoring Albion's first penalty kick against Nottingham Forest in April 1893. He unfortunately left the club under a 'dark' cloud after falling out with the board of directors. Ironically, his League debut for Villa was against Albion on 2 September 1893, and he scored to celebrate the occasion! Almost two years earlier he had made his Albion League debut against his home town club, Blackburn Rovers (home), in Division One in October 1891. He also played in 40 'other' first-team games for Albion. Reynolds died of heart failure at the age of 48.

RICE, Brian

Midfield: 2+1 apps.

Born: Bellshill, Lanarkshire, Scotland, 11 October 1963.
Career: Bellshill & District Schools. Glasgow Youth Club. Whitburn Central FC. Hibernian (junior, 1979, amateur, 1980, professional, October 1980). Nottingham Forest (August 1985). Grimsby Town (on loan, October 1986). ALBION (on loan, January–February 1989). Stoke City (on loan, February 1991). Port Vale (on loan, March–April 1991). Falkirk (August 1991). Dundee (August 1994). Dunfermline Athletic (October 1995). Clyde (August 1997). Morton (assistant manager/coach, March–May 2002).

■ Red-haired Scottish youth and under-21 international Brian Rice, predominantly left-footed, made his Albion debut as a 'sub' in the 2–0 League defeat at Watford in January 1989, having his first start for the club a week later in the 1–1 home draw with Leicester City. He also played in 11 Central League games for the Baggies. Rice gained a lot of experience north of the border, being introduced to League football by Hibs against Motherwell as a 16-year-old. He was a strong, running player who preferred to occupy a position on the left hand side of the pitch.

RICHARDS, Arthur John

Right-back: 1 app.

Born: Knighton, Shropshire, 7 July 1888.
Died: Ludlow, January 1949.
Career: Knighton village & Knighton Schools. St George's Victoria. New Invention. ALBION (professional, April 1910). Kilnhurst (free, May 1911). Knighton Town (August 1914, retired 1919 after service in World War One).

■ A right-back, whose lack of speed was compensated by thoughtful positioning, Arthur Richards had one senior outing for Albion, deputising for Dick Betteley against Bolton Wanderers (away) in Division Two in September 1910. He also played in over 20 second XI games and left the club once Joe Smith had established himself in Albion's first team.

RICHARDS, Geoffrey Mottram

Outside-right: 3 apps. 1 goal.

Born: Bilston, 24 April 1929.
Career: Villers Junior & Wolverhampton Grammar Schools. John Harper's FC (Wolverhampton & District Works League). Albion Works. ALBION (amateur, October 1943, professional, August 1946). Stafford Rangers (July 1952). Bilston Town (player-coach). Hednesford Town (player-manager). Birchen Coppice FC. Nuneaton Borough. Atherstone Town. Hednesford Town (manager, 1962–64). GKN Sankey (as player and part-time coach, August 1965–May 1989). Now lives in Penn, Wolverhampton.

■ Geoff Richards played football until he was 60 years of age. A reserve outside-right at The Hawthorns immediately after World War Two, he first signed for Albion as a 14-year-old in 1943. He did very well in non-League circles, after leaving the Baggies in 1952 when Frank Griffin became first choice. He scored on his League debut against Luton Town (home) in Division Two in December 1946, when

Albion lost 2–1. He was 17 years, seven months and 13 days old and at the time was the youngest player ever to score in a League game for Albion. In November 1954 Tipton-born Alec Jackson, playing against Charlton at The Valley, bettered that record by just two months. He also netted 12 times in 65 Central League games.

RICHARDS, John

Forward: 20 apps. 2 goals.

Born: Martley Hollow, Worcestershire, 15 November 1893.
Died: December 1934.
Career: Wichenford & Berrow Green Schools. Broadheath Rangers. 2nd Battalion Coldstream Guards. City Ramblers FC (London). ALBION (£18, professional, December 1895). Loughborough (free, July 1896). Shepshed Albion (August 1899, retired, May 1906). Later coached in France, North America and Canada.

■ A lively, inventive footballer, John Richards, who was bought out of the Army by Albion, played centre-forward and on both wings. Sadly he failed to hold his form and left the club after barely six months' service. He made his League debut against Small Heath (away) in Division One in December 1895, and, apart from his senior games, he also played in 20 'other' first-team matches for the club.

RICHARDS, Justin

Forward: 0+2 apps.

Born: West Bromwich, 16 October 1980.
Career: Churchfields High School (West Bromwich). Bustleholme Boys FC. ALBION (apprentice, July 1997, professional, January 1999). Bristol Rovers (£75,000, January 2001). Plymouth Argyle (briefly). Stevenage Borough (on loan, December 2002). Colchester United (on loan, October–November 2002). Stevenage Borough (£1,500, March 2003). Woking (August 2004). Dagenham & Redbridge (2005).

■ A reserve striker at The Hawthorns, Justin Richards was an England under-18 squad member who made his Albion debut when called off the bench with just six extra-time minutes remaining of Albion's FA Cup replay with Blackburn

Rovers at Ewood Park in December 1999. Decidedly quick, he found it difficult to establish himself at the club and likewise with struggling Bristol Rovers. He scored eight goals in 47 second XI games for Albion.

RICHARDS, William

Centre-forward: 148 apps. 42 goals.

Born: West Bromwich, 6 October 1874.
Died: West Bromwich, 12 February 1926.
Career: Springfield School (West Bromwich). Wordesley FC. Singers FC (Coventry). West Bromwich Standard. ALBION (professional, July 1894). Newton Heath (£40, April 1901). Stourbridge (free, August 1902). Halesowen Town (September 1904, retired, April 1907). Taken ill before World War One and never recovered full health.

■ Billy Richards was an opportunist centre-forward, always worrying defenders with his quick, decisive thinking and shooting. He was a bustling type of player, loved by the crowd. A comedian in the dressing room but a honest-to-goodness worker on the pitch, he scored consistently well for Albion, finishing up as the club's top marksmen in 1895–96 and again in 1898–99. He led Albion's attack in the 1895 FA Cup final against Aston Villa and besides his senior record for Albion, Richards also played in in more than 80 'other' first-team games (as well as 25 second XI matches) and scored an extra 30 goals. He made his Football League debut for Albion in the Black Country derby against Wolverhampton Wanderers (home) in Division One in September 1894, scoring once in a comprehensive 5–1 win. After leaving The Hawthorns, Richards played nine games for Newton Heath (now Manchester United), before returning to the Midlands, where he wound down his career playing local soccer.

RICHARDSON, Frederick

Centre-forward: 31 apps. 8 goals.

Born: Middlestone Moor, County Durham, 18 August 1925.
Career: Willington & Spennymoor Schools. Durham Boys (1940). Spennymoor United Juniors (1941). Newcastle United (1942). Spennymoor United (1943) Bishop Auckland (1945). Chelsea (professional,

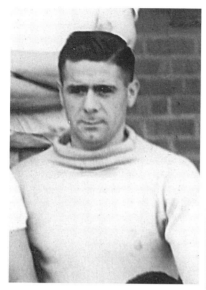

September 1946). Hartlepool United (October 1947). Barnsley (October 1948). ALBION (£7,125 June 1950). Chester (£3,000, February 1952). Hartlepool United (free, November 1952, retired, June 1956). ALBION (scout, in North-Eastern League, 1956–58). Later coached locally in Hartlepool, then Whickham (manager, 1980–82). Now living in the North-East of England.

■ Fred Richardson was a stocky striker who could carve or barge his way though the tightest of defences, aided by a weighty frame. He played for the 'Bishops' in the 1946 FA Amateur Cup final, collecting a runners'-up medal. He then signed 'pro' for Chelsea and embarked on a good career in the Football League, totting up 244 appearances and scoring 66 goals, before retiring in 1957 through injury. Making his Albion debut against Stoke City (home) in Division One in August 1950, he also scored 14 goals in 37 Central League games before joining Chester. As a manager he guided Whickham to victory in the 1981 FA Vase Final at Wembley.

RICHARDSON, Kieran Edward

Midfield: 11+1 apps. 3 goals.

Born: Greenwich, London, 21 October 1984.
Career: West Ham United (junior). Manchester United (apprentice, April 2001, professional, October 2002). ALBION (on loan, January–May 2005).

■ A wide midfielder with excellent all round skills, Kieran Richardson had been under the watchful eye of Albion manager Bryan Robson when he was coaching at Old Trafford. Although restricted to less than a dozen or so senior appearances for Manchester United, when called into action he produced some excellent displays. The recipient of an FA Youth Cup winners' medal with the Reds in 2003, he made his Albion debut as a second-half substitute in the 2-2 home Premiership draw with Crystal Palace in February 2004. He was capped by England at under-21 level, versus Holland and Germany in February/March 2005. He was selected by coach Sven Goran Eriksson to tour the US with the full England Squad in June 2005 and scored twice on his senior debut against the USA on tour three months later, the first goal coming after just four minutes.

RICHARDSON, Samuel

Wing-half: 212 apps. 1 goal.

Born: West Bromwich, 11 August 1894.
Died: West Bromwich, September 1959.
Career: Whitehall Road School (Great

Bridge). Greets Green Prims. Great Bridge Juniors (1909–11). Great Bridge Celtic (August 1912). ALBION (professional, February 1913). Guest for Oldbury Town and Coventry City during World War One. Newport County (£450, August 1927). Aldershot (free, August 1930). Kidderminster Harriers (1931–35). Worked in a factory for several years either side of World War Two.

■ Sammy Richardson, who played in the same Great Bridge United team as future Albion forward Jackie Mann, was a competent wing-half, mainly noted for his workmanlike displays as a defensive rather than attacking player. Physically strong and dominant in the air, he was also a fine passer of the ball and biting in the tackle. He made his Baggies debut against Sheffield United (away) in Division One in January 1915 and was a key member of Albion's League championship side of 1919–20, being virtually a permanent fixture in the team during the first three campaigns after World War One. He lost his place to Tommy Magee in 1923 but returned to the fold as a left-half in seasons 1924–25 and 1925–26. He also played for the reserves in the Birmingham & District League before and after World War One, and scored twice in a total of 143 Central League matches after the hostilities, gaining three championship-winning medals in 1922–23, 1923–24 and 1926–27. He also played for the Football League side and the FA in 1921. He and his brother, Bill Richardson (below), were at The Hawthorns together in 1926–27.

RICHARDSON, William

Centre-half: 352 apps. 1 goal.

Born: Great Bridge, Tipton, 14 February 1908.
Died: West Bromwich, August 1985.
Career: Greets Green Infants & Junior Schools. Whitehall Road Schools (Great Bridge). Greets Green Boys. Greets Green Prims. Great Bridge Celtic. ALBION (professional, November 1926). Swindon Town (£200, May 1937). Dudley Town (free, September 1939). Vono Sports FC (August 1940, retired, June 1941). ALBION (scout, 1950–53). Lived and worked in Hill Top, West Bromwich, until his death at the age of 77.

■ Bill Richardson was a shade casual at

RICHARDSON, William 'G'

Centre-forward: 444 apps. 328 goals.

Born: Framwellgate Moor, County Durham, 29 May 1909.
Died: Perry Barr, Birmingham, 29 March 1959.
Career: Framwellgate Moor & Easington Colliery Schools. Durham Schoolboys. Horden Wednesday FC. United Bus Company (Hartlepool). Hartlepools United (August 1928). ALBION (£1,250 June 1929). Shrewsbury Town (£250, November 1945). ALBION (assistant trainer-coach, June 1946, and was still on Albion's training staff when he collapsed and died

while playing in a Charity Match in Birmingham in 1959). Guest for Derby County and Walsall during World War Two (when free from Army duty).

■ On his day 'W.G.' Richardson had a few equals and no superiors at snapping up half-chances, especially those that flew hard and low across the face of the goal, from either wing, deflected or not. A truly dynamic centre-forward, who depended on his alertness rather than his weight, he was quick, assertive and pretty sharp inside the box. During the 1930s 'W.G.' was seemingly always hitting the headlines and the net. He scored both goals when Albion beat Birmingham to win the 1931 FA Cup final, and he secured the match-winning goal against Charlton Athletic, which ensured Albion would win promotion in that same 1930–31 season to bring them a unique double. He grabbed four goals in five minutes at West Ham in November 1931, hit three in six minutes against Derby County in 1933, set an Albion record with 40 League and cup goals in season 1935–36 (which still holds good today) and he claimed a total of 14 hat-tricks in major League and cup football, including four 'fours' (1933–35). During World War Two 'W.G.' continued to crack in the goals and twice scored six times in matches against Luton Town and the RAF in 1941–42. He notched up five goals against Swansea Town in 1941 and fired in another five against Aston Villa in 1943. His wartime scoring exploits were exceptional: 123 goals for Albion alone in only 106 games, including friendlies (exactly 100 in 'competitive' matches), and he gained a Midland Cup-winners' medal in 1944 (v Nottingham Forest). He also played and scored for the Metropolitan Police, the National Police and Civil Defence teams during the hostilities. After that, he continued to net regularly for Shrewsbury Town, grabbing 55 more goals before returning to The Hawthorns as trainer-coach in 1946. During a brilliant career, hot-seat 'W.G.' Richardson won just one full England cap, lining up against Holland in 1935, but he deserved a lot more. He netted 202 League goals for Albion, a record that stood for over 20 years. He also secured a further 26 goals in the FA Cup. His goal total in approximately 500 games reached the 450 mark, and on top of this he also netted 50 Central League goals for Albion

times, yet all in all he was a splendid pivot, unflagging and especially good in the air. No relation to 'W.G.' but brother to Sammy, he gave Albion 11 years' grand service, making over 350 appearances. He first set foot inside The Hawthorns when the centre-half slot and wing-half positions were causing the management some concern. Richardson buckled down to the task ahead of him, and he settled into the team's style of play without much effort, after making his debut in December 1928. He had 'wee' Tommy Magee on the right and Len Darnell on his left – and, thus, formed a steady, reliable middle line. He also played at right-half and left-half in his first two seasons as a first XI player. From then on Richardson played consistently well, apart from the odd hiccup here and there. He was a popular player and a reliable one too. He played for Albion in both the 1931 and 1935 FA Cup finals, collecting a winners' medal in the former, and he also held together the defence during the promotion campaign of 1930–31. He made his League debut against Middlesbrough (away) in Division Two in December 1928 and also appeared in 62 second XI games (3 goals).

(eight hat-tricks) during his first season with the club, going on to total 83 in only 79 second XI outings. He made his Baggies debut against Millwall (home) in Division Two on Boxing Day in 1929 and scored once in a 6–1 win.

* The 'G' was added to Billy's name to help people distinguish him from the other W. Richardson, who was on Albion's books at the same time. The 'G' stood for ginger (hair).

RICKABY, Stanley

Right-back: 205 apps. 2 goals.

*Born: Stockton-on-Tees, 12 March 1924.
Career: Stockton Grammar School. Stockton & District Schools. South Bank FC (1940). Middlesbrough (amateur, July 1941, professional, July 1946). ALBION (£7,500, February 1950). Poole Town (player-manager, June 1955). Weymouth (1960–61). Newton Abbot Spurs (August 1963, retired, July 1964). Went into accountancy, initially in England, emigrating to Australia in 1969. Still resident in Australia today, living in retirement in North Beach, Perth.*

A strong, accomplished right-back, good in the tackle with a powerful kick, Stan Rickaby was a player that was never flustered. He came to Albion as cover to Jimmy Pemberton, but inside six months he had replaced the injury-stricken right-back and held his place in the side for quite a while afterwards. In contrast, Rickaby was lucky with injuries at Albion, that is until the semi-final of the FA Cup against Port Vale in 1954. He suffered a leg injury that day, which forced him to miss the final against Preston, but, along with 'keeper Norman

Heath, he was awarded a medal, having played in all the previous rounds. Capped once by England against Ireland at Goodison Park in 1953, Rickaby played in over 200 games for Albion, all at right-back. He left the club in 1955, alleging that he had been made a 'soccer slave' and later had a constant battle with the club regarding the way in which he was released. He made his Baggies debut against Manchester City (home) in Division One in April 1950 and also played in six second-team matches.

* Rickaby's autobiography, *Upover and Downunder* was published by Britespot Solutions, Cradley Heath, in 2003.

RIDYARD, Alfred

Centre-half: 34 apps.

*Born: Shafton, Cudworth, 5 March 1908.
Died: West Bromwich, 4 June 1981.
Career: Shafton & Royston Schools. Hemsworth Rovers. South Kirby Boys' club. Barnsley (amateur, June 1929, professional, September 1929). ALBION (£900, June 1932). Queen's Park Rangers (£625, March 1938, retired, May 1948, later assistant manager/coach). Guest for Chelsea, Aldershot and West Ham United during World War Two. Returned to West Bromwich and worked in a factory until he was over 60.*

Alf Ridyard was built like the side of a house. He was a real 'stopper' centre-half, as tough as nails, who acted as reserve to Bill Richardson during his six years' association with the club. He played at Highbury in the 1937 FA Cup semi-final defeat by Preston North End and won three Central League championship medals with Albion during the mid-1930s. Ridyard was milking a cow on a Handsworth farm when a representative from Queen's Park Rangers came along and signed him on the transfer deadline of 1938. He went on to make over 200 appearances for the London club. His Albion debut was against Derby County (away) in Division One in January 1933. Besides his first-team games, he also participated in 125 Central League matches for the Baggies, scoring 8 goals, while gaining three successive championship medals between 1932–35. Ridyard also played for the Civil Defence and the Metropolitan Police, London, during World War Two. He attended

Albion home matches on a regular basis right up until his death.

RILEY, James Harold

Utility half-back: 3 apps. 1 goal.

*Born: West Bromwich, 9 September 1869.
Died: West Bromwich, 1932.
Career: West Bromwich Baptist School. Wednesbury Old Athletic (1887). ALBION (professional, June 1889). Walsall Town Swifts (September 1902, retired through injury, November 1902).*

Jimmy Riley was an everyday 'run-of-the-mill' utility half-back, who filled all three positions in various first XI matches. Having limited experience with Albion, he made his debut for the club against Burnley (away) in Division One in December 1890. He made seven 'other' first-team appearances for the club.

RIX, John

Wing-half: 68 apps.

*Born: Lintz, Bursopfield, 12 July 1908.
Died: West Bromwich, May 1979.
Career: Lintz Day School & Fereday Senior School. Durham Schools. Lintz Colliery. ALBION (professional, November 1927). Lincoln City (£500, with Ernie Hoyland, May 1939, retired, May 1942). Lived and worked in West Bromwich until his death.*

'Jack' Rix was an unspectacular left-half but a worthy one who in essence was a first-class club man, serving Albion for 12 years, during which time he managed nearly 70 senior appearances. A junior international, capped in 1928, he won three successive Central League

championship medals (1932–35 inclusive) and, all told, played in 198 second-team games for Albion (3 goals scored) and hardly ever grumbled about being a reserve! He senior debut was against Port Vale (home) in Division Two in May 1928.

ROBBINS, Walter William

Outside-left: 91 apps. 31 goals.

Born: Cardiff, 24 November 1910.
Died: Swansea, 7 February 1979.
Career: Ely Central & Cardiff City Senior Schools. Cardiff Boys. Ely Brewery FC. Ely United (1927). Cardiff City (professional, September 1928). ALBION (£3,000 April 1932). Newport County (May 1939). Cardiff City (trainer, August 1945). Swansea Town (chief scout, 1958, trainer 1960, later, assistant manager, 1968–71, thereafter, chief scout, retired due to poor health, 1978). During the 1950s he was appointed trainer to the Welsh National side.

■ A highly-efficient and competent outside-left with tree-trunk legs, which enabled him to release a thunderbolt shot, Walter Robbins was once a motor-mechanic and lorry driver in a Welsh brewery. He joined a football club and went on to become a famous Welsh international, winning 11 caps. He joined Albion as deputy to Stanley Wood, but found he had to contest the left-wing position with Wally Boyes as well. In fact, Robbins had a few games at inside-left before finally settling for a more controlled role later in his career as a central-midfielder. He actually had two games at centre-half for Albion in 1938. He had earlier made his Baggies debut against Chelsea (away) in Division One in April 1932. He also netted 38 goals in 86 second-team games for the Baggies, whom he helped win the Central League title for three seasons running in the mid-1930s. Prior to moving to The Hawthorns, Robbins scored 68 goals for Ely United in 1927–28, netted five times for Cardiff City against Thames in February 1932 (to set a League record), toured Canada with the Welsh FA in 1929 and collected a Welsh Cup winners' medal (with Cardiff) in 1930. He was later trainer at Ninian Park when the Welsh club gained promotion to the First Division in 1946–47 and again in 1951–52. For Albion, he was a member of

the Central League side, which carried off their respective championship three seasons running (1932–35), and later, as Swansea's trainer, he sat on the bench when the Welsh club reached the semi-final of the FA Cup in 1964. He played in three different divisions of the Football League with Cardiff. In May 1971 Robbins was granted a well-earned testimonial match by Swansea and Albion were the visitors to The Vetch Field.

ROBERTS, Graham Paul

Defender/midfield: 41 apps. 6 goals.

Born: Southampton, 3 July 1959.
Career: Southampton (associate schoolboy). Southampton & Hampshire Schools. Scholing Sports FC (1975). Bournemouth (apprentice, August 1975). Dorchester Town (on loan, August 1976, signed permanently, October 1976). Portsmouth (apprentice, February 1977, professional, March 1977). Weymouth (August 1979). Tottenham Hotspur (£35,000, May 1990 – after turning down a move to The Hawthorns). Glasgow Rangers (£450,000, December 1986). Chelsea (May 1988, player-coach from November 1989). ALBION (free, November 1990). Enfield (player-manager, March 1992). Chesham United (briefly). Slough Town (1994–95). Stevenage Borough (1995). Yeovil Town (player-manager, January 1995–February 1998). Hertford Town (manager, August 1998). Boreham Wood (manager, February 2001). Carshalton (manager, 2002–03). Soccer coach in Marbella/Spain (2003–05). Clyde (manager, May 2005).

■ A former shopfitter's mate, Graham Roberts started his career as a forward, but as time went by he developed in to a rugged, no-nonsense, hard-tackling midfielder or central defender. He made his League debut for Spurs in October 1980 against Stoke City, the first of 287 appearances for the London club (36 goals scored). He picked up two FA Cup winners' medals (in 1981 and 1982) and also played in the 1982 League Cup final defeat by Liverpool. He won the first of his six England caps against Northern Ireland in May 1983 and 12 months later joyfully lifted the UEFA Cup after Spurs

had beaten RSC Anderlecht in the two leg final. Always a stern, aggressive competitor, he never gave an inch, never shirked a tackle and simply loved to be involved in a tough contest, and he took over from another hard man, Graeme Souness, also a former Spurs player, at Ibrox Park. After helping the 'Gers win both the Scottish Premier League and Skol Cup, he moved back to London to join Chelsea. He quit Stamford Bridge after an argument with chairman Ken Bates and quickly moved to The Hawthorns, making his Baggies debut in a 2–0 League home win over Blackburn Rovers in November 1990, when he slotted into the right-half position (No 4), allowing Gary Robson to switch to right-back. He struggled with injuries during the latter stages of his Hawthorns' career, and after leaving Albion (whom he also served in a handful of second XI games) he became a fairly successful manager at non-League level.

ROBERTS, Jason Andre Davis

Striker: 86+15 apps. 27 goals.

Born: Park Royal, London, 25 January 1978.
Career: Hayes (August 1994). Wolverhampton Wanderers (£250,000, September 1997). Torquay United (on loan, December 1997–February 1998). Bristol City (on loan, March–April 1998). Bristol Rovers (£250,000, August 1998). ALBION (£2 million, July 2000). Portsmouth (on loan, September–December 2003). Wigan Athletic (on loan, January 2004, signed for £1.4 million+, February 2004).

■ Cousin of former Albion star striker Cyrille Regis, Jason Roberts developed into an excellent goalscorer himself. He was signed by Baggies' boss Gary Megson for a club record fee in July 2000, having netted 48 goals in only 93 first-team appearances in two seasons with Bristol Rovers. Partnering Lee Hughes in Albion's attack, Roberts had an excellent first season with the club, claiming 17 goals in 50 outings. However, a couple of foot injuries disrupted his progress in 2001–02 and he only managed seven strikes in 17 appearances, but his efforts during the two-and-a-half months after Christmas helped place the wheels in

motion for automatic promotion into the Premiership. Roberts, who has won six Grenada caps so far, found it hard going in the top flight, having to withstand a fair amount of buffeting from the sturdy defenders. He struggled at times and when Albion were relegated he demanded a transfer. There were no firm offers and eventually he returned to the Premiership by agreeing to join Portsmouth on loan before reverting back to Nationwide soccer with Wigan Athletic, also on loan, early in 2004 – ironically replacing Geoff Horsfield (sold to Albion). Roberts then helped Wigan reach the Premiership in 2005. He also played in four second XI games for Albion (two goals scored).
* Roberts played in a strong Rest of the World side (with Baggies teammate Darren Moore) against an African XI at Bolton in 2002–03.

ROBERTS, Richard James

Winger: 52 apps. 10 goals.

Born: Redditch, Worcs. 22 January 1878.
Died: Birmingham, 8 March 1931.
Career: Studley & District Schools. Redditch Excelsior. ALBION (professional, April 1899). Newcastle United (£150, May 1901). Middlesbrough (£450, April 1904). Crystal Palace (£100, August 1905–08). Worcester City (free, August 1908, retired through injury, April 1909).

■ Dick Richards was a dual-purpose winger, steady, never outstanding, but a

player who gave his all each time he pulled on a jersey. He scored regularly in his 50 plus games for Albion for whom he made his League debut against Bury (home) in Division One in December 1899. Roberts also played in several 'other' first team and in quite a few second XI games for the club. He scored twice when Albion beat Burslem Port vale 5–0 in the final of the Staffordshire Cup in 1900. Roberts worked on munitions during World War One.

ROBERTS, Robert Hugh Clarence

Outside-left: 1 app.

Born: Marchweil near Wrexham, 9 July 1870.
Died: January 1935.
Career: Marchweil & Rhostyllen Schools. Wrexham (trialist, 1889). ALBION (professional, May 1890). Corwen FC (free, April 1891). Played in the Welsh League before retiring in 1902.

■ An amateur left-winger, who was taken 'trialist' by Albion for a season, Bob Roberts played in one League game against Everton (home) in Division One in September 1890.

ROBERTS, Robert John

Goalkeeper: 84 apps.

Born: West Bromwich, 9 April 1859.
Died: Byker, Newcastle-upon-Tyne, 20 October 1929.
Career: Christ Church School (West Bromwich). George Salters Works. ALBION (Strollers) (September 1879, professional, August 1885). Sunderland Albion (free, May 1890). ALBION (free, May 1891). Aston Villa (free, May 1892, retired, June 1893). Married a girl from from the North-East of England and he stayed there until his death.

■ Albion's first international footballer, Bob Roberts was a giant of a man, just the right size for a goalkeeper of that time. He was so well built he could deal comfortably with high crosses and with any robust forward that cared to barge into him! He had a tremendous reach, a big safe pair of hands, he wore size 13 boots (which assisted him in kicking vast distances) and, above all, he had a wonderful temperament. Roberts started

off his playing career as an outfield-player, occupying many different positions, before finally settling down between the uprights. He won three England caps, his first against Scotland in March 1887, and he also played for the Football Alliance and participated in three international trials. Roberts was Albion's custodian in three FA Cup finals in 1886, 1887 and 1888, gaining a winners' medal in the latter against Preston North End when he played exceptionally well against a terrific forward line. In fact, he had two spells with Albion, the second being for a single season, but during his full 12 years with the club he amassed some 400 appearances, including 84 in senior League and cup action, the rest in other local cup competitions and friendlies. A quite magnificent player, he was very popular and, without doubt, an Albion great.

* Roberts is one of the only two players (the other is Ezra Horton) to have featured in Albion's first FA Cup tie against Wednesbury Town at home in November 1883 and in the club's first Football League game against Stoke (away) in September 1888.

ROBERTS, Thomas Frederick

Half-back: 2 apps.

Born: Smethwick, 13 March 1868.
Died: Smethwick, November 1928.

Career: West Smethwick & Cape Hill Schools. ALBION (amateur, January 1890, professional, February 1890). Birmingham St George's (June 1891). Stourbridge (1892). ALBION (January 1894, retired through injury, June 1895).

■ A reserve defender who could play in either centre or left-half position, Tom Roberts had two games for the club in two separate spells before a knee injury ended his career at the age of 27. His League debut was against Bolton Wanderers (home) in Division One in November 1890.

ROBERTSON, Alistair Peter

Defender: 622 + 4 apps. 12 goals.

Born: Philipstoun, Lothian, Scotland, 9 September 1952.
Career: Bridgend Junior & East Lothian Schools. Linlithgow Academy. Uphall Saints. ALBION (apprentice, July 1968, professional, September 1969). Wolverhampton Wanderers (free, September 1986). Worcester City (manager, July 1990). Cheltenham Town (manager, May 1991–May 1992). Now resident in Walsall, he works for a car sales company.

■ After 18 years' service and more than 700 first-team games (626 at competitive level), Ally Robertson said farewell to Albion and joined neighbouring Wolves soon after the start of the 1986–87 season. Told by manager Ron Saunders that he would not fit into his future

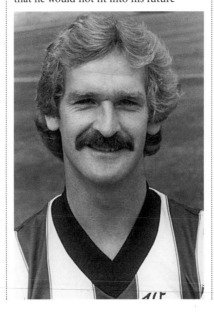

plans, the likeable Scot was given a free transfer. It was a sad occasion for Robertson, who had made his debut against high-flying Manchester United before a 45,000 Hawthorns crowd, back in October 1969, as a 17 year old. 'Robbo' went on to serve Albion through thick and thin, performing as a steady, unobtrusive central-defender, sending in challenges with his powerful shoulders and getting in some crunching tackles, not all of them legal! He drew up a fine understanding with fellow defender John Wile and together the duo appeared in 573 games in Albion colours. They helped the club gain promotion from Division Two in 1976 and reach three major Cup semi-finals, while also containing some of the best strikers in Europe via the UEFA Cup competition. In 1979 Robertson passed Jimmy Dudley's record of 166 consecutive League appearances for Albion, and when he left for Molineux only two players – Tony Brown and Wile – had played in more League games for the Baggies. In fact, Robertson's grand total of 718 + 11 substitute appearances for Albion (all games including friendlies) makes him the second highest appearance maker in the club's history, behind 'Bomber' Brown. He also played in 112 Central League games. When only 18 years of age, Robertson broke a leg playing against Charlton in a League Cup tie at The Hawthorns, but he bounced back in style and went roaring on towards the top, becoming one of Albion's finest defenders. As a youngster he won four Scottish schoolboy caps and added six youth caps to his tally between 1968–70, but he failed to get any full international recognition, hard through he tried. In five seasons (1975–80) he missed only seven League games out of a possible 210, as Albion strove to establish themselves back among the big boys of the First Division. He won Fourth Division championship and Sherpa Van Trophy medals with Wolves in 1987–88 and added a Third Division championship medal to his collection in 1988–89, when he was skipper of the club.

ROBINSON, Bethel

Full-back: 4 apps.

Born: Wheelton, Chorley, 6 July 1858.
Died: December 1934.
Career: Chorley School. Chorley Amateurs.

Preston North End (amateur, August 1881, professional, August 1885). Bolton Wanders (free, September 1887). ALBION (£25, February 1889). Bolton Wanderers (£25, March 1889). ALBION (free, January 1891). Hyde United (free, July 1891). Southport Central (1892–94). Southport Invicta (August 1894). Aughton FC (May 1897, retired, June 1900). Later employed in a factory in Formby, Lancashire.

■ An amateur right-back, who was also the licensee of the Crown and Cushion Inn, Bolton, Bethel Robinson was a thoughtful player bent on achieving his goal – that of safely clearing his lines with a mighty kick. He was a resolute and determined performer who appeared in Albion's FA Cup semi-finals of 1889 and 1891. In fact, his four appearances for the club were, in fact, all in cup ties only, he did not appear in a League game. He was a founder member of Preston North End (1881) and represented The North playing against The South in 1889. He made his Albion debut against Small Heath (away) in the FA Cup, round one, in February 1889.

ROBINSON, Eric Michael

Inside-forward: 1 app.

Born: Manchester, 1 July 1935.
Career: Brooklands School (Manchester). Altrincham (semi-professional, 1953). ALBION (£1,000, March 1957). Rotherham United (£3,000, January 1959). Bangor City (July 1961). Ashton United

(June 1965, retired, c.1969). Now living in Manchester.

■ An inside-forward able to play either side of the park, Eric Robinson promised a great deal when he first came to Albion but did very little. He appeared in 13 League games for Rotherham (one goal scored) and gained a runners'-up medal in the 1964 Welsh Cup final with Bangor City. He made his debut for Albion against Blackpool (away) in Division One in April 1958 and also played in 71 Central League games, scoring 23 goals.

ROBINSON, Ernest Victor

Full-back: 1 app.

Born: Walsall, 12 January 1922.
Career: Wolverhampton Road Junior & Hilary Street Senior Schools Walsall. Hilary Street Old Boys. ALBION (amateur, March 1938, professional, September 1940–May 1948). Shrewsbury Town (free, August 1948, retired through injury, June 1949). Later lived and worked in Dudley and Wolverhampton.

■ A strapping full-back, reserve to Harry White, Idris Bassett and Jimmy Pemberton during his stay with Albion, Vic Robinson joined the Navy during World War Two, going to sea on HMS Bermuda as a torpedoman. He travelled the world and landed in Russia, Algiers, Alexandria, Ceylon, Australia, Shanghai, Hong Kong and the Pacific Islands. He made his senior debut for Albion against Walsall (home) in the Football League North in April 1943.

ROBINSON, Mark James

Midfielder/defender: 2+1 apps.

Born: Oulder Hill, Rochdale, 21 November 1968.
Career: Oulder Hill Senior School. ALBION (schoolboy forms, January 1983, apprentice, July 1985, professional, January 1987). Barnsley (free, June 1987). Newcastle United (£450,000, March 1993). Swindon Town (£600,000, July 1994, retired through injury, January 2002, appointed scout at County Ground, February 2002).

■ Mark Robinson, at age 17, made his League debut for Albion (along with David Burrows) against Sheffield Wednesday at The Hawthorns in April

1986. Despite some impressive displays in the second team (he scored four goals in 43 appearances in total), he failed to establish himself as a player and was duly transferred to Barnsley at the end of the 1986–87 season. He went on to appear in 159 competitive games for the Tykes, 26 for Newcastle and 316 for Swindon, before announcing his retirement due to an aggravating bilateral hernia.

ROBINSON, Paul Peter

Left wing-back: 62+3 apps. 1 goal.

Born: Watford, 14 December 1978.
Career: Watford (apprentice, April 1995, professional, February 1997). ALBION (£250,000+, October 2003).

■ Attacking left wing-back Paul Robinson made well over 250 senior appearances for Watford and gained three England under-21 caps before joining Albion a third into the 2003–04 season. Signed by manager Gary Megson to 'put pressure' on Neil Clement, he is an all-action player, strong and committed in defensive play, and loves to push forward. He accumulated far too many yellow and, indeed, red cards and served several suspensions during his time at Vicarage Road, but since his move to The Hawthorns he has become much more disciplined and helped Albion regain their Premiership status at the end of his first season with the club. His first goal for Albion was a dramatic last minute equaliser against Aston Villa (away) in April 2005 (1-1).

ROBINSON, Ronald

Defender: 1 app.

Born: Sunderland, 22 October 1966.
Career: Sunderland & Wearside Schools. SC Vaux FC (Sunderland). Ipswich Town (apprentice, July 1983, professional, November 1984). Leeds United (free, November 1985). Doncaster Rovers (£5,000, February 1987). ALBION (£80,000, March 1989, with Paul Raven). Rotherham United (£40,000, August 1989). Peterborough United (free, December 1991). Exeter City (£25,000, July 1993). Huddersfield Town (on loan, January 1994). Scarborough (August 1995). Spennymoor United (August 1997–May 1998).

■ Ronnie Robinson's only first-team outing for Albion was at left-back against

Hull City (away) in the final League game of the 1988–89 season. He was never given a chance at The Hawthorns and left after just five months. A reliable, steady defender, he had appeared in 92 first-team games for Doncaster and later had 108 outings for Rotherham, 63 for Posh and 50 for Exeter. He was voted Doncaster's 'Player of the Season' in 1987–88.

ROBSON, Bryan, OBE

Midfielder/defender: 242+7 apps. 46 goals.

Born: Witton Gilbert, Chester-le-Street, County Durham, 11 January 1957.
Career: Chester-le-Street Council & Birtley Comprehensive Schools. Washington & Chester-le-Street Schools. Chester-le-Street Cubs FC. Burnley (trialist, 1971). Coventry City (trialist, 1971). Newcastle United (trialist, 1971). ALBION (apprentice, April 1972, professional, August 1974). Happy Valley FC, Hong Kong (guest, 1980). Manchester United (£1.5 million, October 1981). Middlesbrough (player-manager, May 1994, retiring as a player in May 1997, remained as manager until June 2001). Manchester United (part-time coach, 2001–02). Nigeria (briefly manager/coach, October 2003). Bradford City (manager, November 2003–May 2004). ALBION (manager, November 2004).

■ Bryan Robson became the most costly footballer in Britain when he moved from The Hawthorns to old Trafford in 1981. He captained England (over 60 times) and Manchester United but Albion only spasmodically. He played in 90 senior internationals for his country, scoring 26 goals, including one inside the first half-minute in the 1982 World Cup clash against France in Spain. One of the finest midfield players in world football, he participated in three World Cups for his country and won medals galore with Manchester United including successive Premiership titles (1993 and 1994), three FA Cup final victories (1983, 1985 and 1990) and European Cup-winners' Cup success (1991), also collecting a League Cup runners'-up medal (1991), all this after he had helped Albion win promotion from the Second Division and then, following his departure from Old Trafford, he guided Middlesbrough in to the Premiership. Versatile Robson

occupied the left-back, centre-half, wing-half and inside-forward positions during a superb career. An aggressive competitor with an endless supply of dynamic stamina, he had awareness, was creative, possessed excellent passing skills and a powerful shot, was a superb header of the ball and had an appetite for hard work. He went on to appear in almost 250 first-team appearances for Albion, caretaker manager and former player Brian Whitehouse handing him his Football League debut against York City in a Second Division match in April 1975, in front of just 7,566 spectators at Bootham Crescent. He also played in 58 second XI games and netted 15 goals. He starred in 465 first-team games for Manchester United (100 goals scored), played in 27 senior games for Middlesbrough, whom he twice guided into the Premiership (1995 and 1998) and took them to three domestic Cup finals, sadly losing them all – the FA Cup (1997) and the League Cup twice (1997 and 1998). As 'Boro boss Robson signed some star players, including the Brazilian Juninho, Paul Gascoigne, Nick Barmby, Paul Merson and the Italian Fabrizio Ravanelli. Besides his quota of full England caps, he also appeared in two 'B' and seven under-21 internationals, having earned youth honours as a teenager. He retired with an overall total of 832 competitive appearances under his belt (for club and country) and claimed 172 goals. In November 2004, following the sacking of Gary Megson, Robson, then aged 47, returned to The Hawthorns as Albion manager, signing a one-year rolling contract. His appointment was Albion's 27th managerial change since World War Two and the 20th since winning the FA Cup was won in 1968. He followed Don Howe, Ronnie Allen, Brian Talbot and Bobby Gould as having previously played for and then managed Albion. Robson brought in Nigel Pearson, the former Shrewsbury Town, Sheffield Wednesday and Middlesbrough defender, as his assistant. Ironically, Robson's first game in charge of the Baggies was against his former club Middlesbrough in the Premiership, which Albion lost 2–1. His third was against Manchester United. He finally recorded his first win as Albion boss in a third round FA Cup tie at Preston in January 2005 (his 11th game in charge).

* Robson has been the subject of the TV programme *This Is Your Life,* and he was also a contestant in the BBC's *Super Stars* programme, screened in January 2005.

ROBSON, Gary

Utility: 213+43 apps. 34 goals.

Born: Pelaw, near Chester-le-Street, County Durham, 6 July 1965.
Career: Pelaw Church of England & Pelaw Rosebury Comprehensive Schools. Lumley Juniors. Whitehill Boys FC. Chester-le-Street Boys. Newcastle United (trialist, 1980). ALBION (apprentice, May 1981, professional, May 1983). Bradford City (free, July 1993). Gateshead (player-coach, July 1997). Spennymoor United (August 2000).

■ Younger brother of Bryan, Gary Robson spent 12 years at The Hawthorns, during which time he appeared in more than 250 senior games. A versatile footballer, able to occupy a variety of positions from full-back to outside-left, he made his League debut as a 'sub' against Southampton (home) in May 1983 and played in his last game against Port Vale in February 1993. Later, as a substitute, he sat and watched Albion beat the Valiants 3–0 in the 1993 play-off final at Wembley. A year after that Robson, who also scored 13 goals in

almost 100 Central League appearances for Albion, was rewarded with a testimonial match when Aston Villa visited The Hawthorns.

* He played alongside his brother Justin at Gateshead but never starred in the same team as Bryan (at Albion).

ROBSON, Sir Robert William, CBE

Inside-right/right-half: 257 apps. 61 goals.

Born: Sacriston, County Durham, 18 February 1933.

Career: Waterhouse Secondary Modern School. Langley Park Juniors. Chester-le-Street FC (briefly). Middlesbrough

(amateur, 1948). Southampton (trialist, 1949). Fulham (amateur, April 1950, professional, May 1950). ALBION (£25,000, March 1956). Fulham (£20,000, August 1962, released, June 1967). Oxford University (trainer-coach, 1965–66). Vancouver Royals, Canada (player-manager, August 1967). Fulham (manager, January 1968–November 1968). Chelsea (scout, December 1968–January 1969). Ipswich Town (manager, January 1969–July 1982). England (manager, July 1982–91). England 'B' (team manager, January 1978–July 1982). PSV Eindhoven, Holland (manager, July 1990–May 1992). Sporting Lisbon, Portugal (manager, 1992–93). FC Porto, Portugal (manager,

1994–96). CF Barcelona, Spain (coach-manager, 1996–97). PSV Eindhoven (manager, 1997–99). Newcastle United (manager, September 1999–August 2004).

■ During his initial Fulham days Bobby Robson was part of a very useful inside trio, which included Bedford Jezzard and Johnny Haynes, and after leaving Craven Cottage for Albion in March 1956 (making his Baggies debut in a 4–0 League home defeat by Manchester City) he played alongside a few more fine players, including Ronnie Allen and Derek Kevan. He was successfully converted from a goalscoring inside-right into a creative right-half by Baggies manager Vic Buckingham and went on to gain 20 full caps for England (1957–62), before returning to Fulham where he ended his playing career (1967) with a total of 585 League appearances in his locker. A model competitor whose overall play was full of confidence, Robson's temperament was a shining example to the rest of his teammates. A hard-grafter with great awareness, showing the right spirit at the right moment, he inspired his fellow men and proved a tireless performer wherever he played. Besides his score of England caps, Bobby played five games with the League XI, once for the under-23 team, once for the 'B' team and he also represented the FA XI on tour to South Africa in 1956. He was in the 1958 and 1962 World Cup finals squads, and he netted twice on his England debut against France at Wembley in 1957. He also scored six times in seven Central League games for Albion. In 1962 Robson played for the FA XI against Tottenham Hotspur in the Charity Shield game at White Hart Lane, and as team manager of Ipswich Town he celebrated success in the FA Cup (1978) and the UEFA Cup 1981, as well as winning the Texaco Cup in 1973. He had a near miss in 1981 when Ipswich were pipped for the First Division title by Aston Villa. He was 71 when he lost his job as boss at Newcastle two weeks into the 2004–05, campaign with the Geordies still searching for their first win. In a splendid playing career, Robson amassed a total of 673 senior appearances, scoring 151 goals for his two clubs and for England. As team-manager of his country, he led England to the 1986 World Cup finals in Mexico, celebrating his 50th international in charge in Stockholm in September 1986 when

England met Sweden. A fine cricketer, playing for Sacriston, Worcester Park (London) and West Bromwich Dartmouth, he also enjoys golf and tennis. Awarded the CBE in 1991, 11 years later he was knighted and then handed the Freedom of Ipswich, while being presented with a Special Lifetime Award by UEFA.

RODOSTHENOUS, Michael

Forward: 0+1 app.

Born: Islington, London, 25 August 1976.
Career: Tottenham Hotspur (schoolboy forms, August 1991). ALBION (apprentice, June 1993, professional, August 1996). Telford United (on loan, December 1996–January 1997). Cambridge United (free, non-contract, October 1997–January 1998). Plymouth Argyle (trialist, 1998–99).

■ A reserve striker at The Hawthorns, Michael Rodosthenous made his League debut as a substitute against Bolton Wanderers (away) in March 1997. He also scored twice in over 40 second-team

games for Albion and later spent four months with Cambridge, for whom he made just three senior appearances.

ROGERS, Darren John

Defender: 8+9 apps. 1 goal.

Born: Birmingham, 9 April 1970.
Career: Bartley Green School. ALBION (apprentice, June 1986, professional, July 1988). Birmingham City (free, July 1992). Kidderminster Harriers (on loan, March–April 1993). Lincoln City (trialist, July 1994). Wycombe Wanderers (on loan, November 1993). Walsall (free, July 1994). Stevenage Borough (October 1997). Evesham United (2000–01).

■ Darren Rogers, a utility defender, fast and mobile with a good strong tackle, struggled to hold down a first-team place at The Hawthorns and, indeed, at St Andrew's, but later in his career he did well with Walsall, for whom he appeared in 76 competitive games despite suffering a cruciate ligament injury in 1996. He made his Football League debut for Albion as a 'sub' against Brighton in March 1991, scoring his only goal for the club in a 1–1 home draw with Chester City in April 1992. Rogers played in 150 reserve-team games for the Baggies, netting three goals and earning himself a Pontins League championship medal in 1990–91 with 20 appearances.

ROOKE, Edward John Harold

Centre-half: 42 apps. 1 goal.

Born: Hockley, Birmingham, 18 November 1899.
Died: Perry Barr, Birmingham, January 1974.
Career: Key Hill & Park Road Schools (Hockley). Winson Green Lions. Brierley Hill Alliance (1918). ALBION (professional, May 1921). Nuneaton Borough (June 1929, retired, April 1934). Later worked in a Birmingham warehouse.

■ Teddy Rooke was a quiet but competent centre-half, both creative and firm, who was seldom drawn out of position. He spent eight years with Albion, acting, in the main, as reserve to Fred Reed. He made his League debut against Notts County (away) in Division One in December 1924 and also played in

151 second XI matches, gaining a Central League championship medal in 1923–24, while helping the side win the same title in seasons 1922–23 and 1926–27.

ROSLER, Uwe

Striker: 5 apps. 1 goal.

Born: Attenberg, Germany, 15 November 1968.
Career: Traktor Starken, Germany (1984, professional 1985). Lokomotiv Leipzig, Germany (1986). Chemie Leipzig, Germany (1987). FC Magdeburg, Germany (June 1988). Dynamo Dresden, Germany (August 1991). FC Nurnberg, Germany (August 1992). Manchester City (£375,000, March 1994). FC Kaiserslautern, Germany (free, June 1998). Tennis Borussia FC, Germany (August 1999). Southampton (free, July 2000). ALBION (on loan, October–November 2001). IFC SpVgg Unterhaching, Germany (January 2002). Lillestrom, Norway (2003–05).

■ An East German international (capped five times), Uwe Rosler was a loan signing by Baggies manager Gary Megson at a time when injuries were ruining his choice of strikers. He did a

reasonable job and scored the winning goal against Nottingham Forest in the televised League game at The Hawthorns, having made his Albion debut a week earlier in a 1–0 win at Crystal Palace (October 2001). He netted 64 goals in 177 games for Manchester City but struggled to hold down a first-team place at The Dell. He reached the personal milestones of 125 goals and 400 senior appearances at club level in 2002, the same year he was diagnosed with a form of cancer, but he still continued playing.

ROUSE, Frederick William

Centre-forward: 42 apps. 11 goals.

Born: Cranford, Middlesex, 28 November 1882.
Died: Buckinghamshire, 1953.
Career: Bracknell & District Schools. Southall (1897). High Wycombe (August 1900). Wycombe Wanderers (July 1901). Shepherd's Bush FC (February 1903). Queen's Park Rangers (briefly). Grimsby Town (professional, March 1903). Stoke (£150, April 1904). Everton (£750, November 1906). Chelsea (£1,000, October 1907). ALBION (£250, May 1909). Croydon Common (September 1910). Brentford (August 1911). Slough Town (February 1913, retired, May 1915).

■ A robust player who harried and hassled defenders, Fred Rouse possessed an ability for tricky footwork and had the uncanny ability of being able to stop dead before letting fly with a strong shot. Few defenders could cope with him at his best, but, annoyingly, he tended to have one good day followed by three bad ones, making him a rather inconsistent performer. He played for the Football League in 1905 and 1906 and during his League career averaged a goal every three games, scoring 58 times in 154 outings. He was a huge disappointment at Albion despite making an impressive debut against Stockport County (away) in a Second Division match in September 1909, scoring in a 2–0 win. Rouse was Chelsea's first £1,000 signing when recruited from Stoke in 1907.

ROWLEY, George Arthur

Inside-left: 41 apps. 15 goals.

Born: Wolverhampton, 21 April 1925.
Died: Shrewsbury, 19 December 2002.

Career: Dudley Road & St Peter's Schools, Wolverhampton. Wolverhampton & District Boys. Birmingham County FA (Boys). Wolverhampton Gas Works FC. Manchester United (trialist, 1941). Wolverhampton Wanderers (1942–43). Blakenhall St Luke's. ALBION (amateur, March 1944, professional, May 1944). Guest for Manchester United, Middlesbrough, Brighton and Hove Albion, Lincoln City and Wolves during World War Two. Fulham (December 1948 in exchange for Ernie Shepherd). Leicester City (£14,000, July 1950). Shrewsbury Town (£7,000, June 1958, as player-manager). Sheffield United (manager, July 1968–August 1969). Southend United (manager, March 1970–May 1976). Telford United (assistant manager, 1978–79). Oswestry Town (manager, July 1979–October 1980). He was the first manager in Sheffield United's 80-year history to be sacked (1969).

■ Initially an outside-left, Arthur Rowley was only 16 years and two days old when he made his 'debut' for Manchester United against Liverpool in April 1941, lining up in the same forward-line as his 'big' brother, Jack Rowley. He was subsequently released by Wolves and joined Albion, appearing in his first senior game for the Baggies against Walsall (away) in the Midland Cup, round one (first leg), in April 1944. He scored four goals in 24 League games for Albion (plus a further nine in 16 for the second XI) before his surprise transfer to Fulham. After that he made his own reputation as the most prolific English goalscorer of all-time, netting a record

434 League goals, stretching to 1965, with Shrewsbury Town. It is hard to understand why England 'B' and Football League honours were not followed by a full international cap, as Rowley's marksmanship was so great. He played a leading role in getting first Fulham and then Leicester City promoted to Division One, in 1949 and 1954 respectively, and he had been with Albion in 1948–49 when the Baggies came up with Fulham. He certainly matured with Fulham, developed even greater with Leicester (for whom he rattled in no fewer than 251 goals in 303 League games) and maintained his form at Gay Meadow, netting 152 goals in 236 League appearances, while helping the 'Shrews' win promotion from the Fourth Division in 1959 and playing a vital part in the side that reached the League Cup semi-finals in 1960–61. Even with Southend he gained honours when promotion was forthcoming from Division Four in 1971–72. He was leading scorer in Division Two in 1952–53 and topped the entire League scoring charts in both 1956–57 and 1958–59. His total of 44 in season 1956–57 is still a Leicester record. He was leading scorer for Shrewsbury in five successive seasons and for Leicester on seven separate occasions. He beat Dixie Dean's feat in 1959–60 by scoring 20 or more goals in his 10th successive season – Dean's record was nine (1924–25 to 1932–33 inclusive). How did Manchester United miss him back in 1941 and why did Albion let him go when they did? We shall never know.

RUSHBURY, David Graham

Defender: 31 apps.

Born: Wolverhampton, 20 February 1956.
Career: Tettenhall Road School & St Chad's College, Wolverhampton, ALBION (apprentice, December 1972, professional, July 1974). Sheffield Wednesday (on loan, December 1976, signed for £60,000, January 1977). Swansea City (£60,000, July 1979). Carlisle United (£50,000, August 1981). Gillingham (£15,000, March 1985). Doncaster Rovers (£10,000, July 1985). Cambridge United (on loan, February 1987). Bristol Rovers (February 1987, free transfer, June 1987). Chesterfield (physiotherapist, then caretaker manager, 2001–02 and manager, 2002–03).

Dave Rushbury was a stylish, hard-working defender who occupied positions 2 to 6 inclusive during his professional career. He had one good season with Albion (1974–75) when he replaced Ally Robertson in the middle-line, making his League debut against Millwall (away) in Division Two in October 1974. He also played in 90 Central League games and later helped Swansea City gain promotion from Division Two in 1980–81, and he was with Carlisle when they climbed up from Division Three in 1981–82. He quit senior football in 1987 with around 420 senior appearances under his belt.
* Rushbury's son played for Chesterfield (2002–04).

RUSSELL, Thomas James

Utility forward: 4 apps. one goal.

Born: Walsall, 2 February 1924.
Career: Rushall County School. Brockhouse Works FC. ALBION (amateur, April 1943, professional, August 1944). Kidderminster Harriers (free, October 1948–May 1952). Then local non-League football, retired 1957.

An aggressive player who could fill in any forward position, World War Two certainly disrupted Tom Russell's career with Albion for whom he made his senior debut against Stoke City (home) in the Football League North in November 1943.

RYAN, Reginald Alphonso

Wing-half/Inside-forward: 272 apps. 31 goals.

Born: Dublin, 30 October 1925.
Died: Sheldon, Birmingham, February 1997.
Career: Marino School, Dublin (Gaelic Soccer). Claremont School (Blackpool). Blackpool Boys. Claremont Juniors. Sunbeam Cars FC (Coventry). Sheffield United (trialist, 1941). Jaguar Cars FC (Coventry). Nuneaton Borough. Nottingham Forest (trialist, 1942). Coventry City (amateur, April 1943, professional, August 1944). ALBION (£750, April 1945). Derby County (£3,000, June 1955). Coventry City (September 1958, retired, November 1960). Coventry City (pools organiser 1960–61). ALBION (pools/lottery supervisor, December 1961,

then club's chief scout, September 1962–October 1976). Later scout for Aston Villa, Derby County, Hereford United and Leeds United (up to 1994).

'Paddy' 'Rubberneck' Ryan, who made his Baggies debut against Millwall (away) in the Football League South in November 1945, was a stocky, mobile player, who gave many impressive

displays from both wing-half positions and as an inside-forward for clubs and country. He took time to settle into Albion's team, but once in he stayed and became a very consistent performer, helping the Baggies win promotion from Division Two in 1948–49 and the FA Cup in 1954, when he linked up wonderfully well in centre field with Ray Barlow and Jimmy Dudley. Ryan also scored five

THE WHO'S WHO OF WEST BROMWICH ALBION

goals in 107 Central League games for Albion and after leaving The Hawthorns he skippered Derby County and appeared in 139 games (scoring 31 goals) for the Rams, collecting a Third Division North championship medal in 1956–57. At international level, he won 17 caps (16 for the Republic of Ireland, three goals scored, and one for Northern Ireland) and, all told, in a splendid playing career, he amassed 432 League appearances (234 coming with Albion), registering 70 goals. In 1955 he was in the Third Division North representative side against the South, scoring a penalty in that game. He attended The Hawthorns regularly until his death in 1997.

SAKIRI, Artim

Midfield: 11+22 apps. 1 goal.

Born: Macedonia, 23 September 1973.
Career: Halmstad (1989, professional 1991). Gorica (1992). Melatyaspor (1995). CSKA Sofia (1999). ALBION (£70,000, July 2003). Shanghai Shenhua (on loan, March 2005). Burnley (July 2005).

■ After three months of negotiations, Albion manager Gary Megson finally signed the Macedonian international attacking midfielder Artim Sakiri on a two-year contract (with a 12-month option at the end of that) in July 2003. Having had the pleasure of scoring for his country in a Euro 2004 qualifying game against England at Southampton in October 2002, Sakiri, as captain, gained his 55th full cap in the return fixture against England in September 2003 (later

taking his tally of international appearances to over 65). A strong, powerful competitor with a great engine, Sakiri – owing to minor registration problems (work permit etc.) – had to wait until 16 August 2003 before making his senior debut for Albion, celebrating the occasion with a wonderful equalising goal in a 4–1 televised League home win over Burnley. He was mainly used as a substitute by manager Gary Megson, but played his part in bringing Premiership football back to The Hawthorns. Unfortunately, he did not fit into new manager Bryan Robson's plans and moved to China after making nine first and 33 second-team appearances for Albion.

SAMBROOKE, Clifford Leslie

Inside-centre-forward: 2 apps. 1 goal.

Born: Smethwick, 5 January 1895.
Died: c.1970.
Career: West Smethwick & Shreland Hall Schools. Smethwick Manor. Kidderminster Harriers. Oldbury Town (1914) Coventry City (briefly 1915). Served in the Army during World War One. ALBION (January 1919). Oldbury Town (April 1919). Coventry City (free, August 1919). Nuneaton Town (June 1920). Wellington Town (1921). Stalybridge Celtic (May 1922). Redditch (March 1923). Nuneaton Town (August 1923, retired, May 1924, following a broken leg mishap). Later worked in a Coventry factory.

■ Cliff Sambrooke was a more than useful inside or centre-forward, who broke his right leg playing for Coventry against Blackpool in November 1919. He made his debut for Albion as a guest against Wolves in a Midland Victory League game in March 1919 and went on to score nine goals in 19 League games for Stalybridge. Sambrooke was a private in the Army during World War One.

SANDERS, James Albert

Goalkeeper: 301 apps.

Born: Hackney, London, 5 July 1920.
Died: Tamworth, 11 August 2003.
Career: Hackney Grammar School. North London Boys. Longlands FC (London). Charlton Athletic (amateur, July 1940, professional, September 1941). Guest for

ALBION, Chelsea, Liverpool, Southampton and West Ham United during World War Two. ALBION (£2,250, November 1945). Kettering Town (on loan, 1953). Coventry City (free, June 1958). Hinckley Athletic (August 1959, retired, June 1960). Became a publican, first in Derby, later in Birmingham (Crown and Cushion, Perry Barr), and then ran a hotel in Solihull. He was later confined to a wheelchair.

■ Jimmy Sanders was a very consistent goalkeeper, never acrobatic but always steady and capable. He was something of an expert at stopping penalties, preventing 25 from entering his net during his 19-year career. He was invalided out of the RAF during World War Two after many operational flights as an Air Gunner. In fact, he flew on 120 operations against enemy forces at home and overseas before being shot down. His injuries yielded partly to treatment but he was in terrible pain and thus his RAF days were halted, having been told he would never play football again. 'Nonsense' thought Sanders, and he proved everyone wrong by regaining full fitness inside 18 months. He joined Albion and made his debut against Millwall away in the South League in November 1945 (as a World War Two guest), signing permanently four days later. He went on to appear in almost 400 games for the Baggies, winning an FA Cup winners' medal in 1954, five years after helping the Baggies regain their top flight status as Second Division runners-up. He also played in 101 Central League games and scored one goal – direct from a corner against Derby County reserves in 1946–47. He was at The Valley with the great Sam Bartram but chose to leave Charlton knowing full well that he would never oust such a fine 'keeper. He was right again, as his career from 1945 to 1959 clearly indicates. In later life, Sanders, such a jovial character, always wore a dicky bow and displayed his 1954 FA Cup winning medal on a chain around his neck.

SANDFORD, Edward Albert

Inside-forward: 317 apps. 75 goals.

Born: Handsworth, Birmingham, 22 October 1910.
Died: Great Barr, Birmingham, May 1995.
Career: Wattville Road & Holyhead Road Schools (Handsworth). Tantany Athletic. Overend Wesley. Birmingham Carriage Works FC. Smethwick Highfield. ALBION (amateur, October 1929, professional, May 1930–March 1939). Sheffield United (£1,500). Morris Commercial FC (April 1941, retired, May 1943). ALBION (coach, 1950–57, club scout 1961–67). Ran a café almost next to The Hawthorns for many years. He was the nephew of the former Albion player 'Abe' Jones.

■ Teddy Sandford had 10 fine seasons with Albion. He arrived at the club when there was an abundance of inside-forward talent at The Hawthorns and spent his first term playing with the reserves before making a scoring debut in a 3–2 win at Preston North End in November 1930 (Division Two). The season ended in triumph for both Albion and Sandford with that wonderful FA Cup and promotion double. A quiet player, never flashy, Sandford was, nevertheless, an excellent goalscoring inside-left who was exceedingly quick to pounce and dispossess an opponent and in turn found it hard to get the ball back! He had an enviable physique, which held him in good stead later in his career when he lined up at centre-half, to good effect. An FA Cup winner at Wembley when still only 20 (1931), he collected a runners'-up prize, despite scoring a fine goal against Sheffield Wednesday four years later, and in between times (1932) he was capped by England against Wales. He also scored four goals in 24 Central League games for Albion.

SANKEY, John

Wing-half: 290 apps. 27 goals.

Born: Moulton, Cheshire, 19 March 1912.
Died: Handsworth, Birmingham, January 1985.
Career: Moulton Church of England School. Moulton Wanderers (1927). Winsford United (1928). ALBION (professional, November 1930). Northampton Town (£500, October 1945). Walsall (World War Two guest 1945–46). Hereford United (free, August 1947, retired, May 1953, appointed assistant trainer-coach at Hereford, 1953–54). ALBION (coach, 1955–64, then scout 1965–66). Left football, to work at a cycle factory in Handsworth.

■ 'Jack' Sankey was an industrious and highly efficient wing-half or inside-forward, who let the ball do most of the work. His overall play was characterised by some powerful long-range shooting, and he could defend as well as attack. He made his senior debut in an FA Cup tie away at Chelsea in January 1934, after spending more than three playing in the second team. He eventually took over from Jimmy Edwards in the first XI. From then until the outbreak of World War Two, Sankey's senior outings piled up steadily, and when he left The Hawthorns (in 1945) his total of appearances were close on 300, 130 coming during the hostilities. He also played in 120 second XI games (26 goals scored), gaining a Central League championship medal in 1932–33 and helping the team retain the trophy the following season. He was granted a Testimonial Match (Hereford United against Albion) in 1954 and around 4,500 fans saw the Bulls win 10–5.

SANTOS, Georges

Defender/midfield: 8 apps.

Born: Marseille, France, 15 August 1970.
Career: Toulon, France (professional). Tranmere Rovers (free, July 1998). ALBION (£25,000, March 2000). Sheffield United (free, July 2000). Grimsby Town (September 2002). Ipswich Town (free, July 2003). Queen's Park Rangers (free, August 2004).

■ A rugged 6ft 3in, 14st defender who was a short-term capture by Baggies' manager Gary Megson towards the end of

the 1999–2000 season, Georges Santos played well in the eight games in which he featured, with his debut coming in the 2–1 defeat at Manchester City 48 hours after arriving. Two years later, during Sheffield United's League home game against Albion (March 2002), Santos was sent off soon after coming on as a 'sub' in the notorious abandoned contest, which Albion 'won' 3–0. He was voted Grimsby's 'Player of the Year' in 2002–03.

SAUNDERS, Douglas George

Outside-left: 6 apps. 3 goals.

Born: Winson Green, Birmingham, 22 April 1927.
Career: Dudley Road & Rotten Park Schools. Handsworth Victoria. West Bromwich Hawthorne FC (1941). ALBION (amateur, November 1942, professional, May 1945). Banbury Spencer (free, May 1948).

■ A practical left-winger, proportionately built, Doug Saunders had to contest the number 11 shirt with international Joe Johnson. He made his

Albion debut against Birmingham (home) in the Football League North in May 1945 and later played in one FA Cup tie against Cardiff City (January 1946). He also scored eight goals in 28 Central League games.

SAUNDERS, Sidney

Outside-left: 2 apps.

Born: West Bromwich, 1 June 1872.
Died: Birmingham, April 1939.
Career: Summerfield Park School. Unity Gas FC. ALBION (professional, May 1895). Birmingham Centinels (June 1896).

■ A 'Titch' of a player, Sid Saunders was, in fact, fourth-choice left-winger for Albion during the 1895–96 season, despite playing in two of the first three matches of the League programme. He made his senior debut against Aston Villa (away) in Division One in September 1895.

SAUNDERS, Wilfred William

Goalkeeper: 34 apps.

Born: Grimsbury near Banbury, Oxon, 20 April 1916.
Career: Banbury and Middleton Cheney Schools. Banbury Spencer (May 1935). ALBION (amateur, March 1938, professional, May 1938). Guest for Luton Town and Watford during World War Two. Banbury Spencer (May 1946, retired, 1950).

■ A strong, capable goalkeeper, Bill Saunders deputised for Jimmy Adams during his association with Albion. He

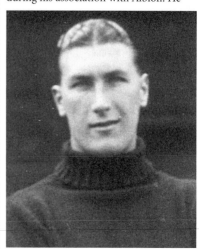

made his League debut against Swansea town (away) in Division Two in December 1938. He also played in 35 Central League games.

SAVAGE, George

Forward: 2 apps.

Born: Aston, Birmingham, 12 August 1903.
Died: Derby, June 1968.
Career: Aston Cross & Rocky Lane Schools. Farm Street Unity (Hockley). West Bromwich United. Willenhall (1920). ALBION (professional, May 1921). Wrexham (£100, April 1922). Alfreton (free, 1924, retired through injury, 1926). ALBION (coach, 1948–49). Thereafter employed as a sportsmaster at a Derbyshire School for over 20 years.

■ A reserve utility player, George Savage could fill in precisely anywhere – even goal! Unfortunately, he failed to impress with Albion, but as a Wrexham player, besides his 111 League outings, he also gained two Welsh Cup winners' medals (1924 and 1925). He made his League debut against Bolton Wanders (home) in Division One in November 1921 and also played in 25 second XI matches, scoring five goals.

SCIMECA, Ricardo

Utility: 30+6 apps.

Born: Leamington Spa, 13 June 1975.
Career: Aston Villa (apprentice, June 1991, professional, July 1993). Nottingham Forest

(£3million, July 1999). Leicester City (free, July 2003). ALBION (£100,000, May 2004).

■ After almost 100 appearances in eight years with Aston Villa, Ricardo Scimeca became David Platt's first signing as manager of Forest and was appointed captain in his first season at The City Ground. Honoured by England at 'B' and under-21 levels (9 caps won for the latter category), he added a further 166 appearances to his tally with the Foxes and after a season with Leicester City he stayed in the premiership by joining Albion for a cut-down fee. A player with excellent skills, good control and an appetite for hard work, he can play in defence or midfield, preferring the former.

SCREEN, John

Full-back: 1 app.

Born: Oldbury, 3 January 1915.
Died: Wolverhampton, 1968.
Career: Causeway Green Junior & Senior Schools (Oldbury). Oldbury Parish Church. Smethwick Highfield. ALBION (amateur, September 1933, professional, May 1934). Wrexham (£250, July 1939). Banbury Spencer (free, October 1946, retired, May 1949). Wolverhampton Wanderers (trainer, 1950s).

■ 'Jack' Screen was a valuable reserve full-back, who won junior international honours for England in 1934. Nicknamed 'Window-Screen', he made his League debut for Albion against Middlesbrough (home) in Division One in January 1935. He also played in 73 Central League games for the Baggies, helping them win the title in 1934–35.

SETTERS, Maurice Edgar

Wing-half/Inside-forward: 132 apps. 10 goals.

Born: Honiton, Devon, 16 December 1936.
Career: Honiton & Cullompton Schools. Bridport Juniors. Exeter City (amateur, June 1952, professional, January 1954). ALBION (£3,000, January 1955). Manchester United (£30,000, January 1960). Stoke City (November 1964). Coventry City (November 1967). Charlton Athletic (January 1970). Doncaster Rovers (manager, July 1971–November 1974). Sheffield Wednesday (coach under Jack

Charlton, 1980). Rotherham United (assistant manager/coach, 1982–84). Newcastle United (chief scout, 1984–85). Republic of Ireland (assistant manager/coach, 1986–89). Now retired, living in Bawtry near Doncaster.

■ With his bandy-legs and crew-cut hair, Maurice 'mo-mo' Setters looked what he was on the field of play, a real terrier, as hard as nails, determined, fearless and even reckless at times. After winning schoolboy honours as a youngster (aged 15), he went on to gain one youth cap for England and 16 at under-23 level, also playing for the FA XI and Young England (1958). He appeared in 120 First Division games for Albion, making his Baggies debut against

Huddersfield Town at Leeds Road in Division One in November 1955. He also had 29 second-team outings and after leaving West Bromwich played in 159 League matches for United. With his other four League clubs he added a further 155 appearances, ending his League career with 500 to his name. He also played in over 70 Cup ties. Setters collected an FA Cup winners' medal with United in 1963, and actually made his senior debut (for Exeter) in March 1954, playing his last game 16 years later with Charlton. He occupied seven different positions during his playing days, but believed he performed best in midfield. He made 500 club appearances during his senior career.

SHAKESPEARE, Craig Robert

Midfield: 120+8 apps. 16 goals.

Born: Birmingham, 26 October 1963.
Career: Walsall (apprentice, September 1979, professional, November 1981). Sheffield Wednesday (£300,000, June 1989). ALBION (£275,000, February 1990). Grimsby Town (£115,000, July 1993). Scunthorpe United (July 1997). Telford United (1998). Blakenhall (August 1999). Solihull Borough (briefly). ALBION (coach, September 1999).

■ Craig Shakespeare played with ex-Albion striker Imre Varadi at Hillsborough and made just 21 appearances for the Owls following his big-money transfer from Walsall. 'Shakey' had earlier appeared in well over 350 games and scored 59 goals for the Saddlers. A positive, hard-working midfielder, he scored on his debut for Albion against Oxford United (away) in February 1990, which they won 1–0, and later became the team's penalty-taker, netting twice from the spot in Albion's first ever Third Division game at home to Exeter City in August 1991 (won 6–3). He lost his place in the side halfway through the 1992–93 season (under Ossie Ardiles' management) and was later re-signed by manager Alan Buckley for Grimsby Town, for whom he made 121 appearances. He also played in 24 Central League games for Albion (one goal).

SHAW, Cecil Ernest

Full-back: 251 apps. 14 goals.

Born: Mansfield, 22 June 1911.
Died: Handsworth, Birmingham, January 1977.
Career: Mansfield & District Schools. Mansfield Invicta. Blidsworth Juniors. Rainworth Church FC. Rufford Colliery FC. Wolverhampton Wanderers (professional, February 1930). ALBION (£7,500, December 1936). Guest for Nottingham Forest and Blackpool during World War Two. Hereford United (free, June 1947, retired, May 1949). Later refereed in Oldbury & District Leagues (1959–61). ALBION (scout, 1961–64).

■ Cecil Shaw was a tough full-back, a resolute and robust tackler, who played in some 183 competitive games for Wolves

before joining Albion for a then record fee of £7,500, which was paid in two installments. He gained a first-team place at Molineux in late 1932, and performed with such consistency and reliability that up to mid-September 1936 he had missed only one senior match, making 126 consecutive appearances in the full-back position. He was skipper at Wolves and their penalty expert. Alas, he missed his first spot-kick for Albion against Coventry in an FA Cup tie in February 1937. A solid man, able to withstand any challenge, Shaw went straight into Albion's League side, making his debut against Liverpool at Anfield in December 1936. He held his place comfortably up until World War Two and partly through the hostilities. He was one of only a handful of players to have served Albion before, during and after the hostilities, between 1939–45. Towards the end of the 1930s Shaw partnered his namesake George Shaw (no relation) at full-back for Albion, and in 1935 he represented the Football League and was reserve for the full England team on two occasions. He also played in 16 Central League games for the Baggies, having earlier helped Wolves gain promotion from the Second Division in 1932–33.

SHAW, Charles Richard

Outside-left: 1 app. 1 goal.

Born: Willenhall, 18 November 1862.
Died: February 1931.
Career: Essington & Willenhall Schools. Willenhall Pickwick. Wolverhampton Wanderers. Walsall Swifts. ALBION (amateur, August–September 1888). Walsall Town Swifts (October 1888–93). Wednesfield Star (1894–95). Became a licensee in Wolverhampton.

■ An eager-beaver left-winger, Charlie Shaw came to Albion on a month's trial, playing just one senior game and scoring a goal against Burnley (home) in Division One in September 1888, (won 4–3). He spent most of his career playing for the Swifts (Walsall) and represented the Staffordshire FA XI and the Birmingham FA XI in 1888–89.

SHAW, George David

Striker: 78+18 apps. 20 goals.
Born: Huddersfield, 11 October 1948.

Career: Rawthorpe Secondary Modern School (Huddersfield). Huddersfield Town (apprentice, July 1965, professional, January 1967). Oldham Athletic (September 1969). ALBION (£77,000, March 1973). Oldham Athletic (on loan, November 1975, signed for £20,000, December 1975, retired through injury, January 1978). Became a publican in Oldham, later a factory worker in Huddersfield.

■ David Shaw was a dangerous striker, full of vim and vigour, but a player who perhaps lacked ball control in tight situations. Nicknamed 'Super-sub' by the Albion fans, he made his Baggies debut against Manchester United (away) in Division One in March 1973, as a substitute. He also scored 10 goals in 18 Central League games for the Baggies. He spent 11 years in the game, having his League debut for Huddersfield against Birmingham City in August 1967. In all he amassed a total of 319 League appearances and scored 109 goals. He helped Oldham win promotion from the Fourth Division in 1970–71, but, after rejoining the Latics, was forced to retire through injury. A testimonial match was arranged for him by Oldham in 1978. He was also a very capable cricketer.

SHAW, George Edward

Full-back: 425 apps. 11 goals.

Born: Swinton, 13 October 1899.
Died: Doncaster, 10 March 1973.

Career: Swinton Schools. Bolton-on-Deane FC (1914). Rossington Main Colliery (1915). Doncaster Rovers (professional, August 1919). Gillingham (March 1920). Doncaster Rovers (September 1922). Huddersfield Town (£1,000, February 1924). ALBION (£4,100, November 1926). Stalybridge Celtic (free, player-manager, May 1938). Worcester City (player-manager, March 1939). FC Foriana. Malta (player-manager/coach, 1948–51). Retired, June 1951. Later worked at Hamworth Colliery near Doncaster.

■ Nicknamed 'Teapot' and the 'Singer', George 'Cocky' Shaw, like several of his

Albion contemporaries, gave long and loyal service to the club. Admirably built for a full-back, he was dominant in the air, strong on the round and decidedly safe and sure with his kicking. He was a grand volleyer of the ball and a useful penalty-taker, as well as a free kick specialist. Shaw was an occasional member of Huddersfield's League championship-winning sides of 1923–24, 1924–25 and 1925–26, making a total of 24 appearances in those three seasons. As an Albion player he gained an FA Cup winners' medal in 1931, a runners'-up prize in 1935, received an England cap against Scotland at Wembley in 1932, had an outing with the Football League XI and went on two FA Tours (to Belgium, France and Spain in 1929, and to Canada in 1931). After making his Albion debut against Sheffield United at Bramall Lane in December 1926 (just 48 hours after signing), Shaw missed only five of the next 300 League games (up to January 1934). When he said farewell to The Hawthorns fans, shortly after the end of the 1937–38 season, his tally of senior appearances for the Baggies was well over the 400 mark. He also played in 32 Central League games (2 goals). He cost Albion a then record fee when signed from Huddersfield and was worth every penny, and more. An ex-Naval man, he loved singing, was also a dab-hand at mat-making and was nicknamed 'Teapot' in the dressing room as he was always seen serving up the tea!

SHEARMAN, Benjamin Walter

Outside-left: 143 apps. 18 goals.

Born: Lincoln, 12 December 1884.
Died: October 1958.
Career: St Mary's School (Lincoln). Sheffield & District Schools. Attercliffe (1899). High Hazels (1900). Worksop Town (1902). Rotherham Town (semi-professional, August 1906). Bristol City (professional, August 1909). ALBION (£100, June 1911). Nottingham Forest (£250, July 1919). Gainsborough Trinity (August 1920). Norton Woodseats (part-time player-trainer-coach, retired, May 1938). Worked briefly for an insurance company after World War Two.

■ Ben Shearman was an elusive outside-left, quick off the mark and strikingly

accurate with his deep crosses, whether hit high or low from the touchline. He replaced Amos Lloyd on Albion's left flank and was a consistent performer, until Howard Gregory and Jack Crisp came along to contest the wide position, pushing Shearman out into the cold. Shearman appeared in over 140 senior games for Albion, including the 1912 FA Cup final and replay against Barnsley. He played for the Football League XI on two occasions (1911) and, during his career, amassed more than 250 games. His Albion League debut was against Notts County (home) in Division One in September 1911, when he scored in a 2–1 win. Sheraman served in the Army (SARB, at the Rammilles Barracks, Aldershot) during World War One.

SHELDON, Arthur Lionel

Full-back: 1 app.

Born: West Bromwich, 17 November 1871.
Died: June 1936.
Career: Walsall Street Schools West Bromwich. Smethwick Carriage Works. ALBION (amateur, July 1892). Worcester Rovers (August 1893). Played cricket, as an all-rounder, for Warwickshire's second team.

■ A stocky, broad-shouldered full-back, Arthur Sheldon had one season with Albion, appearing in one senior game against Stoke (away) in the Bass Charity Cup in March 1893.

SHEPHERD, Ernest

Outside-left: 4 apps.

Born: Wombwell, Yorkshire, 14 August 1919.

Died: 1 March 2001.
Career: Dearne Valley Schools. Bradford City (groundstaff, 1934). Fulham (amateur, August 1935, professional, August 1936). Guest for Bradford City, Brentford and Huddersfield Town during World War Two. ALBION (December 1948, in exchange deal involving Arthur Rowley). Hull City (£4,500, March 1949). Queen's Park Rangers (July 1950). Coached in Iceland (1953–54). Hasting United (July 1956). Bradford Park Avenue (trainer, 1957–58). Southend United (trainer, 1959, then assistant manager 1966–67, general manager 1969–72). Orient (physio-coach and also assistant manager for a while, between 1973–76). Coached in Dubai (mid-1970s) and the United Arab Emirates (from 1977). Retired out of football in 1984, aged 65.

■ Ernie Shepherd was a forceful, goalscoring left-winger, who served Queen's Park Rangers splendidly for six seasons, appearing in 219 League games and netting 51 goals. Earlier in 1948–49 he had helped Fulham, Albion and Hull win promotion from their respective Divisions. He scored with his first kick for Hull after joining the Tigers from The Hawthorns. He made his debut for the Baggies against Nottingham Forest (home) in Division Two in December 1948. He top-scored for Bradford in 1944–45 with 26 goals.

SHEPPARD, Richard James

Goalkeeper: 54 apps.

Born: Bristol, 14 February 1945.
Died: Bristol, 18 October 1998.
Career: Filton Avenue Schools. Bristol Boys. Gloucestershire Schools. ALBION (apprentice, August 1960, professional, February 1963). Bristol Rovers (£2,000, June 1969). Torquay United (on loan December 1973). Fulham (on loan, 1974–75). Weymouth (July 1975). Portway FC, Bristol (Western League, September 1975, retired, October 1975, on medical advice).

■ Dick Sheppard was a capable goalkeeper of sound build and splendid reflexes, who was somewhat unfortunate to be with Albion at the same time as Tony Millington, Ray Potter and John Osborne. He did make over 50 first-team appearances, his senior debut being against Sunderland (home) in Division

One in October 1965. Two years later he collected a runners'-up prize at Wembley when Queen's Park Rangers beat Albion in the 1967 League Cup final. He made 155 second XI appearances for the Baggies before going on to play over 150 times for Bristol Rovers. A fractured skull, suffered in 1973, eventually led to him retiring at the age of 30. He helped Bristol Rovers win the Watney Cup in 1972 and in May 1979 was granted a testimonial (Rovers v Albion).

SHINTON, Frederick

Centre-forward: 68 apps. 46 goals.

Born: Wednesbury, 7 March 1883.
Died: Lancaster, 11 April 1923.
Career: St James's School, Wednesbury. Hawthorn Villa (1898). Moxley White Star (1899). Wednesbury Old Athletic (1900). Hednesfield Town (August 1903). ALBION (professional, April 1905). Leicester Fosse (£150, November 1907). Bolton Wanderers (£1,000, August 1910). Leicester Fosse (£750, January 1911, retired through ill-health, May 1912).

■ Fred Shinton, who weighed 14st 7lb at his peak, was a deadly marksman who scored a goal every 125 minutes of League football for Albion during his eighteen-month association with the club. A very sporting character, he played with dash and tenacity, he had a never-say-die attitude and simply loved scoring goals! Nicknamed 'Appleyard' and 'Tickler' by his teammates, Shinton had perhaps one of the best overall Albion scoring records in terms of goals-per-game. In the first half of season 1906–07 he registered 26 goals in just 21 matches, including three 'fours'. He had a superb knack of finding the net. Recruited by Albion following the problems the club had had with the centre-forward position when no fewer than six different players had been tried there, Shinton fitted in a treat. He became a huge hit with the fans after an excellent display on his debut against his future club Bolton Wanderers (home) in Division Two in April 1905. He also played in a handful of second XI matches. When he left The Hawthorn several hundred supporters were so upset that they rebelled outside the ground. Bob Pailor finally came along to 'replace' Shinton, but not after several

other centre-forwards had been tried, all to no avail. But how do you replace a 'star' overnight? In 1909–10 he was the Second Division's leading scorer with 31 goals in 38 matches for Leicester Fosse.

SHORE, Edward William

Full-back: 5 apps.

Born: Kings Hill, Wednesbury, 12 October 1891.
Died: West Bromwich, 1960.
Career: Kings Hill School. Wednesbury United (1906). Willenhall Swifts (1910). ALBION (£50, March 1913). Stourbridge (free, August 1919–May 1921).

■ A junior international full-back (capped in 1913), Ted Shore was a classy performer, cool in demeanour, who spent six years with Albion as reserve to Joe Smith and the legendary Jesse Pennington. He made his League debut against Liverpool (away) in March 1915. He played over 50 times for the second XI.

SHORT, John Samuel

Inside-forward: 41 apps. 17 goals.

Born: Norbrigg, Chesterfield, 10 May 1903.
Died: January 1955.
Career: St Thomas' School (Newbold). Chesterfield Youth Club (1919). Seamore FC (1922). ALBION (amateur, February 1923, professional, January 1924, retired through injury, May 1931, to become Albion's trainer, staying with the club until 1946).

■ Sammy Short was a goalscoring inside-forward, a shade on the small side, but a player who was always willing to improvise. He made his senior debut against Birmingham (home) in Division One in September 1926, although he first appeared against Bury (home) a year earlier but the match was abandoned because of heavy rain. He netted 103 Central League goals for Albion (in 131 games) and was associated with the club for 23 years, winning junior international honours in 1923 as well as netting 101 goals in 131 Central League appearances, helping the team win the championship in 1923–24 and then gaining a winners' medal in the same competition in 1926–27, when he top-scored with 27 goals in only 20 outings. After retiring, Short was trainer of Albion's second team and occasionally the third team.

SIGURDSSON. Larus Orri

Defender: 114+14 apps. 1 goal.

Born: Akureyri, Iceland, 4 June 1973.
Career: Thor FC, Iceland (professional from 1991). Stoke City (£150,000, October 1994). ALBION (£325,000, September 1999, retired through injury, November 2004).

■ Defender Larus Sigurdsson won 42 full caps for Iceland, plus 16 at under-21 level and five as a youth-team player. A solid, right-footed defender who effectively occupied the right-back or centre-half positions, he made 228 appearances for Stoke before joining Albion where he replaced Daryl Burgess, making his Baggies debut in a 2-2 League home draw with Blackburn Rovers in September 1999. Unfortunately, the 'Iceman' or 'Siggy' was stretchered off in manager Gary Megson's first game in charge at Stockport in March 2000. Diagnosed as a cruciate ligament injury, he fought long and hard to regain full fitness and returned in February 2001. He then appeared in 43 League games the following season as the Baggies gained promotion to the Premiership and in 2002–03, mainly as partner to Darren Moore and Phil Gilchrist at the heart of the defence, he had 29 outings in the top flight. However, he suffered from badly damaged cartilage in his left knee at Crystal Palace in September 2003, came back for one more game in the second XI against Aston Villa in March 2004, but he knew it was to be his last in a Baggies shirt and seven months later called it a day after five years at The Hawthorns. His only goal for the club came in a resounding 5–0 home win over Portsmouth in February 2002. He played in over 20 second-team games for Albion.

SIMMONS, Charles

Centre-forward: 193 apps. 81 goals.

Born: West Bromwich, 9 September 1878.
Died: Wednesbury, 12 December 1937.
Career: Beeches Road School (West Bromwich). Trinity Victoria (1893). Oldbury Town (May 1896). Worcester Rovers (August 1897). ALBION (professional, April 1898). West Ham United (£700, July 1904). ALBION (£600, May 1905). Chesterfield Town (March 1907). Wellington Town. Royal Rovers (Canada, October 1910, retired, 1922). Later returned to West Bromwich where he became a publican, having learned the trade initially in 1909.

■ 'Chippy' Simmons was a regular scorer for Albion from either inside-right or centre-forward. After making his League debut against Burnley (away) in Division One in November 1898, he teamed up splendidly with, first, Billy Bassett and later Jimmy McLean and Fred Buck, and when he returned to The Hawthorns for a second spell he did marvellously well alongside Fred Shinton in Albion's attack. Indeed, in season 1905–06 between them Simmons and Shinton netted no fewer than 34 goals in League competition. A player with a lethal shot, Simmons had plenty of pace and craft and he always seemed to find plenty of space as well. He was a big favourite with the fans, especially the ladies, and it is reported that he had a personal fan club. He scored

75 League goals for Albion (eight seasons), winning a Second Division championship medal in 1902 when he top-scored with a total of 23 goals. This same year he figured in an international trial and later represented The Professionals of the South against The Amateurs of the South (1905). He was an England reserve on three occasions during 1901–02. The first Albion player to score at The Hawthorns, equalising Steve Bloomer's effort for Derby County in the opening League game at the ground on 3 September 1900, Simmons also played several times for the Baggies second XI during the 1906–07 season and he also scored in Albion's 5–0 Staffordshire Cup final victory over Burslem Port Vale in 1900.

SIMPSON, George

Outside-left: 24 apps. 6 goals.

Born: Sheffield, 11 August 1883.
Died: Sheffield, January 1958.
Career: Attercliffe School (Sheffield). Jarrow FC (South Yorkshire). Sheffield Wednesday (amateur, August 1901, professional, March 1902). ALBION (£850, March 1909, signed with Harry Burton). North Shields (£50, October 1910). Served in army during World War One, retired from football on returning home, April 1918. Became a licensee in Sheffield.

■ An outside-left whose chief attributes were speed and a penchant for clever dribbling, George Simpson gained an FA Cup winners' medal with Wednesday, heading the match-winning goal against Everton in the final (1907). Earlier in his career, in 1904, he had collected a First Division championship medal and in seven years' association with the Owls made 142 League appearances and netted 28 goals. He joined Albion with full-back 'Harry' Burton and made his debut against Gainsborough Trinity (away) in the Second Division in April 1909. He played in over 20 second XI games for the Baggies.

SIMPSON, Terence John Norman

Left-half: 77 apps. 4 goals.

Born: Southampton, 8 October 1938.
Career: Park Hall School (Southampton). Southampton & District Boys.

Southampton (amateur, July 1955, professional, June 1957). Peterborough United (£5,000, June 1962). ALBION (£6,000, May 1963). Walsall (£2,000, March 1967). Gillingham (free, July 1968, player-coach, June 1969, retired, May 1971, following a broken leg). Now living in Southampton.

■ Terry Simpson was a durable left-half who later tried his luck at right-back. A strong tackler who loved to go forward, he amassed 226 League appearances during his career, including 50 for Walsall and 45 for Peterborough, as well as 71 for Albion. He scored a total of 16 goals. His Albion debut was against Leicester City (home) on the opening day of the 1963–64 First Division season. He also scored seven goals in 78 Central League games for the Baggies.

SINCLAIR, Frank Mohammed

Defender: 6 apps. 1 goal.

Born: Lambeth, London, 3 December 1971.
Career: Chelsea (apprentice, April 1988, professional, May 1990). ALBION (on loan, December 1991–January 1992). Leicester City (£2 million, August 1998). Burnley (free, June 2004).

■ A Jamaican international defender (22 caps gained by 2003), Frank Sinclair had the misfortune to get himself sent off (at Exeter) in only his second game in an Albion shirt (December 1991), having earlier made an impressive debut against

Bradford City (away). An FA Cup winner with Chelsea (1997) and twice a League Cup winner with Leicester (1998 and 2000), he is strong, determined and resolute. He made 218 appearances for Chelsea and in season 2003–04 reached the milestone of 200 outings for Leicester.

SINFIELD, Marc Russell

Midfielder/forward: 1 app.

Born: Cheshunt, Herts, 24 March 1974.
Career: Rosedale Youth Club. Wimbledon (schoolboy forms, 1989). Cheshunt (March 1990). ALBION (apprentice, June 1990, professional, April 1992, released, May 1993). Later with Enfield (mid-1990s).

■ After a first-team game against Evesham in July 1992, versatile reserve Marc Sinfield made his Albion debut against Mansfield Town (away) in the Autoglass Trophy in January 1993, doing well in a 1–0 win. He also played in 28 Central League games during his three years at The Hawthorns.

SINGLETON, Martin David

Midfield: 16+5 apps. 1 goal.

Born: Banbury, Oxfordshire, 2 August 1963.
Career: Banbury & District Schools. Coventry City (apprentice, July 1979, professional, August 1981). Bradford City (£20,000, December 1984). ALBION (£30,000, December 1986). Northampton Town (free, November 1987). Walsall (free, September 1990–April 1991).

■ A former England youth international (six caps gained and two goals scored between 1981–82), Martin Singleton made 28 appearances for Coventry before moving to Bradford City in 1984. He switched to Albion halfway through the 1986–87 season but found it increasingly difficult to get a game in the first XI. A blonde midfielder, eager and spirited in his play, he played in the Bradford-Lincoln League game in May 1985 when fire savaged Valley Parade. He was a Third Division championship winner that season, appearing in 17 League games. He made his Albion debut against Reading (home) in Division Two in December 1986 and also played in 20 second-team fixtures for the club. He was plagued by injury during the late '80s to the early '90s.

SKOUBO, Morten

Forward: 0+2 apps.

Born: Struer, Denmark, 30 June 1980.
Career: FC Midtjylland, Denmark (semi-professional, August 1997). FC Copenhagan (professional, August 2001). Borussia Moenchengladbach, Germany (£1.7 million, August 2002). ALBION (trialist, December 2003, signed on loan, January–May 2004). Returned to Borussia Moenchengladbach (for season 2004–05).

■ A well-built, 6ft 3in tall and 13st 8lb Danish international striker, with one full and two under-21 caps to his credit, Morten Strouba joined Albion (at the same time as fellow striker Delroy Facey), early in 2004, to boost the first-team squad. He made his 'English' League debut for the Baggies as a second-half substitute in a 3–0 defeat at Preston in

early February and later scored four times in eight second XI games. Prior to his move to The Hawthorns, Skoubo did very well in the Danish Super League, scoring over 30 goals including 24 in 54 games for FC Midtjylland and helping them finish third in 2001. He also played in the UEFA Cup, but his season in the tough and physical German Bundesliga (21 outings) was not a success as he struggled with his form and fitness.

SMITH, Andrew Walter

Inside-forward/centre-half: 81 apps. 22 goals.

Born: Camberwell, London, 4 April 1890.
Died: Dorset, 3 March 1968.
Career: Camberwell & Southwark Council Schools, Langley Green Juniors (Birmingham). Crosswell's Brewery

(1907). Birmingham (amateur, August 1912, professional, April 1914). Manchester City (guest, 1914–18). Birmingham (free, August 1918). ALBION (£100, July 1919). Stoke (£1,500, March 1923). Wigan Borough (free, October 1923). Bournemouth (September 1924, retired, May 1925). Later ran a catering business in Poole.

■ A smart, deliberate inside-right or centre-forward, Andy Smith could also do justice to the centre-half berth where he played as a 'Policeman'. He was a good, clean header of the ball and his ground work was competent and trusty. He won a First Division championship medal with Albion in 1920 and scored both goals when the Baggies beat Tottenham 2–0 in the FA Charity Shield game in London that year. He played over 80 games for Albion, 54 for the Blues and five for Stoke. His League debut was against Oldham Athletic (home) in a First Division game in August 1919.

SMITH, Andrew Wilbour

Forward: 25 apps 8 goals.

Born: Slamanan, Stirlingshire, 15 May 1879.
Died: Glasgow, 7 September 1960.
Career: Slamanan & Cambuslang Schools. East Stirling (1895). Vale of Garron (1897). Stoke (professional, April 1898). ALBION (£50, September 1900). Newton Heath (£75, January 1903). Bristol Rovers (free, September 1903). Millwall (£50, February 1906). Swindon Town (free, August 1906). Leyton (March 1907). Bristol Rovers (briefly). Albion Rovers (trialist). Wednesbury Old Athletic (October 1910). Brierley Hill Alliance (May 1912, retired, May 1914). Returned to Scotland after World War One where he worked for a steel company and also in the docks as a labourer.

■ Andrew 'Scottie' Smith was a grand all-round footballer who could occupy any forward position. Always a hard worker and likely to figure on the scoresheet every game he played, he spent three years with Albion but never really established himself in the first team, although he did score on his debut against Blackburn Rovers (away) in Division One in October 1900. He played in more than 50 'other' first and second XI games for Albion, scoring 24 goals, and in 1905 he gained a Southern League championship medal with Bristol Rovers.

SMITH, Archibald

Outside-right: 10 apps. 2 goals.

Born: West Bromwich, 11 July 1880.
Died: November 1943.
Career: Sandwell Road School. Harvills Hawthorn (1896). Worcester City (May 1900). ALBION (professional, November 1903). Brierley Hill Alliance (free, August 1904–May 1906).

■ Archie Smith was a big, powerfully built right-winger, who could also occupy the three inside berths but seemed to be suited best to the flank. With Albion for a relatively short period, he made his senior debut against Blackburn Rovers (home) in Division One in December 1903 and played in a handful of second team games, collecting a Birmingham & District League championship-winning medal in 1902, before moving to Brierley Hill.

SMITH, Arthur Eric

Outside-left: 52 apps. 13 goals.

Born: Whetstone, Leicester, 5 September 1921.
Career: Whetstone Church of England School. Wolverhampton Wanderers (amateur, March 1938, professional, August 1938). Leicester City (February 1941). Ballymena United (guest, World War Two). ALBION (£5,000, June 1948). Plymouth Argyle (free, August 1952). Crewe Alexandra (free, June 1954, retired, May 1956). Now living in Handsworth Wood, Birmingham.

■ A wing-forward of fair pace, good control and powerful shot, Arthur Smith could also play at inside-left. He served

Leicester (and Ballymena) well throughout the war, winning a League Cup medal with them in 1941. He then helped Albion gain promotion from Division Two in 1948–49 and during a pretty useful career appeared in 198 competitive matches, scoring 61 goals, including a World War Two record with Leicester of 74 outings and 32 goals. He made his Albion debut against Nottingham Forest (away) in the Second Division in August 1948. He also scored 19 goals in 69 second-team outings for the Baggies. He is one of Albion's oldest ex-players.

SMITH, Arthur John

Full-back/wing-half: 62 apps.

Born Aberaman, 27 October 1911.
Died: Weymouth, 7 June 1975.
Career: Aberaman (1926). ALBION (trialist, February–March 1928). Aberdare Athletic (April 1928). Merthyr Town (March 1929). Wolverhampton Wanderers (professional, September 1929). Bristol Rovers (May 1934). Swindon Town (July 1935). Chelsea (March 1938). Guested for Cardiff City, ALBION and Wolverhampton Wanderers during World War Two. Retired as a player, May 1945. Wolverhampton Wanderers (coach, August 1946–April 1948). ALBION (manager, June 1948–April 1952). Reading (manager, May 1952–June 1955). Later a publican and hotelier in Dorset.

■ Jack Smith was a very efficient defender, who guested for Albion during World War Two before becoming the club's first full-time manager in 1948. He appeared in one League game for Merthyr, 30 for Wolves, four for Bristol Rovers, 114 for Swindon and 48 for Chelsea. He also gained one cap for Wales in a wartime international against England in 1940 before his playing career came to an end when a bus (driven by a Wolves supporter) ran over his foot in a Wolverhampton street. He had served as a flight-sergeant in the RAF for four years. He guided Albion to promotion from Division Two in 1948–49 and was in charge for 177 matches (See MANAGERS).

SMITH, Arthur Reginald

Inside-forward: 6 apps. 1 goal.

Born: Guns Village, West Bromwich, 21 September 1878.

Died: West Bromwich, October 1953.
Career: Guns Lane & Swan Village Schools. West Bromwich Baptist (1895). ALBION (professional, August 1898, retired through injury, 1901). Later became a Football League linesman, then referee. Was a JP in West Bromwich from 1939, became a councillor and was appointment Mayor of the town in November 1944.

■ Arthur Smith was a useful inside-forward whose career was cut short by a dislocated left ankle. Brother of Ted and William Smith, who both played for Albion in the 1900s, he was one of eight footballing brothers in a family of 13. He made his League debut for Albion against Sheffield United in a First Division game at Bramall lane in March 1899.

SMITH, Daniel

Outside-left: 7 apps. 1 goal.

Born: Armadale, West Lothian, 7 September 1921.
Died: Scotland, 1998.
Career: Lindsay High School (Lothian). West Lothian Boys' Club. Coltness United (1937). ALBION (amateur, September 1939, professional, May 1945). Guest for Polkemmet Juniors (1944–45). Chesterfield (£1,750, June 1948). Crewe Alexandra (free, August 1949, retired, April 1953).

■ Danny Smith was a left-winger of reasonable skills who acted as understudy to Frank Hodgetts at Albion after he had signed 'pro' forms following his service in the RAF. After leaving The Hawthorns he played in 17 League games for Chesterfield and 110 for Crewe. He made his League debut against Chesterfield (away) in Division Two in October 1947.

SMITH, David

Midfielder/left-back: 91+26 apps. 2 goals.

Born: Stonehouse, Gloucestershire, 29 March 1968.
Career: Coventry City (apprentice, June 1984, professional, July 1986). AFC Bournemouth (on loan, January 1993). Dundee United (trialist, February 1993). Birmingham City (March 1993). ALBION (£90,000, January 1994). Grimsby Town (£200,000, January 1998). Swansea City (free, July 2002, contract terminated, December 2002). Grimsby Town (assistant commercial manager, 2004).

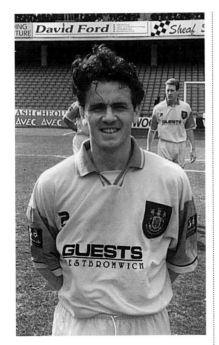

■ An England under-21 international (capped 10 times), David Smith was a good attacking midfielder, a hard and effective worker, who preferred the left flank. Nicknamed 'Smudger', he made over 180 appearances for Coventry, with whom he won England recognition, 44 for Birmingham and 134 for the Mariners. He made his debut for Albion against his future club, Grimsby Town, in February 1994 and two years later helped the Baggies win a penalty shoot-out against his former club, the Blues, in the Anglo-Italian Cup encounter at St Andrew's, netting the crucial fourth spot-kick. He also played in over 60 second XI games for Albion and was an Auto-Windscreen Shield winner with Grimsby in 1998.

SMITH, Edward

Inside-forward: 10 apps. 4 goals.

Born: Old Hill, 12 September 1880.
Died: August 1954.
Career: Saltwell's School (Cradley Heath). Old Hill Wanderers (1897). ALBION (professional, April 1899). Brierley Hill Alliance (free, August 1900). ALBION (free, March 1901). Dudley Town.(free, June 1904). Brockton FC. Halesowen (1910, retired, May 1912).

■ Ted Smith was an honest, hard-working and thoughtful inside-forward whose first-team outings for Albion were restricted considerably owing to the presence of so many other fine players at the club around the same time. He made his League debut against Glossop (away) in Division Two in March 1902, scoring the winner in Albion's 2–1 victory. Smith also scored 12 goals in over 50 second XI games, gaining a Birmingham & District League championship medal in 1902.

SMITH, Graham William Charles

Goalkeeper: 10 apps.

Born: Liverpool, 2 November 1947.
Career: Quarry Bank High School. England Grammar Schools Select XI. Tranmere Rovers (amateur, August 1963). Loughborough College (1964). Loughborough FC, Liverpool (amateur, 1967). Notts County (professional, August 1968). Colchester United (free, June 1969). ALBION (£10,000, November 1971). Cambridge United (free, January 1973, retired, June 1976 with a serious back injury). Went into sports business, became general manager of Adidas Sports (UK). Later director of Chelsea FC (1985–89).

■ Graham Smith was an efficient goalkeeper whose overall performances were hindered at times by his small frame. Albion secured his services after he had played exceedingly well for Colchester in their 1970 FA Cup run and for the 'U's against Albion in the 1971 Watney Cup final. He went on to help Cambridge win promotion from Division Four in 1973 and during his League career 'Smithy' accumulated a

total of 189 appearances (including 94 for Colchester and 85 for Cambridge). He made his Albion debut against Leeds United (away) in Division One in December 1971 and also had 28 outings for the reserve side.

SMITH, Horace

Winger: 2 apps.

Born: Netherton near Dudley, 21 August 1903.
Died: Dudley, February 1954.
Career: Dudley Wood School (Netherton). Hingley's FC (1919). ALBION (professional, November 1922). Blackpool (free, August 1927). Walsall (March 1928). Worcester City (June 1929). Dudley Town (1930, retired through injury, May 1933).

■ A dual-purpose winger, whose footwork at times was most impressive, Horace Smith lacked confidence at times. He won two Central League championship medals with Albion (1923–24 and 1926–27). His brother, Joe, also played for Albion as well as England. His League debut was against Cardiff City (home) in Division One in November 1923.

SMITH, John Gordon

Defender: 1 app.

Born: Nuffield, Birmingham, 15 June 1964.
Career: Shenley Court Comprehensive School, Northfield & South Birmingham Boys, Dunlop Terriers, St Anne's FC, Southern Cross FC and Northfield Thistle (all while still at school). ALBION (apprentice, July 1980, professional February 1982). Telford United (free, June–August 1984). IFK Trellborg, Sweden (free, September–October 1984). Worcester City (November 1984–May 1986).

■ A steady defender who was unlucky to be at The Hawthorns at the same time as Messrs Robertson, McNaught and Bennett, John Smith won a Central League championship medal in 1982–83, before making his only first-team appearance for the Baggies against Millwall in a League Cup round two, first leg, encounter at The Den in October 1983. Smith scored twice in 72 second XI games for the Baggies, gaining a Central League championship medal in 1982–83.

SMITH, Joseph

Right-back: 471 apps.

Born: Darby End, Dudley, 10 April 1890.
Died: Wolverhampton, 9 June 1956.
Career: Halesowen Road Council School (Netherton). Netherton St Andrews (1905). Darby End Victoria (1907). Cradley Heath St Luke's (1908). ALBION (professional, May 1910). Everton (World War One guest 1915–18). Served in Army during World War One. Notts County (guest, 1917–18). Birmingham (free, May 1926). Worcester City (player-manager, May 1929, retired, July 1932). Became 'mine host' at the Red Lion pub in Darby End and stayed in the licensing trade for four years afterwards working at Lloyds Proving House, eventually becoming chief tester.

■ One of the most popular sporting figures in the Netherton area during the first quarter of the century was Joe Smith, a right-back strategist who served Albion for some 16 years, making his League debut against Bolton Wanderers (away) in Division Two in September 1910 and playing in his last game in February 1926 against Bury. He found everlasting fame as a professional footballer, appearing in well over 450 senior games for the Baggies as well as gaining two full England caps and starring in one victory international for his country (after Army service in Bootle, Liverpool). He helped Albion win the Second Division title in 1911 and the First Division crown in 1920, playing a dominant part as full-back partner to the famous Jesse Pennington and later to Billy Adams and Arthur Perry. He was a marvellous positional player, clearing his lines with long, telling kicks. A strong tackler for a relatively small man, he gained a remarkable level of consistency, which was illustrated by the number of League games he played in from 1919–20 to 1924–25 inclusive, 247 out of a possible 252, all in the First Division. He won a junior international cap in 1909 and this honour set him up for a fine career. A wonderful clubman, a studious performer, very well respected and popular local figure, he is Netherton's only international footballer. He died at the Royal Hospital, Wolverhampton, aged 66.

SMITH, Keith Wilson

Striker: 70 apps. 34 goals.

Born: Woodville, Derbyshire, 15 September 1940.
Career: Woodville Junior & Ashby Grammar Schools. Coalville Boys. Wolverhampton Wanderers (trialist, 1956). ALBION (amateur, April 1957, professional, January 1958). Peterborough United (June 1963 in exchange for Terry Simpson). Crystal Palace (free, November 1964). Darlington (free, November 1966). Leyton Orient (free, May 1967). Notts County (free, June 1967). Kidderminster Harriers (free, August 1970). Tamworth (March 1971). Bromsgrove Rovers (player-manager, August 1972, retired, May 1975). Played for West Bromwich Albion All Stars (1969–84). Later worked in the Lottery offices at Aston Villa and Birmingham City and then took employment as a civilian in the West Midlands Police Force, based at the Brierley Hill station.

■ Not ideally built for a striker, being rather small-looking and fragile, Keith Smith was, nevertheless, smart and elusive in and around goal, possessing a fair shot and excellent positional sense. His strike record was first rate for Albion, for whom he scored 43 goals in 100 Central League games, and during his career, which saw him serve with six different League clubs, he netted over 90 goals in a total of 303 competitive matches. Smith actually finished up at left-back, but he did have the pleasure of scoring one of the fastest goals of all-time, netted six seconds after the start of a League game for Crystal Palace at Derby in December 1964. He made his Albion debut against Blackburn Rovers (home) in Division One in April 1960.

SMITH, William Alfred

Outside-right/inside-forward: 22 apps. 3 goals.

Born: Old Hill, 22 November 1882.
Died: May 1916.
Career: Rufford School. Quarry Bank Messengers. West Bromwich Baptist. Old Hill Wanderers (1898). Worcester City (1900). ALBION (professional, November 1902). Brierley Hill Alliance (free, May 1905). Tipton Excelsior (1910, retired, 1914). Later became a local referee, having initially qualified in 1907–08.

■ A strong, muscular player, Billy Smith packed a ferocious shot and was given 22 senior and 34 second XI outings by Albion. He deputised for the likes of Jimmy McLean and Harry Clements, among others, in the first team and made his League debut against Sheffield Wednesday (away) in Division One in April 1903.

SNEEKES, Richard

Midfield: 231+22 apps. 34 goals.

Born: Amsterdam, Holland, 30 October 1968.
Career: DWS, Holland (as a junior from July 1975). Ajax Amsterdam, Holland (amateur, April 1983, professional, October 1986). FC Volendam, Holland (on loan, August 1988–June 1989). Fortuna Sittard, Holland (August 1989). FC Lugano, Switzerland (on loan, August 1993–May 1994). Bolton Wanderers (trialist, July 1994, signed for £200,000, August 1994). ALBION (£400,000, March 1996). Stockport County (free, September 2001). Hull City (free, November 2001). FC Herfolge, Holland (May 2002). Later worked in financial business products and coached Castlefield Athletic (2003–04). Now lives in Sutton Coldfield and runs his own Italian restaurant.

■ When long-haired midfielder Richard Sneekes moved to The Hawthorns in 1996, Albion were deep in relegation trouble. But thanks to the bold and brave efforts of the highly talented Dutchman, whose thumping right-foot shot brought him 10 crucial goals in only 13 games, including one on his debut in a 4–4 home draw with Watford, the Baggies held on to their First Division status. Sneekes, meanwhile, became a cult hero with the fans. Earlier, he had played for Ajax as a

16-year-old in Holland's Premier League, being the youngest player at that time ever to represent the club at senior level – a record later beaten by Clarence Seedorf. Capped 22 times for his country at youth-team level and twice for the under-21 team, he scored 11 goals in 69 games for Bolton, playing for them in the League Cup final (lost 2–1 to Liverpool at Wembley) and helping them gain

promotion to the Premiership in his first season. Released by Albion manager Gary Megson at the end of the 2000–01 campaign, having made over 250 appearances in his five and a half years at The Hawthorns, Sneekes ironically joined Megson's former club, Stockport County, and later signed for Hull where he was reunited with another ex-Albion boss, Brian Little.

SOUTHAM, James Henry

Full-back: 34 apps.
Born: Willenhall, 19 August 1917.
Died Walsall, 1996.
Career: Stowheath Junior & Senior Schools. Shornhill Recreational Centre FC (1938). ALBION (amateur, March 1939, professional, November 1942). Guest for Aberaman, Arsenal, Ipswich Town, Newport County and Colchester United during World War Two. Newport County (£300, May 1946). Birmingham City (free, November 1946). Northampton Town (free, June 1949, retired, May 1955). Walsall (assistant trainer until early 1960s).

■ Jack Southam was a well-groomed, hard tackling full-back, who played a steady game, and was a reliable 90 minute worker, whose senior games for Albion all came during World War Two. He later had eight League outings with Newport, one with the Blues and 145 for Northampton, whom he served for six seasons. He made his Baggies debut against Stoke City (away) in the Football League North in November 1943 and at the end of that season was the recipient of a Midland Cup winners' medal.

SPEEDIE, David Robert

Striker: 9 apps. 2 goals.

Born: Glenrothes, Scotland, 20 February 1960.
Career: Adwick School, Barnsley (apprentice, August 1977, professional, October 1978). Darlington (£5,000, June 1980). Chelsea (£70,000, June 1982). Coventry City (£780,000, July 1987). Liverpool (£675,000, February 1991). Blackburn Rovers (£450,000, August 1991). Southampton (£400,000, July 1992). Birmingham City (on loan, October 1992). ALBION (on loan, January–February 1993). West Ham

United (on loan, March–April 1993). Leicester City (free, July 1993, retired, January 1995, joined coaching staff at Filbert Street). Made a brief comeback with Crook Town (1996–97). Now a football agent.

■ A Second Division championship winner and Full Members Cup winner with Chelsea in 1984 and 1986, David Speedie then helped Blackburn gain promotion from Division Two in 1992 and both Albion and Leicester rise into the First Division and Premiership (via the play-offs) in 1993 and 1994 respectively. A Scottish international (capped once at under-21 level and 10 times by the seniors), he was certainly one of the game's characters. Skilful, occasionally brilliant, aggressive and persistent, and a superb header of the ball for such a small man, he unfortunately had a fiery temper and this often got him into trouble with referees. In a wonderful career, though, he scored 175 goals in 611 games up to May 1994 when he aggravated a previous injury playing for Leicester against Bolton. And although he battled bravely for a year in an effort to get fit, it was to no avail and he quit League soccer at the age of 35. Signed on loan by Albion manager Ossie Ardiles (to add strength to the attack and to assist Bob Taylor), he scored at Bournemouth (won 1–0) and at home to Huddersfield (drew 2–2) after making his debut in a 2–1 home defeat by Stoke City in January 1993.

SPENCER, Geoffrey

Outside-right: 13 apps. 2 goals.

Born: Shavington, 9 November 1913.
Died: 1991.

Career: Shavington & Crewe Schools. Whitchurch FC. Nantwich Victoria (1931). ALBION (£300, March 1933, professional, July 1934). Brighton and Hove Albion (£350, May 1939, retired, May 1940).

■ A lightly-built right-winger, Geoff Spencer's career was cut short by a series of niggling knee injuries and a broken leg, plus two cartilage operations in 1937. A junior international in 1936, he was signed as a possible replacement for Tommy Glidden, but, after a decent enough debut against Burnley (away) in Division Two in September 1938, when he scored in Albion's 3–0 win, World War Two seemingly ruined his career. He scored 19 goals in 50 Central League games for the Baggies.

SPENCER, James Lawrence

Outside-right: 66 apps. 3 goals.

Born: Mosborough, Sheffield, 20 January 1900.
Died: Walsall, March 1979.
Career: Mosborough Junior & Staveley Grammar Schools. Sheffield University. Rotherham Town (1918). Eckington Works FC (1919). Beighton Youth Club (1921). ALBION (professional, August 1922). Aston Villa (free, as a reserve, May 1927). Tamworth (August 1928). Darlaston (December 1930, retired, May 1932). Worked in the leather trade up to World War Two.

■ Jimmy Spencer was a quick and energetic outside-right who was always seeking new ideas. He was only a 'dot' but represented the Football League side in 1924 and the Professional Select XI the same year. He contested the right-wing berth with Tommy Glidden following the departure of Jack Crisp. His Albion debut was against Cardiff City (home) in Division One in December 1922 when he scored in a convincing 3–0 win. He also netted twice in 338 Central League outings.

SPINK, Nigel Philip

Goalkeeper: 24 apps.

Born: Chelmsford, 8 August 1958.
Career: Chelmsford City Schools/Boys. West Ham United (on schoolboy forms). Chelmsford City (semi-professional, August

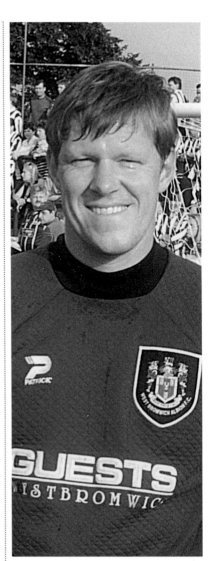

1975). Aston Villa (£4,000, January 1977). ALBION (free, January 1996). Millwall (£50,000, September 1997–May 2000). Employed as a goalkeeping coach in 2000–01 by Birmingham City, Swindon Town and Northampton Town. Forest Green Rovers (August 2001, later appointed joint manager, 2002–03). Birmingham City (goalkeeping coach, again, 2003–04). Currently lives in Sutton Coldfield.

■ Nigel Spink was an apprentice plasterer before becoming a goalkeeper! Quite a few clubs had been seeking his services when Villa stepped in with an offer early in 1977, but when he arrived at the club he found himself third choice behind John Burridge and Jake Findlay, and was soon knocked down to fourth when Jimmy Rimmer arrived. Unperturbed, 'Spinky' battled on in Villa's intermediate and reserve sides before establishing himself as the club's number one 'keeper in 1982. He had only made two senior appearances in the previous five years, his League debut coming in December 1979 against Nottingham Forest followed by an unexpected early appearance in the 1982 European Cup final against Bayern Munich in Rotterdam, after Rimmer had left the field injured. Spink developed into a tremendously effective 'keeper. Powerfully built (6ft 2in tall and weighing 14st 10lb), he could withstand the strongest of challenges, handled the ball exceptionally well, was a fine shot-stopper, had great anticipation and was courageous as well as confident. He gleefully collected his European Cup winners' medal and then added one full England cap to his collection, as a second-half substitute against Australia in 1983, as well as gaining two 'B' caps. In 1988 he helped Villa win promotion to the First Division and was also granted a testimonial. Unfortunately, he lost his place in the team for a short while (to Les Sealey) but regained it and went on to accumulate an exceptionally fine record of 460 senior appearances (361 in the League). In fact, he played in more competitive games than any other Villa goalkeeper, standing between the posts for Villa's first Premiership game against Ipswich Town in August 1992. He joined Albion initially as cover for Stuart Naylor and performed well in the two dozen games he took part in, while also playing roughly the same number of games for the second XI. He actually played his last competitive League match for Millwall at Wigan (Division Two) in January 2000 at the age of 41 years, five months and seven days – and that was his 540th appearance in club and international action before he stepped into Conference soccer with Forest Green Rovers. Spink is also a very competent cricketer.

NB: Spink is the oldest goalkeeper and the second-oldest player ever to appear for West Bromwich Albion. He was 39 years and 19 days old when he starred for the Baggies v Cambridge United in a League Cup tie in August 1997, having earlier made his Albion debut aged 37 years and 179 days against Ipswich Town (away) in February 1996. He is also the second oldest player to serve Millwall.

SPOONER, James

Centre-forward: 2 apps.

Born: West Bromwich, 11 November 1871.
Died: Cannock, November 1950.
Career: George Salter School (West Bromwich). Hednesford Town (1887). ALBION (professional, November 1895). Chadsmoor Swifts (June–October 1896). ALBION (free, November–December 1896). Forced to retire following dislocated knee injury. Became a miner at Hednesford Colliery.

■ Jim Spooner was a darting, sprightly centre-forward and was heading for the big time when a crunching tackle suffered against Derby County in only his second game for Albion virtually ended a promising career. He made two unsuccessful comeback attempts, but in the end he was forced to quit soccer at the age of 25. He made his Albion debut in the Black Country derby against Wolverhampton Wanderers (home) in Division One in November 1895. He was the father of 11 children.

SPROSON, Thomas

Goalkeeper: 9 apps.

Born: Stoke-on-Trent, 9 December 1903.
Died: Kinver, April 1976.
Career: Fenton and Cheadle Schools (Stoke). North Staffordshire Boys. Audley FC (1919). ALBION (amateur, March 1922, professional, March 1923). Port Vale (free, August 1928). Burton United (December 1928). Stone FC (September 1929). Stafford Rangers (August 1931, retired, May 1933).

■ Father of Roy, the future record-breaking Port Vale defender Tom Sproson was a massive 'keeper, often brilliant, who used his weight and height to the full. He was deputy to George Ashmore at Albion and was given only a handful of senior outings, making his League debut against Bolton Wanderers (away) in Division One in October 1925. He also played in 93 Central League games, gaining a championship medal in 1926–27, having helped the reserves claim the same title in 1923–24.

STANTON, JAMES

Full-back/wing-half: 5 apps.

Born: West Bromwich, 18 November 1860.

Died: at sea, August 1932.
Career: Christ Church School (West Bromwich). George Salter Works FC, ALBION (amateur, November 1878). Newton Heath (June 1885). Crosswells Brewery (1886–87). Oldbury Town (August 1887, retired, May 1892).

■ Jim Stanton was a defender of grim men, famed for his hard tackling. As a wing-half he backed his colleagues with superb service, while as a full-back he was never hurried into his clearances. A whole-hearted player, he occupied six different positions during his six years with Albion but preferred a full-back role best of all. Capped six times by Staffordshire in Inter-County matches, he appeared in around 150 games for Albion including five FA Cup ties, the rest in friendlies and domestic Cup fixtures. Stanton played in the club's first ever game against Hudson's Soap Works in November 1878 and made his 'senior' debut against Wednesbury Town (home) FA Cup round one in November 1883.

STATHAM, Derek James

Left-back: 377+1 apps. 10 goals.

Born: Whitmore Reans, Wolverhampton, 24 March 1959.
Career: St Mary's Primary & St Edmund's Junior Schools (Wolverhampton). ALBION (apprentice, July 1975, professional, April 1976). Southampton (£100,000, August 1987). Stoke City (£50,000, July 1989). Aston Villa (trialist, July 1991). Walsall (August 1991–May 1993). Telford United (briefly, 1993–94). King's Lynn (briefly). West Bromwich Albion All Stars (mid-to late 1990s/early 2000s). Now running a café/bar in Marbella, Spain.

■ Derek Statham was perhaps the finest left-back in England during the early 1980s, but he had Arsenal's Kenny Sansom ahead of him at international level and won only three caps for England for all his effort, skill and enthusiasm, against Sansom's tally of 86. In fact, Albion boss Ron Atkinson admitted that Statham was miles better than Sansom, England caps or not. A cheerful, buoyant character, who tackled tigerishly and loved to attack, Statham scored past the famous Peter Shilton when making his Albion debut in December 1976 (won 2–0), having helped the club's youngsters lift the FA Youth

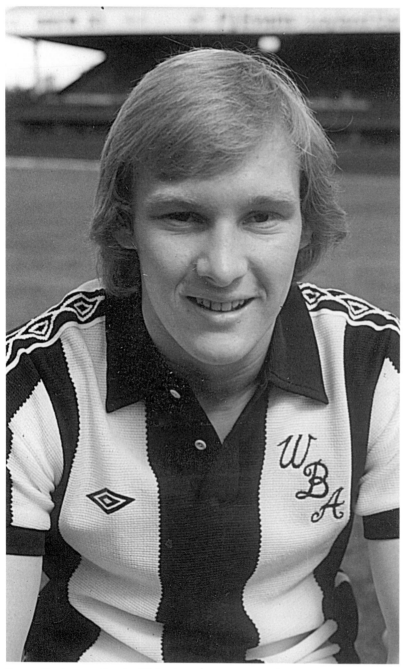

STEELE, Stanley Frederick

Inside-right: 1 app.

Born: Fenton, Stoke-on-Trent, 5 January 1937.

Career: Heron Cross School (Stoke). Stoke City (amateur, June 1953). Port Vale (amateur, February 1954, professional, May 1955). ALBION (£7,000, March 1961). Port Vale (£6,000, July 1961–April 1965). Port Elizabeth City, South Africa (July 1965). Port Vale (trialist, January 1968, released, February 1968). Eastwood FC (briefly). Armitage FC (briefly). Great Harwood (coach). Also coach at Keele University. Now lives in Stoke-on-Trent.

■ Stan Steele was a short, stocky inside-forward, who had the briefest of brief stays at The Hawthorns, precisely 108 days, playing in one League game against Blackburn Rovers (away) in Division One in April 1961. He had already appeared in 189 consecutive matches for Port Vale prior to joining Albion and in his career amassed 336 League outings (90 goals scored), winning a Fourth Division championship medal in 1959 (with Vale) and representing the Third Division North against the Third Division South in 1957, scoring both goals in the 2–2 draw.

STEGGLES, Kevin Peter

Defender: 18 apps.

Born: Ditchingham, Suffolk, 19 March 1961.

Career: Ditchingham & Bungay Schools. Suffolk County Boys. Ipswich Town (apprentice, July 1976, professional, December 1978). Southend United (on loan, February–March 1984). Everton (on loan, December 1985–January 1986). Fulham (on loan, August–September 1986). ALBION (on loan, February 1987, signing permanently, March 1987). Port Vale (£10,000 December 1987–May 1988). Bury Town (August 1988). Later assisted Brantham Athletic, Great Yarmouth and Woodbridge Town. Cambridge United (physiotherapist, 1997–99).

■ Kevin Steggles was a natural 'sweeper' who read the game splendidly. He spent eight years as a 'pro' at Portman Road, never really commanding a first-team place though, appearing in less than 80 senior games. He did, however, help Ipswich to the runners'-up spot in the

Cup earlier that year (beating Wolves in the final). He played for his country at youth team level (seven caps gained), followed up with six appearances for the under-21 side and also representing England 'B', before breaking into the full England team (under Bobby Robson's management) in 1982. Voted the Midland Sportwriter's 'Young Player of the Year' in 1978, Statham struggled at times with injuries during his last two seasons at The Hawthorns and it was perhaps something of a surprise when, in 1987, a proposed £250,000 transfer to Liverpool was called off at the 11th hour following unfavourable medical reports on his fitness. He was transfer-listed at the end of that season and subsequently joined Southampton for a six-figure fee. He went on to appear in over 150 League and cup games after leaving Albion, making his last appearance for Walsall in an Auto-Windscreen Shield encounter against the Baggies at The Hawthorns in 1990. Statham also played in almost 60 second XI matches for Albion.

First Division in successive seasons, 1980–81 and 1981–82, and played in the UEFA Cup semi-final first-leg against FC Cologne in 1981. He made his Albion debut against Derby County (away) in Division Two in February 1987. He also made three appearances for Albion's second XI.

STEPHENS, Kenneth John

Outside-right: 24+3 apps. 3 goals.

Born: Bristol, 14 November 1946.
Career: Speedwell Boys School. Bristol Boys. Phildown Rovers (1961). ALBION (apprentice, December 1962, professional, November 1964). Walsall (£5,000, December 1968). Bristol Rovers (October 1970). Hereford United (October 1977). Gloucester City (February 1980). Almondsbury Greenway (July 1982). Bath City (August 1983). Keynsham RSC (June 1984). Kingswood FC (August 1985). Hanham Athletic (manager, 1986–87). Now lives in Bristol.

■ Kenny Stephens was a useful player who could occupy the right-wing and inside-right berths accordingly, doing himself and the club justice in each one. He was all set to play for Albion in the 1968 FA Cup final but surprisingly, and unaccountably, disappeared! He was subsequently transferred to Walsall and later joined Bristol Rovers, making over 250 senior appearances for the Eastville Stadium club. He dropped into non-League football in 1980 after accumulating a career record in League competition of 314 appearances (17 goals). He helped Bristol Rovers win promotion from Division Three in 1974. His scored on his senior debut for Albion against Manchester City (home) in the League Cup, round three, in October 1966 (won 4–2). He also netted nine goals in 105 second XI games for the club.

STEVENSON, James

Centre-forward/centre-half: 129 apps. 9 goals.

Born: Bonhill, Dumbarton, Scotland, 2 August 1875.
Died: Dumbarton, March 1925.
Career: Bonhill St Augustine's School. Dumbarton Fereday (1891). Dumbarton (1893). Preston North End (professional,

April 1895). Bristol St George (free, August 1898). Preston North End (free, July 1899). ALBION (£150, October 1900). Dumbarton (free, June 1904). ALBION (assistant trainer, August 1914–May 1915). Worked in Leven shipyard after World War One.*

■ Jim Stevenson was a resilient, strong-tackling centre-half who earlier in his career had performed admirably at centre-forward, scoring 27 goals in 81 League games in two spells with Preston North End. Aided by his height and weight, he had good qualities of coolness and precise judgment, and was signed by Albion at a time when the club was at a low ebb. He failed to save them from relegation in 1901, but he was instrumental in helping the Throstles gain promotion in the first attempt when he lined up in all 34 League matches, forming a middle line in between Dan Nurse and Harry Hadley. Stevenson, who commanded the defence, had a wonderful spell with Albion, amassing almost 130 senior appearances, winning, of course, a Second Division championship medal in 1902. He gained a minor representative honour when he played for the Anglo-Scots against Scotland in 1902–03. His Albion debut was against Stoke (home) in Division One in November 1900. He was killed in a tragic accident at the Leven Shipyard.

STRINGER, James

Goalkeeper: 172 apps.

Born: Netherton, Dudley, 12 May 1878.
Died: Llanelli, December 1933.

Career: Netherton. Cradley & Dudley Council Schools. Netherton Rovers (1896). Wolverhampton Wanderers (professional, August 1900). ALBION (free, April 1905). Dudley Town (free, October 1910). Port Talbot (trainer, 1912–16). Retired and remained in South Wales, working as a casual labourer at local slate quarries.

■ Jimmy Stringer, nicknamed 'Joe' and 'Stinker', was a sound, vigilant goalkeeper, whose height and weight enabled him to dominate his area when high crosses looped over or when there was a tight situation near his goal. Albion secured him from neighbours Wolves after he had appeared in 15 League games for the Wanderers in five seasons at Molineux. He arrived to replace 'Ike' Webb and did very well, holding his position for four and a half seasons before handing over his jersey to Hubert Pearson in 1909–10. His Baggies debut was against Leicester Fosse (home) in Division Two in April 1905.

STRODDER, Gary John

Defender: 138+2 apps. 9 goals.

Born: Cleckheaton, 1 April 1965.
Career: Yorkshire Amateurs (1979). Lincoln City (schoolboy forms, January 1980, apprentice, May 1981, professional, April 1983). West Ham United (£100,000, March 1987). ALBION (£190,000, August 1990). Rotherham United (on loan,). Notts County (£145,000, July 1995). Hartlepool United (£25,000, February 1999). Guiseley (July 2001).

■ Gary Strodder was a resolute, no-nonsense central defender, who played 81 games for the Hammers before making a total of 166 for Albion, helping the Baggies win the Second Division play-off Final at Wembley in May 1993. Signed to replace Chris Whyte, he made his debut for Albion at Portsmouth in the opening League game of the 1990–91 season (a 1–1 draw), and, after also playing in almost 40 second XI games, he left The Hawthorns for Notts County five years later, having lost his place to Paul Mardon. In 1998 Strodder gained a Third Division championship medal with County, who were managed at the time by former Albion defender Sam Allardyce. He took his overall first-team appearance tally to a healthy 614 before entering non-League football with

Guiseley in 2001. His rugged, no-nonsense defensive play was much appreciated by The Hawthorns faithful.
* Strodder's father, Colin, played for Boston United, Halifax Town and Huddersfield Town.

STYLES, Arthur John

Wing-half: 1 app.

Born: Smethwick, 29 October 1939.
Career: Brasshouse Infants & Devonshire Junior Schools. James Watt Technical School (Smethwick). Staffordshire Schools. Birmingham & District Schools. Smethwick Boys. ALBION (amateur, March 1956, professional, November 1956). Wrexham (£3,000, March 1960). Hereford United (July 1961). Kidderminster Harriers (player, August 1963, then player-manager, August 1965). Stourbridge (July 1967). Halesowen Town (1968–69). Stourbridge (August 1969 trainer-coach, later manager, 1971–72). Lye Town (manager, 1972–73). Played for West Bromwich Albion All Stars (1969–87). Later employed as a salesman and now lives at Lye near Stourbridge, West Midlands.

■ Reserve left-half (to Ray Barlow and 'Chuck' Drury) Archie Styles, an England schoolboy international trialist, had noticeable skill and an appetite for hardwork. He played only once in Albion's first-team against Fulham (home) in Division One in October 1959 (lost 4–2) but made over 50 Central League appearances and followed up with 20 senior outings for Wrexham, with whom

he gained a Welsh Cup winners' medal in May 1960.

SUGGETT, Colin

Striker/inside-forward/midfield: 165+5 apps. 30 goals.

Born: Washington, County Durham, 30 December 1948.
Career: Washington Grammar School. Chester-le-Street Schools. Durham Boys. Durham Youths (1963). Sunderland (apprentice, July 1964, professional, December 1966). ALBION (£100,000, July 1969). Norwich City (£70,000, February 1973). Newcastle United (£60,000, August 1978, retired, June 1981 to join coaching staff at St James' Park, later reserve team manager, then youth coach, September 1985, and also caretaker manager, October–December 1988, assistant coach, December 1988–February 1994). Bolton Wanderers (scout, February–June 1994). Berwick Rangers (scout and local coach, July 1994–February 1995). Ipswich Town (director of youth, March 1995, later coach and then chief scout at Portman Road).

■ Colin Suggett, nicknamed 'Suggo', was Albion's first and record six-figure signing, and he got off to a flying start with the Baggies, scoring twice on his debut at Southampton in August 1969. He arrived in West Bromwich with a big reputation as a goalscorer and left having

been successfully converted into a highly-efficient midfielder, who also netted twice in 19 Central League games for the Baggies. He had made his League debut for Sunderland in March 1967 and, while at Roker Park, played in the 1966 and 1967 FA Youth Cup finals, the latter against Albion. He won England schoolboy and youth caps (1963–64 and 1966–67 respectively) and later appeared for Albion in the 1970 League Cup final at Wembley (when he missed a sitter, which would have secured victory). As a Norwich player he lined up against Aston Villa in the 1975 League Cup final, and in a lengthy career he appeared in 440 League matches (65 goals scored, 29 coming in his 243 senior outings for the Canaries). For Sunderland his record was 24 strikes in 86 League tussles. A keen golfer, pigeon-fancier, horse-racing fan and greyhound buff, Suggett actually owned a successful greyhound while with Albion, often giving the lads 'tips', which were not always guaranteed!

SUMMERFIELD, Kevin

Striker: 7+4 apps. 4 goals.

Born: Walsall, 7 January 1959.
Career: Alma Street & Joseph Leckie Schools (Walsall). Walsall Town Boys (1974). ALBION (apprentice, July 1975, professional, April 1976). Birmingham City (free, May 1982). Walsall (on loan, December 1982, signed permanently, February 1983). Cardiff City (free, July 1984). Plymouth Argyle (£5,000, December 1984). Exeter City (free, March 1990). Shrewsbury Town (free, October 1990, retired, May 1995 to become assistant manager/coach at Gay Meadow). Plymouth Argyle (youth-team coach, August 1997, caretaker manager, October 2000, then reserve-team coach, assistant manager, then senior coach, 2001–02, caretaker manager, February–May 2004). Southampton (assistant manager/coach, June–September 2004). Sheffield Wednesday (assistant manager/coach, September 2004).

■ A 'string-bean' of a footballer but a skilful one, Kevin Summerfield never really got the opportunity to show his true value with Albion despite playing a key role in the club's FA Youth Cup-winning team of 1975–76. After leaving The Hawthorns he developed into a

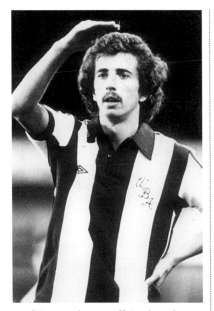

proficient performer, efficiently and effectively piling up his appearances and scoring regularly in the process, including 19 goals in 62 outings for Walsall. As a player he helped Plymouth win promotion to Division Two in 1985–86 and then from the Second Division as assistant manager/coach in 2003–04. He had earlier made his League debut for Albion as a substitute against Derby County (home) in a Division One encounter in March 1979. He also scored over 80 goals in more than 200 Central League appearances for the Baggies. Summerfield certainly did well as a coach in the lower Divisions, especially with Plymouth, and later followed his manager, Paul Sturrock, to Southampton and then to Hillsborough. Summefield's son, Luke, joined Plymouth in July 2005.

SUMMERS, Gerald Thomas Francis

Wing-half: 25 apps.

Born: Small Heath, Birmingham, 4 October 1933.
Career: Coventry Road & Hay Mills Schools. Erdington Albion (1948). ALBION (amateur, April 1950, professional, August 1951). Sheffield United (£3,500, May 1957). Hull City (£14,000, April 1964). Walsall (£10,000 ,October 1965, retired to become coach at Fellows Park, February 1967). Wolverhampton Wanderers (coach, August 1967). Oxford United (manager July 1969–October 1975). Gillingham (manager, October 1975–May 1981).

Southampton (scout, June 1981). ALBION (coach, October 1981–May 1982). Leicester City (coach, October 1982–December 1986). Derby County (chief scout and youth team manager, December 1986–94, now general scout).

■ Gerry Summers was a tireless left-half, unruffled and precise without a hint of robustness. He stepped in to replace Ray Barlow during the 1955–56 season and after two more outings the following season was transferred to Sheffield United. He did extremely well with the Blades, making well over 300 senior appearances before switching to Hull City (59 League games), later having more than 40 games for the Saddlers. In the summer of 1962, Summers toured the Far East with the FA party. He made his Albion League debut against Manchester United (home) in Division One in December 1955. He also netted once in 96 Central League games for the club.

SWAIN, Kenneth

Full-back/midfield: 7 apps. 1 goal.

Born: Birkenhead, 28 January 1952.
Career: Liverpool. Birkenhead & Merseyside District Schools. Kirkby Boys. Bolton Wanderers (schoolboy forms, 1967). Peckham Comprehensive & Streatham Schools. Shoreditch Teachers' Training College (Surrey). South-East Counties Colleges (1971). Wycombe Wanderers (amateur, April 1973). Chelsea (professional, August 1973). ALBION (on loan, November 1978). Aston Villa

(£100,000, December 1978). Nottingham Forest (October 1982). Portsmouth (July 1985). ALBION (on loan, February–March 1988). Crewe Alexandra (August 1988–May 1989, then player-coach, assistant manager). Wigan Athletic (manager, 1993–94). Grimsby Town (reserve team coach, assistant manager, 1995, then caretaker manager, October 1996–May 1997). FA School of Excellence technical director and coach. Scouted for several clubs including Nottingham Forest and Grimsby Town. Senior FA coach (2000–01). Qualified in handicrafts and PE at college.

■ Taken on loan by Ron Atkinson at a crucial period during the 1987–88 season, Kenny Swain's presence in the Albion team, alongside other experienced pro's like Brian Talbot and Andy Gray, certainly gave the Baggies that extra-bit of class to see them through a difficult stage when relegation was looming to the Third Division. A steady, positional player, Swain was originally an orthodox left-winger and was converted into a right-back after moving to Villa Park. He gained League championship, European Cup and Super Cup winners' medals with Villa (1981 and 1982) and helped Pompey win promotion from Division Two in 1987 and Crewe from Division Four in 1989. He had already amassed some 500 League and cup appearances for his previous four clubs prior to

signing for Albion for whom he made his debut against Shrewsbury Town (away) in February 1988. As a youngster he played in the same Kirkby Boys side as Dennis Mortimer (future Albion reserve-team coach and ex-Villa and Coventry midfielder) and he skippered Villa when Mortimer was absent.

SWALLOW, John

Wing-half: 1 app.

Born: Sheffield, 22 February 1860.
Died: Birmingham, 6 June 1917.
Career: Sheffield Schools. Attercliffe FC (1881). Oldbury Town (1882). ALBION (October 1883). Wednesbury Town (August 1884). Became a boilermaker in West Bromwich.

■ John Swallow was a reserve half-back who played in Albion's first ever FA Cup tie against Wednesbury Town in November 1883. A Yorkshireman, he was as tough as they come but failed to make the grade in professional football.

SWIFT, Arthur

Centre-forward: 28 apps. 11 goals.

Born: West Hartlepool, 15 July 1892.
Died: 1964.
Career: West Hartlepool & Billingham Schools. Billingham FC. Hartlepool Expansion FC (1911). ALBION (professional, May 1913). Worcester City (on loan, September–December 1913). Crystal Palace (free, August 1920, retired through injury, May 1921).

■ Arthur Swift played in Crystal Palace's first League season (Division Three) when they were champions, thus gaining promotion. A bustling centre-forward with good control, he could hit a ball with tremendous power and would have surely done exceptionally well at Albion had World War One not intervened when it did. He served with the Labour Corps (British troops) and also with the Lincolnshire Regiment in France during the hostilities (1915–18). He made his League debut against Preston North End (home) in Division One in January 1914. Swift also appeared occasionally in Albion's second XI.

SWINDEN, Sidney Alan

Full-back: 4 apps.

Born: Smethwick, 20 August 1913.
Died: Dudley, 1990.
Career: West Smethwick Junior & St Philip's Senior Schools (Smethwick). Smethwick United (1929). Smethwick Highfield (1930). ALBION (amateur, May 1931, professional, November 1931). Swindon Town (£75, May 1937). Accrington Stanley (June 1939). Oldbury Town (August 1945, retired, May 1948).

■ Sid Swinden was a thoroughly competent reserve full-back, big and strong, who won junior international honours for England in 1934. A product of Birmingham JOC Football, playing with Albion's 'A' team, he was a penalty-expert, and in three seasons (1933–36 inclusive) he scored 19 out of 20 for the reserves and intermediate teams and also netted five times from the spot in 35 Central League games. He made his League debut against Birmingham (away) in Division One in September 1936.

TAGGART, John

Half-back: 93 apps. 5 goals.

Born: Belfast, 3 January 1872.
Died: Walsall, 12 May 1927.
Career: Dundonald & Belmont County Schools (Belfast). Belfast Distillery (semi-professional, July 1889). Middlesbrough (professional, April 1892). ALBION (£150, March 1893). Walsall (free, May 1896, retired, ill-health, March 1903).

■ 'Jack' Taggart was crammed full of football. He played the game methodically from a defensive position, always trying to keep the ball in play rather than hoof it into space. Perhaps his sole blemish on the field was his head-work. He spent just three seasons with Albion, playing in the 1895 FA Cup final. He was capped by Ireland (against Wales) in 1899 when starring for Walsall, appearing in 113 League games for the Saddlers. He made his debut for Albion against Derby County (home) in Division One in April 1893. Taggart also played in more than 60 'other' first-team matches for the club.

TALBOT, Brian Ernest

Midfield: 73+10 apps. 6 goals.

Born: Ipswich, 21 July 1953.
Career: Ipswich & Suffolk Schools. Ipswich Town (amateur, July 1969, professional,

July 72). Toronto Metros (1971 and 1972). Arsenal (£450,000, January 1979). Watford (£150,000, June 1985). Stoke City (£25,000, October 1986). ALBION (£15,000, January 1988, appointed caretaker manager, October 1988, upgraded to manager, November 1988, sacked, January 1991). Fulham (non-contract, March 1991). Aldershot (non-contract, April 1991, later manager, 1991–92). Sudbury Town (player-manager/coach, 1992–93). Hibernians, Malta (player-coach, 1993–97). Rushden & Diamonds (guest, 1996, manager, August

1997). Oldham Athletic (manager, March 2004). Oldham Athletic (manager, March 2004 to March 2005).

■ Brian Talbot was a well-balanced, hard-working, yet very skilful midfielder, who won six full England caps and was an FA Cup winner with both Ipswich Town and Arsenal in successive seasons (1978 and 1979). He made 533 League appearances during a fine career that spanned 22 seasons. Signed by Ron Atkinson from Stoke City, he made his debut against Leeds United in January 1988 and spent three years at The Hawthorns, playing in 20 Central League games (4 goals) and making 83 appearances in the senior side. He immediately brought some fluency and experience to the Baggies midfield, and when player-manager of the team he duly lifted the side to the top of the Second Division table. He lost his job after a shock home defeat by non-League side Woking in the third round of the FA Cup in January 1991. Later, after returning to senior management, he guided Rushden and Diamonds into the Football League as Nationwide Conference winners in 2001 and a year later saw them reach the Third Division play-off final at Cardiff's Millennium Stadium, beaten by Cheltenham Town. In 2004 he took over as boss of Oldham Athletic.

TALBOT, John

Centre-half: 192 + 1 apps. 1 goal.

Born: Headington, Oxfordshire, 20 October 1940.
Career: South Shields Grammar Technical School. South Shields & District Boys. Durham Boys (1955). Burnley (amateur, July 1956, professional, October 1957). ALBION (£30,000 December 1966). KV Mechelen, Belgium (player-manager, May 1971, retired in 1974). Became licensee of the 'Kup Winna' pub in Mechelen, later Leisure Centre proprietor near Brussels. Now living in his native South Shields.

■ John Big 'T' Talbot was a vastly experienced centre-half when Albion secured his transfer halfway through the 1966–67 campaign. He had already played in almost 150 senior games for Burnley and won England caps at both schoolboy (1955) and under-23 levels. He was recruited to The Hawthorns by

manager Jimmy Hagan as a replacement for Stan Jones and proved to be worth every penny of the £30,000 fee invested by the club. He made almost 200 first-team appearances for Albion, collecting a winners' medal in the 1968 FA Cup final and a runners'-up prize two years later in the 1970 League Cup final. His League debut was for Burnley in December 1958 and he played his last game in England with Albion in January 1971, a career spanning just over 12 years, during which time he assembled an appearance record of 323 competitive matches, scoring one goal for Albion against AS Roma in an Anglo-Italian Cup tie at The Hawthorns in May 1970. His debut for the Baggies was on Boxing Day in 1966 in a 3–0 home win over Tottenham Hotspur in Division One, and he also played in 18 Central League games. He entered the Belgium Second Division with KV Mechelen.

TAYLOR, Arthur Sidney

Centre-forward: 4 apps. 5 goals.

Born: Lozells, Birmingham, 14 March 1925.
Career: Gower Street & St Mary's Schools, Birmingham. Aston Boys. Shelley's FC (Handsworth). Handsworth Wood Boys Club (1939). Gower Old Boys (1940). ALBION (amateur, November 1941, professional, May 1947, retired through injury, July 1950). Returned with Llanelli Town (November 1950). Then assisted Hednesford Town (August 1951, retiring for a second time in May 1952).

■ Arthur 'Biff' Taylor was a good, old-fashioned tearaway striker, built to withstand the fiercest of challenges. A promising career was ruined firstly by World War Two and secondly by a knee injury. He began his Albion League career in stupendous style, scoring five goals in four matches when deputising for the injured Dave Walsh at the end of the 1947–48 campaign. He netted on his debut against Nottingham Forest (away) in Division Two in the April and then scored two goals in each of his next two matches against Bradford and Cardiff City. He also netted 17 times in 31 Central League games. Taylor was in the Navy during the war, sailing the Atlantic and Pacific Oceans, sighting Australia, New Zealand, South Africa and China. He played for the Navy against Chinese XI, which later came to England to take part in the 1948 Olympic Games.

TAYLOR, Griffith Alfred

Outside-right: 1 app.

Born: Trehafod near Pontypridd, South Wales, 23 December 1905.
Died: Dudley Road Hospital, Winson Green, Birmingham, 9 October 1978.
Career: Mountain Ash & Gelligaer Schools. Trehafod FC (1919). ALBION (professional, February 1927). Leamington Town (free, March 1929). Merthyr Town. Barry Town (August 1935, retired, May 1937). Returned to the Midlands and worked in engineering in Birmingham until he was 60. Was admitted to the mental unit of Dudley Road hospital in 1975.

■ A junior international, 'Griff' Taylor was a reserve outside-right who suffered an awful lot of injuries during his brief stay with Albion. Slight of build, his only first-team outing was in the third round FA Cup tie against Arsenal (away) in January 1928. He scored once in 34 second team games for the Baggies.

TAYLOR, Harold

Centre-forward: 9 apps. 2 goals.

Born: Dudley, 15 September 1893.
Died: Bristol, 8 March 1974.
Career: Priory Junior & Old Park Senior Schools (Dudley). Dudley Bean FC (1914). ALBION (professional, May 1920). Barrow (free, June 1921). Shrewsbury Town (July 1923). Brierley Hill Alliance (May 1925, retired, July 1927). Went to Pennsylvania,

USA (1928) returning to play the 1930–31 season with Bristol Steel Works FC.

■ A popular, dashing centre-forward, whose style and method upset a lot of steady defences, Harry Taylor deputised for Andy Smith during the second post World War One season, making his Albion debut against Bolton Wanderers (home) in Division One in September 1920.

TAYLOR, Oliver

Goalkeeper: 5 apps.

Born: Wednesfield, 2 February 1880.
Died: July 1938.
Career: Wednesfield and Merridale Schools. Bingley Boys YC. Bilston United (1899). ALBION (professional, May 1901). Coventry City (free, August 1903). Willenhall Pickwick (April 1905, retired through injury, October 1906).

■ Reserve to 'Ike' Webb at Albion, Olly Taylor was a redoubtable 'keeper, stylish and courageous, whose career ended in 1906 when he damaged his back. He played his first League game against Chesterfield (home) in Division Two in September 1901 and also appeared in over 30 second-team games for the club, gaining a Birmingham & District League championship medal in 1902.

TAYLOR, Robert

Striker: 299+78 apps. 131 goals.

Born: Littlethorpe, Easington, County Durham, 3 February 1967.
Career: Horden Comrades Welfare (1982). Horden Colliery Welfare (1983). Newcastle United (trialist, 1983). Hartlepool United (trialist, 1983). Horden Colliery (1984). Leeds United (professional, March 1986). Bristol City (£175,000, March 1989). ALBION (£300,000, January 1992). Bolton Wanderers (free, January 1998). ALBION (£90,000, March 2000). Cheltenham Town (free, August 2003). Tamworth (July 2004).

■ Bob Taylor, without doubt manager Bobby Gould's finest signing for Albion, quickly became a hero at The Hawthorns with his superb marksmanship. He scored on his debut against Brentford and netted eight times in only 19 games during the second-half of that campaign. In his second season (his first full one) 'Super Bob', as he was so-called by his fans, top-

scored with 37 goals, helping Albion win promotion to the First Division via the Wembley play-off final against Port Vale. Named Albion's captain in 1995–96, it was a huge surprise, certainly to all Baggies supporters, when he left The Hawthorns for Bolton Wanderers. He helped the Lancashire club reach the Premiership and then had the pleasure of scoring at Old Trafford in the top flight. Gary Megson, thankfully, brought Taylor back to Albion in March 2000 and once again the supporters took him to their hearts, cheering him to the hilt when he

clinched promotion to the Premiership with the second and deciding goal in the last game win over Crystal Palace in April 2002. Strong and powerful both on the ground and in the air and a perpetual hard-worker, Taylor scored 13 goals in 54 League and cup games for Leeds and followed up with 58 in 126 senior outings for Bristol City. He netted a goal every three games for Albion, who agreed to a well-deserved testimonial being awarded to him in 2003, before his departure to Cheltenham Town and then into non-League football with Tamworth. Taylor is one of only nine players to have scored over 100 League goals for Albion, and he claimed another 17 in 48 outings for the reserve XI. In October 2001 he had the misfortune of getting sent off in the League away game at Barnsley – this becoming the 100th dismissal in the club's history at first-team level.

THOMAS, James Alan

Striker: 1+2 apps.

Born: Swansea, 16 January 1979.
Career: Swansea schoolboy & junior football. Swansea City (trialist, 1994). Blackburn Rovers (apprentice, June 1995, professional, July 1996). ALBION (on loan, August–September 1997). Blackpool (on loan, March–May 2000). Sheffield United (on loan, November–December 2000). Bristol Rovers (on loan, March–April 2001). Swansea City (free, July 2002).

■ Capped 21 times by Wales at under-21 level, James Thomas kept Swansea in the Football League after scoring a hat-trick on the final day of the season (against Hull City) to take his tally of goals for the Welsh club to 15. He had a loan spell at The Hawthorns at the start of the 1997–98 season and made three appearances in the first team, making his debut as a 'sub' in the 0–0 draw at Stoke on 3 September.

THOMAS, John William

Striker: 10+11 apps. 4 goals.

Born: Wednesbury, 5 August 1958.
Career: Everton (apprentice, April 1975, professional, July 1977). Tranmere Rovers (on loan, March–April 1979). Halifax Town (on loan, October–November 1979).

Bolton Wanderers (June 1980). Chester City (August 1982). Lincoln City (£12,500, August 1983). Preston North End (£15,000, June 1985). Bolton Wanderers (£30,000, July 1987). ALBION (£30,000, July 1989). Preston North End (£50,000, February 1990). Hartlepool United (£5,000, March 1992). Halifax Town (free, July 1992–May 1993). Later assisted Bamber Bridge (1997–98).

■ During a wonderful but varied and nomadic career, Black Country-born striker John Thomas (known as 'JT') scored 123 goals in 364 League games, his best efforts coming with Bolton (37 in 95) and Preston (44 in 105). As top-scorer he helped the latter club gain promotion to the Third Division in 1987 and then starred for Bolton when they lifted themselves up from the Fourth Division in 1988, heading the scoring charts with 22 goals. He was also a Sherpa Van Trophy winner with Bolton at Wembley in 1989. An Albion supporter as a lad, he moved to The Hawthorns in the summer of 1989, but failed to hold down a first-team place despite scoring a hat-trick in a splendid 5–3 recovery League Cup win at Bradford City in October 1989. Three months later he made his Baggies debut as a 'sub' against Sheffield United (lost 3–0). Thomas also scored 12 goals in 15 Central League outings.

THOMAS, Michael Reginald

Midfield: 28 apps. 1 goal.

Born: Mochdre, Powys, 7 July 1954.
Career: Mochdre & Newtown Schools. Welshpool District Boys. Pentre Youth Club (1968–69). Wrexham (amateur, August 1969, apprentice, July 1970, professional, April 1972). Manchester United (£300,000, November 1978). Everton (£450,000, player/exchange deal involving John Gidman, August 1981). Brighton and Hove Albion (£400,000 November 1981). Stoke City (£200,000 August 1982). Chelsea (£75,000, January 1984). ALBION (£100,000, September 1985). Derby County (on loan, March–May 1986). Wichita Wings, NASL indoor League (£35,000, August 1986). Shrewsbury Town (August 1988). Leeds United (£10,000, June 1989). Stoke City (on loan, March 1990, signed permanently, free transfer, August 1990). Wrexham (July 1991–May

1993). Conwy United (December 1994). Inter Cardiff (August 1995). Portmadoc (caretaker manager/coach, January 1995). Inter Cardiff (briefly, August–September 1996). Later manager of a soccer coaching School near Wrexham (1997–2000). Also worked as a soccer summariser for Century Radio, Manchester. Rhyl (Director of Football, 2000–02). After leaving Wrexham in 1993 he served an 18-month jail sentence for handling counterfeit money.

■ Mickey Thomas was a hard-working, industrious midfield dynamo, who had been in League football for 14 years when he joined Albion from Chelsea, having made his debut for Wrexham in January 1972. He arrived at The Hawthorns with over 500 senior appearances under his belt, had played on 80 different League grounds, visited 15 countries and cost more than £1.5 million in transfer fees. A Welsh international at three levels – under-21 (2 caps), under-23 (one cap) and full (51 caps) – he was a member of Manchester United's losing FA Cup final side of 1979 and gained a First Division runners'-up medal in 1980. Earlier, with Wrexham, Thomas won three Welsh Cup winners' medals (1972, 1975 and 1978) and also helped the Robins win the Third Division championship in 1978. He was a livewire in midfield when Chelsea gained promotion to the First Division in 1983–84, and two years later, in 1985–86, he helped Derby clinch promotion to Division Two. He left Albion after manager Ron Saunders had decreed that he should live nearer to The Hawthorns than he did. Thomas refused and was subsequently placed on the transfer list, having also played in three Central League games for the club. After a brief association with Derby he joined the North American Indoor Soccer club Wichita Wings on a two-year contract.

THOMPSON, Andrew Richard

Midfield: 21+5 apps. 1 goal.

Born: Featherstone near Wolverhampton, 9 November 1967.
Career: Featherstone Boys (aged 10). Cheslyn Hay High School. Cresswells Boys' Club. Wednesfield Social (1981–82). Featherstone FC (August 1982). Albion (apprentice, June 1984, professional, November 1985). Wolverhampton Wanderers (£70,000 combined fee, which included striker Steve Bull, valued at £65,000, November 1986). Tranmere Rovers (July 1997). Crewe Alexandra (on loan, March–April 2000). Cardiff City (free, August 2000). Shrewsbury Town (on loan, January 2001, signed permanently, March 2002). Hednesford Town (2003–05).

■ All-out endeavour made up for Andy Thompson's lack of height and weight. He strove to make the grade with Albion but was unfortunate that there were so many other midfielders at The Hawthorns at the same time. He gained Fourth Division championship and Sherpa Van Trophy winners' medals with Wolves in 1987–88 and collected a Third Division championship winners' medal

the following season. He went on appear in 451 first-team games for Wolves (43 goals). His Albion debut was against Chelsea (home) in a Full Member's Cup tie in November 1985 when he scored in the penalty shoot-out. 'Thommo' also played in 35 Central League games (4 goals scored).

THOMPSON, Garry Lindsey

Striker: 105 apps. 45 goals.

Born: Kings Heath, Birmingham, 7 October 1959.
Career: Brandwood & Maypole Schools. Coventry City (apprentice, June 1976, professional, June 1977). ALBION (£225,000, February 1983). Sheffield Wednesday (£450,000, August 1985). Aston Villa (£430,000, July 1986). Watford (October 1988). Crystal Palace (March 1990). Queen's Park Rangers (£135,000, August 1991). Cardiff City (free, July 1993). Northampton Town (free, February 1995, retired as a player, May 1997, appointed reserve-team manager/coach). Brentford (coach). Bristol Rovers (coach-assistant manager, July 1999, then caretaker manager, January 2001). Brentford (assistant manager, 2002–03, then caretaker manager to March 2004, coach, August 2004).

■ A tall black striker, powerful in the air, sharp and decisive on the ground, Garry Thompson won six England under-21 caps and scored goals as regular as clockwork throughout his career, ending up with 164 to his name in 614 first-team matches. His form slumped at times,

especially after leaving Albion (this on his own admission), and for the Owls he grabbed just seven goals in 44 games. It must be said that the fans were somewhat annoyed when he packed his bags and left The Hawthorns so soon after his partner up-front Cyrille Regis had departed. He made his Baggies debut against Arsenal (home) in Division One in February 1983 and claimed a goal almost every two games. He also played in one second XI fixture. 'Thommo' helped Villa win promotion to Division One in 1987–88 and Watford to the promotion play-offs in 1988–89. He attended the same school as Paul Dyson.

THOMPSON, John Trevor

Full-back: 22 apps.

Born: North Shields, 21 May 1955.
Career: Linskill School. Northumberland & District Boys. ALBION (apprentice, August 1970, professional, January 1974). Washington Diplomats (guest, 1976). Newport County (£7,500, 1978). Lincoln City (£10,000, December 1979). Gainsborough Trinity (June 1982). Worksop Town (1983–85). Boston United (briefly). Bourne Town (1986). Bostoft FC (player-manager, February–December 1987, retired through ill-health). Returned with Lincoln Moorlands FC (player-manager July 1990–May 1993). Now lives in Lincoln.

■ As a youngster Trevor Thompson was all skin and bone, frail-looking and standing barely 5ft tall. He developed into a capable, stern and surefooted full-back, who appeared in 35 League games for Newport and 80 for Lincoln after being introduced to competitive action by Baggies manager Don Howe, who handed him his senior debut against Bristol City (home) in Division Two in February 1974. Thompson, who also scored 12 goals in 189 Central League games for Albion, helped Lincoln win promotion from Division Four in 1980–81.

THOMPSON, William

Outside-right: 57 apps. 6 goals.

Born: Morpeth, Northumberland, 14 August 1886.
Died: Durham, 20 December 1933.
Career: Morpeth & Ashington Schools.

Byker Boys Club (1901). Grange Town FC (1904). Middlesbrough (professional, August 1905). Morpeth Harriers (August 1906). ALBION (March 1908). Sunderland (free, May 1911). Plymouth Argyle (free, August 1913). South Shields (November 1913). Queen's Park Rangers (1914–15). Served in Army during World War One. Newport County (August 1920). Hartlepools United (July 1921). Jarrow (1922–23).

■ Known to everyone as 'Rubber' for his elastic-type stature and spring-heeled displays down Albion's right-flank, Billy Thompson was brilliant at times but could be so frustrating as well. He spent a little over three seasons at The Hawthorns, making 57 senior appearances and over 30 more in the reserves. After leaving the club he played for the pick of the Southern League in 1914 as an inside-forward, later featuring as a wing-half. He made his Albion debut against Fulham (home) in Division Two in April 1908, scoring in a 3–1 win.

TIGHE, John

Goalkeeper: 1 app.

Born: Aghamore, Ireland, 13 March 1923. Career: County Mayo & Balyhaurus Schools. Aghamore YC (1938). Larkhall Thistle (1943). ALBION (£130, November 1945). Hednesford Town (free, May 1948). Atherstone (1950–52). ALBION (scout, mid-1950s). Later returned to live in Ireland.

■ Sound and sometimes quite brilliant goalkeeper John Tighe could not show off his array of talent to the watching public owing to the dominating form between the posts of Jimmy Sanders. Initially a Gaelic footballer at School, he became a welder in Ireland before joining the Irish Army, playing for his unit and the 10th Army Group during World War Two. He made his League debut against Newport County (home) in Division Two in February 1947.

TIMMINS, George

Left-half/Inside-left: 61 apps. 1 goal.

Born: West Bromwich, 6 February 1858. Died: West Bromwich, August 1926. Career: Christ Church & Beeches Road Schools. George Salter Works. ALBION (September 1879, professional, August

1885). Old Hill Wanderers (May 1891). Newton Heath (trainer, July 1893). Retired out of football, May 1900. Returned as Albion gateman for a number of years prior to World War One.

■ George 'Darkie' Timmins was one of the club's earliest utility players, useful in any half-back or inside-forward position. A skilful and determined footballer, he was a hard, fearless man, who made certain players cringe in the tackle. He lined up at left-half in the 1886, 1887 and 1888 FA Cup finals for Albion, collecting a winners' medal in the latter tie against Preston. He made his senior debut against Wednesbury Town (home) in the opening round of the FA Cup in November 1883 (Albion's first in the competition) and went on to appear in well over 200 games for the club, many in local cup competitions and friendlies. He was one of the marksmen when Albion won their first ever trophy by beating Stoke 3–2 in the final of the Staffordshire Cup in 1883.

TIMMINS, Samuel Roland

Utility: 116 apps. 3 goals.

Born: West Bromwich, 27 June 1879. Died: West Bromwich, August 1956. Career: George Salter School (West Bromwich). Dudley Sports FC. Burnt Tree FC. Dudley Town (1899). Walsall (amateur, 1900). Nottingham Forest (professional, March 1901). ALBION (£50,

August 1906, retired through injury, May 1911). Was licensee of the Old Hop Pole Pub, Carter's Green, West Bromwich (August 1911–29).

■ Sammy Timmins was a short, stocky player, clever and constructive, who always gave a good account of himself no matter what the circumstances. A self-conscious footballer, he had a high regard for discipline. He occupied seven different positions in Albion's first XI, following his senior debut against Blackpool (away) in Division Two in November 1906. He also made over 20 second XI appearances, and prior to his transfer to The Hawthorns he had played in 138 games for Forest. No relation to George Timmins, Sammy served as a Gunner (No 99568) with the 229 Seige Battery in Italy during World War One.

TOWNSEND, Andrew David

Midfield: 17+3 apps.

Born: Maidstone, Kent, 23 July 1963. Career: Welling United (August 1980). Weymouth (March 1984). Southampton (£35,000, January 1985). Norwich City (£300,000, August 1988). Chelsea (£1.2 million, July 1990). Aston Villa (£2.1 million, July 1993). Middlesbrough

(£500,000, August 1997). ALBION (£50,000, September 1999, retired as first-team player in January 2000 to take over as reserve coach at The Hawthorns, a position he held until for six months before being replaced by another ex-Villa player, Gary Shelton). Now a TV soccer pundit.

■ Capped 70 times by the Republic of Ireland at senior level and once by the 'B' team, midfielder Andy Townsend had an excellent career in top-class football. On his day he was an effective, hard-working performer, on par with most of the leading professionals occupying the same position. Before joining Albion he had already made over 100 appearances for Saints, 88 for the Canaries, 138 for Chelsea, 176 for Villa and 88 for Middlesbrough. Townsend gained two League Cup medals with Villa (1994 and 1996), skippering the side in the latter final. He helped 'Boro regain their Premiership status at the end of his first season on Teeside.

* Townsend's father, Don, was a full-back with Charlton Athletic and Crystal Palace.

TRANTER, George Henry

Centre-half: 70 apps.

Born: Yardley, Birmingham, 11 September 1915.
Died: Birmingham, December 1998.
Career: Yardley Wood & Billesley Schools (Birmingham). Jack Mould's Athletic. Shirley Juniors. Birmingham (amateur, September 1930). Evesham Town (1931). Solihull Town (1932). Rover Works FC (Solihull). ALBION (amateur, February 1934, professional, December 1943). Hereford United (June 1947). Birmingham City (coach, 1948–99). Hereford United (August 1950, retired, May 1952).

■ George Tranter started playing football with Albion in 1934 as a right-back. He progressed through the junior and intermediate ranks as an amateur, went to 'war' and returned to The Hawthorns a solid, quite fearless centre-half, decidedly hard in the tackle and strong in the air. Fifty of Tranter's first-team appearances for Albion came between 1944–46. He made his senior debut against Coventry City (home) in the Football League North in September 1944 and also played in 11 second XI matches.

TREACY, Raymond Christopher Patrick

Striker: 24+4 apps. 7 goals.

Born: Dublin, 18 June 1946.
Career: Cabra Roman Catholic School (Dublin). St Catherine's FC. Dublin City Boys. Westland Row CBS. Home Farm. Eire Schools Association (1961). ALBION (apprentice, August 1961, professional, June 1964). Charlton Athletic (£17,500, February 1968). Swindon Town (June 1972). Preston North End (£30,000, December 1973). Oldham Athletic (on loan, March 1975). ALBION (August 1976). Shamrock Rovers (May 1977, appointed player-assistant manager, 1978–80). Toronto Metros, Croatia (1978). Drogheda United (player-manager January 1981–February 1983). Crusaders (manager). Now runs a successful travel agency in Dublin and regularly helps with arrangements for various overseas tours made by the Republic of Ireland soccer party.

■ A bouncy, short striding striker, aggressive at times with good skills and reasonable speed, which he put to good use during a lengthy career, striker Ray Treacy scored with clockwork regularity during his playing days, netting well over 100 goals in more than 350 appearances in competitive soccer. He won 41 caps for the Republic of Ireland (5 goals scored), plus two as a schoolboy, three at youth level and one for the under-23 team. He also played for the Irish XI (in 1971 and 1975) and represented the League of

Ireland on four occasions. Treacy actually won his first full cap before he had made his League debut, that finally came against Sunderland (away) in Division One in October 1966 when he scored in the 2–2 draw. He also scored on his 'second' debut for Albion versus Derby County (away) in Division One in September 1976 (another 2–2 draw). He also played in a handful of second XI games for Albion, plus several more at intermediate level. Between December 1973 and August 1975 he played 30 consecutive games as a striker for Preston and failed to score a single goal. With Shamrock he gained an FAI Cup medal in 1978, scoring a vital match-winning penalty in the final against Sligo. His two spells with Albion came eight years apart. He was granted a testimonial in 1989.

* Treacy, like his fellow countryman and Albion colleague Paddy Mulligan, was granted a testimonial by FAI.

TRENTHAM, Herbert Francis

Full-back: 272 apps.

Born: Chirbury, Salop, 22 April 1908.
Died: Birmingham, June 1979.
Career: Chirbury St John's School. Knighton Town (1923). Knighton Victoria (1924). Knighton United (1925). Hereford United (April 1926). Aston Villa (trial, 1928). ALBION (£600, April 1929). Hereford United (free, May 1937). Darlaston (August 1939, retired, April 1942). Later ran his own ironmonger's business in Ward End, Birmingham.

■ Bert 'Corker' Trentham was a very capable and reliable full-back, able and willing to try anything from either the right or left-hand berths. A model of consistency, he was sound rather than outstanding, and he always had a handkerchief wrapped round his withered right hand. He drew up a fine partnership with his co full-back George Shaw, and together they played in over 230 senior games for Albion during the 1930s, lining up in both the 1931 and 1935 FA Cup finals, being a valuable member of the 'double-winning' side in 1930–31. During a fine career he won junior international honours (1929) and represented the Football League in 1933. He never scored a goal in the 272 appearances for Albion. He did, however,

concede three own-goals! He made his League debut against Blackpool (away) in Division Two in March 1930 and also played in 54 second team games for the club.

TREVIS, Arthur Stanley Sackville Redvers Trevor Boscawen Griffith

Half-back: 1 app.

Born: Blackheath, 23 December 1910. Died: Redditch, 1995. Career: Woodside School. Old Hill Wanderers (1925). Leamington Town (1928). ALBION (amateur, February 1929, professional, April 1931). Chester (£100, May 1936). Worcester City (free, February 1939). Dudley Town (August 1940, retired during latter stages of World War Two). Lived in Redditch for 50 years.

■ 'Bos' Trevis had the distinction of having the longest set of names in League football. He was reserve half-back at Albion for six seasons, appearing in one League game. He was an extremely fit player with enough energy to cover every inch of the pitch. 'Bos' was a perfect tackler and was dedicated to the cause. A junior international (capped in 1931–32 season), he gained a hat-trick of Central League championship medals with Albion in the mid-1930s, making a total of 94 second team appearances in all (5 goals scored). His only League game for Albion was against Liverpool (home) in Division One in April 1934.

TREWICK, John

Midfield: 116 + 18 apps. 12 goals.

Born: Stakeford near Bedlington, Northumberland, 3 June 1957. Career: Bedlington Grammar School. Northumberland Boys (1971–72). ALBION (apprentice, July 1972, professional, July 1974). Newcastle United (£234,000, December 1980). Oxford United (on loan, January 1984, signing permanently, July 1984). Birmingham City (£30,000, September 1987). Bromsgrove Rovers (August 1989). Hartlepool United (October 1989). Bromsgrove Rovers (May 1990). Gateshead (October 1990). Tamworth (briefly). ALBION (youth team coach, 1993, later reserve-team coach and also caretaker manager). Derby County (assistant manager, coach, 2001–02). Cradley Town (assistant manager, coach, 2002–03). Wolverhampton Wanderers (Academy Director, August 2003–May 2004). Hereford United (coach, August 2004). Also coach to Birmingham Festival League side Martini International (1979–80).

■ John 'Tucker' Trewick was a determined midfield-grafter who put in some good performances during his six-year professional career at The Hawthorns. After 134 games for Albion he had 87 outings with Newcastle and then joined Oxford, who successfully converted him into a steady left-back. In 1985 he helped the Us win the Second Division championship and the following year gained a Milk (League) Cup winners' medal when Oxford beat

Queen's Park Rangers 1–0 at Wembley. As a lad, both schoolboy and England youth international honours came Trewick's way and his move to the Blues, in the pre-season of 1987, materialised after he was given a free transfer at the end of the previous campaign. He made his senior debut for Albion against Bristol City (home) in Division Two in November 1974, and he also appeared in over 160 Central League games, scoring 29 goals.

TUDOR, William Henry

Centre-half: 34 apps.

Born: Shotton, Chester, 14 February 1918. Died: June 1955. Career: Shotton & Sealand Road Schools. Llanerch Celts (1933). Lavender FC (Chester). ALBION (amateur, April 1934, professional, April 1935). Guest for Wrexham (four seasons), Nottingham Forest, Darlington and Swindon Town during World War Two. Wrexham (signed for £750, May 1946). Bangor City (July 1949, retired, May 1950).

■ A Welsh schoolboy international (capped in 1933), Bill Tudor lavished a lot of thought to his game. A centre-half who tried to use the ball rather than thump it downfield, he was unlucky in as much as the outbreak of World War Two ruined a most promising career, although he did play through the hostilities and represented the Western Command in 1945. He did play in 56 League games for Wrexham before suffering a nasty knee injury in 1949. He made his League debut against Newcastle United (away) in Division Two in September 1938. Albion lost 5–1 and United's centre-forward, Cairns (marked by Tudor), netted four of those goals! He also made 24 appearances for the Baggies second XI. Bill's father, Tom Tudor, was an Albion reserve in 1906–07.

TURNER, Isaiah

Goalkeeper: 1 app.

Born: Netherton, Dudley, 8 July 1876. Died: Dudley, February 1936. Career: Blowers Green School (Dudley). Netherton Boys' Club. Dudley St James's (1894). ALBION (professional, May 1898). Stourbridge (July 1899). Dudley Town (1902). Kidderminster Harriers (April 1903). Stoke (1906–07). Old Hill

Wanderers (August 1907, retired May 1911).

■ 'Ike' Turner was an acrobatic goalkeeper whose career was more pronounced with Stoke (seven appearances) than it was with Albion (one outing only, against Wolverhampton Wanderers (home) in Division One in October 1898). He did, however, appear in 12 second XI matches.

TURNER, Samuel Isaiah

Inside-left: 1 app.

Born: Langley Green, Oldbury, 7 August 1882.
Died: Dudley, June 1964.
Career: Sprint Street School. Oldbury Town (1898). Darlaston (1902). ALBION (professional, September 1904). Brierley Hill Alliance (August 1905). Coventry City (briefly). Bristol Rovers (1907–08). Dudley Town (May 1911, retired through injury, May 1913).

■ 'Sammy' Turner was a junior international inside-left with a cannonball shot, which sadly he wasn't able to use all that often during his brief spell with Albion – making only one senior appearance against Burslem Port (home) in Division Two on Boxing Day in 1904.

TWIGG, Lewis

Goalkeeper: 2 apps.

Born: Buxton, Derbyshire, 5 August 1921.
Career: Upper End & Burbage Schools. Buxton FC (March 1937). ALBION (November 1945, retired through injury, June 1947, guest for Swansea Town 1945–46). ALBION (scout, 1952–56).

■ Lew Twigg was a grand goalkeeper whose quickness off his line and overall handling of both high and low crosses were features of his game. He made his Albion debut against Cardiff City (home) in the FA Cup third round, second leg, in January 1946. He also played in 32 Central League games. He is one of Albion's oldest living ex-players.

UDEZE, Ifeanyi

Full-back: 7+4 apps.

Born: Kavala Nigeria, 21 July 1980.
Career: Benden Insurance Kavala (1996). PAOK Salonika. Greece (professional,

1998). ALBION (Bosman free transfer, January–May 2003). PAOK Salonika (free, August 2003). FC Kaernton, Austria (August 2004).

■ A Nigerian international with 20 caps to his credit, Iffy Udeze made his Albion debut in the away game against Manchester City (won 2–1) soon after arriving at the club. At times he looked good, attacking down the left flank, but an injured knee set him back.

VALENTINE, Carl Henry

Outside-left: 53 apps. 7 goals.

Born: Manchester, 4 July 1958.
Career: Manchester & District Schools. Trafford Park Boys (1972). Oldham Athletic (apprentice, July 1974, professional, January 1976). Vancouver Whitecaps (March 1979). ALBION (£60,000, October 1984). Wichita Wings, USA Indoor League (January 1986). Cleveland Force, NASL (March 1986). Calgary Kickers (August 1987). Vancouver 69ers (manager, 2000–02). Vancouver Whitecaps (coach, April 2003).

■ A player who hugged the touchline, Carl Valentine showed some clever touches, coupled with a fair turn of speed and improvisation. He looked rather over-weight during his 16 month stay at The Hawthorns. In the NASL championship of 1983–84 he scored a record-breaking 44 goals for the Whitecaps, which prompted two clubs, Las Vegas and Cleveland Force (whom he later joined), to offer him mouth-watering contracts worth £500,000 and £800,000 respectively, which he turned down to come to Albion – signed by his former Whitecaps boss, Johnny Giles. In 1986 Valentine represented his chosen country, Canada, in the World Cup finals in Mexico (three caps gained). He also collected at least two more playing against Wales and England in friendly internationals. He made his Albion debut against Ipswich Town (away) in Division One in October 1984 but went off injured after 25 minutes and 11 seconds. His 'finest' goal for the Albion was the winner against Aston Villa in April 1985 (1–0).

VAN BLERK, Jason

Defender/midfield: 117+4 apps. 3 goals.

Born: Sydney, Australia, 16 March 1968.

Career: Sydney Colts. St George FC, Australia (1987). Blacktown City, Australia (1988–89). Apia Leichardt FC, Belgium (1989–90). K St-Truidense VV, Belgium (1990–91). Apai Leichardt FC (1991–92). Go Ahead Eagles of Deventer, Holland (full-time professional, August 1992). Millwall (£300,000, September 1994). Manchester City (free, August 1997). ALBION (£250,000, March 1998–June 2001). Stockport County (August 2001). Hull City (January 2002). Shrewsbury Town (August 2002). Colwyn Bay (June 2003).

■ A tough defender, Jason Van Blerk was released by Baggies boss Gary Megson at the end of the 2000–01 season and two months later signed for Megson's former club, Stockport (with Richard Sneekes). He made over 120 senior appearances for Albion at senior level and over a dozen for the second team. In 2003 he reached the milestone of 400 appearances in competitive League and cup football (all clubs), having been signed by ex-Albion manager Brian Little for Hull City. Now with 27 full international caps for Australia under his belt, Van Blerk was sent off against Chile in his second international back in February 2000.

VARADI, Imre

Striker: 39+2 apps. 13 goals.

Born: Paddington, London, 8 July 1959.
Career: Paddington & Central London

Schools. Letchworth Garden City. FC 75 of Hitchen (1974). Sheffield United (apprentice, July 1975, professional, April 1978). Everton (£80,000, March 1979). Newcastle United (£125,000, August 1981). Sheffield Wednesday (£150,000 plus David Mills, August 1983). ALBION (£285,000, June 1985). Manchester City (player/exchange involving Robert Hopkins, October 1986). Sheffield Wednesday (in exchange for Carl Bradshaw, September 1988). Leeds United (£50,000, February 1990). Luton Town (on loan, March–April 1992). Oxford United (on loan, January–February 1993). Rotherham United (March 1993). Boston United (May 1995). Mansfield Town (non-contract, August 1995). Scunthorpe United (non-contract, August 1995). Matlock Town (player-manager, November 1995–May 1996). Guiseley (player-coach, late 1996). Denaby United (player-coach, January 1997–May 1998). Stalybridge Celtic (assistant manager/coach, 1998–99). Later became a Football agent and also worked briefly for the PFA.

■ 'Ray' Varadi was a natural goalscorer, hitting the target consistently for every club he served. Fast, alert and keen-eyed, he in fact netted 93 goals at competitive level prior to his move to The Hawthorns in 1985. He then hit the target on his Albion debut against Oxford United (home) in Division One in August 1985 (1–1 draw), and after leaving The Hawthorns he top-scored in 1986–87 for Manchester City with nine goals. He later struck another 60 goals before dropping out of League football in 1995. He had earlier finished up as leading marksman for the 'Owls' when they gained promotion from the Second Division. In May 1986 Varadi was sent off for the first time in his career – playing for Albion's Central League side at Hull. He hit 10 goals in 15 second XI games for the club. Varadi was sent off playing for Rotherham against Albion in 1993.
* His brother, Fernando Varadi, played for Fulham.

VARGA, Stanislav

Full-back: 3+1 apps.

Born: Czechoslovakia, 8 October 1972.
Career: Tretran Presov (1994). SK Slovan Bratislava (1998). Sunderland (£650,000, August 2000). ALBION (on loan, March–May 2002). Celtic (free, January 2003).

■ A Slovakian international, capped 40 times at senior level, Stanislav Varga was recruited by Albion boss Gary Megson as defensive cover as the race for the Premiership hotted up. He played in four League games, making his debut against Crewe Alexandra in March 2002, and he later did exceptionally well with Celtic, helping the Bhoys win the Scottish Premier title in 2004 and the Scottish Cup in 2005.

VARNEY, Herbert

Outside-right: 5 apps.

Born: Belper, Derbyshire, 12 February 1885.
Died: Derby, January 1947.
Career: Belper & Denby Schools. Heanor Miner's Welfare (1900). Belper Town (August 1901). Derby County (March 1902). Belper Town (September 1903). ALBION (professional, October 1905). Belper Town (May 1907, retired, April 1915). Served in the Army during World War One.

■ A well-built and genuine right-winger, Herbert Varney played in five League games for Albion and was on the winning side each time. Signed originally as cover for Jimmy Williams, he made his senior debut against Manchester United (home) in Division Two in October 1905.

VARTY, James William

Wing-half: 3 apps.
Born: Scotswood, Newcastle-upon-Tyne, 2 December 1890.
Died: Hartlepool, 1958.
Career: Shildon Schools. Shildon Athletic (1906). Scotswood Rovers (1909). ALBION (professional, March 1911). Hartlepools United (free, August 1913). Heart of Midlothian (1914–15). Did not figure after World War One.

■ A player who could adapt between playing inside-forward or as a wing-half, Jimmy Varty had loads of skill, could hit a masterly long ball but was sadly dogged by injuries throughout his career, breaking his leg twice. He made his debut for Albion against Woolwich Arsenal (home) in Division One in November 1912 and also played regularly in the club's second XI in 1912–13, collecting a Birmingham & District championship medal in the process.

VERNON, John

Centre-half: 200 apps. 1 goal.

Born: Belfast, 26 September 1919.
Died: Belfast, August 1981.
Career: St Paul's School (Belfast). Springfield Road Juniors (1934). Dundela Juniors (1935). Liverpool (amateur, 1937). Belfast Celtic (professional, August 1938). ALBION (£9,500, February 1947). Crusaders (free, July 1952, retired, June 1954 to continue his father's butchers' business in Belfast, a job he did until his untimely death in 1981). Sadly, his wife died 24 hours later.

■ Without a shadow of doubt, Jack Vernon was one of Albion's greatest centre-halves, fine in defence, supreme in the air and masterful on the ground – a true sportsman of the highest calibre. Albion signed him on a five-year contractual agreement in 1947, handing over a then record cheque to Belfast Celtic. 'Money well spent' said Albion's secretary-manager Fred Everiss. However, owing to the bitterly cold arctic weather that gripped Britain that winter, Vernon had to wait five weeks before making his Baggies debut, and when he did – at West Ham – it was a game he wanted to forget!

The 'Hammers' centre-forward, Frank Neary, bagged a hat-trick as Albion lost 3–2, but, undisturbed, Veron soon settled down into the routine of commanding the back division – a job he did so successfully, not only for Albion but at international level as well. He won 22 caps (two for the Republic of Ireland, 20 for Ireland) and skippered the latter country on 17 occasions. He was also captain of the United Kingdom side against Wales in 1951 and starred at centre-half for the Great Britain XI against The Rest of Europe at Hampden Park in 1947 – an honour that proved he was the game's top pivot at that time. Before he arrived at The Hawthorns, Vernon, who was nicknamed 'Twinkletoes' because of his size 5 feet, won Irish Cup medals in 1941, 1943 and 1944, Irish League championship medals in 1939 and 1940 and represented the Irish FA Select on several occasions while also starring for the Irish Regional League 12 times between 1941–46. He led Albion to promotion in 1948–49 and totalled exactly 200 senior appearances for the Baggies, scoring one goal – a Christmas present against Sheffield Wednesday in 1948. He also played in four second XI matches.

VIGROW, Scott

Inside-left: 1 app.

Born: Muirhead, Angus, Scotland, 20 March 1878.
Died: Scotland 1945.
Career: Muirhead & Callander Schools. Dundee Thistle (1895). Dundee (April 1896). ALBION (£25, October 1896). Airdrieonians (free, July 1897–May 1899). Later with Ayr United (1910). Hamilton Academicals (1912). Did not play after World War One.

■ Scott Vigrow was a clever, all-action forward who was far better suited to the conditions north of the border than he was in the south. He made his Football League debut for Albion against Liverpool (home) in Division One in October 1896.

VINCENT, Edwin Arthur

Wing-half: 1 app.

Born: Tipton, 28 January 1920.
Died: Dudley, 1996.

Career: Jessons Church of England School (Dudley). Toll End Wesley (August 1937). ALBION (amateur, March 1939, professional, August 1944). Worcester City (August 1946). Dudley Town (June 1948, retired, May 1952).

■ A World War Two signing, Ted Vincent never really developed and left soon after peacetime soccer had re-commenced in the mid-1940s. He made his Albion debut against Leicester City (away) in the Football League North in October 1944.

VOLMER, Joost

Defender: 12+6 apps.

Born: Enschede, Holland, 7 March 1974.
Career: FC Twente, Holland (junior, July 1990). AZ Alkmaar, Holland (professional, July 1992). Helmond Sport, Holland (August 1995). VVV (Venlo), Holland (August 1996). MVV Maastricht, Holland (July 1997). Fortuna Sittard (May 1999). ALBION (trialist, May–July 2003, signed August 2003). FC Den Bosch, Holland (September 2004).

■ After playing in pre-season friendly matches against Cheltenham Town and Plymouth Argyle, Albion's 6ft 2in Dutch-born defender Joost Volmer – who was recommended to the club by former Baggies player Romeo Zondervan – made his Football League debut on the opening day of the 2003–04 season, in a 4–1 defeat at Walsall. A solid performer, strong in the air and on the ground, he made over 200 appearances in his home country before agreeing an initial one-year contract with Albion. He made 13 appearances for the Baggies second XI.

WALFORD, Stephen James

Defender: 3+1 apps.

Born: Islington, London, 5 January 1958.
Career: Highgate & North London Schools. Tottenham Hotspur (apprentice, July 1973, professional, April 1975). Arsenal (£25,000, August 1977). Norwich City (£175,000, March 1981). West Ham United (£160,000, August 1983). Huddersfield Town (on loan, October–December 1987). Gillingham (on loan, 1988–89). ALBION (on loan, March–May 1989). Wycombe Wanderers (1990–91). Lai Sun FC, Hong Kong

(1992). Norwich City (coach, June 1995). Leicester City (coach, December 1995). Celtic (coach, July 2000).

■ Steve Walford won England youth honours in 1976 (with John Deehan and Gary Owen) and an FA Cup winners' medal with Arsenal (as a 'sub') in 1979. A good reader of situations with an excellent left 'peg', he appeared in over 300 senior appearances during his professional career that began with Spurs against Liverpool in December 1975. He made his Albion debut against Leeds United (home) in Division Two in March 1989, as a substitute. He played in four second XI matches.

WALKER, David

Forward: 39 apps. 15 goals.

Born: Oakdene, Walsall, 2 July 1884.
Died: October 1935.
Career: Pleck Road Schools (Walsall). Walsall White Star (1899). Birchfield Villa (1902). Wolverhampton Wanderers (professional, September 1904). Bristol Rovers (free, August 1905). ALBION (£100, April 1907). Leicester Fosse (£700, plus Arthur Randle, May 1908). Bristol Rovers (July 1911). Willenhall Swifts (briefly). Walsall (August 1913, retired, April 1920).

■ David Walker was a highly effective utility forward, dangerous near goal, who could bore his way through a defence silkily, requiring little or no space in which to manoeuvre before unleashing a thumping shot. His clever footwork was put to the test after he had left Albion, but he still managed to score regularly. He made his Albion debut against Wolverhampton Wanderers (away) in Division Two in September 1907, scoring in a 2–0 win.

WALKER, Luther

Full-back: 19 apps.

Born: West Bromwich, 6 April 1860.
Died: January 1903.
Career: Christ Church School. West Bromwich Baptists (1876). West Bromwich Standard (1878). West Bromwich Royal (1880). ALBION (amateur, April 1883, professional, August 1885, retired through injury, August 1892).

■ Luther Walker was an excellent full-back, equally adept with his head and both feet and could kick a ball an astronomical distance. Sadly, injuries and ill-health curtailed his career sooner than he had anticipated. He made his senior debut for Albion against Derby Junction (away) in a second round FA Cup tie in November 1886, and besides his 19 senior outings for the club he also played in more than 35 'other' first-team matches.

WALKER, Walter

Centre-forward: 1 app. 1 goal.

Born: Walsall, 21 February 1888.
Died: Walsall, 1968.
Career: Walsall Borough Schools. Walsall Town Swifts (1903). Darlaston (1906). Halesowen (1908). ALBION (professional, May 1910). Willenhall Swifts (June 1911–May 1913). Became a licensee in Wolverhampton after World War One.

■ Wally Walker was a reserve half-back with Albion but got a surprise call-up into the first team as an emergency centre-forward and scored to celebrate the occasion against Lincoln City (home) in Division Two in December 1910 (won 3–0). He also played in over 40 'other' first and second-team matches for the club, netting 10 goals, including an occasion when Burslem Port Vale were defeated 5–0 in the Staffordshire Cup final of 1900 and when the winners against Walsall in the the final of the Birmingham Charity Cup that same year.

WALKER, William Wilfred

Inside-forward: 34 apps. 5 goals.

Born: Horseley Heath, Tipton, 12 December 1879.
Died: West Bromwich, April 1944.
Career: Dudley Port & Coneygreve Schools. Toll End Wesley (1896). ALBION professional, August 1898). Brierley Hill Alliance (May 1903–May 1905).

■ A tireless inside-forward who contested for a first-team place with Billy Richards in 1899–1900, Billy Walker was then switched to the left-wing the following season. He made his League debut against Nottingham Forest (away) in October 1899, finishing on the side that lost 6–1. He also appeared in more than 40 games for the second XI, gaining a Birmingham & District League championship medal in 1902.

WALLACE, John Martin Bokas

Goalkeeper: 76 apps.

Born: Wallyford, Midlothian, 6 September 1935.
Died: 24 July 1996.
Career: Musselburgh Grammar School. South of Scotland Boys. Wallyford Boys' Club. Blackpool (trialist, August 1960). Workington (amateur, July 1951, professional, September 1952). Ashton-under-Lyme (August 1953). Berwick Rangers (1955–56). Airdrieonians (September 1956). ALBION (£10,000 October 1959). Bedford Town (June 1962–May 1964). Hereford United (August 1964–June 1966). Berwick Rangers (player-manager, December 1966–April 1969). Heart of Midlothian (coach-assistant manager, January 1969–April 1970). Glasgow Rangers (trainer-coach, June 1970–May 1972, then manager, June 1972–June 1978). Leicester City (manager, June 1978–July 1982). Motherwell (manager, August 1982-November 1983). Glasgow Rangers (manager, November 1983–May 1986). Seville FC, Spain (manager, May 1986–August 1987). Colchester United (manager, January 1989, resigned December 1989 to become director at Layer Road).

■ Jock Wallace was not the greatest of goalkeepers but was a daring one, who

could be superb at times then blotted his copy-book by dropping a clanger! While with Airdrie he played for the Scottish League against Scotland XI in 1959 – his only representative honour as a player. When boss of Rangers he saw every major Scottish trophy find its way to Ibrox (including the coveted treble twice in three years, in 1976 and 1978). The Scottish Cup was also won in 1973, the First Division championship again in 1975 and the Scottish League Cup clinched for a third time in 1984. He also lifted the Glasgow Challenge Cup, won when he was coach in 1971. In 1977 Rangers finished runners-up in the Scottish Cup, while five years earlier, in 1972, with a certain Willie Johnston scoring twice, Rangers were victorious in the European Cup-winners' Cup, beating Moscow Dynamo in the final. Earlier in his career, when manager of Berwick Rangers, Wallace plotted the downfall of Rangers in the Scottish Cup in January 1967 – and the Ibrox fans never forgot this sensational upset – not even when he moved there in 1970. In later years, when at Leicester, Wallace guided the 'Foxes' to the Second Division championship in 1980 and to the semi-final of the FA Cup in 1982. Certainly a far better manager than a goalkeeper, one might say, he made his Albion debut (with Bobby Cram) against Bolton Wanders (away) in Division One in October 1959, and he also played in 34 Central League games for the Baggies. He was a part-time sportsmaster at Handsworth Technical College (Birmingham) in the 1960s.

WALLWORK, Ronald

Defender/midfielder 53+7 apps. 1 goal.

Born: Newton Heath, Manchester, 10 September 1977.
Career: Manchester United (apprentice, April 1993, professional, March 1995). Carlisle United (on loan, December 1997–January 1998). Stockport County (on loan, March–April 1998). Royal Antwerp (on loan, season 1998–99). ALBION (free, July 2002). Bradford City (on loan, January–March 2004).

■ Brought up with the likes of David Beckham, the Neville brothers, Nicky Butt, Ryan Giggs, Roy Keane and Paul Scholes at Old Trafford, the versatile Ronnie Wallwork made only 28

appearances for Manchester United, mainly performing in midfield. He also had 19 games as a loan player in Belgium at Carlisle and Stockport, before embarking on his career at The Hawthorns, making his Albion debut as a substitute in the club's first ever Premiership victory, 1–0 against Fulham (home) in September 2002. An England youth international, he gained FA Youth Cup (1995) and Premiership (winners' medals with United (2001). He was signed by ex-Baggies star Bryan Robson on loan for relegation-threatened Bradford but returned to The Hawthorns before the end of the deal owing to injury. However, when Robson returned to Albion as the new boss Wallwork was quickly installed into the senior side, and the former Manchester United star duly obliged with his first goal for the club in a 2–0 home Premiership win over Manchester City in January 2005. Besides his first-team appearances he has also played in over 20 second-team games for the Baggies.

* In September 1999 Wallwork had a life time ban for assaulting a referee overturned by a civil court in Belgium.

WALSH, David John

Centre-forward: 174 apps. 100 goals.

Born: Waterford, Ireland, 28 April 1923.
Career: St Joseph's School (Waterford). The Corinthians, Shelbourne (Waterford). Glen Rovers (1941). Limerick (August 1942). Shelbourne (Dublin, on loan during

1942–43). Linfield (August 1943). ALBION (£3,500 May 1946). Aston Villa (£25,000, December 1950). Walsall (July 1955). Worcester City (August 1956, retired, June 1957). Ran a successful sports outfitters at Droitwich, Worcestershire, for many years before retiring to Thurlestone, South Devon, in 1984 (where he still lives).

■ Dave Walsh was the ideal build for a striker – a job he did splendidly for Albion in the immediate post-war years. A player with speed and thrust, he was a consistent goalscorer throughout his career that saw him win 31 caps (11 for Ireland and 20 for Eire with 5 goals scored). He also represented the Irish League twice in 1946 and helped Albion gain promotion from Division Two in

1948–49, netting 23 League goals. As keen as mustard in and around the 'box', Walsh registered over 60 goals for Linfield in 1945–46 when they won the Irish League title, and he also starred, and scored twice, in the Irish Cup final against Distillery that same season. This sort of form attracted the attentions of Albion secretary Fred Everiss and director Claude Jephcott, who travelled over to Ireland and signed Walsh on the spot, the club's first capture after World War Two. The Irishman set off like a house on fire when the English League season started up in August 1946, scoring in each of his first six games – a club record – including two on his debut away at Swansea Town (won 3–2). He ended his career at The Hawthorns with exactly 100 goals to his credit (94 being from 165 League outings), plus three more in second XI games. Afterwards he added another 45 to his tally with Villa and Walsall before drifting into non-League soccer in 1956. Earlier, he had netted 122 goals in Irish football, collecting cup medals in 1944 (runners-up) and 1945 (winners). He was certainly the envy of many Irish footballers when he left the Emerald Isle to join the Baggies for what turned out to be a real bargain fee of just £3,500 – and his first mission with Albion was to represent the FA of Ireland (with his fellow countryman and future Hawthorns star Jack Vernon) against Spain in June 1946.

WARD, Gavin John

Goalkeeper: 1 app.

Born: Sutton Coldfield, 30 June 1970.
Career: Aston Villa (apprentice, June 1986). Shrewsbury Town (professional, September 1988). ALBION (free, September 1989). Cardiff City (free, October 1989). Leicester City (£175,000, July 1993). Bradford City (£175,000, July 1995). Bolton Wanderers (£300,000, March 1996). Burnley (on loan, August–October 1998). Stoke City (free, February 1999). Walsall (free, August 2002). Coventry City (August 2003). Barnsley (on loan, April–May 2004). Preston North End (July 2004).

■ Gavin Ward's only senior appearance

for Albion was in a League Cup game against Bradford City (home) in September 1989 when the Bantams won 3–1. He also played in six Central League matches. However, with Paul Bradshaw and Stuart Naylor ahead of him in the selection stakes, he moved on and developed into a very capable goalkeeper, amassing more than 300 senior appearances while gaining both a Third Division championship and Welsh Cup winners' medal in 1993 and an Autoglass Trophy winners' medal in 2000.

WARD, Robert Andrew

Goalkeeper: 10 apps.

Born: West Bromwich, 4 August 1953.
Career: Manor High School (West Bromwich). Imperial Star FC (1970). ALBION (apprentice, November 1972, professional, March 1973). Northampton Town (on loan, February 1977). Blackpool (£15,000, September 1977). Wigan Athletic (July 1979, retired with a back injury, October 1981). Qualified as a physiotherapist, initially working at Rhyl General Hospital, then taking a similar position with Blackpool (August 1986). Later with Chelsea (as physio, September 1988–May 1995). Middlesbrough (physiotherapist, 1996 to date).

■ Bob Ward acted as understudy to John Osborne and Peter Latchford during his first few years at The Hawthorns. Then Tony Godden arrived and he looked for a change of club, moving to Blackpool after

a brief spell on loan at both Northampton and Blackpool. A competent 'keeper, tall and agile, he had 41 League games with the Seasiders and 46 with Wigan before injury forced him to quit the sport in 1982. A testimonial match was arranged on his behalf – Wigan Athletic against Albion – in March 1983. Ward made his debut for the Baggies against Sheffield Wednesday (home) in Division Two in March 1975. He also played in 130 Central League games for the club.

WATERHOUSE, Frank

Defender: 188 apps. 6 goals.

Born: Langley Green Oldbury, 23 July 1889.
Died: Smethwick, June 1967.
Career: Langley Infants & Junior Schools. Langley St Michael's. Langley St Michael's Guild. Langley Green (1905). Wednesbury Old Athletic (September 1906). ALBION (February 1908). Kidderminster Harriers (free, August 1913). Derby County (£1,000, March 1920). Leeds United (August 1921). Dudley Town (August 1922, retired November 1924). Worked in an Oldbury engineering factory for 20 years either side of World War Two.

■ Frank 'Puffer' Waterhouse gained a junior international cap in 1909 and after that never looked back, going from strength to strength with Albion, appearing in well over 180 first and 50 second XI games, collecting a Second Division championship medal in 1911. A player of sound judgment and all round efficiency, he was a fine tackler and kicker, a stickler for hard work and one who gave opponents little or no room in which to use their ability. He took over the centre-half berth from Ted Pheasant, later switching to right-half in place of George Baddeley. He never really got a chance during his spells with Derby and Leeds. His League debut was against Leicester Fosse (home) in Division Two in November 1909.

WATSON, Arthur

Inside-forward/winger: 30 apps. 3 goals.

Born: Hucknall, Nottinghamshire, 4 July 1868.
Died: Nottingham, April 1937.
Career: Hucknall Town (1885). Mansfield

Invicta (1886). Mansfield Town (1889). Notts County (professional, August 1893). Mansfield Town (September 1894). ALBION (£25, August 1896). Lincoln City (free, December 1898, retired through injury, May 1899).

■ Arthur Watson enjoyed 'fast dribbling' whether down the wing of through the centre, he possessed a long raking stride, powerful right-foot shot and whipped over dangerous centres, high or low. Able to fire in a 'screw shot' using the toe-end of his boot, he made his first appearance for Albion against Preston North End (home) in Division One in September 1896, scoring in a 1–1 draw. He also played in more than 20 'other' first-team games for the club. Prior to moving to Albion, Watson had scored for Notts County in their 1894 FA Cup final victory over Bolton Wanderers.

NB: There was another Arthur Watson playing at the same time as the one associated with Albion. He served with Sheffield United, Rotherham Swifts, Lincoln City and Leeds City – and some reference books have the records of these two players mixed up.

WATSON, Ernest

Right-half: 1 app.

*Born: West Bromwich, 6 December 1901.
Died: March 1980.
Career: St Phillip's School (West Bromwich). Tanfield FC (1919). ALBION (February 1922). Hereford United (March 1923). Kidderminster Harriers (1927–28). Later engaged in the fish and vegetable market.*

■ A reserve half-back who won junior international honours in 1923, Ernie Watson, raven-haired and slender in build, stepped in for Sammy Richardson for his only senior outing in an Albion shirt in May 1922 against Liverpool (home) in Division One, which was also Jesse Pennington's last appearance for the Baggies.

WEBB, Alan Richard

Defender: 23+2 apps.

*Born: Wrockwardine Wood, Salop, 1 January 1963.
Career: Orleton Park School (Telford). Shropshire & District Schools. Admaston FC. Oakengates FC (1977). ALBION (apprentice, July 1978, professional, January 1980). Lincoln City (on loan, March–May 1984). Port Vale (July 1984, retired through injury, June 1992). Later joint manager of Stourbridge.*

■ A solid, forceful defender who can play in either full-back berth or as a sweeper, Alan Webb made his debut for Albion in a European competition against Grasshoppers Zurich (home) in a UEFA Cup second round, second leg, clash in September 1981 as substitute. He always found it hard to establish himself in the senior side at The Hawthorns but later did well with Port Vale, for whom he made 235 senior appearances. He won a Central League championship medal in 1982–83 and played 119 times for Albion's second team (7 goals scored). He was voted Vale's 'Player of the Year' in 1985 and the following season helped the Potteries club gain promotion from the Fourth Division as an ever-present. Again, he was in Vale's promotion-winning side from Division Three in 1988–89. He had to have a blood clot removed from his thigh in November 1987 and suffered a compound fracture of his right leg (against Newcastle) in October 1989, having earlier suffered second-degree burns to his hip, knee and elbow on Preston's artificial pitch in 1987. His career ended after he damaged his cruciate ligaments in his plagued right leg in 1992.

WEBB, Isaac

Goalkeeper: 101 apps.

*Born: Worcester, 1 October 1874.
Died: Winson Green, Birmingham, 12 March 1950.
Career: Worcester Park School. St Clement's Rangers. Berwick Rangers (Worcester League). Worcester Olympic. Evesham Town. Lincoln City (briefly). Mansfield Town. Wellington Town. Evesham Town (1897). Small Heath (free, August 1898). ALBION (£100, May 1901). Sunderland (£250, December 1904). Queen's Park Rangers (November 1906, retired, 1910). Worked in the building trade (London). Made a comeback with ALBION (August 1918, aged 43).*

■ 'Ike' Webb was a goalkeeper of outstanding reflexes and quickness off his

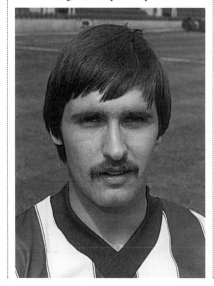

line, being spectacularly agile at times, his actions were usually so perfectly timed, although occasionally he tended to be somewhat casual. It is said that Webb played football at one stage in his career with a fractured skull. He always wore a cap and joined Albion as a replacement for Joe Reader (retired), going on to make over 100 appearances in three-and-a-half seasons at the club before handing over his duties to Fred Cook then Jim Stringer. Webb helped Albion win promotion to the First Division in season 1901–02, playing exceedingly well throughout that campaign, when he conceded just 29 goals in 33 outings. He made his debut against Glossop (home) in September 1901 and served in the Army (Brocton Camp, Stafford) during World War One.

WEBSTER, Herbert

Goalkeeper: 1 app.

Born: Walsall, 5 October 1910.
Career: Fereday Street Council School (Walsall). Beaudesert FC. Burntwood Villa (1926) ALBION (professional, March 1928). Swindon Town (£300, May 1929). Walsall (free, August 1932). Lichfield Rangers (September 1933, retired, 1939). Now living in the Cannock, Hednesford area.

■ Reserve to Harold Pearson and George Ashmore, Bert Webster was a capable goalkeeper, who, after leaving The Hawthorns, conceded 10 goals while playing for Swindon against Manchester City in an FA Cup tie in January 1930. He joined Walsall as cover for Roy John. He made his League debut against Bradford Park Avenue (home) in Division Two in March 1929 and is believed to be the oldest former Albion player alive today.

WEST, Colin

Striker: 72+9 apps. 24 goals.

Born: Wallsend-on-Tyne, 13 November 1962.
Career: Wallsend-on-Tyne & County Durham Schools. Sunderland (apprentice July 1978, professional, July 1980). Watford (£115,000, March 1985). Glasgow Rangers (£180,000, May 1986). Sheffield Wednesday (£150,000, September 1987). ALBION (£250,000, February 1989 in a player exchange deal involving Carlton

Palmer). Port Vale (on loan, November–December 1991). Swansea City (free, August 1992). Leyton Orient (free, July 1993). Northampton Town (on loan, September 1997). Rushden and Diamonds (on loan, December 1997–July 1999). Later coach at Hartlepool United (2000–01). Sheffield Wednesday (assistant manager, 2003–04).

■ Although classed as an out-and-out striker and not always a crowd favourite, Colin West struggled at times to find the net (especially at Hillsborough). Yet during his major professional career, which spanned 18 years, he still managed to score 157 goals in just over 550 senior appearances while serving with nine different clubs. He was sent off playing for Swansea against Albion in the 1993 play-off final second leg, eight years after scoring a hat-trick for Watford against the Baggies in a League game. His debut for Albion was against Birmingham City (home) in Division Two in February 1989. West also scored 20 goals in 33 Central League games for the Baggies.

WHELDON, George Frederick

Inside-forward: 29 apps. 3 goals.

Born: Langley Green, Oldbury, 1 November 1869.
Died: Worcester, 13 January 1924.

Career: Chance's School (Oldbury). Rood End White Star (1885). Langley Green Victoria (1887). ALBION (trialist, April–May 1890). Small Heath (August 1890). Aston Villa (£350, June 1896). ALBION (£100, August 1900). Queen's Park Rangers (£50, December 1901). Portsmouth (free, August 1902). Worcester City (July 1904, retired, January 1907). Worcestershire County cricketer, 1899–1906, scoring 4,938 runs, including three centuries and taking 93 catches as a wicketkeeper. He also played cricket for Carmarthenshire (1910–11).

■ Fred Wheldon demoralised many a defence with his intricate dribbling. Nicknamed 'Diamond', he was brilliant at laying on chances for his colleagues. He gained four England caps (1897–98) and was on the winning side each time, played four times for the Football League side and also won three League Division One championship medals with Aston Villa (1897, 1899 and 1900), as well as receiving an FA Cup medal in 1897 when Villa completed the 'double'. Earlier, with Small Heath, Wheldon won a Second Division championship medal and a year later he helped the Blues win promotion. He appeared in over 130 games for Villa, finishing as the First Division's top scorer in 1897–98 with 21 goals and was appointed captain of Albion on his much-heralded arrival at The Hawthorns, but he was well past his best in the 1900–01 season. He made his debut for Albion in the Black Country derby against Wolverhampton Wanderers (away) in September 1900. Earlier, as a trialist, he played for Albion against his future club Aston Villa in May 1890.

WHELDON, Samuel

Wing-half: 1 app.

Born: Smethwick, 8 February 1865.
Died: Birmingham, December 1930.
Career: St George's School. Langley Green Victoria. Langley Broadway. Langley Swifts. Langley Victoria (1888). ALBION (professional, December 1891). Walsall (May 1892). Erdington Wood (1898), retired, c.1900).

■ A player who could fill in at left-half or as a wing-half, Sam Wheldon was a reserve for Albion in the 1892 FA Cup final, but played only one game during his 10 month stay with the club, against

Accrington (away) in Division One in January 1892. He was the brother of Fred Wheldon.

WHILE, John William

No senior apps.

Born: West Bromwich, 10 March 1861. Died: Lindfield, Victoria, Australia, July 1944.
Career: Christ Church School. George Salter Works. ALBION (August 1880–January 1884). Emigrated to Australia where he became a successful businessman, working in Victoria. He was tragically killed in an accident at the age of 83, being struck by a passing car while boarding a stationary tram. He had plan-ned to revisit England after World War Two.

■ Albion's honorary secretary for two seasons – 1880–82 – and the club's first captain after the Strollers title had been dropped, Jack While was a sound left-half whose career ended when he broke his right leg playing for Albion in the Wednesbury Charity Cup final of May 1883 against Nottingham Forest. He skippered the team to victory in the Staffordshire Cup final of that same year, when Albion won their first ever trophy. He made his debut during the 1880–81 season, playing in numerous local cup ties for Albion until his enforced retirement. He founded Springs FC in Australia in 1885.

WHITE, Harold Arthur

Full-back: 78 apps. 1 goal.

Born: Wednesbury, 16 June 1916. Died: Great Barr, Birmingham, 1981. Career: Kings Hill School (Wednesbury). Shaft Juniors (1932). Darlaston (1935). ALBION (£125, February 1937, professional, September 1937). Worcester City (free, May 1946, with his registration held by Albion for a season, retired, August 1951).

■ Harold White exhibited ability of the highest order from the right-back position, playing in almost 80 first-team games for Albion, 36 in the Football League. During World War Two he was awarded the Military Cross (March 1942). He made his debut for Albion against Sheffield United (home) in Division One in September 1938. He also played in 20 second-team matches.

WHITE, Eric Winston

Forward: 16+2 apps. 1 goal.

Born: Leicester, 26 October 1958. Career: Leicester City (apprentice, April 1975, professional, October 1976). Hereford United (£15,000, March 1979). Bulovga, Hong Kong. Chesterfield (non-contract, September 1983). Port Vale (non-contract, October 1983). Stockport County (non-contract, November 1983). Bury (December 1983). Rochdale (on loan, October–November 1986). Colchester United (February 1987). Burnley (£10,000, October 1988). ALBION (£35,000, March 1991). Bury (non-contract, October 1992). Doncaster Rovers (non-contract, January 1993). Carlisle United (non-contract, February 1993–May 1994). Later bought his own restaurant at Padiham near Burnley.

■ In a 20-year career, soccer journeyman Winston White played for 14 different clubs and appeared in well over 600 games in League and cup competitions, scoring more than 65 goals. His best spell came at Hereford (21 goals in 175 League games), and in two spells at Gigg Lane he netted 11 times in 127 League outings for Bury. He was well past his sell by date when he joined Albion, for whom he made just 18 senior appearances and 22 in the second XI. He made his first-team debut against Charlton Athletic (away) in March 1991. On his day he was a speedy, orthodox winger, exciting to watch and overall a pretty consistent performer.

WHITEHEAD, Clive Robert

Utility: 183 + 13 apps. 9 goals.

Born: Northfield, Birmingham, 24 November 1955.
Career: Alston Junior & Waverley Grammar Schools, Birmingham. Bordesley Green Boys. Northfield Juniors (1970). Wolverhampton Wanderers (trialist, 1971). Bristol City (March 1973, professional, August 1973). ALBION (£100,000 November 1981–July 1987). Portsmouth (free, July 1987). Wolverhampton Wanderers (on loan, January 1986). Exeter City (free, July 1989). Yeovil Town (free, player-manager, October 1990, sacked, April 1991). Bristol City (academy coach-scout, 1990s). Later became a football agent and referee's assessor.

■ Clive Whitehead, a former England youth international (1973), was a good, gritty, unselfish professional, who could perform equally well in any full-back position, as a central-defender or in midfield. At the start of his career he was a skilful left-winger and much sort after by many leading clubs, especially when helping Bristol City win promotion to Division One in season 1975–76, along with Albion. He played 256 games for the Ashton Gate club before joining Albion for a six-figure fee. In season 1982–83 he filled six different positions for the Baggies, but, during his stay at The Hawthorns, always regarded the right-

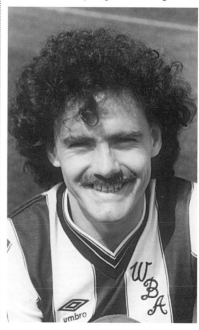

back slot as his best. He was going through a bad patch immediately prior to Ron Saunders taking over as manager in 1986, but the boss confided in him and told him he was the best number '2' in the Football League… if he put his mind to it. At the end of the 1986–87 season 'Scrumpy', as he was called, was released and subsequently joined newly-promoted Portsmouth, thus returning to the First Division much quicker than he had anticipated. He made his Albion debut against Tottenham Hotspur (away) in Division One in November 1981 and played in 14 Central League games (one goal). During his Football League career, Whitehead scored 26 goals in 544 games.

WHITEHEAD, Norman Jarrett

Outside-right: 1 app.

Born: Tamworth, 27 July 1914.
Died: Birmingham, April 1982.
Career: Amington Road & Tamworth Grammar Schools. Tamworth Grammar School Old Boys FC. Birmingham University (from 1929). ALBION (amateur, November 1932). Birmingham (amateur, July 1935, retired, 1937, to become a schoolteacher).

■ Norman Whitehead was a bespectacled right-winger of amateur status, who played for the FA Amateur XI in 1934 and also for England's junior international side in 1935. He still attended Birmingham University while registered with Albion, where he acted as cover for Tommy Glidden, making one senior appearance against Stoke City (away) in Division One on Boxing Day in 1934, while also gaining a Central League championship medal that same season.

WHITEHEAD, Philip Matthew

Goalkeeper: 28 apps.

Born: Halifax, Yorkshire, 17 December 1969.
Career: Halifax Town (apprentice, April 1986, professional, July 1988). Barnsley (£60,000, March 1990). Oxford United (£75,000, November 1993). ALBION (£250,000, December 1998). Reading (£250,000, October 1999). Halifax Town (on loan, March–May 1991). Scunthorpe United (on loan, November–December

1991 and September–October 1992). Bradford City (on loan, November 1992). Tranmere Rovers (on loan, September–October 2002). York City (on loan, April–May 2003). Tamworth (July 2003). Brentford (specialist coach, August 2004).

■ Goalkeeper Phil Whitehead took over from Alan Miller at The Hawthorns. A Yorkshireman, 6ft 3in tall and almost 16 stones in weight, he reached the personal milestone of 400 League appearances in 2002, while also passing the 475 barrier in all competitions. He made his debut for Albion against Bury at Gigg Lane in December 1998.

WHITEHOUSE, Brian

Utility forward: 46 apps. 17 goals.

Born: West Bromwich, 8 September 1935.
Career: Guns Village & George Salter Schools (West Bromwich). Vono Sports (1949). ALBION (April 1950, professional, October 1952). Norwich City (£7,000, March 1960). Wrexham (March 1962). Crystal Palace (November 1963). Charlton Athletic (March 1966). Orient (July 1966). Luton Town (trainer-coach, August 1968). Arsenal (coach, September 1968). ALBION

(coach, July 1971, appointed temporary manager at The Hawthorns, April 1975). Manchester United (coach, July 1981–89). WBA All Stars (1969–79). Later scout for a number of clubs including Aston Villa. Coventry City (chief scout, 1997–98). Now living in Sutton Coldfield.

■ Brian Whitehouse was a versatile forward who was honest, hard-working and sincere to the club. In a long and chequered career, including 10 years at The Hawthorns, he totted up over 350 senior appearances (280 at League level) and scored more than 90 goals, including both for Albion in the 1957 FA Cup semi-final against Aston Villa at Molineux (2–2 draw). Never a regular first-team player with the Baggies (owing to the presence of Messrs Allen, Kevan, Nicholls, Robson and others), he did do superbly well at second-team level, scoring 73 goals in 135 games in the Central League. He then did likewise with his five other clubs, scoring 14 times in 41 League games for Norwich, 19 in 45 for Wrexham, 17 in 82 for Palace, once in 13 for Charlton and six in 52 for Orient. He then became a coach and in 1971 saw Arsenal's youngsters carry off the FA Youth Cup, as well as assisting his old buddy Don How with first-team duties as the Gunners won the coveted League and cup double. As a player, Whitehouse

THE WHO'S WHO OF WEST BROMWICH ALBION

helped Wrexham win promotion from Division Four in 1962 and Norwich escape from Division Three in 1960. He also gained a Welsh Cup runners'-up medal with Wrexham in 1960. He made his Albion debut against Portsmouth (away) in Division One in April 1956.

WHITEHOUSE, James William

Outside-right: 1 app.

Born: West Bromwich, 12 August 1861.
Died: Batley, Yorkshire, June 1933.
Career: Beeches Road & St Phillip's Schools, West Bromwich. Holy Trinity FC. West Bromwich Rovers (1879). ALBION (August 1880, retired, May 1884). Moved to Dewsbury, Yorkshire, where he became a successful businessman.

■ One of Albion's first right-wingers, as hard as nails, 'Jack' Whitehouse put everything into his game and played for the club in several of their early friendly and minor competitive matches, including Albion's first ever FA Cup tie against Wednesbury Town (home) in the FA Cup first round in November 1883 (his senior debut).

WHYTE, Christopher Anderson

Defender: 95+1 apps. 9 goals.

Born: Islington, London, 2 September 1961.
Career: Highbury & District Schools. Highbury Grove FC. Highbury Hill. Islington Boys and Inner London Schools. Arsenal (junior 1976, apprentice, July 1977, professional, September 1979). Crystal Palace (on loan, August–November 1984). New York Express (July 1986). Los Angeles Lazers (1987–88). ALBION (free, August 1988, free transfer). Leeds United (tribunal set fee of £450,000, June 1990). Birmingham City (£250,000, August 1993). Coventry City (on loan, December 1995). Charlton Athletic (March 1996). West Ham United (on loan). Detroit Neon, USA Indoor Soccer League (1996). Leyton Orient (on a non-contract basis, January 1997). Oxford United (February 1997). Rushden and Diamonds (September 1997). Harlow Town (1999–2001).

■ Strong in the air and timely with his on-the-ground interceptions, tall, elegant central defender Chris Whyte made his

Football League debut for Arsenal in 1979. He joined Albion after making over 100 appearances for the Gunners and having a decent spell in America. He made almost a century of appearances during his two seasons at The Hawthorns and later helped Leeds win the Premiership title in 1992, before becoming the backbone of the Blues defence when they won the Second Division championship in 1995. Capped four times by England at under-21 level (all coming as an Arsenal player), Whyte passed the milestone of 500 career appearances in 1996–97 and actually made his debut for Oxford United against his former club, Albion. He was voted Albion's 'Player of the Year' in 1989 and made his senior debut for the club against Peterborough United (away) in the Littlewoods Cup in September 1988 and he also netted once in two Central League outings for the Baggies. He was signed by former Albion manager Brian Talbot for Rushden & Diamonds in 1997.

WILCOX, Edward Evan

Centre-forward: 12 apps. 3 goals.

Born: Blaengarw, Bridgend, South Wales, 24 March 1927.

Career: St Christopher's School (Oxford). Headington Council School. Oxford Boys. Oxford City (August 1946). ALBION (professional, October 1947). Worcester City (free, July 1951, retired, May 1959).

■ Eddie 'Ginger' Wilcox was originally a wing-half, but Albion converted him into a tough, hard-running centre-forward, playing in the first team on dozen of occasions, mainly as deputy to Dave Walsh and then as a stand-in for Cyril Williams (1950–51). He made his League debut against Barnsley (away) in Division Two in December 1948 (wearing the number 11 shirt). He scored 23 goals in 96 Central League games.

WILCOX, Harold Melbourne

Inside-forward: 20 apps. 7 goals.

Born: Hockley, Birmingham, 7 January 1878.
Died: Plymouth, 21 July 1937.
Career: Kings Parish School (Bromsgrove). St David's Youth Club, Small Heath (professional, September 1898). Watford (£500, July 1900). Preston North End (£750, April 1901). Plymouth Argyle (August 1905). Leicester Fosse (August 1906). ALBION (free, November 1907). Plymouth Argyle (May 1908, officially retired, May 1910, but continued to play non-League football until 1920). Later worked at The Barbacon, Plymouth.

■ Harry Wilcox was a gallant inside-forward who played football right up until he was almost 40 years of age. With his heavy moustache, he strutted around the field elegantly and amassed around 400 appearances for his various clubs, scoring 70 goals. He was a member of Preston's Second Division championship side in 1903–04 and as a centre-half, playing for Plymouth, represented the Southern League twice in 1910–11 against the Irish League. He made his Albion debut against Hull City (home) in Division Two in December 1907.

WILCOXSON, George Henry

Inside-forward: 1 app.

Born: Heanor, Derbyshire, 12 January 1925.
Career: Hardwick Council School

(Heanor). Heanor Town (1942). ALBION (amateur, June 1943, professional, November 1943). Mansfield Town (World War Two guest, 1944–45). Heanor Town (May 1946–June 1948).

■ 'Harry' Wilcoxson was a wartime signing by Albion after he had come to The Hawthorns asking for a trial. He played in one competitive game against Birmingham (home) in the Football League North in December 1943.

WILE, John David

Centre-half: 618 + 1 apps. 19 goals.

Born: Sherburn, Co. Durham, 9 March 1947.
Career: Sherburn Secondary Modern School. Eppleton Juniors (Hetton). Hetton Juniors. Durham City (junior, 1962). Peterborough United (trialist, 1963). Sunderland (apprentice, June 1964, professional, June 1966). Peterborough United (free, July 1967). ALBION (£32,000, December 1970). Vancouver Whitecaps (on loan, summer 1982). Rotherham United (briefly as a non-contract player, May 1983). Peterborough United (player-manager August 1983, retiring as a player, March 1986, resigning as manager, November 1986). WBA All Stars (1987–88). Later manager of Solihull Indoor Cricket School. Also Chief Executive of Walsall and Cradley Heath Indoor Cricket Schools. Sutton United (August 1987). ALBION (Chief Executive, March 1997–2002).

■ John Wile's last game for Albion at Sunderland (his former club), in mid-May 1983, was his 500th League appearance for the club. It crowned a magnificent 13-year association with the Throstles, during which time he made many friends, both inside and outside football. He was a fine ambassador in China (May 1978) and proved to everyone what an astute, reliable, commanding, powerful and forthright centre-half he was. Indeed, Wile was acknowledged by the fans as being one of Albion's finest ever pivots. He had the will to win and certainly gave the Baggies everything he had in terms of effort and commitment. Fans still recall his tremendous display in the 1978 FA Cup semi-final against Ipswich Town at Highbury, when he played on with his head swathed in heavy bandages after an

early clash of heads with scorer Brian Talbot. Blood filled his eyes but he bravely battled on, all to no avail as Albion lost 3–1. That was the true essence of John Wile, master centre-half, who was a born fighter, never a quitter and a 90 minute crusader. He retired from first-team football in March 1986 with 831 senior appearances under his belt (Albion and Peterborough). He had 20 outings for Vancouver and during his career also played in a further 140 'friendly' and tour matches, thus bringing his overall tally to around the 1,000 mark. Wile, who was Alan Ashman's last major signing as manager at The Hawthorns, took over the number 5 shirt at Albion from John Talbot. He made his debut against Blackpool at home in a First Division game in December 1970 and was a pillar of strength over the next 13 years before being replaced by Ken McNaught in 1983. During his reign at The Hawthorns, Albion fulfilled 525 League fixtures and 'Wiley' played in 500 of them. He missed only one cup tie in that time and also played in a handful of Central League games. In 1978–79 Albion fulfilled 76 first-team matches and Wile lined up in all but one of them, the most games ever played by an Albion footballer in a single season. He also played more matches at centre-half than any other player in Albion's history, 613, plus one as substitute, and in the League alone he wore the number 5 shirt on 497 occasions. He is the club's third-highest appearance-maker with 714+1 games (behind Tony Brown with 818 and Ally Robertson 729). Unfortunately, he never won a major honour in football. The nearest he came was to play in three cup semi-finals for Albion and in the quarter-

finals of the UEFA Cup, although he did help the team win promotion from the Second Division in 1975–76. An ever-present in seven seasons – an Albion record – there's never been a defensive partnership to equal that of Wile and Robertson. 'Robbo' was, in fact, his skipper's centre-back colleague for most of the time he was at The Hawthorns. Former Albion manager Johnny Giles said of Wile: 'If you could play football from nine in the morning till nine at night, seven days a week, 52 weeks a year, he still wouldn't be satisfied.'
* Wile was Albion's first ever Chief Executive/Director when appointed in 1997.

WILKES, Arthur Graham

Centre-half: 5 apps. 5 goals.

Born: Hagley near Kidderminster, 3 September 1918.
Died: West Bromwich, 1985.
Career: Worcester Road School (Hagley). Hagley Hall Boys. Aston Villa (amateur, 1934). Kidderminster Harriers (1935). Dudley Training College FC (1937). ALBION (amateur, June 1938, professional, May 1939). Guest for Portsmouth and Swansea Town during World War Two. Blackheath (September 1946). Later worked as sportsmaster and woodcraft teacher at George Salter School, West Bromwich (1948–60).

■ The son of the famous Midland photographer Albert Wilkes, Graham Wilkes was a go-ahead centre-forward whose thick black beard made him look more fearsome than he really was. World War Two obviously disrupted his playing career, but during the hostilities he played 24 games for Portsmouth and one for Swansea, top-scoring with 29 goals for Pompey in 1940–41. He made his Albion debut against Manchester United (home) in the third round of the FA Cup in January 1939 and scored four goals in 12 Central League games. He later taught future Albion forward Brian Whitehouse and myself at George Salter school.

WILLETTS, George

Goalkeeper: 1 app.

Born: West Bromwich, 18 August 1920.
Died: West Bromwich, 1992.
Career: Holy Trinity School (West

Bromwich). Clanboro' FC (1936). ALBION (May 1941). Elmore Green Celtic (April 1946). Bilston Town (1948–50).

■ Rather too small to be a first-team goalkeeper, George Willetts was taken on as an amateur by Albion during World War Two, playing once for the first team against Wrexham (home) in a Football League War Cup qualifying round in December 1941, conceding four goals in a 6–4 victory.

WILLIAMS, Cyril Edward

Inside-right: 77 apps. 20 goals.

Born: Bristol, 17 November 1921.
Died: Bristol, 21 January 1980.
Career: Luckwell Road School (Bristol). Bristol Schools, Bristol City (amateur, May 1937, professional, May 1939). Guest for Chelsea, Reading and Tottenham Hotspur during World War Two. Was badly injured at Arnhem while serving in the Airborne Forces. ALBION (player-exchange deal involving Cliff Edwards, plus £500, June 1948). Bristol City (£4,500, August 1951). Chippenham Town (manager, June 1966–February 1967).

■ Cyril Williams was a most capable and efficient inside-right, enthusiastic with a lot of skill. A goalscorer who found the net 20 times in his senior appearances for Albion and four times in 20 second-team games. He made his Baggies debut against Chesterfield (away) in Division Two in

September 1948 and proved to be the vital link in centre-midfield that season as the team battled on gamely to win promotion to the First Division. He returned to Bristol in 1951 and went on to amass nearly 300 League outings (scoring 68 goals), helping City win the Third Division South title in 1955. Williams was tragically killed in a car accident, aged 58.

WILLIAMS, George Owen

Half-back: 18 apps.

Born: Wednesbury, 10 September 1879.
Died: France, 1916.
Career: Kings Hill School (Wednesbury). Monway FC (1894). Oldbury Town (August 1896). Wednesbury Old Athletic (May 1898). ALBION (professional, October 1900). Brierley Hill Alliance (April 1902). Kidderminster Harriers (August 1903). Wrexham (August 1906). Stafford Rangers (July 1908). Willenhall Swifts (February 1911). Walsall (August 1912). Joined King's Royal Rifle Corps (1915).

■ A Welsh international half-back – despite the fact that he was born in England – George Williams was a tough competitor who never shirked a tackle, giving as good as he got, mainly from the pivotal berth. Injuries, however, plagued his career and he made only 40 appearances for Albion at first and second-team levels, being handed his League debut against Notts County (home) in Division One in November

1900. A member of the Baggies' Birmingham & District championship side in 1901–02, Williams is believed to have been killed while serving with his unit on a French battlefield in 1916.

WILLIAMS, Gilbert

Wing-half: 37 apps.

Born: Greets Green, West Bromwich, 12 January 1925.
Died: Wednesbury 1993.
Career: Greets Green. Hill Top Senior

Schools. Hawthorn Juniors (September 1940). ALBION (amateur, September 1943, professional, February 1944). Banbury Spencer (free, July 1949). Wellington Tube Works FC (1951, retired, May 1969). Continued to work at Wellington Tube (West Bromwich).

■ 'Gil' Williams was a small, forceful wing-half, biting in the tackle and vigorous throughout a game. World War Two knocked his career about but he still managed 28 senior appearances during the hostilities, adding a further nine later. He was in the Army during the war (serving with the Pioneer Corps) and played for the 'Pick of the South' and the Army XI in several representative matches. He made his Albion debut against Wolverhampton Wanderers (home) in the Football League North in September 1943. He also scored twice in 58 Central League games. He attended Albion home matches right up until his death at the age of 68.

WILLIAMS, Graham Evan

Full-back: 354 apps. 11 goals.

Born: Hellan near Rhyl, North Wales, 2 April 1938.

Career: Emmanuel Secondary School. Flintshire Boys. Burnley (trialist, 1953). Rhyl Athletic. ALBION (amateur, September 1954, professional, April 1955–April 1972). Weymouth (player-manager, May 1972–June 1975). Sports Klub Kuwait (1975–76). OFI, Greece. (coach, 1976–77). Poole Town (manager, September 1979–June 1981). Cardiff City (coach, then manager, November 1981–March 1982). Newport County (scout, 1983–84). Leopards FC, Nigeria (coach). FC Rovaniemen, Finland (manager, 1987–89). Coaching in Far East, Kuwait and Dubai (1998–99). Newcastle United (scout). Cheltenham Town (chief scout, with ex-Albion manager Bobby Gould, January–October 2003). Appointed West Bromwich Albion ex-Players' Association chairman (August 2003).

■ Graham Williams spent 18 years as a player with Albion, starting out as an orthodox outside-left and finishing up as an international left-back, powerful, determined and courageous. He also put in some sterling displays at left-half, but it was wearing the number 3 shirt where he blossomed best of all, skippering Albion to victory in both the 1966 League

Cup and 1968 FA Cup finals. Williams also played in the 1967 League Cup final (collecting a runners'-up medal) and was in the squad (but didn't play) that lost in the 1970 League Cup final to Manchester City. Capped 26 times by Wales, Williams had two outings at under-23 level and for Albion, his only professional club, he appeared in well over 400 matches, including 314 in the First Division alone, making his League debut against Blackpool (home) in November 1955. He also played in 229 Central League games, scoring 18 goals. It was not until season 1962–63 that he became a firm fixture in Albion's senior side – this after his namesake Stuart had left the club for Southampton. It's interesting to know that the Williamses – himself and Stuart – actually played together at full-back for both Albion and Wales. In 1981 Williams took Poole Town to the final of the Anglo-Italian Tournament. He now lives in Oswestry.

WILLIAMS, James

Outside-right: 35 apps. 1 goal.

Born: Brownhills, Staffs, 10 August 1882. Died: Walsall, 14 June 1936. Career: St Stephen's School (Brownhills). Lichfield City. Brownhills Albion (1902). Aston Villa (professional, August 1904). ALBION (free, March 1905–August 1909). Brownhills Albion (October 1909–May 1911). Served in the Army during World War One.

■ As a right-winger, Jimmy Williams was a most exciting player, fast and clever, who in later years turned his time to defending from the right-back position. He made his League debut for Albion against Bradford City (home) in Division Two in March 1905, and he also played in over 50 second XI matches in four seasons. He did not make the first team at Villa Park.

WILLIAMS, Norman Ernest

Full-back: 1 app.

Born: Wolverhampton, 12 February 1924. Career: High Heath School. Sheffield Villa. Featherstone FC (1942). ALBION (amateur, December 1944, professional June 1945, released, May 1946). Later assisted Bromsgrove Rovers (1947–48).

■ A World War Two signing by Albion, Norman Williams was stylish in his play but never quite fitted the bill at The Hawthorns. He made his senior debut against Tottenham Hotspur (home) in the Football League South in September 1945. He also played in 15 second XI games.

WILLIAMS, Owen

Inside-forward: 19 apps. 9 goals.

Born: Smethwick, 22 November 1874. Died: Birmingham, 4 June 1944. Career: West Smethwick & Queen's Road Schools. Smethwick Centaur (1889). Oldbury Town (1891). ALBION (professional, December 1893). Oldbury Town (November 1895). Worcester Rovers (December 1895). Oldbury Town (1896–1901). Smethwick Centaur (August 1901, retired, May 1910). Was later associated with the church for more than 25 years.

■ An accomplished inside-forward, Owen Williams grafted as well as any man, and his overall play was both versatile and tireless. A spate of niggling injuries ruined a promising career at senior level. He made his League debut as a 19-year-old against Darwen (home) in Division One in December 1893, and, besides his senior appearances, Williams also played in 10 'other' first-team games for Albion.

WILLIAMS, Paul Andrew

Striker: 29+22 apps. 7 goals.

Born: Sheffield, 8 September 1963. Career: Sheffield Schoolboy football. Nuneaton Borough (semi-professional, May 1982). Preston North End (professional, December 1985). Newport County (free, August 1987). Sheffield United (£5,000, March 1988). Hartlepool United (£3,000, October 1989). Stockport County (free, August 1990) ALBION (£20,000, March 1991). Coventry City (on loan, October–November 1992). Stockport County (free, January 1993). Rochdale (free, November 1993). Doncaster Rovers (on loan, March–May 1996). Lincoln City (trialist, 1996–97). Altrincham (1997–98).

■ A tall, black-haired striker, recruited perhaps mistakenly by Albion manager Bobby Gould (the player it should have been was his namesake, Bill), Paul Williams was often the target of the fans for some poor performances. He, nevertheless, appeared in over 50 senior games for the Baggies, scored some good goals and also played in half-a-dozen Central League matches. He gained a full cap for Northern Ireland against the Faroe Islands during his time with Albion, for whom he made his debut against Charlton Athletic (away) in March 1991. He ended his League career with 33 goals to his credit in 169 appearances.

WILLIAMS, Paul Richard Curtis

Left-back: 5 apps.

Born: Leicester, 11 September 1969
Career: Leicester City (apprentice, April 1986, professional, June 1988). Stockport County (free, July 1989). Coventry City (£150,000, August 1993). ALBION (on loan, November–December 1993). Huddersfield Town (on loan, November 1994 and again March–April 1995). Plymouth Argyle (£50,000, August 1995). Gillingham (free, August 1998). Bury (£50,000, November 1998). Ilkeston Town (June 2000). Radcliffe Borough (2001–03).

■ Paul Williams was taken on loan by Albion manager Keith Burkinshaw halfway through the 1993–94 season, when injuries were beginning to disrupt team selection. A positive, attacking player, he made his debut for the club against Nottingham Forest (home) in November 1993 and went on to amass over 300 senior League and cup appearances before leaving Gigg Lane in 2000.

WILLIAMS, Stuart Grenvile

Full-back: 246 apps. 9 goals.

Born: Wrexham, North Wales, 9 July 1930.
Career: Acton Park Junior & Grove Park Grammar Schools. Wrexham Boys. Victoria Victoria Youth Club (1945). Wrexham (amateur, July 1946). Birmingham City (trial). ALBION (amateur, November 1950, professional, February 1951). Southampton (£15,000, September 1962). ALBION (trainer, 1967–69). Aston Villa (trainer, January 1970). Payhaan, Iran (manager, August 1970). Morton (trainer-

coach, 1970–71). Southampton (coach-assistant manager, August 1971–April 1973). Carlisle United (scout, 1973). Stavanger, Norway (manager, 1973–74). Southampton (trainer, 1976–77). Later ran a guest house in Southampton where he lives today.

■ One-time inside-right Stuart Williams – the son of a Wrexham director – was converted by Albion into a grand full-back, who gave the Throstles 12 years' yeoman service, winning a total of 33 Welsh caps during his stay at The Hawthorns – a club record for the most capped player. After leaving Albion, 'Stu' added a further 10 caps to his collection with Southampton. In fact, he teamed up with his clubmate Graham Williams for both his club (Albion) and country – a unique partnership at full-back. He made his senior debut for Albion against Huddersfield Town (away) in Division One in February 1952, the first of 226 in the League for the Baggies, for whom he also starred in 180 second-team games, scoring 11 goals. He followed up with 147 League appearances for Southampton, earlier in his career having made just six for Wrexham. He also appeared in a further 35 cup ties. It seemed likely that he would replace the injured Stan Rickaby in Albion's 1954 FA Cup final team, but at the last minute manager Vic Buckingham left him out in favour of the more experienced Joe Kennedy. He did get to Wembley with Albion later as trainer of the 1968 FA Cup-winning side. * Williams was presented with an award by the Welsh FA in 2003 for services to the game (clubs and country).

WILLIAMS, William

Full-back: 208 apps. 12 goals.

Born: West Smethwick, 20 January 1876.
Died: West Bromwich, 11 January 1929.
Career: Oldbury Road School (Smethwick). West Bromwich Hawthorns FC (1888). West Smethwick FC (1889). Hawthorn Villa (1891). Old Hill Wanderers (1892). ALBION (£20, May 1894, retired, June 1901 with a cartilage injury). ALBION trainer for a short time, later coach at The Hawthorns). Became a licensee of a pub near to the ground.

■ Billy Williams was a brilliant defender, stylish, dedicated and, above all, safe and sure under pressure. He possessed a long,

raking kick and scored quite a few goals from far distances, including one blinder from a full 55 yards against Nottingham Forest in an FA Cup tie in February 1898. He was also an expert with penalty kicks. Williams gained six England caps (1897–99), played for the Football League and also starred for the Professionals XI in various representative matches. He collected a runners'-up medal with Albion after their 1895 FA Cup final defeat by Aston Villa, and, besides his 200 plus senior appearances for the club, he also played in more than 100 'other' first-team games. His enforced retirement was a bitter blow to the club, who suffered relegation for the first time at the end of Williams's 'farewell' season. He had earlier made his League debut against Sheffield United (away) in Division One in September 1894.

WILLIAMS, William Thomas

Centre-half: 1 app.

Born: Esher, Surrey, 23 August 1942.
Career: Esher Schools. Portsmouth (amateur, June 1957, professional, June 1960). Queen's Park Rangers (July 1961). ALBION (£10,500 May 1963–January 1966). Mansfield Town (£10,000). Gillingham (£7,000, September 1967). Maidstone United (July 1972). Durban United, South Africa (August 1973). Durban City, South Africa (1974). Sacramento Gold, NASL (coach, 1979–80).

Atlanta Chiefs, NASL (coach, 1980–81). Maidstone United (manager, November 1981–November 1984). Returned to South Africa, December 1984, to take a job outside football. Came back to England as manager of Maidstone United (July 1986–April 2000). Dover Athletic (manager, 2000–01). Kingstonian (manager, 2001–02). Welling United (manager, 2002–05).

■ A steady, careful centre-half, signed as cover for Stan Jones, Bill Williams won caps for England at schoolboy and youth team levels (at right-back and centre-half) and during his career appeared in well over 300 competitive matches, 269 in in the Football League. He guided Sacremento Gold to the American Soccer League title in 1979. His only outing for Albion was against Nottingham Forest (home) in Division One in January 1965. He did, however, appear in 78 Central League games (2 goals).

WILLIAMSON, Robert

Striker: 45+4 apps. 12 goals.

Born: Glasgow, 13 August 1961.
Career: Clydebank & Govan Schools. Auchengill Boys' Club (Glasgow). Glasgow Boys. Clydebank (amateur, July 1976, professional, August 1978). Glasgow Rangers (£110,000, December 1983).

ALBION (player-exchange deal involving Jimmy Nicholl, August 1986). Rotherham United (free, May 1988). Kilmarnock (£100,000, November 1990, manager, August 1997). Hibernian (manager, March 2002). Plymouth Argyle (manager, from April 2004).

■ Bobby Williamson joined Albion in a straight swap with Jimmy Nicholl at the start of the 1986–87 season and played his first game for Albion in a friendly against Walsall in mid-August, four hours after putting pen to paper! A useful striker, he was a big success with Clydebank, scoring 33 goals in 80 games. He then started off well at Ibrox, the place where he used to stand and support Rangers as a lad, and hit eight goals in 20 outings in his first season, but a fractured leg (suffered on tour in Australia in 1984) knocked him back considerably. He recovered full fitness but, realistically, was never the same player again. He failed to re-establish himself in the Rangers side, hence his move to The Hawthorns, where he had a reasonable first season, hitting eight goals in 35 outings, having made his debut against Hull City (away) in August 1986. He also scored nine goals in just 17 Central League games for the Baggies. In 1988–89 Williamson gained a Fourth Division championship medal with Rotherham, ending up as the Millers top marksman. He later did well on limited resources as manager of both Kilmarnock and Hibernian and his first match in

charge at Home Park coincided with the South Devon club winning the Second Division championship.

WILSON, Charles

Inside-forward: 133 apps. 45 goals.

Born: Heeley, Sheffield, 20 July 1905.
Died: Kidderminster, 8 April 1985.
Career: Netherthorpe Schools (Sheffield). Sheffield Boys. Stonehouse FC. Chesterfield (trialist, May 1919). Sheffield United (trialist, July 1919). Hallam FC (October 1919). ALBION (amateur, December 1920, professional, November 1922). Sheffield Wednesday (£3,000, February 1928). Grimsby Town (March 1932). Aston Villa (August 1933). Coventry City (June 1934). Kidderminster Harriers (July 1935). Worcester City (August 1936). Kidderminster Harriers (May 1937). Guest for Charlton Athletic and Aldershot during World War Two. Played for Kidderminster Police in 1946, retired, summer 1947. Later a Kidderminster licensee (1955–71).

■ Charlie 'Tug' Wilson was an opportunist 'striker' with an unquenchable thirst for goals. He had film-star looks and was a constant threat to opposing defenders, and he could shoot from any angle, seemingly from any distance, with either foot and usually found the target. Curiously, he had a habit of keeping himself clean on the muddiest of pitches, yet was still a worker, who moved back to left-half later on in his career. He had the distinction of being the youngest ever player to appear in a Football League game for Albion, making his debut at Oldham at the age of 16 years and 63 days in October 1921. He gained three Central League championship medals with Albion in the 1920s, scoring a total of 71 goals in 98 games for the club at this level, and he also assisted Sheffield Wednesday in their First Division championship seasons of 1928–29 and 1929–30. He played only a few games at left-back for Grimsby, none for Villa and 12 for Coventry (4 goals). With Albion, Wilson linked up splendidly with fellow front men Stan Davies, George James and Joe Carter, also performing exceedingly well with his left-wing partners, Arthur Fitton and Jack Byers. His best scoring season for Albion was in 1925–26 when he struck 17 goals in 30 League outings. He also scored

THE WHO'S WHO OF WEST BROMWICH ALBION

when Albion beat the Blues in the final of the Birmingham Charity Cup in 1922.

WILSON, Joseph James

Outside-left: 53 apps. 20 goals.

Born: Handsworth, Birmingham, 8 January 1861.
Died: Acocks Green, Birmingham, 20 October 1952.
Career: St Mary's Council School. Handsworth Grammar School. Hamstead Swifts (1877). Aston Unity (1880–85). Stoke (September 1885). Walsall Town (1885–86). Aston Villa (August 1886). Walsall Town (August 1887). ALBION (professional, September 1887–May 1890). Kidderminster Harriers (August 1890). Birmingham St George's (August 1891, retired, April 1892). Later became a Football League referee and linesman (1894–1910). Was a goldsmith by profession and worked in Birmingham's jewellery quarter for 25 years up to World War Two.

■ Albion's first ever Football League goal was scored by Joe Wilson against Stoke (away) on 8 September 1888. Six months earlier he had gained an FA Cup winners' medal when the favourites, Preston North End, were defeated 2–1 at The Oval. He scored half a dozen goals in earlier rounds, including two in the quarter-final victory over Old Carthusians, having made his debut for Albion against Wednesday Old Athletic (home) in the first round of the competition in October 1887, when he also scored twice in a 7–1

win. A year later he claimed two goals in Albion's 10–1 West Bromwich Charity Cup final win over Great Bridge Unity. A smart, unobtrusive left-winger of dashing style and all-out aggression, Wilson kept defences on the alert with his cunning wing play. He formed an excellent partnership and understanding with Tom Pearson and was virtually an ever-present in Albion's first two League campaigns. Besides his senior appearances for the club, Wilson also participated in close on 100 'other' games, and after his playing days were over he did a fine job for some 16 years as a referee and linesman, officiating in both First and Second Division matches, in various FA Cup ties and also at non-League level. He was once placed on standby to run the line in an England international match.

WILSON, Raymond Thomson

Outside-left/left-back: 282+3 goals.

Born: Grangemouth, Stirlingshire, 8 April 1947.
Career: Dundas Primary and Grangemouth High Schools. Stirlingshire Boys. Woodburn Athletic (1962). ALBION (amateur, July 1963, professional, May 1964, retired through injury, March 1977). Later a businessman in Central Birmingham.

■ Ray Wilson, like the player he replaced (Graham Williams), began his career with Albion as an outside-left, but made his name as a competent left-back, gaining Scottish under-23 recognition in 1970, the year he also played in the League Cup final at Wembley, collecting a runners'-up medal when Manchester City won 2–1 after extra-time. A competent player who tackled hard, Wilson had exceptional speed, which enabled him to recover quickly. He loved to over-lap and was a fine 'chipper' of the ball down the line. He established himself in the Albion side at left-back in the late 1960s taking over initially from the aforementioned Williams. His first League game was against Chelsea (home) in October 1965 and his last at Luton in the 1975–76 promotion-winning campaign, when he suffered a shattered knee cap, which resulted in his early retirement. He also played in 134 Central League games (scoring 36 goals). Wilson was rewarded

with a testimonial match at The Hawthorns (Albion v Aston Villa) in May 1975.

WITCOMB, Douglas Frederick

Wing-half: 122 apps. 10 goals.

Born: Cwm near Ebbw Vale, Gwent, 18 April 1918.
Died: Redditch, summer 1995.
Career: Ebbw Vale County School. Cwm Villa (1933). Tottenham Hotspur (amateur, 1934). Northfleet FC (1935). Enfield (March 1936). ALBION (October 1937, professional, November 1937). Guest for Grimsby Town, Leicester City, Swansea Town, Lovells Athletic and Newport County during World War Two. Sheffield Wednesday (£6,500, February 1947). Newport County (November 1953). Llandudno Town (August 1954, retired, June 1956). Redditch (player-coach, 1955–56). Later played football for H.D. Alloys & Alkamatic Works FC (South Wales).

■ Duggie Witcomb was a wing-half of enormous talent. Quick, cunning and a fine distributor under pressure, he tackled hard and possessed a powerful shot. He spent 10 years at The Hawthorns, participating in over 120 games (55 in the League). Making his debut against Burnley (away) in Division Two in September 1938, he went on to score once in 26 second-team games, won 10 caps

for Wales, including wartime internationals, and in 1939 represented the All British team against The Football League at Wolverhampton. In his League career, Witcomb amassed a total of 303 appearances, of which 223 were with Wednesday, whom he helped win promotion from Division Two in 1951–52. He later resided in Halesowen and Redditch and it is understood that he drowned in an accident.

WOLLASTON, William

Outside-right: 26 apps. 3 goals.

Born: Willenhall, 31 December 1889.
Died: 21 November 1933.
Career: Portobello & Arden Hill Schools (Willenhall). Willenhall Pickwick (1905). ALBION (professional, May 1910). Darlaston (May 1913, retired through injury, April 1915).

■ Billy Wollaston was a probing, thrustful right-winger of good value, who suffered two broken legs in as many years, which curtailed a promising career. A junior international in 1910, he gained a Second Division championship medal with Albion the following season, having made his League debut against Hull City (away) in March 1910.

WOOD, Harold Frederick

Inside-forward: 1 app. 1 goal.

Born: West Bromwich, 3 October 1870.
Died: Portsmouth, 3 July 1951.
Career: Spon Lane School West Bromwich. West Bromwich Sandwell. Albion Swifts. Oldbury Town (1888). ALBION (professional, May 1890–June 1893). Walsall Victoria (August 1893). Oldbury Town (September 1898–May 1900). Portsmouth (trainer, 1906–07 and 1910–11).

■ A small, amiable forward, Harry Wood – nicknamed 'Sly' because of the sneaky ways in which he wriggled round the back of the defenders – was an Albion reserve for three seasons, making only one senior appearance against Everton (home) in Division One in October 1892, when he scored in a 3–0 win. Earlier, he netted five goals in 25 minutes of one game playing for Oldbury Town.

WOOD, Matthew Curry

Defender: 17 apps.
Born: Hobson, Bursopfield, County Durham, 19 February 1890.
Died: 12 December 1923, following an appendix operation.
Career: Newton Berry School. Hobson Wanderers (August 1909). ALBION (professional, April 1911–May 1922). Kidderminster Harriers (free, August

1911). *Guest for Aston Villa and Hartlepools United during World War One. Did not figure after the hostilities.*

■ A resolute defender equally at home in the left-back or centre-half positions, Matt Wood was a smart-looking footballer and had a bright future ahead of him until war intervened. He made his League debut against Everton (away) in Division One in April 1912 when players were being rested prior to the FA Cup final replay with Barnsley. Wood, who also played in 50 second-team matches and helped the reserves twice win the Birmingham & District League title in 1913 and 1920, served as a private with the 7th Platoon, B Squad, 2nd Tank Regiment of the Durham Light Infantry, based in France during World War One.

WOOD, Stanley

Outside-left: 281 apps. 66 goals.

Born: Winsford, Cheshire, 1 July 1905.
Died: Halifax, Yorkshire, 22 February 1967.
Career: Meadow Bank School (Winsford Village). Whitegate Victoria. Winsford United (1926). ALBION (professional, April 1928). Halifax Town (free, May 1938, then trainer from 1946 until his retirement in May 1949). Guest for Huddersfield Town (1941–42) and played in every wartime season with Halifax Town.

■ Stan Wood, nicknamed 'Splinter' and the 'Singing Winger', was a wiry, slippery outside-left, whose cleverness stood him in good stead for a decade with Albion. He drew up an impressive record of 256 League appearances (58 goals) and 24 cup ties (8 goals). He starred in the 1931 FA Cup final and a year later represented the Football League, being named as England reserve at the same time. He had his best season with Albion in 1930–31, when that 'unique' double was achieved, playing in 50 competitive matches and netting 17 goals. Wood staked a claim in the side in 1928, taking over the mantle polished by Arthur Fitton before him. He held his place for quite a while until Wally Boyes came along in 1934. After that he was in and out of the side, but he still managed a fair number of outings, especially in 1935–36 and 1936–37. He always gave 100 percent and was a very fine footballer whose League debut was against Notts County (home) in Division Two in September 1928. He also scored 37 goals in 92 second-team games, gaining a Central League championship medal in 1934–35, having helped the side win the same title in the two previous seasons.

WOODHALL, George

Inside and outside-right: 74 apps. 20 goals.

Born: West Bromwich, 5 September 1863.
Died: West Bromwich, 9 September 1924.
Career: Hateley Heath School. West Bromwich Saints. Wednesbury Town (guest, 1882). Churchfield Foresters. ALBION (amateur, May 1883, professional, August 1885). Wolverhampton Wanders (July 1892–May 1894). Berwick Rangers (Birmingham League, August 1894). Oldbury Town (October 1894, retired, May 1898).

■ George 'Spry' Woodhall was well-nicknamed, for he was indeed a sprightly player, figuring prominently at outside-right for Albion in the early days. He could centre with great accuracy and combined well in team work, especially with Billy Bassett as his partner. A regular member of Albion's forward-line for nine seasons, he won two England caps, both in 1888, against Wales at Crewe, when he became the first Black Country-born player to score in a full international, and against Scotland in Glasgow. That same year he also gained an FA Cup medal, notching the deciding goal in Albion's 2–1 win over Preston North End in the final, and was on target in the West Bromwich Charity Cup final when Great Bridge Unity were defeated 10–1. Woodhall also played in the 1886 and 1887 finals and averaged a goal every three and a half games for Albion (appearing in more than 275 first-team fixtures, including many local cup ties and friendlies). With his delightful personality, he was one of the most popular players of the 'Old Brigade', remembered as a generous and wholehearted sportsman by the older generation, who lived to tell the tales of his brilliant play down Albion's right flank. He made his senior debut for the club against Junction Street School, Derby (away), in the first round of the FA Cup in October 1884. He also notched the winning goal against Walsall Swifts in

the replay of the Birmingham Cup final in 1886.
* Richie Woodhall, Britain's Olympic boxing gold winner, is a relative of the former Albion player.

WOOLGAR, Stewart James

Midfield: 3 + 3 apps.

Born: Chesterfield, 27 September 1952.
Career: Chesterfield Grammar School. Derbyshire & District Schools. ALBION (apprentice, October 1968, professional, September 1969). Doncaster Rovers (free, July 1974). Dunstable Town (August 1975–April 1976). Served in the Luton & Bedfordshire Police force (1976–77). Alvechurch (1977–78). Dunstable Town (1978–79).

■ Stewart Woolgar put in many fine performances for Albion's youth and Central League sides but was never really a force to be reckoned with in top company. He made his League debut against Manchester United (home) in Division One in October 1972, coming on as a second half substitute. He also scored 18 goals in almost 100 second XI appearances for the club.

WORTON, Thomas

Inside-left: 75 apps. 23 goals.

Born: Heath Town, Wolverhampton, 4 February 1878.
Died: West Bromwich, 24 July 1940.
Career: Heath Town & Cannock Road Schools (Wolverhampton). Wolverhampton Wanderers (amateur, August 1895,

professional, March 1896). ALBION (free, May 1901, retired through injury, June 1905). Later worked for a firm of solicitors (West Bromwich).

■ Tom Worton spent six years with Wolves, during which time he appeared in 57 League games and scored 11 goals. He joined Albion soon after they had suffered relegation to the Second Division in 1901, and in his first season at The Hawthorns was the brains of the forward line as promotion was achieved straightaway. Worton paced himself superbly, appearing in all 34 matches, scoring 19 vital goals, including three match-winners and a cracking hat-trick against Newton Heath. Both a sharp-shooter and creator of chances, he was also the driving force and instigator in centre-field. He was a fine player of the highest quality, but a knee injury caused him to retire at the age of 27. He made his debut for Albion against Glossop (home) in Division Two in September 1901 and also played in 11 second XI matches.

WRIGHT, Franklin

Defender: 2 apps.

Born: Wednesbury, 22 December 1872.
Died: Oldbury, 1940.
Career: Joseph Edward Cox School (Wednesbury). Darlaston (1888). Halesowen (1891). Wednesbury Old Athletic (August 1894). ALBION (amateur, August 1895). Rowley Star (July 1896, retired, May 1899).

■ A reserve defender who could play with confidence in either wing-half position, Frank Wright made his League debut against Sunderland (home) in Division One on Boxing Day 1895. He made 10 appearances for Albion's second XI.

WRIGHT, Harold Fereday

Inside-forward: 105 apps. 20 goals.

Born: West Bromwich, 12 October 1888.
Died: West Bromwich, 8 September 1950.
Career: Beeches Road and St Phillip's Schools (West Bromwich). West Bromwich St Mark's. ALBION (professional, November 1906). Stourbridge (May 1909). ALBION (free, June 1910). Guest for Oldbury Town and Bilston during World War One. Wolverhampton Wanderers

(£500, November 1919). Newport County (September 1920, retired, May 1922). Later secretary of an allotment association in Handsworth, Birmingham.

■ Harry Wood was an energetic forward who could play, if required, in any position but preferred an inside-berth. A gritty performer, he had two spells with Albion, the first as a raw-boned youngster playing virtually all of his football in the reserves (over 40 games), the second a much more compact and studious footballer. He helped the Baggies win the Second Division championship in 1910–11 and the following season played in the FA Cup final, collecting a runners'-up medal. He had a good scoring record of a goal every five games for Albion (at both senior and reserve-team levels), and he made his Football League debut against Stoke (home) in Division Two in November 1907. In later life he became a useful crown green bowler.

YOUNG, George

Full-back: 16 apps.

Born: Kirkintillock near Dumbarton, Scotland, 16 April 1880.
Died: Worcester, 9 September 1938.
Career: Kirkintillock & Lenzie Schools. Kilsyth Rangers (1896). Dumbarton (professional, April 1897). Glasgow Rangers (August 1900). Portsmouth (July 1901). ALBION (£300, May 1905). West Bromwich Strollers (August 1906). Worcester City (June 1912, retired, April 1914).

■ Reputed to be one of the strongest backs of the period, George Young was a beefy character, a rugged Scot, who was as solid as a rock. He had done very well north of the border (especially with Dumbarton) before switching to Pompey. His brief stay with Albion revealed 16 senior outings before he left under a cloud following internal disagreements. He made his Baggies debut against Burnley (home) in Division Two in September 1905 and also played in a handful of second-team matches.

YOUNG, William Craig

Right-half: 22 apps. 2 goals.

Born: Chadsmor near Hednesford, 12 September 1884.
Died: Evesham, 13 October 1917.
Career: Charney Welfare School. Chadsmoor Celtic. Hednesford Victoria. Hednesford Town (April 1905). ALBION (professional, May 1907–August 1910). Hednesford Town (free, August 1910). Worcester City (April 1913, retired, May 1916 through ill-health).

■ Ex-collier Billy 'Cree' Young showed infinite resource and splendid speed in recovery when playing at right-half. He found it hard to gain a first-team place at The Hawthorns, due to the consistent form of George Baddeley, Sammy Timmins and Jack Manners. His Albion debut was against Blackpool (away) in Division Two in September 1907.

ZONDERVAN, Romeo

Midfield: 93+2 apps. 5 goals.

Born: Paramaribo, Surinam, 4 March 1959.
Career: Velsen School (Holland). Postalia (May 1975). FC Den Haag (professional, August 1976). FC Twente Enschede (£1,500, June 1978). ALBION (£225,000, March 1982). Ipswich Town (£70,000, March 1984). FC Twente Enschede, Holland (youth-team coach, 2000–01). Ipswich Town (scout, based in Holland). Bradford City (scout). Now a football agent in Holland, also a qualified airline pilot.

■ A Dutch international at schoolboy, under-21 and senior levels, gaining his first full cap against Cyprus in a World Cup qualifier in February 1981, Romeo

Zondervan was voted Albion's 'Player of the Year' by the supporters in 1982–83. A talented midfielder, good on the ball, he made his full debut for the Baggies as a substitute left-back against Middlesbrough (away) in Division One in March 1982 (as substitute) and almost immediately lined-up against Queen's Park Rangers in the semi-final of the FA Cup. His best role, however, was on the right side of midfield, where he performed exceptionally well during his two years at The Hawthorns. He left the club when Johnny Giles came back as manager for the second time. Zondervan went on to amass a career record in the English Football League of 258 appearances (84 for Albion).
* It was Zondervan who informed Albion about defender Thomas Gaardsoe.

Wartime Guests

Guest players who assisted Albion during World War One.

IKE WEBB, ex-Albion goalkeeper who played in 1918 at the age of 43. (See under WEBB, Isaac)

ALBERT LINDON, another goalkeeper (recruited from Barnsley), made his Albion debut against Wolves in November 1916. He also played for Birmingham (1910–11), Aston Villa (1911–12), Coventry City (1919–20), Merthyr Town (1920–27) and Charlton Athletic (1927–34). After World War Two he scouted for Arsenal, Cardiff City and Newport County and was manager of Merthyr Town and scout for Swindon Town. He made 321 League appearances in total (250 for Merthyr) and was 85 when he died in 1976.

NB: Several players, including three from Aston Villa – wing-half **JIMMY HAROP**, right-winger **DICKY YORK** and outside-left **FRANK WOOLLEY** – full-back **JOE DAVISON** from Blyth Spartans, wing-half **LEN WALL** of Shrewsbury Town and goalkeeper **BILL NICHOLLS** (Dudley Town) all played in 'mixed' matches for the Albion/Villa or Albion/Birmingham XIs during World War One.

During World War Two over 40 players guested for Albion as follows:

Inside/centre-forward **JACK ACQUAROFF**, whose father was Russian, was recruited from Norwich City in 1944. Formerly with Tottenham Hotspur, Northfleet, Folkestone Town, Hull City (1934–36) and Bury, he moved to Carrow Road in 1939. He later returned to White Hart Lane before emigrating to Tasmania in 1949, playing for Metro FC and Caledonians. He scored twice for Albion in the second leg of the 1944 Midland Wartime Cup final against Nottingham Forest to set up for a 6–5 aggregate win. Born in Chelsea in 1911, he died in Launceston, Tasmania, in November 1987.

Inside-left **MATT ARMSTRONG** arrived from Aberdeen in 1943. He scored 155 goals in 220 games for the Scottish club between 1931–39. He also played for Port Glasgow Juniors, Queen of the South, Elgin City and Peterhead.

Goalkeeper **GEOFF BILLINGSLEY** came from Aston Villa in 1942. He was a registered player at Villa Park from 1939–47.

Centre-half **ALAN BROWN** was acquired from Huddersfield Town in 1942. He later 'defended' for Burnley and Notts County, served Sheffield Wednesday as coach and was later manager of Burnley, Sunderland and Wednesday, while also on the coaching staff at Plymouth Argyle.

Right-half **JIMMY BYE** came from Birmingham in 1943. He also played for local non-League clubs Bournbrook Alliance and Shirley Juniors.

Half-back/inside-forward **DON DEARSON** also 'guested' from Birmingham in 1942. Ex-Barry Town, he later played for Coventry City, Walsall and Nuneaton Borough and during his career won 18 caps for Wales (15 during wartime). He appeared in 136 peacetime and 166 World War Two games for the Blues, scoring a total of 42 goals. He was 76 when he died in Birmingham in 1990.

Inside-right **PETER DOHERTY** was an Albion guest from Manchester City in 1943. A brilliant forward, he also played for Coleraine, Glentoran, Blackpool, Derby County, Huddersfield Town and

Doncaster Rovers (player-manager). He was later Preston North End's assistant boss, managed both Bristol City and Notts County, was Aston Villa's chief scout, Sunderland's assistant manager, a scout with Blackpool and also the Northern Ireland team manager (1957–59). Doherty won the Irish Cup with Glentoran in 1932, the League title with Manchester City in 1937, the FA Cup with Derby in 1946, the Third Division North championship with Doncaster Rovers in 1950 and was capped 16 times for his country (1935–51). He died in Fleetwood, Lancs, in 1990 aged 76.

Outside-right **MAURICE DUNKLEY** guested from Manchester City in 1943. He had two spells with Kettering Town and also assisted Northampton Town and Corby Town as well as playing county cricket for Northamptonshire.

Outside-right **LEN DUNS** assisted Albion from Sunderland in season 1943–44. Unfortunately, he broke his leg playing against Nottingham Forest in March 1944. Previously with Newcastle United, he played at Roker Park until 1952,

making 215 League appearances (45 goals). He died in 1989 at the age of 73.

Inside-forward **GEORGE EDWARDS** was 'signed' from Aston Villa in 1942. An ex-Norwich City player (1935–38), he later served with Bilston United from 1951 after leaving Villa Park. He appeared in 147 League games in total (35 goals) and died in 1993, aged 75.

Outside-left **LESTER FINCH** was born in Hadley, Herts, in 1909. He played for non-League Barnet for 25 years (1928–53), scoring 226 goals in 476 games. He gained an FA Amateur Cup medal in 1946 and a runners'-up medal two years later. He toured South Africa with the FA in 1939, playing in two Test Matches against the South African national XI. He also toured Europe with Athenian League and London FA parties on several occasions, won 16 amateur caps for England, represented Great Britain twice in the 1936 Olympic Games and also played in one Wartime international. Registered with Arsenal briefly in 1933, he assisted Albion from 1942–44 (24 appearances and one goal), gaining a Midland Cup medal in the latter year. He also guested for Chelsea, Wolves, Walsall, Nottingham Forest and Bournemouth during World War Two, when free from serving in the RAF. In 1988 Finch, a printer by trade, published an entertaining memoir of his football career: 'Playing for Fun.' He died on 26 November 1995, aged 84.

Goalkeeper **TED GOODALL**, registered from Bolton Wanderers in 1940, also played for Chesterfield, North Shields and Hull City. He made only 38 League appearances in total and assisted Albion in 1940. He died in 1978, aged 64.

Full-back **JACK GRIFFITHS** (Manchester United) guested for Albion in 1943. He was registered with Wolves from 1929–32 and then played for Bolton Wanderers before moving to Old Trafford in 1934. He made 168 League appearances during his time at Old Trafford and was later player-coach of Hyde United.

Inside/outside-left **BILLY GUEST** 'guested' for Albion from Blackburn Rovers in 1944. He spent 10 years at Ewood Park (1937–47), making 94 appearances and scoring 32 goals. He also played for Birmingham (1928–36),

Walsall (1947–48), Peterborough United, Kidderminster Harriers, Rugby Town and Bilston United. He died in 1994, aged 80.

Arsenal left-back **EDDIE HAPGOOD** was utilised in Albion's defence in 1943. He was a 'Gunner' for 19 years from 1927, having earlier 'defended' for Bristol Rovers and Kettering Town. He later managed Blackburn Rovers, Watford and Bath City and was player-coach of Shrewsbury Town. Capped 30 times by England at senior level and on 13 occasions during World War Two, he made 440 first-team appearances for Arsenal, helping them win the League title five times, the FA Cup twice and the Charity Shield four times. He died in Leamington Spa in 1973, aged 64.

Full-back **GEORGE HARDWICK** came south from Middlesbrough in 1945. He spent 13 years at Ayresome Park (1937–50, making 166 appearances) before joining Oldham Athletic, for whom he starred in 190 games. He returned to 'Boro as coach and also held a similar position with PSV Eindhoven before taking over as manager of Sunderland (1964–65) and Gateshead (1968–70). He won 13 England caps, played for Great Britain against the rest of Europe and helped Oldham win the Third Division North title in 1953. Hardwick died in April 2004, aged 84.

Centre-forward **JIMMY JINKS** was Albion's last World War Two guest, 'signed' from Millwall in March 1946. He was a player at The Den from 1938 until 1948 (scoring 19 goals in 50 games). He later served with Fulham, Luton Town and Aldershot. He died in 1981, aged 65.

Left-half **SAM JONES** was recruited from Blackpool in 1943. Previously with Distillery, he was later employed as assistant secretary at Bloomfield Road. A Northern Ireland international (2 caps), he died in 1993, aged 82.

Inside-right **HARRY LANE** was enticed by Albion from Plymouth Argyle in 1943. A player with Hednesford Town, Birmingham and Southend United, he scored 64 goals in 220 League games for the latter club in two spells up to 1948. He was 68 when he died in 1977.

Tottenham Hotspur's inside-forward, **JIMMY McCORMICK**, served Albion in 1943. Formerly with Rotherham United and Chesterfield and later with Fulham, Lincoln City, Crystal Palace and Sliema

Wanderers of Malta as player-coach, he was also employed as the official coach to the Turkish national team and coached at Wycombe Wanderers, Sheffield United, Walton and Hersham (also manager), and he was also in charge of York City (1953–54) as well as working as assistant trainer at Bramall Lane. Sadly, he was killed in a road accident in Marbella, Spain, in January 1968, aged 55.

Left-winger **JACK McDONALD** arrived from Bournemouth in 1942. Ex-Wolves, he later played for Fulham, Southampton, Southend United and Weymouth. He scored 65 goals in a total of 201 League games.

PETER McKENNAN, guest from Partick Thistle, joined Albion permanently in 1947.

The former Aldershot and Crystal Palace forward **FRANK MANDERS** guested for Albion's reserve side (from Norwich City) during the early part of the war. He drowned in a tragic accident in a Sutton Park Lake in March 1942, aged 28.

Arsenal goalkeeper **GEORGE MARKS** guested for Albion in 1943. He spent 10 years at Highbury up to 1946 (making 131 first-team appearances, 126 during World War Two). He later played for Blackburn Rovers, Bristol City and Reading, then coached at Elm Park. He died in February 1998, aged 84.

Albion's 1941 guest centre-forward **GEORGE MAY** came from Dulwich Hamlet, for whom he continued to play until 1950.

Experienced goalkeeper **GIL MERRICK** – recruited from Birmingham in 1942 –

spent 21 years as a player at St Andrew's (1939–60). He then managed the Blues for four seasons to 1964, taking them to the Fairs Cup final (1961) and then to victory in the 1963 League Cup final. He was also in charge of Atherstone Town. Capped by England 23 times, he was in goal in both games against hungary in 1953 and 1954 when the Magyars won 6–3 at Wembley and 7–1 in Budapest. Merrick appeared in 551 first-team games for the Blues and a further 170 during World War Two. An FA Cup runner-up in 1956, he helped the Blues win the Football League South title in 1946 and the Second Division championship in 1948 and 1955. He was born in January 1922.

Full-back/centre-forward **HARRY PARKES** – a 1945 guest from Aston Villa – was later director at Villa Park (1969–72) and also at Birmingham City (mid-1980s). He made 345 appearances for Villa (1939–55). Parkes, who ran his own sports shop in Corporation Street, Birmingham, for many years, was born in 1920.

Inside/centre-forward **BILLY PRICE** was recruited from Huddersfield Town in 1940. He served the Terriers for 10 years up to 1947 and also played for Reading, Hull City and Bradford City. During his career, Price scored 260 goals in more than 350 matches, including 59 in 131 League outings and 122 in 275 outings for Huddersfield (including wartime). He died in 1995 at the age of 78.

Right-back **WALLY QUINTON** came from Birmingham in 1941, having previously assisted Rotherham United. He later played for Brentford, Southend United and Shrewsbury Town and made 85 League appearances in total. He was 68

when he died in 1996.

Another full-back, **LAURIE SCOTT**, arrived at The Hawthorns from Arsenal in 1943. He spent 14 years at Highbury, from 1937, having previously starred for Bradford City. He was later player-manager of Crystal Palace and then became Hendon's team manager. He appeared in 126 peacetime and 189 World War Two games for the Gunners, gaining a League championship medal in 1948 and an FA Cup winners' medal two years later. He was capped 17 times by England at senior level, played in 16 wartime internationals and collected four 'B' caps, 9 of them as captain. He also represented the Football League on five occasions. He died in 1999, aged 82.

Right-back **JACK SHELTON** found his way to Albion from Walsall in 1943. Ex-Cannock Town and Wolves, he later played with Worcester City and was on the coaching staff at Oxford United. The son of the Wolves FA Cup winner of 1908, Shelton died in Walsall in 1992 at the age of 79.

Centre-forward **HEDLEY SIMMS** (signed from Wellington Town in 1942) also played for Chester and Wellington during his career. He died in 1980, aged 61.

Centre-half or wing-half **TOM SMALLEY** came to Albion from Norwich City in 1943. He had previously played for Wolves (1931–37) and after World War Two served with Northampton Town (1945–50) and then Lower Gornal (as player-coach). He made well over 420 League appearances during his career (179 for Wolves and 200 for the Cobblers). He was also capped once by England. Smalley died in 1984, aged 72.

In 1942 Albion 'signed up' goalkeeper **JACK SMITH** from Sheffield United.

During his career, he also played for Sheffield Wednesday and later worked with the training staff at Bramall Lane. He made 498 appearances for the Blades (1930–49) and played in the 1936 FA Cup final defeat by Arsenal and in United's Second Division promotion-winning side of 1939. He died in 1986, aged 75.

England international outside-left **LESLIE SMITH** – an Albion guest from Aston Villa in 1945 – starred in a pre World War Two FA Amateur Cup final for Wimbledon. He also assisted Brentford (two spells), Hayes and Kidderminster Harriers, the latter as player-coach. He was also a Wolves coach. Smith made 197 League and cup appearances for Villa, played in one senior and 13 wartime and Victory internationals, represented the FA and the Army and helped Chelsea win the League South Cup as a guest in 1945. He died in Lichfield in 1995, aged 77.

Inside-right **BILLY WALSH**, signed from Millwall in 1942, also played for Bolton Wanderers, Oldham Athletic, Hearts and South Shore Wednesday. He scored 48 goals in 79 League games for the Latics and 19 in 42 for Millwall. Walsh died in 1965, aged 56.

Inside-left **TOM WOOD** also arrived at the club in 1942, from Newport County. He was also a player with Walsall, Shrewsbury Town, Aston Villa and Newport County, who later returned to Fellows Park as a trainer. He scored 25 goals in 107 League games for Newport and two in 62 for Villa.

NB: Other guests also served Albion as a player-manager and/or coach either before or after World War Two (see under individual entries).

Managers

(also caretaker managers and assistant managers)

List of Albion's Managers: 1890 onwards

1890–92	Louis Ford
1892–94	Henry Jackson
1894–95	Edward Stephenson
1895–96	Clement Keys
1896–1902	Frank Heaven
1902–48	Fred Everiss
1948–52	Jack Smith
1952–53	Jesse Carver
1953–59	Vic Buckingham
1959–61	Gordon Clark
1961–63	Archie Macaulay
1963–67	Jimmy Hagan
1967–71	Alan Ashman
1971–75	Don Howe
1975–77	Johnny Giles
1977	Ronnie Allen
1978–81	Ron Atkinson
1981–82	Ronnie Allen
1982–84	Ron Wylie
1984–85	Johnny Giles
1985–86	'Nobby' Stiles, MBE
1986–87	Ron Saunders
1987–88	Ron Atkinson
1988–91	Brian Talbot
1991–92	Bobby Gould
1992–93	Ossie Ardiles
1993–94	Keith Burkinshaw
1994–97	Alan Buckley
1997	Ray Harford
1997–2000	Denis Smith
2000	Brian Little
2000–04	Gary Megson
2004–	Bryan Robson, OBE

Albion's Caretaker Managers

Brian Whitehouse*
  7–14 June 1975
John Wile*
  23 December 1977–11 January 1978
Brian Talbot*
  13 October–1 November 1988
Stuart Pearson
  9 January–25 February 1991
Arthur Mann
  21 January–5 February 1997
Richie Barker
  5–12 December 1997
John Trewick*
  13–23 December 1997
Cyrille Regis*/Allan Evans
  6 February–5 March 2000
Cyrille Regis*/John Gorman
  6–8 March 2000
Frank Burrows
  26 October–12 November 2004

* Also played for Albion (see individual entries). Regis had two separate spells as caretaker boss with Evans and Gorman respectively.

Manager's Profiles

Louis Ford, born in West Bromwich in 1845, was a local businessman who was an Albion director for four years between 1892–96. He became a committee member of the club in the late 1880s and was honorary financial secretary for three years from 1887 before his appointment as Albion's general secretary (manager) on 5 June 1890, being deeply involved with team selection. He was, in fact, Albion's first official, paid secretary, receiving a salary of £50 per annum. He was responsible for bringing on some exceptionally fine footballers, including Willie Groves, Roddy McLeod and John 'Baldy' Reynolds. He was an FA Councillor (1890–93), member of the Football League management committee and vice-president of the Football League from 1894 to 1897. In 1900 Ford became a League referee. Prior to that, he worked as secretary of neighbouring Walsall (1896–1900) and before World War One served as secretary of Leicester Fosse (1914–15).

Henry 'Swin' Jackson, born *c.*1850, was a member of Albion's first board of directors, elected on 1 September 1891. He remained a director for two years, taking over as the club's general secretary-manager after his first year and retaining that position for a further 18 months before he handed over his duties to Edward Stephenson. A more than useful Staffordshire and West Bromwich Dartmouth cricketer, Jackson later (like his predecessor Ford) became secretary of Leicester Fosse and after that held a similar position with Luton Town. He later emigrated to Canada where he worked as a parish registrar and postmaster until his death in 1930.

Edward 'Ted' Stephenson, a local man born in West Bromwich *c.* 1852, was appointed Albion's general-secretary-manager in November 1895 but was dismissed for incompetence in January 1895 after having been in office for barely eight weeks. He was an avid supporter and shareholder of the club.

Clement Keys, born *c.*1847, Albion's former financial secretary for three years from 1892, followed Stephenson as the club's secretary-manager in August 1895, remaining in office for just the one season. A member of the famous Keys family, his firm later became the club's accountants, based in the heart of West Bromwich.

W. Frank Heaven, born in Edgbaston, Birmingham, in 1873 and educated at Camp Hill Grammar School (where he refused to play rugby, choosing cricket and football instead), became the first pupil to score a century (116) for his school team (against High Street New School in 1887). He played for South Yardley FC and Belevedere CC, while also playing cricket occasionally for the Warwickshire Club and Ground. In 1894 he joined Smethwick CC and hit 1,200 runs in his first season. On 22 August 1896 he was one of five men who applied for the job as secretary of Albion, three days later he was appointed by the club, earning £104 per annum. In June 1897 Heaven was appointed general financial secretary of Albion on wages of £2.10s (£2.50p) a week, agreeing to a £1-a-week rise, payable from 1 September 1897. He remained in office for a further five years to May 1902, when he was asked to resign his position after a disagreement with the club's directors over policy. The reason for his dismissal was never made public. During his time with Albion, Heaven was a member of the executive committee of the Staffs FA, sat on the Birmingham & District FA Council and spent a few years on the committee of the West Bromwich Wednesday FA. Reaching the portly weight of 17st 2lb at one stage, he helped formulate the plans for Albion's new ground (The Hawthorns) to where they moved in the summer of 1900, and, after seeing the team relegated, he then celebrated the winning of the Second Division championship in 1902. After two years out of the game Heaven returned as secretary of Third lanark, spending one season (1904–05) with the

Scottish Club. He moved back to Worcester where he sadly died on Boxing Day in 1905 when only 32 years of age.

Fred Everiss born in West Bromwich in 1882, was effectively Albion's first manager. Although assuming the title of club secretary-manager in 1902, it was he, in the main, who looked after the team's affairs right up until 1948. While he was 'in charge', Albion played (including both World Wars) well over 1,750 competitive matches.

John 'Jack' Smith, a trialist at The Hawthorns as a 16-year-old, played for Aberaman, Aberdare Athletic, Merthyr Town, Wolverhampton Wanderers, Bristol Rovers, Swindon Town and Chelsea

before World War Two and then guested for Cardiff City, Albion and Wolves during the hostilities. He coached at Molineux before becoming Albion's first ever official manager (appointed on 22 June 1948). He remained in office until 17 April 1952, when he left The Hawthorns to become Reading's boss. He led Albion out of the Second Division in 1948–49 and was in charge for 177 matches – 70 were won and 65 lost. A Welsh wartime international, he was capped against England in 1940 (See SMITH, Arthur John).

Jesse Carver, born in Liverpool on 7 July 1911, was an England schoolboy international centre-half who played for Blackburn Rovers (1929–36, making 143 League appearances), Newcastle United (1936–39, having 70 League outings) and Bury (1939–40) before becoming assistant trainer of Huddersfield Town in 1946–47. He coached FC Xerves (Rotterdam) in 1946, was coach with the Dutch FA in 1947 and Millwall in 1948–49, prior to his appointment as Juventus coach in 1949. He then held similar positions in Italy with Marzotto (1949–50), Inter Milan, Genoa, SCC Lazio and Juventus, before becoming Albion's manager/coach, appointed on 18 April 1952. He stayed at The Hawthorns for less than eight months (19 senior matches, 10 wins) leaving the club on 9 December 1952 to take up a coaching position with Valdagno, later holding similar positions with Torino and AS Roma (coach-manager 1953–55) before moving to Coventry City as manager in June to December 1955. He returned to Lazio as coach (1956–58), was with Inter Milan as coach (albeit briefly) and then Sweden in the 1958 World Cup (under manager George Raynor). He then had a spell with Tottenham Hotspur (as trainer-coach from October 1958 to March 1959), served next with his former club Genoa (also as coach) and then did likewise in both Portugal (1959–61) and the US (1962–63). He guided Juventus to the Italian Serie 'A' title in 1950.

Victor Frederick Buckingham, born in Greenwich, London, on 23 October 1915, played as a full-back for Bromley and Tottenham Hotspur (1934–49), gaining two England wartime international caps. He was Middlesex County FA coach (1946–51), coached the Oxford University side and Pegasus (1951) and became

manager of Bradford Park Avenue (1951–52). He left the Yorkshire club for Albion on 2 February 1953 and held office at The Hawthorns until 18 June 1959, during which time Albion plated 306 League and cup matches, of which 135 were won and 96 lost. He later held managerial appointments with Ajax, Amsterdam (two spells: 1959 to 1961 and 1964–65), Plymouth Argyle (in 1961), Sheffield Wednesday (1961–64), Fulham (1965–68), Ethnikos, Greece (1968–69), FC Barcelona (1969–71) and Sevilla (1972). He led Albion to the runners-up spot in the First Division and to FA Cup glory over Preston North End in 1953–54. He left the club soon after returning from Albion's Canada/US tour in 1959. He died in hospital in Worthing, Sussex, on 27 January 1995, at the age of 79.

Gordon Vincent Clark, born in Guisborough on 15 June 1914, was a rock-solid full-back with Goldthorpe United, Southend United (1935–36), Manchester City (1936–46), Waterford (player-manager) and Hyde United (player-manager), before hanging up his boots to take over as boss of Distillery (1949). He left Ireland for the Football League that same year, when appointed manager of Aldershot, a position he held until 1955 when he became Albion's chief scout. He moved into the manager's chair at The Hawthorns on 9 July 1959 and stayed there until 11 October 1961. In that time Albion played exactly 100 League and cup games, of which 42 were won and 39 lost. After that he served with

Sheffield Wednesday (assistant manager 1961–64), Peterborough United (manager, 1964–67), Arsenal (chief scout, 1976–77), Fulham (assistant manager, 1977–78), Philadelphia Fury (senior coach, 1978–79) and Queen's Park Rangers (assistant manager 1979–80). He joined his former boss, Vic Buckingham, at Hillsborough and took Peterborough United to the League Cup semi-finals in 1965–66, where they lost to Albion over two legs. Clark died on 18 October 1997.

Archibald Renwick Macaulay, born in Falkirk on 30 July 1915, was a Scottish international wing-half (seven full and six wartime caps gained), who played for Camelon Juniors, Glasgow Rangers (1934–37), West Ham United (1937–46), Brentford (1946–47), Arsenal (1947–50) and Fulham (1950–53). Thereafter, he assisted Guildford City (as player-manager 1953–55) and Dundee (as trainer-coach 1955–56) before being named as Norwich City's manager (1957–61). From Carrow Road he moved to Albion as manager on 19 October 1961 and held office until 2 April 1963. The team played 65 competitive games, winning 27 and losing 22. After that he served with Brighton and Hove Albion as manager for five years (1963–68). Macaulay later became a traffic warden in Brighton. As a player, he also represented a Great Britain XI, won a League Cup War medal in 1940 with West Ham and gained League championship and cup medals with Queen's Park Rangers before leading Brighton to the Fourth Division title in 1965. He died on 10 June 1993.

James Hagan, born in Washington, County Durham, on 21 January 1918, was an England schoolboy and full international inside-forward (one senior cap and 16 wartime caps won). Jimmy Hagan was an Albion trialist in 1933 and played for Washington Colliery FC and Liverpool (1932–33) before joining Derby County. He spent five years with the Rams, up to 1938, when he moved to Sheffield United. He had 20 years at Bramall Lane, making 364 League appearances and scoring 118 goals. Hagan then served Peterborough United as manager (1958–62), Albion as manager (10 April 1963–3 May 1967), Manchester City as scout (1968–69), Benfica as manager (1970–73), in Kuwait as a senior professional coach (1974–75)

and was manager of Sporting Lisbon (1975–77), then FC Porto (1978–79), Boavista (1979) and Vitoria Setubal (also in 1979). He guided Peterborough from the Midland League into the Football League and saw Albion twice reach the League Cup final, winning in 1966, losing in 1967. He was in charge at The Hawthorns for 201 senior games, of which 90 were won and 73 lost. Hagan died in Sheffield on 26 February 1998.

George Alan Ashman, born in Rotherham on 30 May 1928, was a centre-forward with Sheffield United (amateur 1946–47), Nottingham Forest (1948–51) and Carlisle United (1951–58). Alan Ashman, a former chicken farmer, then coached Penrith FC (1959–61) and managed his former club, Carlisle (1963–67), before serving as Albion's manager (from 23 May 1967 to 2 July 1971). Albion fulfilled 229 senior games during those four years, winning 79 and losing 79. He then served in turn with the Greek club Olympiakos (manager 1971–72), Carlisle United again (manager 1972–75), Workington (manager 1975–77), Manchester United (scout, 1977–78), Walsall (team manager 1978), Derby County (chief scout 1979 and later as assistant manager 1982) and Hereford United (assistant manager 1983–87), before holding scouting jobs with Plymouth Argyle, Notts County, Mansfield Town, Derby County (again),

Telford United and Aston Villa. Ashman guided Albion to FA Cup glory in 1968 and to runners-up in the 1970 League Cup final. He died in Walsall on 30 November 2002.

Donald Howe, born in Wolverhampton on 12 October 1935, was a player with Wolverhampton Wanderers (amateur 1949–50) before spending 14 years with Albion (1950–64). After leaving The Hawthorns, he served with Arsenal (1964–67 before a broken leg curtailed his career). He gained 23 full caps for England and played in the World Cup. He later became coach and assistant manager at Highbury before serving as Albion's manager from 9 July 1971 to 6 April 1975. Albion won 62 and lost 77 of the 196 competitive games they played under Howe's managership. Howe later coached in Turkey and Saudi Arabia, Leeds United, Arsenal (again), Chelsea and Queen's Park Rangers, also managing at Loftus Road and Coventry City, as well as being a key figure on the England coaching staff (See HOWE, Donald).

John Michael Giles, born in Cabra, Dublin, on 6 January 1940, was initially an outside-right and later a skilful midfielder, who played for the St Columbus School team, Dublin City (later Munster Victoria), Stella Maris, Leprechauns FC and Home Farm, before entering the Football League with Manchester United in 1956. He moved to Leeds United in 1963 and became player-manager of Albion on 19 June 1975, retaining his position for almost two years until 27 May 1977. He was later player-manager of Shamrock Rovers (1977–83), guest for Philadelphia Fury (1978) and coached Vancouver Whitecaps (1980–83), prior to having a second spell as Albion manager from 13 December 1983 to 29 September 1985. In all, Giles was in charge for 187 games, of which 56 were won and 77 lost. He won 60 caps for the Republic of Ireland, whom he also managed (1973–80). He won medals with both Manchester United and Leeds in England and Shamrock Rovers in Ireland and guided Albion to promotion from Division Two in 1975–76 (See GILES, John Michael).

Ronald Allen, born in Fenton, Stoke-on-Trent, on 15 January 1929, was a superb player with Port Vale (1944–50), West Bromwich Albion (1950–61) and Crystal

Palace (1961–65). He later coached and managed Wolverhampton Wanderers (1965–68) and was manager of Atletico Bilbao (1969–71), Sporting Lisbon (1972–73) and Walsall (1973) before returning to The Hawthorns as Albion manager on 22 June, staying albeit for only six months up to 22 December 1977, when he left to take over as coach of the Saudi Arabia national team. In 1980–81 he managed the Greek club Panathinaikos and returned to Albion as team manager on 26 July 1981, holding his job until 30 June 1982, when he took over as general manager at The Hawthorns. In all, Albion played 77 games with Allen as boss, winning 30 and losing 27. Allen later served Albion as a part-time coach (1990s). He won five full England caps and led Bilbao to victory in Spain's King's Cup final of 1969. He died on 9 June 2001, aged 72 (see ALLEN, Ronald).

Ronald Franklin Atkinson, born in Liverpool on 18 March 1939, was a tough-tackling wing-half (or defender) with BSA Tools FC (1954), Wolverhampton Wanderers (as a junior 1955), Aston Villa (as a reserve in 1956–59) and Headington United/Oxford United (1960–1971). He then became player-manager of Kettering Town (1971–74), manager of Witney Town (1974) and also of Cambridge United (1974–78) before taking over the reins at Albion on 12 January 1978, remaining in charge until 9 June 1981. He then 'transferred' his duties to Manchester United (1981–86), served Bolton Wanderers (as a coach in 1986) and returned to The Hawthorns as manager for the second time on 3 September 1987, staying this time until 12 October 1988. Albion played a total of 232 competitive games with 'Big Ron' in charge, 95 were won and 63 lost. After leaving the club (second time round) he served with Atletico Madrid (as coach 1988–89), Sheffield Wednesday (manager 1989–91), Aston Villa (manager 1991–94), Coventry City (manager 1995–96 – he won the 'Manager of the Month' award after just 44 days in charge at Highfield Road), Sheffield Wednesday (manager, again: 1997–98) and Nottingham Forest. As a player he helped Oxford win two Southern League titles (1961 and 1962) and gain Football League status and the climb up from the Fourth to the Second Division in double-quick time. As a

football boss, he guided Cambridge to the Fourth Division championship in 1977, and he assembled a superb Albion side, which reached the FA Cup semi-final in 1978, finished third in the First Division and also qualified for the UEFA Cup quarter-finals. He won two Wembley FA Cup finals with Manchester United (in 1983 and 1985), was successful with Sheffield Wednesday first time round over Manchester United in the 1991 League Cup final, as well as winning promotion with the Owls to the First Division. He then guided Aston Villa to victory, again over his former club, Manchester United, in the 1994 League Cup final. Unfortunately, he didn't have a happy

time in Spain as, although on a contract worth half-a-million pounds, he was dismissed after just 96 days in office, despite taking Bilbao to third spot in the League. He did, however, receive the princely sum of £100,000 in compensation following his dismissal by Manchester United in November 1986. Atkinson now works for ITV Sport as a soccer analyst and summariser. Atkinson played once in Albion's first team as a centre-forward against Kettering Town (away) in April 1988.

Ronald Maurice Wylie, born in Glasgow on 6 August 1933, was an inside-forward with Clydesdale Juniors (1946–47), Notts

County (1948–58), Aston Villa (1958–65) and Birmingham City (1965–70), before becoming a coach at Villa Park and then Coventry City, later taking over as assistant manager at Highfield Road. After that, he worked as a soccer adviser in Cyprus and served in Bulova (Hong Kong) as team manager in 1981–82 before taking over as Albion's manager on 27 July 1982, retaining the position until 13 December 1983. Albion won 30 and lost 34 of the 80 games played during Wylie's reign as manager. Thereafter, Wylie returned to Villa Park as reserve team coach-manager (1986–87) and scouted for several clubs during the late 1980s. He was appointed Community Officer at Aston Villa in 1990. Wylie won both the Second Division championship (1960) and League Cup (1961) with Villa and was voted 'Midland Footballer of the Year' in 1965. He failed to do the business with Albion!

Nobert Peter Stiles, MBE, born in Manchester on 18 May 1942, was a terrific wing-half with Manchester United (1957–71), Middlesbrough (1971–73) and Preston North End (1973–74), who became manager at Deepdale (1974–78) and later assisted his brother-in-law Johnny Giles at Vancouver Whitecaps (1981–83), before becoming Albion's coach, then assistant manager and finally manager on 15 October 1985 and remaining in the hot-seat until 14 February 1986. Albion won four and lost 11 of the 23 games played under Stiles, who later returned to Old Trafford as coach under Alex Ferguson. Stiles, who guested for Albion against Leeds United in Giles's testimonial match in October 1975, gained 28 England caps, was a World Cup winner in 1966, collected a European Cup winners' medal two years later and also gained both League and FA Cup medals at club level with Manchester United. In July 2002, then working as an after-dinner speaker and charity committee member, he suffered a mild heart attack, but, with a smile on his face, he said: 'Don't panic… I'm okay!'

Ronald Saunders, born in Birkenhead on 6 November 1932, was an England youth international centre-forward, as hard as nails. A prolific goalscorer with Birkenhead and Liverpool Schools, Everton (1951–56), Tonbridge (1956–57), Gillingham (1957–58), Portsmouth

(1958–64), Watford (1964) and Charlton Athletic (1965–67), he became general manager of Yeovil Town (1967–68) and then took charge of Oxford United (1969), Norwich City (1969–73), Manchester City (1973–74), Aston Villa (1974–82) and Birmingham City (1982–86) before holding office at The Hawthorns from 14 February 1986 to 1 September 1987. He led a trio of clubs – Norwich, Manchester City and Villa – to Wembley League Cup finals in successive seasons (1973,74,75) but only Villa won the trophy, playing against his former club, Norwich. He did, however, lead the Canaries to the Second Division title in 1972. He also guided Villa to the Football League championship in 1981. He failed at Albion, who won only 14 and lost 34 of the 67 games played during his reign in charge, and there is no doubt that The Hawthorns fans will certainly never forgive him for selling Tipton-born striker Steve Bull (and to a certain extent Andy Thompson) to Wolves. Indeed, Bully went on to score over 300 goals for Albion's arch-rivals. As a marksman himself, Saunders netted 207 goals in 392 League appearances for his five senior clubs.

Brian Ernest Talbot (born Ipswich, 21 July 1953) was a highly talented midfield player with Ipswich Town (1968–79), Toronto Metros (1971 and 1972), Arsenal (1979–85), Watford (1985–86) and Stoke City (1986–88), who joined Albion for £15,000 in January 1988. He was appointed caretaker manager at The Hawthorns on 13 October 1988 and was

upgraded to team manager on 2 November of that same year. Unfortunately, he lost his job on 8 January 1991, soon after Albion had been dumped out of the FA Cup by non-League side Woking. Albion won 39 and lost 44 of the 121 games played under Talbot, who went on to assist Fulham (as a player), Aldershot (manager in 1991), Sudbury Town (1992) and Hibernians (Malta, 1993–96), before taking over as manager of Rushden and Diamonds, whom he successfully guided into the Football League (as Nationwide Conference winners in 2001) and a year later saw them reach the Third Division play-off final at Cardiff's Millennium Stadium (beaten by Cheltenham Town) and then Oldham Athletic as manager from March 2004. He won six full England caps and was also an FA Cup winner with both Ipswich and Arsenal in successive seasons (1978 and 1979). He made a total of 533 League appearances during a fine career, netting six goals in his 83 first-team outings for Albion (see TALBOT, Brian Ernest).

Robert Anthony Gould, born in Coventry on 12 June 1946, was a tough-nut centre-forward who served with Coventry City (1962–68), Arsenal (1968–70) and Wolverhampton Wanderers (1970–71) before joining Albion for the unusual fee of £66,666 in September 1971. He remained at The Hawthorns until December 1972 when he switched his allegiance to Bristol City. He later served with West Ham United (1973–75), Wolves again (1975–77), Bristol Rovers (1977–78) and Hereford United (1978–79). He also assisted FC Aalsund of Norway (player-coach 1978), Charlton Athletic (coach 1979), Chelsea (assistant manager 1979–81), Wimbledon (non-contract player-coach 1981), Aldershot (assistant manager 1981), Bristol Rovers (team manager 1981–83), Coventry City (manager 1983–84), Bristol Rovers (again manager 1985), Wimbledon (manager 1987–90), Queen's Park Rangers (coach 1990–91) and then back to Albion as manager from 26 February 1991 to 5 May 1992, during which time the Baggies slipped into the Third Division for the first time in the club's history! Albion won 24 and lost 22 of the 69 games played under Gould's managership. After leaving The

Hawthorns, Gould returned to Coventry City as manager (1992–93) and was then the Welsh national team manager from 1995–98, having former Albion skipper Graham Williams as his assistant for a time. He then went on to manage Cheltenham Town (2003) before becoming manager Barry Fry's aide at Peterborough United. As a player, Gould was an FA Cup winner with West Ham (1975) and Second Division championship victor with both Coventry (1967) and Wolves (1977). As a manager, he led Wimbledon to FA Cup glory (against Liverpool) in 1988. He scored 19 goals in 60 senior appearances for Albion (see GOULD, Robert Anthony).

Osvaldo Cesar Ardiles, born in Cordoba, Argentina, on 3 August 1952, was a brilliant midfield player who starred for South American clubs Red Star (Cordoba), Instituto de Cordoba (1975) and FC Huracan (1975–78) before being signed by Tottenham Hotspur for £325,000 in the summer of 1978. During his 10 years at White Hart Lane he was adored by the fans and appeared in 416 first-team matches for the London club. He also assisted Paris St Germain and Blackburn Rovers on loan while a Spurs player and he served with Queen's Park Rangers and Fort Lauderdale Strikers in the late 1980s before managing Swindon Town from 1989–91. He was then Newcastle United's manager in 1991–92 before taking charge of West Bromwich Albion, a position he held from 8 May 1992 to 18 June 1993. In that time Albion played 59 games, of which 33 were won and only 15 lost. He returned to Tottenham as team manager for seasons 1993–95, then coached the Mexican club Deportiv Guadelajara, returning as manager of Shimizu S-Pulse of Japan in 1996 and after that taking the reins at Croatia Zagreb, Yokohama F Marinos (Japan) from December 1999 to June 2001 and then Al Ittihad (Saudi Arabia) from July 2001. In the summer of 2002 Ardiles, who is now a qualified lawyer, returned to his homeland to take charge of the Argentine champions, Racing Club Buenos Aries. Capped 52 times at senior level by his country, Ardiles was a World Cup winner with Argentina in 1978, twice an FA Cup winner with Spurs (1981 and 1982) and he guided Albion to promotion from Division Two via the Wembley play-off final in 1993.

Keith H. Burkinshaw, born in Higham on 23 June 1935, played for Denaby United, Wolverhampton Wanderers (amateur), Liverpool (1953) and Workington (1957) before taking over as manager of the latter club in 1964–65. He then managed Scunthorpe United in 1965–66 before coaching in Zambia (1968). Next he was assistant coach and then first-team coach at Newcastle United, and in 1975 he was appointed coach at Tottenham Hotspur, moving into the manager's office in 1976 and retaining his position for eight years. After coaching appointments in Bahrain and Portugal (with Sporting Lisbon) and spells as manager of Gillingham and chief scout at Swindon Town, he became Albion's assistant manager (to Ardiles) in May 1992, taking over as team manager on 2 July 1993 (when Ardiles left) and retaining his post until 16 October 1994. In that time Albion played 61 games, of which 17 were won and 35 lost. In 1997 he went as an aide to the Scottish club Aberdeen. Burkinshaw led Spurs to the Second Division championship in 1978, two FA Cup final triumphs (1981 and 1982), League Cup success (also in 1982) and to UEFA Cup glory in 1984. He is now with Watford as an assistant-manager to former Albion youth/intermediate team coach Adrian Boothroyd, since March 2005.

Alan Peter Buckley, born in Mansfield on 20 April 1951, was a goalscoring forward with Nottingham Forest (1966–73), Walsall (1973–78 and 1979–86) and Birmingham City (1978–79), who served as player-manager of the Saddlers from 1982–85, becoming manager at the club in 1986. Thereafter, he played briefly for Stourbridge and Tamworth before taking over as manager of non-League side Kettering Town (1986–88). From there he switched to Grimsby Town, managing the Mariners for six years from 1988. He left Blundell Park to become boss at Albion (appointed on 20 October 1994) and he left on 20 January 1997. Albion won 41 and lost 46 of the 124 games played under Buckley, who rejoined Grimsby Town in mid-1997 and guided the Mariners to victory in the 1998 Auto-Windscreen Shield final versus AFC Bournemouth at Wembley. Earlier, he had steered Grimsby from the Fourth to the Second Division(now the Championship) in successive seasons (1990–91). He was

sacked by Albion after a horrible run of home results. Buckley returned to his former club Grimsby Town (1997–2000) and later held the position of manager of Lincoln City (February 2001–May 2002) and then Rochdale (from May 2003). Buckley played in one first-team game for Albion, a friendly against Cheltenham Town (away) in May 1995.

Raymond Thomas Harford, born in Halifax, Yorkshire, on 1 June 1945 and died on 9 August 2003, was a central defender with Charlton Athletic (junior, June 1962, professional, May 1964), Exeter City (from January 1966), Lincoln City (from July 1967), Mansfield Town (from June 1971), Port Vale (from December 1971) and Colchester United (from January 1973). He retired in May 1975 after more than 400 senior appearances, 354 in the Football League, including 161 for Lincoln and 107 for Colchester. Thereafter, his managerial career took him to Fulham (1984–86), Luton Town (1987–89),Wimbledon (1990–91), Blackburn Rovers (1995–96), West Bromwich Albion (from 6 February to 4 December 1997) and Queen's Park Rangers, whom he joined directly on leaving The Hawthorns. Harford has also worked as a coach and/or assistant manager at Colchester United, Fulham, Luton Town, Oxford United, Wimbledon and Blackburn Rovers, prior to taking over as team boss at each of the last four clubs. He has also held coaching positions at Swindon Town, Reading, Fulham, Queen's Park Rangers, Millwall and Luton Town (his last club in 2002–03). As manager of Luton, he guided the Hatters to League Cup glory in 1988, to League Cup runners-up in 1989 and to victory in the Simod Cup final, also in 1988. As coach at Ewood Park (1991–95), he helped Blackburn win promotion from the First Division and then helped them win the Premiership title. He failed to gain any honours as a player. He did pretty well during his short time at The Hawthorns, pushing Albion into top spot (albeit briefly) early on in the 1997–98 season, but then, perhaps surprisingly, he quit The Hawthorns after barely 10 months in charge to take over the reins at Queen's Park Rangers. Albion won 20 and lost 17 of the 44 games played under his control. Harford died in 2003 at the age of 58, after a three-year battle against cancer.

Denis Smith, born in Meir, Stoke-on-Trent, on 19 November 1947, was one of the greatest defenders ever to play for Stoke City. He was certainly a fine servant to the Potters, whom he served for 17 years, during which time he amassed 493 appearances and scored 41 goals while overcoming countless injuries. A pupil at Queensbury Road School, he joined Stoke as a junior in 1965, turning 'pro' in 1966. It was not until he was almost 21 that he made his debut against Arsenal (away) in a First Division match in 1968. He became a permanent fixture in the side in 1969, partnering Alan Bloor. He won Football League honours but never a full England cap. He helped Stoke win the League Cup in 1972 and retired in May 1982, having been on the Potters coaching staff in his last season. He then became manager of York City, holding office at Bootham Crescent for five years until 1987 when he took over at Sunderland. He stayed at Roker Park for four years and in 1992 was put in charge of Bristol City. He left Ashton Gate rather quickly to take charge of Oxford United (in September 1993), and in December 1997 he quit his post at The Manor Ground to become Albion's boss, appointed on Christmas Eve. His first win as the Baggies chief was a 3–1 FA Cup victory over his former club, Stoke, in January 1998. Unfortunately, after some poor results, Smith left The Hawthorns on 27 July 1999, Albion having won 22 and lost 32 of the 74 games played in that time. He later returned to football as manager of hard-up Oxford United (2000) and then took over the reins of struggling Wrexham in October 2001, replacing Bryan Flynn at The Racecourse Ground. He guided Wrexham to victory in the LDV Vans

Trophy in April 2005, but he failed to save the Welsh club from relegation to League Division Two.

Brian Little , born in Peterlee, County Durham, on 25 November 1953, was an inside-forward with Aston Villa, whom he served (from an apprentice) for a total of 13 years (1969–82). A trialist with several clubs including a spell at The Hawthorns in 1968, Stoke City, Newcastle United, Leeds United and Manchester City, Little went on to score 82 goals in 301 first-team appearances for Villa, helping them win the League Cup in 1977 when he scored two goals in the second replay against Everton at Old Trafford. He was also an FA Youth Cup winner in 1972 and was a member of Villa's Second Division championship-winning side of 1975, as well as gaining one full England cap (as a late substitute against Wales in 1975). A proposed £600,000 transfer to St Andrew's broke down in 1979–80 on medical grounds. On his retirement (alas through injury) Little became a coach at Villa Park, later taking a similar position with Wolves, where he also acted as caretaker manager for a while, prior to the arrival of Graham Turner in 1986. From Molineux, Little went to Middlesbrough as a coach,

he then managed Darlington from 1989–91 and was in charge of Leicester City for three years to 1994, before returning to Villa Park as boss where he remained until 1998. Prior to taking over at The Hawthorns, Little managed Stoke City where, ironically, he was replaced by Gary Megson! He was officially appointed as Albion's manager on 11 August 1999 (with ex-Villa colleague Allan Evans as his assistant), but, after a run of disappointing results, he was sacked on 6 February 2000. Indeed, Albion won only nine and lost 15 of the 42 games played with Little in charge. He later managed Hull City (from April 2000 to February 2002) before taking over as the new boss of Tranmere Rovers in October 2003.

NB: Little was one of three former Albion men to lose their managerial jobs in 2002, the other two being Garry Thompson (Bristol Rovers) and Alan Buckley (Lincoln City).

Gary Megson, born in Manchester on 2 May 1959, is the son of Don Megson, the former Sheffield Wednesday left-back and skipper who played in the 1966 FA Cup final. Megson junior was a hard-working, aggressive midfielder who played, in turn, for Plymouth Argyle (signed as a professional in May 1977), Everton (December 1979), Sheffield Wednesday (August 1981), Nottingham Forest (albeit briefly, August–November 1984), Newcastle United (November 1984), Sheffield Wednesday, again (December 1985), Manchester City (January 1989),

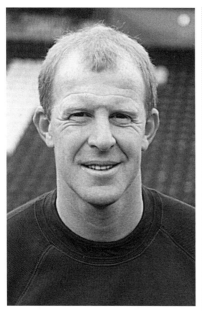

Norwich City (August 1992), Lincoln City (non-contract, August 1995) and finally Shrewsbury Town (September 1995, retiring, October 1995 with 588 competitive matches and 50 goals to his credit). He quickly took a coaching position with Bradford City before becoming manager at Carrow Road, later taking over the reins at Blackpool (1996–97), Stockport County (1997–99) and Stoke City (briefly, also in 1999). Named Albion's new manager on 9 March 2000, he did an excellent job by keeping the Baggies in the First Division and then lifting the club into the Premiership in April 2002, only to drop back down after just one campaign with the big boys. However, after some very disappointing performances and results during the first three months of the 2003–04 season, Megson was sacked by the club after he had written a letter to chairman Jeremy Peace stating that he would leave The Hawthorns at the end of the campaign. Overall, Megson's record as Albion's manager was good, they played 222, won 96, drawn 70 and lost 66.

NB: Megson was handed the Freedom of West Bromwich at a mediaeval-style presentation evening at the Botanical Gardens, Birmingham, in October 2002, with the title Lord of the Manor of West Bromwich.

Bryan Robson, OBE, born in Witton Gilbert, Chester-le-Street, County Durham, on 11 January 1957, had trials with Burnley, Coventry City and

Newcastle United before joining Albion as an apprentice in 1972, turning professional two years later. Over the next seven years he appeared in 249 senior games for Albion, scoring 46 goals before transferring to Manchester United for a record fee of £1.5 million. He did exceedingly well at Old Trafford, skippering United on many occasions and helping them win successive Premiership titles (1993 and 1994), three FA Cup finals (1983, 1985 and 1990) and lift the European Cup-winners' Cup (1991). He netted 100 goals in 465 appearances for United, took his total number of England caps to 90 and led his country more than 60 times. On leaving Old Trafford in 1994, he took over as player-manager at Middlesbrough. He retired as a player in 1997 but remained as manager until 2001. He then returned to Manchester United as a part-time coach, was boss of the Nigerian national side (briefly in 2003) and then took charge of Bradford City (November 2003-May 2004) before turning full circle and returning to The Hawthorns as manager in November 2004, bringing in Nigel Pearson, the former Shrewsbury Town, Sheffield Wednesday and Middlesbrough defender, as his assistant, who was also on England's coaching staff and Director of Football at Carlisle United as well as coach at Hillsborough. (see ROBSON, Bryan, OBE)

Caretaker Manager's Note-pad:

Allan James Evans, born in Polbeath near Edinburgh on October 1956, was a rugged no-nonsense defender who played for Dunfermline Athletic, Aston Villa (1977–89), Leicester City, Brisbane United (Australia) and Darlington. He later worked as assistant to his former playing colleague, Brian Little, at Leicester, Stoke City, Villa Park and Albion, the latter from 1999–2000, during which time he acted briefly as joint caretaker boss with Cyrille Regis. In June 2000 Evans himself went into management with the Scottish club Morton but was sacked after a humiliating cup defeat at the hands of Peterhead in January 2001. He appeared in 469 games for Villa (60 goals scored) and helped them win the League title, both the European and Super Cups in 1982, and he also gained four caps for Scotland. He once scored six goals in a Central League game for Villa against Sheffield United in 1978.

John Gorman, also born near Edinburgh in the town of Winchburg on 16 August 1949, was a full-back who played for Celtic, Carlisle United, Tottenham Hotspur and Tampa Bay Rowdies before becoming Gillingham's trainer/coach. Afterwards he served in the same capacity with Leyton Orient before becoming manager Glenn Hoddle's assistant at Swindon, later moving with his former playing colleague to Tottenham Hotspur and Southampton, while also having a spell as assistant manager/coach at The Hawthorns, during which time he, along with Cyrille Regis, looked after the affairs of the first XI on a caretaker basis. Gorman was also Hoddle's right-hand man when the former Spurs midfielder was boss of England.

Stuart James Pearson, born in Hull in June 1949, was a fine centre-forward who, after leaving School in East Riding, played for Hull City (amateur 1966, professional, 1968), Manchester United (signed for £200,000 in May 1974) and West Ham United (a £220,000 buy in August 1979). He retired from League football in 1982 (with a knee injury) but continued to play at a lower level, in South Africa and the NASL. He also had a spell with Sale Rugby Club. He then became Stockport County's coach (1985–86), was Northwich Victoria's manager (for the first half of 1986–87 season) and then arrived at West Bromwich Albion as coach-assistant manager in 1988, remaining at The Hawthorns until 1992. He was caretaker manager for a time in 1991. After that Pearson served as Bradford City's assistant manager (1992–94). He was Manchester United's leading marksman in 1974–75, when the Second Division championship was won, he played in the FA Cup final defeat by Southampton in 1976 and scored the opening goal in the 1977 FA Cup victory over Liverpool. Nicknamed 'Pancho', he was also an FA Cup winner with the Hammers in 1980 and a League Cup finalist 12 months later (as a substitute). Capped once by England at under-21 level, Pearson went on to win a total of 15 full caps during 1976 and 1977, scoring four goals. He played 180 games for Manchester United and netted 66 goals. He played once for Albion's first team as a substitute against Wigan Athletic (away) in March 1988.

Arthur Fraser Mann, born in Falkirk, Scotland, in January 1948, played as a full-back for Manchester City against Albion in the 1970 League Cup final at Wembley. He started his career with Hearts before moving to Maine Road in 1968. Spells with Blackpool (on loan), Notts County, Shrewsbury Town and Mansfield Town followed before he quit top-line football in 1982 with over 450 League and cup appearances under his belt. He later teamed up as assistant to team manager Alan Buckley at Grimsby Town and then Albion. He acted as caretaker boss at The Hawthorns during January and February 1997. He played one first-team game for Albion in a friendly at Cheltenham in May 1995.

NB: Mann was tragically killed in a Birmingham factory accident involving a stacking-truck on 4 February 1999.

Richie Barker was born in Derby on 23 November 1939. He did not enter League football until he was 28, having played 13 years at a lower level with Morris Sports FC, Burton Albion (two spells), Loughborough, Matlock Town and the Canadian side Primo Hamilton (on loan). He joined Derby County as a professional in October 1967 and later assisted Notts County and Peterborough United before moving into management as assistant to Alan Durban at Shrewsbury. When Durban left for Stoke he became boss at Gay Meadow and after

that served as assistant manager to John Barnwell at Wolves. In 1981 he took charge of Stoke City, became manager of Notts County in 1984, coached the Greek club Ethnikos and the Egyptian side FC Zamalek prior to becoming Ron Atkinson's assistant at Sheffield Wednesday (1989). Barker was appointed Albion's chief scout in the summer of 1997 and he acted as caretaker manager at The Hawthorns (albeit briefly in December of that year), before becoming assistant manager at Halifax Town (2000).

Frank Burrows, placed in temporary charge after the sacking of Gary Megson in October 2004, made over 500 senior appearances (409 in the Football League) between 1962 and 1974, serving with Raith Rovers, Scunthorpe United, Swindon Town and Mansfield Town. He then became assistant manager of Swindon before taking over as senior coach at Portsmouth in 1978, holding the manager's job at Fratton Park from 1979–82. Spells as a coach with Southampton and Sunderland then preceded his appointment as manager of Cardiff City in 1986, a position he held until 1989 when he returned to Portsmouth as assistant boss to John Gregory, taking over as team manager in 1990. A year later he switched to Swansea City as manager, remaining at The Vetch Field until 1995. He returned later for a second spell in charge of Cardiff City (1998 and 1999). Burrows was a League Cup winner with Swindon Town (v Arsenal) in 1969, and as a manager twice gained promotion from Division Four, in 1980 with Portsmouth and 1988 with Cardiff. Burrows, who was born in Larkhall near Glasgow on 30 January 1944, became the oldest man to 'manage' Albion at the age of 60.

Albion assistant managers

Since the 1970s the manager of Albion has seemingly always had an assistant, who was also listed as a coach at The Hawthorns, among them were Brian Whitehouse/George Wright (to Don Howe), Sam Allardyce (to Brian Talbot/Bobby Gould), Colin Addison and Mick Brown (to Ron Atkinson), Gerry Summers (to Ronnie Allen), Nobby Stiles (to Johnny Giles), Stuart Pearson (to

Malcolm Crosby and Denis Smith

Brian Talbot), Keith Burkinshaw (to Ossie Ardiles), Arthur Mann (to Alan Buckley), John Trewick (to Ray Harford and Denis Smith), Malcolm Crosby (to Denis Smith), Cyrille Regis (to Ray Harford), John Gorman (to Denis Smith), Allan Evans (to Brian Little), Frank Burrows (to Gary Megson) and Nigel Pearson (to Bryan Robson).

Colin Addison had a long career in football, playing in more than 400 competitive games and scoring over 230 goals (1955–74) for York City, Nottingham Forest, Arsenal, Sheffield United and Hereford United, managing the latter club (two spells), Merthyr Tydfil, Derby County, Durban City (South Africa), Celta Vigo (Spain), Atletico Madrid and Cardiff City, Yeovil Town, Swansea City and Forest Green Rovers, and he was also assistant manager at Notts County and Atletico Madrid, coach in Kuwait (Al Arabi), Qatar and Spain (Cadiz and Atletico Madrid). He is now a respected scout in the Midlands area.

Nigel Pearson, born in Nottingham on 21 August 1963 and initially a semi-professional with Heanor Town, developed into a solid defender who amassed a total of 544 League and cup appearances while playing for Shrewsbury Town (1981–87), Sheffield Wednesday (1987–94) and Middlesbrough (1994–98). He was a League Cup winner in 1991 with Wednesday and skippered Middlesbrough (under Robson) when they twice reached the Premiership and qualified for three Cup finals.

Coaches

West Bromwich Albion's first official coach was former left-back Albert Evans, who was appointed in 1910.

Since then several other ex-players have held the position as Albion coach, also referred to as trainer, including the following: Billy Bassett (on an unpaid basis), Billy Williams (pre World War One), Jesse Pennington (1922–23), Tommy Glidden (1936–39), Teddy Sandford and Jack Sankey (during World War Two), Frank Hodgetts, Harold Pearson and Cecil Shaw (1950s), 'W.G.' Richardson (1946–59, who also acted as assistant trainer until his death), Arthur Fitton (1950s), George Lee (1959–63), Graham Williams (1970–72), Brian Whitehouse (1971–75). Tony Brown (1984–86), John Trewick (1993–96) and Ronnie Allen (1990s).

Since the early 1990s Albion have also employed a goalkeeping coach and they have included: Tony Parks, ex-Tottenham Hotspur, Oxford United, Gillingham, Brentford, Fulham, West Ham United, Stoke City, Blackpool, Falkirk, Burnley and Doncaster Rovers, who played in more than 150 League and cup games between 1980 and 1998 and won the UEFA Cup with Spurs.

Gerry Peyton, who was capped by the Republic of Ireland on 33 occasions at senior level and amassed over 600 League appearances while serving with Burnley, Fulham, Southend, Bournemouth, Everton, Bolton Wanderers, Chelsea and West Ham United.

Eric Steele, formerly of Peterborough United, Brighton & Hove Albion, Watford, Cardiff City, Derby County, Southend United and Mansfield Town, started his professional career with Newcastle United in 1972 and appeared in almost 350 League matches.

Fred Barber was another nomadic 'keeper, whose professional clubs were Darlington, Everton, Walsall, Peterborough United (three spells), Chester City (two spells), Blackpool, Colchester United, Luton Town, Ipswich Town, Blackpool and Birmingham City. He was a League professional for 15 years (1981–96) and made over 450 senior appearances.

And, finally, big **Joe Corrigan**, ex-Manchester City, Brighton & Hove Albion, Norwich City and Stoke City, whose career spanned 18 years (1967–85) and realised more than 600 League and cup appearances. He won nine full, one under-23, three under-21 and 10 'B' caps for England, represented the Football League, an England XI and the FA and also coached the international team. He was appointed by Albion in November 2004 in succession to Barber.

Club Secretaries

Albion's secretaries: 1880–1996

1880–81	John Bisseker
1881–82	John While
1882–83	Arthur E. Eld and F. Seymour (joint secretary)
1883–84	Arthur E. Eld (Hon secretary). Joseph Hughes (Hon financial secretary)
1884–90	Thomas Smith (Hon general secretary)
1884–85	John Homer (Hon financial secretary)
1885–87	Thomas Foster (Hon financial secretary)
1887–90	Louis Ford (Hon financial secretary)
1890–92	Louis Ford (general secretary). W. Pierce Dix (Hon financial secretary)
1892–94	Henry 'Swin' Jackson (general secretary)
1892–95	Clement Keys (financial secretary)
1894–95	Edward Stephenson (general secretary)

John Westmancoat

1895–96	Clement Keys
1896–1902	W. Frank Heaven
1902–48	Fred Everiss
1948–60	Ephriam 'Eph' Smith
1960–80	Alan Everiss
1980–84	Anthony E. Rance
1984–85	Gordon H. Dimbleby
1985–86	John Westmancoat
1986–89	Gordon Bennett
1989 to date	Dr John Evans, PA PhD (Wales)

Notepad

■ Albion's first treasurer was Joseph Hughes who was followed by William Bisseker (1882–84) and then James Couse (1884–85).

■ Albion's assistant secretaries have included: 'Eph' Smith (1911–48), Alan Everiss (1948–60), Fred Horne (1960–74) and Ray Fairfax (1974–79).

■ Tom 'Razor' Smith represented Albion at a number of important football meetings in London during the 1880s, and he had a big say in the introduction of professionalism. He travelled 4,000 miles in 1886–87 on Albion business. A George Salter's employee, he was also a player for the club in the early days.

■ W. Pierce Dix was a leading figure in Sheffield footballing circles between 1875 and 1888 and a referee of note, who, in 1883, when a vice-president of the Football Association, umpired the Staffordshire Cup final (with Lionel King) between Albion and Stoke.

■ Albion's first full-time, paid general secretary (with a salary of £50 a year) was Louis Ford (appointed in 1890). Ford was responsible for bringing many fine players to the club, including Willie Groves, Roddy McLeod and John Reynolds. An Albion committee member and then director (1892–96), he was an FA Councillor (1890–93), member of the Football League management committee and vice-president of the League from 1894 to 1897. In 1900 he became a League referee. He was also secretary of Walsall (1896–1900) and Leicester Fosse (1914).

■ 'Swin' Jackson was a Staffordshire and West Bromwich Dartmouth cricketer who was later secretary of Leicester Fosse and Luton Town before emigrating to Canada, where he became a parish registrar and postmaster until his death in 1930.

W. Frank Heaven was also a Dartmouth cricketer who gave the Albion six years' unstinting service, before he resigned over a disagreement with the directors in 1902. He was just 23 when he was appointed secretary in 1896. He spent the 1904–05 season with Third Lanark, but on returning south he died tragically on Boxing Day in 1905, when still only 32 years of age.

Clement Keys (1895–96) was the first Albion secretary placed in sole charge of the club's administration.

Between 1902 and 1980 the position of Albion secretary was held by three members of the same family – Fred Everiss, 'Eph' Smith (Fred's brother-in-law) and Alan Everiss (Fred's son).

Tony Rance was commercial manager and secretary of Bristol City before joining Albion and later he became assistant secretary and general manager of Wrexham.

Gordon Dimbley served (as secretary-commercial manager etc.) with Northampton Town, Hull City, Wolverhampton Wanderers and Chelsea.

John Westmancoat held the secretary's job at Walsall, Birmingham City and Port Vale. He died in January 1992.

Gordon Bennett was employed by Bristol Rovers as secretary and later managing director before moving to Albion. He left to become Youth Development Officer at Norwich City, later assuming the title Chief Executive at Carrow Road.

Dr John Evans, a former Schoolteacher, was secretary of Nuneaton Borough prior to his appointment at Albion. He was also part-time secretary of Northampton Town (1986–89). He was appointed as an Albion director in July 2002, thus becoming the first ever secretary-director of the club.

EVERISS, ALAN, JP

Born in West Bromwich in 1918, Alan Everiss was introduced to office work at The Hawthorns by his father Fred in August 1933, earning £1-a-week as a 14-year-old junior. Like his father, he made rapid progress and duly carried on the family name and tradition of long service magnificently. After serving his apprenticeship in the 'office', he was

made assistant secretary in 1948 to Ephraim Smith (who was his brother-in-law incidentally), and, when Smith retired in May 1960, Alan was upgraded to secretary, a position he held for 20 years, until 1980, when Tony Rance took over. He compiled most of the text for the Albion programme throughout the 1960s and was a great help to me when I first started my research in readiness for the publication of my first *A-Z of Albion* and then the *Complete Record*. Following in the footsteps of his father, Alan also became a Justice of the Peace in West Bromwich (1968) and was chairman of the Football League Secretaries', Managers' and Coaches' Association. After retiring he served as a director of the club (1981–86), also becoming a Life Member of West Bromwich Albion in August 1980. He died in 1999, aged 81.

EVERISS, Frederick, JP

Fred Everiss, born in Spon Lane, West Bromwich, in May 1882, joined the Albion staff as an office boy in September 1896. He was put in charge of compiling the team-sheets as well as doing general duties. He acquitted himself so well that the directors had no hesitation in appointing him secretary at the age of 20 in 1902, a tremendous responsibility for one so young, which he shouldered magnificently. He became a much-admired and loved figure in the game, and, with the assistance of Billy Bassett and Harry Keys in particular, he brought great respectability to the Albion club. In 1926 an unusual tribute was paid to Fred Everiss by past and present Albion players, who presented him with an illuminated address as a tangible token of the high regard in which he was held. From 1927 he was secretary of the Football League Secretaries' and Managers' Association and later he became its chairman. During World War Two he had to combine the jobs at The Hawthorns of secretary-manager, typist, telephonist, office-clerk, part-time groundsman and ARP night watchman! In October 1946 he was presented with a silver casket and a second illuminated address, this time on the occasion of his completing 50 years' service with Albion. For the last three years of his life, Fred Everiss JP was on the Board of Directors and when he passed away in 1951 he had

served the club for over 54 years. He was undoubtedly one of the greatest names in the history of West Bromwich Albion Football Club.

Chairmen

Albion first appointed a chairman in 1885 – six years before the club became a Limited Company. The full list of chairmen who have been in office is:

1885–88	Henry Jackson
1888–90	Edward W. Heelis
1891	Henry Jackson
1891–95	George Salter
1895–99	T. Harris Spencer
1899–1903	Harry Keys
1903–05	A.E.J.M. 'Jem' Bayliss
1905–08	Harry Keys
1908–37	William I Bassett
1937–47	L.J. 'Lou' Nurse
1947–63	Major H. Wilson Keys
1963–74	'Jim' W. Gaunt
1974–83	F.A. 'Bert' Millichip
1983–88	J. 'Sid' Lucas
1988–92	John G Silk
1992–94	Trevor J. Summers
	'Tony' B. Hale
1997–2002	Paul Thompson
2002 to date	Jeremy Peace

In The Chair

Harry Keys was a blunt, outspoken man, who called a spade a spade and sometimes a sanguinary shovel. He was nicknamed 'John Bull' by the players and resigned as Chairman after a disagreement with his fellow directors in 1903. He returned as Chairman two years later and was immediately elected on to the Football League Management Committee, becoming its vice-President in 1910, a position he held until his death in 1929. He was also an FA Councillor and member of the International Selection Committee. Two of his brothers were also closely associated with Albion, W Hall Keys as a director and Clement Keys as secretary and auditor. Major H. Wilson Keys, son of Harry, joined the Albion board shortly after his father's death.

George Salter, educated at Malvern College, was a goalkeeper with West Bromwich FC (1881–82) and a West Bromwich Dartmouth cricketer, who was forced to retire from soccer through injury. An avid Albion supporter, he was, like so many Albion directors, a prominent Freemason, and in 1891–92 and again in 1895–97 he was sworn in as Lord Mayor of West Bromwich. He was also Albion's first president in 1882.

■ 'Jem' Bayliss was the first ex-Albion player to join the board of directors. Bayliss was, in fact, the first former player to become chairman of the Club, having earlier served on the selection committee (from 1886). He resigned as chairman in 1905 when financial troubles within the club were coming to a head.

■ Louis Nurse was the brother of Dan Nurse, who played in Albion's 1901–02 Second Division championship-winning side. Lou had been an Albion scout for many years before his election to the board in 1922. He became an FA Councillor in 1941.

■ H. Wilson Keys spent 10 years as Albion's vice-chairman before taking over as chairman in 1947. A very influential

figure at The Hawthorns, like his father before him, he was also a leading light in FA circles, eventually becoming FA vice-president in 1969. No one has yet served on the Albion board of directors longer than the Major, his term being 35 years between 1930–65.

■ Jim Gaunt, 11 years Albion's chairman, was elected president of the club on his retirement in 1974. He died in April 1989.

■ Sir 'Bert' Millichip was a partner in Sharp and Millichip, High Street, West Bromwich, for many years solicitors to the Albion club. He became a director at The Hawthorns in 1964, replacing W.H. Thursfield, and in 1969 he was elected to the FA Council. A year later he was made Albion's vice-chairman, moving up to chairman in 1974. He resigned in 1983 because of the pressure from his FA commitments. When he left the Albion

board in 1984 he was elected club president and in 1991 was knighted for his services to football. Sir 'Bert' retired as chairman of the FA in the summer of 1996, shortly before his 82nd birthday.

■ Sid Lucas became an Albion director in 1975, moving into the vacancy caused by the untimely death of former player Tommy Glidden. A local businessman, and one-time terrace supporter on the Birmingham Road End, he was chairman for five years (from 1983) and then stayed on as a director for another three years, before being elected vice-president. He died in July 1991.

■ John Silk was elected a director in August 1984. A local solicitor, also with business interests in West Bromwich and Brierley Hill, John Silk was born in West Bromwich. He has been an Albion shareholder since 1948.

■ Trevor Summers was born and educated in West Bromwich. A former Chairman of West Bromwich Dartmouth CC, he had interests in the timber business. Elected a director in August 1984, he became chairman in 1992.

■ Tony Hale was elected to the board in August 1988 to fulfil a lifetime ambition. A Birmingham man, born in Moseley, he built up a business involving car component spares and became Albion chairman in 1994. Thereafter, he was a major shareholder who was closely involved in the re-structuring of the club's shares in the mid 1990s. He left the club in 1999 to be replaced by Paul Thompson.

■ Paul Thompson was in office as Albion chairman from 24 December 1999 until early July 2002, when he resigned.

The company's second largest shareholder with 23.2 percent of the club shares, he qualified as a Chartered Accountant with Coopers and Lybrand in 1976. One of the founders of Sanderson Group Plc (on 5 February 1983), he later held the position as chairman of that company for 12 years until 14 January 2000. He was elected as a director of the Football League in March 2002.

■ Jeremy Peace became a paid and full-time Albion director on 8 December 2000, and just 18 months later he was

appointed chairman. He has a background in stockbroking and corporate finance and is a director of Thomas Potts Plc, London Town Plc, e-prime-financial Plc and Galahad Capital Plc.

Directors

West Bromwich Albion Football Club became a Limited Liability Company in June 1891. The first board of directors (under chairman George Salter) took office in September 1891. Prior to this the club itself was run by a committee, and it is interesting to know that from 1878 to 1986 there was an ex-Albion player on the club's committee/board of directors. This sequence (unique in football) was broken when Cliff Edwards left the Board in 1986.

Albion directors elected between 1891 and 1910:
William Bache (1891–92), James 'Jem' Bayliss (1891–1905), James Couse (1891–92 & 1895–96), Edward W.W.

Heelis (1891–95), Henry S. Jackson (1891–93), James Lavender (1891–92), John Phillips (1891–93), Dr Robert Rees (1891–95), George Salter (1891–95), Louis Ford (1892–96), Harry Roberts (1892–97), Enoch Wood (1892–95), Dr Isaac Pitt (1893–1904), J.A. Fellows (1896–99), T. Harris Spencer (1895–1902 & 1905–07), W. Hall Keys (1896–97). Harry Keys (1896–1903, 1905–08 & 1919–29), Charles Perry (1896–1902), Harry Powell (1896–1904), Thomas Brennand (1897–1900), Joseph Lones (1900), George W. East (1901–05), George Mason (1902–05), Joseph S. Round (1903–05 & 1927–40), Thomas Hedges (1904–05), Richard Mason (1904–05), J W.B. Stephens (1904–05). William I. Bassett (1905–37), Charles Couse (1905–10), James V. Webster (1907–08), Major (later Lt Col) Harold Ely (1909–27), Daniel Nurse (1910–27), Albert Seymour (1910–22).

Albion directors elected after World War One:
Louis J. Nurse (1922–48), Walter W. Hackett (1927–37), Major H. Wilson Keys (1930–65), James Everiss (1930–32), A. Claude Jephcott (1934–50), W. Horace Thursfield (1937–64), Norman W. Bassett (1937–52), W. Ellery Jephcott (1941–53), Frederick Everiss, JP (1948–51), Thomas W. Glidden (1951–74), James W. Gaunt (1951–76), Samuel R. Shepherd (1952–63), Leonard Pritchards (1953–71), Clive H. James (1963–70), Sir Frederick A. 'Bert' (1964–79), Thomas H. Silk (1965–80), E. John Gordon (1970–79), Clifford I. Edwards (1971–86), J. Sidney Lucas (1975–91), D. Brian Boundy (1976–88), Alan E. Everiss, JP (1981–86), John G. Silk (1984–92), Trevor J. Summers (1984–96), Joseph W. Brandrick (1986 to date), Michael McGinnity (1986–92), Anthony B. Hale (1988–96), Clive M. Stapleton (1991–99/1999–2002), Terry K. Guy (1992–96), Barry Hurst (1992–99/1999–2002), Paul Thompson BSc FCA (1996–2000), Robert E. McGing (1997–2000), John D. Wile (1997–2002), P. Owen (1999), D. Colston (1999), J. Driscoll, MBE (1999). J. Peace (2000 to date). Brendon M. Batson, MBE (2002–03). Michael O'Leary (2002–04, as chief executive), Dr John Evans, BA PhD (2002), Jeff Farmer (2004 to date), Mark Jenkins (financial, 2004 to date)

■ John Wile was Albion's first ever chief executive/director, appointed in March 1997.

Other Players
Most of these appeared for Albion at first-team level, other than in League, major European and domestic cup, Charity Shield and competitive Wartime fixtures. The date and opposition, if known, after the player's name, indicates when he made his first-team debut for Albion.

ADAMS, Ross I. July 1999. 'Sub' against Halesowen, Albion apprentice, professional, 2001.

ALLEN, Albert December 1891. Outside-right against Wednesbury Old Athletic.

ALLEN, Russell December 1972. Inside-forward against Walsall. He was born in Smethwick in January 1954 and is the son of Ronnie Allen. He left The Hawthorns in 1973 for Tranmere Rovers and later Mansfield Town. He scored 62 goals in 272 League games for the latter two clubs, having failed to make it with Albion, for whom he scored 15 goals in 45 second XI matches.

ANDERSON, John November 1978. Left-half against Stafford Rangers. Born near Dublin, 7 November 1959, he played for Stella Maris then Albion from 1976–79 (92 Central League appearances), Preston North End, Newcastle United, for whom he made 299 League appearances, was honoured by the Republic of Ireland at schoolboy, youth and under-21 levels, and he won 16 full caps before retiring in 1992.

ARMSTRONG, Jack December 1879. Outside-left against Bullocks Club.

ASHTON, Sir Hubert, MP A versatile player, who could occupy the leftback, centre-half and centre-forward positions, he was born in Calcutta, India, on 13 February 1898 and died in Essex in May 1979. Amateur with the Corinthians, Bristol Rovers, Clapton Orient, Albion (1919–20), Corinthians, he scored 20 goals in 16 games for the famous Corinthians and retired to live in Brentwood, Essex.

ASHTON, Mark January 1989. Goalkeeper against SC Caen, later conceded six goals playing against Real

Madrid. Born in West Bromwich in October 1971, he first joined Albion as a 13-year-old, then professionally in 1988–90. Later with Willenhall Town, Dudley Town, Halesowen Town, Halesowen Harriers and Moor Green, he returned to The Hawthorns as youth-team coach, then the club's 'Football in the Community' Manager. He became commercial executive of Watford in August 2004.

ATKISS, Jeffrey May 1941. Outside-left against RAF West Bromwich. He was ex-George Salter FC and signed professional forms in May 1940.

BAGNALL, Albert September 1896. Right-half against Walsall. He was ex-Wordsley FC and later with Singer's FC, Redditch and Gravesend United.

BAKER, Albert C. September 1892. Inside-left against Wrexham. Born in Dudley in 1870, he moved to Brierley Hill Alliance in 1893.

BANNER, Albert E. November 1896. Inside-left against Great Marlow. He later played for Burton Swifts.

BARLOW, Robert January 1883. Left-half against Wellington. He was born in Halesowen in March 1863.

BARNES, John C.R. MBE May 1999. Midfield against Jamaica, Tony Brown's testimonial. Born in Jamaica in November 1963, he was an England international (79 caps full and three under-21 caps), played for Sudbury Court, Watford (1981–87), Liverpool to 1997, Newcastle United and Charlton Athletic, retiring in 1999 with 739 club appearances to his credit and 198 goals. Later he was assistant manager/head coach with Celtic and won FA Youth Cup, FA Cup, League Cup, First Division championship and FA Charity Shield medals.

BASSETT, Harry April 1893. Outside-right and brother of Billy Bassett whom he partnered against Birmingham & District, also played on the right-wing the following season (2 games).

BAVERSTOCK, Herbert September 1903 Right-back against Burton United. He signed in May 1903 from Dudley, previously with Netherton and Dudley St James, and later played for Brierley Hill Alliance, Bolton Wanderers (1905–21), making 388 League and cup appearances, and Blackpool.

BEDWORTH, Thomas 1880s. Played as an inside-forward (1880–82). He was born in Nuneaton in 1859.

BELL, William April 1900. Centre-half against Small Heath. He was signed from Burton Swifts in May 1899 and left Albion in May 1901.

BENNETT, George April 1882. Centre-half against Walsall Alma Athletic, he also played for West Bromwich FC.

BENNION, Alan September 1894. Full-back against Wolves, ex-Newport County, later Newport again and Leicester Fosse (1899), he was born in Newport in 1873. He was with Albion in 1894–96.

BIDDULPH, F. Robert 1882–84. A Utility forward, he played several games. Born in West Bromwich in 1860, he was an ex-George Salter Works employee who retired in December 1883, on doctor's orders .

BLAKE, Mosiah May 1999. 'Sub' against Rotherham United and apprentice with Albion until 2002.

BLOSS, Philip August 1973. 'Sub' against Rhyl. Born in Dovercourt in January 1953, he was ex-Colchester United, an Albion trialist and later with Wimbledon.

BODELL, Anthony August 1989. 'Sub' midfield trialist against Newcastle Town. He was son of then chief scout Norman Bodell and later sustained a serious injury playing for Albion reserves against Wolves, which ended his career.

BORE, Edward November 1916. Outside-right against Wolves.

BOWMAN, Darren M. October 1997. 'Sub' midfielder against Kidderminster Harriers at Albion for three seasons as a youth and reserve-team player. He made over 30 appearances for the second XI, later with Ramsbottom United, Rossendale United, Grantham Town, Radcliffe Borough, Leigh RMI and Stalybridge Celtic (July 2002).

BRADBURY, Arthur G. December 1882, against Notts Rangers, played in 12 first-team games for Albion up to 1888. Born in West Bromwich in 1860 and ex-Christ Church School, he was later with Birmingham Excelsior, Crosswells Brewery and Oldbury Town.

BRADBURY, William April 1899. Outside-right against Walsall. He signed in August 1898 and was later with Stourbridge.

BRADFORD, David December 1976.

Outside-right against Kettering Town. Born in Manchester in February 1953, he played for Blackburn Rovers, Sheffield United, Peterborough on loan, Albion from December 1976 to June 1978 (scored 5 goals in 40 second XI games), Detroit Express, Washington Diplomats, Coventry City, Tulsa Roughnecks, Seattle Sounders, Barrow and Rossendale United in a 15-year career.

BRADLEY, William February 1883. Outside-right against Birmingham Heath. He was an ex-Wednesbury Old Athletic and Burton Swifts player and moved to Crosswells Brewery in 1886. Born in Wednesbury in 1860, he was the brother of Fred Bradley and died in July 1902.

BRIGGS, Mark J. July 2002. Striker against Halesowen, regular youth and reserve-team player for three seasons. He made over 20 second XI appearances. Born in Wolverhampton in February 1982, he was later associated with Herfolge BK (Denmark), Bilston United and Notts County.

BRODIE, Jack Brant July 1886. Inside-left against Aston Villa. He was an England international (3 caps) and also played for Wolves (1877–92), who died on 16 February 1925.

BROWN, Arthur April 1899. Centre-forward against Small Heath. He signed from Tamworth in September 1898.

BROWN, Edward G. August 1919. Outside-left against Aston Villa, signed from Stourbridge in 1914, later played for Merthyr Town.

BROWN, Simon May 2003. 'Sub' midfielder against Bryan Robson's XI – Bob Taylor testimonial, youth and reserve-team player at The Hawthorns, 2000–04. Born in West Bromwich on 18 September 1983, he went on loan to Kidderminster Harriers, March–May 2004 and August–December 2004, and he joined Mansfield Town for £50,000 a week after returning from his second spell at Aggborough. He scored eight goals in 17 reserve-team games for Albion.

BUCKLEY, Simon J. July 1996. 'Sub' inside-forward against Kidderminster Harriers. Born in Stafford in February 1976, he is the son of Albion manager Alan Buckley and brother to Adam. He was an apprentice with Grimsby Town (1994–95) and Albion (1995–97) (2 goals in 37 reserve games) and was also

associated with Rugby Town (1997–98) and Lincoln City.

BULLOCH, William August 1973. 'Sub' against Colchester United, centre-forward. Born in Motherwell in February 1955, he joined Albion from Garrison Academy in 1971, turned 'pro' in 1973 and left in 1975 and later played in South Africa for Durban City.

BUNN, Abraham February 1883. Inside-forward against Birmingham Heath. He died on 22 December 1903 and is a member of the famous Bunn family.

BURKE, Stephen J. August 1986. Midfield against Bristol City. He was an England youth international trialist, born in Nottingham on 29 September 1960, previously with Nottingham Forest, Queen's Park Rangers, Millwall, Notts County, Lincoln City and Brentford, later with Doncaster Rovers, Stockport County, Shepshed Charterhouse and Grantham Town.

BURTON, Henry December 1891. Left-back against Wednesbury Old Athletic, formerly of Brierley Hill Alliance.

BUTLER, Eric A. April 1899. Right-half against Walsall. He was signed in February 1899 and born in West Bromwich.

BUTLER, Jack October 1890. Centre-forward against Wolves. He was a Welsh international centre-forward (3 caps won) who also played for Bolton Wanderers as a trialist, Chirk and Wrexham. He died in October 1956.

BUTLER, Kenneth August 1942 Outside-left against Northampton Town. He was recruited from Birmingham University.

CAMPBELL, Gary February 1989. Inside-left against Torquay United. Born in Belfast in April 1966 he was an Arsenal junior, then with Leyton Wingate, Albion on loan January– February and November– December 1989 and Leyton Orient.

CARLISLE, David February 1982. 'Sub' goalkeeper against Dudley Town. Born in Abbot's Langley in November 1963, he was a trialist with Watford as a centre-half, played for Garston FC, Watford Boys XI and Hertfordshire Youths, Albion from 1977–83 and also a loan spell with Birmingham City.

CARPENTER, Arthur December 1888. Defender against Cambridge University.

He was later with Oldbury Town and Brierley Hill Alliance.

CHAPMAN, Campbell March 1989. 'Sub' against Irthlingborough Diamonds. The son of Wolves manager Sammy and brother of Cavan Campbell, he was born in Mansfield in June 1963 and was previously with Peterborough United, Stamford Town, Derby County, Crewe Alexandra, Bilston Town, Wolves (1984–86), Preston North End trialist, Birkirara (Malta), after Albion played for Keps (Finland), Willenhall Town player-manager 1992–93 and Chasetown.

CHARLTON, Sir Robert October 1975. Guest inside-forward against Leeds United in Giles' testimonial match. Born at Ashington in October 1937, he was brother to Jack. He scored 217 goals in 606 games for Manchester United, whom he served from 1953 to 1974, winning League, FA Cup and European Cup winners' medals as well as gaining a then record 106 England caps, netting 49 goals, he later managed Preston North End, was a director at Wigan Athletic and is now on the board at Old Trafford.

CHURCHLEY, Walter October 1891. Half-back against Wolves, ex-Causeway Green FC, later with Coles Farm Unity.

CIARDI, Marco Midfield against Wigan Athletic. He was Italian-born trialist.

CLANSEY, Sidney November 1892. Right-half against Walsall Town Swifts, signed from Brierley Hill.

CLARKE, Brian May 1977, centre-half against Swansea City, reserve defender. An FA Youth Cup winner in 1976 and ex-Phoenix Comprehensive School, Telford, he played for Albion until 1978 and later assisted Exeter City, Telford, Newtown and Shifnal Town.

CLARKE, Stuart August 1995. 'Sub' midfielder against Birmingham City. Born in Leamington Spa in March 1977, he was released in June 1996 and was later a Worcester City trialist.

CLEVERLEY, Jay May 1995. 'Sub' against Cheltenham Town. Born in Bristol in February 1978, he joined Bath City in 1996 and was later with Cheltenham Town.

COLCOMBE, Scott March 1990. 'Sub' winger against Elmore. Born in West Bromwich in December 1971, he was with Albion in 1989–91, Pontins League championship in 1990–91, and later with Torquay United, Doncaster Rovers and Willenhall Town.

COLLINS, Matthew May 2001. 'Sub' against Newcastle United in Daryl Burgess's testimonial. Born in Hitchin in February 1982, he was an Albion reserve-team player in 2000–03 and joined Nuneaton Borough in 2003–05.

COLLINS, Thomas April 1903. Goalkeeper against Small Heath, he signed in March 1903 and left in 1904.

COOPER, Anthony November 1978. 'Sub' against Stafford Rangers, reserve right-back. Born in Crewe in January 1958, he was with Albion for five years to 1979.

CRANE, Daniel May 2003. 'Sub' goalkeeper against Bryan Robson's XI, Bob Taylor's testimonial. He played in Albion's second XI in 2002–03, joined Burton Albion in 2004, and wears size 13 boots!

CRAVEN, Dean October 1997. 'Sub' against Kidderminster Harriers, he spent three years at The Hawthorns playing youth and reserve-team football, making over 20 appearances for the second XI, and was later with Stafford Rangers, Hereford United and AFC Telford (under ex-Albion midfielder Bernard McNally).

CREANEY, Gerard T. July 1998. Striker against Hereford United. Born in Coatbridge in April 1970, he played for Celtic, Portsmouth, Manchester City, Oldham Athletic, Ipswich Town, Burnley and Chesterfield before assisting Albion and scored more than 100 goals in 265 competitive games, was later trialist with Tampere IF (Finland) and was capped by Scotland 11 times at under-21 level and once for the 'B' team.

CROW, Kevin July 1985. 'Sub' centre-half against Rotherham United. USA international (7 caps) trialist at The Hawthorns, he also played for San Diego Sockers and the American 1988 Olympic soccer team. He was born in the US in September 1961.

CUTLER, Neil August 1993. Goalkeeper against West Ham United. He played for Albion's second team in 1994 and 1995 (11 games) and also assisted Cheltenham Town, Coventry City, Tamworth and Chester City, all on loan, Crewe Alexandra in 1996, Leek Town (two spells on loan, 1997), Chester twice more,

Aston Villa in 1999, Oxford United, Stoke City in 2001, Swansea City in 2003 and Stockport County in 2004. He was an FA School of Excellence graduate, capped by England at schoolboy, under-16 and under-17 levels, born in Birmingham in September 1976.

DADFORD, Thomas November 1891. Right-half against Aston Villa.

DANKS, Philip March 1980. 'Sub' against Barnet, reserve defender. He was born in Kidderminster in June 1961, played for Albion from 1977 to 1982 and was later with Shrewsbury Town, Manchester United as a trialist, Kidderminster Rovers and Bromsgrove Rovers.

DAVIES, Joseph September 1889. Half-back against Warwick County. He was a Welsh international (7 caps), ex-Newton Heath, and later Wolves and Druids and died on 7 October 1943.

DAVIES, Robert cost £50,000 when signed from Wrexham as a 16-year-old in August 2003. Albion will pay more if and when he plays for Wales.

De CLER, Tim July 2002. 'Sub' defender against Stoke City. A Dutchman, trialist from Ajax, he was later associated with FC Alkmaar (Holland).

DEXTER, Arthur April 1893. Left-back against Small Heath. He was a trialist from Oldbury Town.

DIABETE, Lassina July 2003. Midfielder against B1909 (Denmark). He was a trialist with Albion for one month.

DICKETTS, Arthur March 1892. Left-half against Wrexham. He was a Welshman from Ruabon.

DOUGAN, A. Derek October 1975. Striker against Leeds United in Johnny Giles's testimonial. 'Doog' was an Irish international (43 full caps gained), and he played for Distillery, Portsmouth, Blackburn Rovers, Peterborough United, Aston Villa, Leicester City and Wolverhampton Wanderers in a nomadic career that spanned 20 years. He scored 123 goals in 323 League games and also represented his country at schoolboy, youth, amateur and 'B' team levels, he later returned to Molineux as Chief Executive in the early 1980s and was also the PFA chairman.

DOWLER, Frederick March 1884. Right-half against Wednesbury Old Athletic, he was later an Albion steward

DWIGHT, Arthur November 1899. Left-half against Kaffirs. He was an ex-Burton Swifts amateur, born in Derby in 1878.

ELD, Arthur Edwin 1881–83. Goalkeeper, then Albion's joint secretary in 1882 and honorary secretary in 1883–84.

ELFORD, George December 1917. Outside-right against Aston Villa.

ELLEMAN, Arthur November 1890. Outside/inside-right against Warwick County. A Belfast-born Irish international (2 caps), he also served with Cliftonville, Notts County and Grimsby Town, briefly.

EVANS, Ernest November 1878. Inside-forward against Hudsons.

EVANS, Harold November 1878. Half-back against Hudsons.

EVANS, Sidney November 1878. Inside-forward against Hudsons.

EVES, Melvyn James December 1988. Inside-forward against Newquay Town. Born in Wednesbury on 10 September 1956, he scored 53 goals in 214 games for Wolves (1973–84) and also played for Huddersfield Town, Manchester City (non-contract), Sheffield United, Gillingham, Mansfield Town, Telford United, Old Wulfunians and also had four Central League games for Albion. He is now a footballer's agent and was capped by England 'B' while at Molineux.

FARMER, John July 1972. Goalkeeper against Kalmar FF. Born in Biddulph in Staffs on 31 August 1947, he was on loan to Albion in July–August 1972 from Stoke City and also played for Leicester City on loan and Northwich Victoria, made 185 appearances for the Potters and was an England under-23 international and later manager of a crisp factory in Cheadle.

FARRINGTON, Geoffrey September 1904. Centre-forward against Wolves. Brother of Samuel, he was signed from North Staffordshire FC, left Albion in 1904 and later played for Preston North End.

FERGUSON, Glen A. December 1983. 'Sub' outside-right against BSR (Stourbridge). Born in Carlisle on 17 February 1966, he played for Albion in 1982–84.

FITZPATRICK, James November 1900. Outside-right against Past WBA XI. He was ex-George Salter FC, signed in August 1900. He was born in West Bromwich.

FLETCHER, Jack December 1892. Outside-left against Aston Villa. He was a trialist from Army football.

FORRESTER, James November 1878. Right-half against Hudsons FC.

FOULKE, Wilfred March 1896. Goalkeeper against Liverpool. He signed from Wellington and was brother of Billy 'Fatty' Foulke, former Sheffield United, Chelsea and England 'keeper.

FRAIN, Peter March 1983. 'Sub' against Wigan Athletic. He played for the England youth international team as inside-forward, Albion (1981–84) – Central League Championship in 1982–83, Mansfield Town on loan and was later with Oldbury Town, Solihull Borough and player-manager at Knowle and manager of Alevechurch. He was Born in Birmingham on 18 March 1965.

FREW, Angus October 1895. Outside-right against Dundee. He was an amateur from Steventon Thistle.

GARBUTT, Thomas March 1891. Goalkeeper against Sheffield Wednesday. He also played for Oldbury Town, Birmingham St George's and Worcester Rovers. He was born in Bromsgrove.

GARDNER, Nathan May 1995. 'Sub' full-back trialist against Cheltenham Town. He was ex-Walsall and later played for Telford United.

GARRITY, Michael July 1999. 'Sub' against Halesowen. He played in over 30 second-team games for the club before suffering a broken leg.

GERMAINE, Gary May 1994. 'Sub' goalkeeper against Aston Villa. Born in Birmingham in August 1976, he played for Albion in 1994–97 (30 second XI games) and also played for Telford United, Scunthorpe United (on loan), Shrewsbury Town (on loan) and Tennasse Rhythm (US).

GILES, Michael August 1984. Right-back against Walsall. He was son of the manager, Johnny, born in 1965, and was previously with University College Dublin, Shamrock Rovers and later with Bradford City (briefly), Oldbury United and Worcester Rovers.

GLASS, Stuart May 1990. Left-back trialist against Cheshunt.

GODLEY, Sidney May 1925. Goalkeeper 'sub' against Aston Villa. He played for both teams in the match and conceded

nine goals in total.

GORAM, Andrew L. April 1981. Goalkeeper against Aldershot. Born in Bury on 13 April 1964, he signed for Albion in 1980, was released to Oldham Athletic in 1981, was later with Hibernian, Glasgow Rangers, Notts County, Sheffield United, Motherwell, Manchester United, Coventry City, Oldham Athletic again and Queen of the South, as well as coaching in Brazil. He made well over 700 appearances at club level, including 219 for the Latics and 260 for Rangers, won 43 caps for Scotland, as well as under-21 honours, and collected 10 domestic League and cup winners' medals during his time at Ibrox Park in 1991–98. He also represented his country at cricket.

GOULD, Jonathan March 1992. 'Sub' goalkeeper against Gibralter Select. He was born in Paddington, London, on 18 July 1968. Son of Bobby Gould, he played in 17 second XI games for Albion, served with Derby County (briefly), Halifax Town, Coventry City, Bradford City, Gillingham (on loan), Celtic (for whom he made 158 senior appearances) and Preston North End. He was sent off playing for the latter club against Albion in 2003.

GREEN, Charles 1881–83. Utility defender. He was born in West Bromwich.

GREEN, Ronald April 1984. 'Sub' goalkeeper against Aston Villa. Born in Birmingham on 3 October 1956, he had a nomadic career with Alvechurch, Walsall (1977–84), Albion briefly, Shrewsbury Town, Bristol Rovers, Scunthorpe United, Wimbledon, Shrewsbury again, Manchester City, Walsall (1989–91), Kidderminster Harriers, Cambridge United, Colchester United, Bromsgrove Rovers, Happy Valley (Hong Kong), Paget Rangers, Hereford United, Redditch United, Moor Green, made 230 League appearances for Walsall and was Commercial Liaison Officer with Coventry City (1997–98).

GREIG, Walter December 1896. Inside-left against Kettering Town.

GRIFFITHS, William December 1943. Right-back against Birmingham City. He was also a Bury guest and was hospitalised in 1945 with injury suffered during wartime action.

GROBBELAAR, Bruce August 1978. Goalkeeper against Motherwell (Joe Wark testimonial). Born in Durban, South Africa, on 6 October 1957, he played for Inyazura Police, Salisbury Callies, Matabeland Highlanders, Hamilton High School, Bulawayo, Chibuku Shumba (Salisbury), Salisbury Callies again, Durban City, Amazulu (guest), Albion (three months as a trialist, July–September 1978, making one Central League appearance), Bournemouth (trialist), Vancouver Whitecaps, Crewe Alexandra, Liverpool (1981–94), Stoke City, Southampton and Plymouth Argyle. He made 440 League and 188 cup appearances during his time at Anfield, winning medals galore, a Rhodesian and Zimbabwean international and he also represented the Football League and later coached Manning Rangers (South Africa).

HACKETT, Walter W. April 1916. Right-half against Aston Villa. He signed from Cradley Heath St Luke's in 1912, won a Birmingham & District League championship medal in 1913 and later was an Albion director.

HALL, Harold January 1898. Right-back against Small Heath.

HALLOWS, Jack May 1926. Left-half against Fred Morris's XI. He joined Albion from Bluecoat FC in February 1922, moved to Grays Thurrock in 1927 and later scored 76 goals in 163 League games for Bradford City in 1930–36, ending his career with Barnsley.

HAMPTON, James late 1870s/early 1980s. Local-born centre-forward.

HANMER, Gareth Craig July 1996. Left-back against Kidderminster Harriers. Born in Shrewsbury on 12 October 1973, he signed from Newtown, played 21 Central League games for Albion, assisted Shrewsbury Town (1991–92 and 1997–2001) and was later with Telford United.

HANNAH, Andrew B. September 1888. Right-back against Wolves. A guest from Renton with whom he won two Scottish Cups, he also played for Everton (League champions, 1891), Liverpool (Second Division winners 1894), Rob Roy and was a Scottish international (one cap). Born in Renton in September 1864, he died in June 1940.

HARRIS, William F. October 1904. Centre-forward against Clapton. A Rugby FC amateur, he also played for Warwickshire CCC.

HARTLAND, Henry April 1919. Inside-right against RAF XI. He signed in January 1919.

HATFIELD, Sidney November 1916. Centre-half against Wolves.

HAYNES, Harry G. 1888–89. Reserve outside-left. He was born in Smethwick.

HAYTER, Robert August 1995. 'Sub' defender against Real Oviedo, YTS. He was released in June 1996 after scoring seven goals in 25 second-team games for Albion.

HAZELWOOD, Frederick late 1870s/early 1980s. Outside-left. He was born in West Bromwich.

HEASELGRAVE, Sidney September 1895. Inside-left against Aston Villa.

HEATH, Lloyd May 1889. Inside-right against Hyde.

HEMMINGS, George October 1884. Left-half against Aston Villa.

HEMMINGS, A. Franklin September 1907. Left-back against Barnsley. He was ex-Langley St Michael's, signed in October 1905, and was later with Shrewsbury Town and Brierley Hill. He was born in Oldbury.

HIPKISS, R. Kenneth May 2003. 'Sub' against Bryan Robson's XI at Bob Taylor's testimonial, Albion's official club chaplain.

HODGETTS, Dennis May 1886. Inside-left against Preston North End and England international (6 caps). He was born in Birmingham on 28 November 1863 and died on 25 March 1945. He also played for Aston Villa, Mitchell St George's and Great Lever and was twice an FA Cup winner.

HODGETTS, Harold July 1886. Outside-left against Aston Villa. He was a guest from Villa.

HODGSON, Vernon February 1979. 'Sub' against Portsmouth as a full-back. Ex-Birmingham City, he played for Albion for two years (1978–80) and was later with Oldbury United. He was born in West Bromwich on 11 February 1960.

HOLT, John May 1887. Half-back against Wednesbury Old Athletic and played until 1889.

HOYLE, Colin May 1990. Trialist midfielder against Walsall. Born in Wirksworth near Derby on 15 January 1972, he was released by Arsenal and also

played for Chesterfield (on loan), Barnsley (1991–92), Bradford City (1992–94), Notts County (1994–96), Mansfield Town on loan (1994) and later with Burton Albion and Worcester City.

HUDSON, John W. May 1926. Left-back against Fred Morris's XI. He was signed from Bromsgrove Rovers in March 1926 and Born in Worcester.

HUGHES, Arthur H. September 1907. Inside-left against Barnsley. He was a Welsh international at amateur and senior levels, also played for Chirk, Wrexham Whitchurch and Llangollen, where he was born in July 1884 and died in August 1970.

HUGHES, Barry September 1958. Centre-half against Port Vale. Born in Carmarthen on 31 December 1957, he played for Rhyl, Flintshire and Wales Schools XIs, signed amateur forms for Albion in June 1953, turned 'pro' in December 1954 and was later with Dutch clubs Blaauwit (1960–63), Alkmaar (1963–65), Harlingen as coach, FC Haarlem (1970), manager (1972–80), then commercial manager (1989–90), Go Ahead Deventer manager (1970–71), Sparta Rotterdam coach (1980 and 1986–88), FC Utrecht coach (1983), MVV Maastricht coach (1984), Volendam coach (1985) and later Belgian club Beerschot as coach (1988).

HUGHES, Joseph 1880–81. Reserve centre-half. He was Albion's first official treasurer, appointed in 1880, then financial secretary (1883–84).

HUNT, Herbert Outside-right or left, reserve at The Hawthorns. Born in West Bromwich in July 1916, he signed for Albion in 1933 and left in 1935 for Walsall. He made six League appearances for the Saddlers, later assisted Darlaston, is listed as being one of Albion's oldest former players and is now living in Tipton.

IEZZI, Massamiliano July 1999. Forward against Halesowen. Born in Rome in February 1981, he was with Albion from 1999–2002 (scoring 8 goals in almost 40 second XI games) and later with Benventa (Italy).

INGRAM, Godfrey P. August 1988. 'Sub' inside-forward against Wolverton Town, England schoolboy and youth international, played for Luton Town (1977), New York Cosmos (1979),

Northampton Town (1980), San Jose Earthquakes (1982), Cardiff City (1982–83), Golden Bay Earthquakes (1983–84), Minnesota Strikers (1984). He was born in Luton in October 1969.

JOHNSON, Cory March 1988. 'Sub' against Whitby Town as an inside-forward. He was born in Stoke in November 1969 and played for Wolves as a schoolboy and was later with Willenhall Town, Stafford Rangers, Rhyl Athletic, Leek Town, Burton Albion, Rocester (three spells), Knypersley Victoria, Armitage, Leicester United, Sutton Coldfield Town (two spells) and Redditch United. He made almost 60 appearances for Albion's second XI (1985–89).

JOHNSTONE, Jack December 1879. Half-back against Black Lake Victoria. He was born in West Bromwich.

JOHNSTONE, Frank January 1893. Centre-forward against Notts County.

JONES, Charles May 1942. Inside-right against Walsall.

JONES, Colin M. February 1982. Outside-left against Dudley Town. He was born in Selly Oak, Birmingham, on 30 October 1963, and was ex-Broadmeadow FC, Northfield Thistle and Dunlop Terriers and was later with FK Trelleborg (Sweden) and Mansfield Town.

JONES, Bernard February 1883. Inside-left against Birmingham Heath.

JONES, Graham P. August 1973. 'Sub' against Colchester United. He was born in Sedgley on 18 October 1955 and was an England schoolboy international who joined Albion in 1971 and left in 1974. He later played for Dudley Town, Stourbridge and Kidderminster Harriers.

JONES, Joseph W. September 1903. Outside-right against Burton United. He signed in May 1903 from Wolves.

JONES, Sidney November 1878. Outside-left against Hudsons FC.

JONES, Thomas April 1889. Centre-forward against Birmingham St George's. He was ex-Birmingham Carriage Works.

JONES, Thomas November 1901. Right-back against Reading. He won a Birmingham & District championship medal with Albion in 1902 and later played for Shrewsbury Town, Bristol Rovers, Hull City and Wigan County.

JONES, Walter November 1878. Inside-forward against Hudsons FC.

JOYCE, William December 1917. Inside-right against Aston Villa.

KATALINIC, Ivan August 1979. Goalkeeper against Ajax. He was a trialist from Crvena Zvezda (Red Star Belgrade) and a Yugoslavian international (17 caps). He was born in Belgrade on 17 May 1951 and was also with Hajduk Split, Derby County (trialist), Southampton (1980–83) and Hajduk Split again.

KEBLE, Patrick May 1893. Inside-left against Ulster. He was an Irish-born trialist.

KERSHAW, Albert October 1881. Outside-left against The Grove.

KEYS, Solomon January 1885. Goalkeeper against Walsall Swifts.

KNIGHT, Lee K. July 1996. 'Sub' defender against Kidderminster Harriers. He later served with Solihull Borough, Willenhall Town and Evesham. Born in Birmingham in April 1978, he played in almost 40 second XI games for Albion.

LACEY, Andrew February 1982. Left-back against Dudley Town. Born in Wednesfield in March 1965, he played for Albion (1981–83) and later Rushall Olympic and Bilston Town.

LAVENDER, Tom August 1885. Inside-left against Small Heath Alliance. He played in several 'other' first-team games for Albion and his father was an Albion director (1891–92).

LEAKE, Gary February 1988. 'Sub' goalkeeper against Tottenham Hotspur. Born in Hucknall in January 1970, he later played for Chester, Huddersfield Town (1989–90) and Eastwood Town, and he made almost 40 Central League appearances for Albion.

LINES, William May 1885. Half-back against District XI. He played until May 1886, appearing in 12 'other' first-team matches. He was the brother of Charlie Lines, who also played for Albion in a handful of 'other' games before becoming a Football League and international-class referee.

LITTLEJOHN, Adrian August 1987. 'Sub' in midfield against Mansfield Town. Born in Wolverhampton on 26 September 1970, he played for Albion (1987–89, scoring four goals in 32 second XI games) and later played for Walsall, Sheffield United, Plymouth Argyle (signed for £100,000 in 1995) Oldham Athletic, Bury,

in China and the US, Port Vale, Barnsley (trial) and Lincoln City (from 2004). He also represented England GM National School XI and England's youth team and scored 29 goals in 110 League games for Plymouth, whom he helped win promotion via the Wembley play-off final in 1996.

LOVE, Alistair August 1973. 'Sub' Inside-left against Rhyl. Born in Edinburgh on 9 May 1955, he was ex-Melbourne Thistle, a Glasgow Rangers trialist and signed 'pro' forms for Albion in July 1973. He was later with Southend United, Newport County, Partick Thistle, Ayr United and Falkirk.

LOVERIDGE, John May 1978. 'Sub' against Don Rogers' XI at Swindon. Born in Wolverhampton on 28 February 1959, he was with Albion from 1975–80 and later played for Walsall, Alvechurch and Dudley Town. He scored 12 goals in 164 Central League games for Albion and was an FA Youth Cup winner in 1976 (versus Wolves).

McCABE, William March 1893. Outside-right against Burslem Port Vale, he was an Irish international from Middlesbrough and ex-Ulster.

McCARTNEY, Richard October 1894. Centre-forward against Wolves.

MacGOWAN, John February 1990. 'Sub' midfielder against Ryde Sports. Born in Glasgow, he was ex-Southport Boys and qualified as a physiotherapist at Nottingham University. He was on the Albion staff in July 1989-March 1992.

McLAREN, Stewart August 1973. Left-half against Colchester United. He was born in Larkhall, Scotland, in April 1953, he captained Lanarkshire Boys and Scotland under-15 Grammar Schools. He signed apprentice forms for Albion in July 1969, turned 'pro' in April 1970 and later played for Motherwell (1974–78), Dundee (1978–81) and Heart of Midlothian (1981–84).

MAIN, Brian September 1958. 'Sub' against Port Vale. Born in Pegswood on 5 November 1940, he played for Pegswood Rangers, signed amateur forms in May 1958, turned 'pro' in September 1958 and was released in May 1959.

MAJOR, John September 1889. Full-back against Great Bridge Unity, he was also a Warwickshire cricketer. He died in 1931.

MARSHALL, Frank May 1890. Outside-left against Aston Villa and guest from Birmingham St George's. He was born in Smethwick.

MASON, Charles May 1886. Full-back against Preston North End. He was an England international (3 caps) and also played for Wolves and Albion again in 1888. He died in February 1941.

MASON, Lionel December 1903. Outside-left against Aston Villa. He signed from Dudley in May 1903 and was later with Brierley Hill Alliance.

MEESE, Alfred April 1903. Centre-half against Wolves, he signed in August 1901.

MIOTTO, Simon July 2004. 'Sub' goalkeeper in 2–0 tour win over Fredericia in Denmark. Born in Tasmania on 5 September 1969, he served with Riverside Olympic, Blackpool (1994–98 – no senior appearances), Hartlepool United (5 League games), Raith Rovers (9 outings) and St Johnstone (one game) before joining Albion in 2003. He turned down offers to play in Australia and Sweden in 1998 and was placed on the transfer list by Albion in December 2004. He used to play Aussies Rules football at school and in 1990 made the training squad for the Commonwealth games as a triple jumper, he had moved from Tasmania to Canberra in 1988 to work at The Institute of Sport.

MKANDAWIRE, Tamika July 2002. 'Sub' midfielder against Bromsgrove Rovers. A regular in Albion's youth team before enjoying success in the second team in 2002–03, he went on to appear in over 70 second-team games for Albion, signed on loan for Hereford United in October 2003 and again in March 2004 before joining for the Bulls full-time in June 2004. He turned down the opportunity to play for Malaysia in season 2003–04.

MOORE, William February 1897. Inside-left against Everton (WBCC). West Bromwich-born, he was a regular in Albion's second XI (1897–98).

MORRIS, Elliott July 2000. Goalkeeper against Naestved, Denmark. Born in Belfast in May 1981, his crucial penalty saves won Albion's youngsters the Football League Alliance Cup at Wembley in April 2000. He moved to Glentoran after spending three years at The Hawthorns.

MORTIMER, Denis March 1990. Midfield against Elmore. Born in

Liverpool in April 1952, he had an excellent career with Coventry City, Aston Villa, Sheffield United, Birmingham City, Brighton and Hove Albion, Kettering Town, Redditch United as player-manager, then Albion community officer, later coach, making 590 League appearances, all told. He led Villa to League championship and European Cup glory in 1981 and 1982, was capped by England at youth, 'B' and under-21 levels, was later West Midlands FA regional coach and also manager of Wolves' Ladies team (2002–04).

MORTON, Arthur December 1892. Half-back against Aston Villa. He was a Yorkshire-born trialist from Sheffield.

MUMFORD, William September 1897. Left-back against Walsall. He was later with Brierley Hill Alliance.

MUZINIC, Drazen August 1980. Inside-left against Swindon Town. A Yugoslavian international (36 caps), he was born on 25 January 1953. He was a trialist with Albion from Hajduk Split and later played for Norwich City (1980–82) then opened his own wine bar and restaurant in Brac, Yugoslavia.

NAPPI, Marco July 1998. Forward against Cardiff City, scored twice. He was an experienced Italian trialist with Albion, who, in a fine career, played for Urbe Tevere, Cesena, Ravenna, Vis Pessaro, Arezzo, Genoa, Brescia, Fiorentina, Udinese, Spal, Atalanta and Trenana (2004), all in his home country of Italy.

NEALE, Walter W. October 1885. Inside-forward against Stafford Road. He also played for West Bromwich Victoria.

NOBLE, Daniel January 1898. Right-half against Small Heath. He signed in May 1898.

PAINTER, Jimmy February 1883. Half-back against Birmingham Heath. Ex-West Bromwich FC, later on he was on Albion's training staff.

PANGBOURNE, Oscar September 1895. Centre-forward against Walsall. He signed from Worcester Rovers and was born in Ludlow.

PARRETT, Jack September 1899. Centre-forward against Burton Swifts and ex-Brierley Hill Alliance.

PATTERSON, Darren J. August 1987. Defender against Bristol City. Born in

Belfast on 15 October 1969, he played for Albion (1986–89, made 61 Central League appearances), then Wigan Athletic, Crystal Palace, Luton Town, Preston North End, Dundee United, Oxford United (released by the latter in April 2002) and was also capped by Northern Ireland at youth, 'B', under-21 and senior levels, playing 10 games in the latter category.

PEERS, Ernest September 1895. Right-back against Wolves. Ex-Wednesfield Rovers, he was later with Walsall, Nottingham Forest and Burton United.

PERKINS, Charles November 1891. Centre-half against Wednesbury Old Athletic and a Royal Scots Fusilier player.

PHILLIPS, Gary C. December 1980. Goalkeeper against Barnet. Born in St Albans on 20 September 1961, he played for Hillingdon Borough, Barnet, Albion (1980–81), Barnet again, Brentford, Reading, Barnet (on loan), Hereford United, Barnet (for a fourth time), then manager at Underhill, player-coach at Aylesbury United (July 1995) and later assistant manager of Stevenage Borough.He was capped by England at semi-professional level with Barnet.

PIKE, Martin February 1982. Right-half against Dudley Town. Born in South Shields in October 1964, he played for Albion in 1981–83 (scored once in seven Central League games), then Peterborough United, Sheffield United, Tranmere Rovers, Bolton Wanderers, Fulham (for whom he had 190 League outings) and Rotherham United to 1995. He also assisted Durham City from July 1996, Blyth Spartans and was later scout for Fulham (2002–05).

PITTAWAY, Alex October 1899. Left-back against Aston Villa. He signed in September 1899.

PLAYFAIR, Ronald September 1904. Outside-left against Wolves. He was ex-Newtown, released in January 1905, and was born in Smethwick in 1884.

PRICE, Douglas April 1899. Left-back against Walsall. He signed in April 1898 and was later goalkeeper with Druids FC (Ruabon).

PRILASNIG, Gilbert August 2001. Left-back trialist against Sunderland. Born in Austria, he was a trialist at The Hawthorns, having already played for

Sturn Graz and was later with Aris Salonika, Greece.

PURDY, Richard August 1990. 'Sub' full-back against Shelbourne. He was a trialist from Home Farm, a Republic of Ireland youth international and was later capped at under-21 level.

RASMUSSEN, Kasper July 2000. Right-back against Naestved, Denmark. Austrian-born, he was a trialist at The Hawthorns from Randers FC, Austria.

RAWLINGS, Charles March 1953. Left-half against Wolves. Known as 'Tim', he signed as an amateur from Erdington Albion in May 1949, turned 'pro' in March 1950, made 105 second XI appearances for Albion, later played in 207 senior games for Walsall (1956–63) and also served with Port Vale and Nuneaton Borough. He was Born in Coleshill on 4 November 1932.

READER, Arthur September 1897. Outside-right against Leicester Fosse.

REYNOLDS, Hubert April 1880. Half-back against Hearts of Oak.

REYNOLDS, James June 1883. Inside-forward against Wednesbury Old Athletic, he played until May 1885, making over 90 first-team appearances for the club.

RICKUS, James April 1892. Centre-half against Bristol Association.

ROBERTS, John October 1883. Half-back against Stoke and ex-Chester College.

ROBERTS, William T. August 1918. Centre-forward against Wolves, he scored three goals. Born in Handsworth in November 1898, he played for Kentish Rovers (Smethwick), Soho Villa, Leicester Fosse and Southport Vulcan before serving in the Army in World War One, then Preston North End (FA Cup finalist, 1922), Burnley, Tottenham Hotspur and Chorley between 1919–31. He also gained two caps for England in 1924. Later a licensee in Preston, he died in 1973.

ROBERTSON, Michael May 1981. Forward against International Select XI. A 21 year old West Bromwich-born supporter who won a competition to play in John Wile's testimonial match at The Hawthorns, he scored to celebrate the occasion. He also played and scored for WBA All Stars.

ROBINSON, James September 1903. Centre-forward against Burton United.

ROBSON, Justin May 1994. Midfielder

against Aston Villa. He is the brother of Bryan and Gary and was a guest for Albion in Gary's testimonial match. He also played for Gateshead United.

ROSE, Arthur November 1900. Right-half against Cambridge University, he signed from Halesowen.

ROSE, William Crispin May 1890. Goalkeeper against Aston Villa. He was an England international (5 caps), guest from Wolves and also played for Small Heath, London Swifts, Preston North End, Loughborough Town and Stoke.

ROUND, William December 1879. Inside-forward against Bullocks Club.

SALMON, Harry May 1930. Inside-right against Winsford United as a trialist.

SAMBROOK, Christopher L. March 1919. Centre-forward against Wolves, ex-Oldbury Town and later played for Coventry City and Nuneaton.

SECK, Mamadon July 2001. Defender against Cheltenham Town. A trialist who played for Ajaccio FC (Corsica), Toulouse and Olympique Nimes in France, he also played in Senegal, Africa, and rejoined Ajjaccio in 2003.

SEYMOUR, George November 1916. Left-half against Wolves. Some references have his surname as Seylour.

SHAW, Sidney H. November 1899. Outside-left against Kaffirs and ex-Burton Swifts.

SHELDON, Arthur November 1892. Right-back against Walsall Town Swifts. He signed from Smethwick Carriage Works and was later with Worcester Rovers.

SHEPHERD, John S. May 1930. Outside-right against Winsford United. Born in Stoke, he was subsequently signed by Albion from Congleton Town in June 1932.

SHILTON, Jack E. September 1891. Left-back against Northwich Victoria. He also played cricket for Warwickshire and was later an Albion umpire. Born in October 1861, he died an alcoholic in September 1899 after serving a prison sentence.

SHIPLEY, Thomas April 1899. Outside-right against Swindon Town.

SIDDALL, Barry J. August 1990. 'Sub' against Swansea City. Born in Bromborough in September 1954, he was a nomadic goalkeeper, whose career spanned some 26 years (1970–96), during

which time he served with Bolton Wanderers, Sunderland, Darlington, Port Vale, Blackpool, Stoke City, Tranmere Rovers, Manchester City, Blackpool, Stockport County, Hartlepool United, Albion as a trialist, Carlisle United, Mossley, Chester City, Horwich RMI, Northwich Victoria, Preston North End, Bury, Lincoln City, Burnley and Birmingham City, and he was also an England youth international. He made 614 League appearances in total.

SIDDONS, James November 1878. Outside-right against Hudsons FC.

SILVESTER, Alfred November 1890. Right-half against Warwick County.

SIMPSON, Arthur November 1883. Left-half against Walsall Swifts.

SLABBER, Kevin May 1984. 'Sub' goalkeeper against Oxford United. Born in Bristol in October 1965, he also played for Knowle Boys, West Town and Bristol City and was at Albion in 1983–84.

SLIM, Horace October 1894. Outside-left, played against Everton (WBCC).

SMITH, Dennis 1880s. Utility forward, with Albion in 1880–81, 1883–87 and 1888–89. He made over 40 first-team appearances for the club and also played for Great Bridge Unity (1887–88).

SMITH, Edward T. December 1879. Inside-forward against Black Lake Victoria.

SMITH, Thomas December 1879. Right-half against Black Lake Victoria. Later he was Albion's honorary general secretary (1884–90).

SMITH, William January 1920. Centre-forward against Corinthians. He was a trialist from Hingley's FC, cousin of Albion's international Joe Smith and also played for Great Bridge Juniors (1910–12).

SNAPE, John J. February 1982. Right-back against Dudley Town. Born in West Bromwich in October 1963, he was an ex-local YMCA player, with Albion in 1980–83 and later served with Bromsgrove Rovers, Sutton Town, Halesowen, Stourbridge and Worcester City, the latter in 2003–04.

STADDON, Philip March 1990. 'Sub' goalkeeper against Elmore, the home 'keeper played for both clubs in this game.

STAVROS, Stavrou April 1988. 'Sub'

midfielder against Kettering Town. Born in Islington, London, he was with Albion in 1987–89 and later with Burton Albion and Armitage Town.

STEVENS, George January 1880. Right-back against St Phillip's FC.

STEWART, David November 1978. Goalkeeper against Stafford Rangers. He was a Scottish international (one cap) and played for Kilsyth Rangers, Ayr United and Leeds United before joining Albion as cover for Tony Godden, making no League appearances but playing in 36 second XI games. He was later with Swansea City and Ryoden (Hong Kong) to 1982, when he became a goldsmith, residing on the Gower Peninsula. He was Born in Glasgow in March 1947.

STOCKLEY, Harry April 1893. Outside-left against Small Heath. He was later with Oldbury Town and Worcester Rovers.

STOKES, John T. November 1878. Inside-right against Hudsons FC. He also played centre-half and was with Albion until 1883. He died in January 1936.

STOVELL, Adrian May 2001. 'Sub' against Newcastle United in Daryl Burgess's testimonial match. He was an apprentice who played for Albion's youth team (2000–02).

SUAVE, Alexis January 1890. Centre-forward against Notts Rangers, he scored three goals. He was born in Gibraltar.

SUTTON, John March 1897. Left-back against Oldbury Town. He was ex-Oldbury Town and later returned there. He also played for Hereford Thistle (1898–99).

SWINNERTON, Alf March 1896. Inside-forward against West Norwood.

TARANTINI, Alberto May 1979. Left-back against Cyrille Regis' XI in Len Cantello's testimonial. He was a guest from Birmingham City, a World Cup winner with Argentina in 1978, played initially for Boca Juniors, Talleres Cordoba, River Plate, Bastia (Corsica), Toulouse (France), Urania (Switzerland) and Platense (Argentina). He was born in Buenos Aires on 3 December 1955 and capped 59 times by his country.

THOMPSON, Dennis May 1933. Centre-half against Winsford & District. He signed from Wrexham in October 1932 and returned there in June 1935.

TIERNAN, Andrew May 2003. 'Sub' against Bryan Robson's XI in Bob Taylor's testimonial and was a first year YTS at the time.

TORTOLANO, Joey May 1984. Left-back against Oxford United. Born in Stirling on 6 April 1966, he played for Tullibody Hearts Boys before Albion (1982–85), then afterwards with Hibernian (222 League appearances) and Falkirk. He won Scottish under-21 honours.

TOVEY, Arthur C. April 1903. Inside-left against Wolves. He was later with Coventry City.

TURNER, Edward G. December 1879. Centre-half against Bullocks Club.

TURNER, John April 1899. Centre-half against Walsall. He signed August 1898.

TURNER, Matthew July 2002. Striker against Bromsgrove Rovers. He scored once and also played in 14 second-team games for the club. Born in Nottingham in December 1981, he was an England youth international signed from Nottingham Forest. He also played for Herfolge Boldklub of Denmark (on loan) and Hednesford Town (2004–05).

TWIST, Hubert December 1879. Right-back against Black Lake Victoria.

WARRENDER, Donald F. May 1941. 16-year-old right-back against RAF (West Bromwich). Born in Cannock in July 1925, he played initially for Elmore Green.

WATERFIELD, Thomas November 1878. Left-half against Hudsons FC.

WHITE, George May 1888. Inside-left against Blackburn Rovers. He was a guest from Great Bridge Unity.

WHITEHOUSE, Arthur March 1884. Right-back against Wednesbury Old Athletic.

WHITEHOUSE, Carl January 1985. Goalkeeper against Tunisia XI. He was an amateur trialist from Darlaston and later played for Sutton Town, Halesowen, in Sweden and the Faroe Islands, GI Orkney, Bridgnorth Town and Blakenall Town.

WHITEHOUSE, Philip May 1988. Left-back against Wolverton Town. He also played in 1989–90 and was later with Walsall and Telford United. He was born in Wolverhampton in March 1971.

WILLIAMS, Ernest September 1897. Right-half against Walsall.

WILSON, Alex November 1895. Outside-left against Everton and atrialist from Glasgow University.

WILSON, James 1880–81. Reserve outside-left. He was born in West Bromwich.

WINTERBOTTOM, Harold October 1887. Inside-right against Notts County.

WITHE, Jason April 1988. 'Sub' inside-forward against Kettering Town. Born in Liverpool in August 1971, he was the son of Peter Withe, ex-Aston Villa and England, and left Albion in 1989. He later played for Huddersfield Town, Burnley (trialist), Stafford Rangers, Crewe Alexandra, Telford United, Coleshill Town, Evesham United, Redditch United, Birmingham City Commercial Department and Stratford Town.

WOOD, Brian T. May 1960. Centre-half against George Salter's XI. Born in Hamworthy on 8 December 1940, he played for Bournemouth Schools, Albion (amateur, August 1957, 'pro', January 1958), Crystal Palace (1961–66), Leyton Orient (1966–68), Colchester United (1968–70) and Workington (1970–76), making a total of 476 League appearances, including 204 for Workington.

WOOD, George May 1990. Goalkeeper against Walsall. He was a guest from Cardiff City. Born in Douglas in September 1952, he played, in turn, for East Stirlingshire, Blackpool (1972–77), Everton, Arsenal, Crystal Palace, Cardiff (1988–90), Blackpool (on loan), Hereford United, Merthyr Tydfil, Mid-Cardiff FC, Inter-Cardiff as player-manager and was capped four times by Scotland and made over 500 League appearances in total.

WOOD, Harry March 1885. Outside-left against Derby St Luke's. He was an England international (3 caps) and also played for Wolves, Southampton, Walsall and Wednesbury Town. He was later Portsmouth trainer.

WOOD, Samuel A. October 1893. Outside-left against Wolves. He played in a total of 20 'other' first-team games for Albion.

WOOD, Sidney March 1891. Inside-forward against Sheffield Wednesday. He was later with Stourbridge and Oldbury Town.

WOODBINE, James February 1890.

Inside-right versus Burton Wanderers, he scored a hat-trick.

WOODHALL, Solomon March 1884. Goalkeeper against Wednesbury Old Athletic.

WOODHOUSE, Ben May 1925. Goalkeeper against Aston Villa XI. He was a guest from Cradley Heath St Luke's and died in February 1963.

WOODWARD, Oscar September 1899. Outside-right against Burton Swifts.

WRIGHT, Arthur J. April 1951. Right-half against Swindon Town. Ex-Bethel United, he signed as an amateur in November 1949 and professional in February 1950. He was later with Bilston United and Stourbridge and born in Dudley on 25 November 1926.

YARNALL, Norman September 1897. Goalkeeper against Leicester Fosse and ex-Smethwick Rovers.

ZAJAC, Marcin July 2004. Midfield trialist against Stoke City and Bristol City in away friendlies. He was a Polish international, born in Warsaw in 1975, and was a former Glasgow Rangers trialist.

Albion Players Who Got Away!

Scores of players failed to make Albion's first XI and subsequently left the club for pastures new. Here are some of those players (not listed previously in this book), who prospered elsewhere:

Gerry Adair (Hibernian, Dunfermline Athletic, Cowdenbeath, Meadowbank Thistle). Russell Allen (Tranmere Rovers, Mansfield Town). Billy Arch (Newport County, Grimsby Town, Hartlepools United). Dave Barnett (Barnet, Walsall, Birmingham City). Gary Bell (Cardiff City, Hereford United, Newport County). Jack Beynon (Halifax Town, Rotherham United, Doncaster Rovers, Aberdeen). Jack Bridgett (Walsall). Arthur Brookes (Halifax Town). Chris Buckley (Arsenal, Aston Villa, Brighton & Hove Albion, Manchester City). Dave Butler (Shrewsbury Town, Workington, Seattle Sounders). Bill Chambers (Burnley, Halifax Town, Bolton Wanderers, Chester, Oldham Athletic, Shrewsbury Town). Bruce Collard (Scunthorpe United).

Barry Cooke (Northampton Town). Frank Costello (Southampton, West Ham United, Bolton Wanderers). Mark Cowan (Airdrieonians). Vic Crowe (Aston Villa, Peterborough United, Wales, also manager at Villa Park). Jack Devey (Aston Villa, England). Bobby Downes (Peterborough United, Rochdale, Watford, Barnsley, Blackpool). Jack Draper (Northampton Town). Jack Driscoll (Sheffield Wednesday). Ted Duckhouse (Birmingham City, Northampton Town). Jack Edwards (Aberystwyth Town, Wales). Jack Ellis (Bristol Rovers, Clapton Orient, Hull City, Wolves). Jack Flavell (Walsall and also Worcestershire & England cricketer). Ron Floyd (Crewe Alexandra). Jimmy Fowler (Falkirk). Bill Gallier (Walsall). Mike Gibson (Shrewsbury Town, Bristol City, Gillingham). Sid Glidden (Sunderland, Port Vale, Reading). John Glover (Blackburn Rovers, New Brompton, Birmingham). Tom Grosvenor (Birmingham, Sheffield Wednesday, Bolton Wanderers, England). Harry Haddington (Walsall). Ian Hathaway (Mansfield Town, Rotherham United, Torquay United). Pat Hewson (Gateshead). George Hickman (Halifax Town). Pat Hilton (Brighton & Hove Albion, Blackburn Rovers, Gillingham, Aldershot). Peter Hilton (Swindon Town). Jim Holton (Shrewsbury Town, Manchester United, Sunderland, Coventry City, Scotland). John Honour (Hartlepool United). Derek Hood (Hull City, York City, Lincoln City). Alf Horne (Lincoln City, Manchester City, Mansfield Town, Preston North End, Southend United). Stan Horrocks (Swindon Town). Dennis Jennings (Grimsby Town, Birmingham City, Huddersfield Town). Dick Jones (Crewe Alexandra). Tom Jones (Hull City). Tommy Jones (Blackpool, Burnley, Grimsby Town, Accrington Stanley). Dean Kiely (York City, Bury, Charlton Athletic, Republic of Ireland). Ernie King (Brighton & Hove Albion). Willie Lammus (Nelson, Wolverhampton Wanderers). Keith Lawrence (Brentford). Mark Leetion (Meadowbank Thistle, East Stirling). Gary Leonard (Shrewsbury Town, Bury, Stockport County, Hartlepool United). Jack Lewis (Crystal Palace, Bournemouth, Reading). John Lewis (Mansfield Town). Colin Lyman (Tottenham Hotspur, Northampton Town, Notts County, Nottingham Forest,

Port Vale). Mark McCarrick (Birmingham City, Crewe Alexandra, Lincoln City, Tranmere Rovers). Mick McCartney (Carlisle United, Southampton, Plymouth Argyle, Gretna). Stewart MacLaren (Motherwell, Dundee, Heart of Midlothian). Tudor Martin (Newport County, Wolverhampton Wanderers, Swansea Town, West Ham United, Southend United, Wales). Billy McDonald (Glasgow Rangers, Partick Thistle). John McIlvenny (Bristol Rovers, Reading). Bill Morris (Wolverhampton Wanderers, England). John Morris (Walsall). Albert Newman (Walsall, Aston Villa). Ernie Pattinson (Rotherham United, Doncaster Rovers). Ted Peers (Walsall, Nottingham Forest, Burton United, Swindon Town, Coventry City). Eric Perry (Coventry City). Jack Pitt (Bristol Rovers). Eli Postin (Cardiff City, Bristol Rovers, Wrexham). Jack Quantick (Hull City). Robert Roberts (Rhosllanarchongog, Wrexham, Crewe Alexandra, Wales). Stuart Romaines (Berwick Rangers, Falkirk, Raith Rovers, Alloa Athletic). Alec Ross (Crystal Palace). Ray Russell (Shrewsbury Town, Crewe Alexandra). Alan Scarrott (Reading). Wilf Smith (Blackpool). Ronnie Stockin (Wolverhampton Wanderers, Cardiff City, Grimsby Town). Billy Taylor (Cardiff City, Aberdare Athletic, Hull City, Norwich City). Billy Thomas (Falkirk, Hamilton Academical, Morton). Jack Thomas (Crystal Palace). Luke Tinkler (Plymouth Argyle, Walsall). Joey Tortolano (Hibernian). Arthur Turner (Stoke City, Birmingham City, Southport, also manager of Oxford United and Birmingham City). Geoff Turton (Gillingham. Crystal Palace). Keith Vickers (Portsmouth, Gillingham). Wilf Vickers (Brighton & Hove Albion, Aldershot). Frank Warrilow (Millwall, Barnsley). Tom Watson (Gateshead). Trefor West (Walsall). Ray Whale (Southend United). Frank White (Coventry City, Newport County). Jim Whitehouse (Walsall, Rochdale, Carlisle United). Jimmy Whitehouse (Reading, Coventry City, Millwall). Gordon Wills (Notts County, Leicester City, Walsall) and Jasper Yeull (Portsmouth).

New signing for 2005-06

CARTER, Darren Anthony

Midfield

Born: Solihull, 18 December 1983
Career: Birmingham City (apprentice, April 2000, professional, November 2001), ALBION (£1.4 million, June 2005)

■ A regular for the England under-20 side, 6ft 2in tall left-footed Darren Carter is a box-to-box player with a terrific engine. He scored a dramatic spot-kick that beat Norwich City and so earned Birmingham a place in the Premiership in the penalty shoot-out in the 2003 play-off final at Cardiff. In all he made well over 50 senior appearances for the Blues before switching to The Hawthorns to give Bryan Robson more midfield options.

KIRKLAND, Christopher

Goalkeeper

Born: Leicester, 2 May 1981
Career: Coventry City (apprentice, June 1997, professional, May 1998), Liverpool (£6 million, August 2001), ALBION (season long loan from June 2005)

■ An England youth international, 6ft 6in tall goalkeeper Chris Kirkland gained eight under-21 caps as a Coventry player before his big-money move to Liverpool. Initially understudy to the Polish star Jerzy Dudek, he suffered finger, wrist and leg injuries at Anfield but did make the 'subs' bench for England's full international v. Poland in February 2004. A brave, confident 'keeper, he was signed by Albion boss Bryan Robson as further cover for Russell Hoult.

WATSON, Stephen Craig

Utility

Born: North Shields, 1 April 1974
Career: North Shields schoolboy football, Newcastle United (apprentice, June 1990, professional, April 1991), Aston Villa (£4 million, October 1998), Everton (£2.5 million, July 2000), ALBION (free, July 2005).

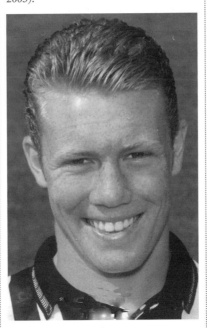

■ A consistent and versatile footballer, strong-running with a terrific engine, Steve Watson is calm under pressure and prior to joining Albion had amassed 450 appearances at club level and scored over 30 goals, perhaps performing best at Newcastle (14 goals in 263 outings). An England international with three Youth, one 'B' and 12 Under-21 caps to his credit, Watson, who is at home in either the full-back or midfield positions (and occasionally in attack), scored a hat-trick in 25 minutes from the right side of midfield playing for Everton against Leeds United in the Premiership in September 2003.

KAMARA, Diomansy

Forward

Born: Paris, France, 8 November 1980.
Career: Red Star 93 (1998). Catanzaro, Italy (October 1999). Modena, Italy (August 2002). Portsmouth (£2.5m, August 2004). ALBION (£1.5m, July 2005).

Bibliography

Other than checking references in the previous books I have written/compiled on West Bromwich Albion FC, I have also referred to several other publications to clarify statistics, facts and figures, birth dates and deaths and individual players' details and, indeed, stories and match reports from past seasons. There are some conflicting facts, statistics and certain other information in these sources and I have made judgement as to what is likely to be correct.

Davies, G.M. and I. Garland, Welsh International Soccer players, Wrexham, Bridge Books, 1991

Farror, M. and D. Lamming, A Century of English International Football, 1872-1972, London, Robert Hale & Co., 1972

FA Yearbook (1951-2000, published annually), London, The Football Association

Gibbs, N., England: The Football Facts, Exeter, Facet Books, 1988

Gibson, A. and W. Pickard, Association Football And The Men Who Made It (4 vols), London, Caxton Publishing Company, 1906-06

Goldsworthy, M., The Encyclopaedia of Association Football, London, Robert Hale & Co, 1969

Goldsworthy, M., We Are The Champions, London, Pelham Books, 1972

Horsnell, B. and D. Lamming, Forgotten Caps, Harefield, Middlesex, Yore Publications, 1995

Hugman, B.J., (ed) PFA Footballers' Factfile 1996-97 to 2000-01, Hertfordshire, Queen Anne Press, 1996-2000

Hugman, B.J., (ed) PFA Footballers' Factfile 2001-02, Basildon, AFS, 2001

Hugman, B.J., (ed) PFA Footballers' Factfile, 2002-03 to 2004-05, Hertfordshire, Queen Anne, Press, 2002-2004

Hugman, B.J., (ed) PFA Premier and Football League Players' Records: 1946-1998, Hertfordshire, Queen Anne Press, 1998

Johnson, F., Football Who's Who, London, Associated Sporting Press, 1935

Joyce, M., Football League players' Records: 1888-1939, Nottingham, Tony Brown/Soccer Data, 2002

Lamming, D., Who's Who of Scottish Internationalists: 1872-1982, Basildon, AFS, 1982-83

Morris, Peter, West Bromwich Albion: Soccer in the Black Country: 1879-1965, London, William Heinemann, 1965

Pringler, A. and M. Fissler, Where Are They Now? London, Two Heads Publishing, 1996

Rollin, J,. Soccer At War: 1939-45, London, Willow Books Collins, 1985

Spiller, R., (ed) AFS Football Who's Who: 1902-003, 1903-04, 1907-08, 1909-10, Basildon, AFS 1990

Whitney, S., The Ultimate Book of Non-League Players: 2002-03, Newcastle, Baltic Publications, Ltd., 2003

Williams, T., (ed) Football League Directory: 1992-1995, London, *Daily Mail*, 1992-95

Other Publications
West Bromwich Albion official programmes: 1905-2005
West Bromwich Albion handbooks, reviews, magazines, supporters guides, 1954-2005
AFS Bulletins (various)
Rothmans Yearbooks (1970-2004), 35 vols. 1-34 (various editors)
Charles Buchan Football Monthly: 1951-1969
Sports Argus Football Annuals: 1949-68
Sports Argus Newspapers (various: 1935-2005)
Sporting Star Newspapers (various: 1949-2005)
Goal Magazine: 1966-78
Soccer Star Magazine: 1963-67
Shoot Magazine: 1990-2004

I have also referred to several other newspapers, various club histories and Who's Who books, autobiographies and biographies of players and managers, scores of general football books and magazines and hundreds of assorted programmes.

Subscribers

Charles E. Allen

Michael R. Allen

Robert D. Allen

Alex Anderson

Franc Andrews

Gary Ashman

Ian Atkins

Thomas Bagley

David Arthur Ball

Alan Michael Bastable

Adam P. Bates

Laura L. Bates

Dr John Batham

Arran Baxter

Jane Baxter

Michael Baxter

Peter Baxter

Trevor Baxter

Michelle Bennett

Matthew Bevan

Alex J.A. Bissell

Clive Blake

Mark Blaney

John Bradley

Robert S. Bradley

Steve Bradley

Ted Bradshaw

Karl Brealey

Keith Brealey

Sam Broad

Mike Browning

Mike Buckland

Chris Cadman

Steve Cannon

Tom Charles

Anthony Clarke

Nicholas Clarke

Abigail Clay

Michelle Clay

Steven Clay

Lew Clews

Peter Collins

Natalie Davies

Paul John Davies-Abingdon

George Deakin

Luke Deakin

Mike Deakin

Scott Deakin

David Derricott

Anthony Clive Evans

Clive Evans

John G. Evans

Keith Evans

Shaun-Pierre Evans

Daniel D. Ford

Chris Foxall

Keith Godfrey

Michael J. Godwin

Brian Goredema-Braid

Jim Grant

Michael Green

Neil Griffin

Patrick Grinham

John F. Groarke

Jack Daniel Guest

Ryan James Guest

John H. Habberley

Lewis Bradley Harbon

Simon Emile Harris

Paul Harrison

Paul Benjamin Hart

William Hayward

Chris J.E. Hextell

Linda Higgs

Neil Hipkiss

John Joseph Homer

Anthony 'Hoppo' Hopkins

Ian Hoult

Ian Hoverd

Hazel D. Hughes

Michael Igoe

Stephen Knott

Dave Langran

Harry Lewis DOB (28/10/1919)

Jonathon Lloyd

Peter Lofthouse

Jamie McVicar

Tony Matthews

Margaret Matthews

Daisy Miles

Noah Miles

Robert L. Mills

Daniel Molloy

Helen Moore

J.A. Morris

R.G. Morris

Ian Murphy

Geoffrey Charles Nevey

Christopher Nickless

Michael North - Number 1 Dad

Simon Osborne

Tim Page

Darren Partridge

Matthew Patrick

Anthony Perkins

Lynne Phipson

Bradley Poole

Richard Powell

Martyn Pratley

Alan Price

John Pye

Leigh Raybould

Charlie Reynolds

Neil Reynolds

Martyn Ridout

Alan Roberts

Ian Alan Roberts

Joseph Alan Roberts

Malcolm Rose

Jonathan Clive Round

Ray Rouse

Julian Rowe

Jonathan Russel

Johnathan Sketchley-King

Stuart Sketchley-King

Alan G. Smith

G.T. Smith

Kenneth James Smith

Paul Geoffrey Smith

Phil Allan Smith

Robert Smith

T.S. Smith

Reginald Stephens

Julie L. Stevens

Philip Stevenson

Robin Stokes

Stephen Straw

Scott Swingler

David J. Taylor

Michael Thomas

Lisa Tranter

Terence Tumelty

Pauline E. Tyler

Darren Underwood

David Velemir

David Vincent

Martin Waite

Dale Walker

Mark Walker

Daniel James Weston

Daniel Wildman

John Paul Wilks

Adrian Woodcock

Ben Woodcock

Tom Woodcock

Emily Woodhall

Karen Wright

Keith Young

*Mick***Doohan**

Mick
Doohan

Thunder from Down Under by Mat Oxley

For Julian

© Mat Oxley 1999

First published in April 1999

British Library Cataloguing in Publication Data:
A catalogue record for this book is available from the British Library

ISBN 1 85960 635 0

Library of Congress catalog card no. 98-75398

Haynes North America, Inc.
861 Lawrence Drive, Newbury Park,
California 91320, USA

Haynes Publishing, Sparkford, Nr Yeovil, Somerset, BA22 7JJ.
Tel: 01963 440635 Fax: 01963 440001
Int. tel: +44 1963 440635 Fax: +44 1963 440001
E-mail: sales@haynes-manuals.co.uk
Web site: http://www.haynes.com

Typeset by G&M, Raunds, Northamptonshire, England
Printed and bound by Imprimerie Pollina s.a., Luçon, France n° 76499

Contents

Acknowledgements

It is difficult to do justice to a racer of Mick's stature in mere words but I'd like to thank him for letting me try, and for his time and commitment to this project.

Thanks also to the Interswill crew. Love ya work!

And big ups to: Chuck Aksland, Daryl Beattie, Jerry Burgess, Dr Claudio Costa, Bob Cowley, Don Cox, Col Doohan, Scott Doohan, Michael Dowson, Honda Racing Corporation, Ken and Colleen Johnstone, Kevin Magee, Niall Mackenzie, Jon MacGillivray, Mike Porter, Rob Phillis, Wayne Rainey, Repsol, Michael Scott, Kevin Schwantz, Selina Sines, Brad and Eden Thomas, Warren Willing, Ken Wootton and *Australian Motor Cycle News*.

Mat Oxley tests Doohan's '92 NSR500 at Suzuka, Japan. (Koichi Ohtani)

You don't need to know the details of our operations

'**E**h, Sid! Sid, I've just checked the boat's cold store and could only find about 30 cartons of turps [Aussie for beer]. Are you sure we've got enough for the trip?'

Brad Thomas recoils in a rage of laughter, takes another slug of Castlemaine and looks to the horizon, where the deep blue sea perfectly meets the deep blue sky, azure overkill punc-

A million miles away from the madness – Mick at the helm, Dick Smart and Selina man the jet-skis. It's a hard life, eh? (Doohan archive)

tured here and there by sunburnt sub-tropical islets. Paradise.

Mick Doohan grins and turns back to steer *Majestic*: 59-foot, two 1,150-horse-power MTU marine engines, sleeps ten, heaps of leather and chrome, you know the kind of thing. It's James Bond territory – you half expect Blofeld to emerge from below, malevolently stroking his pussycat.

Sid is Mick's middle name, something only his good mates get to call him. There's another nickname too: Hoppy. Why? 'Because he limps, of course!'

This is Mick's kick-back yin to his racing yang, and there's a simple significance to the scene. He's on a boat off the Great Barrier Reef with his mates, the people he likes to hang out with, old mates from the days before Fame and Fortune rumbled into his life, not shiny new celeb friends, collected in the bars and restaurants of Monaco. And like all real mates, they don't take each other too seriously.

They're a bunch of Gold Coast party heads into bikes, racing and having a good time, loosely calling themselves the Interswill Conglomerate: 'Inter' for

The Interswill Conglomerate takes its fun seriously – you gotta keep your beer cool, mate. And how do you spell aviation? (Gold & Goose)

international, and 'Swill' for, well, you work it out…

Mick got to know them way back, when he'd only been racing a few months; the gang name followed later when he started racing abroad. Their slogan 'You don't need to know the details of our operations' implies a certain shadiness, and it's meant to. In fact the details are simple: watch some racing, sink a few tinnies, have a laugh.

The Interswill crew are just about the only people who get to see the real Mick Doohan. When he's mucking about in boats, a million miles from his racing universe, he undergoes a seismic transformation. He looks and sounds different, he seems another person, not just the same person in a different mood, but someone else, completely.

The flared eyes and gritted teeth – the face he presents to the outside world – are gone, his face softens. Sitting in a pub on Hamilton Island he's drinking beer, feet up on the bar and looking five years younger. You'd hardly recognise him. And when he says 'No worries', it sounds like he means it, which it doesn't when he's in a racing environment.

Witnessing Mick in this other world forces you to reconsider your perceptions of the man. The face we see in the pits, around the paddock, at motorcycle happenings around the globe, is a facade. It's a hard-edged race face, forged to present an impenetrable mask to his rivals, to cope with the pressures of a life of high-octane brinkmanship.

So what are the details of *his* operation? What makes Mick tick? What has driven him to win five world championships and more than 50 grands prix, to become the greatest motorcycle racer of modern times – some would argue ever?

There are so many ingredients that go towards making a successful bike racer: talent, determination, bravery, instinct, intelligence, competitiveness, the desire

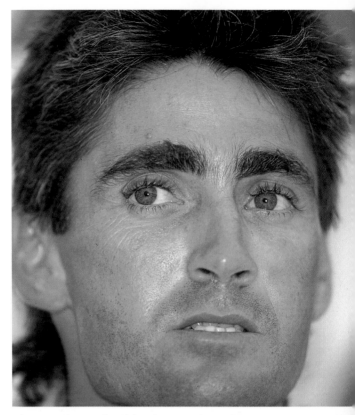

The two faces of Mick: the morning after on Hamilton Island, and facing the press at a GP. Which would you prefer to meet? (Eden Thomas/ Gold & Goose)

to take risks, the ability to withstand pain, even the knack of being in the right place at the right time and, most certainly, a little luck.

As you look back over a racer's life you dig deep to work out how someone came to possess those characteristics. Some may have been there from birth, DNA imprints – others will have been formed from life experiences. And then there's another question, the big one: why? Why race motorcycles?

The psychology of this sport is deep and bewildering, but to understand a racer you must first grasp his psyche. Mental fortitude is undoubtedly the principal factor in Mick's success – he uses psychology to do great things and to undo his rivals.

These were the subjects I wanted to get into when I hooked up with him a couple of days after he'd wrapped up his fifth straight world title. We were heading out to Hamilton Island, his favourite holiday haunt, and that morning I'd been woken at 6am as he prepared for a

60km bicycle ride; no consideration for his championship hangover.

Mick has never liked talking about himself. For one who has been around so long, under the unblinking, all-seeing eye of the television camera, people know remarkably little about the man. He likes it like that.

He's opening up though, lately appearing more at ease with his towering achievements and with the celebrity he once found so irksome. Waiting for our flight at Brisbane airport he's incessantly disturbed by fans wanting autographs, photos. It's the same on the plane, and in the island's restaurants and bars. He handles it well, although his shyness is still apparent. As he signs the back of another fan's boarding pass, I ask him why he doesn't like being worshipped.

'I understand it a bit more nowadays.

One boat for comfort, one for speed: Mick's had 175kph out of this 600-horsepower Douglas Skater. (Doohan archive)

I could always see why people went "wow!" if they saw a rock star, but I could never imagine why anyone would want to worship someone in my league. I just see myself as somebody who races a motorcycle; I find it hard to understand why anyone would want to backslap me.'

A telling final few words. One of Mick's greatest attributes in life, in his racing career, is his inner drive. He is totally self-motivated – he doesn't need backslaps or the cheers of the crowd for encouragement. He'd be just as driven if the grandstands were empty and the cameras down. Psychologists might suggest an explanation for this: Mick lost his father at an early age, so he grew up without those paternal words of encouragement.

'My father's death meant I missed out on a lot of things, but it helped me other ways – I could always get around without having someone holding my hand.'

So the loss hardened him for the rigours of life, made him determined to transcend the loss. And that's exactly what he's done, using toughness, determination and commitment as the cornerstones of his success.

'Determination is the number one thing in racing: without that you've lost before you've started. Riding skill and understanding what's going on, knowing why you're going quick, they're important too. At world level everyone's got natural talent – the difference comes from who's prepared to work to make the most of that ability. I never had to work to be fast, I picked it up pretty quick, but there's a lot of people who can get to that point, and that's when the real work begins.'

Indeed. Mick's commitment is phenomenal, to the point of psychosis. Who

else would be training at the crack of
dawn, two days after winning another
world championship? Eldest brother
Colin – a graduate in human movement
studies – was dragged out riding with
him that morning.

'He's got such a work ethic. I've only
met a couple of top sportsmen with his
aptitude to train. Mick won't cut corners
– if anything he'll go the other way. Say
he's out on a long ride and he comes to a
cross-roads, one way giving the easy way
home and the other the hard way, he
wouldn't even hesitate, he'd take the
hard way just to make sure he's done
that little bit more. I think he really
enjoys it all – he's a pretty straight-up
guy, he just enjoys the training, the riding, the competition, the winning, the
whole scene.'

The non-stop preparation is only one
rather visible aspect of Mick's commitment. His whole approach to racing is
shot through with an obsession to eliminate anything that might be a factor in
him getting beaten. It's a mindset thing:
if he doesn't trust the food at a racetrack,
he'll eat dry bread, just to make sure he
doesn't get sick; when racing takes him
far from his Monaco base, he flies in a
few days earlier than his rivals, just to
make sure he doesn't suffer from jet lag.

His family doesn't always remember
him like that; his dedication seems to
have shone through later, once he was
doing something he loved. Perhaps it
derives from a fierce competitive instinct,
born out of his status as the youngest of
three bike-mad brothers. Or maybe it's a
genes thing.

'I can't remember my father that well,
but from what I believe and what I've
heard from other people he was fairly
stubborn and had his own way of doing
things – he was a bit of an independent

*He's only looking worried because the beer's about
to run out. Mick and the gang cut loose on*
Majestic, *early '98. (Lou Martin)*

thinker. That led him to be pretty successful at what he did, and that's the same with my mother.

'I don't know where I get the determination from – I just hate losing, I've always been like that. I did a lot of swimming when I was a kid – I was house captain and I wanted to win. I wouldn't cry if I lost but I'd be pissed. It was the same when I was messing around on bicycles as a kid. I wanted to jump higher, do crazier things than everyone else.'

Mick recognises that he wasn't quite a normal kid. 'There was a definite bend in the rails somewhere. My first school was run by nuns, the next by catholic brothers – maybe you end up with a different way of doing things. I guess I was a bit off the rails for a while. I've never considered myself a rebel, but motorcycle racing isn't your lawn bowls kind of sport, although the danger itself has never appealed to me. I used to think you needed rocks in your head to race on tarmac. Then I didn't want to get into racing high-powered bikes because they're dangerous. I still think the same.'

Mick's tenacity – a decade at the top and still going strong – takes on a new edge if you consider what he and his closest rivals have been through. Motorcycle racing is a dangerous sport and he's never been allowed to forget that: he's come close to having a leg amputated and will limp for the rest of his life. The guy who was world champion before him retired early, suffering from physical injury and mental torment, because the guy who was champion before that ended up in a wheelchair.

To understand what drives these men you have to own up to the dangers: there's no point pretending they're the glittering heroes in thrilling tales of derring-do. Bike racing is hardcore. You have to consider how the human psyche

The evolution of a master: Mick exits Ossebroeken at Assen in '89, '94 and '98. Faster, neater and more deadly with every year. (All Lou Martin)

can feel that it's important to race around in circles faster than anyone else, risking life and limb apparently for the sake of ego; or, as Mick puts it, 'for the instant gratification of winning'.

Is there a more dangerous competitive sport? Car racing? Boxing perhaps? Boxers face the prospect of brain damage, even death in the most extreme circumstances, and so do car racers. But they don't break arms, legs and wrists with sickening regularity. Neither are they so likely to get killed. You choose: one round with Mike Tyson or a 220kph highside, bike racing's nastiest, most bone-crunching crash.

'The danger does put it in a different arena to other sports: you've almost got to have a bit of a crazy streak to get involved. You have to make the fear work for you. A lot of riders can't control their aggression, they can't get the fear to work for them. They'll keep pushing to get through the fear, and that's why they crash.'

Never take the easy road home: Mick and brother Col (behind) hook into a 60km cycle ride. (Lou Martin)

In other words, a racer should use fear and intelligence ahead of fearlessness and aggression as he attempts to overcome the forces of physics. Denying gravity, after all, is what motorcycle racing is all about.

'That's how you use fear to your advantage. You take that fear to your limit and you work as close as possible to that limit. Once you go past that you're not in control any more. Or if fear goes out of your mind, that's when you crash.

'There's not a race or a test session that I go into thinking I won't get injured. I try and make that work for me; I realise I'm putting myself in danger, so I try and eliminate the risks as much as possible. That goes into the preparation of the bike with my guys and making myself 100 per cent focused. I've actually crashed on slow-down laps because I wasn't concentrating.'

Falling off is compulsory in bike racing; as they say, if you don't fall off now and again, you're not trying hard enough.

The art is to minimise the risk factor. That's the attraction: not the risk itself, but the control of that risk. Then there's the speed, the buzz of rockin' on and bending those laws of physics just as far as they'll go, keeping the bike skating on the edge of control, half a degree from disaster. You're out there, just you and Isaac Newton, dancing on the precipice, like you own the whole world.

Mick knows all about these feelings; he's warped those laws more than anyone. And while he's not the kind of guy to intellectualise racing, he speaks best when he stops fielding questions about contracts, rivals and team-mates and starts discussing what he does on the racetrack. When he talks about riding you realise why he races and why he's still racing after all these years – he gets a massive buzz from riding a 500.

What he does on a bike is magical, hunched over the front, juggling throttle, clutch, front and rear brakes, shifting body weight between the handlebars, footpegs and seat. It's a dance: 'You steer a lot with the footpegs; you can tell because the pegs make big holes in the soles of your boots.' Then there's that 185bhp kick up the arse: 'A 500 will spin the rear tyre no matter what gear you're in. Like, there's a fifth-gear, 200 kays left-hander at Phillip Island and as soon as you bend it in there, the motor picks up revs and the bike steps out sideways.'

Top racers sometimes describe how they can move into an altered state of consciousness when they're really on it, like moving into a fourth dimension. In fact, it's the other way round – their inner self, their subconscious, is taking over. Divine F1 talent Ayrton Senna once stopped his car during Monaco qualifying because he felt he was no longer driving; he was going quicker than ever but was somehow watching himself from outside the car. Mick knows the scenario, but reckons that kind of tale only encourages hero worship.

'Riding fast is a subconscious thing – you go quickest, you're most in control and least likely to make any mistakes when you don't have to think about anything.'

When he talks about racing he's most enthusiastic about real racetracks – Phillip Island, Hockenheim, Salzburgring – not those modern motorsport facilities designed to contain the flight of the F1 car, all second-gear turns, yawning gravel traps and bouncy castle barriers. At heart he's a real racer, who needs to feel he's really moving, not just riding round a go-kart track. He adores Hockenheim: 'It's awesome fun – you're smoking along close on 320 kays and the bike's getting lively, you're bending it over because the fastest straight isn't even straight and

Mick's been a big jet-ski fan since his teens. Check the skin graft on his right ankle – just one of many reminders of Assen '92. (Lou Martin)

you're riding through an endless tunnel of trees and Armco.'

Most of all, he loves Austria's Salzburgring – a lethal 300kph ribbon of tarmac nestling deep in an alpine valley, straight out of *The Sound of Music*. It's an incongruous place for a racetrack, but Mick is glad someone put it there.

'It's got my all-time favourite corner – where you come over the top of the hill overlooking the pits. I know it's dangerous but to me it's everything racing is about.

'You're in sixth gear at over 300 kays, the bike is just about revving out and it doesn't want to turn. You flick it left and you run past a bank really fast. As you go through the left you're over the brow of the hill and the track starts to fall away and there's a little dip in the road there too. The bike also unloads the suspension as you go from one angle of lean to the other. The steering suddenly goes light and the back breaks away – the whole bike is loose. It's breaking loose and sliding at close to top speed, then while that's happening you knock it down two gears for the next right. To me, riding a bike like that at those speeds is why I like racing.'

I'm a sly racer – I go about things as quietly as possible

Then again, Mick can have a lot of fun at walking pace in the paddock. He's a racer, but he believes racing is 90 per cent psychology, so he carefully controls his demeanour to intimidate and confuse the opposition.

'It's just screwing with people's minds – you can read a lot from someone's vibe, so I try to give out the same vibe all the time. People may take that as arrogant or uninteresting, but I'm not in racing to win friends; I don't think my friends are in the paddock anyway. When I'm outside that atmosphere I'm a totally different person, which is why I try and get away from it. People I know who haven't seen me at a race before can't believe how serious I become.'

The race face takes over on Thursdays, sometimes Wednesdays, according to Selina Sines, his girlfriend since '95 and now expecting their first child. From Thursdays he's a different person. Big brother Scott agrees: 'You've got to think before you open your mouth – ask him a silly question and he jumps down your throat.'

Mick knows he's hard to deal with, but that's the way it has to be. 'If someone talks to me and my mind appears to be elsewhere it's because I'm mentally occupied, I'm focused. I might have Oprah Winfrey on the TV in the motorhome but I'm not watching it – I'm looking at time sheets, checking what the other guys are doing. Racing is all I'm thinking about.'

He spends a lot of time gathering intelligence on his rivals. 'It's like if you're in business, you want to know everything about your competitor. Every day I'm thinking about their weak points and their strong points, about doing things different from them, about how we can make the bike better or what's going to be the best plan of attack for the race.'

Mick probably sleeps better on Saturday nights than anyone else in the paddock. Invariably he knows he's got them beat, but he never, ever shows it at the time. 'I don't like people who are boisterous. [Wayne] Gardner was like that, [Max] Biaggi's like that, and it just fires me up, so I try to be more subtle in the way I intimidate people. I don't feel comfortable saying stuff like "I'm going to win the race easy".'

And the mind games continue after the finish – on the podium, in the press conference: 'I'll be playing Mr Cool

Giving it some sideways action at Catalunya, '98. (Christian Lacombe)

16

because I don't want to give those other guys any extra reasons to want to beat me. It's part of the whole game plan. I'm a sly racer: I go about things as quietly as possible, tiptoe through the bush and then boooof! I attack.'

It's a strategy that has worked well. Until Biaggi arrived on the scene in '98, none of the new generation of 500 riders had got themselves really fired up to overthrow the master. Criville and Co have taken up residency on the lower steps of the podium – with the occasional exception – and seem resigned to await his abdication, like little princes; you can almost hear their sighs of despair every time Mick announces that he will contest another season.

Personal enjoyment is his aim, not fame and fortune

One wonders if he is perhaps hooked on racing. Addiction is a recurring theme in the paddock, and while I was researching this book well-known GP technician George Vukmanovich asked me: 'Do you know any heroin addicts? Because that's the closest you'll get to these guys – they're addicted and, like heroin addicts, they're not sure why.'

Some years after his crippling accident in '93, three-time 500 world champion Wayne Rainey admitted he was an addict, he needed that victory hit, the moment of glory coursing through his veins, and he needed it pretty much every weekend, until he couldn't live without it. So is Mick the same? 'I know I am. It's a shame because I never think about the sporting side of racing. Whenever I think I'll go out and enjoy myself and not worry about where I finish, it never works out like that. Once the race starts there's only one possibility and that's winning.'

Beyond addiction and commitment there are other reasons why Mick has kept going so long, longer than the Americans who dominated before him. Guys like '93 500 champ Kevin Schwantz never grew up like other kids; they just raced through childhood into adulthood, burned themselves out. Mick drifted in and out of competition before his teens, grew up and partied. He's had a life beyond motorcycles.

And since he got serious about racing he's been religious about one thing: keep it simple. Mick is clever enough to maintain a straightforward, uncomplicated approach, steering well clear of outsmarting himself, channelling his energies instead into mental focus and physical training. As friend and fellow 500 rider Daryl Beattie explains: 'Mick and his whole team are very natural, that's what's so good about them. He just goes at it; there's none of that American bullshit – you've got to push the front this way or drift the rear that way. It's "give me the motorcycle and I'll ride it".'

The simplicity extends beyond the riding; Mick has kept the same people around him pretty much throughout his career, although of course that kind of loyalty cuts both ways. His manager is the guy who gave him his first decent ride way back in '85; he's worked with crew chief Jerry Burgess and mechanic Dick Smart since he first rode 500s in '89; and during his entire professional career he's only ridden for two teams. Oh, and he's only had two long-term girlfriends in the last ten years. His best friends are still his oldest mates, and if you judge people by the company they keep, some of Mick's closest friends in racing have been Beattie and former 500 rider Niall Mackenzie, two of the nicest, most genuine people you'd ever meet in a GP paddock.

Mick likes to keep racing stripped to its bare elements, not easy when the

Mick and Selina in Monaco, looking forward to a new life together: 'Hey, Sel, did you remember to get the nappies in?' (Gold & Goose)

sport has become a global high-speed corporate ad site. Beyond riding he has other commitments, to the media, to sponsors, to the fans, and you get the feeling that he would have preferred racing in the '60s when life was less complicated: travel to racetrack, race, sink a few beers with the boys, go home.

He's never courted attention from the media, since self-satisfaction is his aim, not fame and glory. Like he says, he understands the fame thing better nowadays and he deals with the press more effectively than he used to, but he'd rather have peace and quiet any day: 'Being private is still easier for me.'

Of course, he likes the corporate pay cheques (at the end of '98 he became the first bike racer to buy a private jet), but he's hardly bothered about maximising his earning potential with advertising and endorsement deals outside racing: 'I'd rather have a holiday with Selina than earn 50 grand – if I didn't have that time off from racing I'd burn out a lot quicker.'

But he is corporate-aware. He does his own contract negotiating, buys the *Financial Review* and talks of laying the foundations so he can make money from his racing profile long after he retires. And he's aware of that profile. In a racing environment he dresses smartly and speaks international English (he once admonished me for using slang in the column I ghost for him: 'I don't want you making me out to look like a yob,' he grinned. 'Even though I am one.'), while out on Hamilton Island he wears T-shirt and shorts, and his conversation is liber-ally sprinkled with Aussie strine: 'Good on ya' and 'No worries'.

Yes, he's still the man he always was – not a yob, but a straight-up Aussie bloke. 'Deep down he's still the Mick I met in '86,' says Beattie. 'I'm glad I get to see him that way, because he's not the real Mick at races. If you're famous you can't keep everyone happy, you have to have a defence, to protect yourself from certain people, the media and so on. For me the fame was the worst thing in the world, and I think he's the same; he's not really happy in the limelight. Away from that he's got a heart of gold, he's a giver, and he still likes to go out and have a laugh. It's a shame people don't get to see him like that.'

Mick has never had the cult popularity of, say, Schwantz, because he's not a showman, he doesn't play to the crowd. That's given him a tough run with the media, who like their heroes big and brash, but it's endearing to find a great talent who doesn't need his ego massaging.

'His attitude is different from most riders,' says Burgess. 'He's not doing it for anything other than his personal enjoyment. He does it because he wants to: he loves riding the bike, he thrives on the challenge, he enjoys winning and he doesn't like losing. He's a phenomenon, he works very hard at it and the harder it gets the harder he works.'

Simple really. Well, kind of...

Mat Oxley
London, England
January 1999

chapter one

Blame it on big brother

The Nudgee dump is a strip of messy sub-industrial scrubland, caught between the concrete runways of Brisbane airport and the sprawling east side of Queensland's state capital. Mick only gets to see it nowadays when he helicopters into the airport, en route to his favourite playground, the Great Barrier Reef.

Back in the mid-'70s the dump was

Three brothers racing – Mick (aged two), Scott and Col Doohan in '67. It was Col who got the bros into bikes. (Doohan archive)

the focus of his life – the training ground where he laid the foundations of his riding genius. It was the place his parents took him and his elder brothers, where they could thrash around without getting bothered by the police.

Nudgee was 15 minutes drive from the Doohan family home in West Chermside, north Brisbane. Colin and Colleen Doohan set up camp in the smart, leafy suburb soon after the birth of second son Scott in 1963. Today, West Chermside has been swallowed up in the suburban sprawl of the sunshine state's capital, but back then it was a new estate

Colleen and Colin Doohan get hitched, February 1958. (Doohan archive)

on the outskirts, houses backing on to bushland and forest. Next stop, the outback.

Brisbane was booming in the '70s, had been for 20 years or so, as newcomers flocked to the area attracted by a land offering golden opportunities.

Colin Doohan's father, also Colin, had been a postmaster but married into the hotel business. Originally from County Clare in western Ireland, the Doohans had joined the Irish exodus in 1862. During the decade that preceded their emigration, around 40 per cent of County Clare's population fled abroad, driven away by the potato famine and British Protestant oppression. Mum can trace her ancestry back to Jeremiah Buckley, a 14-year-old from Cork and convict number 606, banished to the faraway penal colony in 1823 for stealing a handkerchief.

The two sides of the family did well in Australia: there are pioneering tales of fortunes made in gold, sheep and cattle, and squandered in gambling dens and casinos. The Doohans had a particular talent for marrying well – grandfather Colin wedded into a string of hotels and licensed premises. Dad Colin met Colleen in one of the family establishments in Tumbulgum, 100km south of Brisbane, and they were married two years later in February 1958.

Motorcycles were already a part of the Doohan household. The couple courted on Colin's Triumph, and later aboard a Harley. And it seems that Colin was possessed of the same youthful mischief that was such a feature of Mick's early years.

'My parents didn't know Colin had a motorbike – they wouldn't have liked that,' remembers Colleen. 'He used to hide it down the road when he came to pick me up. We had to make up a few stories, like when I got my skirt caught in the Triumph's chain.'

And there were other signs of the Doohan spirit we now know so well…

Like the day Colin came limping home after losing control of a wheelie. He'd been performing in front of a busload of 'admirers' in Coolangatta – they'd probably never even seen a wheelstand before.

Bikes disappeared from their lives when Colleen became pregnant in 1959. The Harley was traded in for a Ford Prefect, and that would've been that if the couple's first-born hadn't fallen in with a gang of minibiking kids 12 years later.

'I used to hang around with a couple of school friends who lived up the road,' recalls Col Jnr. 'One of their houses backed on to some forest and they both had boxframes – real basic motorcycles made with lawnmower motors, box frames and tiny wheels. I used to bludge rides off them, then I started pestering my parents for a bike, and I didn't stop pestering until I got one.'

Colin Snr was a generous dad and bought his eldest son an Aussie-built 80cc Dexon Eagle minibike, with inevitable results. Scott (born four years after Col in May '63) and Mick (born 4 June '65) also wanted a ride, and the only way to end the ensuing garden riots was to add another two-wheeler to the family stable. Within a few years the brothers had some 13 motorcycles, in varying states of dilapidation.

To start with, Scott and Mick shared a boxframe, powered by a Victor lawnmower motor. That, too, led to feuds, so Colin capitulated and bought Mick a brand-new Honda MR50 and Scott a new Honda XR75. Both machines were fruits of the booming US minibike market.

'The XR was the gun minibike at the time,' says Col. 'And I put up enough of a bitch to get a new bike for myself – a six-speed Indian 80.' So the stable grew again.

Mick – eight years old when the MR came into his life – had already shown

Using all the road and a little bit more, Mick was bouncing off the kerb from the age of five. (Doohan archive)

early signs of a love of speed. The family home in Tyrone Street sat atop a hill and Mick used to scare Colleen half to death by trundling off down the slope, first on a tricycle, later on a scooter, as fast as his little legs would take him. It was the same with the MR. 'The bushland we used to ride around was half a kilometre away by road,' he says. 'So we used to ride it and pretty often we'd get pulled up by the police. That's when our parents decided

The riding style is already familiar – hunched over the front and hanging on for dear life. (Doohan archive)

Thrashing the guts out of the MR50 at the Nudgee dump, aged eight. (Doohan archive)

that it was best to get us on a racetrack.'

The Doohan offsprings joined the North Brisbane minicycle club en masse and began competing at the Nudgee dump. Pretty soon the family household was taken over by bikes. And not only their own. Colin Snr had moved out of the hotel business into earthmoving, and a large trailer used for hauling chains was pressed into weekend service. With a bit of a squeeze it could carry ten bikes.

Racing transport '70s-style: half the neighbourhood's bikes would fit on dad Doohan's trailer. (Doohan archive)

'Every Sunday morning you'd hear all these bikes coming to our place from all over the neighbourhood – like bumblebees,' says Mick. 'We'd put them on the trailer and take off.'

Dad Doohan relished his return to motorcycling, devoting his evenings to preparing the boys' bikes for next weekend's racing, and moving on to selling minibike tune-up parts from the garage. But no one was more deeply bitten by the two-wheel bug than Mick. All he wanted to do was go bush riding (or 'missing trees', as fellow Aussie prodigy Kevin Magee dubbed the pastime).

'I enjoyed riding the whole time. I'd hardly ever take my helmet off all day – just run the bike till it needed fuel and start over. I was playing football before, but I lost interest in that pretty quickly. From then on it was pretty much racing and swimming. I used to hammer swimming pretty hard.'

School hardly got a look in. Colleen: 'Michael never wanted to go to classes, he just wanted to get out into the bush. He was on the go all the time. Scott would sit down and read a book, but not Michael – he was always up to tricks.'

'Missing trees' soon became the serious game. Mick, his brothers and the rest of the local bike kids would turn bush tracks into unofficial race circuits. Their parents weren't so keen on letting their boys ride unsupervised, and with good reason: Mick broke a wrist when he flipped the MR50, and was lucky to survive a head-on with no more than a gash to his forehead.

The bush bashing wasn't doing his riding talent any harm, though. Mick won the 50cc North Brisbane club championship in his first season, although 'there wasn't a lot of competition around then; Brisbane was a pretty small city in those days'.

Most of the time he raced Aussie dirt track, not US-style ovals but tracks with left and right-hand turns and maybe the occasional motocross jump thrown in.

Meanwhile father was getting sucked deeper into the bike business. A serious car crash back in '69 had left him badly hurt, with two broken legs and facial injuries. Unable to continue in earth-moving, he did the obvious thing: mort-gage the house and buy a motorcycle shop. Doohan's Honda opened for business in nearby Zillmere Road in early '72.

With dad's shop came a flood of go-faster goodies, mainly Flying Machine Factory gear from the USA, via Melbourne importer Alf Bond, who became a family friend. Bond made sure the boys got the latest gear, fresh in from California.

'FMF stuff was pretty gun equipment at the time,' remembers Col. 'Alf was always sending us motors and other bits and pieces – we loved that. There was some very trick stuff, like a three-valve head with a camshaft running in roller bearings for Scott's XR. In those days that was pretty outrageous.'

By now the Doohans were racing every Saturday and Sunday – dirt track one weekend, motocross the next. And Mick just kept getting faster. In '76 he ran second in the Queensland 10–12 flat track championship, riding a hand-me-down Yamaha YZ80, previously used and abused by Col.

Life was good for the Doohan family: the shop was going well, the kids were happy, totally absorbed in doing what they loved. Then Colin died in April '77. He had never fully recovered from that car accident.

Colin and his love of bikes had been the centre of the boys' lives – his death hit desperately hard. Suddenly Mick didn't care about racing any more. And anyway, from a purely practical point of view Dad was no longer around to fix the bikes and take the kids to meets. Mick rode in that year's Australian junior flat track championship but 'the interest

wasn't there at all. I pretty much got out of racing.'

As the youngest, he was probably most affected by the tragedy. He was 11, going on 12, when his father passed away, while Scott was 14 and Col 17. Life was toughest of all for Colleen – working full-time, making ends meet and raising three sons all on her own. Not always the easiest of children either, admits Mick: 'I was probably a bit of a shit of a kid after my father died.'

Over the next few years he drifted in and out of bikes. He would take up riding again, then give it away, try his hand

Mick gets taken for a ride on holiday in Singapore, circa '72. (Doohan archive)

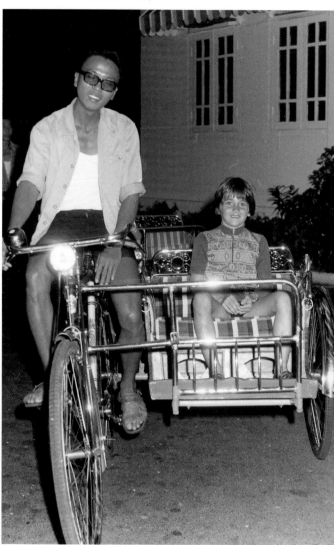

at BMX, then give that up. The driving force was no longer there.

Colin's death had other far-reaching effects: the family had to sell the shop, since Honda Australia refused to allow Colleen to take the reins – they didn't want a woman running a bike dealership. Col (by then studying engineering at Brisbane University) took a year out from college to manage the business, but in '78 it finally had to go.

Two years later Mick got back into racing on another Col hand-me-down, this time a Honda CR125 motocrosser, specially adapted to fit his tiny body. Mick was a wee lad until he hit 18, and even at 15 the cut-and-shut CR was way too big. Nevertheless he rode the bike to third in the Queensland state dirt track series.

He'd lost his licence five times by the age of 20

According to people on the scene, Mick wasn't a stand-out rider in those early years, just one of a bunch of crazy teen tearaways. But it was around this time that Col began to think that Mick might be something a bit special.

'I've a vivid memory of my first realisation that Mick was good,' he says. 'He was racing a motocross event and it was the first time we'd seen a full minibike motocross circuit, with quad jumps and so on. All through the heats and the first final everyone was taking the quad jumps one at a time. Then along came Mick in the second final: bang, bang, taking them two at a time. He won the race by a huge margin. I asked him what made him think he could do that. He just said he'd seen it on TV. That's pretty special – to watch something on TV and then just go and do it.'

Col's own race career ended in late '79 when he was 19. Earlier that year he'd won the Brisbane Solo Cup speedway title and had been considering going pro

in England. But a first international outing in Brisbane changed his mind.

'There were loads of top guys like Ole Olsen (former world champion) and I got my ass kicked. I had a bit of a dummy spit. Rather than get my head down and work harder – like Mick would – I quit and went surfing.'

Scott had also stopped for now, finding racing too much like hard work. He went out and bought himself a Kawasaki Z650 road bike, the machine that gave Mick his first taste of tarmac (though Scott didn't know it at the time).

Mick quit school in 1981. He had never been a model pupil, rebelling against the fierce regime of a Catholic school he attended in his early years and taking little interest in classroom activities from then on. He was often in trouble, sometimes for truancy, other times for daydreaming in class, drawing pictures of motorbikes on school books, stuff like that.

Freed from the confines of the education system, Mick had more time than ever to get out and about. And he had plenty of exploring to do. In June 1980 Colleen remarried, to Ken Johnstone, an affable Scot whose accent is as strong today as it was when he emigrated Down Under in '67. The family moved to the Gold Coast, where Ken was a senior constable and where Mick started getting into boats. He and his mates would blast their tinnies – small, outboard-powered aluminium dinghies – around the Coast's labyrinthine network of waterways, jumping wakes and generally having a blast. It didn't matter what he was up to, so long as it was fast.

And once again he drifted back into racing. In '81 he hooked up with an old school mate for a return to the 80 class – the little bikes still fitted him better than that CR. With his friend's father providing vital transport and back-up, Mick was soon back to racing every week – motocross one weekend, dirt track the next. It was a good year, with plenty of wins. And his famed aggression was beginning to show…

'I got disqualified from a Gold Coast motocross meeting that year. There was this girl racer – she was pretty hard and we were going head to head in the finals. She won the first, I won the second. In the third race we locked together in mid-air and she came in crying, saying she was going to take me out in the last race. So I got to her before she got to me.'

Now 16 going on 17, and a young man out for a good time, Mick was getting into the usual kinds of mischief that teenage speed freaks get into. Nothing too serious, mind, but enough to have copper Ken shuddering at the memories. Mick was often to find out that having a cop as a step-dad had its compensations…

If he wasn't 'borrowing' his brothers' bikes and practising wheelies, he'd nick their cars. Scott remembers: 'I had this V8 and I used to wonder why the thing was chewing so much gas. Of course, Mick kept stealing it. One day I saw him driving it around, so I told him: "Mate, I don't mind you taking the thing, just stick some gas in it now and again".'

Not long before he turned 17 and qualified for his road licence, Mick bought a Honda XR250 enduro bike for bush bashing. 'It ended up getting nicked and Scott told me I should get a road bike. I wasn't into it – I thought anyone who rode street bikes was crazy.'

Big brother's advice won the day and the insurance money went on a year-old Yamaha RD250LC, the legendary two-stroke that launched a thousand race careers in the early '80s. Pretty soon Mick had revised his opinion on road bikes and was starting to explore the LC's limits. Legal limits were another thing entirely – he would lose his licence

Dad Doohan's Brisbane Honda dealership in '74, selling all the latest gear: CB400s, CB750s and tricked-up minibikes, of course. (Doohan archive)

five times before he was 20, for speeding, pulling wheelies, the usual LC lunacy. 'I never raced the thing, but I enjoyed messing around and scraping the footpegs.'

So was he immediately a tarmac god, faster than his mates? 'I had a lot more experience; I'd already done ten years on bikes so I was more confident than them. I used to try out stuff, like how far you can go in the wet – like the day I was going for a job interview. It was raining and I was going round corners, thinking this doesn't feel bad, so I pushed a bit harder at the next corner and slid down the road, skinning my hands. I think the guy was impressed I'd made it, so I got the job.'

But that wasn't his last crash on the LC, oh no. Easter '83, and Mick set off with a bunch of mates to spectate at the annual Bathurst bike races, a 900km ride into New South Wales. Back then Bathurst was Australia's biggest race,

Acquiring the secret of throttle-to-rear-tyre relationship: Brisbane 10–12 dirt track finals. (Doohan archive)

staged around the picturesque but daunting Mount Panorama street circuit. The event had a reputation for trouble; harmless stuff really – just bikies hooning around, getting drunk, doing wheelies, doughnuts, burning each others' bikes, that kind of thing.

The trip started badly and got tragically worse. 'I was on my way to meet some mates and this guy pulled up next to me at the lights on a Kawasaki Z1000. I thought I'd impress him with a wheelie but I went too far, over the back and down the road into the gutter.'

Bathurst was wild that year: a phalanx of riot police fighting pitched battles with hundreds of bikies up on the hill. Mick, his legs still hurting from his endo, was sleeping it off in a tent.

'Then Col stuck his head inside and told me to come out and have a look – everyone was throwing stuff at the police. It was like a game: the people would throw stuff, then the police would make a charge. Just as I got to where it was all happening, the police charged us. I started running but I wasn't too flash. I tripped over some tent ropes and went down, so I was lying there hoping they'd miss me. I watched them pull some guy out of a tree and lay into him with their batons. It was pretty wild.'

The long journey home was undertaken in sheeting rain, and two of the gang were killed when a car ploughed into them. Next day Mick smashed into the side of another car when he got sideways entering a gas station. 'It was still raining and my rear tyre was shot.'

By the time he made it home the LC was a wreck, so he traded it in for one of the just-out YPVS RZ350s. He made a deal with his local shop: he would buy the bike so long as they'd fix '250' stickers to the side-panels. Mick didn't have a full motorcycle licence, so he couldn't ride anything bigger than a 250. 'Ken was in the police force, and mum would've freaked if I came home with a 350.'

And this was the bike that was to change his life.

I thought I'd impress him with a wheelie but I went too far

chapter two

Babes, beaches and beer. Or bike racing?

As a good-looking teenager, it wasn't difficult for Mick to have a good time on the Gold Coast. In fact, he found it pretty easy. And he liked it.

A few months after the Bathurst trip Mick turned 18 – real man at last. By now he was earning money, fixing swimming pools, doing factory jobs: 'Like making guttering: pump sheet metal into a machine, take it out the other end, pack it up and start again.' And he had pretty much moved out of home. He'd tried moving back to Brisbane, working as a builder with Scott, but couldn't stomach the early-morning starts. It wasn't that Mick was lazy as such, he just didn't often make it into bed until the early hours. So he returned to the Gold Coast, moving in with a gang of mates in Burleigh Head, then to the infamous squat on Miami beach in Surfers Paradise, returning to Ken and Colleen's only when he needed a good feed or some washing done. Just a normal teenager, then.

What do you want to do – race bikes or party?

Life was easy, and there was no reason why Mick should concentrate on anything else than the things he was good at: babes, beaches and beer. Oh, and honing the art of performing wheelies on his RZ350. He couldn't wring bikes out of his system, and now he had a new motorcycle, another machine with which to explore the outer limits, and a racetrack where he could do just that for ten bucks a day.

Surfers Paradise raceway is still there today, in a tumble-down kind of way. The growing multitudes of Japanese tourists seeking paradise on Surfers beach and playing the local golf course precipitated its closure in '87. Mick is still bitter about that.

He'd turn up on his RZ and hustle round all day. Apparently it was quite a sight. 'He never used to check the tyre pressures or anything,' says Scott. 'He'd be sliding around because he only had 15psi in the tyres, with his shirt hanging out between his two-piece leathers. He was a bit loose in those days – it was just all good fun.'

Not so much fun for everyone. Another Surfers regular at the time was Michael Dowson, a lean, lanky west coaster from Perth and one of the nation's best racers of the era. An official Yamaha rider, and several times national champion, Dowson was somewhat alarmed to find this nutty street kid keeping up with him.

Mick's style wasn't typical 250 production stuff. With treaded tyres and 40 horsepower, the accepted technique was keep the power down and the wheels in line. For a kid brought up on the dirt, that didn't feel right at all.

'I got hooked pretty quick and I actually found it easier than the dirt. I guess I always expected the back end to step out when I flicked into a turn, so when that happened it didn't bother me. The only thing I wasn't keen on was the front brake, because it's not so important on a dirt bike.'

Sure enough, word got around about Mick's days out at Surfers. Local dealer and racing patron Bob Cowley – boss man at Gold Coast Motorcycle Wreckers – was one of many who got to hear about this young lair who could ride an RZ sideways. Cowley already knew of Mick: he'd watched him race dirt as a kid, although 'he never stood out then – there were better kids'.

Cowley still runs a couple of bike shops on the Gold Coast. They're old style – no fawning, besuited salesmen, just the smell of dirt, oil and a passion for speed. He's a grass-roots, salt-of-the-earth type, still known for helping youngsters get into racing – he reckons it's a great way of keeping young crazies out of trouble, giving them a focus to their lives.

'I'd seen Mick ride on the road and I thought it'd be good to get him off it. But he didn't have any money – he was a bit of a struggler. I just wanted to give him some encouragement.'

Cowley got his chance one day in August '84. Mick had recently bought a Honda XR500 enduro – however much he loved thrashing round Surfers he still missed the dirt – and was getting ready to head into the bush. A mate rolled by and asked for a go on the RZ. He reap-

peared a while later with the bike bent and mangled; a car had got in the way and he'd gone through a fence.

Mick headed to Cowley's for second-hand parts. 'I used to hang around there a bit, buy second-hand tyres, that kind of stuff. I went in looking for parts and Bob said he'd fix the bike for nothing if I'd do a race on the thing. That sounded like a fair deal to me, so I did the next race at Surfers a few weeks later.'

His entry fee paid by Bob, Mick finished his first race in second place. No big deal – this wasn't exactly a landmark event. Fulfilling his role as the laid-back beach bum, Mick didn't make it over to

How cool does he look? Mick gets it on aboard the Team Camo RZ500 in '85. The army overalls were Jonno's idea. (Doohan archive)

Jonno and a puffy-faced Mick. 'He was still a bit of a hippy back then,' said Rob Phillis. (Doohan archive)

Cowley's shop until the next Tuesday, when his patron gave it to him straight: 'What you want to do? Race bikes or party?'

A simple question maybe, but going racing wasn't really an option for Mick. He had no money – well, just enough to keep partying – and he wasn't about to give that away to race motorcycles.

'I told Bob I'll race bikes if I've got an interest, so he went over the road to Donny Pask Motorcycles, who had been given one of the new RG250s by the Queensland Suzuki importer. Someone must've put a word in, because they gave me the bike.'

The RG wasn't the tool of the moment, but Mick made it work for him. Cowley remembers his first sight of the man racing on tarmac at Surfers: 'Someone took him out on the warm-up lap and he got back to the grid so embarrassed because he'd bent the bars. Then

he went and lapped the entire field.'

Despite Mick's full-on hedonistic lifestyle – photos from that period show him puffy eyed and overweight, a sure sign of excess alcohol intake – his high-intensity race face was already in place. Cowley: 'Some people told me his eyes were so intense they reckoned he must be on drugs.'

Few drugs are more powerful than adrenaline and Mick's adrenal pump was locked on max. Always has been. A few weeks later he won his second race on the Suzuki, then the relationship imploded after a profane encounter between rider and sponsor.

Mick remembers: 'Donny was a bit of a fiery sort of person and the RG was taking up too much room in his workshop. He went off the dial, then I spat the dummy and told him he could stick his bike wherever it'd fit.' End of deal and end of Mick's racing career. No worries, though – there was plenty of partying that needed doing. And Mick was as dedicated as ever in that respect.

Eight months passed before news of

this guy's riding spread further afield, thanks to the still-awed Dowson, and via Rob Assink of local dealers Gaythorne Yamaha. In between times Mick had returned to Bathurst for the Easter '85 meet, where Jeff Hardwick – now involved in a GP team with Mick – had promised him a run in the 250 proddie race. 'The bike didn't arrive, so I went from potential racer to potential drunk.'

Dowson had introduced himself to Mick a few months earlier, convinced that the man deserved a helping hand. He got his chance when 'a bunch of Assink's maniac mates contacted me. They'd got an RZ500 and they wanted to put a young rider on it.

'I remember standing on the roof of my Transit van at Surfers to watch this guy some more. He was going quicker and quicker and quicker. He goes into this big, fast, sweeping turn and I'm thinking, "Nah, he's not going to make it." He's zinging in there, drifting both tyres and he's hit the kerb with such force that it's twisted him around and highsided him. The bike and him endoed for ages. I thought. "If you get out of that alive, good on ya." That's the crash that gave him the collarbone like a spotlight bracket. I said to Assink's boys, "This is the guy."'

Mick didn't prove an easy man to nail down. He was always out and about, having a good time. And when he started getting messages to call some mate of Dowson's, he thought this guy was after him for 50 bucks he'd been loaned. He didn't call back.

Finally communication was established with Jon MacGillivray, the guy who owned the RZ500 and who would become Mick's friend, confidant and manager. Jonno had bought the bike earlier that year to ride on the street, but it was spending too much time in the garage. After a chat with motocross mate Eden Thomas at the Cauldron night club in Sydney's infamous King's Cross, they

decided they'd find someone to race the thing. The plan was simple: find a fast youngster and split the costs five ways, between Jonno, Eden, Assink, Cas Mischaleic and the rider. A second opinion, confirming Dowson's, came from Cowley: 'I told Jon this guy would be world champion one day.'

Mick was rapt. 'The deal sounded perfect. They asked me up to a meeting at Gaythorne. I borrowed my girlfriend's car and went up with her. They told me they wanted someone who wasn't going to throw it down the road every weekend. Then they asked me to bring my girlfriend inside so they could have a look. I realised then that these guys were a bit out there.'

A bit out there indeed. When Mick won first time out on the RZ at Surfers in September, he didn't realise what lay in store with this crew from Brisbane.

'They wanted to spray the bike in

It didn't matter, just so long as it had two wheels. (Doohan archive)

Still a mischievous-looking teenager, Mick at Scott's wedding in '85. Col on the left, Scott on the right. (Doohan archive)

camouflage and put camo overalls over my leathers – I used to blow up like a Michelin man. Jonno and the guys would erect this big army tent in the paddock, with camo netting over the top. They'd hang out there, invite all their mates, bring some bottles and get a barbecue going. They'd drink beer and carry on – that's how it worked.'

Thus was born Team Camo, prototype for the Interswill Conglomerate. There was, however, a serious motive behind the military posturing. MacGillivray: 'We were chasing sponsors and I firmly believed that if we stood out, we'd be well ahead.' Sure, the team pulled in sponsors, but that probably had more to do with the results.

'Mick kept winning and winning, then all these people started giving us stuff for free. We loved it.'

The team blossomed. And everyone got on famously – hardly surprising con-sidering their mutual interest in similar off-track pursuits. The Team Camo patrons weren't all pose and party though. Jonno and Eden, both former dirt riders, co-ordinated the effort and did basic maintenance, while Rob would tune the engine, undertake rebuilds and so on.

Jonno: 'We would all pitch in money for the team, and if you'd had a tough month someone would kick in for you. Mick came to us with a reputation as someone who could ride a motorcycle. He was a bit rough, but he could ride. He didn't mind if there was a problem with the bike, he'd just ride around it.

'He was still a C or D grader then, but he'd make them look stupid, and when he moved up to the B grade he made them look pretty silly too. Within four months he was an A grader. It was obvious he was a natural. We would run out of rear tyres at a meeting, so we'd have to run second-hand stuff. You could see him out on the track having a hell of a time – the moment he leaned into a corner and got on the gas the thing would

go sideways but it didn't faze him. He'd have it sideways all over the place, as if nothing was wrong. RZs were notorious for tankslappers but he just kept it nailed the whole way.'

Fellow future star Kevin Magee, who was a year or two ahead of Mick but also headed for 500s, found his style captivating. 'He was a loose unit back then. I was watching him during practice at Surfers because I didn't know the place. He'd bury the bike into turns and just hang on. It looked unethical but it was quick.' Very quick.

And the more he won, the better the parties. 'I wouldn't say they were legendary,' says Jonno. 'But they were pretty well attended. We were all after a good time, and a good time meant doing well and having some fun afterwards.'

Early in 1986 Mick ventured to race outside Queensland for the first time. So far he'd only raced at the local Surfers and Lakeside tracks. Now he was flying south to take up a reserve rider slot with a couple of racers contesting the presti-

Cigarettes and alcohol – Jonno and Mick celebrate his 21st, June '86. (Doohan archive)

gious Castrol Six Hour race at Oran Park, outside Sydney. The connection came via their sponsor STP. Mick had won the STP Stars of Tomorrow at Lakeside and the company was funding this pair's Suzuki GSX-R750.

'They nearly spat the dummy when they heard I'd never raced at Oran Park. As reserve rider I got a little practice and ended up going faster than them, moving them up the pecking order. I had a pretty good run in the race – opened a few eyes.'

Team Camo had already had their eyes opened. They reckoned Mick deserved another bike, so they built an RZ250 from bits. Others were also starting to take notice, and the Queensland Yamaha distributors supplied one of the new five-valve FZ750s at cost price. Mick's first four-stroke, though he never got on with it.

chapter three

Young gun, Super Angel

Motorcycle racing still hadn't got a hold of Mick Doohan. Sure, he was having a ball thrashing around on the FZ and the two RZs, but the sport still came in second to partying. So long as he

Team Camo (now sans army chic and renamed Gaythorne Yamaha) crack open a few tinnies after the '86 Surfers 3-hour. Mick is in the middle, Jon MacGillivray on the RZ250 (right), Rob Assink and Cas Mischaleic (with beard) behind the RZ500. (Doohan archive)

could fit both into his life, things would be cool.

'He was still a surfie beach bum back then,' remembers future Supers rival Rob Phillis. 'He was a bit of a hippie, just living on the beach with his mates, fixing the odd swimming pool.'

At the time Mick shared a notorious squat with a bunch of mates, right on the beach in Surfers. The dilapidated hang-out would ultimately fall to the bulldozer and be replaced by million-dollar apart-

ments. Fellow Gold Coast racer Daryl Beattie will never forget the place. 'It was a dirty old house – half the place didn't have electricity. Mick would be there smoking Winfield Blues and drinking beer. You'd go upstairs and he'd say 'Go careful down the hallway', and there'd be a dirty great hole in the floor. You'd have to jump over it, or there'd be planks around. It was a beaut spot, right on the beach. We had jet-skis and that's all we did – every hour of the day we'd go jet-skiing.'

So, the living was easy. But that trip to the '86 Castrol Six Hour had got him thinking. He'd never even seen Oran Park before, but he'd run well among some of the most competitive riders on the national scene. Perhaps he could get some results at other tracks. It had to be worth a go.

Towards the end of the year Mick borrowed Jonno's ute, strapped in the RZ250 and headed out to contest the Swann series 250 production support races. Back then the Swann was Australia's biggest international championship, attracting a bunch of foreign GP riders who used the fiercely competitive racing to stay sharp during their off-season. British Marlboro Yamaha man Rob McElnea and rising Aussie star Kevin Magee were the main men that year, duking it out on a couple of YZR500 GP bikes, sent over from Europe.

Sure, Mick wouldn't be racing against these guys, but he'd be sharing the same paddock. No big deal, just another small step up the ladder.

The 250 proddie racing would be competitive enough anyway, attracting the category's top exponents from all over Australia. The class was coming to be recognised as the breeder-feeder system for the national Superbike series. Anyone who looked hot on a 250 streetbike would mark themselves as a potential Supers graduate. Magee had shown the way: the Victorian had started out on a 250LC and was now Australian's Next Big Thing. From there he was on a fast track to 500s: proddie 250s to 500 GPs via Aussie Supers – it became a well-worn trail, followed by Doohan, Beattie, Peter Goddard, Mat Mladin, Anthony Gobert and Troy Corser.

Mick started off the Swann with a

Hustling along on the Gaythorne Yamaha RZ250 in 1986. (Doohan archive)

home advantage, taking third at Surfers. Then he turned south to contest rounds at Oran Park and Calder Park, outside Melbourne.

He may not have won any of the races, but there were important people watching trackside, racing's movers and shakers, and his demonic style on the RZ could hardly go unnoticed.

'I'd get the thing sliding with the momentum, then have it bouncing around. All the top guys were passing me down the straights and I'd be passing them back in the turns. I was leaving black lines, hanging it out.'

The sight left a severe impression on one Japanese Yamaha official and a big-time bike dealer from Tokyo, who could hardly wait to get back home and tell colleagues about this madly talented maniac. Word would spread.

His demonic style on the RZ could hardly go unnoticed

Dowson was never less than amazed. 'Most riders grind their knee-sliders in one place; Mick's had grind marks from two different angles. He'd push the bike into a turn, lose the front, dig in a knee to save the slide, then keep dragging the scraper till it was dust. He was always sending leathers to be repaired. Even on the RZ250 he had this crazy style he'd got from dirt riding – all the emphasis on the front. He just let the rear look after itself. That's why I never spent much time dicing with him when we were team-mates in '88 – he'd come past and disappear.'

By now Mick's crew had dropped the camo paint-job (much to his relief) and were running Gaythorne's blue and white livery. Very orthodox, but the team no longer had to scream for attention.

Mick won plenty of races in '86, although he was beginning to realise he enjoyed riding the 250 more than anything else. The FZ never felt quite right and the RZ500 had had its day. That year

he also got his first ride on slicks, aboard a hybrid open-class racer: a TZ250 with a third cylinder grafted on, housed in an RG500 chassis. 'That's the bike I had my first real highside on. I was leading a race at Lakeside and wicked it up out of this slow turn. Over the bars I went.'

For '87 Mick decided that he wanted to concentrate on 250 proddie racing, using Yamaha's latest weapon, the TZR. 'I never wanted to race anything quicker – anything faster than 200 kays was too stupid!'

The TZR Yamaha Cup was his priority for the new year and he was up front right away. 'The other main guy was Graham Morris – we'd fight it out. I was outright quickest, but he had the experience so he'd end up out-smarting me.'

The pivotal event turned out to be that Easter's Bathurst meet. Mick got beaten again, this time by an ex-dirt tracker from Sydney, Peter Goddard. 'After the race I was sitting around when this Japanese guy comes up and asks me if I want to do the Suzuka Eight Hours. I said sure, sounds pretty trick.' This was the Yamaha official who had been dazzled by Mick at Surfers. The other witness to his young talent on that occasion had been Kouzou Morinaga, one of Tokyo's richest bike dealers and boss of the Super Angel team. Now Morinaga had sent his friend to get Mick.

This was the Big Time knocking at his door, and a good moment for fate to play its hand. Michael Dowson crashed at Lakeside and broke a leg, leaving his Marlboro Yamaha FZR750 vacant.

The team's manager, Warren Willing, already knew about Mick – Dowson had pointed him out some while before – and he'd also heard about the Eight Hour offer. Concerned that the youngster would be making a dangerously big

A sweet-looking bunch, considering they're rock-hard roadracers: Mick at the '87 Swann series with mates (from left) Michael Dowson, Briton Rob McElnea and Kevin Magee. (Doohan archive)

jump (from a 250 streetbike to a full-on Superbike in the world's biggest race), Willing offered him a ride on Dowson's FZR at Winton, the next Aussie Superbike round.

Willing had been one of Australia's top international riders in the mid to late '70s, until his career was curtailed by a horrendous crash at an Irish street circuit in '79. Now he was back home, running Magee and Dowson in the Marlboro Yamaha Dealer team. A racer and self-taught engineer with a fine intellect, Willing was always on the hunt for new talent.

If anything, he got too good at his job, for whoever he nurtured would be moved on to bigger and better things. Magee was already headed towards a GP career, and soon Willing would earn the mantle 'Kingmaker'.

Needless to say, Mick accepted the offer. Willing collected him at Melbourne airport and drove to Winton, using the 2-hour drive to get into the boy's head.

'I wanted to see what his attitude was. He was reasonably hard to talk to, reserved I guess. But he came across as serious about what he was doing and the intelligence was there – that's what I was after. His reputation back then was as a bit of a wild guy on a bike, but after talking to him I realised he wasn't a complete nutter.'

Mick had plenty to get used to at Winton: in particular 100 extra horsepower and slick tyres. And a nice hotel, too, instead of dossing in the back of the ute.

'It was all pretty exciting. I found the FZR quite an easy thing to ride compared to a production bike because it seemed to do everything you wanted.'

The ride that changed everything – celebrating with Super Angel after grabbing third at the '87 Sugo F1 world round. (Doohan archive)

He did indeed make it look easy – fifth overall in his first Superbike ride.

Another Yamaha cup win on the TZR, then off to Japan and into the big time. Kind of. The Yamaha FZR he shared with fellow Aussie Rod Cox was a dog. They qualified 38th out of 50 teams and exited the race when the gearbox failed, ejecting Cox through the windscreen.

The Eight Hours scene blew Mick's mind. This was his first trip abroad since he'd been a little boy, when his parents took him to Singapore and he'd got his kicks riding the hotel lifts with Scott. Now he was right there at Suzuka, sharing a grid with Wayne Gardner, Kevin Schwantz and Wayne Rainey, the world's fastest 500 riders imported for this 8-hour slog in Japan's high summer – 35–40 degrees and 80 per cent humidity.

Back then the Eight Hours was an insane event – racing as market-led pantomime. The late-'80s Japanese racing scene was raging out of control, fuelled by an overheating economy. Team budgets for this most important of races were obscene, bolstered by the factories, desperate to raise market share with a high-profile victory, and by big business, bloated beyond reason by the consumer boom to end all consumer booms.

In the midst of life-sized corporate-liveried cartoon characters and tottering Suzuka race queens – looking more like prep-school porn stars – Mick tried to learn from the experience. In this world he was very much a beginner, anxious to acquire race knowledge any way he could, even snooping on Kenny Roberts as the king advised his riders of the hot line round Suzuka.

Beginner, maybe, but fast. Fast enough to encourage Morinaga to invite him back for the following month's Japanese round of the TT F1 world championship at Sugo. Once again, the

On the ill-fated FZR at the '87 Suzuka Eight Hours. The bike broke, but Mick's riding impressed the Japanese. (Koichi Ohtani)

entry list looked serious.

'It was like "Wow', I'm gonna be in a race with Joey Dunlop" [famed Irish street circuit racer].' He was shocked when he out-qualified the established names, and amazed when he finished the race third behind winner Magee, who'd followed him spellbound in practice. 'Mick was going through the hairpin and flip-flop doing everything absolutely right, the same every lap, and Right On The F*****g Limit. That's when I knew he could ride – he was a definite gun.'

Mick remembers Sugo for different reasons. 'I got a wedge of prize money, paid on the day – how good was that!' Now he was really getting to like this racing business. Earlier that year he had quit his job, convinced he could at least scrape a living by riding bikes. Pretty soon Colleen would be finding bundles of prize money stuffed around his bedroom at home.

He had two further appointments with Super Angel: the end-of-season Fuji F1 event, aboard the same FZR Superbike he'd used at Sugo, and the Castrol Six Hour proddie race at Oran Park, sharing an FZR1000 with John Pace (a former GP privateer). He was fifth at fog-bound Fuji, behind four factory F1 bikes led by Schwantz, Dowson and Magee. There were nine factory bikes behind him.

At Oran Park he led from Dowson until his motor broke. 'That's the race he really started standing out and making waves with us guys,' recalls Phillis. 'He was on the gas, riding like there was no tomorrow, but he was still a hippie.'

Following another guest ride for Marlboro Yamaha at the Lakeside Swann round in December, Willing offered him a full-time ride for '88. The next day he was back home and in court – for giving an off-duty cop the finger while pulling a wheelie. Almost a factory rider and still a high-street hoon. Endearing.

Mick's career had now started its wild

The jet-set, headache lifestyle: heading home with a hangover after another international ride, late '87. (Doohan archive)

acceleration curve: in less than five months he'd gone from 250 proddie head-banger to official Superbike rider. Another ten months and he'd signed his first 500 contract.

During this period Willing's knowledge and experience would play a crucial role. Proddie racing hadn't taught Mick much about bike set-up, since streetbikes don't allow wide-ranging adjustments. Not that Willing wanted to blind him with science. Like fellow Aussie Jerry Burgess, who would later fettle Mick's 500s, his approach was straightforward: don't try and reinvent the wheel, just get the job done.

'I had no idea – Warren helped me understand what I needed. I'd just tell him what the bike was doing and he'd get it working. Since then I've never tried to out-smart myself with bike set-up – I just relay what's going on. I can give the guys an idea what the bike is doing

250 proddie racing was always madly close – the perfect arena to hone an aggressive edge. (Lou Martin)

and what it needs, but if you get into "two clicks off that and a smidge off this", you start to out-smart yourself.'

Of course, Mick didn't come to the party empty-handed. He would combine everything he had learned on the dirt and in proddie racing, mixing it up to create a style that would dominate the world's premier race series for over half a decade.

The art of rear-wheel steering had come into road racing during the late '70s, fetched over from the US dirt ovals. The Americans subordinated everything to the all-important corner exit, since momentum gained there is maintained all the way down the next straight.

Confined by poor chassis and tyre performance, they knew of only one way to make those fast corner exits: force the rear tyre beyond its limit of adhesion, get it spinnin' and smokin', 'cookin' up a barbecue', as Mick likes to call it.

Mick could do all that stuff. He just rewrote the first half of the Yanks' mantra – 'In slow, out fast' – shifting the emphasis from the rear tyre to both tyres, and trading 'in slow' for mightily fast corner-entry and mid-corner speed.

Phillis: 'He used to tail slide everywhere, but we all used to do that shit in Australia. Proddie bikes taught guys like Mick and me to race. You had to ride through the corners faster, drift both ends so you got the maximum out of both tyres. He's still got that rolling speed that most other guys don't have on 500s. They just stop it, turn it and gas it.'

chapter four

Into the feeding frenzy

Just look at our young hero now: the simple Gold Coast lifestyle is about to recede, to be replaced by a corporate-financed, high-stress roller coaster ride to international fame and fortune. He doesn't know it yet, but the eyes of the world are already upon him.

Mick lined up for the 1988 season with his first real contract: a one-year deal with the Marlboro Yamaha Dealer squad alongside Michael Dowson.

Duties: Australian Endurance series (later renamed the Superbike series) aboard FZR750s, plus irregular Formula One outings for the Yamaha factory in Japan, aboard YZF750s. He was a real racer on a real salary. He could hardy believe it. And he was still on the juice.

Winning came easy in '88, almost too easy: Marlboro men Mick and Dowson celebrate their victory in the Arai 500km race at Bathurst. (John Pryke)

Mick rode his FZR750 harder than anyone else knew how in '88. But he still missed out on the Aussie Superbike crown. (Lou Martin)

'My lifestyle probably wasn't the ideal guideline for a racer: I was still on the beer, podgy and puffy-eyed. It wasn't a big thing to have a few beers the night before a race – I was young and it still hadn't really dawned on me what was happening. I was taking racing a bit more seriously but it was still only a laugh. I didn't realise how far I was going to go – I hadn't even thought about 500s.'

Booze and babes were still a real theme. Jonno MacGillivray remembers one particular nightlife incident. 'It was at the Tunnel Club in Surfers and I think it may have involved a girl…Mick got into a heated discussion with this guy and I ended up getting punched and thrown out of the club. While I was lying there gathering my thoughts another body landed on top of me. It was Mick.

He had a classic shiner and he was racing a couple of days later. We told everyone he'd been hit by a jet-ski.'

Mick was having too much fun all round: 'I was just blown away by the whole thing: me and my mates would look in magazines and reckon how trick it'd be to ride one of those factory Superbikes. And here I was. John Pace knew the lifestyle I was living and got me training before the season started. It was the first time I'd done any and it didn't last long.'

Not to worry, he was still racing on pure talent, and for the moment that would be enough. His main rivals for the Superbike crown were expected to be Dowson and two gritty, craggy-faced veterans: Kawasaki's Rob Phillis and Honda's Mal Campbell. The six-round championship would be tough, for there were few national race scenes as viciously competitive. Australia produced a special breed of racer in those days: super-fast and ultra-macho, the 'rostrum or hospital' mentality. Guys like Dowson, Phillis and Campbell all proved themselves in world championship racing at some stage in their careers. Mick wouldn't find the series a pushover.

But he was fast, mightily fast. 'He put the fear of God into people,' remembers Dowson. 'You always knew he'd go quicker every time he rode the bike. So even if you were faster in qualifying you wouldn't sleep well Saturday night, because you knew he'd be faster tomorrow.'

He was particularly adept at the front-tyre drift, the true mark of a master, since the edge of disaster is far, far narrower than a rear-end slide and rescue bids are unreliable. When Mick went to GPs he would be marked out not by his sideways corner exits, but by the way he shunted his NSR into turns, with such shocking violence and speed he must surely crash. Dowson again: 'When we raced together he ran softer-compound front tyres because he didn't mind a bit of front-end push, whereas I was probably a bit of a woos and didn't like it. He was able to ride through problems other guys couldn't.'

Luckless as ever, Dowson broke a wrist

in pre-season testing, and the race for the title fell to Mick and Phillis. First round was at Sandown Park, Victoria, another track Mick had never seen before. He turned up, qualified on the front row and ran away with the race.

'Again, it was "Wow!". Warren seemed pretty happy and things seemed to be going to plan.' At least until the racing moved to Baskerville, Tasmania, where Mick crashed out of the lead. Phillis won the race and the next round, then fell at Adelaide, swinging the advantage back to Mick, until his FZR motor broke a few laps later. The battle raged all season, with Mick jetting off here and there to pursue his growing international commitments. By the end of the series he had won seven of the 11 races, but old-man Phillis took the crown on his GPX750.

Phillis – nine years Mick's senior and a tough bastard on any day – found he had few answers to the young upstart from the Gold Coast. They both have distinct

Mick's first 100 per cent factory race bike, the YZF750 he shared with Tadahiko Taira at the '88 Eight Hours. Once again his speed stunned Yamaha bosses. (Koichi Ohtani)

memories of that year's Easter Bathurst meet, when they went head-to-head in the waterlogged 1000cc event, both men aboard Superbikes.

'Rob thought I was mad. He was probably the age I am now, while I was pretty young and loose – I was passing him through the fast turns over the mountain. I got so sideways one lap that he could read all the names on my fairing.'

Phillis was shaken by the youngster's determination around the wall-lined circuit: 'I thought he was willing to die to win that race. Bathurst is such a dangerous track – I'd lost three or four mates there. It was pissing rain and he rode unreal – I just wasn't prepared to go that far. But he rode faultlessly; he didn't do anything stupid. I still thought he was crazy, though.'

I thought he was willing to die to win that race

In June Warren packed Mick off to Europe – Assen, to be precise – so he could show his face to the GP paddock. By now people surely had to be interested. Mick arrived at Yamaha Europe's Amsterdam HQ and headed into the city's infamous centre with Team Roberts computer guru Tom O'Kane. It was to be a surprising introduction to the Big Bad World.

'We were having a few drinks, carrying on, and everyone was trying to sell us drugs and other stuff. Tom ends up telling this guy to f**k off and the guy pulls out a pretty serious looking gun. I didn't know what make it was, but it was machine-gun style and the guy puts it in Tom's stomach. We got to walk away very slowly. That was my main memory of the trip.'

While at Assen Mick slept on the couch in Kevin Magee's motorhome, had his hair cut by Rainey's mom and made contact with Giacomo Agostini (then chief of Yamaha's number one 500 team)

and Suzuki race boss Mitsuo Itoh. But no one from Honda.

Then back to Australia for more national racing and on to Suzuka for the Eight Hours – his first ride on a 100 per cent hand-made factory F1 machine, a YZF750 shared with Japanese race god Tadahiko Taira. The pair were running third with 15 minutes to go when the engine stopped. No result, but Yamaha chiefs liked what they saw and he was invited to race the YZF again at the end-of-season Sugo and Fuji internationals.

Suzuka was the first time I came across Mick. We met at the hairpin during final qualifying, me on a private RC30, him on his factory tool. He swept through at warp speed, slammed the bike on its side, heaved it upright and jumped on the throttle, smoking the rear tyre out to the kerb as he burned a thick arc of rubber on the tarmac. From there he kept the rear spinning, steering the bike by weighting each footrest. Through the next fourth-gear right-hander he was still smokin' that tyre. Jesus H. Christ, I'd never seen anything like it.

A month later he returned to Japan for a landmark event – the Sugo round of the new World Superbike Championship on 28 August. By now Mick was well aware of his talent. He had won a lot of races at home, his confidence was swelling and he knew that Sugo was a crucial race – a chance to show what he could do right under the eyes of the factory race overlords. The pressure was on, and it showed.

'I got a bit cocky at Sugo, probably because I'd been winning so much at home – that's another reason why I never get too confident nowadays. I crashed a couple of times in qualifying and Warren was at me: "What are you doing? You've got to settle down."'

Dowson remembers Willing calling

The stress wrinkles are yet to come but the grey hairs are already on their way. (John Pryke)

Oran Park World Superbike, September '88 – Mick wasted the championship regulars and suddenly everyone wanted him in 500 GPs. (Lou Martin)

him at home that weekend. 'Warren was pissed off big time. Mick had trashed two bikes, just going quicker and quicker and quicker until he crashed. The factory guys were concerned, and I thought, "Great! The guy isn't so good after all."'

Willing's advice fell on deaf ears. Mick tore away at the start of the wet first race, took the lead and crashed through the

fast sweeper before the chicane. He remounted, fought his way back to third. And fell again. Next time out he heeded Willing's wise words and swept to an 8-second victory. He was that good, after all.

Now the offers started coming. Suzuki made the first approach through its former world champ Barry Sheene, now a Gold Coast neighbour. Sheene told Mick that Suzuki wanted him to partner Schwantz in its 1989 Pepsi-backed 500 outfit. Sheene's line of chat must have been convincing, for Mick signed a letter of intent.

'It wasn't something I wanted to do but Sheeney was pushing me into it. Then Wayne Gardner called not long after that. He asked me if I had any interest in going 500s because Honda were interested in me.'

Honda wanted Mick badly. Digger Gardner had won the title aboard an NSR in 1987 but wasn't getting any younger. The factory needed to introduce new blood to its 500 ranks.

Honda flew some Honda Racing Corporation personnel to the next round of the World Superbike series at Oran Park on 25 September, where Mick destroyed the opposition. He beat team-mate Dowson in both races by over 20 seconds, with the series full-timers over half a minute down. He still rates those two rides with his best GP races. Now Honda wanted him even more, and told him so during a meeting in Melbourne a few days later.

In October the talks moved to Japan where Mick was to race the YZF at Sugo and Fuji. He ruled Sugo and met up with Eddie Lawson, the reigning 500 champ, who, unbeknown to Mick, was struggling to agree terms with Yamaha for 1989. The Californian was one of Mick's heroes, a thinking man's racer, smooth as you like, hence the nickname Steady Eddie. He was *the* racer's racer, and the rider upon whom Mick would model himself.

'I didn't know Eddie but he was a super-hero to me – it was him and Freddie [Spencer] who I was into when I got interested in road racing. I tried to pick his brains about what I should do. He said Suzuki wasn't the way to go and that if he was me, he'd jump on the Honda. That night we went out and got pretty drunk. We ended up breaking into a go-kart circuit and driving around holding torches.'

From there he headed to Yamaha's Iwata HQ for contract talks. The factory was obviously keen to hold on to its new talent, although Mick was dismayed to learn that he was expected to stay on four-strokes in '89. Nevertheless he was allowed his first ever 500 ride at Yamaha's Fukuroi test track. It turned out to be a typical introduction to the joys of 500 racing.

'I tested a factory Superbike, then the 500. I was enjoying myself – wheelspinning out of the chicane on to the back straight. I'd already gone as quick as Taira's lap record and I was trying to get a good drive and a good slide out of the chicane.'

As Mick changed direction through the right-left, lifting himself off the seat to shift his body weight and pressure the footpegs, while also steering with his hands, he involuntarily gave the YZR more throttle. The combined effect of dialling in extra horsepower while removing weight from the rear tyre was instant and inevitable: 'The thing spun up and threw me off big time. That's when I realised 500s are a bit different.'

Limping badly, Mick said goodbye to Yamaha and took the Shinkansen to Tokyo where he was met by HRC people and escorted to their mightily impressive workshops at Asaka. Erv Kanemoto was there, plus Gardner's crew chief Jerry Burgess. No doubt Honda hoped that HRC's facilities – light years ahead of Yamaha's race shop – would seduce Mick, and they did.

'The whole HRC thing was a wow, and I'd always had the feeling that Honda would be the place to go. The problem with Yamaha was that they had so many riders: Lawson, Magee, Rainey, Sarron – pretty much anyone who was anyone in 500s was on a Yamaha, plus they had

The best way forward seemed to be with Honda

Chasing hard bastard Phillis at Winton. Mick won most of the '88 Aussie Superbike rounds, but Phillis won the title on his Kawasaki GPX. (Lou Martin)

guys like Kocinski coming up. Suzuki had Schwantz and he was the same age as me, while Honda had WG, six years older than me. I was looking at the future and the best way forward seemed to be with Honda.'

First of all, though, he wanted out of the Suzuki deal.

'A letter of intent is fairly binding, but if you don't want to ride for somebody it's difficult for them to force you to ride. Barry came up with this idea: he told them I'd got a load of superstitions about riding Suzukis. They must've been shaking their heads, going "This guy's weird, best get rid of him".'

From Asaka, Mick travelled to Fuji where he won again on the YZF, while continuing negotiations with both factories. Jonno had flown over from Australia a few days earlier to assist in the final dealings. As is usual in racing – indeed in any hard-line business – the young hotshot and his manager were trying to raise the stakes by playing the two sides against each other.

'I admit I didn't have much of an idea of what I was doing back then – but we weren't naive,' remembers Jonno. 'We'd been approached by a lot of teams, so we knew Mick was hot property and we were never backward in asking for what we wanted. We couldn't reach agreement with Yamaha, then we met with Honda at Fuji, in a caravan on the evening before the race. We decided what we

wanted before we went in and Honda gave us what we wanted.'

The caravan agreement covered two years – to give Mick a chance to get acquainted with a 500 and the world championship circuits – and the dollars sounded good.

In the meantime Yamaha had offered a 500 ride, in a one-man factory team outside the existing outfits run by Agostini, Kenny Roberts and Yamaha Motor France. They'd not done that for anyone since Roberts's racing days, but it was too late: Mick had made up his mind to join the Rothmans-backed Honda factory crew alongside Gardner, the feisty New South Welshman who always seemed to ride on a wing and a prayer. The next day Honda dropped its bomb-shell – that Lawson would also ride a

Honda, also in Rothmans colours, but in a satellite team run by Erv Kanemoto. Gardner – loyal Honda servant for years – was outraged that his employers had signed his bitter rival. But there was nothing he could do about it.

With his immediate future decided, Mick jetted back home to complete his final duties for Marlboro Yamaha: the Winton round of the Aussie Superbikes championship and the 1988 Swann Insurance series.

Honda sent Jerry Burgess down to Winton to keep an eye on its new boy. JB had already been told that he would be looking after Mick in '89, after spending the past three years heading Gardner's crew and winning the '87 500 title. An affable, sanguine, down-to-earth Adelaide man who raced Down Under

ABOVE LEFT: *Mick, Dowson and Mal Campbell at the Swann series, November '88. Mick had the title in the bag, until it all went wrong for the final race.* (Lou Martin)

ABOVE RIGHT: *Mick's two mentors: Honda's Jerry Burgess (right) chats with Yamaha's Warren Willing at Winton, late '88.* (Lou Martin)

before travelling to Europe to spanner for Randy Mamola, Ron Haslam and Freddie Spencer, Burgess wasn't convinced at first. But pretty soon he was. According to Dowson, Burgess was amazed by his new charge: 'JB had been around long enough to see this guy was a bit different; he hooked on to him and

wasn't going to let him go. He was like a kid at Christmas.'

The six-race Swann series started at Oran Park, moved to Lakeside and ended at the recently re-opened Phillip Island circuit in southernmost Victoria. Mick led on points going into the final race, then his clutch blew on the grid.

'I later found out the bike wouldn't have finished the race anyway, because the guys hadn't put in enough fuel [an allegation vehemently denied by the team]. Yamaha wanted Dowson to win the series because they knew I was going to Honda. That left a bitter taste in my mouth.'

Goodbye Yamaha, hello Honda.

chapter five

Fire in his belly, pain in his soul

Mick was a rocket man – in the space of 18 months he'd gone from 250 proddie headbanger to 500 GP rider, from 40 horsepower to 180 – whoa!

Now he had almost two months off before his first test on Honda's NSR500 – a chance to get into some serious training. Yeah, right: 'If anything I was partying harder towards the end of '88, because everything was coming so easy.'

Not for much longer, mate.

His first appointment with the notorious NSR was set for Suzuka in early January – mid-winter in Japan, not an ideal moment to make your acquaintance with the world's most evil race bike.

The evil sonofabitch '89 NSR. Probably the nastiest, scariest race bike ever built – 310kph and it didn't steer or stop. (Koichi Ohtani)

JAPAN, SUZUK

With Gardner at Suzuka, March '89: already looking in different directions. (Gold & Goose)

'It was pretty cold, I was riding the '88 NSR, which wasn't real good, and the Fukuroi thing happened again. I gave it a fistful going through the esses and as I shifted my weight from right to left the rear just lit up. The thing had me off the side so I was hanging on to the handlebars with both knees dragging on the ground. I ran off the track and slammed into one of the big rubber bales they use at Suzuka. My face ended up in the dirt while the bike got me in the back of the head. The impact broke my helmet open.

'That was my first wake-up call. It was like, "Wow! So they call this a motorcycle do they?" I realised then that the Honda wasn't like the Yamaha. The Yamaha was just another motorcycle, whereas the Honda definitely wasn't. I could see why WG was always getting spat off.'

Next time out in Brazil Mick got to ride the '89 NSR, the bike Lawson would later describe thus: 'Riding the Honda was like death – every time you flicked into a turn you didn't know if you'd make it out.'

The '89 model was an improvement but still a real beast. HRC had changed the firing order, from an even 90 degrees to a semi-big-bang 180 degrees, to calm the V4's maniacal power delivery. By the end of the Goiania session he was less than a second slower than Gardner. 'I was still wary of the thing, but I thought my times weren't too bad. It was pretty hot down there so the racetrack had some feel – I could feel what the rear was doing.'

HRC's final pre-season outings at Phillip Island and Suzuka were backward steps. Mick was considerably slower

ABOVE RIGHT: *Hooking into it at Phillip Island and grinding his knee-slider to atoms. His left hand was next.* (Gold & Goose)

RIGHT: *Grimly hanging on, Mick nails the NSR at Misano.* (Gold & Goose)

than Gardner and Lawson in Australia and he fell again at Suzuka. But all this was only a mildly painful overture to a horribly gory first 500 season that would force him to ask *that* question for the first time: is it all worth it?

By the time he got back to Suzuka for the season-opening Japanese GP he was already having to wise up.

'I wasn't 100 per cent happy with the way things were going and I didn't know whether it was me or the bike. I wasn't getting a lot of feel and I'd been thrown down the road a few times. I was already thinking I've got to change the way I do things. I was feeling a bit cocky after the past couple of years. I probably wasn't preparing myself in the best way to go racing. I wasn't 100 per cent dedicated.'

They became such mates the paddock named them 'the sisters'

Mick may not have been up to speed on fitness but he did look deadly cool when he rolled up for his 500 debut at Suzuka. He had a new helmet design: a shock of red and blue ziggy-zag lines streaking across his Arai, like he'd just got into acid house. You might've known it though – this was MacGillivray again, trying to make his man stand out from the crowd.

'Everyone had symmetrical helmet designs so we wanted to get away from that,' Jonno recalls. 'I went down the local library to look at some pop art books and came across a painting by Jackson Pollock [famed abstract expressionist painter who died in '56]. My brother is a graphic artist so I got him to make it look good on a helmet.'

Flash lid or not, The Debut didn't go great. Sixth in qualifying was good, but his crankshaft broke eight laps into the race.

Back home for round two and the first ever Australian GP, at Phillip Island.

Mick was up there doing his bit for pre-race publicity with fellow Aussies Gardner and Magee. Both were GP winners, but Mick was just a raw novice, out to do his best in front of an expectant home crowd. Instead, things just got worse.

During Friday afternoon qualifying he crashed at Southern Loop, a sweeping left-hander that runs close to the Island's coastline, overlooking the Bass Strait to Tasmania.

'I got my hand caught under the handlebar and ground away the little finger and the finger beside that. I could see the bone, with gravel rash in it, and the tendon had been torn away.

'Right then, I was thinking, what the hell am I doing here? Maybe I'm in a bit too deep. I realised I was on to a completely different playing field where everyone was quick and strong, not just for one lap but the whole way through. I really hadn't been hurt up until then – I'd got away with a lot of stuff. I thought about the whole deal and decided to keep going.'

That day Mick made an acquaintance that would serve him well a few years down the line – GP medic Dr Claudio Costa patched up his hand. Skin grafts were advised but they would sideline him for several races. He declined and had some stitches removed on Sunday morning so he could race. Using a specially adapted clutch lever, and without the comfort of pain-killers, he winced his way to eighth.

En route from Japan, Lawson had stayed *chez* Mick at Surfers; now Eddie returned the compliment, inviting his new friend to Lake Havasu during the break between Phillip Island and the US round at Laguna Seca.

It seemed only natural that Mick and Eddie should strike up a friendship.

Jet-skiing had made Mick strong, but not strong enough for a 500. (John Pryke)

They were similar characters, and similar racers: reserved in public, fun-loving at home, both immensely talented, dedicated riders who hate the bullshit that goes with racing. And there was plenty Mick could learn from Eddie – just about all he needed to know, if the American was willing. For his part, Eddie could use the partnership to destabilise arch-rival Gardner. They became such inseparable mates that the paddock nicknamed them 'the sisters'.

There was also the question of Mick's lack of friendship with Gardner, who was anxious to protect his position as Australia's number one hero. Kevin Magee had felt the same chill winds from WG when he got into GPs in '88; now it was Mick's turn.

'I guess WG felt threatened. He didn't like the idea of other Australians coming through – he wanted to be the home-town hero. I liked Eddie because he was pretty laid back – he wasn't a racer when he was away from the racetrack, while

'The sisters' in action: Eddie Lawson and Mick were constant companions in '89. (Gold & Goose)

Wayne was. He was always reminding you he'd been world champion.'

On Lake Havasu the sisters mucked about in Eddie's boat, while Mick watched his hand reconstruct itself. By Laguna time the wound was 'just starting to grow a film of meat'.

Laguna didn't prove to be a turning point. The Californian track magnified the NSR's deficiencies and Gardner ran into Mick during practice, knocking him to the ground and ripping the virgin flesh from his mangled left hand. Sadly, that wasn't the worst of Laguna '89. Rainey won, Schwantz got second and Lawson took third just ahead of Magee, who vented his frustration with a slow-down lap burn-out. GP newcomer Bubba Shobert rode into the stationary Yamaha and never raced again.

Mick finished eighth then headed to Europe for the Spanish GP at Jerez. The hand was still a mess – bad enough to put a couple of journalists off their lunch as they watched Mick get ready for qualifying. He prepared the wound for each outing with a protective smearing of gelatine and a surgical glove. And pretty

much every outing seemed to be an appointment with the guard rail. This time he lasted three laps.

'I'd been trying different things in qualifying and on the fourth lap of the race I changed up another gear through the fast rights behind the paddock. The thing just spun up and sent me straight into the hay bales. That didn't do the hand any favours.'

The long drive to Misano in Italy for round three was his first trip across Europe in his new motorhome. Plenty of time for thinking. 'First time I ever met Eddie I remember him saying a lot of people can get on a 500 and go fast straight away. Then they have one crash, two crashes, three crashes and they take a big backward step. I've never heard a truer word.

'My confidence had been knocked about and I actually feared hopping on the motorcycle. Every time I heard the boys revving it up in the pits, it was like, "Oh my God, have I really got to throw a leg over this thing?"'

As it happened, Misano didn't even count. Mick joined a riders' strike when rain made the patchwork racetrack too treacherous. Hockenheim and its Honda lanes were next. The German track suited the NSR well because it's all straights and few corners. Mick got third behind title duellists Rainey and Lawson: 'That was a little bit of brightness. I was up there on the podium thinking that Rob McElnea [burly British 500 rider and a new friend] has raced all his career and never made the top three, so at least I've got a podium if I do nothing else.'

Then a bit of fun. Mick, Eddie, Schwantz and Mamola blagged a bunch of Porsches and thrashed them down to the Salzburgring. They managed several minor accidents; Eddie ended up sticking his in a ditch. Oh, how they laughed.

He was coping well with the lifestyle upheaval, the undoing of so many other Bright Young Things new to the European scene. 'Everything was foreign but I'd never been much of a home boy since my father died – I was always out and about, so I didn't feel that uncomfortable in Europe.' Nevertheless he quickly established himself a base in Monaco: relatively central for European races and by the sea.

By now his furious efforts on the NSR were starting to attract notice and comment, and not all of it flattering. There were people in the paddock who thought he was trying too hard, that his riding style was just too wild, that he was going to get himself hurt. The little-known nickname 'Dead by June Doohan' started doing the rounds in the press room.

On 4 June (his 24th birthday) Mick raced at the Salzburgring for the first time. There's no other GP circuit like it: the track rushes up and down an alpine valley in the shadow of rocky crags and greener-than-green alpine pastures, and it's shrouded in Armco. Picturesque, yet deadly.

My confidence was knocked – I actually feared riding the 500 now

'It was a daunting place. The bike wasn't steering too well and I ran off the track. I was heading for the wall thinking, "Here goes – it's all going to end on the same day I was born."' He stayed on this time and was happy to finish eighth again.

That night he celebrated his survival with a few beers, or maybe more – at least that's the way Rainey remembers it: 'Mick was shit-faced; he had my Marlboro jacket on and he was after my sister. He was always in the thick of parties.' These were the dying days of paddock hedonism. GP racing was about to get far too serious for all that – the sponsor's dollar would grow to demand total dedication. 'Back then we just wanted to know who's motorhome we'd be partying in on Sunday night. Back in Australia we'd be out all night before a race. It was a lot of fun back then.'

Distractions aside, at least Honda was working to improve the NSR. Mick received a revised chassis in Austria, the second of four that he would run during the year. Lawson meanwhile used no fewer than 11 different chassis in his ultimately successful battle to beat Rainey to the title.

Deep inside I knew that talent wasn't enough – I had to focus

'The main thing was you couldn't feel the front tyre until it was tucked and you couldn't feel the rear until it was way out there. The balance of the thing was all wrong.' And there was worse.

'Back in those days HRC used to make everything from the handlebar grips to the footpegs, the brakes too, and they were so bad. At Phillip Island the bike would spread the callipers through the fast turns before Lukey Heights; you'd have to pump the brakes every lap. I kept telling JB that Yamaha streetbikes don't do that. I told him Yamaha streetbikes handle better than Honda race bikes, and he just said, "This isn't a streetbike or a Superbike, this is a 500 and this is the way it is." I thought fair enough, maybe it is. And he kept referring to WG all the time: WG this, WG that, which was fine because I was the new boy.'

Team morale was collapsing: Mick was in awe of the bike and his crew was getting fed up with the crashes and lack of results. Perhaps he really wasn't ready for 500 GPs; doubts began to set in, doubts, doubts, doubts.

Assen, however, *was* a turning point:

An age of heroes: Rainey (3), Schwantz (34), Lawson (1), Spencer (19), Kocinski (behind Spencer) and Mick charge out of La Source hairpin at Spa '89. (Gold & Goose)

'JB was doing his WG bit and I spat the dummy: do I look like WG? Are my initials WG? From that day we got on better, I think he realised there's a bit of fire in this kid so maybe he had to work towards what I wanted.'

Looking back at that crash-happy first season JB is more complimentary, now he's able to pinpoint the earliest signs of later greatness. He says Mick conformed to that old racing adage: if you're fast and crash a lot, don't worry, you can learn to stop crashing but you can't learn to be fast. Speed is either in you or it isn't.

From Assen to Spa in Belgium, another fast, daunting, Armco-lined racetrack. And another fast, daunting crash, this time when 500 first-timer John Kocinski rode into him. 'By now I'd just lost confidence in the whole show. I knew Yamaha had a 500 that felt like a motorcycle. I was thinking I'd done the wrong thing in signing with this lot.'

Honda's 500 may have been a mess but the factory's four-stroke RVF750 was the bike to beat at the Suzuka Eight Hour. Now Mick was jetting east to partner Gardner in the world's biggest motorcycle race aboard an RVF. He'd already smashed the four-stroke lap record in testing. This might just turn his season around.

In some ways it did, in some ways it didn't. In withering, steamy conditions Mick and Gardner smoked everyone, including Yamaha's Rainey and Magee (also taking a break from their day jobs – riding 500s for the Lucky Strike Team Roberts outfit). With 3 hours to go they held a comfortable lead…

'Then I came up to lap Phillis on one of the factory Kawasakis – I was going round the outside when he picked his bike up and the exhaust caught the little

Helmet by Jackson Pollock, hand wrecked by Phillip Island, Laguna and Jerez. The surgical glove protects his mangled fingers. (Gold & Goose)

finger on my left hand. I crashed and the finger got chopped off below the top knuckle – I found the top bit still in the glove.'

Japanese surgeons reattached the stub with a couple of pins and Mick flew home to Australia where a specialist tidied things up (minus the middle knuckle). In some ways it would've been easier to amputate the whole finger; certainly he would have been able to return to racing sooner. But right now he needed a rest.

'I'd never really raced under any pressure before '89 and I was getting worried; I was wondering what the team was thinking of me. This was the real wake-up call. I needed to change my lifestyle – I was all right to race a 500 for eight laps, but after that I'd start to fade.

'I was having a major crisis in myself. I decided I'd give racing 100 per cent, so I'd either make a career of it, or I'd know I'm not good enough. I stayed with mum and Ken back on the Gold Coast and that's when the fitness thing really started. I ran every day to lose the weight I'd been carrying from my party years. Deep inside I knew talent wasn't enough – I had to make some sacrifices. I'd still be able to party after racing. When my father died I went off in a different direction – I wasn't riding so much, just partying. I had to go back, get some focus.'

Mick knew the alternatives to racing – he'd already tried making a living from good, honest back-breaking work: 'I realised how hard it is to earn a dollar by digging holes, so I know what a dollar is worth.'

There were, however, good things to be remembered from Suzuka. 'I'd shown myself I could do it on a four-stroke – not a problem. To me Rainey was the man on a 500 and I'd been pulling away from

And you should've seen his finger… Mick's RVF750 stands wrecked at the Suzuka Eight Hour, July '89. (Gold & Goose)

him and I'd been faster than Gardner and Magee too. It was some light at the end of a long, dark tunnel. I knew I could be fast when I understood a machine; I just had to come to terms with the 500.'

His return was pencilled in for the season-ending Brazilian GP in mid-September, eight weeks after the Eight Hours. During that time Mick turned his lifestyle upside down. He would never be the same again, at least not during his race career. No booze (well, maybe the occasional beer), no burgers, just running, running, running, with the Lucky Strike roundel on Rainey's leathers in his mind's eye. Rainey had only come into 500s the previous year but was already

Back from his Eight Hour injury for the Brazilian season finale, Mick is all crossed up but now he's got the NSR tamed. (Gold & Goose)

battling with Lawson for the title. Super-aggressive, a master of tail-happy riding and unerringly consistent, Mick knew he'd be the man to beat. 'He was the guy I was focusing on, he was the man of the moment.'

Meaner and plenty leaner, Mick flew to Goiania, went for a jog and nearly took the top off that oh-so-horrible little finger. 'The pins were still sticking out the top and I caught them in my shorts when I got on a bit of a sprint. It pulled the end of the finger half off; I didn't know whether to pull it right off or what. It stayed loose for the rest of that weekend.' Refusing pain-killers, he went out to play.

No one else knew what this race meant to Mick. Bloodied and battered, he had come close to buckling under the strain of his first 500 season. Now he was back, psychologically transformed and

physically stronger than ever, wobbly little finger aside.

The NSR had bitten him many times too often in '89; now he desperately needed to prove to himself that he could tame the beast. He did so in spectacular fashion, executing wild, smokin' power-slides during practice. No one had ever managed that kind of thing with Michelin's unforgiving slicks and survived. Here was proof that ol' Dead by June could ride a bit.

'I was doing it because it was fun, but also because I could feel where the bike was at when it was sideways. At last I was getting some feel.'

Schwantz won the race, while Eddie took second to clinch the title from Rainey. Mick was next in fourth. Not as good as third in Germany, but actually much better. 'I'd conquered another psychological barrier by beating everyone except the top three. It felt good and it meant more than Hockenheim, because Goiania isn't all straights. I also beat Gardner and that was a big motivation for me.'

He had completed his first GP season ninth overall, despite missing three races. But the year was not over yet. Unfortunately. From Goiania he headed north to Eddie's mansion in Upland, just hanging out and dirt riding. Then back home to have that troublesome little pinkie screwed together once and for all. Then to Suzuka in early December – mid-winter in Japan and freezing cold.

'It was 5pm and I had to do a few more laps to test some more stuff. This was in the days before tyre warmers, and coming out of turn one the thing spun up in a straight line as I changed into second. It spat me over the bars and I broke my left arm between the shoulder and the elbow – I could feel the bones grinding together.'

Mick flew home to have the bone plated and told Honda that he would never again test in Japan between November and March. 'Once I was home, I was just happy the year was over.'

He really had to prove that he could tame the beast

A view to the crown

In several ways Mick had been lucky to survive 1989. Physically, psychologically, emotionally he'd had a terrible time. But as they say in racing, if it don't kill ya, it'll make ya stronger. And it did.

He went into 1990 knowing what to expect. After his grisly Eight Hour accident he had made a pivotal career decision: sacrifice everything to make the grade or give up and get out. A couple of beers on New Year's Eve and he was into training for his second 500 season: training, training, training.

I began to understand the 500, how to ride it properly

That fourth place in Brazil the previous September had been a crucial psychological turning point, but Mick was still rather scared of the NSR, and his broken left arm was still weak, delaying his first tests until early February.

'I wasn't looking forward to hopping on the bike, although at least I knew what I was in for. The 1990 NSR looked a lot more pleasant, but once you rode it you realised it wasn't a great deal different. It still had that hereditary understeer, and that's when the single-crank theory came up.'

The single-crank theory supposed that the NSR's wayward handling was due to the engine, not the chassis. While rival V4s – Suzuki, Yamaha and Cagiva – ran counter-rotating twin crankshafts, the NSR used a single crank. Honda's design offered less friction losses and therefore more horsepower, but the torque reaction of the single crank was reckoned to lift the front wheel, sending it off line at every corner.

With a season's 500 experience behind him, Mick now wanted the opportunity to offer his own input into HRC's development programme. He had his own ideas about solving the NSR's handling woes, but most of all he wanted some decent brakes. Kind of a priority on something that can run 310kph.

'The bike still had Honda brakes and the callipers would spread, so I was telling HRC they should try Brembo. They just said it was their policy to build the whole machine.' Two massive accidents would soon change that policy.

Suzuka once again ushered in a new

Over the hill at Laguna – 260kph and both tyres just skimming the tarmac. No run-off either. (Lou Martin)

season with its own special atmosphere: foreboding, a chill of apprehension, ever so slightly scary. And the race heralded the Rainey/Team Roberts domination that would become the theme of the year. With new backers Marlboro, Kenny Roberts had assembled his 'Evil Empire', the best road race team ever: Rainey and reigning champ Lawson (who had defected from Honda back to Yamaha), plus big-talkin' young punk John Kocinski on a 250. And they'd switched to Michelin too. Suzuki had picked up Roberts's cast-offs – the Lucky Strike sponsorship and Magee as team-mate to Schwantz, the wildly talented Texan whose past, present and future always seemed to lie in the hay bales. Rothmans Honda were back to two men: Mick and WG, although HRC also leased 'production' NSRs to double-250-champ Sito Pons and Italian hothead PierFrancesco Chili.

Rainey bolted from the start leaving Mick contesting second with Gardner, Schwantz and Lawson. It was close stuff, typical of the majestic Suzuka track. Too close, in fact.

'I was having trouble with my brakes again – the lever was coming into the bar so I was pumping it. I didn't realise but the callipers were leaking fluid – HRC had made the brakes with extra-strong seals to stop them spreading, and the seals were just too stiff.'

On lap five Mick was chasing the bunch down Suzuka's long back straight. As he approached the third-gear left he went for the brakes at around 300kph, and found nothing. He grabbed another handful and the bike stood on its nose, rear wheel sailing through the air at 270-ish.

'I tipped it back down and into the turn – it was either that or run head first

There's only one way to keep a 500 pointed where you want it pointed – fight it all the way. Assen, 1990. (Gold & Goose)

into the trackside barrier. I was way too fast for the corner though – the front folded and I ran into Eddie.'

The two friends careered into the gravel trap and as the dust settled Lawson picked himself up, walked over to Mick and apologised. 'He said, "Sorry, man" – he thought he'd highsided and taken me out.'

Next stop Laguna and things were starting to come together, for Mick at least. For racing as a whole, the US GP was another nightmare event – Magee was helicoptered away in a coma, Lawson smashed a heel when his (Nissin) brakes failed at top speed, and Schwantz broke a wrist chasing winner Rainey. Mick inherited a best-ever second, albeit half a minute behind the local hero.

Jerez proved to be a real breakthrough – his first pole position. No coolness under fire in those days, though, and Mick fluffed the start. He finished fourth but made up for that with third at

After a dodgy start in '89, JB and Mick were getting on fine now, and finding the answers to the NSR's problems. (Gold & Goose)

Misano, just 8 seconds down on winner Rainey. And apart from his infamous formation highside with Chili at the Nurburgring, he was starting to put together some consistent results: third at the Salzburgring, fourth at Rijeka, Assen, Le Mans, Donington and Anderstorp, and sixth at soaking Spa. Ninth at Brno followed a first-lap tumble, his last fall of the year – compare that to '89. And in between all this, a quick diversion east for the Suzuka Eight Hour. Partnering Gardner again, this time they ran out of fuel.

'I was starting to understand the 500, how to ride it. JB was working towards what I wanted, not what WG wanted, so I was getting confident. We were getting a good combination together – the biggest problem was front-end push.'

HRC was starting to listen too. When Pons's brakes failed during pre-Jerez testing, resulting in a massive crash, Brembo callipers were ordered. And a new chassis arrived mid-season. From there JB and the crew started experimenting with castor angle, swapping the coned inserts in the NSR's steering head

as they searched for the ideal set-up. The steering geometry they came up with is pretty much identical to what Mick runs today. Interestingly, he also quit his crashing habit at this point. JB: 'Prior to that the angle was too steep for him; now the bike did what he wanted it to do.'

Mick was also working at improving other aspects of the NSR. He had started the year as number two in the Rothmans Honda team, and now believed that his results merited equal treatment. Tyres were a different problem. During 1990 Michelin offered their best 'A grade' rubber only to the chosen few: Lawson, Gardner, Schwantz and Rainey. Mick had to earn them in practice – the fastest B grader would be offered top rubber for the final session, or maybe only race-morning warm-up. A poisoned chalice. 'We used to complain a lot. You'd practice on Bs, then you'd get the good tyres, which would throw all your settings out. You'd have to re-adjust everything because you had so much more grip.

'The pecking order thing with WG started getting to me too. I was ahead on points and he still had all the trick stuff. I started asking HRC for the same gear, so I could do the best possible job for Honda. They just said, "You're young, you've got plenty of time."'

He didn't like that one bit. Young he may have been but he wasn't in the mood for hanging around, quietly awaiting his turn. So he started talking to Suzuki about riding alongside Schwantz in '91. His first two-year contract with Honda was drawing to a close, and maybe this would be a good time to leave – the RGV certainly outshone the NSR in a lot of respects. On the other hand, Mick seemed unlikely to get equal status with Suzuki golden boy Schwantz. Proof, perhaps, that he was still politically green.

Or maybe not. When Mick told HRC he'd been talking with Suzuki, things started happening; at Brno his NSR had all the trick gear. And he was on pole for

'Hungary was the turning point … now I could run with them and beat them.' Mick wins his first GP in September '90 and gets a drowning from Schwantz. (Gold & Goose)

the next race at the Hungaroring, behind the recently collapsed Iron Curtain.

'The place was bumpy and that suited me because it wasn't so much a case of set-up, and bike set-up is the game in 500s. With the bumps, you just had to ride the thing. I felt confident I could win the race, then I heard rain on the motorhome roof on Saturday night, and thought, "Shit, it isn't going to happen."'

And it nearly didn't. The old pole-position nerves struck again and he blew the start. Rainey, crowned world champion at the previous race and already a seven-time winner, got away fast and in front. That wasn't the plan at all.

Mick hunted down the Yamaha and swept ahead mid-race to win easily, his first GP success and his first triple crown: pole, victory and lap record. On the podium he looked bemused, almost embarrassed to be the centre of attention. It was a demeanour we'd get used to.

Celebrations? There were none – Mick was digging deeper and deeper into himself and was fully teetotal for 1990. He wasn't even going to let his guard slip to toast his maiden GP win. Anyway, he was high on something much more potent: adrenaline.

'Hungary was the turning point. I'd been the best of the rest and now I'd got equal equipment I could run with them and beat them. It was a fantastic moment. The adrenaline was still pumping when I arrived at Phillip Island.'

At home for the final GP of the year he was on pole again. And very fired up. The race was another classic, just like 1989, a bare-knuckle fight. He pitched back and forth with wild-man Gardner, Rainey and Schwantz. Teetering on the edge of disaster, the four men made up ground, lost it, rallied, then dropped back again. Gardner got the winning break when Schwantz went down big time at the end of the start–finish, costing the others valuable time. Mick crossed the line 0.8 down, but knew he could've won it. 'Australia was another turning point: I knew I had what it takes to be a consistent front-runner.'

He signed with HRC the next week while attending a group test session at Sydney's brand-new Eastern Creek venue. This time the numbers looked even better: a 100 per cent pay raise for 1991. Neat.

A GP salary buys proper toys: Mick and Beattie in the Eliminator. Towards the end of '90 Mick wrecked it at 150kph. (John Pryke)

The increase demonstrated Honda's growing attachment to its up-and-comer. HRC was taking him very seriously now, and when the time came to develop the 1991 NSR, it was to him that the engineers turned, not Gardner.

Initially both men travelled to Japan to commence testing a number of different chassis. 'We tested frame after frame, with different geometry, different engine positions, everything, and I found a chassis that wasn't so bad. Then HRC asked me to stay on in Japan, not WG. I guess that was a significant moment. Until then I'd just been working my way through – Wayne had been the world champion.'

Burgess could also see Mick in the ascendance. 'He knew what he wanted. No disrespect to WG, but Wayne didn't really know how a motorcycle worked,

he just wrestled it around. Honda built a good bike in '87 and WG ran away with the title, but they got way off the rails in '88 and '89 – there was heaps more power but the chassis didn't handle. Mick has had a lot to do with turning the Honda into a good motorcycle.'

More money also meant more toys – in this case an Eliminator speedboat, just like Eddie's. Powered by two 250-horse-power outboards, it could move a bit. Back home from the tests, Mick discovered that the boat also had a bit of a steering problem and flipped it at around 150kph, with a couple of friends on board.

'I went out through the side of the boat, taking an 18-foot section of hull with me. It was the week after I'd had the plate removed from the arm I broke in November '89 and I couldn't feel the arm. I was in the water but I was more worried by the smell of fuel and the sparks from the motor – they could fix the arm but I didn't want to burn to death. I got back on the boat, turned the electrics off, then started looking for people. Thankfully nobody got hurt.'

Now he was going into a new season wholly uninjured on a much-improved motorcycle and couldn't help but feel confident. He kept that very much to himself, of course, and ultimately with good reason, since there were to be other problems that would stand in his way to the crown. Nevertheless this would be the first year that he made a serious challenge for the title. From now on, *everyone* would take him seriously, very seriously indeed.

Team line-ups hadn't altered radically for the new year: Gardner, Rainey and

Schwantz stayed where they were, while 250 champ Kocinski joined Rainey on 500s at Team Roberts. Lawson – nearing retirement – succumbed to the lure of the lira and hooked up with Cagiva.

There was one crucial change for 1991, however: Michelin had announced its withdrawal from GPs in July '90, but HRC opted to run the French firm's production slicks during the new season. Team Roberts switched back to Dunlops, taking Suzuki with them. Tyres would be the story of the year.

Mick voiced his concerns about running over-the-counter rubber and, it turned out, with good reason. He did, however, start off right where he reckoned he'd be: up front but with plenty of company. Suzuka '91 was an all-time classic, a stunner of a race in an era of heroes: Mick, Schwantz, Rainey and Kocinski duking it out, burning rubber and getting kinda squirrely. Schwantz came from behind to win, two-tenths up on Mick. The Texan and the Dunlops had blundered their way through pre-season tests but were now working well together – scarily well, in fact.

Rainey, of course, had run the Anglo-Japanese tyres in '88 and '89, so it was no big surprise when he wasted everyone at Eastern Creek two weeks later. Mick got second after a slow getaway; ninth on lap one, he swept past Schwantz, Gardner and Kocinski with ease.

Rainey ruled again at Laguna – as was his habit – and Mick was second again: three runner-up finishes in a row, after another start-line clutch problem forced him to miss the warm-up lap and start the race on cool tyres. In those circumstances the result augured well, but there were early warnings of the problems that would ultimately cost him the title.

'The front was wandering a lot, I couldn't get the grip, so I was always run-

The best GP race ever? Schwantz, Mick, Rainey and Kocinski fight it out at Suzuka '91. (Gold & Goose)

ning wide.' The problem was so bad that Mick even tested a grooved front slick, designed to work heat into the rubber.

Then to Europe for the start of the Ground War (Rainey's nickname for the Continental campaign, a Gulf War analogy). Dunlop had won the first three races, but at Jerez and Misano it was Rainey who was deep in rubber trouble. His front tyre collapsed in Spain, where he limped to third, and his rear fell apart at the Adriatic track, forcing him to take the unprecedented step of pitting for a replacement. Mick won both races comfortably and led the world championship for the first time. 'Dead by June' Doohan was starting to look like a world champ, a superstar.

The GP season was going awry by now, but he did win the Suzuka Eight Hours for the first, and only, time with Gardner (right). Much respected HRC boss Yoichi Oguma (in fluorescent-peaked cap behind Mick) oversees this pit stop. (Koichi Ohtani)

Not that he behaved like that. Intense as ever and growing more dedicated by the race, he could still be endearingly humble. I'd done some work for him that year and was first to reach him after he took the chequer at Misano. He pulled off his helmet and said: 'I owe you some dollars – I'll sort you out back at the motorhome.' Imagine that: you've just won the third grand prix victory of your career, you're leading the world championship by 14 points, and you're chatting about a couple of hundred bucks you owe a journo. This certainly was a very unusual guy.

He would've won at Hockenheim too, except this time it was his turn for tyre disasters. First, he fell in qualifying, testing an ultra-hard rear slick designed to survive sustained high-speed torture, then his rear tyre flew apart in the race as he cranked along the track's 310kph Honda lanes, fighting to escape Schwantz and Rainey. Braving potential

disaster, he eased home third while Schwantz acted out the most remarkable overtaking manoeuvre of his career. On the last lap he threw himself past Rainey into the lead, his RGV skipping ludicrously sideways into the Nuremberg-esque stadium. A famous victory.

This was turning out to be one maniac-fast season. Lap records were getting trashed everywhere, down almost 3 seconds at Hockenheim, and this despite the minimum weight limit having been raised by 15kg to 130kg (one of the FIM's knee-jerk reactions to the crash-happy 1990 season).

The rash of new lap records, many of which stood until recently, was thanks to Dunlop tyres providing massive grip, albeit briefly. Dunnies stuck like hell for a few laps, but Michelins usually lasted best. And while Dunlop riders struggled with rear traction, Michelin men looked vainly for front grip.

Mick got the worst of the tyre trade-

Sussing out his biggest rivals at Laguna, April '91. Mick's just finished second to Rainey, Schwantz was third. (Gold & Goose)

off, for while most pros happily live with lurid rear-end scares, there's nothing more harrowing than a front-end moment. And Mick was having plenty of those.

Now both companies redoubled their efforts to fix their respective weak points, Michelin recommencing full development. The major teams – already running exhaustive test programmes – were forced into a gruelling schedule of race, test, race, test, race…There had never been a GP season like it, and the spectre of a damaging escalation in costs forced a rule change for '92: testing at world championship circuits was banned, excepting a nominated test track for each team.

OVERLEAF: *Hunting for front-end grip, Mick skates home third at Mugello.* (Gold & Goose)

Dunlop worked hard, although Schwantz seemed less able to take advantage of the improvements than Rainey; Michelin meanwhile made little progress. Nevertheless Mick continued to trade blows with Rainey as the action moved from Hockenheim's dark forests to the alpine valleys of the Salzburgring and thence to the hot and dusty plains of Jarama, outside Madrid (replacing Rijeka in war-torn Yugoslavia).

The real deal was beating Rainey, anyhow, anywhere, even at jogging

Mick won by a fraction in Austria after a hectic, high-speed duel between the Armco barriers, and one or two scary front-end slides. Rainey returned the compliment in Spain, his Dunlops loving the heat. Half-distance in the championship and Mick led by 12 points, with Schwantz lagging a further 28 points adrift. From the outside things looked good, but the writing was already on the wall.

Assen would be the turning point for his title aspirations, and not for the last time. The Dutch track is the last street-based GP circuit and therefore unlike any other, its thin ribbon of tarmac darting this way and that, demanding inch-perfect lines at very high speeds. Mick had never liked the place and would grow to hate it.

Chasing Rainey, with Schwantz on his tail, his front Michelin skipped across the ripples in the fast left preceding the chicane, and let go. He bounced across the damp grass run-off at barely diminished speed and slammed into a stack of hay bales. Motionless for a moment, he was stretchered away: 'I was a bit ga-ga. I'd been having front-end slides all year, but that time it pushed to the point of no return.

'The front tyre was the only reason we didn't win the championship in '91 – it would push everywhere and then fade as the race went on. Some of the slides I had were unbelievable – I was leaving black marks in a lot of places.'

Rainey should've won at Assen, but made a rare error entering the chicane for the final time, allowing an ecstatic Schwantz through for the win. He was blazing angry afterwards, even though he'd moved back into the championship lead.

From there things just got worse for Mick. He didn't win another GP all year, although his trademark consistency was beginning to come together: apart from his Assen DNF he finished on the podium at every race. An important signal to the future.

The next two races were particular nightmares. At France's Circuit Paul Ricard and the UK's Donington Park he had no answer to the improving Dunlops. Second and third places were the best he could do, while Rainey piled on the points with another first and a second, Schwantz winning in Britain. 'The Dunlop guys were taking off – at Donington I had no feel from the front at all. I can't remember how many times I nearly crashed that weekend.'

One week before Donington Mick had travelled back to Japan for the Eight Hours, a race he was growing to hate. This time he won along with Gardner, after a race-long tussle with Yamaha's Magee and American Doug Chandler. He could have taken the victory as a good omen, but he didn't. For Honda the event is the most important one-off race in the world (hence its inclusion in his HRC contract); for Mick it was just an unwanted distraction from the real deal.

The real deal was beating Rainey, anyhow, anywhere, even out jogging. The hard-training Californian remembers them running together at Donington, where his rival ran him to the point of collapse: 'I knew then Mick was trying

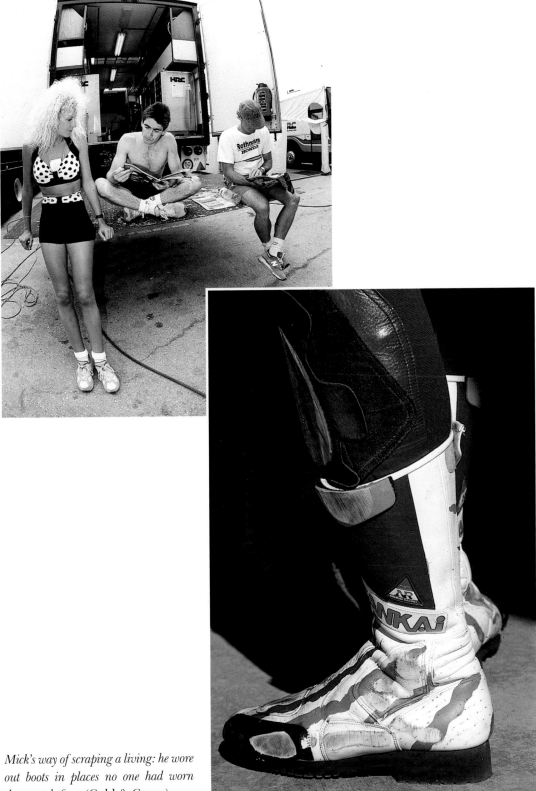

Time out at Jarama '91 – Mick hangs with Kelly and big brother Col. (Lou Martin)

Mick's way of scraping a living: he wore out boots in places no one had worn them out before. (Gold & Goose)

hard – he was thinking about what he had to do.'

Michelin had been spurred to greater efforts by that humiliating defeat on home tarmac in France. New front slicks started filtering through from Clermont Ferrand, but Dunlop and Rainey had built up some serious momentum, and now Schwantz was sneaking up from behind. The pair again relegated Mick to third at Mugello, winner Rainey stretching his championship lead to 15 points.

He was now established as a serious world title contender

During Czech GP practice Mick had another major front-end horror, this time his backside on the tarmac before he pulled back from the brink. He harassed Rainey as best he could in the race, but it was obvious he was fighting a losing battle. Rainey did everything he could to exploit his rival's Achilles' heel: 'I kept showing him my front wheel, so he'd use up his front tyre'. Mick crossed the line 3 seconds and 18 points down.

So the title had almost slipped away as the series returned to France, this time to Le Mans for a hastily arranged replacement for the cancelled Brazilian GP. This was Mick's last stand – the penultimate race of the year – and he had to beat Rainey to keep his championship hopes alive.

As had so often been the case that year, he tested at Le Mans before the event. But the session only deepened his crisis of confidence. Barrelling into the track's sweeping 260kph turn one – the corner that would later end Alberto Puig's career – he had the mother of all front-wheel slides. 'I thought, "Oh no, not here." It left a 100-metre rubber mark that was still there when we turned up for the race a week later. The Michelin guys couldn't believe it.'

The race turned out to be a five-way fight: Mick, Schwantz, Rainey, Kocinski and Gardner. Schwantz won in the end, the dead-stop turns suiting his desperate late-braking style (the Texan's braking mantra: 'See God, then brake'). Mick was less than two-tenths down, with Rainey just beating Kocinski. So the American was world champ again.

The year was due to end where it had started – out east. Asia's tiger economies were in full swing now and wanted in on the GP show. Malaysia's chosen venue was the extravagantly named Shah Alam Motorsports Paradise, carved out of steamy jungle outside Kuala Lumpur. But a pre-race open test session was a disaster: Rainey fractured his right femur while Schwantz broke a hand.

Kocinski ran away with the race, Mick out of control as he wobbled and weaved his way to a distant third behind Gardner. His team's official explanation for his handling problems suggested that a broken tyre-warmer thermostat had over-cooked his rear tyre. A creative excuse – the truth emerged much later: his team had fitted a new swinging-arm pivot bolt before the race, and the bolt didn't match the pivot bearings.

A disappointing end to an ultimately disappointing year. Mick had believed he could win the championship but had been failed by below-par equipment. He had, however, established himself as a serious title contender, a world champion in waiting. All he needed was a better-handling motorcycle and a grippier front tyre. These things would come to him.

chapter seven

Then we went to Assen...

Mick had come tantalisingly close to winning the 1991 world championship. He had ended the season a handful of points behind Rainey and wasn't going to let that happen again. Something had to be done.

Since his earliest days at Honda he had appealed to HRC engineers for less top-end power and more mid-range. The concept is simple: you only use top speed once a lap, but you use mid-range out of every corner. Yet Honda has always worshipped at the altar of horsepower – HRC engineers were proud that their machines always led the top-speed sheets.

As the title slipped away during '91 Mick and JB stepped up their demands for a more rideable motorcycle. JB used some history to convince the Japanese. He reminded them of 1983, when Freddie Spencer had used Honda's NS500 triple to beat Kenny Roberts, despite giving away 15 horsepower to Roberts's fiery V4.

'We wanted the HRC guys to think in that direction, rather than being blinded by top speed,' says JB. 'We told them we needed acceleration between corners.'

Honda had lost the title two years in a row, so finally they were prepared to lis-ten. Their answer was a revised engine configuration with bunched-together power pulses. This motor didn't make great numbers on the dyno, but, HRC argued, it would work on the racetrack because it gave the rear tyre an easier time.

When Mick and Gardner first tested the new motor at Eastern Creek in January, trackside spies reported a droning engine note and a marked absence of the hazy, crazy wheelspin that had always been the NSR's trademark. The big-bang engine had been born.

There was, in fact, nothing new about the big-bang concept. Years before, US dirt track tuners had re-jigged Harley motors to fire both cylinders simultaneously, softening traction breakaway under acceleration. Suzuki tried the concept in '79 with its RG500 GP bike, but it never got beyond the dyno, where it destroyed gears and primary drives with depressing regularity. Honda ran into the same problems, but simply beefed up the engine internals.

Mick wasn't over-impressed when he

We said we needed acceleration between corners

first tried the motor – lap times were no better than before, and it's fast lap times that win races. Well no, it isn't actually, it's fast race times that win races, and over race distance the big-bang motor was better, because it didn't fry rear tyres.

'At the first few tests I was quicker on the '91 bike; it wasn't until our last test that the new bike was faster. Wayne liked it more than I did because it suited his style. He didn't carry any corner speed and the big-bang motor let him do want he wanted – park the bike in a turn, pick it up and give it a handful. The old motor wouldn't accept that.'

He wanted to win so bad, and had now worked out what it takes

Gardner may have preferred the engine, but remember, this motorcycle had been built for Mick. Honda's development programme was now framed entirely around the world number two. In fact, HRC hadn't even planned to field Gardner in '92. They wanted to replace him with latest Aussie hotshot Daryl Beattie, a friend of Mick's from the Gold Coast who had spent the previous year racing 500s and F1 for HRC in Japan.

Perhaps talk of team-mates is irrelevant – Mick didn't need that kind of support for the job ahead. With three 500 seasons behind him, he knew the bikes, he knew the tracks, he knew his rivals and he knew he had the talent and determination to be world champion. As Rainey says: 'He came out smokin' – he wanted to win so bad and he'd figured out what it takes'.

He was training harder than ever. During the off-season, brother Col hooked him up with triathlon world champion Miles Stewart. The pair trained together and Mick's cardiovascular fitness was right up there with Stewart's.

'I guess it's a mental thing – you've got to do more than you did last year. Back then I was training seven days a week. I'd swim a kilometre, or a kilometre and a half, and I'd run anywhere up to 10 kilometres, every day.'

Michelin had been hard at work too. The French firm had finally built a good front tyre, although the rubber roundabout had turned again during the off-season, with both Suzuki and Team Roberts returning to Michelin. So Rainey and Schwantz would be on the same tyres, but that wasn't a problem – Mick could handle that.

Rivals-wise, the two Americans would surely be his main concern again; perhaps Kocinski too, now in his second 500 season with Team Roberts, and just maybe Doug Chandler, Schwantz's new team-mate at Suzuki. Lawson had stayed on with Cagiva, the Italian V4 much improved thanks to Eddie's input, but unlikely to challenge for the title. Then there was clown prince Randy Mamola, back on a YZR after a season's absence.

None of these men had any idea what was about to hit them. They'd heard rumours about the droning Honda, but HRC hadn't attended any open test sessions, so no one knew just how good it might be.

To Japan for round one, and Suzuka was even more miserable than usual for March. The rain came down all through Friday, and although Saturday dawned dry, dark rain clouds threatened again as the 500s lined up for the crucial final qualifier. It stayed dry for just two laps, during which Schwantz and everyone else went like hell in anticipation of the coming downpour. Except Mick, who was running in new pistons.

By the time the rain came he hadn't

Mick (2) started '92 with a big bang – winning by a mile in the Suzuka rain. He raced past Gardner (5), Chandler (10) and Schwantz (34) like they weren't even there. (Gold & Goose)

Getting busy with the champagne at Eastern Creek, April '92. Mick won, while Beattie got third in his GP debut. (Gold & Goose)

gone fast enough to qualify. He had the most potent weapon in the paddock and he might not make Sunday's grid. The task looked hopeless – to get within the regulation 110 per cent of Schwantz's dry time on a soaking track. But he had to give it a go.

Under the gaze of worried Honda officials his team fitted intermediates, but Mick couldn't find enough grip. He returned to the pits and had his crew mount a set of wets. Still not fast enough. By now he was just praying that race officials might bend the rules and let him start from the back of the grid. Then the rain slackened and with 10 minutes to go he eased himself into the top ten. Big sigh of relief.

No such worries in the race. The rain lashed down throughout as Mick took off after Schwantz and Chandler, then moved into the lead and disappeared through the spray. With the big-bang engine he could find grip where apparently there was none, laying down the power and pulling wheelies while everyone else slipped and slithered. Mick sailed effortlessly onward as his rivals crashed and burned all around. Gardner slid off on lap two, followed immediately by Rainey (his first race crash in over two years), then Kocinski. WG remounted and, enjoying the same miraculous grip as Mick, charged his battered NSR through the pack en route to his date with destiny. He went from 19th to sixth, then fell at speed, badly breaking his right leg against an unyielding Armco barrier.

Mick crossed the finish line 28 seconds ahead of Chandler's Suzuki, and while Honda celebrated a first 500 win at its own track, there were worried frowns in the Yamaha and Suzuki pits as crews packed crates for round two in Australia. This new Honda really was something else.

Rival race engineers were quickly on the trail of the NSR's secret. At Suzuka they'd recorded the bike's exhaust note at every opportunity. These tapes were rushed to Hamamatsu (home to Suzuki and Yamaha) and Varese (Cagiva's HQ), then played against an oscilloscope to reveal the distance between each exhaust pulse, and hence the firing interval. Easy, but it would take them longer to build their own big-bang motors, and still longer to keep them from blowing apart.

Australia underlined the urgency of their task, for Mick was again unbeatable, this time before an adoring home crowd at Eastern Creek. On pole by over four-tenths from Rainey, and a 7-second win over the world champ. Beattie came in third on Gardner's NSR – 21 years old and a podium finish in his first 500 GP.

Gardner was there of course, with his

right leg plastered, enjoying the sympathy of the Aussie media and fanning the mutual hatred smouldering between himself and the championship leader. The papers went big on his comments suggesting that the big-bang had been his idea all along and Mick was being flattered by the new bike. Mick fumed, channelling his anger into another devastating victory. On the podium he looked ill at ease as the crowd held an impromptu party on the start-finish.

But maybe he wasn't unbeatable. Rainey was still unfit after a lazy off-season recovering from that broken femur and he'd fallen again in pre-season tests, losing the top off the little finger of his left hand. A Mick replica. He had chased hard at the Creek and maybe, just maybe, he'd be able to beat the Honda once 100 per cent fit.

Not in the suffocating heat of Shah Alam, though. Mick was on pole again and ahead in the race when a sub-tropical downpour halted proceedings. In the damp restart it was the same story, Mick picking his way into the lead, Rainey well back until another cloudburst brought the race to a final close.

Three races down, three wins and a yawning 29-point lead over Chandler. Mick was on a roll: 'Riding the new bike felt like riding a Superbike: I felt confident, everything clicked and I was dominating like I'd done on Superbikes.'

Not that he played Mr Confident at the time. The media was already treating him as world champ, more a case of when than if, but he wouldn't have it that way. He worked hard to play down his superiority; he didn't want to fire up his rivals by trumpeting his domination.

On to Europe and Jerez, and another overwhelming win, this time 18 seconds ahead of a visibly demoralised Rainey. Mick's only worry now was complacency – winning too easily doesn't suit someone

Doohan fever hits the Creek. Now he was a bona fide Aussie superstar. (Gold & Goose)

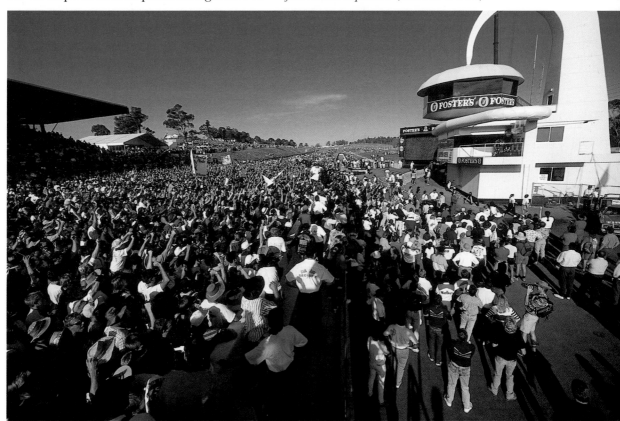

from a school of racing that believes when the going gets tough, the tough get going.

The Jerez win also marked the opening of an important new chapter in Mick's career – for the first time he was taking on the role of history-maker. Record watchers at Jerez pointed out that this was the first time anyone had won the opening four races of a season since 1972, when Italian heart-throb Giacomo Agostini ruled the 500 class on his MV Agusta. Such historical comparisons – usually with Ago or Briton Mike Hailwood – would haunt him over the coming years. Mick is no history scholar and gets no satisfaction from being compared with riders from an era that means nothing to him, even if they are legends.

Anyway, talk of legends was perhaps a bit premature, for the Mighty Mick steamroller was finally halted at Mugello two weeks later. Not by Rainey, though; he ended his race in the dirt, pushing way beyond the limit in a bitter last-ditch bid to beat that sonofabitch Honda. Instead the glory went to Schwantz, after Mick got a rare dud Michelin and limped to second.

Rainey's crash was significant. All season the American had complained about Michelin's front slicks, and Mugello's numerous off-camber turns exaggerated their deficiencies. Finally he'd had enough of holding back; now he decided to push on through the fear barrier. He was running away with the race when the front folded, just like he'd expected.

Deep down in the dumps, Rainey now slipped to third in the championship, a whole 50 points off Mick and 7 down on Schwantz. His bid for a title hat-trick was surely over.

Mick loved it. The front-tyre nightmares that had been his alone last year were now haunting Rainey and

Schwantz. There was no doubt in his mind he had lost the '91 crown because of those problems, and Rainey had enraged him by suggesting that his style was all wrong – too much for any front tyre. 'Biggest load of bullshit I've ever heard,' was Mick's unusually forthright response. 'The guys from Michelin had built a better front for '92 but it still wasn't giving Wayne and Kevin the grip they'd had with the Dunlops in '91. Wayne just got frustrated at Mugello – he flicked it in like he did on Dunlops and it threw him down the road.'

Years later Rainey would admit: 'What I said sure upset him and that's why I said it.'

There was indubitable evidence to support Mick's point of view: the stopwatch. Lap records had been pulverised in '91 when Rainey and Schwantz lavished in the Dunlop front's (admittedly ephemeral) grip. Now those records stood fast.

Honda's NSR was transformed for '92 – the most complete 500 GP bike ever built. (Gold & Goose)

On to Catalunya – Barcelona's new racetrack born out of Spain's bike racing boom but unfortunately situated in a depressing industrial-park landscape, uncomfortably close to the local abattoir. Mick was on pole again, his fifth in a row, almost a whole second ahead of Kocinski, with local hero Criville third and Rainey a woeful 1.3 seconds off the pace. Criville's sole lightning-fast lap was a sign of things to come. He had achieved the time by grimly hanging on to Mick's tail, a situation both men would get used to over the coming years. Being the tow truck was a new experience for Mick, and already he didn't like it. 'It's not nice thinking that if you fall down, someone's going to run over you.'

On Sunday it was Rainey's turn to stick grimly to the NSR's tailpipes. Until the last-but-one lap. Then the Yamaha slipped ahead, holding its advantage to the line by half a bike's length, the world champion's first win in nine months.

'I wouldn't have won that race unless the wind had changed just before the start,' says Rainey. 'We had a front-end

feel problem and I knew the wind would help by pushing the front of my bike on to the ground. The only way I could hope to win was by out-thinking him.'

At Hockenheim Rainey resorted to Mugello mode. He was riding way out there, chasing Mick during qualifying in a hopeless attempt to overcome a 1.4-second deficit. 'I just didn't want to lose the championship. That was the biggest downfall of my career – I couldn't accept losing any more.' Tail-sliding out of the Sachs kurve – the left side of his tyres still cool after the long run through the forest – Rainey was spat hard into the dirt. Barely able to walk, he pulled out of the next day's race while Mick meanwhile produced another disappearing act, 24 seconds ahead of Schwantz.

Seven rounds down, six to go and Mick was on 130 points, 53 up on Schwantz and exactly double Rainey's score. In the media room journalists calculated that he could wrap up the title in Hungary, with four rounds remaining. Mick maintained his usual line: a couple of DNFs and the rest would be right with him.

Assen next. And now Rainey did give up. Still battered from his German get-off, the champ had woken up to reality. He wobbled round for eight laps in first practice, then flew home to California to lick his wounds. He departed on a note of apparent defiance: 'The championship ain't over till it's over – all Doohan needs is one big crash'. Oh, if only he'd known.

Well, he kind of did. Racing at this level is a vicious business. He didn't want Mick to get hurt bad, just a small flesh wound, a few weeks out of racing. Hard bastard? Not really. This is the way riders' minds work: 'I was thinking me not being there might change things, maybe something could happen. We didn't have a hope any other way.'

Strange things always happened at Assen – still do. It's one of those weirdo events. The track is grippy, massively grippy, but complicated by an old-fashioned surface profile. While most race-tracks are dead flat, Assen is crowned liked a highway, delivering no fewer than four camber changes as riders enter and exit each turn.

Not that the camber was blamed for the string of disasters that befell final qualifying. Mick had been predictably fastest in the opening session, then Lawson (using a big-bang motor for the first time, the second NSR 'copy', Suzuki having run one at Hockenheim) went quicker in the final outing. At the time Mick was busy running in new pistons, just two laps, then he'd go for it and chase down Eddie's time.

'It was my first flying lap and exiting the first turn the rear lit up in a place it never usually does. The bike flicked me off and I was going up the road at 160 kays with the bike on top of me. It was getting warm, so I tried to spin my body round. Everything moved except my right leg. As soon as we stopped I knew I'd broken it – I could feel the bones grinding – so I hollered for a marshal.'

He had sustained spiral fractures at the base of his right tibia and fibula, although he wasn't the only faller in that session. Not by far. Schwantz, Gardner, Mamola, Criville and Niall Mackenzie had also tumbled.

The session was red-flagged after Mick's fall, allowing an ambulance to ferry him to the paddock Clinica Mobile while JB, the crew, Ken and girlfriend Kelly Trundley looked anxious in the

Bits of the leg were dying – it smelled like a bad butcher's shop

OVERLEAF: *Not quite unbeatable: Champ Rainey finally got to defeat Mick at Catalunya, May '92, six races into the season.* (Gold & Goose)

pits. Inside Dr Costa's A&E the scene was somewhat chaotic.

'Costa, Dr Richards [an FIM doctor], Dean Miller [Team Roberts's physical fixer] and a whole bunch of people were standing around discussing things. Costa said the break wasn't that bad – they could either put the leg in plaster and I'd be back for Brazil in eight weeks, or they'd pin it and I could ride in Hungary in three weeks. Brazil seemed too far off. Dean wanted me to go to the States to get it pinned; Dr Richards said I should get it done in the UK. Then someone said the leg would heal better if I had the operation within 8 hours. So I asked this Dutch guy who's the best surgeon in Assen, and he told me, "We're all the same, we all went to the same school." I thought that was a bit strange.'

His pit crew were appalled – Mick was grey, wasted and haggard

Nevertheless Mick opted to go under the knife there and then. A surgeon screwed and plated the tibia that afternoon at Assen's Wilhelmina Hospital.

The following morning Mick was in serious discomfort. At around 6am Costa entered the ward to check on his progress and didn't like what he saw. As he removed the bandages he was thrown out by hospital security; the Italian wasn't licensed to work in a Dutch hospital. Now things got nasty.

'As the day went on things deteriorated. The leg was swelling up and shutting down the circulation. They call it compartment syndrome, but it's quite a common thing with broken legs; most doctors have got a grip on it. I guess they weren't worried. They did the operation then parked me in a corner. That evening they wheeled me back into theatre and cut open the leg from the back of the knee to the heel, and from the front of the ankle to the toes, to let the muscles expand and let the blood flow. The wound on the back of the leg must've been 12cm wide. And there had already been some damage to the nerves and muscle from lack of circulation.

'A couple of days passed and I knew things weren't looking good for getting back for Hungary. Two days and they hadn't even changed the bandages. Bits of the leg were dying, like it was gangrenous, and it started smelling like a bad butcher's shop. I asked them to change the bandages and they wheeled me down to the emergency room. The doctor came in and while he removed the bandages he told me he'd been speaking with Costa. He said Costa would be coming to pick me up on Thursday – this was Tuesday. Then he said he had told Costa that if the leg didn't improve within 24 hours he'd have to amputate. The bandages were stuck really bad with all the blood and the guy said there's only one way to take them off. I said, "What's that – soak them in water?" Then he just ripped them off, pulling a load of flesh off the back of the leg. That was the first time I was in pain and they had to knock me out. I think they used two bags of blood just changing the bandages.'

Costa turned up in a hurry the next day, chartering a Lear jet ambulance from Verona to rescue Mick and Schwantz, who had also been languishing at Wilhelmina's after coming together with Lawson while disputing the lead in Saturday's race. The Texan had fractured his left forearm and dislocated a hip. He wanted out too.

The pair were wheeled into the Lear jet at Emmen airport and flown down to Italy. Back at the Villa Albi clinic in Bologna, Costa set to work immediately. Mick was in serious danger of losing the leg, and who's ever heard of a one-legged motorcycle world champion?

Desperate measures were called for. 'There wasn't much oxygen getting to

the injury. Costa even tried wrapping a plastic bag around the leg, sealing it up and then pumping in oxygen.'

Mick was also making daily visits to a hospital in Ravenna to use a hyperbaric (decompression) chamber, typically used for divers suffering from the bends and for old people with circulation problems. The idea was to oxygenate his body. He hated the daily trip, at the mercy of a wild Italian driver.

'The drive down there was the biggest nightmare, plus it was a stinking hot summer and I'd be in the chamber for an hour and a half. I'd come out drenched in sweat.'

Costa had other things on his mind too. The Dutch had dramatically thinned Mick's blood in a bid to improve circulation, and there was concern that his liver and kidneys might shut down.

'About this time I started noticing black spots where the leg was festering and dying. Another doctor came in one day with this scoop thing and started chipping away at the black bits. He could dig until he got to the bone and tendons.'

Plastic surgeons were called in and shook their heads when they saw the biggest wound – the size of a fist. They reckoned it would be several months before they could do anything. Not in Mick's plans at all. 'All this time I was pushing, pushing: can we go racing, can we go racing? But I still didn't understand what was going on: I'm in Italy, I can't speak Italian, Costa can't speak English, and the other doctors just aren't saying anything.'

An exploratory skin graft was attempted, transferring flesh from his backside to the leg. But the blood circulation

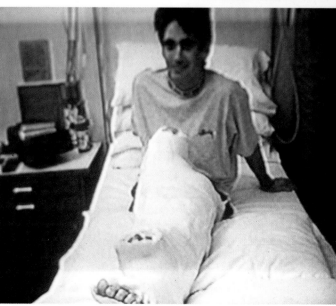

…the next he was wasted and green in hospital, his legs sewn together. (Gold & Goose)

wasn't up to it, so the graft died.

Two weeks after Mick's arrival in Bologna, Costa decided there was only one option left: sew both legs together, using the left leg as a donor to feed blood to its neighbour.

According to Costa, Mick cried after that operation, and when his pit crew came visiting they were appalled by what they saw: their champion turned grey, wasted and haggard. Would he ever ride again?

Mick spent more than two weeks with the legs sewn together and bound with Scotchcast. On the 16th night surgeons spent 8 hours grafting quarter-inch-deep chunks of flesh from his quads to the old wounds, then the legs were separated the following morning and further grafts applied to the donor sites.

'That was a big relief, just for general things like going to the toilet. Both legs had withered away a lot: I couldn't put any weight on them. The last two weeks were better – I stayed at the Molino Rosso hotel where I could swim. I realised then I'd have a problem with the rear brake because the ankle wasn't moving, and I've always used a lot of rear brake to keep the bike stable on the brakes, to help it turn and to smooth things out when I get on the gas.'

Mick insists that even during his bleakest moments he never considered quitting, and that's frightening enough in itself. 'There were times when I was wondering what the hell's going on, but I never lost sight of what I wanted to do, I always wanted to keep going.'

Pretty soon he was riding slow laps of the nearby Imola circuit on a bicycle. Then Costa borrowed an Aprilia street bike from a local dealer, so he could do static exercises, shifting his weight from one leg to the other.

And all this time his apparently indomitable 57-point lead was getting whittled away. He watched every GP on TV: Assen didn't count, since neither Rainey nor Schwantz scored. In Hungary the weather was on his side –

Mick mid-pack at the start of the most disappointing ride of his career. He finished a pointless 12th at Sao Paulo while Rainey won. Now the crown was nearly gone. (Gold & Goose)

Lawson scored Cagiva's first ever GP win on a damp track, Rainey down in fifth and Schwantz fourth – a superhuman comeback from his Assen injuries. A week later, at Magny-Cours, Schwantz fell again, effectively ending his title aspirations, but Rainey won. The gap was down to 37 points. A fortnight later at Donington Rainey was a hard-charging second to Gardner, the Aussie's final GP win. Twenty-two points and counting.

But the aftermath of that race gave Mick a glimmer of hope – his turn to get malicious. 'There was a track invasion and Wayne got knocked off his bike. It looked like he might've hurt the leg he broke at the end of '91. That gave me some inspiration – if he missed one race I might be in with a chance. Maybe that's not the way to look at it, but I'm sure Wayne felt the same way when I broke my leg.' Damn right.

Three weeks later, Mick arrived in Brazil, a shadow of his former self. Even rock-hard Rainey was shocked by what he saw: 'he was a mess'. During that weekend it was spirit alone that kept Mick going. 'I'd lost 6 kilos and I'd been pretty lean to start with; I was run down, beat up and on some pretty strong pills.'

Sao Paulo had never been used for bike racing before and should never have been used for bike racing then. Perched on a hillside next to a sprawling slum, the track was way too dangerous. From the moment the riders clapped eyes on the place there was talk of a boycott. Perfect for Mick – a strike would put the title out of Rainey's reach.

Strike talk simmered all weekend but the race went ahead. Rainey and Doohan kept out of the debate, although Lawson was enraged when his fellow Californian failed to fulfil his role as leading light of rider safety. Lawson stormed out of a crisis meeting, fuming, 'The trouble with you guys is you haven't got enough balls.'

It says much for Mick's sense of fair play that he didn't agitate for a boycott. 'I

Doctor Costa offers some words of pre-race encouragement in the Sao Paulo pits. An hour later the doc was in tears. (Gold & Goose)

chatted with Wayne, told him we could run two races in South Africa instead. I was disappointed with him because up till then he'd been very strong on safety. But I'd probably have done the same as him in that situation.'

Rainey won the race, Mick struggled to 12th, two places out of the points. Fate was against him – '92 was a unique year, with points only to 10th instead of the usual 15. Now the gap stood at 2 points. The post-race scene in Mick's pit was ugly. Costa – an emotional guy at the best of times – was in tears.

'It was my worst ever race, but I was happy I'd finished. I got back to the pits and Costa and another doctor were crying. It was pretty emotional. I almost wanted to get those guys out of there; I didn't need it, but that's the way Costa is.'

Yes indeed. Four years later, in much happier times, the Italian doctor would pen a gushing eulogy to Mick's triumph over these weeks of agony and the months and years of struggle that would follow. It went like this: 'As you lay suffering on a bed of thorns, wounded by fate and the conceit of mankind, and as tears streamed from your eyes, glinting in the twilight of your hospital room, we thought those tears would never suffice to fill the abyss of your stress or soothe the suffering of your affliction... Then all of a sudden the casket of treasures which every human being carries inside of himself opened itself and you, Michael, saw all of yourself, from the crypts of the soul to the light of reason. You were the champion of the world.' Right.

I wanted him to know I admired him for what he'd been through

There are those in the paddock who believe the doc is nuts, although Mick doesn't agree: 'He's a little bit eccentric and a bit of a philosopher but he's fantastic – what he's done for me and the sport is great.'

Back to Italy for two weeks of intensive therapy, staying at Costa's family home; the room Mick used during that period is still kept ready for him even today. Then to the dark continent for the final showdown.

'I was a lot stronger for South Africa, but I could still hardly walk. I qualified third and reckoned we needed a top-four finish to beat Wayne for the championship. I got sixth and Wayne got third so he won the title by 4 points. I was pretty bummed out, wondering what I had to do to win one of these things.' Well, he would've won if the FIM had retained its 'drop your worst two results' system from '91.

A while after the podium ceremony three-times champ Rainey entered the deadly quiet HRC pit to offer condolences.

'I was still in my leathers and we'd been celebrating,' Rainey remembers. 'It was strange. I wasn't sorry for winning the championship, but I wanted him to know I admired him for what he'd been through. I'd been calling him after every race while he was out, because I was concerned for his health – I really felt for him. In Brazil I realised this guy's as hungry as I ever was. He'd just about crippled himself and I felt a lot of it was my fault because he'd been trying to beat me.'

Rainey's sympathy was undoubtedly genuine. The two rivals shared huge respect for each other and had built as close a friendship as is possible between world title rivals. Anyway, they had other people to hate. 'Mick and I always got on good because we weren't from the same country – I had my battles with Schwantz, he had his with Gardner.'

Back home in Australia the year ended on a bitter note. Gardner had visited the Adelaide Formula 1 GP, where a Melbourne journalist overheard him chatting with Tom Walkinshaw, technical director of Michael Schumacher's Benetton team. Amongst other things WG opined that he'd been faster than Mick during pre-season tests and his words made headlines.

'He was saying stuff like how I'd blown the championship. I guess he forgot to mention he blew it at Suzuka. I'd just had enough of him trying to stay on top when he wasn't. I put out a press release saying he's full of shit, and a TV crew came to interview myself, Daryl and Magee about the whole thing. Daryl said if you believe everything Gardner says, the rest of us wouldn't be bike racers, we'd be bricklayers.'

At least 1992 was over. Only 1993 would be so much worse for racing.

chapter eight

Tales of no ordinary madness

There's a moment in a highside crash when things don't seem so bad after all. The rear tyre has slid, gripped and ejected the rider from his motorcycle. Now he's flying and it's kinda quiet and peaceful up there. Then he descends into the fiery pit of hell – his bowels loosen in expectation of the horrors to come and he collapses on to the tarmac like he jumped out of a first-floor window. He's seeing earth-sky-earth-sky-earth-sky, he can taste blood and he's desperately trying to catch sight of his bike, now self-destructing somewhere in mid-air. Not because he's worried about the bastard thing. He just doesn't want it to land on top of him.

This was Mick's second ride since Kyalami. Still without a contract for '93, he was back on a bike in early December. A two-day HRC session at Phillip Island passed without incident, then the following week he suffered a massive 200kph get-off at Eastern Creek.

'The leg just wasn't strong enough, so I was using too much upper body strength to change direction – the front wheel tucked, then the back came around and flicked me over the top.'

He had already been into hospital once following Kyalami, when the leg had become badly infected, now he was back again because the crash had loosened the metalwork. Surgeons removed the pins and plates, cleared up the infection and worked on the ankle tendons, opening a few degrees of movement.

Three weeks after breaking his wrist, Mick's at the Eastern Creek season opener, March '93. The short little finger (missing its middle knuckle) is a souvenir from the '89 Suzuka Eight Hours. (Gold & Goose)

Once out he wasted no time getting back to his physio programme, based around static cycling and gym work, since he could no longer do what he really loved doing – running. He was to push so hard over the coming months that the lower leg bent like a banana. Few people saw Mick walk in '93; he'd use a scooter for the shortest trips, and would always put his left foot down first as he rode his NSR into the pits.

He had proved he could still ride a motorcycle at Kyalami the previous September, even without a rear brake. But did he still want to race? He had come so close to being a cripple – those Dutch doctors had been within 24 hours of amputating the leg. And surely another bad crash would be the end of the withered, scarred limb?

All this was playing on Mick's mind. The doubts he hadn't allowed himself to consider while he lay helpless in Costa's clinic now began to eat into his dedication. While he considered his future,

Mick and JB had plenty of talking to do in '93 – Honda had let development of the NSR500 get badly off-track. (Gold & Goose)

HRC was also wondering what to do with him. There were those within the company who believed that he'd never be strong enough to win a world title. For some while there was no contract on offer.

'Because of the leg I didn't have a deal for '93. Gardner still wanted to stay on and the Japanese wanted letters from Costa and other doctors to say I could still ride a motorcycle. Kenny Roberts was on my side. He said he'd find something for me if things didn't work out with Honda.'

While he recuperated from the Eastern Creek fall, his new Rothmans Honda team-mates undertook pre-season testing duties. Beattie had finally won a full-time upgrade from Japanese racing, along with former Japanese 500 champion Shinichi Itoh.

Mick was still undecided: 'The way things were going I felt I was wasting my time; maybe I should find something else to do. Racing just didn't seem worth all the garbage. Had I won the title I think I would've given it away and done something different.' There was also the option of taking a year off – wait for the

leg to improve – but he didn't believe it would get better any faster off the bike and, anyway, it might be hard to get a ride after a year out.

He stumbled through this period of uncertainty, grimly considering his future. Then came another milestone moment. Just as he'd done after his accident at the '89 Eight Hours, he determined to redouble his efforts and narrow his focus still further. This was the moment that Mick Doohan transformed himself into Superman.

MacGillivray: 'The things I saw him endure, they served to strengthen his will to succeed. There was a lot of frustration that his body wouldn't do what he wanted it to do, and that just made him incredibly determined, incredibly strong. The accident made Mick into Superman.'

So the fire still burned: 'I still wanted to win. I was winning quite easily when I was strong, so I knew I could win races again if I could get anywhere near that mark.' During February he signed another one-year deal with HRC.

In early March he travelled to Malaysia for a final three-day test session. The opening GP was only three weeks away, and no longer in Japan but on home tarmac at Eastern Creek.

Mick wasn't impressed by what he found at Shah Alam. Without his guidance, HRC engineers had returned to their old ways, chasing maximum horsepower at the expense of just about everything else.

'The first time I rode the new bike it was a piece of junk and I told them so. The development had gone off track; the bike had just become a test bed, with fuel injection and all this other stuff. Itoh would always say everything was great and Daryl didn't have the experience to enforce his ideas.'

And that wasn't all. On the final day of the session Mick crashed again, breaking the tiny yet notoriously troublesome scaphoid bone in his left wrist (tucked deep inside the wrist, the scaphoid gets little blood, so takes ages to heal). The fuel injection pump had leaked gas on to the rear tyre. 'I bashed the leg and thought I'd broken it again. I think that crash weakened the bones and helped them bend.'

Mick flew home to have the scaphoid screwed and two weeks later arrived at Eastern Creek for a final IRTA test session before the following weekend's season opener. He struggled through testing and practice, never stringing more than a handful of laps together. The Aussie media wanted to know the wrist would be a problem for the race: 'It'd be OK if I was just riding down the shops to get some milk.'

This was the moment he transformed himself into Superman

There were obviously bigger questions that needed asking: could he race full-time without a rear brake, since the ankle would never recover anything like full movement? Had his spirit been crushed? Would the leg ever be strong enough to win again?

And this being the first race of the year there were all the usual early-season uncertainties. Wild boys Gardner and Lawson had retired, their places taken by Beattie and Doug Chandler, the drawling Californian moving from Suzuki to Cagiva. Roberts had sacked Kocinski, replacing him with double-250-champ Luca Cadalora, and putting his team back on Dunlops again. Schwantz, with fiery Brazilian Alex Barros as his new partner, was looking stronger than ever after an impressive run of pre-season tests.

The race was a three-way dogfight that belied the Creek's follow-your-leader layout, but Mick had no part in it. Schwantz, Rainey and Chandler monopolised the podium, while he retired with an engine misfire. Only later would HRC admit he'd been using experimental fuel injection.

At the next GP in Malaysia HRC chief Yoichi Oguma allowed Mick and Daryl to junk the PGM-FI and run carburettors; Itoh would continue to play the role of injection guinea pig. Rainey won the race, Mick was fourth, 20 seconds down and really missing a rear brake.

For round three at Suzuka JB fashioned a hand-operated rear brake: a decompression lever sitting above the clutch, worked by the index finger (the foot lever stayed for now, just in case). It wasn't so bad but his fingers were too busy. 'If the rear tyre starts to spin I use the clutch to drain the power – if you just shut the throttle you're too late. But I couldn't get to the clutch if I had one finger on the brake.'

How true: another gut-wrenching highside during practice highlighted the problem. Rainey's wife, Shae, saw the harrowing crash on the pit-lane TV monitors and burst into tears. 'She thought I'd broken the leg again, but luckily I bounced.' Shae's upset was nothing unusual. Riders' loved ones share a kind of group grief, like that experienced back in the '50s by the families of USAF test pilots in the Mojave Desert: even if your man doesn't get it, he might be next…

During the race – while Rainey, Schwantz, Itoh and Beattie battled for the lead well ahead – Mick got thinking: how about a thumb-operated brake? Good idea, but the more immediate problem was a gloomy seventh-place finish; now it was obvious he wasn't up to fighting for the title. Would he ever be? Rumours soon whipped round the paddock that Mick would be sent home, his place filled by Lawson.

By the time the circus had moved to

The turning point: Mugello produced Mick's first win since Hockenheim '92. (Gold & Goose)

Europe JB had created a jet-ski-style thumb brake. It worked well first-time out at Jerez, although fourth place was still well short of where he wanted to be.

'I need to sort out my riding,' he said at the time. 'I'm not getting into the corners as deep as I should, and I need to get on it harder out of the turns.' Just a confidence thing.

Salzburgring and Hockenheim next, where the NSR's straight-line speed would surely be a help. It was; Mick chased winner and series leader Schwantz in Austria to score his first podium in a year, and was leading in Germany before his rear Michelin flew apart again.

After Wayne's accident I asked myself again: is it all worth it?

'I was starting to get it together but the bike still wasn't right; it was making all its power right at the top. We went testing before Assen and tried some '92 cylinders and a different rear shock, so it started to feel like a motorcycle again, instead of an engineer's test bench.'

Mick was getting back to normal now, or at least adapting his style to suit his physical deficiencies. Around this time Scott came visiting from Australia and was horrified by the state of the leg: 'It was a shocker; Mick asked me if I thought the leg was bending. It was just about broken off but I didn't say anything.'

At Assen he was on pole for the first time since his accident there the previous June, and racing Schwantz and Barros for the win. His hatred for the track has made the Dutch GP a special event. People don't expect him to win there, for surely he must be scared of the place. But it doesn't work like that.

'I wanted to do well, to show the doctor who did my leg I could still ride, despite the mess he'd made. That year I still wasn't confident though – I wasn't going to throw it down the road. I was just ecstatic to get second; it gave me confidence because it's a physical track, and I shouldn't have gone well there.'

After another second place at Catalunya, Mick sensed the big breakthrough: 'I felt like it'd be perfect to win at Mugello – with Costa and his family there it was almost like a home GP to me. And we had tested there.'

On pole again, he raced for the lead with Schwantz until his NSR snapped sideways, flicking him overboard. In normal circumstances he would've landed back on the seat and carried on regardless. What happened next was a scary reminder of the leg's weakness: his left leg slipped off its footpeg, and without enough strength in the bad leg to recover the situation, he started to slide on to the tarmac at around 190kph. Schwantz swept ahead as he desperately hauled himself back on board, then set off in successful pursuit. Yes, he could still win races.

Then from Mugello glory to Donington ignominy. Mick arrived in Britain straight from the mid-season diversion of the Suzuka Eight Hours. He hadn't won the race but he had signed a new contract, a significant moment showing that HRC had reaffirmed its faith.

At Donington he didn't even make the first lap. Chasing Rainey, Barros and Schwantz towards the dead-stop chicane, he cannoned into the Brazilian, then skittled the Texan. 'Sure it was my fault, but I think Suzuki team orders had something to do with it. Barros hit the brakes big time to let Schwantz through – I had nowhere to go.'

Mick limped horribly back to the pits, aware that he'd just blown the championship wide open. Schwantz had led Rainey comfortably on points; now the Californian had moved to within 3 points of the series lead after riding to second behind team-mate and first-time-500-

His right ankle made useless by the Assen crash, Mick resorted to a thumb-operated rear brake, mounted beneath the left handlebar. (Gold & Goose)

winner Cadalora. Rainey won next time out at Brno, Mick third; then to Misano...

This was the race that changed racing, that forced everyone to reappraise their belief in this boyish game of 'I can go faster than you'. Sensing his fourth title, Rainey led, riding looser than ever – front wheel airborne, rear tyre burning rubber.

When the world champ fell at turn one, Mick was recovering from a bodged start. 'I saw someone had crashed, but I thought it was Luca. Then I passed Kevin and got right up with Luca, so I realised it must've been Wayne who'd gone down.'

Of course, Mick was oblivious to Rainey's fate. He just kept up his attack on leader Cadalora, losing out by a fraction on the final lap. Only afterwards would he hear that Rainey had been paralysed from the chest down. So it goes.

Racing had lost another of its wild boys. 'That hit me really hard; I felt physically ill for a week. It was another point when I asked myself: is it all worth it? I'd nearly lost a leg, now Wayne had

lost the use of both his legs.'

This was a sickening moment for everyone in GP racing, and there was no time to mourn – just a westward dash for next Sunday's US GP at Laguna Seca, right in Rainey's back yard.

Mick only knew of one way to deal with the trauma. Forget the horrors and concentrate on what he does best: going round in circles faster than anyone else. And that's exactly what he did: pole position over Kocinski, whom Cagiva had just brought back to 500s.

The race looked to be going the same way: Mick ahead of the American until his NSR got sideways exiting the Corkscrew, Laguna's infamous 'chicane on a hill'. 'I was still steering the thing too much with the handlebars – that's

OVERLEAF: *Real horror show: Mick's dodgy leg lets him down while leading Laguna, September '93. Too weak to save the slide, he gets thrown overboard, runs off the track, crashes and breaks his right shoulder. (All Nick Cedar)*

why she stepped out on me'. The weak leg crumpled as he fought to regain control; he ran wide and ricocheted off a row of trackside bales, ending up on his back in the middle of the track, bikes racing past uncomfortably close. He tried to stand, but the leg folded again, visibly flexing under the strain. Real horror show.

The crash had broken Mick's right shoulder but, hey, look on the bright side: now he could miss the season-ending Jarama GP, stay in the US and make an early start to further corrective surgery.

Back in May he had sought advice from several eminent US surgeons, some of whom suggested re-breaking and resetting the bones, others who suggested using radical Ilizarov surgery.

Each day he would tighten the bolts straightening his wonky leg

'At first I'd been told I'd have to take a year off to do the Ilizarov thing, so that was out of the question. Then Arthur Ting [surgeon to the San Francisco 49ers and various top American racers] told me about Dr Kevin Louie. I went to see him before Laguna and he said he could do it in three to four months.'

Mick headed to Frisco immediately after Laguna and had the Ilizarov gantry installed by Dr Louie.

The Ilizarov contraption consisted of three carbon-fibre rings circling the leg, held together by sets of threaded bolts and smaller pins embedded in the tibia bone. Each day Mick would tighten the bolts, gradually straightening his wonky leg. Then the gantry was relocated and the leg compressed, then stretched again to encourage extra calcification around the breaks.

Basing himself in a serviced apartment for three months, Mick kept himself busy with gym work and swimming pool exercises. Later on he headed south to visit Rainey in his LA hospital, then spent Christmas with Lawson. In January he flew back to the Gold Coast to prepare for 1994. And have some fun.

Niall Mackenzie, long-time friend and fellow 500 rider until the end of '94, will never forget a boating trip he took with Mick, Beattie, Mamola and Marlboro Team Roberts team manager Chuck Aksland that Easter.

'It was the most frightened I've ever been, because I don't really know about boats and the sea. We'd gone to an island north of Brisbane for lunch and we didn't come back for three days. We were in a harbour on some island, there was a storm brewing and these big fishing boats were running for cover. These hardy fishermen types were saying, "Don't even think about going out in that thing." Mick said, "Nah, it's a boat, it floats, that's what it's for." The swells were huge and the boat got pretty wrecked. I just sat in a corner, shitting myself. I'd not been a father long and I wanted to see my son again. I was wearing a lifebelt but I knew the sharks would get us if anything bad happened.'

And that wasn't the end of it. After that scare Mick took Aksland for a ride in his speedboat. 'We must've been doing 160 kays,' Aksland recalls. 'He floored it to jump a wake from a big boat, just missing this post sticking out of the water. It was pretty scary, but with guys like Mick you know they're well ahead of the situation. Anybody else driving and I would've been real scared.'

Aksland was on the Gold Coast getting to know new signing Beattie, the man Kenny Roberts had chosen to replace Rainey after he'd failed to steal Mick from Honda.

The Californian soon noticed that Mick maintained an aura of psychological superiority over his young friend. 'We thought Daryl would win some races that year, but you could see Mick already had his number; he didn't see him as a threat. It was like when Kenny was racing in the States and Skip Aksland [highly talented racer and Chuck's uncle] looked like he could go all the way. Kenny just didn't see him as a problem; he had him beat before they even started.'

There was every reason to be optimistic about the coming year, his sixth on 500s: the leg was now straight (if still nasty to behold) and after his '93 experience he had asked HRC to leave the bike untouched while he recuperated in the States. Testing started Down Under in late February.

'Straight away I felt better on the bike. But I was pretty tentative; with the amount of operations I'd been through I didn't want to injure myself again.'

This was to be the first post-Rainey season, although there had been surprisingly few team reshuffles to fill the gaping void left by the American. Title-winner Suzuki retained its '93 line-up while Yamaha replaced Rainey (who bravely travelled to the season-opening Australian GP to launch his 250 team) with Beattie. The young Aussie had been mysteriously let go by Honda, who instead took the fast but erratic Criville into its official squad alongside Mick and Itoh. The team's NSRs looked very different this year, liveried in red, white and blue after Honda had failed to replace the Rothmans millions, now invested in the Williams Formula 1 car team (Mick wasn't unhappy about that – it meant less PR work). Last but not least, big bad John Kocinski was now a full-timer at Cagiva, alongside the disgruntled Chandler.

But for all his optimism, Mick left the Creek unhappy and confused. Third place hadn't been the plan, especially 9 seconds off Kocinski's flying Italian V4. On to Shah Alam and the same problem – a lack of suspension balance. Mick couldn't work it out; the bike hadn't changed from '93 but it was behaving so

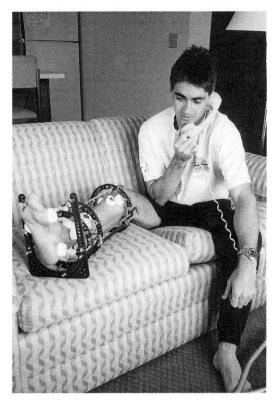

A mal-union in the bone had bent Mick's still-healing right leg like a banana. An Ilizarov gantry bent it straight in time for '94. (Rich Adams)

differently. He only just made the front row.

Race day worked out better – first win of the year, thanks to an inspired overnight rethink: 'We couldn't keep any corner speed so we geared the bike down, so I could put it into a turn, park it, stand it up and accelerate.'

Suzuka next, and still the same suspension problems. But the race provided valuable clues. While he battled for the lead with Schwantz and wild local Norick Abe (just 18 years old and reigning Japanese 500 champ), he noticed that Abe's '93 NSR was getting drive where his couldn't, at least until the long-haired loon dumped it, leaving Schwantz to win by 3 seconds.

A pre-Spanish GP test session at Jarama, near Madrid, revealed the truth. 'They kept telling me I was running '92 suspension, but I was a second faster once we fitted '92 forks, and the front tyre didn't chew up any more. I was pissed off; that took some of the trust out of our relationship.'

Mick may have been outraged but at least he'd got his problems fixed. At Jerez he was bursting with confidence and aiming to deal a morale-busting defeat to Schwantz. Although Kocinski was still closer on points, he reckoned that the Texan would be his real rival over the long haul.

'I knew it'd be psychologically good to beat Schwantz there. It'd bum him out because Jerez isn't a horsepower track, and after that we were going to two horsepower circuits.'

The pair fought an epic duel, the pace increasing throughout, Mick easing home a fraction ahead after both men had shattered the record on the final lap. Going into '99 that record still stands. On the podium they bullied Kocinski, sending him staggering to Costa's Clinica Mobile, blinded by stinging champagne.

Mick didn't talk about the title – no way was he about to forget '92

Mick was right about the next two races: he used his NSR's speed to twice demolish Schwantz, by 12 seconds at the Salzburgring and by 14 at Hockenheim, his mind concentrated by some foul weather during German GP qualifying: 'The straights there aren't straights. You're out in the forest through the rain, bent over all the time, getting wheelspin at 290 kays as you brake into the next turn.' Bravery over skill, just the way Mick doesn't like it.

And talking of bravery, Assen was next: Schwantz's favourite racetrack and the circuit Mick loves to hate. Both men fell heavily during practice underlining the treacherous nature of the sinuous Dutch venue. Mick hobbled away from his 225kph get-off, and although the American also walked from a nasty high-side, he was in agony with a broken left wrist.

Already 28 points ahead, with Kocinski nursing a broken finger from Germany, Mick was already looking like the new world champion. But he'd been here before, hadn't he?

Anyway, Schwantz is made of sterner stuff, with a frightening capacity to overcome pain. Costa moulded him a special cast and he raced to fifth at Assen. Very brave, but the ride was to cause permanent damage to the wrist, precipitating his retirement the following year.

Up front, Mick was on a roll. The bike was doing exactly what he wanted it to do, whatever the track. He was all-dominant, just like he'd been in '92. And his first Assen win was particularly sweet: 'I wanted to stick that to the doctor who messed up my leg and hopefully spoil his evening.'

Now 42 points up on Schwantz, he extended his winning streak to six victories with relatively untroubled successes in Italy and France, Barros chasing hard at Assen and Cadalora giving cause for minor concern at Mugello. Then at Le Mans he almost undid himself. Twice.

'I'd not been getting good starts all year, because we'd been running lighter clutch springs, so I could work the clutch and the thumb brake at the same time.'

He bogged the motor off the line and tried to ride round the outside of a dozen riders at the first esses. But someone was in the way. 'It was like, "Oh shit, next plan...let's panic!"' Taking to the dirt at speed, his NSR kicking dirt and stones in all directions, he was lucky to regain the track without a major collision. Eight laps later he was in the lead. Amazing.

No one could ever accuse Mick of flamboyance, of putting style over substance, but back then he liked to save a final-lap flourish for those occasions when he made everyone else look silly. And this was certainly one of those moments. He used to get his last-lap kicks laying 'blackies' – oily arcs of scorched rubber intended to spotlight his mastery of throttle control.

'Three corners from the flag I threw the bike sideways for the people watching in the stands. The bike went straight on to full lock and chucked me out the seat. I was lucky I still had my finger on the clutch – I grabbed the lever, drained the power and the bike pulled itself back into line.' That was his last celebratory blackie.

Going into the following weekend's British GP he had amassed a 76-point lead over Schwantz, who had slid off on the final lap at Le Mans. Mick still didn't even want to talk about the title, though, and anyone who brought the subject up would regret it. No way was he about to forget '92.

But he was close enough to think of racing for points, not wins. At Donington he took the safe option on tyres, going soft to eke some feel from the skaty sur-

face, and he had no answer to hero Schwantz, recovering from a high-flying practice fall to take his final GP victory. Second was fine anyway.

This year Mick had finally talked HRC into excusing him from riding duties at the Suzuka Eight Hours. Instead he attended the event in flesh-pressing mode, taking the opportunity to hunker down with HRC and sign another one-year deal. '1995 was the first year the Eight Hours wasn't in my contract. I told them I didn't want to lose the championship by throwing it down the road over there. Oguma was one of the few guys who could see that kind of thing.'

Four races to go and the title would be his if he won in Czecho. Mick wanted it over and done with and eased away to win ahead of Itoh. Schwantz was nowhere, his Suzuki flummoxed by

Mick chased by the Suzukis of Schwantz and Barros at Jerez. A crucial change to his NSR's suspension won him a pivotal victory. (Gold & Goose)

On a roll and on his way to the title, Mick leaves Puig, Criville, Cadalora, Schwantz and Barros stranded at the Salzburgring, May '94. (Gold & Goose)

Brno's off-camber turns.

Climbing the podium to the strains of 'Waltzing Matilda' and wearing his HRC 'No Worries' world champion's T-shirt, he grinned and grinned. Not a tear was shed though. 'I'm not a crying, emotional type of person – what made me happy was seeing the rest of the team so happy.'

In the post-race press conference he made an ominous announcement: 'I know my determination won't dwindle; I feel I've got to win another title to make the point.' If only he'd known how much trouble that would cause him.

The party started in the paddock with outlandish HRC boss Oguma leading the celebrations. Mick shouldn't even have been there – he was booked on a flight that evening, not daring to believe he'd have a reason to stick around. From the paddock the party moved to Brno's Hotel Bobby, the kind of men's establish-

ment that always does good business over a grand prix weekend. The sun was already up as the revellers headed for the Austrian border and Vienna airport. And from there to the US of A.

Champion or not, Mick was determined to beat the Americans on home ground. American riders had won every 500 race since the first Laguna GP in '88, and victory would go some way to avenging that brat Kocinski for his Australian GP win back in March. Not a chance, though. The NSR never worked at Laguna and he skated home to a distant third. Cadalora won, his Dunlops working just perfectly.

During '94 Mick had seen luck turn his way, at last. He'd got away with a few rapid tumbles, pushing Schwantz (who had fallen again at Laguna, putting himself out for the year) to remark: 'Why's it always me that gets hurt?'

Now Lady Luck was about to change her mind again, turning on the new world champ in the most horrible way. After Laguna Mick and brother Col trav-

No worries, he's world champion at last. Cadalora gives Mick a victory bath at Brno, August '94. Itoh keeps his magnum for later. (Gold & Goose)

elled to Road Atlanta to watch Scott – now a top Aussie Supers rider – contest a round of the AMA Superbike series.

'Two corners from the end this other guy ran into him, pushing him into a concrete wall at 180 kays. Me and Col were the first people to get to him and I was surprised he was still alive. He looked like he was going to pass away and when I got to the hospital I expected them to tell me he was dead. He wasn't but he was in fairly bad shape: he'd broken both his arms, a wrist and a shoulder and he'd punctured his lungs.'

Mick stayed as long as he could, until the time came to head to Argentina for the penultimate race of the year. En route to Buenos Aires he asked himself *that* question again. 'I thought about what had happened to me, what had happened to Rainey, and now my brother, lying in a medically induced coma. It was another of those moments – should I keep going or should I stop?'

Maintaining regular contact with the hospital, Mick worked his way through the chaotic South American event. On the dirty track he changed his style, sacrificing corner speed for the less graceful 'stop it, turn it, then ride it till it spins' approach. He won, way ahead of Chandler's Cagiva, and dedicated the victory to his critically ill brother.

One more race – well, two in fact – then he could kick back and let the reality of the championship sink in, so long as Scott was getting better…

At the final GP at Catalunya in Spain he was beaten again by Cadalora, who secured second overall, on just over half the points Mick had scored. Then another trek to Japan for the traditional non-championship Sugo event and another win, followed by a 'good on ya' tour, palm pressing with Honda's top brass.

Returning to Europe via the States, where he underwent further surgery on his right ankle, he found Scott out of danger. Thank God for that.

chapter nine

The trail of the lonesome tow truck

Mick hadn't just won the championship in '94, he had assumed an over-powering mastery of 500 racing: he had won two-thirds of the races and started from the front row and finished on the podium at every round. Now he wanted to do better than that, much better.

'I'd always told myself that if I won a championship, I'd have to win two. A lot of people can win one title on luck, but it's hard to get lucky twice, back to back. That was when I started training harder, pushing harder, and with that came more pressure.

'I was still training seven days a week, working harder than ever. I even had an exercise bicycle on the boat. I only rested when I was on a plane. It's a mental thing – you've got to do more than you did last year.'

As Mick began honing himself into an obsessive winning machine incapable of contemplating defeat (rather like that Rainey guy), racing continued its shift through the generations. The Wild Boys were almost all gone now. Gardner and Lawson had disappeared at the end of '92, Rainey in '93 and Schwantz was on his way out.

There was new blood, of course. Beattie had moved to Suzuki, as under-study to the Texan after a grim and gory year with Team Roberts. Cadalora was still improving and joined by a growing band of surprisingly rapid Europeans – Alex Criville, Alberto Puig, Loris Capirossi and Carlos Checa – all on production versions of Mick's user-friendly NSR. A few years back these men would've hopelessly fumbled and tumbled on a 500.

Mick had played his part in this transition. A dirt tracker by nature, he had nevertheless moved the emphasis away from the rear tyre, and where he went, the technicians followed. Better front slicks and improved chassis performance allowed riders to employ high corner speed as a go-fast tool, instead of relying solely on the tail-end slide. This suited the Europeans, who only knew one way to go fast on their 125s and 250s – corner speed, and lots of it. Further assistance came from the big-bang engine, moderating the V4's vicious 180-horsepower kick, so former 125 and 250 riders could survive where previously they would've fried.

It would take some years to learn to be loved by his people

When he wasn't crashing, Mick spent '95 playing tow truck to the new generation of European 500 riders. It wasn't what he called racing. (Gold & Goose)

Sponsors were delighted. GP racing had always been funded from its European heartland and sponsors had only imported Americans and Australians because they were the men to tame the old 500s. Now their services were no longer required. Spanish sponsors could hire Spanish riders, Italian companies could hire Italians.

One day the Europeans would learn to spin the rear tyre with confidence. Not yet, though. Mick was thus sure-fire title favourite, since doubts clouded Suzuki's new American/Australian line-up; Schwantz had already announced that this would be his last year, while new boy

Beattie had lost all the toes from his left foot in a bloody accident at Le Mans '94. The happy-go-lucky Gold Coaster was still easing himself back into action, although not without a sense of humour: 'Hangin' five in '95' was his motto for the year.

So this should've been a towering season, a confirmation of everything Mick had done in '94 (and the first half of '92). And yet he rates '95 as his worst year, during which the enjoyment vanished from racing, encouraging sweet thoughts of retirement.

It all started well enough, with a resounding home success at Eastern Creek, way ahead of Beattie, Mick's NSR wearing the colours of new HRC sponsor Repsol for the first time. The podium ovation was deafening – Doohan worship was swinging Down Under – yet it would take him some years to get used to it, to learn to be loved by his people. A one-two repeat in Malaysia, and by the time the paddock assembled at Suzuka people were already laying bets: could he win all 14 GPs?

Their answer came on Sunday. In sodden conditions Mick moved steadfastly into the lead chased by Beattie. Halfway through the final lap he was far enough ahead. 'I was getting a bit cocky, I was enjoying spinning it up, and this time the thing snapped sideways big time. It was my fault for messing around – I wouldn't have done that now, I would've kept it cool.'

RIGHT: *Mick ran away with the season opener at Eastern Creek, and the Aussie fans repaid him the only way they know how – hero worship. (Gold & Goose)*

BELOW: *Three races into '95 and things are about to go badly wrong. Mick rides into the Suzuka spray with Beattie (4), Itoh (7), Cadalora (2) and Puig (6). This was Schwantz's last race. (Gold & Goose)*

Running off the track at 180kph, he was lucky to find the Suzuka heli pad at his disposal. But by the time he'd regained the circuit, Beattie was past and heading for a first win on his RGV, no longer understudy to the off-colour Schwantz. 'I'm pissed off I made a mistake,' said Mick. 'But happy I finished.' Not next time, sunshine.

On Saturday evening at Jerez he was back where everyone expected him to be – on pole for the fourth time in a row, his Suzuka blunder already forgotten. In the race he'd carefully established a 6-second lead when his NSR flicked him again, this time deep into the dirt. He blamed the fall on a critical change in track temperature, but now admits: 'I felt I could go quicker than I went with Schwantz in '94 – I was focusing on the wrong thing.'

The press pored over the apparent unravelling of a legend

The self-imposed pressure was getting to him. He was trying too hard, he'd lost sight of the logical, simplistic approach to racing that had served him so well. But he didn't cop on yet.

The German GP was back at the Nurburgring: a dull modern circuit replacing Hockenheim's wild run through the forests. It was cold too, dead cold, the track like a skating rink, marshals and medics kept busy all weekend.

Mick didn't even make it through Friday. He fell and broke a finger, his mind still elsewhere: 'I knew it'd be easy to crash there.' He reappeared on Saturday, finger in a mini-cast and clutch lever shortened to avoid snagging. Refusing Dr Costa's mesotherapy jabs with the immortal words, 'I'm not a painkiller type of person', he went out and reclaimed pole. Hard.

He did need to win here, for Beattie had moved into the title lead at Jerez – serious pressure. 'I was still feeling pret-ty good. I caught and passed Daryl, then the front tucked into the next left. I had the bike on my knee trying to get it back and the slide went on for ever. I couldn't believe I'd crashed again, it was like, "What was that one all about?"' I was pretty pissed off.'

Indeed. Almost halfway into the championship and he languished 29 points behind Beattie, the youngster riding well and his fickle Suzuki improving. It wouldn't be easy to eat through that advantage.

Worst of all, Mick couldn't explain that last fall, and that plays badly on a racer's mind – if you don't know why you crashed, there's every chance you'll do it again. Visibly shaken, he turned his back on the whole show and headed to the States for some R&R with new girlfriend Selina.

'Maybe it wasn't the best time to take a break; I could already feel the pressure for the next race – I was putting myself down. Then Dupasquier [Michelin's GP chief] faxed me, telling me to slow down. He said I'm quicker than the other guys – I should just win at the slowest possible speed.'

Back in Europe at Mugello and he wasn't out of the hole just yet. 'I was ahead of Daryl with the front wheel up in the air as I was about to hit the brakes for turn two. By the time I'd got the wheel down I'd missed my turn-in point, so I ran it off into the grass.'

Mick gathered himself together and set off after the Suzuki. He won the race but was still 24 points down. Time for more soul-searching. 'The pressure was hitting home. I knew I had to keep things together or the championship wouldn't happen. And the press were giving me a hard time.'

Mick had been suspicious of the media since his arrival in GPs. 'I got to see the bad side of the press because I didn't exactly set the world on fire in '89, just a few bikes. Then you start winning and

they want to be your friend.'

The media, of course, would argue that its job is to write about winners, or winners who start losing. Losers who lose don't make headlines, so Mick hadn't been headline news in '89.

Journalists frenzied over his mistakes, poring over the apparent unravelling of a legend. But there was more to it than that. Schwantz hadn't raced since Suzuka, and turned up at Mugello to announce his retirement, citing lingering injury problems. Later he would admit that his racing impulse had never recovered from the shock of Rainey's paralysis back in '93.

So now Mick was the last of the Wild Boys, up there on a pedestal, all alone under the limelight. Just the way he didn't like it.

'I guess the press were missing the old riders; there was bitterness that I was still there. The press would always ask me what would I do if Schwantz was here, if Rainey was here. I just got fed up with it. It was the same in Formula 1 when Mansell retired and Senna crashed. I was caught in a transition period. Nowadays everyone's used to Criville, Checa and guys like that.'

Mick would certainly get used to them. At Assen Criville took his first pole, proof that he was finally getting a handle on the 500. Mick heeded Dupasquier's advice for the race, hanging with Criville and Puig and just beating them to the line. The win put him back into the series lead – Beattie had fallen during practice, breaking a collarbone.

Le Mans next, and his easiest win of the year, over 20 seconds ahead of

Cadalora. He looked in cruise mode, but if that was the case his rivals were in trouble trying to keep up. The impressive Puig crashed horribly while chasing down Mick's pole time. He fell at 265kph entering turn one, shattering a leg, the beginning of the end of his career. Other Spaniards would suffer similar bloody fates as they were bequeathed the chase, urged on by a flag-waving national media.

At the British GP Mick's relationship with the press hit rock bottom. He had been interviewed at Le Mans by the sensationalist *Motor Cycle News*, who quoted him saying: 'Racing is as boring as shit right now.' He denied he'd said any such thing, prompting gleeful *MCN* to run the taped conversation on a phone-in hotline. Mick back-pedalled, insisting that the quote had been taken out of context.

If he lost, the press savaged him – if he won, it was all 'too cushy'

In fact he was pretty much right to say that racing was boring. Watching him ride to another lonely win wasn't what we wanted after witnessing the golden years: Schwantz, Rainey, Gardner, Lawson and Mick trading fairing paint in every race. Yet his isolation at the top would gradually acquire a certain splendour. As the records fell one by one his name would be mentioned in the same breath as all-time legends Mike Hailwood and Giacomo Agostini. He would win more races than any other rider of the modern era, and, hey, it wasn't his fault that the other guys were no longer around.

All this was yet to come, though. For the moment Mick had worked himself into a no-win situation: if he messed up, as he'd done earlier in the year, the press ate him alive; if he won with ease, as he did at Donington, they said he was having it too cushy. Which he was. Even

Beattie seemed to know that he was beaten, although he insists that wasn't the case: 'I always knew he was beatable and all I wanted to do was beat him.'

The pair had become firm friends after meeting on Daryl's 16th birthday nine years earlier. Now they were competing for racing's biggest prize, so how did that affect their relationship? 'During '95 we didn't talk so much because we were competitors, but he was always open to me as a friend,' says Beattie. 'He'd ring me in Monaco and get me to go training. How many winners do you find on the GP circuit, who's opposition but still trains with you?'

Mick stretched his points advantage at Brno and Rio despite getting beaten by Cadalora, on new Dunlops and on a mission, Beattie third and fourth.

Bike racing hadn't been back to Brazil since its unhappy visit to Sao Paulo in '92, and Rio was no less chaotic. But within the air-conditioned containers that serve as paddock offices, order was being made of one particular piece of chaos.

Since pre-season tests Mick had been negotiating a move to Yamaha. He had been approached by Rainey, who was establishing a 500 team in '96 with backing from Marlboro, the cigarette brand financing Kenny Roberts's 500 outfit. Then everything went weird.

'Chuck Aksland came into my motorhome at Donington and offered me a two-year deal on more money than Wayne was offering. I went to see Wayne

INSET: *Beattie's leading the championship and piling on the pressure at Mugello, June '95. Mick made another cock-up but still won – his first victory in four races.* (Gold & Goose)

MAIN PICTURE: *Mick pitches into Le Mans's 265kph turn one, way ahead of runner-up Cadalora. With no serious competition in '95, Mick wasn't enjoying himself out on the track.* (Gold & Goose)

and told him – it seemed like the same job on more money in a different office. He wasn't happy.'

Roberts was talking big bucks and was desperate to ink a deal. Despite a win here and a win there, his team had floundered since Rainey's downfall and he rated Mick head and shoulders above his peers.

Philip Morris – owner of the Marlboro brand – now found itself in a bizarre situation, with two team owners, employing the same business manager and using its money to outbid each other for the same rider. And there was an added edge: if Roberts failed to get his man, he might lose the Marlboro millions to Rainey and his enormous squad would collapse.

In the end, it seems, everything just got too complicated, and when Honda bettered Roberts's offer on the eve of Rio, Mick gladly accepted: 'It was easier to stay than get into a bunfight'. But this wouldn't be the last time he'd get sucked into Machiavellian paddock schemings.

After a few crashes and plenty of soul searching, title number two was finally his. And now he was just getting into his stride. (Gold & Goose)

Every team manager was now painfully aware that there was no one else around close to his talent – so they'd have to slug it out with open chequebooks to get the only man that mattered. Mick was now earning more than any rider before him, but the figures would get a whole lot fatter over the next few years.

Money wasn't the only thing on his mind, though. Unimpressed with team-mate Criville, he wanted him replaced for '96 with an up-and-coming Aussie youngster, name of Anthony Gobert, then making a name for himself as a wild but desperately fast Superbike racer. Later Goey would become more famous for dyeing his hair the full rainbow of colours, stripping on the podium and smoking dope.

'I thought it'd be good to have another Aussie coming through. I'd met him and he seemed all right and eager to do well; that's before it all went to his head. Alex wasn't doing much until he got wind of me trying to oust him; I think that's what fired him into life in '96. Now I guess it's a godsend Anthony didn't happen.'

On to Argentina, where he finally put

Beattie out of his misery, wrapping up the title with a seventh win. The season ended on a low-ish note back in Europe – fourth at Catalunya behind winner Criville, his NSR proving unwieldy on full fuel load. It was his first finish off the podium in 31 races, since Spain '93. Wow.

Even so, it hadn't been a great year, at least not the kind of year Mick had wanted. He'd won that second championship and from now on everything else would be a bonus, oh yeah. But he wasn't having fun.

So into '96 with a new frame of mind. 'I was tired after '95. Mentally it had been my hardest season. I realised I had to get back to winning races, because that's what makes me happy; thinking about championships doesn't make me happy. I needed more enjoyment, so I had to change my whole approach or

The '96 500 season was the closest ever in GP history. Mick is just ahead of the pack at Suzuka, chased by Barros, winner Abe, Criville, Fujiwara and Okada. (Gold & Goose)

that'd be the end of it – I'd stop at the end of '96.'

Changing his whole approach opened a chink in his armour as 'more enjoyment' became 'less work'. 'I didn't push myself too hard for '96 – it was win the laziest way. I'd only do 40 minutes on a static bike or do some easy stuff in the gym.' The idea was to hit cruise mode and just win at the slowest possible speed.

As Mick slackened the pace (hey, he had hit the big three-zero the previous June), that new generation of 500 riders was shifting up a gear or two. Some of them would even get quick enough to find him a soft target on occasions.

Cadalora certainly looked dangerous. He had defected from Roberts's beleaguered Yamaha squad to Erv Kanemoto's crew and said that he was 99 per cent to win the title now he had a Honda and Michelins. How unwise. At Suzuki Beattie had worked hard to eliminate the RGV's shortcomings and much was expected of team-mate Scott Russell's first full 500 campaign. Rainey had wound up with former 125 *wunderkind* Loris Capirossi, the Italian apparently keen to learn his master's ways after a fast but fraught debut 500 season on a Honda. Roberts's best shot was heavy metal dude Norick Abe, while Carlos Checa had won himself a full-time ride after some rapid outings as Puig's stand-in. Criville had diligently devoted his off-season to fitness training and dirt tracking...

Rejecting the gizmos, he'd rather rely on his skills to get things right

The ghosts of Rainey and Schwantz weren't ready to be laid to rest, but they would fade during '96. And while there were no new giants just yet, there was a new-found strength in depth, with which the stopwatch concurred: this would be 500 racing's closest ever season.

Maybe Mick could afford to throttle back, since his decision to stick with Honda for an eighth successive season had saved him the risky adventure of building a relationship with another motorcycle. He had long been utterly at one with his NSR. The bike had been tailored around him since '91 and his crew had gigabytes of set-up data to which they referred at every racetrack. Since '92 year-on-year changes had been negligible, as neither Suzuki nor Yamaha had caught up, so his crew could start practice at each GP with the bike already halfway set up, a big advantage since it allowed him to concentrate on fine tuning and the crucial art of tyre choice.

This hadn't happened by chance – Mick and JB's policy had always been keep it simple, and they had even turned HRC away from its wildest flights of technical fancy.

Over the past few years HRC engineers had toiled away in their Asaka labs, concocting new technology to make 500s even more rideable. They had created a traction control device, semi-active suspension, fuel and water injection and an easy-start system to stifle time-wasting start-line wheelies.

One by one Mick rejected them all, even the ubiquitous quick shifter, considered a must-have by rivals. JB: 'Perhaps he would have had a greater margin of error if he had used the devices, but he prefers to put the effort back on to himself to make sure he gets things right. He just told HRC to give the stuff to Criville and Itoh, and if they start beating him, he'd try it.'

You could argue that Mick's contempt for hi-tech gizmos single-handedly killed off this dubious line of development. If he had adopted the HRC trickery, surely every other rider and every other factory would have followed.

Burgess greatly appreciates Mick's effort, perfectionism and professionalism. They match his own, based on his dad's simple but worthy racing maxim: 'the five Ps' ('perfect preparation prevents poor performance').

'If I could compare him with any of the guys I've worked with it would be Freddie [Spencer, the only rider in history to win simultaneous 250 and 500 titles]. Mick's the same – he uses the bike as a tool, he doesn't dick around. He's here to do a job. He knows the target, the kind of lap times we need to do, and he wants to go straight there. There's a lot of guys who like to play with their motorcycles, but there's no time at races. If there's a problem we fix it, if there isn't we don't play with things.

'He's the same when testing: he won't

ride around all day on the off-chance of finding something better. He's a very direct kind of guy – if there's ten tyres to test, each tyre gets six laps and we get the information. He's not prepared to be a development rider and that's good. Factories need development riders but you want your number one guy to be honed into winning GPs.

'He's very straightforward at races. He doesn't come into the pits at 8.30 like Criville does; he comes in ten minutes before practice starts, then he comes back at the end of the session and tells us what's wrong. After that he doesn't fiddle around in the pits: he's gone in 15 minutes and to me that's perfect.'

JB's respect for his man is enormous, but he carefully avoids becoming close friends with riders. 'There's no point falling in love because if you do that you can't kick their asses when you have to. Plus it's a high-risk sport; if anything really bad happens…'

During their ten-year partnership

Seconds away from disaster: Criville and Doohan dodge through the Jerez track invasion, but only one of them would make it to the flag. (Gold & Goose)

there have inevitably been disagreements. 'Everyone in the team has copped a salvo off him at one time or another, but they only happen when he's frustrated, because he knows what he wants and we're having trouble giving it to him.'

There were no raised voices after the first race of '96 at Shah Alam. Mick stood there, glistening with sweat and leaning against a pile of HRC cargo crates. 'Shit happens,' he mumbled with a shrug of the shoulders. Indeed it had. He'd been narrowly leading a thriller of a race from Cadalora when his rear slick blistered – tortured by the 40-degree track temperature. He limped home fifth, Mr 99 per cent certain taking an ominous debut victory on his NSR.

The Italian may have won but he wasn't the real star of the meeting – that was class newcomer Tadayuki Okada, whom HRC had promoted from 250s to ride its all-new NSRV500 twin. Okada had out-qualified everyone and led the race before crashing out. The V4 men were worried; even Mick contemplated switching to the light 'n' nimble bike at tighter tracks.

Shit had also happened for the man expected to be his biggest rival. Beattie had fallen heavily when his RGV seized during private tests at Shah Alam. He suffered head injuries that effectively ended his GP career.

At Sentul the class status quo was restored. Mick won from Barros (now riding for Capirossi's old Pileri Honda team), using a strategy he had devised for shrugging off the 500 parvenus. He would wait until the tyres began to lose certain grip, then push harder, spinning and sliding ahead, safe in the knowledge that these upstarts couldn't spin with confidence. Not yet anyway.

He knew his status gave him some sort of responsibility

At Suzuka he copped a front-tyre puncture and nursed his NSR home, this time in sixth. Wild man Abe won from 11th on the grid, astonishing himself, Roberts and pretty much everyone else.

Back in Europe the Spanish were already hyping things up for Jerez. Criville, they believed, was now ready to beat Mick head to head. Qualifying suggested he might just do that – he was less than a tenth down on the world champ. And he led the race, Mick watching and waiting. Then the unthinkable happened. Confused by the hysterical trackside commentary, fans poured on to the track to celebrate a home win. But there was still a lap to go. The two NSRs weaved past startled spectators, Mick going for the kill at the final corner, as he'd planned all along. Alex counterattacked, then highsided a few hundred metres from the line. Outraged Spanish fans stoned the victor on the slow-down lap and booed him on the podium. No worries: 'It just made me laugh.'

He was into his stride now, winning in Italy, France and Holland. But Criville was a constant shadow, and was only beaten at Assen when he ran wide into the final chicane. Was the Spaniard getting faster or was Mick just winning at the slowest possible speed?

In Germany he did get beaten, but not by his team-mate. It was a rookie's mistake – unable to see his own pitboard, he mis-read the trackside lap counter, expecting another lap when the chequered flag appeared. Cadalora won. Not a problem: eight races down, seven to go and he led Criville by 57 points.

Most important of all, he was enjoying racing again and now decided to continue into '97. But who with? There were three choices this time: stick with Honda, go to Yamaha with Rainey, or join Kenny Roberts's ambitious self-build project. The American had finally tired of dealing with the Japanese and was creating his own 500, using British Formula One expertise.

'Chuck Aksland asked me in Japan. I told him what I wanted and he said "Wow". He gave me a contract at Jerez and I read it on the plane home. I'm not a lawyer but I could see so many flaws, no way was I going to sign it. Chuck tried to press me into signing in Italy; he told me "Take it or leave it", so I said "See ya". I'd been speaking with Wayne too, but I agreed with Honda at Assen – the other offers had helped the Honda deal and I signed in Germany. It was a good deal – I don't think there were many F1 drivers on bigger contract fees.'

Mick hadn't only been talking money with HRC. However uncomfortably he

The track, the kerb and a little bit more. Mick charges through a Jerez corner, thumbing the rear brake to tighten his line. (Gold & Goose)

wore his crown as 500 overlord, he was aware his status gave him some kind of responsibility. And for a while he had been aware that the 500 class was under attack. Lap times had been going nowhere over the past few years, so 250s and Supers were getting uncomfortably close – in fact, Aussie Troy Corser had just broken the Donington 500 record on a Ducati Superbike. Something had to be done if the 500 class was to remain inviolate.

What he wanted was a new engine. While big-bang motors made 500s more rideable, they lacked the missile-like acceleration of their fiery forebears. He reckoned it was time to return to a pre-big-bang engine configuration. Power delivery would be more aggressive, but he could live with that, and, perhaps more to the point, the others might not. Big-bang motors hadn't only allowed 250s and Superbikes to catch up, they'd also helped his rivals close the gap, and he believed that a more vicious engine might allow him to better exploit his mastery of the tail-end slide. Dirt-track training had quickly taught Criville to rear-wheel steer, but could he handle Mick armed with a fiercer weapon?

He'd show them just how devastating he was if backed into a corner

In Britain (his 100th GP start) Criville was right there again but not quite close enough. And didn't Mick look strange on the podium, his head shaved in a pre-race stunt that raised £3,000 for charity. The skinhead didn't suit, but it sure got rid of all those grey hairs. Not that Mick seemed concerned about ageing; he'd just swapped his Ferrari for a Mercedes. 'The Ferrari was a bit lairy; I prefer something a bit more subtle.' No longer a boy, then.

He was still a skinhead when he turned up at the A1-Ring, Austria's new GP track, a renamed and sadly emasculated version of the glorious (but dangerous) Osterreichring.

And now he was in for a shock. Two, in fact. As a storm rolled off the Alps and lashed the circuit on Saturday morning, Mick's umbrella was struck by lightning as he scootered to the flooded pits. Worse was to come on race day as Criville beat the world champ in a breathtaking last-lap duel, his first head-to-head defeat at the hands of the new generation. The pair touched at least once as Mick battled to keep his wayward NSR on track – he'd gambled incorrectly on tyre choice after losing much of practice to the stormy weather.

He was gracious enough in defeat: 'Congratulations to Alex. He's been pushing me all year and it was his turn to win.'

In other words, he didn't expect to get beaten again, at least not in the next race. But Mick had now exhausted the full range of tactics he'd developed to cope with the troublesome Spaniard. Alex had finally got wise to them all: in France Mick had slowed to let the youngster ahead, then spent the remainder of the race on his back, until Criville cracked under the pressure. In Italy he had slowed fractionally, dropping into Criville's comfort zone, then speeding up again, leaving his understudy unable to lift himself back on to the ragged edge. All these had worked, but not any more.

At Brno it was the same deal: the two Repsol Hondas way ahead, Mick the tow truck. All Criville had to do was hang in there and match the leader's moves one by one. He'd been doing it all year, and Austria had proved that anything was possible. Exiting the last turn Alex went for the outside. At the finish line he was 10cm and two-thousands of a second ahead – the closest finish in 500 history.

This time Mick wasn't gracious at all. He wore a face of thunder on the podium, and in the post-race press conference laid into his nemesis, the man he had wanted out of Honda 12 months earlier: 'Racing with Alex isn't like racing with Rainey or Schwantz – I'm just a tow truck. It's very frustrating because he can't get out in front and go by himself; he's a second slower when he's ahead.'

Later he would admit that he'd been too complacent at the last corner: 'I was covering the wrong side – I'd messed up. That's another reason I was mad.'

The only reason Criville was saved the ire that Mick would later direct toward Max Biaggi is his quiet-as-a-mouse aspect. The neatly coiffured Catalan hardly ever says a word about anyone or anything. 'He lets his results do the talking, so I've respect for that; if anything he's too quiet. The only reason I fell out with Biaggi was his mouth.'

Mick got plenty of stick for his moodiness at Brno, but you could see what he meant. He wanted a bit of cut and thrust, some real racing. He didn't get any at Imola. Unflustered by his master's harsh words, Criville stuck with the same tactics, but this time rain stopped play with Mick just ahead.

Back to Spain now, where the national media was running out of control. Even the King was coming on Sunday. It was all good stuff, though – the packed grandstands erupting every time Mick or Alex rode out on to the track, boos for the foreigner, cheers for the home hero.

Neither won, Checa announcing his arrival amongst the elite with a first victory, Mick second, a fraction ahead of you know who. And that was enough to secure world title number three.

His dominance may have been dented over the past few months (just two wins from six races) but he was about to show the kids just how devastating he can be when backed into a corner. The place was Rio and Mick reckons this was one of his greatest rides ever.

He was racing with Abe and Criville when the trio happened upon a

Victim of many a close shave, Mick did this for charity at Donington in '96. Selina seems to approve. (Doohan archive)

dawdling backmarker. Abe panicked, ran off line, forcing Mick on to the dirt and apparently gifting the win to Criville. The Spanish press corps – a large and noisy party in the Rio media centre – were in raptures. Then they fell silent. With a handful of laps remaining and a 3-second deficit to overcome, Mick got serious. His Michelins skipping on the brink, he zeroed in on Criville, whose pitboard told the tale of a winning lead evaporating in the space of a few laps. With half a lap to go he swept ahead. It was a sobering experience, and not only for the vanquished – the whole paddock was reeling.

Criville wasn't for giving in, though. The season finale at Eastern Creek was a perfect and final opportunity to avenge

Criville's just beaten the tow truck by two-thousandths of a second and thinks it's hilarious. Mick is well unhappy, while third-home Scott Russell is just goofy. (Gold & Goose)

that unhappy ending at Jerez. And avenge it he did, unleashing a final-lap suicide attack at the hairpin. Both men crashed, remounting to finish eighth and sixth, Mick's first fall of the year.

Then a strange thing happened. Following the official top-three podium ceremony Mick made an unbidden appearance, above a sea of Aussie flags. He wore a broad grin and waved enthusiastically at his fans, apparently delighted with what had happened. And in a way he was. It justified all he'd said about his rival, and Criville ended the year as the villain. 'It showed he was desperate – whenever he tried to overtake he was always out of control.'

Even worse, Criville had refused to shake hands back in the pits, deepening Mick's resolve to raise himself on to a higher level in '97 and remind people that the new generation may be quick,

but not that quick.

The first move in that direction came the very next day, when HRC began its off-season test programme at the track. Mick and the new NSR engine – dubbed 'the screamer' for its high-pitched exhaust note – got on famously, lapping well inside the record. Then Criville had a go and got spat off at high speed, unable to tame the engine's fierce power delivery.

It had been a great year, oh yes – a hat-trick of championships equalling fellow greats Roberts and Rainey. He'd also surpassed Lawson's total of 31 500 wins, making him the third most successful 500 rider in history behind legends Hailwood and Agostini. And for the second year running he had won the Australian male athlete of the year award (in '95 he'd beaten golfer Greg Norman). He'd even received the Order of Australia in the Queen's Birthday Honours list.

A demi-god for sure. Now he was ready to take the next step.

chapter ten

Becoming god

The heat at Shah Alam beats down like a thousand hammers – 38 degrees and 85 per cent humidity. You don't breathe, you gasp. The haze seeps out of the surrounding jungle, jolted aside every few seconds by a motorcycle and rider, boiling their way towards another qualifying lap. The motorcycles are fast, deadly fast, but their exhaust notes drone like they're sickly scooters. Now here comes Mick and his screamer, singing out of a turn, rear tyre scrabbling for grip as he disappears into the steaming fog, having fun, fun, fun. It sounds like it too – the screamer lays down a hairy, scary wail. Just like the old days.

Big-bang motors had been great for riders but bad for race fans: no smokin' rubber, no aural entertainment. Mick had got bored of the things too; he wanted something a bit more exciting for the weekend, something fiery, something to drill the opposition deeper into the ground: 'Winning at the slowest possible speed hadn't really worked in '96, now the plan was to demoralise everyone in every practice session, every race.'

And that's pretty much what he did. This was to be his most successful season: 12 wins (including 10 in a row), 12 pole positions and age-old records broken every other race. The history books would never look the same again. Not that Mick seemed to care, but like it or not he was now right up there with the sport's all-time greatest two riders.

The record-breaking was relentless. Deep breath: during '97 he broke Agostini's record for the most wins in a season, Freddie Spencer's record for the most poles in a row, and Spencer's and Wayne Gardner's record for the most poles in a year; he also equalled his own and Rainey's record for the most podiums in a season and broke his own record for the most points scored in a year. Most important of all he eclipsed Hailwood's total of 37 wins to become the second most successful 500 rider in history, and open the possibility of beating Ago's 68-win record. Just one year earlier the Italian's tally had been emphatically pronounced 'unbeatable'.

His most outstanding year coincided with his rejection of the tried and tested big-bang engine and the adoption of the self-styled screamer, HRC returning to its pre-1992 180-degree firing order,

> **The youngsters were closing in – he'd try anything to hold them off**

with updated cylinders and trimmings. This meant spacing out the V4's power pulses and possibly returning to the crazy, rubber-shredding wheelspin that had once been the NSR's signature. That's what his rivals were hoping, anyway.

Pre-season tests had gone very well, for improvements in engine and tyre technology had tempered the engine's wild ways. Yet Mick and his crew were still wary and kept a big-bang motor in the back of the pits at the first three races, just in case.

He didn't get pole in Malaysia (that honour went to Okada, now on a V4), but he destroyed everyone on race day, dealing a morale-busting defeat to distant runner-up Criville, who now had his eyes firmly on the world title, nothing less. The screamer was a winner and tyre wear wasn't a problem, even in the searing Asian heat. The opposite, in fact.

'I was spinning less than the other guys. When the tyre spun I could roll off the throttle and get the tyre to hook up without losing drive. The big-bang would lose acceleration if you backed off. We'd got back a direct relationship between the throttle and the rear wheel.'

JB soon realised there were other important advantages: 'The big-bang motor has a lot of engine braking, which upsets the motorcycle into corners, then when you open the throttle you get this sudden pulse of power, which again upsets the suspension. Mick's secret is corner speed, so he needs the bike to be smooth, and the 180-degree engine is much smoother than the big-bang.'

There was another important aspect that had nothing to do with crankshafts, suspension or tyre wear. It was psychology. This was an area Mick was getting

into more deeply. He knew he could still beat anyone on riding talent alone, but the new generation was closing in and he'd try anything to keep them at bay.

Repsol Honda team-mates Criville and Okada had both tested the screamer but couldn't handle its light-the-blue-touch-paper power delivery. The message seemed simple, and it ate away at them: Mick's a better rider, he's on a higher level.

Mick moved his riding on to a new level in '97 and '98. Using HRC's new screamer engine, he completed both seasons without once finishing lower than second. (Lou Martin)

'I wanted to play a psychological game – they'd always be wondering if it was me or the engine that was beating them. It would play on their minds.'

There was no one else to worry about. This was the year that Honda assumed complete control of the 500 class – HRC's three V4 riders winning all 15 GPs, and Hondas invariably filling the first four or five places. Dejection ruled in the Suzuki and Yamaha pits, and

nowhere more so than under the withering gaze of factory bosses at Suzuka, where Mick chased down early leader Okada, then fended off a last-gasp attack from Criville, who came worryingly close to repeating the Eastern Creek pile-up at the final chicane.

The Spaniard got his revenge at home, his victory crowned on the podium by King Juan Carlos. The usually impassive Criville even shed a tear as all

hell broke loose on Jerez's crowded, dusty hillsides: Mexican waves, singing, shouting, screaming, firecrackers, thunder-flashes, blow-up dolls. Bedlam.

Victory was sweet, and just as well, for this would be his last in five months, and he only won because the champ's NSR had snapped a power-valve linkage.

Now Mick launched into his greatest run of wins. He went unbeaten as the GP circus moved to Mugello, the A1-Ring, Paul Ricard, Assen, Imola, Nurburgring, Rio, Donington, Brno and Catalunya. Ten races undefeated – no one had done that since the early '70s. He was a colossus – no, he'd been one of those for a while. Any advance on gargantuan? The press was running out of superlatives. Bored of their own negativity, journalists were now building him into a legend, exalting his Leviathan domination of the sport.

Bored of its negativity the press now built him into a legend

Not everyone was convinced, though. Rainey: 'I don't think I could've done what Mick has done these last few years – riding against guys who might beat him once or twice. I needed competitors who could beat me every race. I guess it comes down to the fact that he enjoys riding a motorcycle more than anything else; he enjoys being on the racetrack so much he doesn't even need anyone else out there.'

Rainey's arch-rival Schwantz shares Mick's point of view: 'That leg injury would've put most people out of the sport, but he got over it and became untouchable. I bet he just wishes he never broke that leg, because if he hadn't it may have been a whole different story. I may never have won a world championship.'

Some races he did indeed have the track to himself. He won by over 20 seconds at the A1-Ring, more than 10 at Mugello, Brno and Assen. Runaway victories, but the numbers tell a bit of a lie. Okada, Criville, Checa and Nobuatsu Aoki (an impressive 250 graduate running Mick's '96 NSRs) took turns in pursuit, only to find that they were in way too deep and crash, run off the track or come perilously close to disaster. The plan to demoralise his opponents was working perfectly: they were throwing themselves after him with ever-increasing desperation and he was just toying with them. Their various downfalls became as much the story of the year as Mick's remorseless march through the history books.

The smiling Okada, lone family man of the 500 elite, was the most impressive of his pursuers. The Japanese took pole at the first three GPs, then broke a wrist in saving a highside while duelling with Mick at Mugello. He crashed his way through the next two races, then came within a fraction of winning at Rio and Donington. He fought like a demon at Brno too, tumbling on the final lap; Mick, incidentally, rates that as one of his own best races, proof of his respect for the Japanese. Those near successes inspired optimism and Tady succumbed to Mick's mind games – he raced the screamer at Catalunya, struggling to his worst result in five races. But his reward would come.

Criville came to pieces pretty quickly after Jerez, once he realised that he wasn't going to carry on from where he'd left off in '96. At Mugello, the A1-Ring and Ricard he either ran wide or ran off the track while giving chase. Then he too fell into Mick's trap, testing the screamer again, only to discover he still wasn't man enough. That must've been the final insult. During qualifying at Assen he fell at horrifying speed – around 245kph – as he switched back and forth through the track's high-speed kinks, rupturing an artery and almost severing a thumb. It was a chillingly bloody fall and threatened to end his career. Yet the meek and mild Spaniard made a heroic comeback just two months later, and he too would get his reward.

Meanwhile more rivals fell by the wayside. Beattie had suffered further head injuries in France, which sidelined him for much of the year then pushed him into retirement. Mick's one-time protégé Anthony Gobert, brought into 500s for '97 by Suzuki, didn't even make it to the end of the season – the Aussie wild child tested positive for marijuana and was dismissed by his team, who only five months earlier had proclaimed him to be the new Schwantz. During his brief spell in the paddock Goey made plenty of waves, politically, socially and in the swimming pool erected outside his motorhome: racer as rock star.

In France the rainbow-haired youngster made an undignified attack on Mick after the pair almost collided during qualifying, later claiming on Aussie TV that he wanted to beat the champ so bad 'he could almost taste it'. Mick wisely rose above it all. Well, he didn't need to do anything else since Gobert wasn't attack-

ing from a position of strength; he'd so far done nothing on a 500. Then suddenly he was gone – a tragedy, for he was the entertainer the sport needed.

Mick secured his fourth straight title at Donington in August, with four races to go. Early, even by his standards. The celebrations were uncharacteristically joyful – a helmetless victory lap, smiling and waving, grey hair streaked back by the wind. He was starting to enjoy being a hero.

And here he was, a four-time champion, right up there with Lawson, Hailwood, Geoff Duke and John Surtees, a part of history. After the race he had bad news for his rivals: 'I'm definitely racing next year and I'm enjoying myself more than ever now; the new engine has really inspired me. I think I can still get better as a rider too – I'm still learning.' Very true – his riding was now reaching new levels of perfection.

Pre-season testing '97, and Mick, JB, Dick Smart and Pete 'Buddha' Luczkowski know they're already on to a good thing with the screamer motor. (Lou Martin)

Criville had been Mick's main rival in '96 but fell apart in '97, then suffered a bloody crash at Assen in June. (Gold & Goose)

There was bad news also for Yamaha, who had been conducting its annual 'Get Mick' operation since January. By now it was tempting to consider this yearly performance as no more than pantomime, or perhaps just Mick's way of jacking up his Honda pay cheque. Things had certainly worked out that way in '95 and '96. But this time Yamaha seemed prepared to go to any lengths, having come to the inevitable conclusion that it absolutely had to have him. He wouldn't come cheap – Yamaha would have to pay much, much more than it had ever paid any other rider – but the factory was already spending millions going nowhere. So was Suzuki, who hadn't won a race since early '95.

'Suzuki called and made me an offer, but I told them I was already on more money at Honda. My '97 sign-on fee was pretty hefty so I'd asked Wayne [Rainey] for only 10 per cent more. Yamaha didn't have a sponsor but they committed to that, then Honda matched them, so then I went back to Yamaha and told them if you want me, this is what I want.'

Then he had another idea: he was becoming increasingly frustrated with HRC's policy of furnishing other NSR riders with his '96 set-up data, making life much easier for Okada and Aoki, who had no previous experience of the bike. 'We'd try to keep our secrets to ourselves but it was impossible, so I'd end up racing guys who had used my data to get their bikes right.'

After Rio he flew to Tokyo, where he asked HRC if he could establish his own team with his own sponsor. 'They said go ahead, so I called a few people and pretty soon I'd found a budget for a one-rider team. But in the end Repsol wouldn't allow Honda to let me go it alone.'

Now the numbers spiralled. 'Honda had to buy me out of that deal, so my contract fee ended up increasing by about 40 per cent. But I still would've made more if I'd done my own team.'

Yamaha – suspicious that they'd been stitched up again – didn't give up easily. At Donington Rainey made a public plea:

'You'll prove you're a great rider if you sign with Yamaha.' What he meant was that Mick's talent had been bolstered by the best machinery; the world could only judge his true merit if he rode another machine. But Mick doesn't need to prove anything to anyone; hadn't he said all along that he did this for himself and no one else?

Certainly a move to Yamaha would have been great for racing. And if this had been F1 cars, you can't help but think that Bernie Ecclestone would've stepped in to ease the transition; Bernie knows that it's not good box office sense to put the best man on the best machine. Sadly, bike racing lacks that autocracy, and pretty soon Mick seemed destined to stick with Honda. The last two races of the year would at least prove he wasn't unbeatable on an NSR.

'I was feeling more invincible with every win. I was pushing harder and harder and harder and not making mistakes, so when I finally did get beat it was hard to take – I was like a spoilt kid.'

Dogged Okada, stung by his miserable performance on the screamer at Catalunya, finally got his reward in Indonesia. He borrowed Criville's tactics to win on the final lap and Mick was furious, just like he'd been at Brno a year earlier, rudely saluting the Japanese with a flick of the wrist as they crossed the line.

'I just wish it had been fair and square, rather than Tady hanging in my draught and then going desperate on the last lap; I think he was lucky to stay upright.' Okada admitted his pass had been a bit hard – but what was the alternative?

The media once again scalded Mick for his churlishness, then quickly came to this conclusion: he's a bad loser and that's what makes him such a great winner.

Now he had a chance to make

Mick parks his Sunseeker in Monaco harbour. He'd quite like a really big boat next, like the one in the background. (Gold & Goose)

amends, of a sort, by playing the home-coming hero at the season finale. The Australian GP was back at Phillip Island for the first time in seven years and Mick seemed keener than usual to win in front of the Aussie fans. Faced with their wor-ship a few years earlier he had felt awk-ward – now he felt he owed them for their support.

First of all he had to deal with a media firestorm, whipped into life by 15-times world champion Agostini, an Island visi-tor, and Rainey, smarting at Mick's rejec-tion. Ago's opinions made headlines: 'Mick is lucky because he's got no oppo-sition' – a bit rich coming from a man who won most of his 500 titles on thun-dering MVs, racing against a bunch of antiquated Nortons. Rainey fanned the flames: 'Back when I was racing with Mick, Schwantz, Lawson and Gardner you never knew who'd win; now we all wake up thinking "Who's gonna get sec-ond?"' Mick had a simple answer to that one: 'I've raced Rainey, Schwantz, Lawson and Gardner and I was domi-nating those guys until I broke my leg in '92.'

The cold, gloomy weekend didn't get any better. On Saturday he suffered his first fall of the year and threw away a commanding race lead the following day, leaving Criville the lucky winner. He was mortified, the fans were mortified, the Aussie media was mortified.

'I was riding along, thinking "How easy is this?" – I was thinking about other things. It was one of my biggest disap-pointments – my bottom lip was hanging out for the next week.'

That rare moment of complacency

had shown he was human – a glimmer of hope for his rivals for '98, but also a reminder to himself – keep it together and work even harder.

The work started soon enough at the end-of-season Sugo international. HRC now had three engines on offer: the big-bang, the screamer, and a new ultra-screamer, with equally spaced 90-degree firing order. Honda had run a 90-degree V4 in '88 and it was an evil sonofabitch, with a spine-chilling yowl. But late-90s technology had again made all the difference.

He used the ultra-screamer to win Sugo, but the motor proved less effective on higher gearing at other tracks. It was also more unreliable, so JB concentrated off-season testing on the big-bang, only committing to the screamer after arriving at Suzuka for the season opener.

I'd won ten races in a row – what else was I going to do?

By then Mick may have suspected that he was in for a tough year. New regulations had dictated a switch to 'green' unleaded fuel, and the new gas blunted power output. This had two knock-on effects: Mick now found his beloved NSR unchallenging to ride – 'a truck' he called it – while his rivals found their bikes easier to master. For these reasons the 1998 championship would be the closest, most exciting in years.

One man in particular was making it all look rather easy, and he'd never even ridden a 500 before. He was Max Biaggi, charismatic – nay, arrogant – 250 ace, who'd logged four straight 250 titles while Mick was dealing it up in 500s. Biaggi would be the first member of the new generation who didn't seem to subconsciously stoop to Mick's superiority. Unlike Beattie, Criville and Okada, Biaggi's ego allowed him to believe the unbelievable – that he could topple the king from his castle. His team cap even carried a '#1' logo, well earned in 250s, but not yet in 500s. Cheeky. He claimed he had come to 500s on Mick's recommendation – that his presence would add excitement to the class. It certainly added brightness: Biaggi's appropriation of superstardom, his desire for high-profile girlfriends culled from the worlds of film, TV and modelling, not to mention his eccentrically adjusted facial hair, added a certain glitz and glamour that had been missing from 500s. It also put him at direct odds with Mick.

As rulers of racing's two major categories the pair had known each other for some years, and as Monaco residents they socialised on occasion. But otherwise they had nothing in common: Mick is your straight-talking Aussie, who learned to ride in the bush and made his name on big, bruising Superbikes. Max carries a jet-set profile, spent his youth promenading around Rome on scooters and became famous riding rapier-sharp 250s. Their rapidly worsening relationship would dominate the coming season.

Biaggi's pace came as a bit of a shock. In the weeks preceding the first GP he travelled from one track to the next, obliterating lap records: Jerez, Catalunya, then Suzuka. Riding a production NSR, fettled by legendary tuner Erv Kanemoto and funded by Marlboro, Biaggi fulfilled his promise by taking pole and a runaway win in Japan; the first man to win first-time out on a 500 in 25 years.

Mick never even finished. He had started the race with an extra-heavy fuel load (the unleaded gas was proving less economical) and ran off the track while making up ground after a lacklustre start. He rejoined third from last, then his crank broke (another legacy of the new fuel – engines were wearing out at twice the usual rate).

After that he was certain he'd have to revise his tactics. In the past Mick had been happy to make steady starts, safe in the knowledge that he could move to the front at will. Not any more.

'I knew my starts would be critical from then on. I felt I could ride the old bikes better than the other guys, but the '98 bikes were more docile, so it closed things up and everyone was running pretty similar lap times. I knew I could no longer afford to go out there and catch them after ten laps.'

The media greeted Suzuka as a watershed: the birth of Max, the death of Mick, although perhaps he had brought some of that upon himself, seeming grim and moody all weekend: 'I'm starting to feel old,' he said. 'I rode my first race in '74 and sometimes I feel like I've been racing too long.'

Yet he didn't appreciate the media writing him off and he liked Biaggi's boastfulness even less. Normal service was resumed at Johor in Malaysia two weeks later, with pole position and victory, and he didn't waste the moment: 'A lot of people said Mick Doohan was finished after Japan, that I'm too old and too tired. Hopefully this has showed them I'm not too slow.'

Deep down, though, he was still unhappy, unfulfilled and somewhat burned out: 'I ran out of steam going into '98, because I didn't give myself a break. I kept training through Christmas, and it was hard to get motivated after '97. I'd won ten races in a row – what else was I going to do?' And the bike was still garbage, 'like a big 250, not a 500', which went some way to explaining Biaggi's speed. By the time he arrived at Mugello for round four he was ready to announce his retirement.

'I wasn't even happy when I won in Malaysia, so I felt like calling it quits. Like Schwantz once said – you've got pocketfuls of motivation and then it's gone.'

He seemed to be searching for a new buzz: before Mugello he tested (and crashed) Jacques Villeneuve's Williams F1 car, the drive arranged by Winfield cigarettes, a new personal sponsor and Williams's principal backer. After the Italian GP he volunteered for a run in a 230kph Class One offshore speedboat.

When they were still mates: Mick and Max Biaggi (left) out for a beer with Ken Johnstone (second left), JB and Dick Smart. (Doohan archive)

He wished he hadn't – he was utterly terrified by the experience. At the same time he became an enthusiastic supporter of a much-discussed plot to ditch 500s and replace them with 1,000cc four-strokes, more in line with most factories' streetbikes.

Rapid Roman rookie Max Biaggi (6) brought new fire to the 500 class in '98, making Mick and Criville work harder than ever. (Gold & Goose)

But beating Biaggi in front of the Italian's home crowd was a joy, so he decided to keep going. Criville meanwhile had quietly moved into the series lead, narrowly beating Mick at Jerez and Ricard, leading him by 2 points as the circus moved to dusty, decrepit Jarama. There he agreed terms with HRC for '99. 'I told them I wasn't interested in speaking to anyone else – I'd had enough of all the talking over the last few

years. Anyway, Honda always came back and beat the other offers.'

The Jarama race, however, was a disaster. He got punted wide by Biaggi in a turn-one mêlée and knocked down by Simon Crafar, a recent graduate to GPs from World Superbike. Who to blame – the New Zealander, with whom Mick sometimes trains on the Gold Coast, or Biaggi, with whom he was due to share a private plane to Monaco that evening?

Mick blamed Crafar: 'He was on the outside, so he should've been ready to move. I always go mid-track into a first-turn hairpin, so I'm ready to pick up if anyone comes up the inside, too late on the brakes.'

Biaggi would later make fun of Mick's complaints about maniacs who try to win races on the first lap. Hadn't he complained two years ago about riders who try to win races on the last lap? Exactly

which lap would he like his rivals to make their move?

Whatever, the championship situation looked bleak: he had slipped to fourth now, 13 points down on Criville. Well, it would've been bleak for anyone else. While Criville faltered, Mick won in Holland and Germany and took second place in Britain to put him ahead on points for the first time all year.

Not for long, though. The front-end grip problems that had bothered him earlier in the season returned big time at Brno. JB suspected the NSR's '98 suspension or even the lead-free gas: 'The power is really flat now, so when the rider cracks open the throttle mid-turn, it doesn't take the weight off the front tyre like it used to.'

Mick had already tumbled during private tests at Catalunya before the Czech GP, testing different suspension solutions. Then he fell again chasing leader Biaggi on the very first lap of the race. Doh!

There's only one way to go from here – you can't win forever

Even before he won at Brno, Biaggi's confidence was growing to dangerous levels. At a cheerful press conference on race eve he announced: 'Mick used to say 500 racing was boring. I don't hear him saying that any more.'

Too true. Biaggi's second 500 success put him back into the series lead, Mick sliding to third behind Criville, 13 points down and just four races to go; now he really thought he'd blown it. JB still kept the faith, though: 'Max was still a bit of an unknown quantity but I knew the others would snap like carrots – you wouldn't want to be leading a world championship with Mick breathing down your neck.'

But why had he fallen? Had he panicked when he'd seen Biaggi out front, then tried too hard on cool tyres and a full fuel load? 'No, I just turned in a bit

deep to get a good drive round the outside of Max – I already had a lot of lean angle so the front folded, no warning.'

Back on top, Biaggi had redoubled his efforts to destabilise Mick with more well-aimed boasts to the press. The media is a game the Roman plays well, and something Mick hadn't had to get involved with since Gardner had been around. Biaggi was the first man in years prepared to risk the champion's wrath by teasing and provoking him. Hadn't Mick himself said that racing is 90 per cent psychology? Biaggi had simply taken lessons from the master and added his own Machiavellian twist. It had to be worth a go.

And maybe it was working; even JB was concerned that Mick might be getting emotionally involved: 'He was talking about Max a lot, losing his focus, and once you do that you're opening a hole in your armour. I think we had a little boil over with Max.'

Mick says no, but at the next race he did something he hadn't done since the Gardner days: he launched into Biaggi, using the Italian press to label his goateed rival a preening prima donna.

'Max loves himself too much,' he said. 'He thinks too much about his appearance. He's more of a product than a person – he's plastic. He just comes up with excuses and lies, and cries so much he should be sponsored by Kleenex.'

For someone who doesn't usually play this game he was proving pretty handy. But perhaps that only encouraged his assailant some more – during the Imola post-qualifying press conference Mick had a go at Biaggi for his out-of-control Brno victory wheelie, which had the Italian frighteningly close to a 230kph loop-the-loop. Max rejoined quick as a flash: 'I think it's OK to crash after the

Looking for a new buzz – Mick got to test Jacques Villeneuve's Williams Renault F1 car at Catalunya. And crashed it. (Both Winfield/ICN)

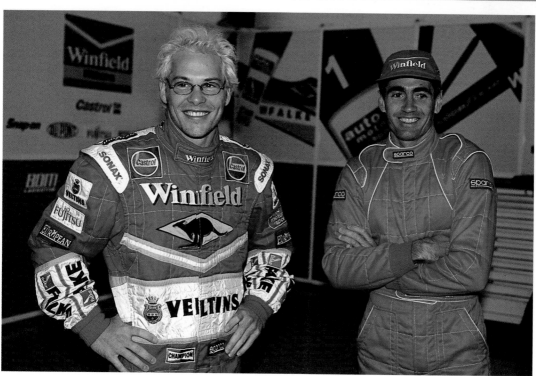

The champ goes down: Mick gets taken out at Jarama, June '98, after clashing with Biaggi and Simon Crafar. (Eric Celis, Moto Revue)

finish line, but not before.' Sniggers all round.

This was vintage stuff – better than Schumacher and Hill, Senna and Prost – and it generated the headlines bike racing had lacked for years.

Next day Mick was back to doing what he does best: winning races, destroying Criville and Biaggi in a display of utter dominance. And he was superbly eloquent at the post-race press conference, neatly placing the pressure back on his rivals: 'I've always known I've got to lose the title one day, so there's no pressure on me. I've won the championship four times and there's only one way to go from here – you can't win for ever.'

Then some final words of defiance: 'I tell you, Max isn't making things any easier for himself by saying all this stuff – he's just making me more determined.' Biaggi's game was about to go badly wrong.

Mick, Selina and Biaggi shared a private jet to races from Monaco in '98. The in-flight chit-chat got less as the year went on. (Lou Martin)

On to Catalunya, just 7 points separating Biaggi (189), Mick (185) and Criville (182), the closest title contest in living memory. The Spanish were apoplectic in support of their home-town hero. Check out this eulogy from some pre-race press material: 'This and no other is Criville's meeting with destiny. We are privileged to witness the most epic, mythical challenge of our time. Nothing is closer to a horse than a motorcycle, nothing closer to a hero than a motorcyclist.' Eh?

There's more: 'Men, heroes and only one God, the champion, Mick Doohan. Where Mick lives there is only room for one. It is true that today we still don't know if tomorrow Alex will have a real, mathematical chance of becoming God.' The piece ended thus: 'Not winning means losing.' Oh, how true, how true.

Criville didn't win or lose on Sunday – he just got buried in the turn-one gravel trap, sent flying by a wayward Katsuaki Fujiwara. Local fans were so enraged at the Suzuki rider they stoned the ambulance ferrying him to the medical centre. Bike racing gone football.

And then the whole championship fell apart. Biaggi and Barros duelled up front, Mick hunting them down after a sluggish start. But the two leaders had been spotted overtaking under a yellow flag, shown to indicate danger at the scene of the first-turn accident. Max – gloriously arrogant as ever – ignored signals to enter the pits for a stop-and-go penalty and was subsequently excluded from the results. Mick won and couldn't conceal his delight at his rival's ruin; in his eyes justice had been done, and poetic justice at that. Australia and Argentina to go and he led by 21 points.

A win at Phillip Island would give him his fifth straight world title in front of his home crowd. He absolutely had to do it, especially since his '97 Island goof still hurt.

Mick was devastating all weekend, honing the art of going super-quick from the first lap out of the pits, a risky tactic on coolish tyres that Spencer and Rainey had used to deadly effect years before. 'It was a psychological thing – to show these guys I'm not finished just yet and to put me in

a good frame of mind for next year.'

On lap one he opened a crushing 1.5-second lead, moving him safely clear of a desperate slipstreaming battle for second place. Beattie, spectating in the pits, was so choked by that first lap he cried. Then something else we'd not seen before – three corners from the flag he was waving to the crowd, allowing himself a tiny moment of self-indulgence. Not the Mick we know at all.

He was full of it on the podium too, the mask discarded perhaps for the first time to share his joy with the beered-up swamp of Aussie fans. He even, dare we say it, did a bit of showing off: 'I know I'm getting to the end of my career, so I thought I better make the most of it.'

Championships number four and five had made all the difference to Mick Doohan. He finally seemed at ease with himself, wholly comfortable with his achievements, which he certainly hadn't

Biaggi's attempts to destabilise Mick with a war of words backfired badly. 'He's just making me more determined to beat him.' (Gold & Goose)

Now he's enjoying it! Milking the Phillip Island crowd after the devastating home win that secured his fifth straight title. (Gold & Goose)

been before, almost as if three world titles weren't enough to prove his greatness.

He repeated the demolition strategy at Buenos Aires, bolting from the green light, leaving his rivals floundering in his wake. Another little something to work on their minds during the off-season.

Just one more assignment before he could head back to Australia and kick back on Hamilton Island: a Superbike race at Sugo, his first race on a four-stroke in over five years. The traditional end-of-season race had always been a 500 affair, but this year there wasn't time to get the bikes back to Japan. Mick would race an RC45 Superbike alongside Okada, a bunch of World Superbike regulars and the local hot shots. Perhaps this would answer the oft-posed question: are GP riders better than Superbike riders?

Mick wasn't looking forward to the race. He reckoned he had everything to lose on a dangerous track packed with Japanese desperados aching for a chance to stuff the master, whatever the consequences: 'I knew I'd be a target and the race didn't hold any importance for me; all I could do there was injure myself'.

He got just a couple of hours of practice and finished the race third, 2 seconds down on winner Okada, who had raced the RC45 at the past few Eight Hours, and Aaron Slight, Honda's top World Superbike man. Most significantly the race was much faster than a World Superbike round staged at the track a few weeks earlier.

Michael Dowson, the man who got Mick his first break in '85, had watched the year's final two GPs on TV back home in Australia, enthralled by the latest developments in Mick's tactics.

'It's not just watching him race, it's wondering what the hell he's going to do next. He knows the other guys are learning his tricks so you're watching for what he's experimenting with to go faster. He's just playing with the other guys all the time, messing with their minds. Now he knows he can blow them away by going fast right from the start, so he'll do it every race from now on. The fire in his belly is mind-boggling – he's had it from the first day he sat on a race bike, and it's inextinguishable. The others lack that.'

Too right, mate, too right.

Mick Doohan: career statistics

Abbreviations:
DNF – did not finish; DNS – did not start;
FL – fastest race lap; mech – machine failure

1984–1987

Various production and Superbike events

Bikes: Yamaha RZ250LC/TZR250/ RZ500LC/FZ750/FZR750/Suzuki RG250

Period results analysis: 57 starts, 26 wins, 9 seconds, 8 thirds, 3 fourths, 3 fifths, 2 sixths, 1 eighth, 1 tenth, 4 DNFs
Period win rate: 45.6 per cent

1988

Shell Australian Endurance (Superbike) Championship

Bikes: Marlboro Yamaha FZR750/ Yamaha YZF750

After round one, all events featured two legs

Date		Grid	Race
21.2	Sandown, Victoria	4th	1st
20.3	Baskerville, Tasmania	2nd	DNF, crash/ 2nd
1.5	Wanneroo, Western Australia	pole	1st/2nd
8.5	Adelaide, South Australia	4th	2nd/DNF, mech
7.8	Oran Park, New South Wales	2nd	1st/1st
4.9	Lakeside, Queensland	pole	1st/1st

Overall championship position: 2nd
(winner: Rob Phillis, Kawasaki GPX750)

Swann Insurance Series

Date		Grid	Race
20.11	Oran Park, New South Wales	pole	2nd/3rd
27.11	Lakeside, Queensland	*	1st/2nd
4.12	Phillip Island, Victoria	*	DNF, mech/2nd

Overall championship position: 2nd
(winner: Michael Dowson, Marlboro Yamaha FZR750)

* grids arranged according to championship points

World Superbike Championship

All events feature two legs

Date		Grid	Race
28.8	Japanese round, Sugo	5th	DNF, crash/1st
25.9	Australian round, Oran Park	pole	1st/1st

1988 results analysis: Australian/Word Superbike and Japanese F1 events: 27 starts, 15 wins, 5 seconds, 2 thirds, 1 fourth, 4 DNFs
Season win rate: 55.5 per cent

(Gold & Goose)

1989

500 World Championship
Bike: Rothmans Honda NSR500

Date		Grid	Race
26.3	Japanese GP, Suzuka	6th	DNF, mech
9.4	Australian GP, Phillip Island	12th	8th
16.4	US GP, Laguna Seca	12th	8th
30.4	Spanish GP, Jerez	11th	DNF, crash
14.5	Italian GP, Misano	9th	DNF, riders' strike
28.5	German GP, Hockenheim	6th	3rd
4.6	Austrian GP, Salzburgring	10th	8th
11.6	Yugoslav GP, Rijeka	10th	6th
24.6	Dutch GP, Assen	13th	9th
2.7	Belgian GP, Spa Francorchamps	3rd	8th
16.7	French GP, Le Mans	8th	8th
6.8	British GP, Donington Park	DNS, injured	
13.8	Swedish GP, Anderstorp	DNS, injured	
27.8	Czech GP, Brno	DNS, injured	
17.9	Brazilian GP, Goiania	8th	4th

Overall championship position: 9th
(winner: Eddie Lawson, Rothmans Honda)

1990

500 World Championship
Bike: Rothmans Honda NSR500

Date		Grid	Race
25.3	Japanese GP, Suzuka	5th	DNF, crash
8.4	US GP, Laguna Seca	2nd	6th
6.5	Spanish GP, Jerez	pole	4th/FL
20.5	Italian GP, Misano	3rd	3rd
27.5	German GP, Nurburgring	2nd	DNF, crash
10.6	Austrian GP, Salzburgring	3rd	3rd
17.6	Yugoslav GP, Rijeka	5th	4th
30.6	Dutch GP, Assen	7th	4th
7.7	Belgian GP, Spa Francorchamps	4th	6th
22.7	French GP, Le Mans	5th	4th
5.8	British GP, Donington Park	7th	4th
12.8	Swedish GP, Anderstorp	6th	4th
26.8	Czechoslovak GP, Brno	5th	9th
2.9	Hungarian GP, Hungaroring	pole	1st/FL
16.9	Australian GP, Phillip Island	pole	2nd

Overall championship position: 3rd
(winner: Wayne Rainey, Marlboro Yamaha)

1991

500 World Championship
Bike: Rothmans Honda NSR500

Date		Grid	Race
24.3	Japanese GP, Suzuka	2nd	3rd
7.4	Australian GP, Eastern Creek	3rd	2nd
21.4	US GP, Laguna Seca	4th	2nd
12.5	Spanish GP, Jerez	3rd	1st
19.5	Italian GP, Misano	5th	1st
26.5	German GP, Hockenheim	pole	3rd
6.6	Austrian GP, Salzburgring	pole	1st
16.6	GP of Europe, Catalunya	3rd	2nd
29.6	Dutch GP, Assen	4th	DNF, crash
21.7	French GP, Circuit Paul Ricard	2nd	2nd
4.8	British GP, Donington Park	6th	3rd
18.8	San Marino GP, Mugello	2nd	3rd
25.8	Czechoslovak GP, Brno	2nd	2nd
8.9	GP du Vitesse de Mans, Le Mans	2nd	2nd/FL
29.9	Malaysian GP, Shah Alam	3rd	3rd

Overall championship position: 2nd
(winner: Wayne Rainey, Marlboro Yamaha)

1992

500 World Championship
Bike: Rothmans Honda NSR500

Date		Grid	Race
29.3	Japanese GP, Suzuka	5th	1st/FL
12.4	Australian GP, Eastern Creek	pole	1st/FL
19.4	Malaysian GP, Shah Alam	pole	1st
10.5	Spanish GP, Jerez	pole	1st/FL
24.5	Italian GP, Mugello	pole	2nd
31.5	GP of Europe, Catalunya	pole	2nd/FL
14.6	German GP, Hockenheim	pole	1st/FL
27.6	Dutch GP, Assen	2nd	DNS, injured
12.7	Hungarian GP, Hungaroring		DNS, injured
19.7	French GP, Magny-Cours		DNS, injured
2.8	British GP, Donington Park		DNS, injured
23.8	Brazilian GP, Interlagos	14th	12th
6.9	South African GP, Kyalami	3rd	6th

Overall championship position: 2nd
(winner: Wayne Rainey, Marlboro Yamaha)

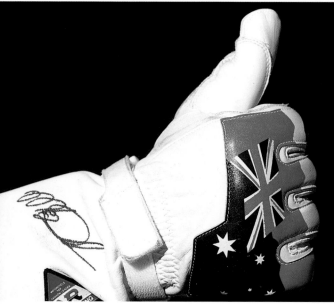

1993

500 World Championship
Bike: Rothmans Honda NSR500

Date		Grid	Race
28.3	Australian GP, Eastern Creek	8th	DNF, mech
4.4	Malaysian GP, Shah Alam	5th	4th
18.4	Japanese GP, Suzuka	4th	7th
2.5	Spanish GP, Jerez	7th	4th
16.5	Austrian GP, Salzburgring	2nd	2nd/FL
13.6	German GP, Hockenheim	2nd	DNF, mech/FL
26.6	Dutch GP, Assen	pole	2nd
4.7	GP of Europe, Catalunya	pole	2nd
18.7	San Marino GP, Mugello	pole	1st/FL
1.8	British GP, Donington Park	3rd	DNF, crash
22.8	Czech GP, Brno	2nd	3rd
5.9	Italian GP, Misano	5th	2nd/FL
12.9	US GP, Laguna Seca	pole	DNF, crash
26.9	FIM GP, Jarama		DNS, injured

Overall championship position: 4th
(winner: Kevin Schwantz, Lucky Strike Suzuki)

1994

500 World Championship
Bike: Honda NSR500

Date		Grid	Race
27.3	Australian GP, Eastern Creek	3rd	3rd
10.4	Malaysian GP, Shah Alam	4th	1st/FL
24.4	Japanese GP, Suzuka	2nd	2nd
8.5	Spanish GP, Jerez	3rd	1st
22.5	Austrian GP, Salzburgring	pole	1st/FL
12.6	German GP, Hockenheim	pole	1stFL
25.6	Dutch GP, Assen	pole	1stFL
3.7	Italian GP, Mugello	3rd	1st
17.7	French GP, Le Mans	pole	1st/FL
24.7	British GP, Donington Park	pole	2nd
21.8	Czech GP, Brno	2nd	1st
11.9	US GP, Laguna Seca	pole	3rd
24.9	Argentine GP, Buenos Aires	2nd	1st/FL
9.10	GP of Europe, Catalunya	2nd	2nd/FL

Overall championship position: 1st

(Mat Oxley)

(Gold & Goose)

1995

500 World Championship
Bike: Repsol Honda NSR500

Date		Grid	Race
26.3	Australian GP, Eastern Creek	pole	1st/FL
2.4	Malaysian GP, Shah Alam	pole	1st/FL
23.4	Japanese GP, Suzuka	pole	2nd/FL
7.5	Spanish GP, Jerez	pole	DNF, crash
21.5	German GP, Nurburgring	pole	DNF, crash/FL
11.6	Italian GP, Mugello	pole	1st/FL
24.6	Dutch GP, Assen	2nd	1st
9.7	French GP, Le Mans	pole	1st/FL
23.7	British GP, Donington Park	pole	1st/FL
20.8	Czech GP, Brno	2nd	2nd
17.9	Rio GP, Circuit Nelson Piquet	pole	2nd
24.9	Argentine GP, Buenos Aires	2nd	1st
8.9	GP of Europe, Catalunya	2nd	4th

Overall championship position: 1st

1996

500 World Championship
Bike: Repsol Honda NSR500

Date		Grid	Race
31.3	Malaysian GP, Shah Alam	3rd	5th
7.4	Indonesian GP, Sentul	pole	1st/FL
21.4	Japanese GP, Suzuka	7th	6th
12.5	Spanish GP, Jerez	pole	1st
26.5	Italian GP, Mugello	pole	1st
9.6	French GP, Circuit Paul Ricard	2nd	1st
29.6	Dutch GP, Assen	3rd	1st/FL
7.7	German GP, Nurburgring	2nd	2nd/FL
21.7	British GP, Donington Park	pole	1st
4.8	Austrian GP, A1-Ring	pole	2nd
18.8	Czech GP, Brno	2nd	2nd
1.9	City of Imola GP, Imola	pole	1st
15.9	Catalunyan GP, Catalunya	pole	2nd
6.10	Rio GP, Circuit Nelson Piquet	pole	1st/FL
20.10	Australian GP, Eastern Creek	3rd	8th

Overall championship position: 1st

1997

500 World Championship

Bike: Repsol Honda NSR500

Date		Grid	Race
13.4	Malaysian GP, Shah Alam	2nd	1st/FL
20.4	Japanese GP, Suzuka	2nd	1st/FL
4.5	Spanish GP, Jerez	2nd	2nd
18.5	Italian GP, Mugello	pole	1st/FL
1.6	Austrian GP, A1-Ring	pole	1st/FL
8.6	French GP, Circuit Paul Ricard	pole	1st/FL
28.6	Dutch GP, Assen	pole	1st
6.7	City of Imola GP, Imola	pole	1st/FL
20.7	German GP, Nurburgring	pole	1st/FL
3.8	Rio GP, Circuit Nelson Piquet	pole	1st
17.8	British GP, Donington Park	pole	1st/FL
31.8	Czech GP, Brno	pole	1st/FL
14.9	Catalunyan GP, Catalunya	pole	1st/FL
28.9	Indonesian GP, Sentul	pole	2nd
5.10	Australian, Phillip Island	pole	DNF, crash/FL

Overall championship position: 1st

1998

500 World Championship

Bike: Repsol Honda NSR500

Date		Grid	Race
5.4	Japanese GP, Suzuka	4th	DNF, mech
19.4	Malaysian GP, Johor	pole	1st/FL
3.5	Spanish GP, Jerez	5th	2nd
17.5	Italian GP, Mugello	pole	1st/FL
31.5	French GP, Circuit Paul Ricard	pole	2nd
14.6	Madrid GP, Jarama	pole	DNF, crash
27.6	Dutch GP, Assen	pole	1st/FL
5.7	British GP, Donington Park	2nd	2nd
19.7	German GP, Sachsenring	3rd	1st
23.8	Czech GP, Brno	pole	DNF, crash
6.9	City of Imola GP, Imola	3rd	1st
20.9	Catalunyan GP, Catalunya	4th	1st
4.10	Australian GP, Phillip Island	pole	1st
25.10	Argentine GP, Buenos Aires	pole	1st

Overall championship position: 1st

GP results analysis: 135 starts, 54 wins, 30 seconds, 10 thirds, 58 pole positions, 44 fastest laps, 16 DNFs
Win rate: 39.5 per cent

Suzuka Eight Hours, Japan

Year	Partner	Machine	Result
1987	Rod Cox	Yamaha FZR750	DNF
1988	Tadahiko Taira	Yamaha YZF750	DNF
1989	Wayne Gardner	Honda RVF750	DNF
1990	Wayne Gardner	Honda RVF750	DNF
1991	Wayne Gardner	Honda RVF750	1st
1993	Daryl Beattie	Honda RVF750	4th

Awards/honours

Australian Male Athlete of the Year	1995/96/97
Australian Sports Hall of Fame Honour Roll	1994/95/96
Australian Sports Personality of the Year	1998
Order of Australia	1996
Freeman of the City of Brisbane	1998

Records (all 1997)

Most 500 GP wins in a season	12
Most 500 GP poles in a season	12
Most 500 successive poles	12
Most 500 GP points in a season	340

Mick's place in history

Riders with most 500 world championship titles

Rider	Titles	Years
Giacomo Agostini (Italy)	8	1966/67/68/69/70/71/72/75
Mick Doohan (Australia)	5	1994/95/96/97/98
Eddie Lawson (US)	4	1984/86/88/89
Mike Hailwood (GB)	4	1962/63/64/65
John Surtees (GB)	4	1956/58/59/60
Geoff Duke (GB)	4	1951/53/54/55
Wayne Rainey (US)	3	1990/91/92
Kenny Roberts (US)	3	1978/79/80

Riders with most 500 GP wins

Rider	Wins	Years
Giacomo Agostini (Italy)	68	1965–76
Mick Doohan (Australia)	54	1990–98
Mike Hailwood (GB)	37	1961–67
Eddie Lawson (US)	31	1984–92
Kevin Schwantz (US)	25	1988–94
Wayne Rainey (US)	24	1988–93
Geoff Duke (GB)	22	1950–1960

Index